BRAKE SYSTEM DIAGNOSIS AND REPAIR

President	Dean F. Morgantini, S.A.E.
Vice President–Finance	Barry L. Beck
Vice President–Sales	Glenn D. Potere
Executive Editor	Kevin M. G. Maher
Production Manager	Ben Greisler, S.A.E.
Project Managers	Michael Abraham, George B. Heinrich III, S.A.E., Will Kessler, A.S.E., S.A.E., Richard Schwartz
Schematics Editor	Christopher G. Ritchie
Editor	Richard J. Rivele

CHILTON™ Automotive Books

PUBLISHED BY **W. G. NICHOLS, INC.**

Manufactured in USA
© 1998 W. G. Nichols
1020 Andrew Drive
West Chester, PA 19380
ISBN 0-8019-8945-0
Library of Congress Catalog Card No. 98-70666
1234567890 7654321098

Contents

Contents

SAFETY NOTICE

Proper service and repair procedures are vital to the safe, reliable operation of all motor vehicles, as well as the personal safety of those performing repairs. This manual outlines procedures for servicing and repairing vehicles using safe, effective methods. The procedures contain many NOTES, CAUTIONS and WARNINGS which should be followed, along with standard procedures, to eliminate the possibility of personal injury or improper service which could damage the vehicle or compromise its safety.

It is important to note that repair procedures and techniques, tools and parts for servicing motor vehicles, as well as the skill and experience of the individual performing the work, vary widely. It is not possible to anticipate all of the conceivable ways or conditions under which vehicles may be serviced, or to provide cautions as to all possible hazards that may result. Standard and accepted safety precautions and equipment should be used during cutting, grinding, chiseling, prying, or any other process that can cause material removal or projectiles.

Some procedures require the use of tools specially designed for a specific purpose. Before substituting another tool or procedure, you must be completely satisfied that neither your personal safety, nor the performance of the vehicle, will be endangered.

Although information in this manual is based on industry sources and is complete as possible at the time of publication, the possibility exists that some vehicle manufacturers made later changes which could not be included here. While striving for total accuracy, NP/Chilton cannot assume responsibility for any errors, changes or omissions that may occur in the compilation of this data.

PART NUMBERS

Part numbers listed in this reference are not recommendations by Chilton for any product brand name. They are references that can be used with interchange manuals and aftermarket supplier catalogs to locate each brand supplier's discrete part number.

SPECIAL TOOLS

Special tools are recommended by the vehicle manufacturer to perform their specific job. Use has been kept to a minimum, but, where absolutely necessary, they are referred to in the text by the part number of the tool manufacturer. These tools can be purchased, under the appropriate part number, from your local dealer or regional distributor, or an equivalent tool can be purchased locally from a tool supplier or parts outlet. Before substituting any tool for the one recommended, read the SAFETY NOTICE at the top of this page.

ACKNOWLEDGMENTS

A special thanks to the fine companies who supported the production of this book. Hand tools, supplied by Craftsman, were used during all phases of vehicle teardown and photography. A Rotary lift, the largest automobile lift manufacturer in the world offering the biggest variety of surface and inground lifts available, was also used.

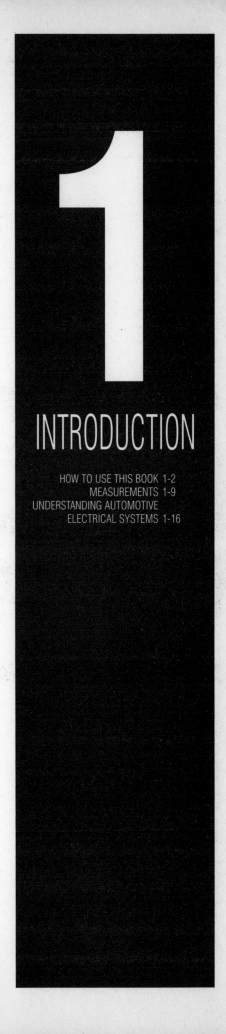

1

INTRODUCTION

HOW TO USE THIS BOOK

Brake work is certainly not the hardest job you can do on a vehicle, but it is certainly the most important.

All other systems on a vehicle are concerned with getting you going. Only the brake system has as its job, getting you stopped.

Brake work requires, above all, concentration. No matter what brake component you're working on, it is of the utmost importance that you keep attention to all the details and finish the job correctly. Mistakes made during brake system work can result in very unpleasant consequences.

On the lighter side, brake work is one of the few jobs on a vehicle that a do-it-yourselfer can perform while sitting down.

The fact that you're looking at this book means that you're fairly comfortable in your ability to work on your own vehicle. In most cases, people decide to replace brake components as part of routine maintenance, not out of necessity. If you've planned the job as a scheduled project, you'll probably do a better job than if you are working under the pressure of replacing a faulty parts in a vehicle that you are forced to do without in the meantime. The more relaxed and less hurried you are the better the job you do will be. Things that may go wrong will have less of an impact since you'll have time to correct them. Delays won't be as stressful.

We've tried to gear the writing of this book towards the average do-it-yourselfer who has no specialized mechanical knowledge. An experienced mechanic in a well-equipped shop doesn't need this book.

We'll explain what things are called and how things work. We will prepare you for the job, take you through it step-by-step and make sure that you complete your work successfully.

89549P35

Fig. 1 Although brake work may seem intimidating to the uninitiated, careful step-by-step work will allow even the novice to accomplish it

Can You Do It?

Probably the first real question you're asking yourself is, "Can I really do this?" The answer is, sure, why not?

You don't have to be an experienced mechanic to service the brakes on your vehicle. Really! If you have a basic set of hand tools, and a few, readily available and inexpensive brake tools, and are at all familiar with their use, you should have few, if any, real problems.

Physical strength doesn't have much of a bearing on your ability to complete the job either. There is not a lot of heavy lifting involved. And most work can be performed without any help. Although, a friend is always helpful for brake bleeding.

Where to Begin

Before removing any bolts, read through the entire procedure. This will give you the overall view of what tools and supplies will be required. There is nothing more frustrating than having to walk to the bus stop on Monday morning because you were short one bolt on Sunday afternoon. So read ahead and plan ahead. Each operation should be approached logically and all procedures thoroughly understood before attempting any work.

This book contains adjustments, maintenance, removal and installation procedures, and in some cases, repair or overhaul procedures. When repair is not considered practical, we tell you how to remove the part and then how to install the new or rebuilt replacement. In this way, you at least save the labor costs. Backyard repair of some components is just not practical.

Avoiding Trouble

Many procedures in this book require you to "label and disconnect . . ." a group of lines, hoses or wires. Don't be lulled into thinking you can remember where everything goes—you won't. If you reconnect or install a part incorrectly, the vehicle's brakes will operate poorly, if at all. If you hook up electrical wiring incorrectly, you may instantly learn a very expensive lesson.

A piece of masking tape, for example, on a hose and a piece on its fitting will allow you to assign your own label such as the letter A or a short name. As long as you remember your own code, the lines can be reconnected by matching similar letters or names. Do remember that tape will dissolve in gasoline or other fluids. If a component is to be washed or cleaned, use another method of identification. A permanent felt-tipped marker can be very handy for marking metal parts. Remove any tape or paper labels after assembly.

SAFETY is the most important thing to remember when working on a vehicle, especially on the brake system (since the whole purpose of a brake system is your safety). Be sure to read the information on shop safety in Section 2 of this book.

Maintenance or Repair?

Proper maintenance is the key to long and trouble-free vehicle life, and the work can yield its own rewards. A properly maintained vehicle performs better than one that is neglected. As a conscientious owner and driver, set aside a Saturday morning, say once a month, to check or replace items which could cause major problems later. Keep your own personal log to jot down which services you performed, how much the parts cost you, the date, and the exact odometer reading at the time. Keep all receipts for parts purchased, so that they may be referred to in case of related problems or to determine operating expenses. As a do-it-yourselfer, these receipts are the only proof you have that the required maintenance was performed. In the event of a warranty problem, these receipts will be invaluable.

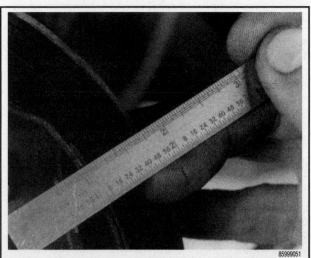

85999051

Fig. 2 Periodic inspection will give you piece of mind that your vehicle's brakes are up to their task . . .

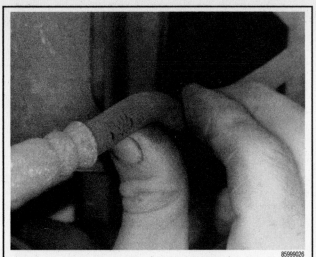

Fig. 3 . . . and it could reveal trouble, such as an impending brake hose failure, before it becomes dangerous

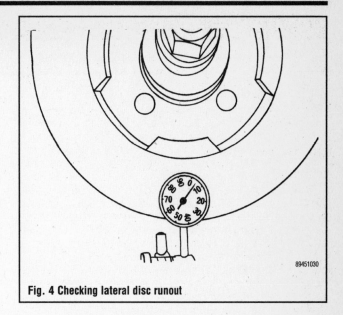

Fig. 4 Checking lateral disc runout

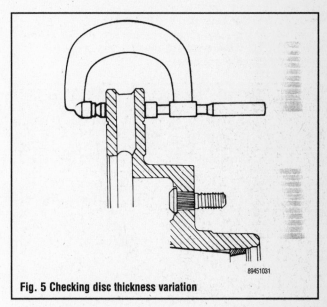

Fig. 5 Checking disc thickness variation

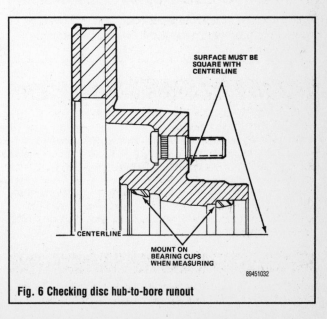

Fig. 6 Checking disc hub-to-bore runout

The literature provided with your vehicle when it was originally delivered includes the factory recommended maintenance schedule. If you no longer have this literature, replacement copies are usually available from the dealer, or, you can purchase a Chilton Repair Manual that is written just for your vehicle.

It's necessary to mention the difference between maintenance and repair. Maintenance includes routine inspections, adjustments, and replacement of parts that show signs of normal wear. Maintenance compensates for wear or deterioration. Repair implies that something has broken or is not working. A need for repair is often caused by lack of maintenance. Example: draining and refilling the brake fluid is maintenance recommended by the manufacturer at specific mileage intervals. Failure to do this can impair the operation of the brake system, requiring very expensive repairs. While no maintenance program can prevent items from breaking or wearing out, a general rule can be stated: MAINTENANCE IS CHEAPER THAN REPAIR.

Two basic mechanic's rules should be mentioned here. First, whenever the left side of the vehicle is referred to, it is meant to specify the driver's side. Conversely, the right side of the vehicle means the passenger's side. Second, most screws and bolts are removed by turning counterclockwise, and tightened by turning clockwise. An easy way to remember: righty, tighty; left loosey. Corny, but effective.

Safety is always the most important rule. Constantly be aware of the dangers involved in working on a vehicle and take the proper precautions. See the information in this section regarding SERVICING YOUR VEHICLE SAFELY and the SAFETY NOTICE on the acknowledgment page.

Professional Help

We're not suggesting a psychiatrist. It's just that there are some things in automotive work that are beyond the realm of the do-it-yourselfer. As far as brake work goes, there are 2 areas in which we advise taking the job to a professional, qualified technician. They are, brake drum and rotor machining, also called, turning, and most anti-lock brake system diagnosis and repair, specifically procedures involving the ABS electronics.

MACHINING

Drum and rotor machining requires a large and expensive milling machine, not practical for the DIYer. The braking surface on drums and rotors is supposed to be as flat and even as possible. A flat, even surface for the pads and shoes to contact gives the maximum braking effect.

As drums and rotors wear during normal usage, the surfaces wear unevenly, warp and groove. The principle culprits are heat and foreign matter. At every brake lining change, the drums and rotors should be checked. If you feel a pulsation in the brake pedal during braking, the braking sur-

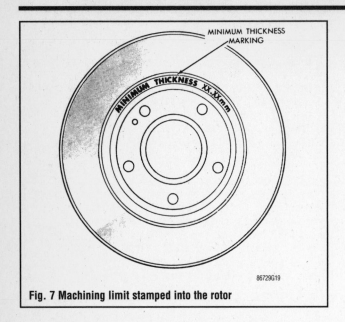

Fig. 7 Machining limit stamped into the rotor

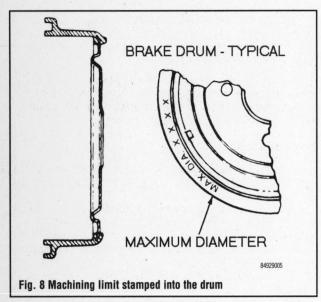

BRAKE DRUM - TYPICAL

MAXIMUM DIAMETER

Fig. 8 Machining limit stamped into the drum

Fig. 9. Some DIYer code scanners are available which can help you troubleshoot ABS systems

faces of the rotors and/or drums could be at fault. Very often, you can feel grooving and, sometimes, even warping by hand. But, for a complete check, dial indicators and micrometers are necessary.

If necessary, the braking surfaces can be restored to a like-new condition. This is the function of machining. The technician mounts the rotor or drum on the machining lathe. The lathe removes material from the braking surface as the drum or rotors turns slowly. This process continues until a flat surface it achieved.

The problem is, the lathe removes material. A drum or rotor has a machining limit. As material is removed, the drum or rotor gets thinner. There is a point beyond which you can't go. A drum or rotor that is too thin can overheat, stress, crack and fail. The machining limit is cast into each drum and rotor. The technician will measure the thickness of the part before machining and determine if the part is salvageable. If not, you'll have to get a new one.

ABS DIAGNOSIS & REPAIR

ABS systems are very complicated computer controlled, high pressure systems. Diagnosis requires expensive electronic devices and a lot of technical training. While non-hydraulic work on ABS systems is pretty much the same

as on non-ABS systems, most repair procedures requiring the opening of the ABS hydraulic system involve special tools and skill beyond the capabilities of a DIYer. For that reason, this book deals with non-ABS systems and ABS procedures, which we think, can be performed by the average person. All other ABS procedures should be referred to a professional, qualified technician.

Avoiding the Most Common Mistakes

Pay attention to the instructions provided. There are 3 common mistakes in mechanical work:

1. Incorrect order of assembly, disassembly or adjustment. When taking something apart or putting it together, performing steps in the wrong order usually just costs you extra time; however, it CAN break something. Read the entire procedure before beginning disassembly. Perform everything in the order in which the instructions say you should, even if you can't immediately see a reason for it. When you're taking apart something that is very intricate, you might want to draw a picture of how it looks when assembled at one point in order to make sure you get everything back in its proper position. We will supply exploded views whenever possible. When making adjustments, perform them in the proper order; often, one adjustment affects another, and you cannot expect even satisfactory results unless each adjustment is made only when it cannot be changed by any other.

2. Overtorquing (or undertorquing). While it is more common for overtorquing to cause damage, undertorquing may allow a fastener to vibrate loose causing serious damage. Especially when dealing with aluminum parts, pay attention to torque specifications and utilize a torque wrench in assembly. If a torque figure is not available, remember that if you are using the right tool to perform the job, you will probably not have to strain yourself to get a fastener tight enough. The pitch of most threads is so slight that the tension you put on the wrench will be multiplied many times in actual force on what you are tightening.

A good example of how critical torque is can be seen in the case of brake line-to-caliper fittings. Many of these fittings are equipped with copper gaskets. Too little torque can fail to crush the gasket, causing leakage. Too much torque can damage the threads or distort the gasket, also causing leakage.

Another example is of a very obvious, but often overlooked component, the wheel lugs. Now, we know that most people don't routinely torque the wheel lugs. However, what most people don't realize is the importance of wheel lug torque. On modern vehicles, wheel lug torque can be critical. Overtorquing wheel lugs can distort brake rotors and, believe it or not, can even affect wheel alignment on some vehicles with shim-type alignment procedures. Undertorquing wheel lugs can have the obvious result of wheels coming loose while driving. Besides, overtorquing wheel lugs can lead to the very frustrating experience of not being able to change a flat tire with the factory supplied lug wrench.

There are many commercial products available for ensuring that fasteners won't come loose, even if they are not torqued just right (a very common brand is Loctite®). If you're worried about getting something together tight enough to hold, but loose enough to avoid mechanical damage during assembly, one of these products might offer substantial insurance. Before choosing a threadlocking compound, read the label on the package and make sure the product is compatible with the materials, fluids, etc. involved.

3. Crossthreading. This occurs when a part such as a bolt is screwed into a nut or casting at the wrong angle and forced. Crossthreading is more likely to occur if access is difficult. It helps to clean and lubricate fasteners, then to start threading with the part to be installed positioned straight in. Always, start a fastener, etc. with your fingers. If you encounter resistance, unscrew the part and start over again at a different angle until it can be inserted and turned several times without much effort. Keep in mind that many parts have tapered threads, so that gentle turning will automatically bring the part you're threading to the proper angle, but only if you don't force it or resist a change in angle. Don't put a wrench on the part until it has been tightened a couple of turns by hand. If you suddenly encounter resistance, and the part has not seated fully, don't force it. Pull it back out to make sure it's clean and threading properly.

Always take your time and be patient; once you have some experience, working on your vehicle may well become an enjoyable hobby.

Storing Parts

Above all, we can't emphasize too strongly the necessity of a neat and orderly disassembly. Even if you are an experienced mechanic, parts can get mislaid, misidentified and just plain lost.

Start with an indelible marker, lots of cans and/or boxes and tags. Each time a part is removed, label it and store it safely. "Parts" includes all fasteners (bolts, nuts, screws, and washers). Bolts and nuts may look the same and not be alike. Similar looking bolts may be different lengths or thread count. Lockwashers may be required in some places and not in others. Everything should go back exactly from where it came.

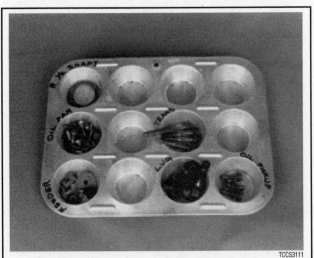

TCCS3111

Fig. 10 Don't laugh, but that old muffin baking tray can be very helpful in the garage once its life is over in the kitchen

Fasteners

The term, fasteners, refers to the bolts, nuts, screws, pins, and washers that hold everything together. These components come in all sizes, shapes and grades. It is extremely important to have the correct size and grade fastener for the job.

REPLACING FASTENERS

Whenever you remove a bolt, screw or nut, check its condition. Wipe it off with a shop rag and clean it up with a wire brush or brush wheel. Check the threads for signs of stripping, stretching or breakage. Check the shaft of the bolt or screw for rust, cracks or pitting. If everything looks okay, the fastener can be used again. If you are at all suspicious of the condition of any part, fasteners included, replace it. When replacing a fastener, always use the exact same size and type.

NEVER use a substitute bolt or screw of a lower grade or unknown grade. Markings on the bolt head will tell you what the grade is. The grading indicates the bolt's strength.

Often, the length of a particular bolt or screw is critical. Never replace a bolt or screw with one that is longer. A lot of bolts and screw are threaded into blind holes. A bolt that is too long won't secure the part. Worse still, a bolt that is a few threads too long may look or feel tight but actually won't be, resulting in trouble later.

When removing a fastener, consider how long it's been in place. If it's been in there a while it's bound to be rusted and/or seized. Always use a liberal amount of penetrating oil on and around a rusted fastener, or for that matter, all the fasteners from an old vehicle.

Keep in mind that old, rusted fasteners will probably be hard to remove, even with all your preparation. So, don't get impatient and force something that doesn't want to move. When trying to unscrew a stubborn, old bolt, use the breaker bar and apply gradually increasing force until the bolt or nut begins to move. At this point, apply a little more penetrating oil. The oil can now get under the bolt head and maybe onto the threads. WEAR HEAVY GLOVES for when the bolt or nut breaks free.

➡**Before any assembly takes place, always clean up (chase) the threads of any fastener or threaded hole with your tap and die set. This simple procedure makes assembly much easier and reduces the risk of crossthreading, stripping or breaking.**

Broken Bolts or Studs

I'm sure this won't happen to you, but if you know anyone who happens to come across a broken bolt or stud or who is unfortunate enough to break one, here's what to do.

There are tools called stud extractors. If, after breakage, there is a piece of the bolt or stud still visible, the stud extractors can grab a hold of it and continue the unscrewing process.

Or, if the shaft of the bolt or stud is thick enough, you can file a notch in the end for a screwdriver.

Or, you may be able to grab the shaft of the bolt or stud with a pair of locking pliers, such as ViseGrips®.

However, if the bolt or stud is broken off flush with the surface of the part, a tool kit called screw extractors or "Easy-Outs" is available. These tools are coarsely threaded reamers with left-hand threads. To use them, you drill a tap hole down through the shaft of the offending bolt or stud and screw the extractor into it. The extractor tightens in the direction of bolt loosening, thus turning the bolt out.

If all the above methods don't work, which sometimes happens, your only recourse is to completely drill out the stud or bolt, CAREFULLY! Don't over-drill! Usually when you drill out enough of the bolt or stud the rest will come out easily. What will probably happen as a result of all this drilling is that you'll do some damage to the threads in the hole. If the damage isn't too severe, you can clean up the threads with a tap and die set, using the proper sized tap. If the threads are completely destroyed, you'll have to repair them.

REPAIRING DAMAGED THREADS

Several methods of repairing damaged threads are available. Heli-Coil® (shown here), Keenserts® and Microdot® are among the most widely used. All involve basically the same principle—drilling out stripped threads, tapping the hole and installing a prewound insert—making welding, plugging and oversize fasteners unnecessary.

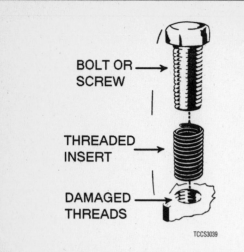

Fig. 11 Damaged bolt holes can be repaired with thread insert kits

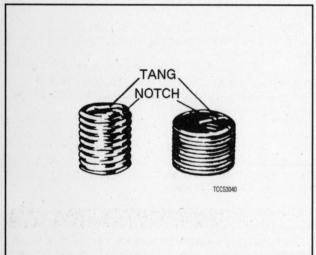

Fig. 12 Standard thread repair insert (left) and spark plug thread insert (right)

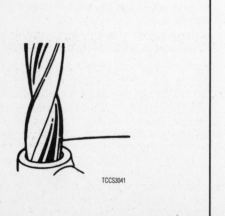

Fig. 13 Drill out the damaged threads with specified drill. Drill completely through the hole or to the bottom of a blind hole.

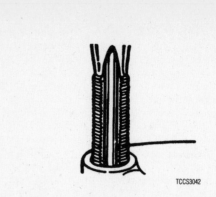

Fig. 14 With the tap supplied, tap the hole to receive the thread insert. Keep the tap well oiled and back it out frequently to avoid clogging the threads.

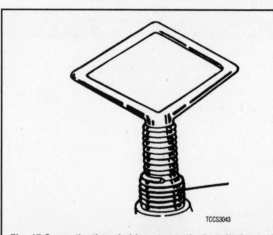

Fig. 15 Screw the threaded insert onto the installation tool until the tang engages the slot. Screw the insert into the tapped hole until it is ¼-½ turn below the top surface. After installation break off the tang with a hammer and punch.

Two types of thread repair inserts are usually supplied: a standard type for most—Inch Coarse, Inch Fine, Metric Course and Metric Fine thread sizes and a spark lug type to fit most spark plug port sizes. Consult the individual manufacturer's catalog to determine exact applications. Typical thread repair kits will contain a selection of prewound threaded inserts, a tap (corresponding to the outside diameter threads of the insert) and an installation tool. Spark plug inserts usually differ because they require a tap equipped with pilot threads and a combined reamer/tap section. Most manufacturers also supply blister-packed thread repair inserts separately in addition to a master kit containing a variety of taps and inserts plus installation tools.

Before effecting a repair to a threaded hole, remove any snapped, broken or damaged bolts or studs. Penetrating oil can be used to free frozen threads. The offending item can be removed with locking pliers or with a screw or stud extractor. After the hole is clear, the thread can be repaired, as shown in the series of accompanying illustrations.

Parts

It's your vehicle and it's your life. So, the quality of the parts you buy is up to you. We recommend that you buy only name brand parts (you've heard of them before). You can be cheap with some things, but brake parts isn't one of them.

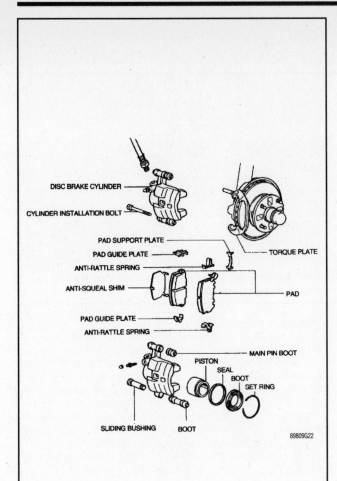

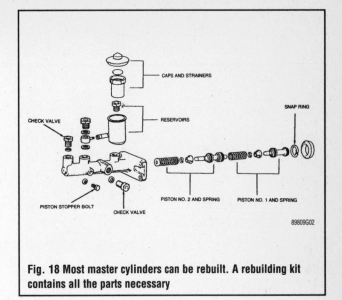

Fig. 18 Most master cylinders can be rebuilt. A rebuilding kit contains all the parts necessary

Disc brakes use stopping devices call brake pads. Drum brakes use brake shoes.

Most brake shoe or pad replacement jobs involve not just the pads or shoes, but also the related hardware. This hardware takes the form of pins, springs, clips and fasteners.

Whenever you do a brake job, it makes good sense to purchase brake hardware kits. These kits contain all the hardware parts that need to be replaced. Hardware kits are readily available at all auto parts stores and are relatively inexpensive, in most cases.

Additionally, it may become necessary to replace certain hydraulic parts. One alternative to replacement is overhauling. Master cylinders, calipers and wheel cylinders can, in most cases, be rebuilt (overhauled). There are rebuilding kits available for this purpose. Before deciding on rebuilding, check the price difference between a kit and a new part. If it's not much cheaper to rebuild, go with the new part.

Friction Materials

Brake shoes and pads are constructed in a similar manner. The pad or shoe is composed of a metal backing plate and a friction lining. The lining is either bonded (glued) to the metal, or riveted. Generally, riveted linings provide superior performance, but good quality bonded linings are perfectly adequate.

Friction materials will vary between manufacturers and type of pad and may be referred to as; asbestos, organic, semi-metallic and metallic compounds. The difference between these compounds lies in the types and percentages of friction materials used, material binders and performance modifiers.

❋❋ WARNING

Asbestos was used in friction lining compounds for many years because of its ability to withstand heat, but became less popular as health concerns arose. It may still be found in different types of pads and, unless you personally placed the last set of brakes on your vehicle, for safety reasons, you should assume that a compound containing asbestos may have been used.

Generally speaking, organic and non-metallic asbestos compound brakes are quiet, easy on rotors and provide good feel. But this comes at the expense of high temperature operation, so they may not be your best choice for heavy duty use. In most cases, these linings will wear somewhat faster than metallic compound pads, so you will usually replace them more often. But, when using these pads, rotors tend to last longer.

Semi-metallic or metallic compound brake linings will vary in performance based on the metallic contents of the compound. Again, generally speaking, the higher the metallic content, the better the friction material will

Fig. 16 An exploded view of a typical brake assembly showing all the parts which may need servicing. All these parts are available at your local auto parts store

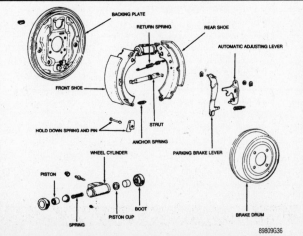

Fig. 17 An exploded view of a typical drum brake assembly. There are more parts here than with disc brakes, but all are available for replacement

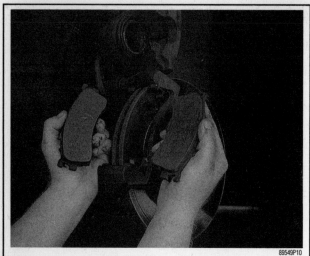

Fig. 19 When purchasing brake pads (and shoes) remember that in the end, they are the only things stopping your vehicle

Fig. 20 When filling the master cylinder, use only clean, fresh fluid specified for your vehicle

resist heat. This makes them more appropriate for heavy duty applications, but at the expense of braking performance before the pad reaches operating temperature. The first few applications on a cold morning may not give strong braking. Also, metallics and semi-metallics are more likely to squeal. In most cases, metallic compounds last longer than non-metallic pads, but they tend to cause more wear on the rotors. If you use metallic pads, expect to replace the rotors more often.

When deciding what type of brake lining is right for you, keep in mind that today's modern cars have brake materials which are matched to the expected vehicle's performance capabilities. Changing the material from OEM specification could adversely affect brake feel or responsiveness. Before changing the brake materials, talk to your dealer or parts supplier to help decide what is most appropriate for your application. Remember that heavy use applications such as towing , stop and go driving, driving down mountain roads, and racing may require a change to a higher performance material.

Some more exotic materials are also used in brake linings, among which are Kevlar® and carbon compounds. These materials have the capability of extremely good performance for towing, mountain driving or racing. Wear characteristics can be similar to either the metallic or the non-metallic linings, depending on the product you buy. Most race applications tend to wear like metallic linings, while many of the street applications are more like the non-metallics.

Brake Fluid

✷✷ WARNING

Clean, high quality brake fluid is essential to the safe and proper operation of the brake system. You should always buy the highest quality brake fluid that is available. If the brake fluid becomes contaminated, drain and flush the system, then refill the master cylinder with new fluid. Never reuse any brake fluid. Any brake fluid that is removed from the system should be discarded.

At first, vehicles used mechanically actuated brakes. Simple and easy, the system worked okay until vehicles started going more than 10 miles per hour on a regular basis. At this point, the idea for hydraulically actuated brakes came up.

A liquid, for all practical purposes, can't be compressed. So, if you fill a sealed system with liquid and try to compress it, say, with a master cylinder, the liquid exerts equal force on all other parts of the system, for instance, calipers and wheel cylinders. Get the idea?

Vehicle manufacturers recognized the need for a fluid that resists high temperatures, has lubricating capabilities, has a low freezing point and resists corrosion.

Almost all vehicles on the road today use brake fluid designated DOT 3 or DOT 4. DOT stands for Department of Transportation. The DOT established the standards by which brake fluid, among other things, is regulated.

Some vehicles have been built using a silicone-based brake fluid, but these are few and far between. DOT 3 and 4 fluids are petroleum based liquids. Silicone fluids are, of course, not petroleum based and are completely incompatible with other types and may cause damage to the rubber seals if added to systems that are not designed for Silicone fluid. There are 2 chief advantages to silicone based brake fluid. For one thing, it has a superior ability to withstand heat. And for another, it does not share the petroleum based fluid's tendency to absorb moisture. However, petroleum based fluids are perfectly able to withstand the heat generated by just about all modern vehicles. If you maintain the DOT 3 or 4 fluid in your brake system through periodic changes, and keep the system sealed to protect it from dirt or moisture, silicone based fluids are unnecessary.

Brake fluid is a specialized liquid and should never be mixed with any other type of fluid, such as mineral oil. Also, brake fluid has the ability to absorb moisture from the air, so, it can become contaminated simply by age. Over the years, you'll be removing the master cylinder cap or disconnecting brake lines. During the time that the system is open, the brake fluid will absorb small amounts of moisture, thereby reducing its effectiveness. Brake fluid contaminated with moisture will cause rust in the system as well as losing its ability to stand up to heat.

Therfore, it is recommended by most professionals that the brake fluid system be flushed and refilled every 2 years. This is especially true on vehicles with ABS systems.

When adding brake fluid to your vehicle's brake system, use brake fluid that is fresh and kept in a small, sealed container. If your brake fluid jar has been sitting around for a while, get new stuff. It's not expensive and is critical to the performance of the braking system. Don't forget, use only approved DOT 3 or 4 fluid. If you're in doubt about the fluid recommendation for your vehicle, check your owner's manual.

Used fluids such as brake fluid are hazardous wastes and must be disposed of properly. Before draining any fluids, consult with your local authorities; in many areas waste oil, etc. is being accepted as a part of recycling programs. A number of service stations and auto parts stores are also accepting waste fluids for recycling.

Be sure of the recycling center's policies before draining any fluids, as many will not accept different fluids that have been mixed together.

A final note . . . brake fluid should be handled with care. Brake fluid is a nasty and poisonous substance. Keep it out of your eyes and of your skin. Also, remember that it is an excellent paint remover. If you don't care for your personal safety, think of your vehicle. If brake fluid gets on your vehicle's paint, wipe if off immediately and rinse the area with water. It is probably not a bad idea to also clean the area with a gentle household cleaner or car wash detergent.

MEASUREMENTS

Most of the world uses the metric system. So, if you have an imported vehicle, you can be pretty certain that it was built with metric fasteners and put together using metric measured clearances and adjustments.

In the United States, most people still use the English system, which nowadays should be called the U.S. system. However, if your U.S. made vehicle was built after 1980, most, if not all, of the fasteners and measurements are metric. So, we have included the following conversion charts for your convenience.

ENGLISH TO METRIC CONVERSION: MASS (WEIGHT)

Current mass measurement is expressed in pounds and ounces (lbs. & ozs.). The metric unit of mass (or weight) is the kilogram (kg). Even although this table does not show conversion of masses (weights) larger than 15 lbs, it is easy to calculate larger units by following the data immediately below.

To convert ounces (oz.) to grams (g): multiply th number of ozs. by 28
To convert grams (g) to ounces (oz.): multiply the number of grams by .035

To convert pounds (lbs.) to kilograms (kg): multiply the number of lbs. by .45
To convert kilograms (kg) to pounds (lbs.): multiply the number of kilograms by 2.2

lbs	kg	lbs	kg	oz	kg	oz	kg
0.1	0.04	0.9	0.41	0.1	0.003	0.9	0.024
0.2	0.09	1	0.4	0.2	0.005	1	0.03
0.3	0.14	2	0.9	0.3	0.008	2	0.06
0.4	0.18	3	1.4	0.4	0.011	3	0.08
0.5	0.23	4	1.8	0.5	0.014	4	0.11
0.6	0.27	5	2.3	0.6	0.017	5	0.14
0.7	0.32	10	4.5	0.7	0.020	10	0.28
0.8	0.36	15	6.8	0.8	0.023	15	0.42

ENGLISH TO METRIC CONVERSION: TEMPERATURE

To convert Fahrenheit (°F) to Celsius (°C): take number of °F and subtract 32; multiply result by 5; divide result by 9

To convert Celsius (°C) to Fahrenheit (°F): take number of °C and multiply by 9; divide result by 5; add 32 to total

Fahrenheit (F)		Celsius (C)		Fahrenheit (F)		Celsius (C)		Fahrenheit (F)		Celsius (C)	
°F	°C	°C	°F	°F	°C	°C	°F	°F	°C	°C	°F
−40	−40	−38	−36.4	80	26.7	18	64.4	215	101.7	80	176
−35	−37.2	−36	−32.8	85	29.4	20	68	220	104.4	85	185
−30	−34.4	−34	−29.2	90	32.2	22	71.6	225	107.2	90	194
−25	−31.7	−32	−25.6	95	35.0	24	75.2	230	110.0	95	202
−20	−28.9	−30	−22	100	37.8	26	78.8	235	112.8	100	212
−15	−26.1	−28	−18.4	105	40.6	28	82.4	240	115.6	105	221
−10	−23.3	−26	−14.8	110	43.3	30	86	245	118.3	110	230
−5	−20.6	−24	−11.2	115	46.1	32	89.6	250	121.1	115	239
0	−17.8	−22	−7.6	120	48.9	34	93.2	255	123.9	120	248
1	−17.2	−20	−4	125	51.7	36	96.8	260	126.6	125	257
2	−16.7	−18	−0.4	130	54.4	38	100.4	265	129.4	130	266
3	−16.1	−16	3.2	135	57.2	40	104	270	132.2	135	275
4	−15.6	−14	6.8	140	60.0	42	107.6	275	135.0	140	284
5	−15.0	−12	10.4	145	62.8	44	112.2	280	137.8	145	293
10	−12.2	−10	14	150	65.6	46	114.8	285	140.6	150	302
15	−9.4	−8	17.6	155	68.3	48	118.4	290	143.3	155	311
20	−6.7	−6	21.2	160	71.1	50	122	295	146.1	160	320
25	−3.9	−4	24.8	165	73.9	52	125.6	300	148.9	165	329
30	−1.1	−2	28.4	170	76.7	54	129.2	305	151.7	170	338
35	1.7	0	32	175	79.4	56	132.8	310	154.4	175	347
40	4.4	2	35.6	180	82.2	58	136.4	315	157.2	180	356
45	7.2	4	39.2	185	85.0	60	140	320	160.0	185	365
50	10.0	6	42.8	190	87.8	62	143.6	325	162.8	190	374
55	12.8	8	46.4	195	90.6	64	147.2	330	165.6	195	383
60	15.6	10	50	200	93.3	66	150.8	335	168.3	200	392
65	18.3	12	53.6	205	96.1	68	154.4	340	171.1	205	401
70	21.1	14	57.2	210	98.9	70	158	345	173.9	210	410
75	23.9	16	60.8	212	100.0	75	167	350	176.7	215	414

TCCS1C01

ENGLISH TO METRIC CONVERSION: LENGTH

To convert inches (ins.) to millimeters (mm): multiply number of inches by 25.4

To convert millimeters (mm) to inches (ins.): multiply number of millimeters by .04

Inches		Decimals	Milli-meters	Inches to millimeters inches	mm		Inches		Decimals	Milli-meters	Inches to millimeters inches	mm
	1/64	0.051625	0.3969	0.0001	0.00254			33/64	0.515625	13.0969	0.6	15.24
1/32		0.03125	0.7937	0.0002	0.00508		17/32		0.53125	13.4937	0.7	17.78
	3/64	0.046875	1.1906	0.0003	0.00762			35/64	0.546875	13.8906	0.8	20.32
1/16		0.0625	1.5875	0.0004	0.01016		9/16		0.5625	14.2875	0.9	22.86
	5/64	0.078125	1.9844	0.0005	0.01270			37/64	0.578125	14.6844	1	25.4
3/32		0.09375	2.3812	0.0006	0.01524		19/32		0.59375	15.0812	2	50.8
	7/64	0.109375	2.7781	0.0007	0.01778			39/64	0.609375	15.4781	3	76.2
1/8		0.125	3.1750	0.0008	0.02032		5/8		0.625	15.8750	4	101.6
	9/64	0.140625	3.5719	0.0009	0.02286			41/64	0.640625	16.2719	5	127.0
5/32		0.15625	3.9687	0.001	0.0254		21/32		0.65625	16.6687	6	152.4
	11/64	0.171875	4.3656	0.002	0.0508			43/64	0.671875	17.0656	7	177.8
3/16		0.1875	4.7625	0.003	0.0762		11/16		0.6875	17.4625	8	203.2
	13/64	0.203125	5.1594	0.004	0.1016			45/64	0.703125	17.8594	9	228.6
7/32		0.21875	5.5562	0.005	0.1270		23/32		0.71875	18.2562	10	254.0
	15/64	0.234375	5.9531	0.006	0.1524			47/64	0.734375	18.6531	11	279.4
1/4		0.25	6.3500	0.007	0.1778		3/4		0.75	19.0500	12	304.8
	17/64	0.265625	6.7469	0.008	0.2032			49/64	0.765625	19.4469	13	330.2
9/32		0.28125	7.1437	0.009	0.2286		25/32		0.78125	19.8437	14	355.6
	19/64	0.296875	7.5406	0.01	0.254			51/64	0.796875	20.2406	15	381.0
5/16		0.3125	7.9375	0.02	0.508		13/16		0.8125	20.6375	16	406.4
	21/64	0.328125	8.3344	0.03	0.762			53/64	0.828125	21.0344	17	431.8
11/32		0.34375	8.7312	0.04	1.016		27/32		0.84375	21.4312	18	457.2
	23/64	0.359375	9.1281	0.05	1.270			55/64	0.859375	21.8281	19	482.6
3/8		0.375	9.5250	0.06	1.524		7/8		0.875	22.2250	20	508.0
	25/64	0.390625	9.9219	0.07	1.778			57/64	0.890625	22.6219	21	533.4
13/32		0.40625	10.3187	0.08	2.032		29/32		0.90625	23.0187	22	558.8
	27/64	0.421875	10.7156	0.09	2.286			59/64	0.921875	23.4156	23	584.2
7/16		0.4375	11.1125	0.1	2.54		15/16		0.9375	23.8125	24	609.6
	29/64	0.453125	11.5094	0.2	5.08			61/64	0.953125	24.2094	25	635.0
15/32		0.46875	11.9062	0.3	7.62		31/32		0.96875	24.6062	26	660.4
	31/64	0.484375	12.3031	0.4	10.16			63/64	0.984375	25.0031	27	690.6
1/2		0.5	12.7000	0.5	12.70							

ENGLISH TO METRIC CONVERSION: TORQUE

To convert foot-pounds (ft. lbs.) to Newton-meters: multiply the number of ft. lbs. by 1.3

To convert inch-pounds (in. lbs.) to Newton-meters: multiply the number of in. lbs. by .11

in lbs	N-m	in lbs	N-m	in lbs	N-m	in lbs	N-m	in lbs	N-m
0.1	0.01	1	0.11	10	1.13	19	2.15	28	3.16
0.2	0.02	2	0.23	11	1.24	20	2.26	29	3.28
0.3	0.03	3	0.34	12	1.36	21	2.37	30	3.39
0.4	0.04	4	0.45	13	1.47	22	2.49	31	3.50
0.5	0.06	5	0.56	14	1.58	23	2.60	32	3.62
0.6	0.07	6	0.68	15	1.70	24	2.71	33	3.73
0.7	0.08	7	0.78	16	1.81	25	2.82	34	3.84
0.8	0.09	8	0.90	17	1.92	26	2.94	35	3.95
0.9	0.10	9	1.02	18	2.03	27	3.05	36	4.0

ENGLISH TO METRIC CONVERSION: TORQUE

Torque is now expressed as either foot-pounds (ft./lbs.) or inch-pounds (in./lbs.). The metric measurement unit for torque is the Newton-meter (Nm). This unit—the Nm—will be used for all SI metric torque references, both the present ft./lbs. and in./lbs.

ft lbs	N-m	ft lbs	N-m	ft lbs	N-m	ft lbs	N-m
0.1	0.1	33	44.7	74	100.3	115	155.9
0.2	0.3	34	46.1	75	101.7	116	157.3
0.3	0.4	35	47.4	76	103.0	117	158.6
0.4	0.5	36	48.8	77	104.4	118	160.0
0.5	0.7	37	50.7	78	105.8	119	161.3
0.6	0.8	38	51.5	79	107.1	120	162.7
0.7	1.0	39	52.9	80	108.5	121	164.0
0.8	1.1	40	54.2	81	109.8	122	165.4
0.9	1.2	41	55.6	82	111.2	123	166.8
1	1.3	42	56.9	83	112.5	124	168.1
2	2.7	43	58.3	84	113.9	125	169.5
3	4.1	44	59.7	85	115.2	126	170.8
4	5.4	45	61.0	86	116.6	127	172.2
5	6.8	46	62.4	87	118.0	128	173.5
6	8.1	47	63.7	88	119.3	129	174.9
7	9.5	48	65.1	89	120.7	130	176.2
8	10.8	49	66.4	90	122.0	131	177.6
9	12.2	50	67.8	91	123.4	132	179.0
10	13.6	51	69.2	92	124.7	133	180.3
11	14.9	52	70.5	93	126.1	134	181.7
12	16.3	53	71.9	94	127.4	135	183.0
13	17.6	54	73.2	95	128.8	136	184.4
14	18.9	55	74.6	96	130.2	137	185.7
15	20.3	56	75.9	97	131.5	138	187.1
16	21.7	57	77.3	98	132.9	139	188.5
17	23.0	58	78.6	99	134.2	140	189.8
18	24.4	59	80.0	100	135.6	141	191.2
19	25.8	60	81.4	101	136.9	142	192.5
20	27.1	61	82.7	102	138.3	143	193.9
21	28.5	62	84.1	103	139.6	144	195.2
22	29.8	63	85.4	104	141.0	145	196.6
23	31.2	64	86.8	105	142.4	146	198.0
24	32.5	65	88.1	106	143.7	147	199.3
25	33.9	66	89.5	107	145.1	148	200.7
26	35.2	67	90.8	108	146.4	149	202.0
27	36.6	68	92.2	109	147.8	150	203.4
28	38.0	69	93.6	110	149.1	151	204.7
29	39.3	70	94.9	111	150.5	152	206.1
30	40.7	71	96.3	112	151.8	153	207.4
31	42.0	72	97.6	113	153.2	154	208.8
32	43.4	73	99.0	114	154.6	155	210.2

TCCS1C03

ENGLISH TO METRIC CONVERSION: FORCE

Force is presently measured in pounds (lbs.). This type of measurement is used to measure spring pressure, specifically how many pounds it takes to compress a spring. Our present force unit (the pound) will be replaced in SI metric measurements by the Newton (N). This term will eventually see use in specifications for electric motor brush spring pressures, valve spring pressures, etc.

To convert pounds (lbs.) to Newton (N): multiply the number of lbs. by 4.45

lbs	N	lbs	N	lbs	N	oz	N
0.01	0.04	21	93.4	59	262.4	1	0.3
0.02	0.09	22	97.9	60	266.9	2	0.6
0.03	0.13	23	102.3	61	271.3	3	0.8
0.04	0.18	24	106.8	62	275.8	4	1.1
0.05	0.22	25	111.2	63	280.2	5	1.4
0.06	0.27	26	115.6	64	284.6	6	1.7
0.07	0.31	27	120.1	65	289.1	7	2.0
0.08	0.36	28	124.6	66	293.6	8	2.2
0.09	0.40	29	129.0	67	298.0	9	2.5
0.1	0.4	30	133.4	68	302.5	10	2.8
0.2	0.9	31	137.9	69	306.9	11	3.1
0.3	1.3	32	142.3	70	311.4	12	3.3
0.4	1.8	33	146.8	71	315.8	13	3.6
0.5	2.2	34	151.2	72	320.3	14	3.9
0.6	2.7	35	155.7	73	324.7	15	4.2
0.7	3.1	36	160.1	74	329.2	16	4.4
0.8	3.6	37	164.6	75	333.6	17	4.7
0.9	4.0	38	169.0	76	338.1	18	5.0
1	4.4	39	173.5	77	342.5	19	5.3
2	8.9	40	177.9	78	347.0	20	5.6
3	13.4	41	182.4	79	351.4	21	5.8
4	17.8	42	186.8	80	355.9	22	6.1
5	22.2	43	191.3	81	360.3	23	6.4
6	26.7	44	195.7	82	364.8	24	6.7
7	31.1	45	200.2	83	369.2	25	7.0
8	35.6	46	204.6	84	373.6	26	7.2
9	40.0	47	209.1	85	378.1	27	7.5
10	44.5	48	213.5	86	382.6	28	7.8
11	48.9	49	218.0	87	387.0	29	8.1
12	53.4	50	224.4	88	391.4	30	8.3
13	57.8	51	226.9	89	395.9	31	8.6
14	62.3	52	231.3	90	400.3	32	8.9
15	66.7	53	235.8	91	404.8	33	9.2
16	71.2	54	240.2	92	409.2	34	9.4
17	75.6	55	244.6	93	413.7	35	9.7
18	80.1	56	249.1	94	418.1	36	10.0
19	84.5	57	253.6	95	422.6	37	10.3
20	89.0	58	258.0	96	427.0	38	10.6

TCCS1C04

ENGLISH TO METRIC CONVERSION: LIQUID CAPACITY

Liquid or fluid capacity is presently expressed as pints, quarts or gallons, or a combination of all of these. In the metric system the liter (l) will become the basic unit. Fractions of a liter would be expressed as deciliters, centiliters, or most frequently (and commonly) as milliliters.

To convert pints (pts.) to liters (l): multiply the number of pints by .47
To convert liters (l) to pints (pts.): multiply the number of liters by 2.1
To convert quarts (qts.) to liters (l): multiply the number of quarts by .95

To convert liters (l) to quarts (qts.): multiply the number of liters by 1.06
To convert gallons (gals.) to liters (l): multiply the number of gallons by 3.8
To convert liters (l) to gallons (gals.): multiply the number of liters by .26

gals	liters	qts	liters	pts	liters
0.1	0.38	0.1	0.10	0.1	0.05
0.2	0.76	0.2	0.19	0.2	0.10
0.3	1.1	0.3	0.28	0.3	0.14
0.4	1.5	0.4	0.38	0.4	0.19
0.5	1.9	0.5	0.47	0.5	0.24
0.6	2.3	0.6	0.57	0.6	0.28
0.7	2.6	0.7	0.66	0.7	0.33
0.8	3.0	0.8	0.76	0.8	0.38
0.9	3.4	0.9	0.85	0.9	0.43
1	3.8	1	1.0	1	0.5
2	7.6	2	1.9	2	1.0
3	11.4	3	2.8	3	1.4
4	15.1	4	3.8	4	1.9
5	18.9	5	4.7	5	2.4
6	22.7	6	5.7	6	2.8
7	26.5	7	6.6	7	3.3
8	30.3	8	7.6	8	3.8
9	34.1	9	8.5	9	4.3
10	37.8	10	9.5	10	4.7
11	41.6	11	10.4	11	5.2
12	45.4	12	11.4	12	5.7
13	49.2	13	12.3	13	6.2
14	53.0	14	13.2	14	6.6
15	56.8	15	14.2	15	7.1
16	60.6	16	15.1	16	7.6
17	64.3	17	16.1	17	8.0
18	68.1	18	17.0	18	8.5
19	71.9	19	18.0	19	9.0
20	75.7	20	18.9	20	9.5
21	79.5	21	19.9	21	9.9
22	83.2	22	20.8	22	10.4
23	87.0	23	21.8	23	10.9
24	90.8	24	22.7	24	11.4
25	94.6	25	23.6	25	11.8
26	98.4	26	24.6	26	12.3
27	102.2	27	25.5	27	12.8
28	106.0	28	26.5	28	13.2
29	110.0	29	27.4	29	13.7
30	113.5	30	28.4	30	14.2

TCCS1C05

ENGLISH TO METRIC CONVERSION: PRESSURE

The basic unit of pressure measurement used today is expressed as pounds per square inch (psi). The metric unit for psi will be the kilopascal (kPa). This will apply to either fluid pressure or air pressure, and will be frequently seen in tire pressure readings, oil pressure specifications, fuel pump pressure, etc.

To convert pounds per square inch (psi) to kilopascals (kPa): multiply the number of psi by 6.89

Psi	kPa	Psi	kPa	Psi	kPa	Psi	kPa
0.1	0.7	37	255.1	82	565.4	127	875.6
0.2	1.4	38	262.0	83	572.3	128	882.5
0.3	2.1	39	268.9	84	579.2	129	889.4
0.4	2.8	40	275.8	85	586.0	130	896.3
0.5	3.4	41	282.7	86	592.9	131	903.2
0.6	4.1	42	289.6	87	599.8	132	910.1
0.7	4.8	43	296.5	88	606.7	133	917.0
0.8	5.5	44	303.4	89	613.6	134	923.9
0.9	6.2	45	310.3	90	620.5	135	930.8
1	6.9	46	317.2	91	627.4	136	937.7
2	13.8	47	324.0	92	634.3	137	944.6
3	20.7	48	331.0	93	641.2	138	951.5
4	27.6	49	337.8	94	648.1	139	958.4
5	34.5	50	344.7	95	655.0	140	965.2
6	41.4	51	351.6	96	661.9	141	972.2
7	48.3	52	358.5	97	668.8	142	979.0
8	55.2	53	365.4	98	675.7	143	985.9
9	62.1	54	372.3	99	682.6	144	992.8
10	69.0	55	379.2	100	689.5	145	999.7
11	75.8	56	386.1	101	696.4	146	1006.6
12	82.7	57	393.0	102	703.3	147	1013.5
13	89.6	58	399.9	103	710.2	148	1020.4
14	96.5	59	406.8	104	717.0	149	1027.3
15	103.4	60	413.7	105	723.9	150	1034.2
16	110.3	61	420.6	106	730.8	151	1041.1
17	117.2	62	427.5	107	737.7	152	1048.0
18	124.1	63	434.4	108	744.6	153	1054.9
19	131.0	64	441.3	109	751.5	154	1061.8
20	137.9	65	448.2	110	758.4	155	1068.7
21	144.8	66	455.0	111	765.3	156	1075.6
22	151.7	67	461.9	112	772.2	157	1082.5
23	158.6	68	468.8	113	779.1	158	1089.4
24	165.5	69	475.7	114	786.0	159	1096.3
25	172.4	70	482.6	115	792.9	160	1103.2
26	179.3	71	489.5	116	799.8	161	1110.0
27	186.2	72	496.4	117	806.7	162	1116.9
28	193.0	73	503.3	118	813.6	163	1123.8
29	200.0	74	510.2	119	820.5	164	1130.7
30	206.8	75	517.1	120	827.4	165	1137.6
31	213.7	76	524.0	121	834.3	166	1144.5
32	220.6	77	530.9	122	841.2	167	1151.4
33	227.5	78	537.8	123	848.0	168	1158.3
34	234.4	79	544.7	124	854.9	169	1165.2
35	241.3	80	551.6	125	861.8	170	1172.1
36	248.2	81	558.5	126	868.7	171	1179.0

TCCS1C06

ENGLISH TO METRIC CONVERSION: PRESSURE

The basic unit of pressure measurement used today is expressed as pounds per square inch (psi). The metric unit for psi will be the kilopascal (kPa). This will apply to either fluid pressure or air pressure, and will be frequently seen in tire pressure readings, oil pressure specifications, fuel pump pressure, etc.

To convert pounds per square inch (psi) to kilopascals (kPa): multiply the number of psi by 6.89

Psi	kPa	Psi	kPa	Psi	kPa	Psi	kPa
172	1185.9	216	1489.3	260	1792.6	304	2096.0
173	1192.8	217	1496.2	261	1799.5	305	2102.9
174	1199.7	218	1503.1	262	1806.4	306	2109.8
175	1206.6	219	1510.0	263	1813.3	307	2116.7
176	1213.5	220	1516.8	264	1820.2	308	2123.6
177	1220.4	221	1523.7	265	1827.1	309	2130.5
178	1227.3	222	1530.6	266	1834.0	310	2137.4
179	1234.2	223	1537.5	267	1840.9	311	2144.3
180	1241.0	224	1544.4	268	1847.8	312	2151.2
181	1247.9	225	1551.3	269	1854.7	313	2158.1
182	1254.8	226	1558.2	270	1861.6	314	2164.9
183	1261.7	227	1565.1	271	1868.5	315	2171.8
184	1268.6	228	1572.0	272	1875.4	316	2178.7
185	1275.5	229	1578.9	273	1882.3	317	2185.6
186	1282.4	230	1585.8	274	1889.2	318	2192.5
187	1289.3	231	1592.7	275	1896.1	319	2199.4
188	1296.2	232	1599.6	276	1903.0	320	2206.3
189	1303.1	233	1606.5	277	1909.8	321	2213.2
190	1310.0	234	1613.4	278	1916.7	322	2220.1
191	1316.9	235	1620.3	279	1923.6	323	2227.0
192	1323.8	236	1627.2	280	1930.5	324	2233.9
193	1330.7	237	1634.1	281	1937.4	325	2240.8
194	1337.6	238	1641.0	282	1944.3	326	2247.7
195	1344.5	239	1647.8	283	1951.2	327	2254.6
196	1351.4	240	1654.7	284	1958.1	328	2261.5
197	1358.3	241	1661.6	285	1965.0	329	2268.4
198	1365.2	242	1668.5	286	1971.9	330	2275.3
199	1372.0	243	1675.4	287	1978.8	331	2282.2
200	1378.9	244	1682.3	288	1985.7	332	2289.1
201	1385.8	245	1689.2	289	1992.6	333	2295.9
202	1392.7	246	1696.1	290	1999.5	334	2302.8
203	1399.6	247	1703.0	291	2006.4	335	2309.7
204	1406.5	248	1709.9	292	2013.3	336	2316.6
205	1413.4	249	1716.8	293	2020.2	337	2323.5
206	1420.3	250	1723.7	294	2027.1	338	2330.4
207	1427.2	251	1730.6	295	2034.0	339	2337.3
208	1434.1	252	1737.5	296	2040.8	240	2344.2
209	1441.0	253	1744.4	297	2047.7	341	2351.1
210	1447.9	254	1751.3	298	2054.6	342	2358.0
211	1454.8	255	1758.2	299	2061.5	343	2364.9
212	1461.7	256	1765.1	300	2068.4	344	2371.8
213	1468.7	257	1772.0	301	2075.3	345	2378.7
214	1475.5	258	1778.8	302	2082.2	346	2385.6
215	1482.4	259	1785.7	303	2089.1	347	2392.5

TCCS1C07

UNDERSTANDING AUTOMOTIVE ELECTRICAL SYSTEMS

Every automotive brake system uses electricity, whether it is to activate the brake lights and warning lights on the dash or to run portions of the Anti-Lock Brake System (ABS). A do-it-yourselfer is eventually going to have face the seemingly dark mysteries of electricity. But, the good news is that it is really easier than most people fear. The following section is designed to help lift some of the fog that often worries people when they are dealing with electrical problems.

Basic Electrical Theory

For any 12 volt, negative ground, electrical system to operate, the electricity must travel in a complete circuit. This simply means that current (power) from the positive terminal (+) of the battery must eventually return to the negative terminal (-) of the battery. Along the way, this current will travel through wires, fuses, switches and components. If, for any reason, the flow of current through the circuit is interrupted, the component fed by that circuit will cease to function properly.

Perhaps the easiest way to visualize a circuit is to think of connecting a light bulb (with two wires attached to it) to the battery—one wire attached to the negative (-) terminal of the battery and the other wire to the positive (+) terminal. With the two wires touching the battery terminals, the circuit would be complete and the light bulb would illuminate. Electricity would follow a path from the battery to the bulb and back to the battery. It's easy to see that with longer wires on our light bulb, it could be mounted anywhere. Further, one wire could be fitted with a switch so that the light could be turned on and off.

The normal automotive circuit differs from this simple example in two ways. First, instead of having a return wire from the bulb to the battery, the current travels through the chassis of the vehicle. Since the negative (-) battery cable is attached to the chassis and the chassis is made of electrically conductive metal, the chassis of the vehicle can serve as a ground wire to complete the circuit. Secondly, most automotive circuits contain multiple components which receive power from a single circuit. This lessens the amount of wire needed to power components on the vehicle.

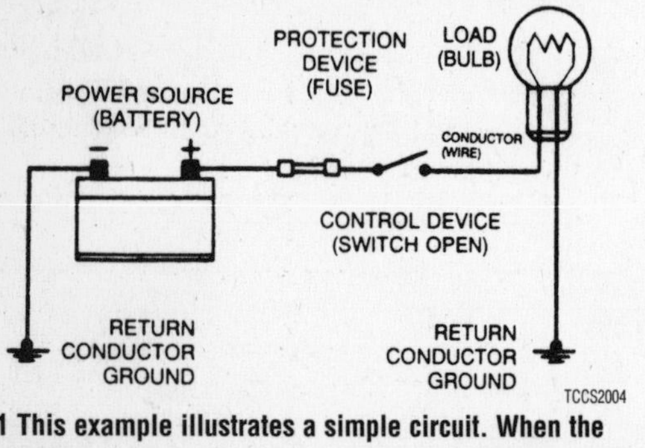

Fig. 21 This example illustrates a simple circuit. When the switch is closed, power from the positive (+) battery terminal flows through the fuse and the switch, and then to the light bulb. The light illuminates and the circuit is completed through the ground wire back to the negative (-) battery terminal. In reality, the two ground points shown in the illustration are attached to the metal chassis of the vehicle, which completes the circuit back to the battery.

THE WATER ANALOGY

Electricity is the flow of electrons—hypothetical particles thought to constitute the basic "stuff" of electricity. Many people have been taught electrical theory using an analogy with water. In a comparison with water flowing through a pipe, the electrons would be the water.

The flow of electricity can be measured much like the flow of water through a pipe. The unit of measurement used is amperes, frequently abbreviated as amps (a). When connected to a circuit, an ammeter will measure the actual amount of current flowing through the circuit. When relatively few electrons flow through a circuit, the amperage is low. When many electrons flow, the amperage is high.

Just as water pressure is measured in units such as pounds per square inch (psi), electrical pressure is measured in units called volts (v). When a voltmeter is connected to a circuit, it is measuring the electrical pressure. The higher the voltage, the more current will flow through the circuit. The lower the voltage, the less current will flow.

While increasing the voltage in a circuit will increase the flow of current, the actual flow depends not only on voltage, but also on the resistance of the circuit. Resistance is the amount of force necessary to push the current through the circuit. The standard unit for measuring resistance is an ohm (W or omega). Resistance in a circuit varies depending on the amount and type of components used in the circuit. The main factors which determine resistance are:

- Material—some materials have more resistance than others. Those with high resistance are said to be insulators. Rubber is one of the best insulators available, as it allows little current to pass. Low resistance materials are said to be conductors. Copper wire is among the best conductors. Most vehicle wiring is made of copper.
- Size—the larger the wire size being used, the less resistance the wire will have. This is why components which use large amounts of electricity usually have large wires supplying current to them.
- Length—for a given thickness of wire, the longer the wire, the greater the resistance. The shorter the wire, the less the resistance. When determining the proper wire for a circuit, both size and length must be considered to design a circuit that can handle the current needs of the component.
- Temperature—with many materials, the higher the temperature, the greater the resistance. This principle is used in many of the sensors on the engine.

OHM'S LAW

The preceding definitions may lead the reader into believing that there is no relationship between current, voltage and resistance. Nothing can be further from the truth. The relationship between current, voltage and resistance can be summed up by a statement known as Ohm's law.

Voltage (E) is equal to amperage (I) times resistance (R): $E = I \times R$
Other forms of the formula are $R = E/I$ and $I = E/R$

In each of these formulas, E is the voltage in volts, I is the current in amps and R is the resistance in ohms. The basic point to remember is that as the resistance of a circuit goes up, the amount of current that flows in the circuit will go down, if voltage remains the same.

Electrical Components

POWER SOURCE

The power source for 12 volt automotive electrical systems is the battery. In most modern vehicles, the battery is a lead/acid electrochemical device consisting of six 2 volt subsections (cells) connected in series, so that the unit is capable of producing approximately 12 volts of electrical pressure. Each subsection consists of a series of positive and negative plates held a short distance apart in a solution of sulfuric acid and water.

The two types of plates are of dissimilar metals. This sets up a chemical reaction, and it is this reaction which produces current flow from the battery when its positive and negative terminals are connected to an electrical load. The power removed from the battery is replaced by the alternator, which forces electrons back through the battery, reversing the normal flow, and restoring the battery to its original chemical state.

GROUND

Two types of grounds are used in automotive electric circuits. Direct ground components are grounded through their mounting points. All other components use some sort of ground wire which is attached to the body or chassis of the vehicle. The electrical current runs through the chassis of the vehicle and returns to the battery through the ground (-) cable; if you look, you'll see that the battery ground cable connects between the battery and the body or chassis of the vehicle.

→It should be noted that a good percentage of electrical problems can be traced to bad grounds.

PROTECTIVE DEVICES

It is possible for large surges of current to pass through the electrical system of your vehicle. If this surge of current were to reach the load in the circuit, it could burn it out or severely damage it. To prevent this, fuses, circuit breakers and/or fusible links are connected into the supply wires of the electrical system. These items are nothing more than a built-in weak spot in the system. When an abnormal amount of current flows through the system, these protective devices work as follows to protect the circuit:

• Fuse—when an excessive electrical current passes through a fuse, the fuse "blows" (the conductor melts) and opens the circuit, preventing the passage of current.

• Circuit Breaker—a circuit breaker is basically a self-repairing fuse. It will open the circuit in the same fashion as a fuse, but when the surge subsides, the circuit breaker can be reset and does not need replacement.

• Fusible Link—a fusible link (fuse link or main link) is a short length of special, Hypalon high temperature insulated wire that acts as a fuse. When an excessive electrical current passes through a fusible link, the thin gauge wire inside the link melts, creating an intentional open to protect the circuit. To repair the circuit, the link must be replaced. Some newer type fusible links are housed in plug-in modules, which are simply replaced like

a fuse, while older type fusible links must be cut and spliced if they melt. Since this link is very early in the electrical path, it's the first place to look if nothing on the vehicle works, but the battery seems to be charged and is properly connected.

※※ CAUTION

Always replace fuses, circuit breakers and fusible links with identically rated components. Under no circumstances should a component of higher or lower amperage rating be substituted.

SWITCHES & RELAYS

Switches are used in electrical circuits to control the passage of current. The most common use is to open and close circuits between the battery and the various electric devices in the system. Switches are rated according to the amount of amperage they can handle. If a sufficient amperage rated switch is not used in a circuit, the switch could overload and cause damage.

Some electrical components which require a large amount of current to operate use a special switch called a relay. Since these circuits carry a large

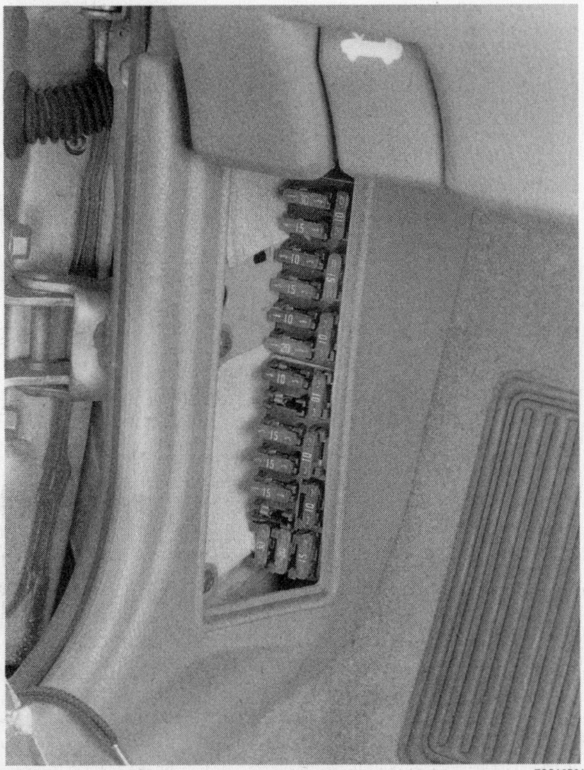

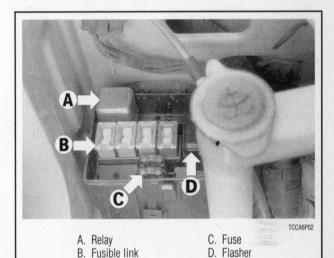

A. Relay   C. Fuse
B. Fusible link   D. Flasher

Fig. 23 The underhood fuse and relay panel usually contains fuses, relays, flashers and fusible links

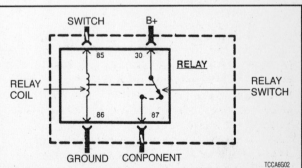

Fig. 24 Relays are composed of a coil and a switch. These two components are linked together so that when one operates, the other operates at the same time. The large wires in the circuit are connected from the battery to one side of the relay switch (B+) and from the opposite side of the relay switch to the load (component). Smaller wires are connected from the relay coil to the control switch for the circuit and from the opposite side of the relay coil to ground.

Fig. 22 Most vehicles use one or more fuse panels. This one is located in the driver's side kick panel

amount of current, the thickness of the wire in the circuit is also greater. If this large wire were connected from the load to the control switch on the dashboard, the switch would have to carry the high amperage load and the dash would be twice as large to accommodate the increased size of the wiring harness. To prevent these problems, a relay is used.

Relays are composed of a coil and a switch. These two components are linked together so that when one operates, the other operates at the same time. The large wires in the circuit are connected from the battery to one side of the relay switch and from the opposite side of the relay switch to the load. Most relays are normally open, preventing current from passing through the circuit. Additional, smaller wires are connected from the relay coil to the control switch for the circuit and from the opposite side of the relay coil to ground. When the control switch is turned on, it grounds the smaller wire to the relay coil, causing the coil to operate. The coil pulls the relay switch closed, sending power to the component without routing it through the inside of the vehicle. Some common circuits which may use relays are the horn, headlights, starter, electric fuel pump and rear window defogger systems.

LOAD

Every complete circuit must include a "load" (something to use the electricity coming from the source). Without this load, the battery would attempt to deliver its entire power supply from one pole to another. The electricity would take a short cut to ground and cause a great amount of damage to other components in the circuit by developing a tremendous amount of heat. This condition could develop sufficient heat to melt the insulation on all the surrounding wires and reduce a multiple wire cable to a lump of plastic and copper.

WIRING & HARNESSES

The average automobile contains about 1/2 mile of wiring, with hundreds of individual connections. To protect the many wires from damage and to keep them from becoming a confusing tangle, they are organized into bundles, enclosed in plastic or taped together and called wiring harnesses. Different harnesses serve different parts of the vehicle. Individual wires are color coded to help trace them through a harness where sections are hidden from view.

Automotive wiring or circuit conductors can be either single strand wire, multi-strand wire or printed circuitry. Single strand wire has a solid metal core and is usually used inside such components as alternators, motors, relays and other devices. Multi-strand wire has a core made of many small strands of wire twisted together into a single conductor. Most of the wiring in an automotive electrical system is made up of multi-strand wire, either as a single conductor or grouped together in a harness. All wiring is color coded on the insulator, either as a solid color or as a colored wire with an identification stripe. A printed circuit is a thin film of copper or other conductor that is printed on an insulator backing. Occasionally, a printed circuit is sandwiched between two sheets of plastic for more protection and flexibility. A complete printed circuit, consisting of conductors, insulating material and connectors for lamps or other components is called a printed circuit board. Printed circuitry is used in place of individual wires or harnesses in places where space is limited, such as behind instrument panels.

Since automotive electrical systems are very sensitive to changes in resistance, the selection of properly sized wires is critical when systems are repaired. A loose or corroded connection or a replacement wire that is too small for the circuit will add extra resistance and an additional voltage drop to the circuit.

The wire gauge number is an expression of the cross-section area of the conductor. The most common system for expressing wire size is the American Wire Gauge (AWG) system. As gauge number increases, area decreases and the wire becomes smaller. An 18 gauge wire is smaller than a 4 gauge wire. A wire with a higher gauge number will carry less current than a wire with a lower gauge number. Gauge wire size refers to the size of the strands of the conductor, not the size of the complete wire. It is possible, therefore, to have two wires of the same gauge with different diameters because one may have thicker insulation than the other.

12 volt automotive electrical systems generally use 10, 12, 14, 16 and 18 gauge wire. Main power distribution circuits and larger accessories usually use 10 and 12 gauge wire. Battery cables are usually 4 or 6 gauge, although 1 and 2 gauge wires are occasionally used.

It is essential to understand how a circuit works before trying to figure out why it doesn't. An electrical schematic shows the electrical current paths when a circuit is operating properly. Schematics break the entire electrical system down into individual circuits. In a schematic, no attempt is made to represent wiring and components as they physically appear on the vehicle; switches and other components are shown as simply as possible. Face views of harness connectors show the cavity or terminal locations in all multi-pin connectors to help locate test points.

CONNECTORS

Three types of connectors are commonly used in automotive applications—weatherproof, molded and hard shell.

• Weatherproof—these connectors are most commonly used in the engine compartment or where the connector is exposed to the elements. Terminals are protected against moisture and dirt by sealing rings which

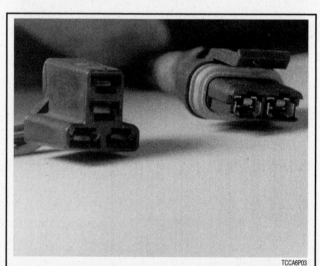

Fig. 25 Hard shell (left) and weatherproof (right) connectors have replaceable terminals

Fig. 26 Weatherproof connectors are most commonly used in the engine compartment or where the connector is exposed to the elements

provide a weathertight seal. All repairs require the use of a special terminal and the tool required to service it. Unlike standard blade type terminals, these weatherproof terminals cannot be straightened once they are bent. Make certain that the connectors are properly seated and all of the sealing rings are in place when connecting leads.

• Molded—these connectors require complete replacement of the connector if found to be defective. This means splicing a new connector assembly into the harness. All splices should be soldered to insure proper contact. Use care when probing the connections or replacing terminals in them, as it is possible to create a short circuit between opposite terminals. If this happens to the wrong terminal pair, it is possible to damage certain components. Always use jumper wires between connectors for circuit checking and NEVER probe through weatherproof seals.

• Hard Shell—unlike molded connectors, the terminal contacts in hard-shell connectors can be replaced. Replacement usually involves the use of a special terminal removal tool that depresses the locking tangs (barbs) on the connector terminal and allows the connector to be removed from the rear of the shell. The connector shell should be replaced if it shows any evidence of burning, melting, cracks, or breaks. Replace individual terminals that are burnt, corroded, distorted or loose.

Test Equipment

Pinpointing the exact cause of trouble in an electrical circuit is most times accomplished by the use of special test equipment. The following describes different types of commonly used test equipment and briefly explains how to use them in diagnosis. In addition to the information covered below, the tool manufacturer's instructions booklet (provided with the tester) should be read and clearly understood before attempting any test procedures.

JUMPER WIRES

✳✳ CAUTION

Never use jumper wires made from a thinner gauge wire than the circuit being tested. If the jumper wire is of too small a gauge, it may overheat and possibly melt. Never use jumpers to bypass high resistance loads in a circuit. Bypassing resistances, in effect, creates a short circuit. This may, in turn, cause damage and fire. Jumper wires should only be used to bypass lengths of wire.

Jumper wires are simple, yet extremely valuable, pieces of test equipment. They are basically test wires which are used to bypass sections of a circuit. Although jumper wires can be purchased, they are usually fabricated from lengths of standard automotive wire and whatever type of connector (alligator clip, spade connector or pin connector) that is required for the particular application being tested. In cramped, hard-to-reach areas, it is advisable to have insulated boots over the jumper wire terminals in order to prevent accidental grounding. It is also advisable to include a standard automotive fuse in any jumper wire. This is commonly referred to as a "fused jumper". By inserting an in-line fuse holder between a set of test leads, a fused jumper wire can be used for bypassing open circuits. Use a 5 amp fuse to provide protection against voltage spikes.

Jumper wires are used primarily to locate open electrical circuits, on either the ground (-) side of the circuit or on the power (+) side. If an electrical component fails to operate, connect the jumper wire between the component and a good ground. If the component operates only with the jumper installed, the ground circuit is open. If the ground circuit is good, but the component does not operate, the circuit between the power feed and component may be open. By moving the jumper wire successively back from the component toward the power source, you can isolate the area of the circuit where the open is located. When the component stops functioning, or the power is cut off, the open is in the segment of wire between the jumper and the point previously tested.

You can sometimes connect the jumper wire directly from the battery to the "hot" terminal of the component, but first make sure the component uses 12 volts in operation. Some electrical components, such as fuel injectors, are designed to operate on about 4 volts, and running 12 volts directly to these components will cause damage.

TEST LIGHTS

The test light is used to check circuits and components while electrical current is flowing through them. It is used for voltage and ground tests. To use a 12 volt test light, connect the ground clip to a good ground and probe wherever necessary with the pick. The test light will illuminate when voltage is detected. This does not necessarily mean that 12 volts (or any particular amount of voltage) is present; it only means that some voltage is present. It is advisable before using the test light to touch its ground clip and probe across the battery posts or terminals to make sure the light is operating properly.

✳✳ WARNING

Do not use a test light to probe electronic ignition spark plug or coil wires. Never use a pick-type test light to probe wiring on computer controlled systems unless specifically instructed to do so. Any wire insulation that is pierced by the test light probe should be taped and sealed with silicone after testing.

Like the jumper wire, the 12 volt test light is used to isolate opens in circuits. But, whereas the jumper wire is used to bypass the open to operate the load, the 12 volt test light is used to locate the presence of voltage in a circuit. If the test light illuminates, there is power up to that point in the circuit; if the test light does not illuminate, there is an open circuit (no power). Move the test light in successive steps back toward the power source until the light in the handle illuminates. The open is between the probe and a point which was previously probed.

The self-powered test light is similar in design to the 12 volt test light, but contains a 1.5 volt penlight battery in the handle. It is most often used in place of a multimeter to check for open or short circuits when power is isolated from the circuit (continuity test).

The battery in a self-powered test light does not provide much current. A weak battery may not provide enough power to illuminate the test light even when a complete circuit is made (especially if there is high resistance in the circuit). Always make sure that the test battery is strong. To check the battery, briefly touch the ground clip to the probe; if the light glows brightly, the battery is strong enough for testing.

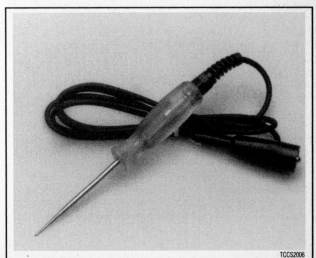

TCCS2006

Fig. 27 A 12 volt test light is used to detect the presence of voltage in a circuit

→A self-powered test light should not be used on any computer controlled system or component. The small amount of electricity transmitted by the test light is enough to damage many electronic automotive components.

MULTIMETERS

Multimeters are an extremely useful tool for troubleshooting electrical problems. They can be purchased in either analog or digital form and have a price range to suit any budget. A multimeter is a voltmeter, ammeter and ohmmeter (along with other features) combined into one instrument. It is often used when testing solid state circuits because of its high input impedance (usually 10 megaohms or more). A brief description of the multimeter main test functions follows:

• Voltmeter—the voltmeter is used to measure voltage at any point in a circuit, or to measure the voltage drop across any part of a circuit. Voltmeters usually have various scales and a selector switch to allow the reading of different voltage ranges. The voltmeter has a positive and a negative lead. To avoid damage to the meter, always connect the negative lead to the negative (-) side of the circuit (to ground or nearest the ground side of the circuit) and connect the positive lead to the positive (+) side of the circuit (to the power source or the nearest power source). Note that the negative voltmeter lead will always be black and that the positive voltmeter will always be some color other than black (usually red).

• Ohmmeter—the ohmmeter is designed to read resistance (measured in ohms) in a circuit or component. All ohmmeters will have a selector switch which permits the measurement of different ranges of resistance (usually the selector switch allows the multiplication of the meter reading by 10, 100, 1,000 and 10,000). Since the meters are powered by an internal battery, the ohmmeter can be used as a self-powered test light. When the ohmmeter is connected, current from the ohmmeter flows through the circuit or component being tested. Since the ohmmeter's internal resistance and voltage are known values, the amount of current flow through the meter depends on the resistance of the circuit or component being tested. The ohmmeter can also be used to perform a continuity test for suspected open circuits. In using the meter for making continuity checks, do not be concerned with the actual resistance readings. Zero resistance, or any ohm reading, indicates continuity in the circuit. Infinite resistance indicates an opening in the circuit. A high resistance reading where there should be none indicates a problem in the circuit. Checks for short circuits are made in the same manner as checks for open circuits, except that the circuit must be isolated from both power and normal ground. Infinite resistance indicates no continuity to ground, while zero resistance indicates a dead short to ground.

✵ WARNING

Never use an ohmmeter to check the resistance of a component or wire while there is voltage applied to the circuit.

• Ammeter—an ammeter measures the amount of current flowing through a circuit in units called amperes or amps. At normal operating voltage, most circuits have a characteristic amount of amperes, called "current draw" which can be measured using an ammeter. By referring to a specified current draw rating, then measuring the amperes and comparing the two values, one can determine what is happening within the circuit to aid in diagnosis. An open circuit, for example, will not allow any current to flow, so the ammeter reading will be zero. A damaged component or circuit will have an increased current draw, so the reading will be high. The ammeter is always connected in series with the circuit being tested. All of the current that normally flows through the circuit must also flow through the ammeter; if there is any other path for the current to follow, the ammeter reading will not be accurate. The ammeter itself has very little resistance to current flow and, therefore, will not affect the circuit, but it will measure current draw only when the circuit is closed and electricity is flowing. Excessive current draw can blow fuses and drain the battery, while a reduced current draw can cause motors to run slowly, lights to dim and other components to not operate properly.

Troubleshooting Electrical Systems

When diagnosing a specific problem, organized troubleshooting is a must. The complexity of a modern automotive vehicle demands that you approach any problem in a logical, organized manner. There are certain troubleshooting techniques which are standard:

• Establish when the problem occurs. Does the problem appear only under certain conditions? Were there any noises, odors or other unusual symptoms?

• Isolate the problem area. To do this, make some simple tests and observations, then eliminate the systems that are working properly. Check for obvious problems, such as broken wires and loose or dirty connections. Always check the obvious before assuming something complicated is the cause.

• Test for problems systematically to determine the cause once the problem area is isolated. Are all the components functioning properly? Is there power going to electrical switches and motors. Performing careful, systematic checks will often turn up most causes on the first inspection, without wasting time checking components that have little or no relationship to the problem.

• Test all repairs after the work is done to make sure that the problem is fixed. Some causes can be traced to more than one component, so a careful verification of repair work is important in order to pick up additional malfunctions that may cause a problem to reappear or a different problem to arise. A blown fuse, for example, is a simple problem that may require more than another fuse to repair. If you don't look for a problem that caused a fuse to blow, a shorted wire (for example) may go undetected.

Experience has shown that most problems tend to be the result of a fairly simple and obvious cause, such as loose or corroded connectors, bad grounds or damaged wire insulation which causes a short. This makes careful visual inspection of components during testing essential to quick and accurate troubleshooting.

Testing

OPEN CIRCUITS

1. Isolate the circuit from power and ground.
2. Connect the self-powered test light or ohmmeter ground clip to a good ground and probe sections of the circuit sequentially.
3. If the light is out or there is infinite resistance, the open is between the probe and the circuit ground.
4. If the light is on or the meter shows continuity, the open is between the probe and end of the circuit toward the power source.

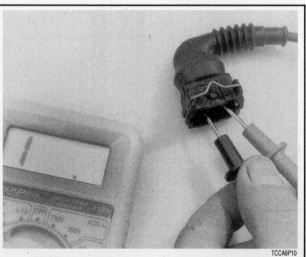

TCCA6P10

Fig. 28 The infinite reading on this multimeter (1 .) indicates that the circuit is open

SHORT CIRCUITS

➡ **Never use a self-powered test light to perform checks for opens or shorts when power is applied to the electrical system under test. The 12 volt vehicle power will quickly burn out the light bulb in the test light.**

1. Isolate the circuit from power and ground.
2. Connect the self-powered test light or ohmmeter ground clip to a good ground and probe any easy-to-reach test point in the circuit.
3. If the light comes on or there is continuity, there is a short somewhere in the circuit.
4. To isolate the short, probe a test point at either end of the isolated circuit (the light should be on or the meter should indicate continuity).
5. Leave the test light probe engaged and sequentially open connectors or switches, remove parts, etc. until the light goes out or continuity is broken.
6. When the light goes out, the short is between the last two circuit components which were opened.

VOLTAGE

This test determines voltage available from the battery and should be the first step in any electrical troubleshooting procedure. Many electrical prob-

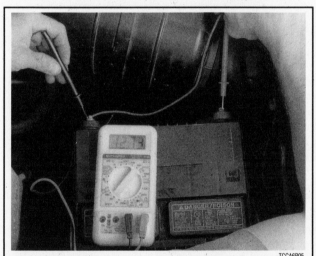

Fig. 29 Using a multimeter to check battery voltage. This battery is fully charged

Fig. 30 Testing voltage output between the alternator's BAT terminal and ground. This voltage reading is normal

lems, especially on computer controlled systems, can be caused by a low state of charge in the battery. Excessive corrosion at the battery cable terminals can cause poor contact that will prevent proper charging and full battery current flow.

1. Set the voltmeter selector switch to the 20V position.
2. Connect the multimeter negative lead to the battery's negative (-) post or terminal and the positive lead to the battery's positive (+) post or terminal.
3. Turn the ignition switch **ON** to provide a load.
4. A well charged battery should register over 12 volts. If the meter reads below 11.5 volts, the battery power may be insufficient to operate the electrical system properly.

VOLTAGE DROP

When current flows through a load, the voltage beyond the load drops. This voltage drop is due to the resistance created by the load and also by small resistances created by corrosion at the connectors and damaged insulation on the wires. The maximum allowable voltage drop under load is critical, especially if there is more than one load in the circuit, since all voltage drops are cumulative.

1. Set the voltmeter selector switch to the 20 volt position.
2. Connect the multimeter negative lead to a good ground.
3. Operate the circuit and check the voltage prior to the first component (load).
4. There should be little or no voltage drop in the circuit prior to the first component. If a voltage drop exists, the wire or connectors in the circuit are suspect.
5. While operating the first component in the circuit, probe the ground side of the component with the positive meter lead and observe the voltage readings. A small voltage drop should be noticed. This voltage drop is caused by the resistance of the component.
6. Repeat the test for each component (load) down the circuit.
7. If a large voltage drop is noticed, the preceding component, wire or connector is suspect.

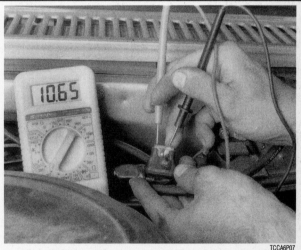

Fig. 31 This voltage drop test revealed high resistance (low voltage) in the circuit

RESISTANCE

WARNING

Never use an ohmmeter with power applied to the circuit. The ohmmeter is designed to operate on its own power supply. The normal 12 volt automotive electrical system current could damage the meter!

TCCA6P08

Fig. 32 Checking the resistance of a coolant temperature sensor with an ohmmeter. Reading is 1.04 kilohms

1. Isolate the circuit from the vehicle's power source.
2. Ensure that the ignition key is **OFF** when disconnecting any components or the battery.
3. Where necessary, also isolate at least one side of the circuit to be checked, in order to avoid reading parallel resistances. Parallel circuit resistances will always give a lower reading than the actual resistance of either of the branches.
4. Connect the meter leads to both sides of the circuit (wire or component) and read the actual measured ohms on the meter scale. Make sure the selector switch is set to the proper ohm scale for the circuit being tested, to avoid misreading the ohmmeter test value.

Wire and Connector Repair

Almost anyone can replace damaged wires, as long as the proper tools and parts are available. Automotive wire and terminals are available to fit almost any need. Even the specialized weatherproof, molded and hard shell connectors are now available from aftermarket suppliers.

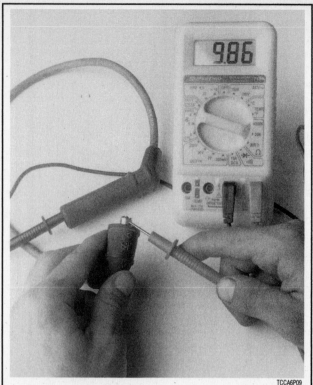

TCCA6P09

Fig. 33 Spark plug wires can be checked for excessive resistance using an ohmmeter

Be sure the ends of all the wires are fitted with the proper terminal hardware and connectors. Wrapping a wire around a stud is never a permanent solution and will only cause trouble later. Replace wires one at a time to avoid confusion. Always route wires exactly the same as the factory.

→**If connector repair is necessary, only attempt it if you have the proper tools. Weatherproof and hard shell connectors require special tools to release the pins inside the connector. Attempting to repair these connectors with conventional hand tools will damage them.**

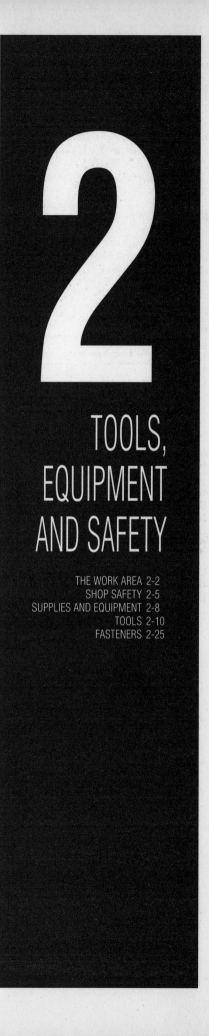

2

TOOLS, EQUIPMENT AND SAFETY

THE WORK AREA

Floor Space and Working Height

The average one car garage will give you more than enough workspace. A floor plan of 16 ft. X 12 ft. is more than sufficient for shelving, workbenches, tool shelves or boxes and parts storage areas. 12 X 16 works out to 192 square feet. You may think that this sounds like a lot of room, but when you start building shelves, and constructing work benches almost most half of that can be eaten up!

Also, you may wonder why a lot of floor space is needed. There are several reasons, not the least of which is the safety factor. You'll be working around a large, heavy, metal object—your vehicle. You don't want to be tripping, falling, crashing into things or hurting yourself, all because your vehicle takes up most of your work space. Accidents can happen! You can easily trip over a jack handle or work stand leg or drop a heavy part or tool. You'll need room to take evasive action!

Fig. 2 Typical homemade wood shelves, crammed with stuff. These shelves are made from spare $5/4$ x 6 in. pressure treated decking

TCCA1P18

Fig. 1 Example of an engine stand—you won't need it for brake work, but they're great to have around

Most garages have concrete floors. Your creeper rolls best on a smooth surface. If your garage floor has cracks with raised sections or blocks with deep grooves, you may have a problem. The wheels can hang up on these cracks or grooves causing you to get stuck under the vehicle.

As for working height, overhead clearance is a problem, only if you have a tall vehicle, such as an RV or sport utility vehicle, or, if you're doing more than brake work. If doing engine work, for example, you might need an engine crane. To lift an engine from or install an engine in a vehicle, the crane cane needs as much as 10 ft. overhead.

87933020

Fig. 3 Modular plastic shelves, such as these are inexpensive, weatherproof and easy to assemble

Storage Areas

SHELVES

You can't have enough shelf space. Adequate shelf space means that you don't have to stack anything on the floor, where it would be in the way.

Shelves aren't tough. You can make your own or buy modular or prefab units. The best modular units are those made of interlocking shelves and uprights of ABS plastic. They're lightweight and easy to assemble, and their load-bearing capacity is more than sufficient. Also, they are not subject rust or rot as are wood and metal shelves.

Probably the cheapest and best shelves are ones that you make yourself from one inch shelving with 2 X 4 uprights. You can make them as long, wide and high as you want. For at least the uprights, use pressure treated wood. Its resistance to rot is more than worth the additional cost.

TOOL CHESTS

There are many types and sizes of tool chests. Their greatest advantage is that they can hold a lot of tools, securely, in a relatively small area. If you decide that you need one, make sure that you buy one that's big enough and mobile enough for the work area. Remember, you get what you pay for, so purchase a good brand name, and it should last a lifetime.

Fig. 4 These shelves were made from the frame of old kitchen cabinets

There are several things to look for in a tool chest, depending on how much you plan on using it, and just how many tools you plan to stuff in it. Check the overall construction. In general, bolted-together chests are stronger than riveted or tabbed, because they are sturdier. Drawers that ride on ball bearings are better than compound slide drawers, because they can hold more and are easier to open/close. Heavy-duty, ball bearing casters are better than bushing type wheels, because they will roll better and last longer. Steel wheels are better than plastic, as they are less prone to damage. Compare different boxes, you'll have to make up your own mind exactly what style is best for you.

Fig. 5 Different types of mobile, steel tool chests

Fig. 6 A good tool chest has several drawers, each designed to hold a different type tool

WORK BENCHES

As with the shelving, work benches can be either store-bought or home-made. The store-bought workbenches can be steel or precut wood kits. Either are fine and are available at most building supply stores or through tool catalogs.

Homemade benches, as with the shelves have the advantage of being made-to-fit your workshop. A freestanding workbench is best, as opposed to one attached to an outside wall. The freestanding bench can take more abuse since it doesn't transfer the shock or vibration to wall supports.

A good free-standing workbench should be constructed using 4 X 4 pressure treated wood as legs, 2 X 6 planking as header boards and ¾ inch plywood sheathing as a deck. Diagonal supports can be 2 X 4 studs and it's always helpful to construct a full size ¾ inch plywood shelf under the bench. Not only can you use the shelf for storage but also it gives great rigidity to the whole bench structure. Assembling the bench with screws rather than nails takes longer but adds strength and gives you the ability to take the whole thing apart if you ever want to move it.

87933023

Fig. 8 At least two of this type of twin tube fluorescent light is essential

87933512

Fig. 7 Homemade workbenches

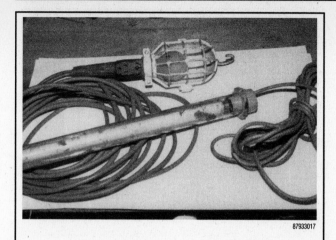

Fig. 9 Two types of droplights. Incandescent and fluorescent

LIGHTING

The importance of adequate lighting can't be over emphasized. Good lighting is not only a convenience but also a safety feature. If you can see what you're working on you're less likely to make mistakes, have a wrench slip or trip over an obstacle. On most vehicles, everything is about the same color and usually dirty. During disassembly, a lot of frustration can be avoided if you can see all the bolts, some of which may be hidden or obscured.

For overhead lighting, at least 2 twin tube 36 inch fluorescent shop lights should be in place. Most garages are wired with standard light bulbs attached to the wall studs at intervals. Four or five of these lights, at about a 6 foot height combined with the overhead lighting should suffice. However, no matter where the lights are, your body is going to block some of it so a droplight or clip-on type work light is a great idea. These lights can be mounted on the engine stand, or even the engine itself.

VENTILATION

At one time or another, you'll be working with chemicals that may require adequate ventilation. Now, just about all garages have a big car-sized door and all sheds or workshops have a door. In bad weather the door will have to be closed so at least one window that opens is a necessity. An exhaust fan or regular ventilation fan is a great help, especially in hot weather.

HEATERS

If you live in an area where the winters are cold, as do many of us, it's nice to have some sort of heat where we work. If your workshop or garage is attached to the house, you'll probably be okay. If your garage or shop is detached, then a space heater of some sort—electric, propane or kerosene—will be necessary. NEVER run a space heater in the presence of flammable vapors! When running a non-electric space heater, always allow for some means of venting the carbon monoxide!

ELECTRICAL REQUIREMENTS

Obviously, your workshop should be wired according to all local codes. As to what type of service you need, that depends on your electrical load. If you have a lot of power equipment and maybe a refrigerator, TV, stereo or whatever, not only do you have a great shop, but your amperage requirements may exceed your wiring's capacity. If you are at all in doubt, consult your local electrical contractor.

SHOP SAFETY

It is virtually impossible to anticipate all of the hazards involved with automotive maintenance and service but care and common sense will prevent most accidents.

The rules of safety for mechanics range from "don't smoke around gasoline" to "use the proper tool for the job." The trick to avoiding injuries is to develop safe work habits and take every possible precaution.

Do's

• Do keep a fire extinguisher and first aid kit handy.
• Do wear safety glasses or goggles when cutting, drilling, grinding or prying, even if you have 20–20 vision. If you wear glasses for the sake of vision, wear safety goggles over your regular glasses.

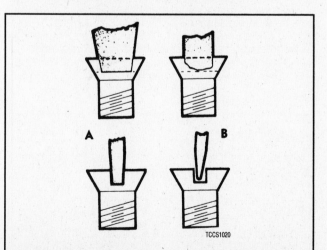

Fig. 10 Screwdrivers should be kept in good condition to prevent injury or damage that could result if the blade slips from the screw

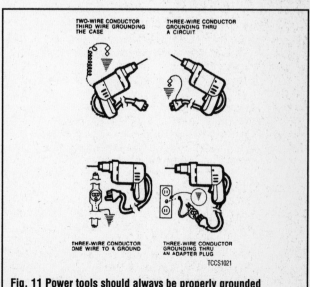

Fig. 11 Power tools should always be properly grounded

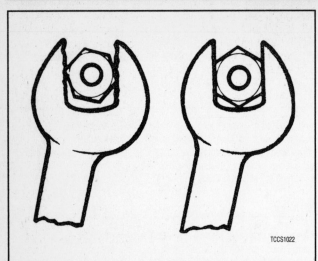

Fig. 12 Using the correct size wrench will help prevent the possibility of rounding-off a nut

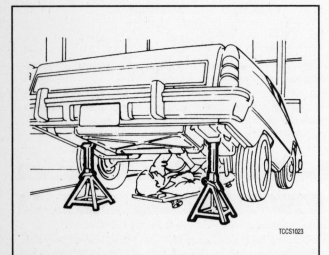

Fig. 13 NEVER work under a vehicle unless it is supported using safety stands (jackstands)

• Do shield your eyes whenever you work around the battery. Batteries contain sulfuric acid. In case of contact with the eyes or skin, flush the area with water or a mixture of water and baking soda, then seek immediate medical attention.

• Do use safety stands (jackstands) for any undervehicle service. Jacks are for raising vehicles; jackstands are for making sure the vehicle stays raised until you want it to come down. Whenever the vehicle is raised, block the wheels remaining on the ground and set the parking brake.

• Do use adequate ventilation when working with any chemicals or hazardous materials. Like carbon monoxide, the asbestos dust resulting from some brake lining wear can be hazardous in sufficient quantities.

• Do disconnect the negative battery cable when working on the electrical system. The secondary ignition system contains EXTREMELY HIGH VOLTAGE. In some cases it can even exceed 50,000 volts.

• Do follow manufacturer's directions whenever working with potentially hazardous materials. Most chemicals and fluids are poisonous if taken internally.

• Do properly maintain your tools. Loose hammerheads, mushroomed punches and chisels, frayed or poorly grounded electrical cords, excessively worn screwdrivers, spread wrenches (open end), cracked sockets, slipping ratchets, or faulty droplight sockets can cause accidents.

• Likewise, keep your tools clean; a greasy wrench can slip off a bolt head, ruining the bolt and often harming your knuckles in the process.

• Do use the proper size and type of tool for the job at hand. Do select a wrench or socket that fits the nut or bolt. The wrench or socket should sit straight, not cocked.

• Do, when possible, pull on a wrench handle rather than push on it, and adjust your stance to prevent a fall.

• Do be sure that adjustable wrenches are tightly closed on the nut or bolt and pulled so that the force is on the side of the fixed jaw.

• Do strike squarely with a hammer; avoid glancing blows.

• Do set the parking brake and block the drive wheels if the work requires a running engine.

Don'ts

• Don't run the engine in a garage or anywhere else without proper ventilation—EVER! Carbon monoxide is poisonous; it takes a long time to leave the human body and you can build up a deadly supply of it in your system by simply breathing in a little every day. You may not realize you are slowly poisoning yourself. Always use power vents, windows, fans and/or open the garage door.

• Don't work around moving parts while wearing loose clothing. Short sleeves are much safer than long, loose sleeves. Hard-toed shoes with neoprene soles protect your toes and give a better grip on slippery surfaces. Jewelry such as watches, fancy belt buckles, beads or body adornment of any kind is not safe working around a vehicle. Long hair should be tied back under a hat or cap.

• Don't use pockets for toolboxes. A fall or bump can drive a screwdriver deep into your body. Even a rag hanging from your back pocket can wrap around a spinning shaft or fan.

• Don't smoke when working around gasoline, cleaning solvent or other flammable material.

• Don't smoke when working around the battery. When the battery is being charged, it gives off explosive hydrogen gas.

• Don't use gasoline to wash your hands; there are excellent soaps available. Gasoline contains dangerous additives which can enter the body through a cut or through your pores. Gasoline also removes all the natural oils from the skin so that bone dry hands will suck up oil and grease.

• Don't service the air conditioning system unless you are equipped with the necessary tools and training. When liquid or compressed gas refrigerant is released to atmospheric pressure it will absorb heat from whatever it contacts. This will chill or freeze anything it touches. Although refrigerant is normally non-toxic, R-12 becomes a deadly poisonous gas in the presence of an open flame. One good whiff of the vapors from burning refrigerant can be fatal.

• Don't use screwdrivers for anything other than driving screws! A screwdriver used as a prying tool can snap when you least expect it, causing injuries. At the very least, you'll ruin a good screwdriver.

• Don't use a bumper or emergency jack (that little ratchet, scissors, or pantograph jack supplied with the vehicle) for anything other than changing a flat! These jacks are only intended for emergency use out on the road; they are NOT designed as a maintenance tool. If you are serious about maintaining your vehicle yourself, invest in a hydraulic floor jack of at least a 1½ ton capacity, and at least two sturdy jackstands.

SAFETY EQUIPMENT

Fire Extinguishers

There are many types of safety equipment. The most important of these is the fire extinguisher. You'll be well off with two 5 lbs. extinguishers rated for oil, chemical and wood.

First Aid

Next you'll need a good first aid kit. Any good kit that can be purchased from the local drug store will be fine. It's a good idea, in addition, to have something easily accessible in the event of a minor injury, such a hydrogen peroxide or other antiseptic that can be poured onto or applied to a wound immediately. Remember, your hands will be dirty. Just as you wouldn't want dirt entering a brake system that has been opened, you certainly don't want bacteria entering a blood stream that has just been opened!

Fig. 14 Three essential pieces of safety equipment. Left to right: ear protectors, safety goggles and respirator

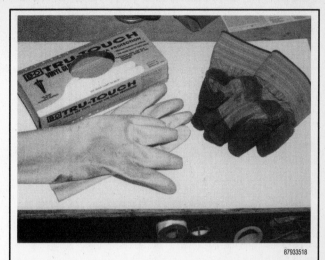

Fig. 16 Three different types of work gloves. The box contains latex gloves

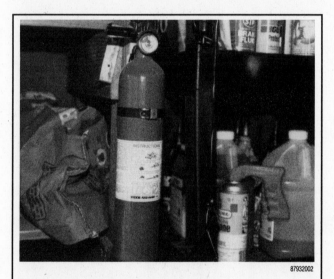

Fig. 15 A good, all-purpose fire extinguisher

Work Gloves

Unless you think scars on your hands are cool, enjoy pain and like wearing bandages, get a good pair of work gloves. Canvass or leather are the best. And yes, we realize that there are some jobs involving small parts that can't be done while wearing work gloves. These jobs are not the ones usually associated with hand injuries.

A good pair of rubber gloves such as those usually associated with dish washing is also a great idea. There are some liquids such as solvents and penetrants that don't belong on your skin. Avoid burns and rashes. Wear these gloves.

And lastly, an option. If you're tired of being greasy and dirty all the time, go to the drug store and buy a box of disposable latex gloves like medical professionals wear. You can handle greasy parts, perform small tasks, wash parts, etc. all without getting dirty! These gloves take a surprising amount of abuse without tearing and aren't expensive. Note however, that it has been reported that some people are allergic to the latex or the powder used inside the gloves.

Work Boots

It's up to you, but I think that a good, comfortable pair of steel-toed work boots is a sensible idea. Primarily because heavy parts always get dropped sooner or later. A brake rotor or drum can do significant damage to a sneaker-clad foot.

Good work boots also provide better support,—you're going to be on your feet a lot—are oil-resistant, and they keep your feet warm and dry.

To keep the boots protected, get a spray can of silicone-based water repellent and spray the boots when new, and periodically thereafter.

Eye Protection

Don't begin this, or for that matter, any job without a good pair of work goggles or impact resistant glasses! When doing any kind of work, it's all too easy to avoid eye injury through this simple precaution. And don't just buy eye protection and leave it on the shelf. Wear it all the time! Things have a habit of breaking, chipping, splashing, spraying, splintering and flying around. And, for some reason, your eye is always in the way!

If you wear vision correcting glasses as a matter of routine, get a pair made with polycarbonate lenses. These lenses are impact resistant and are available at any optometrist.

Ear Protection

Often overlooked is hearing protection. Power equipment is noisy! Loud noises damage your ears. It's as simple as that!

The simplest and cheapest form of ear protection is a pair of noise-reducing ear plugs. Cheap insurance for your ears. And, they even come with their own, cute little carrying case.

More substantial, more protection and more money is a good pair of noise reducing earmuffs. They protect from all but the loudest sounds. Hopefully those are sounds that you'll never encounter since they're usually associated with disasters or rock concerts.

Work Clothes

Everyone has "work clothes". Usually this consists of old jeans and a shirt that has seen better days. That's fine. In addition, a denim work apron is a nice accessory. It's rugged, can hold some tools, and you don't feel bad wiping your hands or tools on it. That's what it's for.

If you're so inclined, overalls are a superb work garment. They're rugged and are equipped with numerous pockets, loops and places to put stuff. When bending or reaching, you won't have to worry about your shirt pulling out. Also, they cover your shirt like a work apron.

When working in cold weather, a one-piece, thermal work outfit is invaluable. Most are rated to below zero (Fahrenheit) temperatures and are ruggedly constructed.

Jacking

Your vehicle was supplied with a jack for emergency road repairs. This jack is fine for changing a flat tire or other short term procedures not requiring you to go beneath the vehicle. If it is used in an emergency situation, carefully follow the instructions provided either with the jack or in your owner's manual. Do not attempt to use the jack on any portions of the vehicle other than specified by the vehicle manufacturer. Always block the diagonally opposite wheel when using a jack.

A more convenient way of jacking is the use of a garage or floor jack.

Never place the jack under the radiator, engine or transmission components. Severe and expensive damage will result when the jack is raised. Additionally, never jack under the floorpan or bodywork; the metal will deform.

Whenever you plan to work under the vehicle, you must support it on jackstands or ramps. Never use cinder blocks or stacks of wood to support the vehicle, even if you're only going to be under it for a few minutes. Never crawl under the vehicle when it is supported only by the tire-changing jack or other floor jack.

➡**Always position a block of wood or small rubber pad on top of the jack or jackstand to protect the lifting point's finish when lifting or supporting the vehicle.**

Small hydraulic, screw, or scissors jacks are satisfactory for raising the vehicle. Drive-on trestles or ramps are also a handy and safe way to both raise and support the vehicle. Be careful though, some ramps may be too steep to drive your vehicle onto without scraping the front bottom panels.

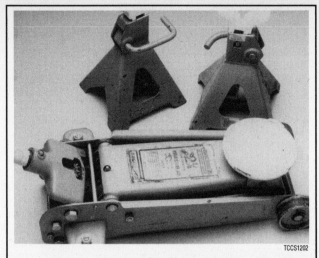

TCCS1202

Fig. 17 Do yourself a favor, if you plan to work on your vehicle, buy a good quality floor jack and set of jackstands

Never support the vehicle on any suspension member (unless specifically instructed to do so by a repair manual) or by an underbody panel.

JACKING PRECAUTIONS

The following safety points cannot be overemphasized:
• Always block the opposite wheel or wheels to keep the vehicle from rolling off the jack.
• When raising the front of the vehicle, firmly apply the parking brake.
• When the drive wheels are to remain on the ground, leave the vehicle in gear to help prevent it from rolling.
• Always use jackstands to support the vehicle when you are working underneath. Place the stands beneath the vehicle's jacking brackets. Before climbing underneath, rock the vehicle a bit to make sure it is firmly supported.

SUPPLIES AND EQUIPMENT

Fluid Disposal

Used fluids such as engine oil, transmission fluid, antifreeze and brake fluid are hazardous wastes and must be disposed of properly. Before draining any fluids, consult with your local authorities; in many areas waste oil, etc. is being accepted as a part of recycling programs. A number of service stations and auto parts stores are also accepting waste fluids for recycling.

Be sure of the recycling center's policies before draining any fluids, as many will not accept different fluids that have been mixed together.

Chemicals

There is a whole range of chemicals that you'll need. The most common types are, lubricants, penetrants and sealers. Keep these handy, on some convenient shelf.

When a particular chemical is not being used, keep it capped, upright and in a safe place. These substances may be flammable or irritants or caustic and should always be stored properly, used properly and handled with care. Always read and follow all label directions and wear hand and eye protection!

LUBRICANTS & PENETRANTS

In this category, a well-prepared automotive shop should have:
• Clean engine oil. Whatever you use regularly in your engine will be fine.
• Lithium grease.
• Chassis lube

87933516

Fig. 18 A variety of penetrants and lubricants is a staple of any DIYer's garage

- Assembly lube
- Silicone grease
- Silicone spray
- Penetrating oil

Clean engine oil is used to coat most bolts, screws and nuts prior to installation. This is always a good practice since the less friction there is on a fastener, the less chance there will be of breakage and crossthreading. Also, an oiled bolt will give a truer torque value and be less likely to rust or seize. An obvious exception would be wheel lugs. These are not oiled.

Lithium grease, chassis lube, silicone grease or a synthetic brake caliper grease can all be used pretty much interchangeably. All can be used for coating rust-prone fasteners and for facilitating the assembly of parts that are a tight fit. Silicone and synthetic greases are the most versatile and should always be used on the sliding areas of slider-type calipers or on the pins with pin-type calipers. It's also a good lubricant for the mounting pads on drum-type brake backing plates. The main advantages of silicone grease are that it's slipperier than most similar lubricants and it has a higher melting point. You don't want a grease melting and possibly contaminating the friction surfaces of your brakes.

➡**Silicone dielectric grease is a non-conductor that is often used to coat the terminals of wiring connectors before fastening them. It may sound odd to coat metal portions of a terminal with something that won't conduct electricity, but here is it how it works. When the connector is fastened the metal-to-metal contact between the terminals will displace the grease (allowing the circuit to be completed). The grease that is displaced will then coat the non-contacted surface and the cavity around the terminals, SEALING them from atmospheric moisture that could cause corrosion.**

Silicone spray is a good lubricant for hard-to-reach places and parts that shouldn't be gooped up with grease.

Penetrating oil may turn out to be one of your best friends during disassembly. The most familiar penetrating oils are Liquid Wrench® and WD-40®. These products have hundreds of uses. For your purposes, they are vital!

Before disassembling any part, check the fasteners. If any appear rusted, soak them thoroughly with the penetrant and let them stand while you do something else. This simple act can save you hours of tedious work trying to extract a broken bolt or stud.

Engine assembly lube. There are several types of this product available. Essentially it is a heavy-bodied lubricant used for coating moving parts prior to assembly. For engine work, the idea is that is stays in place until the engine starts for the first time and dissolves in the engine oil as oil pressure is achieved. This way, expensive parts receive needed protection until everything is working. For non-engine work, it comes in handy for assembling tight-fitting parts.

SEALANTS

Sealants are an indispensable part of almost all automotive work. The purpose of sealants is to establish a leak-proof bond between or around assembled parts. Most sealers are used in conjunction with gaskets, but some are used instead of conventional gasket material in newer engines.

The most common sealers are the non-hardening types such as Permatex® No.2 or its equivalents. These sealers are applied to the mating surfaces of each part to be joined, then a gasket is put in place and the parts are assembled.

One very helpful type of non-hardening sealer is the "high tack" type. This type is a very sticky material that holds the gasket in place while the parts are being assembled. This stuff is really a good idea when you don't have enough hands or fingers to keep everything where it should be.

The stand-alone sealers are the Room Temperature Vulcanizing (RTV) silicone gasket makers. On many newer vehicles, this material is used instead of a gasket. In those instances, a gasket may not be available or,

Fig. 19 Sealants are essential. These four types are all that you'll need

because of the shape of the mating surfaces, a gasket shouldn't be used. This stuff, when used in conjunction with a conventional gasket, produces the surest bonds.

It does have its limitations though. When using this material, you will have a time limit. It starts to set-up within 15 minutes or so, so you have to assemble the parts without delay. In addition, when squeezing the material out of the tube, don't drop any glops into the engine. The stuff will form and set and travel around the oil gallery, possibly plugging up a passage. Also, most types are not fuel-proof. Check the tube for all cautions.

CLEANERS

You'll have two types of cleaners to deal with: parts cleaners and hand cleaners. The parts cleaners are for the vehicle; the hand cleaners are for you.

There are many good, non-flammable, biodegradable parts cleaners on the market. These cleaning agents are safe for you, the parts and the environment. Therefore, there is no reason to use flammable, caustic or toxic substances to clean your parts or tools.

As far as hand cleaners go, the waterless types are the best. They have always been efficient at cleaning, but left behind a pretty smelly odor.

Fig. 20 Three types of cleaners. Some are caustic; some are not. Always read and follow label instructions

Fig. 21 This is one type of hand cleaner that not only works well but smells pretty good too

Fig. 22 The best thing to clean up all types of spills is "kitty litter"

Recently though, just about all of them have eliminated the odor and added stuff that actually smells good. Make sure that you pick one that contains lanolin or some other moisture-replenishing additive. Cleaners not only remove grease and oil but also skin oil.

One other note: most women know this already but most men don't. Use a hand lotion when you're all cleaned up. It's okay. Real men DO use hand lotion!

SHOP TOWELS

One of the most important elements in doing shop work is a good supply of shop towels. Paper towels just don't cut it! Most auto parts stores sell packs of shop towels, usually 50-100 in a pack. They are relatively cheap and can be washed over and over. Always keep them handy.

One of the best shop towels known to science, is the old-fashioned cloth diaper. They're highly absorbent and rugged, but, in these days of disposable diapers, are hard to find.

Fig. 23 A pack of shop towels

TOOLS

Every do-it-yourselfer loves to accumulate tools. So gathering the tools necessary for engine work can be real fun!

When buying tools, the saying "You get what you pay for" is absolutely true! Don't go cheap! Any hand tool that you buy should be drop forged and/or chrome vanadium. These two qualities tell you that the tool is strong enough for the job. With any tool, power or not, go with a name that you've heard of before, or, that is recommended buy your local professional retailer. Let's go over a list of tools that you'll need.

Most of the world uses the metric system. So, if you have an imported vehicle, you can be pretty certain that it was built with metric fasteners and put together using metric measured clearances and adjustments.

In the United States, most people still use the English system, which nowadays should be called the U.S. system. However, if your U.S. made vehicle was built after 1980, most, if not all, of the fasteners and measurements are metric.

So, accumulate your tools accordingly. Any good DIYer should have a good set of both U.S. and metric measure tools. Don't be confused by terminology. Most advertising refers to "SAE and metric", or "standard and metric". Both are misnomers. The Society of Automotive Engineers (SAE) did not invent the English system of measurement; the English did. The SAE likes metrics just fine. Both English (U.S.) and metric measurements are SAE approved. Also, the current "standard" measurement in automotive building IS metric. So, if it's not metric, it's U.S. measurement.

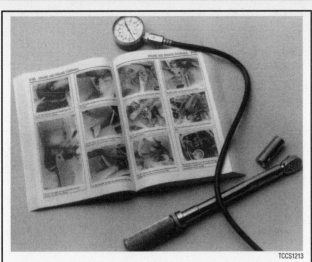

TCCS1213

Fig. 24 The most important tool you need to do the job is the proper information, so always have a Chilton manual handy

Hands Tools

SOCKET SETS

Socket sets are the most basic, necessary hand tools for automotive work. For our purposes, socket sets basically come in three drive sizes: ¼ inch, ⅜ inch and ½ inch. Drive size refers to the size of the drive lug on the ratchet, breaker bar or speed handle.

You'll need a good ½ inch set since this size drive lug assure that you won't break a ratchet or socket. Also, torque wrenches with a torque scale high enough are usually ½ inch drive. The socket set that you'll need should range in sizes from ⁷/₁₆ inch through 1 inch for older American models, or 6mm through 19mm on imports and late-model American vehicles.

A ⅜ set is very handy to have since it allows you to get into tight places that the larger drive ratchets can't. Also, this size set gives you a range of smaller sockets that are still strong enough for heavy duty work.

¼ inch drive sets aren't usually necessary or applicable for brake work, but they're good to have for other, light work around the vehicle or house. Besides, they're tools . . . you NEED them!

As for the sockets themselves, they come in standard and deep lengths as well as standard and thin walled, in either 6 or 12 point.

87932513

Fig. 25 The well-stocked garage pegboard. Pegboards can store most tools and other equipment for ease of access. Besides, they're cool looking

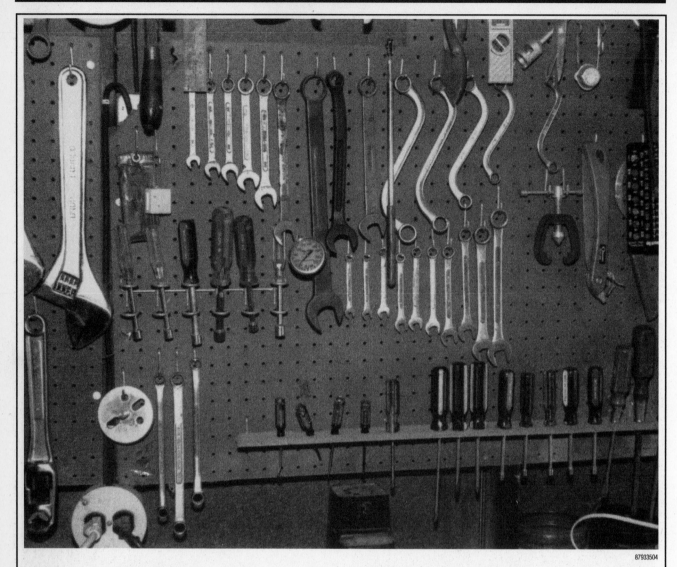

87933504

Fig. 26 You can arrange the pegboard any way you like, but it's best to hang the most used tools closest to you

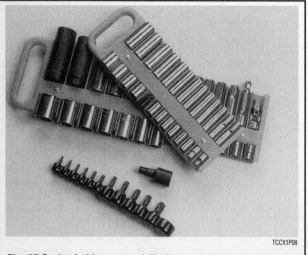

TCCX1P08

Fig. 27 Socket holders, especially the magnetic type, are handy items to keep tools in order

87932007

Fig. 28 A good set of handy storage cabinets for fasteners and small parts makes any job easier

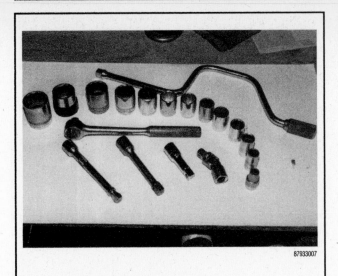
Fig. 29 A good half inch drive socket set

Fig. 32 Two types of drive adapters and a swivel (U-joint) adapter

Fig. 30 Left, a hex drive socket; right, a Torx® drive socket

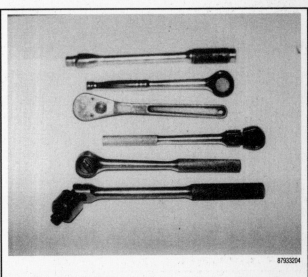
Fig. 33 Ratchets come in all sizes from rigid to swivel-headed

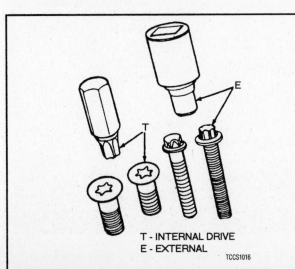

T - INTERNAL DRIVE
E - EXTERNAL

TCCS1016

Fig. 31 Internal and external Torx® fasteners are becoming more and more common on modern vehicles

Standard length sockets are good for just about all jobs, however, some stud-head bolts, hard-to-reach bolts, nuts on long studs, etc., require the deep sockets.

Thin-walled sockets are not too common and aren't usually needed in most work. They are exactly what you think, sockets made with thinner wall to fit into tighter places. They don't have the wall strength of a standard socket, of course, but their usefulness in a tight spot can make them worth it.

6 and 12 points. This refers to how many sides are in the socket itself. Each has advantages. The 6 point socket is stronger and less prone to slipping which would strip a bolt head or nut. 12 point sockets are more common, usually less expensive and can operate better in tight places where the ratchet handle can't swing far.

Many manufacturers use recessed hex-head fasteners to retain caliper pins. These fasteners require a socket with a hex shaped stud or a large sturdy hex key. To help prevent torn knuckles, we would recommend that you stick to the sockets and leave the hex keys for lighter applications. Hex stud sockets are available individually or in sets just like conventional sockets. Any complete tool set should include hex stud sockets.

More and more, manufacturers are using Torx® head fasteners, which were once known as tamper resistant fasteners (because many people did not have tools with the necessary odd driver shape). They are still used on parts of the vehicle where the manufacturer would prefer only knowledgeable technicians or advanced Do-It-Yourselfers (DIYers) be working. One automotive example would be some headlight adjustment screws, though it is possible to find these fasteners just about anywhere.

There are currently three different types of Torx® fasteners; internal, external and a new tamper resistant. The internal fasteners require a star-shaped driver. The external fasteners require a star-shaped socket. And, the new tamper resistant fasteners use a star-shaped driver with a small hole drilled through the center. The most common are the internal Torx® fasteners, but you might find any of them on your vehicle. For example, certain GM models use external Torx® fasteners to retain wheel cylinders on their rear drum brakes.

Torque Wrenches

In most applications, a torque wrench can be used to assure proper installation of a fastener. Torque wrenches come in various designs and most automotive supply stores will carry a variety to suit your needs. A torque wrench should be used any time we supply a specific torque value for a fastener. A torque wrench can also be used if you are following the general guidelines in the accompanying charts. Keep in mind that because there is no worldwide standardization of fasteners, the charts are a general guideline and should be used with caution. Again, the general rule of "if" you are using the right tool for the job, you should not have to strain to tighten a fastener" applies here.

BEAM TYPE

The beam type torque wrench is one of the most popular types. It consists of a pointer attached to the head that runs the length of the flexible beam (shaft) to a scale located near the handle. As the wrench is pulled, the beam bends and the pointer indicates the torque using the scale.

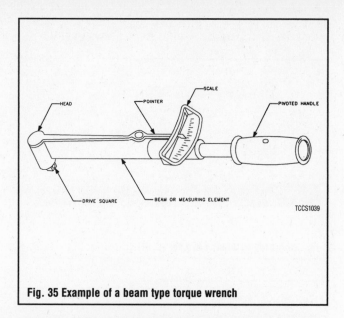

Fig. 35 Example of a beam type torque wrench

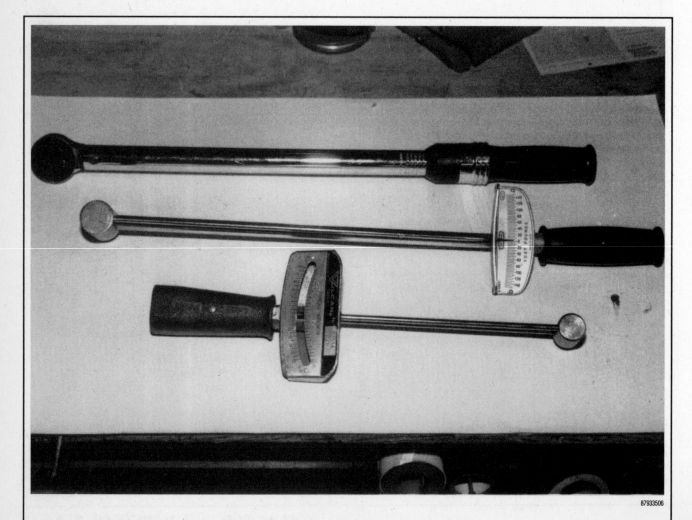

Fig. 34 Three types of torque wrenches. Top to bottom: a ½ inch drive clicker type, a ½ inch drive beam type and a ⅜ inch drive beam type that reads in inch lbs.

CLICK (BREAKAWAY) TYPE

Another popular design of torque wrench is the click type. To use the click type wrench you pre-adjust it to a torque setting. Once the torque is reached, the wrench has a reflex signaling feature that causes a momentary breakaway of the torque wrench body, sending an impulse to the operator's hand.

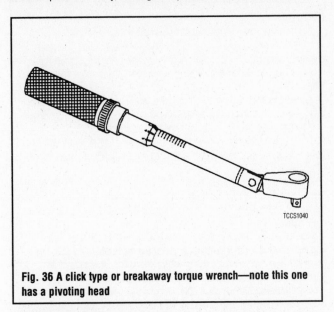

Fig. 36 A click type or breakaway torque wrench—note this one has a pivoting head

PIVOT HEAD TYPE

Some torque wrenches (usually of the click type) may be equipped with a pivot head that can allow it to be used in areas of limited access. BUT, it must be used properly. To hold a pivot head wrench, grasp the handle lightly, and as you pull on the handle, it should be floated on the pivot point. If the handle comes in contact with the yoke extension during the process of pulling, there is a very good chance the torque readings will be inaccurate because this could alter the wrench loading point. The design of the handle is usually such as to make it inconvenient to deliberately misuse the wrench.

➡It should be mentioned that the use of any U-joint, wobble or extension would have an effect on the torque readings, no matter what type of wrench you are using. For the most accurate readings, install the socket directly on the wrench driver. If necessary, straight extensions (which hold a socket directly under the wrench driver) will have the least effect on the torque reading. Avoid any extension that alters the length of the wrench from the handle to the head/driving point (such as a crow's foot). U-joint or wobble extensions can greatly affect the readings; avoid their use at all times.

RIGID CASE (DIRECT READING)

A rigid case or direct reading torque wrench is equipped with a dial indicator to show torque values. One advantage of these wrenches is that they

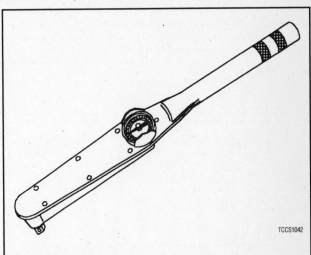

Fig. 38 The rigid case (direct reading) torque wrench uses a dial indicator to show torque

can be held at any position on the wrench without affecting accuracy. These wrenches are often preferred because they tend to be compact, easy to read and have a great degree of accuracy.

Torque Angle Meters

Because the frictional characteristics of each fastener or threaded hole will vary, clamp loads which are based strictly on torque will vary as well. In most applications, this variance is not significant enough to cause worry. But, in certain applications, a manufacturer's engineers may determine that more precise clamp loads are necessary (such is the case with many aluminum cylinder heads). In these cases, a torque angle method of installation would be specified. When installing fasteners that are torque angle tightened, a predetermined seating torque and standard torque wrench are usually used first to remove any compliance from the joint. The fastener is then tightened the specified additional portion of a turn measured in degrees. A torque angle gauge (mechanical protractor) is used for these applications.

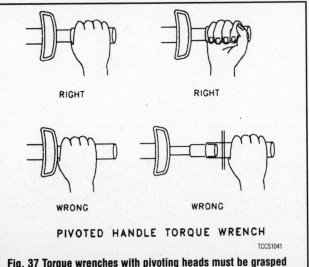

PIVOTED HANDLE TORQUE WRENCH

Fig. 37 Torque wrenches with pivoting heads must be grasped and used properly to prevent an incorrect reading

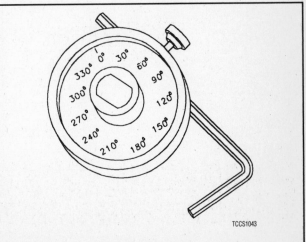

Fig. 39 Some assembly procedures (mostly on engines not brakes) require the use of a torque angle meter (mechanical protractor)

Breaker Bars

Breaker bars are long handles with a drive lug. Their main purpose is to provide extra turning force when breaking loose tight bolts or nuts. They come in all drive sizes and lengths. Always wear gloves when using a breaker bar.

Speed Handles

Speed handles are tools with a drive lug and angled turning handle that allow you to quickly remove or install a bolt or nut. They don't, however

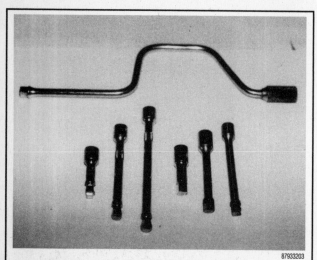

87933203

Fig. 40 A speed driver and extensions. The 3 on the left are called "wobbles" since they allow some lateral movement

have much torque ability. You might consider one when installing a number of similar fasteners such as brake backing plate bolts or nuts.

WRENCHES

Basically, there are 3 kinds of fixed wrenches: open end, box end, and combination.

Open end wrenches have 2-jawed openings at each end of the wrench. These wrenches are able to fit onto just about any nut or bolt. They are extremely versatile but have one major drawback. They can slip on a worn or rounded bolt head or nut, causing bleeding knuckles and a useless fastener.

Box-end wrenches have a 360° circular jaw at each end of the wrench. They come in both 6 and 12 point versions just like sockets and each type has the same advantages and disadvantages as sockets.

Combination wrenches have the best of both. They have a 2-jawed open end and a box end. These wrenches are probably the most versatile.

As for sizes, you'll need a range of ¼ inch through 1 inch. As for numbers, you'll need 2 of each size, since, in many instances, one wrench holds the nut while the other turns the bolt. On most fasteners, the nut and bolt are the same size.

One extremely valuable type of wrench is the adjustable wrench. An adjustable wrench has a fixed upper jaw and a moveable lower jaw. The lower jaw is moved by turning a threaded drum. The advantage of an adjustable wrench is its ability to be adjusted to just about any size fastener. The main drawback of an adjustable wrench is the lower jaw's tendency to move slightly under heavy pressure. This can cause the wrench to slip. Adjustable wrenches come in a large range of sizes, measured by the wrench length.

INCHES	DECIMAL	DECIMAL	MILLIMETERS
1/8''	.125	.118	3mm
3/16''	.187	.157	4mm
1/4''	.250	.236	6mm
5/16''	.312	.354	9mm
3/8''	.375	.394	10mm
7/16''	.437	.472	12mm
1/2''	.500	.512	13mm
9/16''	.562	.590	15mm
5/8''	.625	.630	16mm
11/16''	.687	.709	18mm
3/4''	.750	.748	19mm
13/16''	.812	.787	20mm
7/8''	.875	.866	22mm
15/16''	.937	.945	24mm
1''	1.00	.984	25mm

87933106

Fig. 41 Comparison of U.S. measure and metric wrench sizes

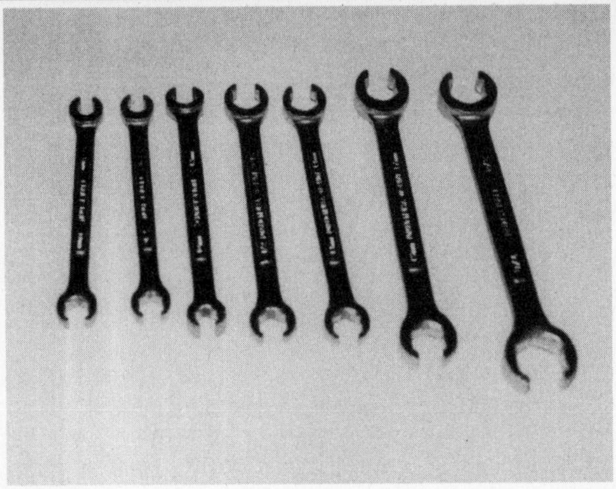

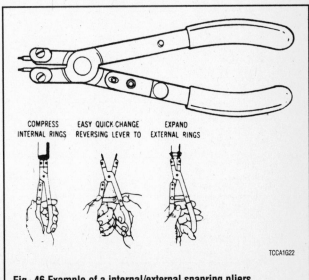

Fig. 42 Flarenut wrenches are critical for brake lines or tubing, to make sure the fittings do not become rounded

PLIERS

At least 2 pair of standard pliers is an absolute necessity. Pliers are simply mechanical fingers. They are, more than anything, an extension of your hand.

In addition to standard pliers there are the slip-joint, multi-position pliers such as ChannelLock® pliers and locking pliers, such as Vise Grips®.

Slip joint pliers are extremely valuable in grasping oddly sized parts and fasteners. Just make sure that you don't use them instead of a wrench too often since they can easily round off a bolt head or nut.

Locking pliers are usually used for gripping bolt or stud that can't be removed conventionally. You can get locking pliers in square jawed, needle-nosed and pipe-jawed. Pipe jawed have slightly curved jaws for gripping more than just pipes. Locking pliers can rank right up behind duct tape as the handy-man's best friend.

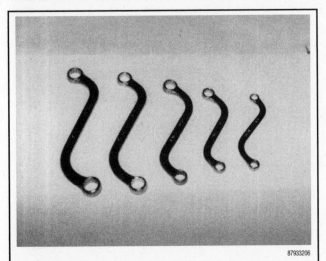

Fig. 43 These S-shaped wrenches are called obstruction wrenches

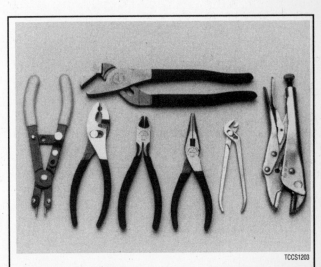

Fig. 45 Pliers and cutters come in many shapes and sizes. You should have an assortment on hand

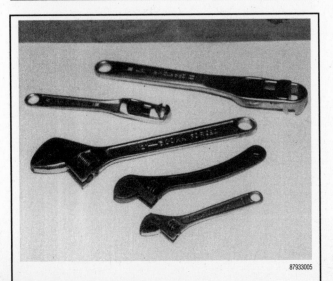

Fig. 44 Several types and sizes of adjustable wrenches

COMPRESS INTERNAL RINGS   EASY QUICK-CHANGE REVERSING LEVER TO   EXPAND EXTERNAL RINGS

Fig. 46 Example of a internal/external snapring pliers

SCREWDRIVERS

You can't have too many screwdrivers. Screwdrivers are either standard or Phillips. Standard blades come in various sizes and thicknesses for all types of slotted fasteners. Phillips screwdrivers come in sizes with number designations from 1 on up, with the lower number designating the smaller size. Screwdrivers can be purchased separately or in sets.

HAMMERS

You always need a hammer—for just about any kind of work. For most metal work, you need a ball-peen hammer for using drivers and other like tools, a plastic hammer for hitting things safely, and a soft-faced dead-blow hammer for hitting things safely and hard.

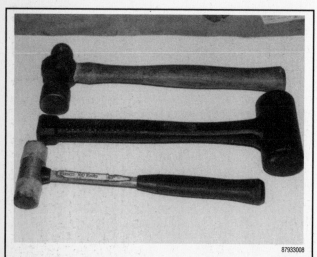

87933008

Fig. 47 Three types of hammers. Top to bottom: ball peen, rubber dead-blow, and plastic

OTHER COMMON TOOLS

There are a lot of other tools that every workshop should have for automotive work. They include:

- Chisels
- Punches
- Files
- Hacksaw
- Bench Vise
- Tap and Die Set
- Flashlight
- Magnetic Bolt Retriever
- Gasket scraper
- Putty Knife
- Screw/Bolt Extractors
- Prybar

Chisels, punches and files are repair tools. Their uses will come up during the rebuilding operation.

Hacksaws have just one use, cutting things off. You may wonder why you'd need one for something as simple as brake work, but you never know. Among other things, guide studs for parts installation can be made from old bolts with their heads cut off.

A large bench vise, of at least 4 inch capacity, is essential. A vise is needed to hold anything being worked on.

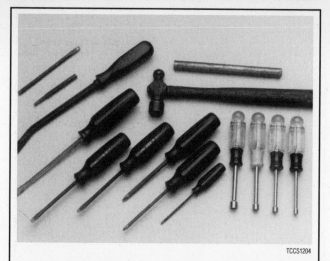

TCCS1204

Fig. 48 Various drivers, chisels and prybars are great tools to have in your box

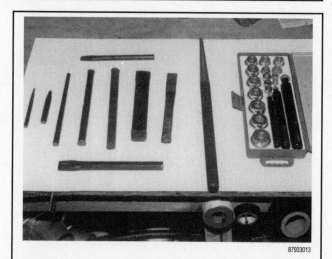

87933013

Fig. 49 Punches, chisels and drivers can be purchased separately or in sets

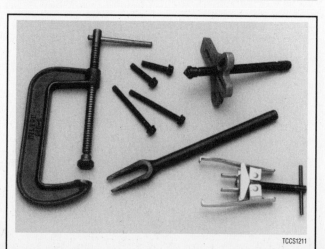

TCCS1211

Fig. 50 An assortment of pullers, clamps and separator tools are also needed for many larger repairs (especially engine and suspension work)

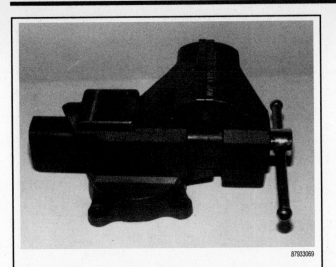

Fig. 51 A good quality, heavy-duty bench vise, like this 5½ in. type, with reversible jaws, is ideal for shop work

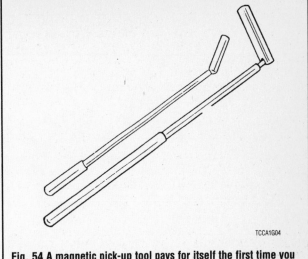

Fig. 54 A magnetic pick-up tool pays for itself the first time you need it

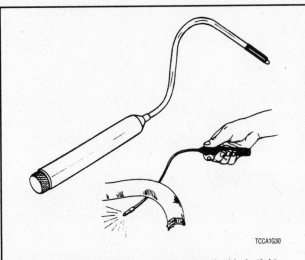

Fig. 52 A flexible flashlight can become invaluable in tight places

Fig. 55 Two good tap and die sets; US measure (left) and metric

Fig. 53 A telescoping mirror is also great for tight places

A tap and die set might be something you've never needed, but you will eventually. It's a good rule, when everything is apart, to clean-up all threads, on bolts, screws and threaded holes. Also, you'll likely run across a situation in which stripped threads will be encountered. The tap and die set will handle that for you.

Gasket scrapers are just what you'd think, tools made for scraping old gasket material off of parts. You don't absolutely need one. Old gasket material can be remove with a putty knife or single edge razor blade. However, putty knives may not be sharp enough for some really stuck gaskets and razor blades have a knack of breaking just when you don't want them to, inevitably slicing the nearest body part!

Putty knives really do have a use in automotive work. Just because you remove all the bolts from a component sealed with a gasket doesn't mean it's going to come off. Most of the time, the gasket and sealer will hold it tightly. Lightly driving a putty knife at various points between the two parts will break the seal without damage to the parts.

A small—8-10 inches long—prybar is extremely useful for removing stuck parts such as cylinder heads, timing cases, intake manifolds, etc. NEVER, NEVER, use a screwdriver as a prybar! Screwdrivers are not meant for prying. Screwdrivers, used for prying, can break, sending the broken shaft flying!

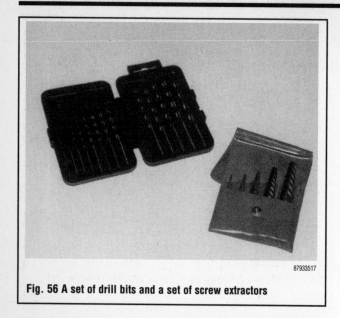

Fig. 56 A set of drill bits and a set of screw extractors

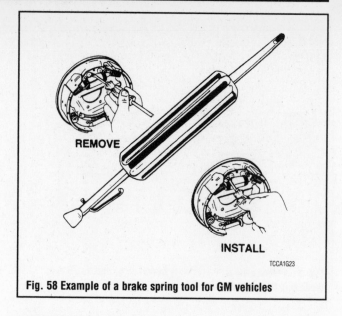

Fig. 58 Example of a brake spring tool for GM vehicles

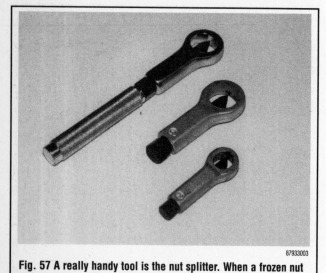

Fig. 57 A really handy tool is the nut splitter. When a frozen nut simply won't budge, use one of these

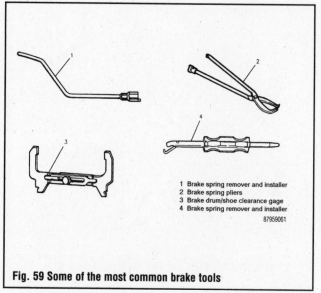

1 Brake spring remover and installer
2 Brake spring pliers
3 Brake drum/shoe clearance gage
4 Brake spring remover and installer

Fig. 59 Some of the most common brake tools

Screw/bolt extractors are used for removing broken bolts or studs that have broke off flush with the surface of the part.

BRAKE TOOLS

In addition to the common hand tools, there are a number of tools designed specifically for automotive brake work. They are:

- Brake pad spreader
- Caliper piston depressor
- Brake spring tools for return and hold-down springs
- Caliper dust boot installer
- Seal puller
- Brake adjusting spoon
- Wheel cylinder piston clamp
- Brake cylinder hone
- Bleeder screw wrench

Some of these tools are more necessary than others. The caliper piston depressor, brake spring tools and adjusting spoon are the most helpful. The hone is necessary only if you intend to rebuild your wheel cylinders or master cylinder.

On vehicles with anti-lock brakes, many brake system problems can be diagnosed only with code scanners. These scanners plug into the vehicle's

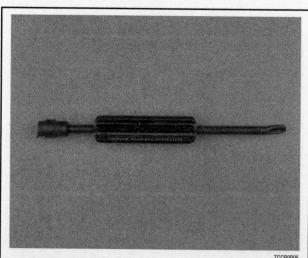

Fig. 60 Brake spring tools such as this will help tremendously in drum brake service

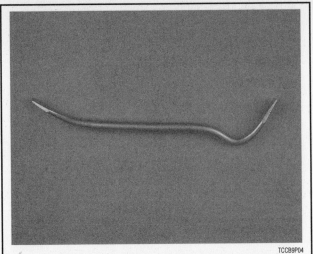

Fig. 61 A brake adjusting spoon can be used to set the drum brakes with the wheel installed

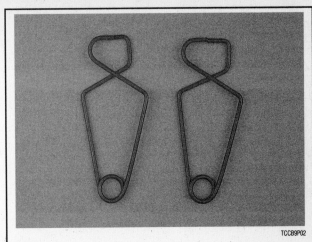

Fig. 64 A pair of wheel cylinder piston holding clamps will help keep the cylinder pistons from dislodging while the shoes are removed

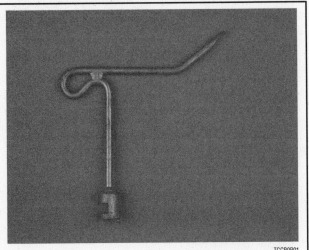

Fig. 62 This tool is a combination brake spring holder and brake adjusting spoon

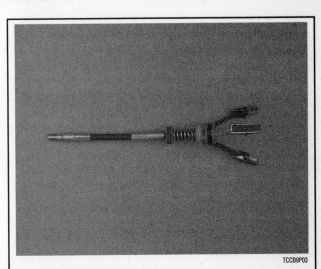

Fig. 65 A brake cylinder hone can be used restore damaged cylinder bores

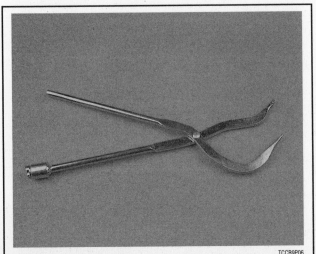

Fig. 63 This pair of brake spring pliers can be used to install drum brake return springs

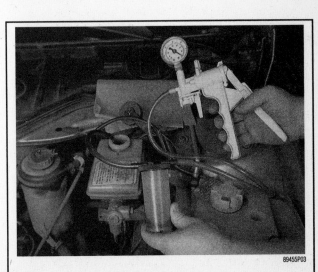

Fig. 66 A hand-held vacuum pump can be used for bleeding, or to remove unwanted fluid from the reservoir

Fig. 67 Code scanners are available for many of the major vehicle manufacturers

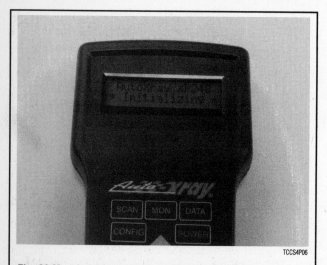

Fig. 68 Most hand-held scanners, like this AutoXray®, read engine codes, as well as ABS codes on some vehicles

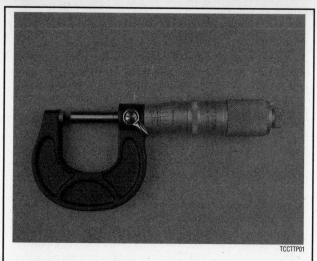

Fig. 69 Outside micrometers can be used to measure bake components including rotors, pads and pistons

A micrometer is an instrument made up of a precisely machined spindle which is rotated in a fixed nut, opening and closing the distance between the end of the spindle and a fixed anvil.

To make a measurement, you back off the spindle until you can place the piece to be measured between the spindle and anvil. You then rotate the spindle until the part is contacted by both the spindle and anvil. The measurement is then found by reading the gradations in the handle of the micrometer.

Here's the hard part. I'll try to explain how to read a micrometer. The spindle is threaded. Most micrometers use a thread pitch of 40 threads per inch. One complete revolution of the spindle move the spindle toward or away from the anvil 0.025 in. ($\frac{1}{40}$ in.).

The fixed part of the handle (called, the sleeve) is marked with 40 gradations per inch of handle length, so each line is 0.025 in. apart. Okay so far?

Every 4th line is marked with a number. The first long line marked 1 represents 0.100 in., the second is 0.200 in., and so on.

The part of the handle that turns is called the thimble. The beveled end of the thimble is marked with gradations, each of which corresponds to 0.001 in. and, usually, every 5th line is numbered.

Turn the thimble until the 0 lines up with the 0 on the sleeve. Now, rotate the thimble one complete revolution and look at the sleeve. You'll see that one complete thimble revolution moved the thimble 0.025 in. down the sleeve.

To read the micrometer, multiply the number of gradations exposed on the sleeve by 0.025 and add that to the number of thousandths indicated by the thimble line that is lined up with the horizontal line on the sleeve. So, if you've measured a part and there are 6 vertical gradations exposed on the sleeve and the 7th gradation on the thimble is lined up with the horizontal line on the sleeve, the thickness of the part is 0.157 in. (6 x 0.025 = 0.150 . Add to that 0.007 representing the 7 lines on the thimble and you get 0.157). See?

If you didn't understand that, try the instructions that come with the micrometer or ask someone that knows, to show you how to work it.

electrical system and read trouble codes that are stored in the on-board computer's memory. Since these scanners are relatively expensive, we don't recommend that you purchase a scanner unless you intend to use it on a regular basis. If you intend to do extensive work on a computer controlled vehicle, a scanner may be worthwhile since it can be used to read codes associated with all operating systems, not just brakes. See the Chilton Total Car Care manual for your particular vehicle when using a scanner.

MICROMETERS & CALIPERS

Outside Micrometers

Outside micrometers are used to check the diameters of such components as the pistons from a caliper or wheel cylinder, and the thickness of a rotor. The most common type of micrometer reads in 1/1000 of an inch. Micrometers that use a vernier scale can estimate to 1/10 of an inch.

Micrometers and calipers are devices used to make extremely precise measurements. The success of any rebuild is dependent, to a great extent on the ability to check the size and fit of components as specified by the manufacturer. These measurements are made in thousandths and ten-thousandths of an inch.

Inside Micrometers

Inside micrometers are used to measure the distance between two parallel surfaces. In brake rebuilding work, the inside mike measures caliper, master cylinder or wheel cylinder bore wear. Inside mikes are graduated the same way as outside mikes and are read the same way as well.

Remember that an inside mike must be absolutely perpendicular to the work being measured. When you measure with an inside mike, rock the mike gently from side to side and tip it back and forth slightly so that you span the widest part of the bore. Just to be on the safe side, take several readings. It takes a certain amount of experience to work any mike with confidence.

Metric Micrometers

Metric micrometers are read in the same way as inch micrometers, except that the measurements are in millimeters. Each line on the main scale equals 1 mm. Each fifth line is stamped 5, 10, 15, and so on. Each line on the thimble scale equals 0.01 mm. It will take a little practice, but if you can read an inch mike, you can read a metric mike.

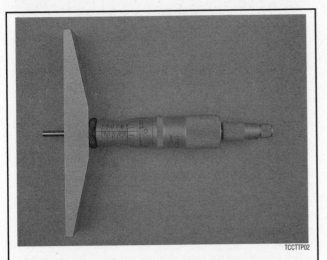

TCCTTP02

Fig. 70 Depth gauges, like this micrometer, can be used to measure the amount of pad or shoe remaining above a rivet

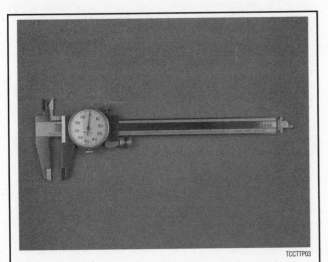

TCCTTP03

Fig. 71 Outside calipers are fast and easy ways to measure pads or rotors

Inside and Outside Calipers

Inside and outside calipers are useful devices to have if you need to measure something quickly and precise measurement is not necessary. Simply take the reading and then hold the calipers on an accurate steel rule.

DIAL INDICATORS

A dial indicator is a gauge that utilizes a dial face and a needle to register measurements. There is a movable contact arm on the dial indicator. When the arms moves, the needle rotates on the dial. Dial indicators are calibrated to show readings in thousandths of an inch and typically, are used to measure end-play and runout on camshafts, crankshafts, gears, and so on.

Dial indicators are quite easy to use, although they are relatively expensive. A variety of mounting devices are available so that the indicator can be used in a number of situations. Make certain that the contact arm is always parallel to the movement of the work being measured.

TELESCOPING GAUGES

A telescope gauge is used to measure the inside of bores. It can take the place of an inside mike for some of these jobs. Simply insert the gauge in the hole to be measured and lock the plungers after they have contacted the walls. Remove the tool and measure across the plungers with an outside micrometer.

PLASTIGAGE®

Plastigage is a sort of soft plastic that will flatten out to predetermined widths when subjected to torquing. These widths will equal a specific clearance. Plastigage is only used in engine rebuilding to check main and rod-bearing clearance. It is sold in a paper sleeve that also doubles as the scale upon which it is measured. The scale reads out in thousandths of an inch. The most common type is green Plastigage that is used to measure clearances from 0.001 to 0.003 in.

Special Tools

Normally, the use of special factory tools is avoided for repair procedures, since these are not readily available for the do-it-yourself mechanic. When it is possible to perform the job with more commonly available tools, it will be pointed out, but occasionally, a special tool was designed to perform a specific function and should be used. Before substituting another tool, you should be convinced that neither your safety nor the performance of the vehicle would be compromised.

Special tools can usually be purchased from an automotive parts store or from your dealer. In some cases special tools may be available directly from the tool manufacturer.

Electric Power Tools

Power tools are most often associated with woodworking. However, there are a few which are very helpful in automotive work.

The most common and most useful power tool is the bench grinder. You'll need a grinder with a grinding stone on one side and a wire brush wheel on the other. The brush wheel is indispensable for cleaning parts and the stone can be used to remove rough surfaces and for reshaping, where necessary.

87933006

Fig. 72 Three types of common power tools. Left to right: a hand-held grinder, drill and impact wrench

Fig. 73 The bench grinder can be used to clean just about every part removed from the vehicle

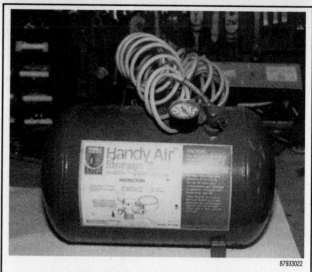

Fig. 75 An air storage tank

Almost as useful as the bench grinder is the drill. Drills can come in very handy when a stripped or broken fastener is encountered.

Power ratchets and impact wrenches can come in very handy. Power ratchets can save a lot of time and muscle when removing and installing long bolts or nuts on long studs, especially where there is little room to swing a manual ratchet. Electric impact wrenches can be invaluable in a lot of automotive work, especially wheel lugs and axle shaft nuts. They don't have much use on brakes, though.

Air Tools and Compressors

Air-powered tools are not necessary for brake work. They are, however, useful for speeding up many jobs and for general clean-up of parts. If you don't have air tools, and you want them, be prepared for an initial outlay of a lot of money.

The first thing you need is a compressor. Compressors are available in electrically driven and gas engine driven models. As long as you have electricity, you don't need a gas engine driven type.

The common shop-type air compressor is a pump mounted on a tank. The pump compresses air and forces it into the tank where it is stored until you need it. The compressor automatically turns the pump on when the air pressure in the tank falls below a certain preset level.

Fig. 74 This compressor operates off ordinary house current and provides all the air pressure you'll need

There are all kinds of air powered tools, including ratchets, impact wrenches, saws, drills, sprayers, nailers, scrapers, riveters, grinders and sanders. In general, air powered tools are much cheaper than their electric counterparts.

When deciding what size compressor unit you need, you'll be driven by two factors: the Pounds per Square Inch (PSI) capacity of the unit and the deliver rate in Cubic Feet per Minute (CFM). For example, most air powered ratchets require 90 psi at 4 to 5 cfm to operate at peak efficiency. Grinders and saws may require up to 7 cfm at 90 psi. So, before buying the compressor unit, decide what types of tools you'll want so that you don't short-change yourself on the compressor purchase.

If you decide that a compressor and air tools isn't for you, you can have the benefit of air pressure rather cheaply. Purchase an air storage tank, available in sizes up to 20 gallons at most retail stores that sell auto products. These storage tanks can safely store air pressure up to 125 psi and come with a high pressure nozzle for cleaning things and an air chuck for filling tires. The tank can be filled using the common tire-type air compressor.

Jacks and Jackstands

Jacks and safety stands (jackstands) will be needed for just about anything that you'll do on the lower end of a vehicle.

Your vehicle was supplied with a jack for emergency road repairs. This jack is fine for changing a flat tire or other short-term procedures not requiring you to go beneath the vehicle. For any real work, you MUST use a floor jack.

Never place the jack under the radiator, engine or transmission components. Severe and expensive damage will result when the jack is raised. Additionally, never jack under the floorpan or bodywork; the metal will deform.

Check your owner's manual or a Chilton Total Car Care for proper jacking and support locations on your vehicle. Many vehicles have crossmembers at the front and rear of the sub-frames that are suitable for jacking, but be careful not to mistake a thin metal skid plate or plastic trim piece as a crossmember.

There are usually reinforced pinch welds along the sides of the vehicle (just in front of the rear wheel and just behind the front wheel) that are used with the vehicle's emergency jack and can be used to raise the vehicle or that can be used with a pair of jackstands. In this case, a block of wood with a cut down the middle in order to cradle the pinch weld will help prevent stress or damage to the metal.

If you have a truck or an older framed vehicle, jackstands can be used almost anywhere along the frame for support. Always use a pair of stands directly across from each other (no closer to the front or rear of the vehicle than the other stand) to help keep the vehicle properly balanced.

Fig. 76 Floor jacks come in all sizes and capacities. Top is a large 2¼ ton models; underneath is a compact 2 ton model

Fig. 77 Jackstands are necessary for holding your vehicle up off the ground. Top are 6 ton models; bottom are 4 ton models

✳✳ WARNING

Always position a block of wood or small rubber pad on top of the jack or jackstand to protect the lifting point's finish when lifting or supporting the vehicle.

Whenever you plan to work under the vehicle, you must support it on jackstands or ramps. Never use cinder blocks or stacks of wood to support the vehicle, even if you're only going to be under it for a few minutes. Never crawl under the vehicle when it is supported only by the tire-changing jack or other floor jack.

✳✳ CAUTION

Refer to the jacking precautions and the safety information earlier in this chapter before attempting to raise or support the vehicle. Failure to follow proper jacking procedures could result in severe injury or death.

Small hydraulic, screw, or scissors jacks are satisfactory for raising the vehicle. Drive-on trestles or ramps are also a handy and safe way to both raise and support the vehicle. Be careful though, some ramps may be too steep to drive your vehicle onto without scraping the front bottom panels. Never support the vehicle on any suspension member (unless specifically instructed to do so by a repair manual) or by an underbody panel.

FASTENERS

Although there are a great variety of fasteners found in the modern vehicle, the most commonly used retainer is the threaded fastener (nuts, bolts, screws, studs, etc). Most threaded retainers may be reused, provided that they are not damaged in use or during the repair. Some retainers (such as stretch bolts or torque prevailing nuts) are designed to deform when tightened or in use and should not be reinstalled.

Whenever possible, we will note any special retainers which should be replaced during a procedure. But you should always inspect the condition of

POZIDRIVE

PHILLIPS RECESS

TORX®

CLUTCH RECESS

INDENTED HEXAGON

HEXAGON TRIMMED

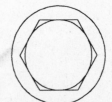

HEXAGON WASHER HEAD

TCCS1037

Fig. 78 Here are a few of the most common screw/bolt driver styles

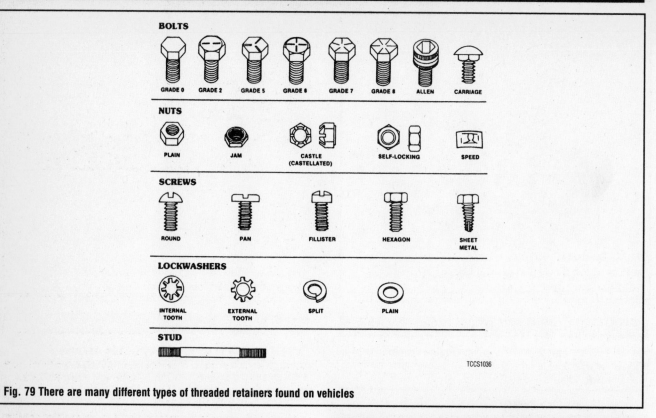

Fig. 79 There are many different types of threaded retainers found on vehicles

a retainer when it is removed and replace any that show signs of damage. Check all threads for rust or corrosion that can increase the torque necessary to achieve the desired clamp load for which that fastener was originally selected. Additionally, be sure that the driver surface of the fastener has not been compromised by rounding or other damage. In some cases a driver surface may become only partially rounded, allowing the driver to catch in only one direction. In many of these occurrences, a fastener may be installed and tightened, but the driver would not be able to grip and loosen the fastener again. (This could lead to frustration down the line should that component ever need to be disassembled again).

If you must replace a fastener, whether due to design or damage, you must ALWAYS be sure to use the proper replacement. In all cases, a retainer of the same design, material and strength should be used. Markings on the heads of most bolts will help determine the proper strength of the fastener. The same material, thread and pitch must be selected to assure proper installation and safe operation of the vehicle afterwards.

Thread gauges are available to help measure a bolt or stud's thread. Most automotive and hardware stores keep gauges available to help you select the proper size. In a pinch, you can use another nut or bolt for a thread gauge. If the bolt you are replacing is not too badly damaged, you can select a match by finding another bolt that will thread in its place. If you find a nut that threads properly onto the damaged bolt, then use that nut to help select the replacement bolt. If however, the bolt you are replacing is so badly damaged (broken or drilled out) that its threads cannot be used as a gauge, you might start by looking for another bolt (from the same assembly or a similar location on your vehicle) which will thread into the damaged bolt's mounting. If so, the other bolt can be used to select a nut; the nut can then be used to select the replacement bolt.

In all cases, be absolutely sure you have selected the proper replacement. Don't be shy, you can always ask the store clerk for help.

❋ WARNING

Be aware that when you find a bolt with damaged threads, you may also find the nut or drilled hole it was threaded into has also been damaged. If this is the case, you may have to drill and tap the hole, replace the nut or otherwise repair the threads. NEVER try to force a replacement bolt to fit into the damaged threads.

Bolts and Screws

Technically speaking, bolts are hexagon head or cap screws. For the purposes of this book, however, cap screws will be called bolts because that is the common terminology for them. Both bolts and screws are turned into drilled or threaded holes to fasten two parts together. Frequently, bolts require a nut on the other end, but this is not always the case. Screws seldom, if ever, require a nut on the other end.

Screws are supplied with slotted or Phillips heads. For obvious reasons, screws are not generally used where a great deal of torque is required. Most of the screws you will encounter will be used to retain components, such as brake hose connection clamps, where strength is not a factor.

Threaded retainers (such as bolts and screws) come in various sizes, designated as 8-32, 10-32, or ¼-32. The first number indicates the minor diameter, and the second number indicates the number of threads per inch (or distance between threads in mm).

Nuts

Nuts have only one use: they simply hold the other end of the bolt or stud and, thereby, hold the two parts together. There are a variety of nuts used on vehicles, but a standard hexagon head (six-sided) nut is the most common.

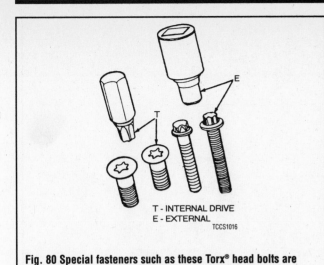

Fig. 80 Special fasteners such as these Torx® head bolts are used by manufacturers to discourage people from working on vehicles without the proper tools

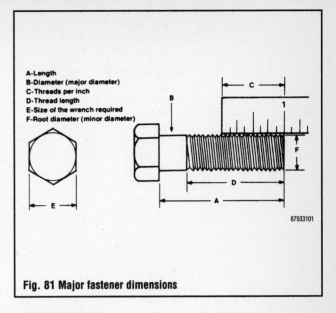

Fig. 81 Major fastener dimensions

Castellated and slotted nuts are designed for use with a cotter pin and are usually used when it is extremely important that the nuts do not work loose (in wheel bearings, for example). Other nuts are self-locking nuts that have a slot cut in the side.

When the nut is tightened, the separated sections pull together and lock the nut onto the bolt. Interference nuts have a collar of soft metal or fiber. The bolt cuts threads in the soft material that then jams in the threads and prevents the nut and bolt from working loose.

A jam nut is a second hexagon nut that is used to hold the first nut in place. They are usually found where some type of adjustment is needed; parking brake cables, for instance.

Pawlnuts are single thread nuts that provide some locking action when they have been turned down on the nut.

Speed nuts are simply rectangular bits of sheet metal that are pushed down over a bolt, screw, or stud to provide locking action.

Studs

Studs are simply pieces of threaded rod. They are similar to bolts and screws in their thread configuration, but they have no heads. One end is turned into a threaded hole and the other end is generally secured by same type of nut. Unless the nut is self-locking, a lockwasher or jam nut is generally used underneath it.

Lockwashers

Lockwashers are a form of washer. They may be either split or toothed, and they are always installed between a nut or screwhead and the actual part being held. The split washer is crushed flat and locks the nut in place by spring tension. The toothed washer provides many edges to improve the locking effect and is usually used on smaller bolts and screws.

Screw and Bolt Terminology

Bolts and screws are identified by type, major diameter, minor diameter, pitch or threads per inch, class, length, thread length, and the size of the wrench required.

MAJOR DIAMETER

This is the widest diameter of the bolt as measured from the top of the threads on one side to the top of the threads on the other side.

MINOR DIAMETER

This is the diameter obtained by measuring from the bottom of the threads on one side of the bolt to the bottom of the threads on the other side. In other words, it is the diameter of the bolt if it does not have any threads.

PITCH OR THREADS PER INCH

Thread pitch is the distance between the top of one thread to the top of the next. It is simply the distance between one thread and the next. There are two types of threads in general use today. Unified National Coarse thread, and Unified National Fine. These are usually known simply as either fine or coarse thread.

Anyone who has been working on vehicles for any length of time can tell the difference between the two simply by looking at the screw, bolt, or nut. The only truly accurate way to determine thread pitch is to use a thread pitch gauge. There are some general rules to remember, however.

Coarse thread screws and bolts are used frequently when they are being threaded into aluminum or cast iron because the finer threads tend to strip more easily in these materials. Also, as a bolt or screw's diameter increases, thread pitch becomes greater.

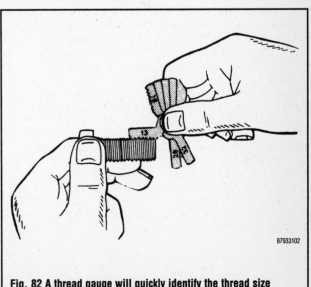

Fig. 82 A thread gauge will quickly identify the thread size

THREAD CLASS

Thread class is a measure of the operating clearance between the internal nut threads and the external threads of the bolt. There are three classes of fit, 1, 2, or 3. In addition, there are letter designations to designate either internal (class A) or external (class B) threads.

Class 1 threads are a relatively loose fit and are used when ease of assembly and disassembly are of paramount importance.

Class 2 bolts are most commonly encountered in automotive applications and give an accurate, but not an overly tight, fit.

Class 3 threads are used when utmost accuracy is needed. You might find a class 3 bolt and nut combination on an airplane, but you won't encounter them very often on a vehicle.

LENGTH & THREAD LENGTH

Screw length is the length of the bolt or screw from the bottom of the head to the bottom of the bolt or screw. Thread length is exactly that, the length of the threads.

TYPES OR GRADES OF BOLTS & SCREWS

The tensile strength of bolts and screws varies widely. Standards for these fasteners have been established by the Society of Automotive Engineers (SAE). Distinctive markings on the head of the bolt will identify its tensile strength.

These outward radiating lines are normally called points. A bolt with no points on the head is a grade 1 or a grade 2 bolt. This type of bolt is suitable for applications in which only a low-strength bolt is necessary.

On the other hand, a grade 5 bolt is found in a number of automotive applications and has double the tensile strength of a grade 2 bolt. A grade 5 bolt will have three embossed lines or points on the head.

Grade 8 bolts are the best and are frequently called aircraft grade bolts. Grade 8 bolts have six points on the head.

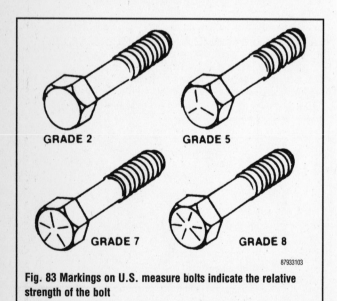

Fig. 83 Markings on U.S. measure bolts indicate the relative strength of the bolt

METRIC BOLTS

While metric bolts may seem to be the same as their U.S. measure counterparts, they definitely are not. The pitch on a metric bolt is different from that of an U.S. measure bolt. It is entirely possible to start a metric bolt into a hole with U.S. measure threads and run it down a few turns. Then it is going to bind. Recognizing the problem at this point is not going to do

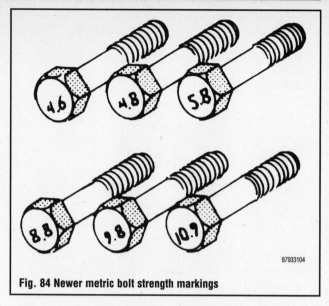

Fig. 84 Newer metric bolt strength markings

much good. It is also possible to run a metric nut down on an U.S. measure bolt and find that it is too loose to provide sufficient strength.

Metric bolts are marked in a manner different from that of U.S. measure bolts. Most metric bolts have a number stamped on the head. This metric grade marking won't be an even number, but something like 4.6 or 10.9. The number indicates the relative strength of the bolt. The higher the number, the greater the strength of the bolt. Some metric bolts are also marked with a single-digit number to indicate the bolt strength. Metric bolt sizes are also identified in a manner different from that of U.S. measure fasteners.

If, for example, a metric bolt were designated 14 x 2, that would mean that the major diameter is 14 mm (.56 in.), and that the thread pitch is 2 mm (.08 in.). More important, metric bolts are not classified by number of threads per inch, but by the distance between the threads, and the distance between threads does not quite correspond to number of threads per inch. For example, 2 mm between threads is about 12.7 threads per inch.

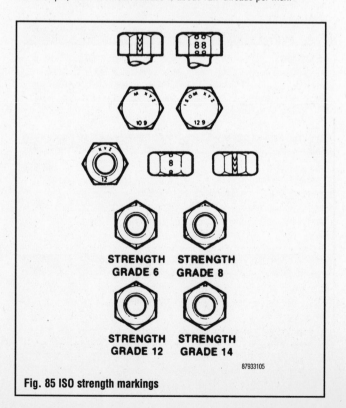

Fig. 85 ISO strength markings

	Mark	Class		Mark	Class
Hexagon head bolt	Bolt head No. 4 / 4— 5— 6— 7— 8— 9— 10— 11—	4T 5T 6T 7T 8T 9T 10T 11T	Stud bolt	No mark	4T
	No mark	4T			
Hexagon flange bolt w/ washer hexagon bolt	No mark	4T		Grooved	6T
Hexagon head bolt	Two protruding lines	5T			
Hexagon flange bolt w/ washer hexagon bolt	Two protruding lines	6T	Welded bolt		4T
Hexagon head bolt	Three protruding lines	7T			
Hexagon head bolt	Four protruding lines	8T			

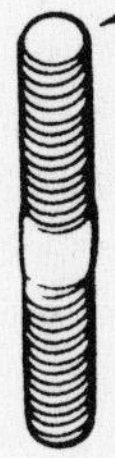

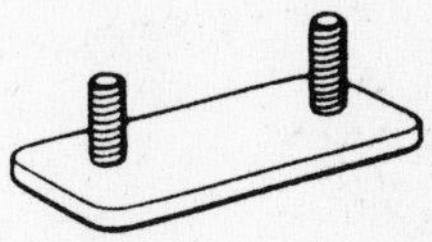

TCCS1240

Fig. 86 Metric bolt strength indicator marks

Class	Diameter mm	Pitch mm	Specified torque					
			Hexagon head bolt			Hexagon flange bolt		
			N·m	kgf·cm	ft·lbf	N·m	kgf·cm	ft·lbf
4T	6	1	5	55	48 in.·lbf	6	60	52 in.·lbf
	8	1.25	12.5	130	9	14	145	10
	10	1.25	26	260	19	29	290	21
	12	1.25	47	480	35	53	540	39
	14	1.5	74	760	55	84	850	61
	16	1.5	115	1,150	83	—	—	—
5T	6	1	6.5	65	56 in.·lbf	7.5	75	65 in.·lbf
	8	1.25	15.5	160	12	17.5	175	13
	10	1.25	32	330	24	36	360	26
	12	1.25	59	600	43	65	670	48
	14	1.5	91	930	67	100	1,050	76
	16	1.5	140	1,400	101	—	—	—
6T	6	1	8	80	69 in.·lbf	9	90	78 in.·lbf
	8	1.25	19	195	14	21	210	15
	10	1.25	39	400	29	44	440	32
	12	1.25	71	730	53	80	810	59
	14	1.5	110	1,100	80	125	1,250	90
	16	1.5	170	1,750	127	—	—	—
7T	6	1	10.5	110	8	12	120	9
	8	1.25	25	260	19	28	290	21
	10	1.25	52	530	38	58	590	43
	12	1.25	95	970	70	105	1,050	76
	14	1.5	145	1,500	108	165	1,700	123
	16	1.5	230	2,300	166	—	—	—
8T	8	1.25	29	300	22	33	330	24
	10	1.25	61	620	45	68	690	50
	12	1.25	110	1,100	80	120	1,250	90
9T	8	1.25	34	340	25	37	380	27
	10	1.25	70	710	51	78	790	57
	12	1.25	125	1,300	94	140	1,450	105
10T	8	1.25	38	390	28	42	430	31
	10	1.25	78	800	58	88	890	64
	12	1.25	140	1,450	105	155	1,600	116
11T	8	1.25	42	430	31	47	480	35
	10	1.25	87	890	64	97	990	72
	12	1.25	155	1,600	116	175	1,800	130

TCCS1241

Fig. 87 Determining the strength of metric fasteners

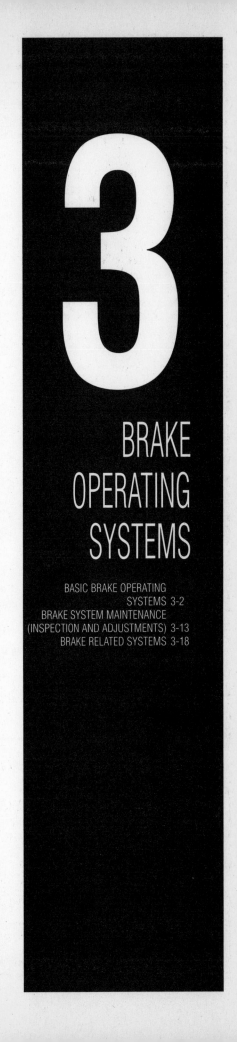

3

BRAKE
OPERATING
SYSTEMS

BASIC BRAKE OPERATING SYSTEMS

Drum Brake Systems

GENERAL INFORMATION

Drum brakes employ two brake shoes mounted on a stationary backing plate. These shoes are positioned inside a circular drum that rotates with the wheel assembly. The shoes are held in place by springs. This allows them to slide toward the drums (when hydraulic force is applied) while keeping the linings and drums in alignment. The shoes are actuated by a wheel cylinder. The cylinder is mounted at the top of the backing plate.

➡**On some older vehicles, 2 cylinders were used, one at the top and one at the bottom. Rather than using a single cylinder with 2 pistons, each cylinder contained one piston with the other end of the cylinder acting as an anchor point for the shoes.**

When the brakes are applied, hydraulic pressure forces the wheel cylinder's actuating pins outward. Since these pins bear directly against the top of the brake shoes, the tops of the shoes are then forced against the inner

Fig. 1 Drum brakes basically work by pivoting the brake shoes outward against the drum

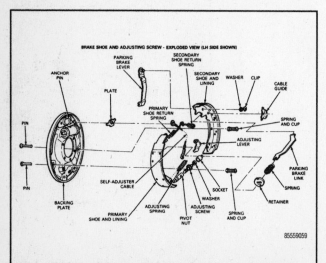

Fig. 2 This is what most common drum brake assemblies look like. Don't be concerned. It's not as complicated as it looks

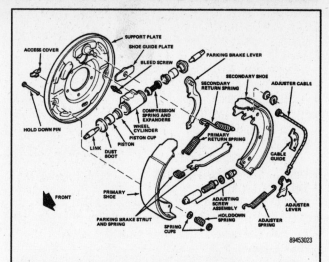

Fig. 3 An exploded view of another common drum brake assembly

side of the drum. This action forces the bottoms of the two shoes to contact the brake drum by rotating the entire assembly slightly (known as servo action). When pressure within the wheel cylinder is relaxed, return springs pull the shoes back away from the drum.

Most modern drum brakes are designed to self-adjust during application when the vehicle is moving in reverse. This motion causes both shoes to rotate very slightly with the drum, rocking an adjusting lever, thereby causing rotation of the adjusting screw. Some drum brake systems are designed to self-adjust during application whenever the brakes are applied. This on-board adjustment system reduces the need for maintenance adjustments and keeps both the brake function and pedal feel satisfactory.

Disc Brake Systems

GENERAL INFORMATION

Instead of the traditional expanding brakes that press outward against a circular drum, disc brake systems utilize a disc (rotor) with brake pads

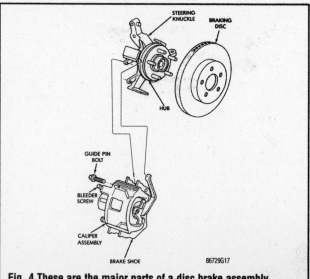

Fig. 4 These are the major parts of a disc brake assembly

Fig. 5 Disc brakes work by using a caliper to squeeze pads against the brake rotor

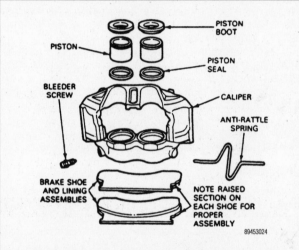

Fig. 6 An exploded view of a heavy duty sliding caliper setup. This type is most often used on light trucks

positioned on either side of it. When you step on the brake pedal, the pads are squeezed onto the rotor, slowing its motion.

The disc (rotor) is a casting, sometimes equipped with cooling fins between the two braking surfaces. This enables air to circulate between the braking surfaces making them less sensitive to heat buildup and more resistant to fade. Dirt and water do not drastically affect braking action since contaminants are thrown off by the centrifugal action of the rotor or scraped off the by the pads. Also, the equal clamping action of the two brake pads tends to ensure uniform, straight line stops. Disc brakes are inherently self-adjusting. There are 3 types of disc brake:

- A fixed caliper
- A floating caliper
- A sliding caliper

The fixed caliper design uses pistons mounted on either side of the rotor (in each side of the caliper). The caliper is mounted rigidly and does not move.

The sliding and floating designs are quite similar. In fact, these two types are often lumped together. In both designs, the pad on the inside of the rotor is moved into contact with the rotor by hydraulic force. The caliper, which is not held in a fixed position, moves slightly, bringing the outside pad into contact with the rotor. There are various methods of attaching floating calipers. Some pivot at the bottom or top, and some slide on mounting bolts. In any event, the end result is the same.

Hydraulic Brake Systems

GENERAL INFORMATION

Hydraulic systems are used to actuate the brakes of virtually all modern passenger cars and light trucks. The system transports the power required to force the frictional surfaces of the braking system together from the pedal to the individual brake units at each wheel. A hydraulic system is used for two reasons.

First, fluid under pressure can be carried to all parts of a vehicle by small pipes and flexible hoses without taking up a significant amount of room or posing routing problems.

Second, a great mechanical advantage can be given to the brake pedal end of the system, and the foot pressure required to actuate the brakes can be reduced by making the surface area of the master cylinder pistons smaller than that of any of the pistons in the wheel cylinders or calipers.

The components in a modern vehicle's hydraulic system are:
- The master cylinder
- The calipers (disc brakes)
- The wheel cylinders (drum brakes)
- The control valves, which are usually a proportioning valve (sometimes called a metering valve) and a pressure differential valve.
- Anti-Lock Brake System (ABS) control valves (when equipped)

The master cylinder consists of a fluid reservoir along with a double cylinder and piston assembly. Double type master cylinders are designed to separate brake system into two parts. Some vehicles have the system zoned front and rear; other vehicles have their systems separated diagonally, that is, one front brake and one rear brake on opposite sides. Whichever your vehicle has, the advantage is simple. If the case of a leak, at least half of your vehicle's system will work, enabling you to stop (slower, but albeit, safely).

The master cylinder converts mechanical motion from the pedal into hydraulic pressure within the lines. This pressure is translated back into mechanical motion at the wheels by either the wheel cylinder (drum brakes) or the caliper (disc brakes).

Steel lines carry the brake fluid to a point on the vehicle's frame near each of the wheels. The fluid is then carried to the calipers and wheel cylinders by flexible tubes in order to allow for suspension and steering movements.

In drum brake systems, each wheel cylinder contains two pistons, one at either end, which push outward in opposite directions and force the brake shoe into contact with the drum.

In disc brake systems, the cylinders are part of the calipers. At least

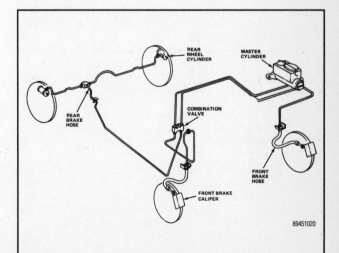

Fig. 7 This is a typical, non-ABS hydraulic system which is split front and rear

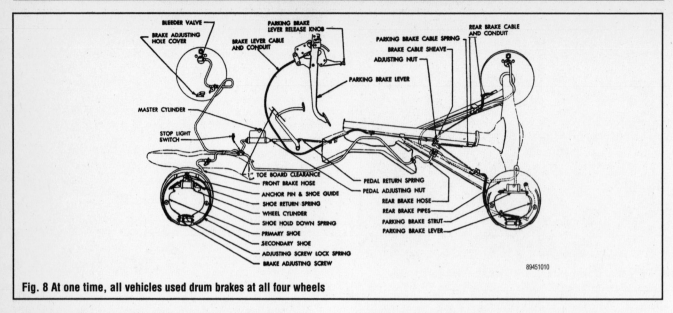

Fig. 8 At one time, all vehicles used drum brakes at all four wheels

one cylinder in each caliper is used to force the brake pads against the disc.

All pistons employ some type of seal, usually made of rubber, to prevent fluid leakage. A rubber dust boot seals the outer end of the cylinder against dust and dirt. The boot fits around the outer end of the piston on disc brake calipers, and around the brake actuating rod on wheel cylinders.

The hydraulic system operates as follows: When at rest, the entire system, from the piston(s) in the master cylinder to those in the wheel cylinders or calipers, is full of brake fluid. Upon application of the brake pedal, fluid trapped in front of the master cylinder piston(s) is forced through the lines to the wheel cylinders. Here, it forces the pistons outward, in the case of drum brakes, and inward toward the disc, in the case of disc brakes. The motion of the pistons is opposed by return springs mounted outside the cylinders in drum brakes, and by spring seals, in disc brakes.

Upon release of the brake pedal, a spring located inside the master cylinder immediately returns the master cylinder pistons to the normal position. The pistons contain check valves and the master cylinder has compensating ports drilled in it. These are uncovered as the pistons reach their normal position. The piston check valves allow fluid to flow toward the wheel cylinders or calipers as the pistons withdraw. Then, as the pads or shoes return to the released position, any fluid that has leaked out of the system will be replaced through the compensating ports.

Dual circuit master cylinders employ two pistons, located one behind the other, in the same cylinder. If a leak develops in one of the two hydraulic portions of the system, the remaining part will be available to stop the vehicle using 2 of the wheel's brakes.

All dual circuit systems use a switch to warn the driver when only half of the brake system is operational. This switch is usually located in a valve body that is mounted on the firewall or the frame below the master cylinder. A hydraulic piston receives pressure from both circuits, each circuit's pressure being applied to one end of the piston. When the pressures are in balance, the piston remains stationary. When one circuit has a leak, however, the greater pressure in that circuit during application of the brakes will push the piston to one side, closing the switch and activating the brake warning light.

In modern brake systems, this valve body also contains a metering valve and, in some cases, a proportioning valve. The metering valve keeps pressure from traveling to the front brakes until the brakes on the rear wheels have contacted the discs or drums, ensuring that the front brakes will never be used alone. The proportioning valve controls the pressure to the rear brakes to lessen the chance of rear wheel lock-up during very hard braking.

➡**On some ABS systems, the Anti-Lock Control Valves may serve the purpose of the metering or proportioning valves, eliminating the need to use mechanical valves in the system.**

Warning lights may be tested by depressing the brake pedal and holding it while opening one of the wheel cylinder bleeder screws. If this does not cause the light to go on, substitute a new lamp, make continuity checks, and, finally, replace the switch as necessary.

The hydraulic system may be checked for leaks by applying pressure to the pedal gradually and steadily. If the pedal sinks very slowly to the floor, the system has a leak. This is not to be confused with a springy or spongy feel due to the compression of air within the lines. If the system leaks, there will be a gradual change in the position of the pedal with a constant pressure.

Check for leaks along all lines and at wheel cylinders. If no external leaks are apparent, the problem is inside the master cylinder.

Master Cylinder

The master cylinder, in modern vehicles, is a device consisting of a fluid reservoir and a pressure body in which is a dual acting piston. This type of master cylinder is designed to separate either the front and rear braking systems or the diagonal paired wheels hydraulically in case of a leak. This is an advantage if one of the wheel's or lines develops a leak. For example, if a rear brake wheel cylinder develops a leak on a front and rear split system, the front brakes will still act effectively, and vise-versa. If the right rear develops a leak on a diagonally split system, then the front right and rear left wheels will still brake normally.

➡**A brake system would most likely never be split by side of the vehicle, because if a leak occurred and the brakes only operated on one side, the vehicle would dive toward the side on which the brakes still during braking. This could lead to a loss of control.**

Older vehicles used a single chamber master cylinder with a single-acting piston. This is obviously not desirable because the entire braking system could be disabled in the event of a leak at any point.

Dual circuit master cylinders employ two pistons, located one behind the other, in the same cylinder. The pistons are equipped with seals and return springs. The primary piston is actuated directly by mechanical linkage from the brake pedal through the power booster. The secondary piston is actuated by fluid trapped between the two pistons. If a leak develops in front of the secondary piston, it moves forward until it bottoms against the front of the master cylinder, and the fluid trapped between the pistons will operate the rear brakes. If the rear brakes develop a leak, the primary piston will move forward until direct contact with the secondary piston takes place, and it will force the secondary piston to actuate the front brakes. In either case, the brake pedal moves farther when the brakes are applied, and less braking power is available.

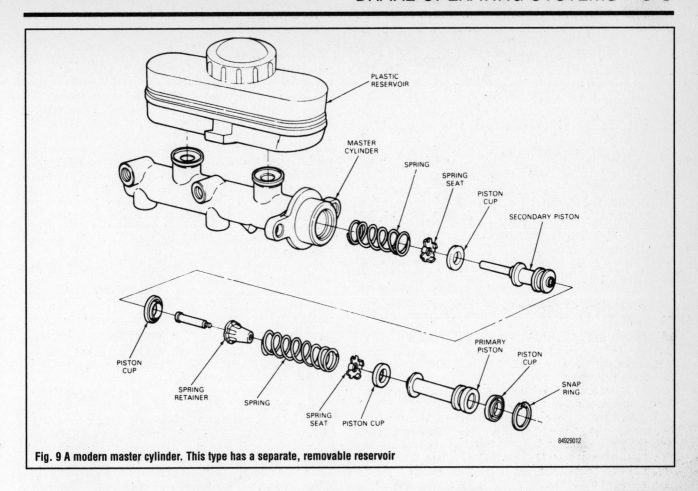

Fig. 9 A modern master cylinder. This type has a separate, removable reservoir

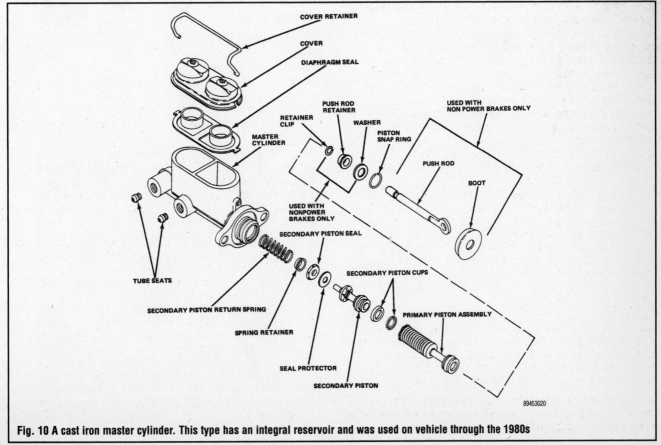

Fig. 10 A cast iron master cylinder. This type has an integral reservoir and was used on vehicle through the 1980s

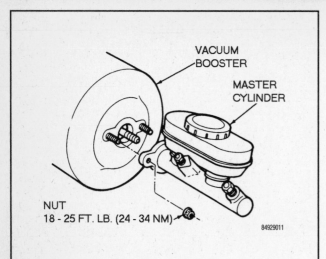

Fig. 11 The master cylinder is mounted to the power booster on most modern vehicles

shoes return to the released position, any fluid that has leaked out of the system will be replaced through the compensating ports.

Wheel Cylinders

Wheel cylinders are the devices that actuate drum brakes. They are mounted on backing plates along with the brake shoes. A brake line screws directly into the back of the wheel cylinder.

As its name suggests, this device is a cylinder in which, on modern vehicles, are two pistons, each of which has a seal. Between the pistons is a coil spring. Each end of the cylinder is capped with a dust boot. On some older vehicles, wheel cylinders contain a single piston. These vehicles use two wheel cylinders mounted opposite each other on the backing plate.

When pressurized brake fluid is applied to the wheel cylinder, the pistons are forced outward. The upper end of each brake shoe bears either directly on the pistons or on pins that bear on the pistons. The shoes are forced outward against the brake drums.

When braking action is released, return springs, mounted on the shoes, force the pistons back into the cylinder.

Most wheel cylinders are rebuildable. Kits containing all seals, pistons and boots are available at auto parts stores.

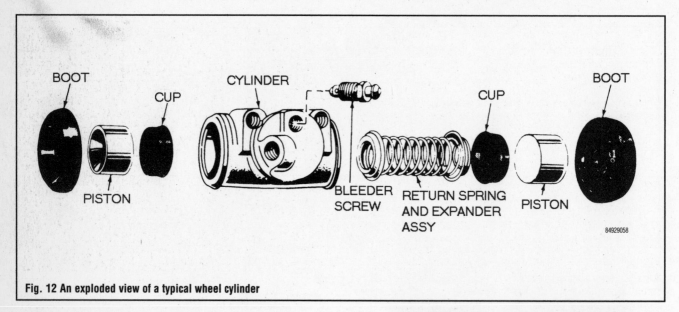

Fig. 12 An exploded view of a typical wheel cylinder

On most modern vehicles, the master cylinder is mounted in the engine compartment, usually on the firewall in front of the driver. It is connected, either directly to the brake pedal linkage in the case of non-power brakes, or, is connected to the power booster, in the case of power assisted brakes. Almost all modern vehicles are equipped with power assisted brakes.

On some older vehicles, the master cylinder can be found mounted on the frame, under the floor on the driver's side. This type is accessed through a removable plate on the floor, in front of the driver's seat.

When the brake pedal is depressed, hydraulic pressure is created in the master cylinder body. This pressure is transferred, through the brake lines, to the proportioning and differential valves. These valves transfer the pressure, through the brake lines to the wheel cylinders and calipers. At this point, the hydraulic pressure is turned into mechanical energy through the caliper and wheel cylinder pistons. This mechanical energy applies the brakes.

Upon release of the brake pedal, a spring located inside the master cylinder immediately returns the master cylinder pistons to the normal position. The pistons contain check valves and the master cylinder has compensating ports drilled in it. These are uncovered as the pistons reach their normal position. The piston check valves allow fluid to flow toward the wheel cylinders or calipers as the pistons withdraw. Then, as the pads or

Fig. 13 A wheel cylinder pushes the brake shoes outward against the drum—this shows a dual cylinder

Fig. 14 The wheel cylinder is used to actuate the brake shoes

89709P23

89549P05

Fig. 16 This is a single piston, floating caliper (which is the most common style used today)

Calipers

The caliper is a large metal casting which contains a fluid chamber and, depending on the vehicle, one to four pistons. Most modern vehicles use the single piston design.

When you depress the brake pedal, brake fluid, under pressure, forces the piston(s) out of their chamber(s) against the brake pad(s). All of these parentheses can be explained. There are two basic types of calipers: ones that move and ones that don't move. The ones that don't move are called, fixed calipers. The ones that move are called, floating or sliding calipers, depending on their design.

Fixed calipers are rigidly mounted on the steering knuckle or adapter. These calipers always employ more than one piston. When the pistons are forced out of their chambers by pressurized brake fluid, they tend to center the brake pads on the rotor by equalizing the pressure from side-to-side. The major drawback of this system is the tendency to transmit any irregularities in the brake rotor surface back to the brake pedal in the form of pulsation.

Sliding and floating calipers use a single piston. Floating calipers are mounted on pins and sliding calipers are mounted on machined surfaces. In both types, when the piston is forced out of its chamber, the whole caliper moves, either on the pins or machined surfaces, equalizing the braking action. Unlike fixed calipers, the movable caliper absorbs most pulsation.

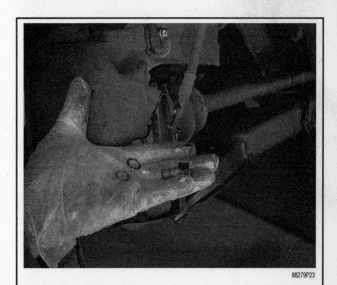

88279P23

Fig. 17 Banjo fitting bolt and washers

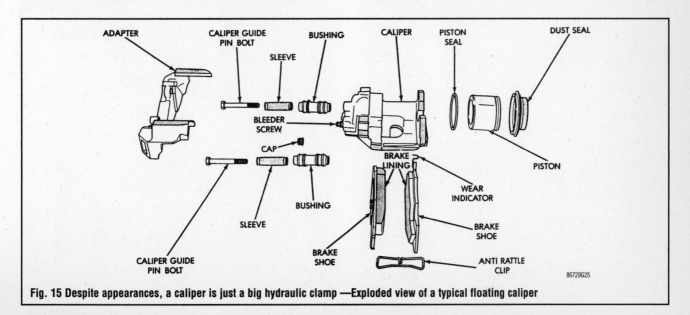

86729G25

Fig. 15 Despite appearances, a caliper is just a big hydraulic clamp —Exploded view of a typical floating caliper

The piston is equipped with one or two seals that hold the brake fluid in, and is covered with a dust boot, which keeps dirt and moisture out.

The brake line is attached to the caliper, usually, with what is called a "banjo" fitting. This type of fitting takes the form of a brass block with a hollow bolt attaching the block to the caliper. Brake fluid flows through the bolt and into the caliper. The banjo fitting is equipped with crushable brass or copper washers on either side to keep the fluid in. These washers are not reusable and must be replaced any time the line is removed. On some calipers, the brake line threads directly into the caliper housing. On this type, no sealing washers are used.

The caliper is fitted with a bleeder screw to expel air.

Most calipers are rebuildable. Kits are available at auto parts stores that contain all seals and dust boots.

Control Valves

When you step on the brake pedal, you're forcing pressurized brake fluid to all points in the hydraulic system. Sounds like a great idea, especially if you want all 4 wheels to slow down at the same time. But, since, in most cases, you're traveling forward, the vehicle's momentum creates a lot of energy in that direction. Applying the brakes will cause all that energy to be shifted forward, moving the vehicle's center of gravity forward and giving the front wheels an advantage when it comes to available traction for braking. Because of this, the front brakes will take most of the braking action. If you are applying braking pressure equally to all 4 wheels and the brakes at all wheels are equally capable, you will have one of 2 problems. Either the front wheels will not receive enough pressure to fully utilize their braking potential, or you will lock the rear wheels (slide the vehicle sideways and die in a horrible ball of fire . . .).

Ok, so let's not get carried too away here. The point is, that you don't actually want even brake pressure applied to both the front and rear wheels (unless the manufacturer balanced the brake system with different size/types of brakes at the rear wheels than the front wheels). To help correct this problem, manufacturers have come up with metering and proportioning valves, usually combined into one unit called, a combination valve.

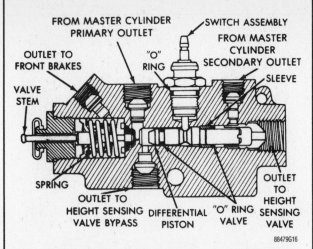

Fig. 18 Cutaway view of a combination warning switch/hold-off/proportioning valve assembly

The metering valve keeps pressure from traveling to the disc brakes on the front wheels until the brake shoes on the rear wheels have contacted the drums, ensuring that the front brakes will never be used alone. The proportioning valve controls the pressure to the rear brakes to lessen the chance of rear wheel lock-up during very hard braking.

Most modern vehicles have these valves in the brake system, but not all. Some manufacturers balance and tune the brake system by using different hydraulic and/or mechanical components on the rear wheels than that which were used on the front wheels. In these cases, even fluid pressure at all 4 wheels will not produce even braking force and therefore will not tend to lock the rear. Also, it is important to note that some modern vehicles use the ABS control valves to take the place of the metering or proportioning valve.

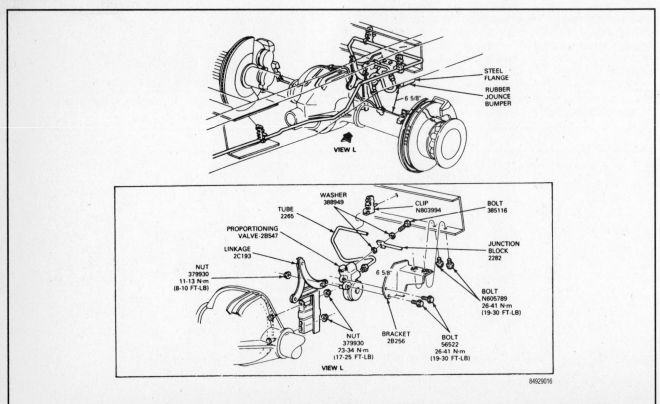

Fig. 19 An example of a height sensing proportioning valve system. You'll find these mainly on light trucks that carry varying loads

On most vehicles (who are equipped with a hydraulic control valve), this valve is mounted in the system, below the master cylinder. Usually it's found on the frame rail or firewall. On some vehicles, however, the proportioning valve part is integral with the master cylinder and is replaced with it.

➡️**The metering valve is also known as a hold-off valve because it "holds-off" full pressure to the front discs until the rear brake shoes are in full contact with the drum.**

A height sensing proportioning valve regulates the front-to-rear braking balance based upon vehicle load conditions. The valve senses vehicle loads through variations in rear suspension height. With a light load on the rear axle, the valve reduces hydraulic pressure to the rear brakes. As the load increases, more hydraulic pressure is released to the rear brakes.

Brake Warning Switch

Most vehicles use a hydraulically split brake system, to help make sure that only half of the system could fail from a single point leak. On these vehicles, both systems are routed through, but hydraulically separated by a pressure differential switch. The function of this switch is to alert the driver to a malfunction in one of the hydraulic systems. Since the brake system is split, a failure in one part of the brake system does not result in failure of the entire hydraulic brake system. The brake warning light on the instrument panel will come **ON** if one of the brake systems should fail after the brake pedal is depressed. The warning light switch is the latching type. It will automatically re-center itself after the repair is made and the pedal is depressed.

The instrument panel bulb can be checked each time the ignition switch is turned to **ON** or **START** or the parking brake is set.

The brake warning light is lit only when the parking brake is applied with the ignition key turned **ON**. The same light will also illuminate should 1 of the 2 service brake systems fail.

To test the service brake warning system, raise the vehicle on a hoist and open a wheel cylinder bleeder while a helper depresses the brake pedal and watches the warning light. If the light fails to light, check for a burned out bulb, disconnected socket or a broken or disconnected wire at the switch. If the bulb is not burned out and the wire continuity is uninterrupted check the service brake warning switch operation with a test light between the switch terminal and a voltage source.

If the light still fails to light, disconnect the brake tubes from the valve assembly and install a new valve assembly. If a new is installed, bleed the system. The warning switch is not serviced separately. Do not remove the switch or attempt to repair.

After repairing and bleeding the brake system applying the brakes with moderate force will hydraulically re-center the valve's piston and automatically turn off the warning light. Do not disassemble to reset the piston.

Power Boosters

Virtually all modern vehicles use a power assisted brake system to multiply the braking force and reduce pedal effort. There are two types of power assist used. The most widely used, by far, is the vacuum assist booster. The other is the hydraulically assisted booster.

VACUUM ASSISTED BOOSTERS

Most modern vehicles use a vacuum assisted power brake. This system was likely developed because, on all internal combustion engines, except diesels, vacuum is always available when the engine is operating, making the system is simple and efficient.

With diesel engines, vacuum is created and stored by way of a belt-driven vacuum pump and reservoir. In either case, the operation of the vacuum assist is the same.

A vacuum diaphragm is located on the front of the master cylinder and assists the driver in applying the brakes, reducing both the effort and travel he must put into moving the brake pedal. The vacuum diaphragm housing is normally connected to the intake manifold by a vacuum hose. A check valve is placed at the point where the hose enters the diaphragm housing, so that during periods of low manifold vacuum brake assist will not be lost.

Depressing the brake pedal closes off the vacuum source and allows

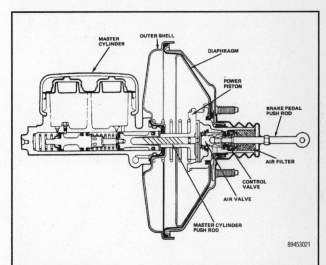

Fig. 21 An cutaway view of a single diaphragm vacuum-type power booster

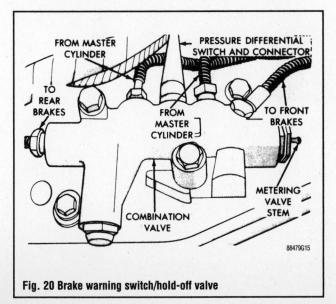

Fig. 20 Brake warning switch/hold-off valve

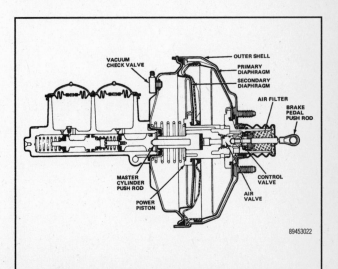

Fig. 22 An cutaway view of a dual diaphragm vacuum-type power booster

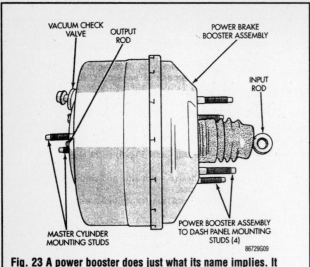

Fig. 23 A power booster does just what its name implies. It boosts the power applied by your foot on the pedal

atmospheric pressure to enter on one side of the diaphragm. This causes the master cylinder pistons to move and apply the brakes. When the brake pedal is released, vacuum is applied to both sides of the diaphragm and springs return the diaphragm and master cylinder pistons to the released position.

If the vacuum supply fails, the brake pedal rod will contact the end of the master cylinder actuator rod and the system will apply the brakes without any power assistance. The driver will notice that much higher pedal effort is needed to stop the vehicle and that the pedal feels harder than usual.

If you think this is the case you can check it as follows:

Operate the engine at idle without touching the brake pedal for at least one minute.

Turn **OFF** the engine and wait one minute. Test for the presence of assist vacuum by depressing the brake pedal and releasing it several times. If vacuum is present in the system, light application will produce less and less pedal travel. If there is no vacuum, air is leaking into the system.

With the engine **OFF**, pump the brake pedal until the supply vacuum is entirely gone. Put light, steady pressure on the brake pedal. Start the engine and let it idle. If the system is operating correctly, the brake pedal should fall toward the floor if the constant pressure is maintained.

HYDRAULICALLY ASSISTED BOOSTERS

Used on some large cars and light trucks, the unit is fed hydraulic fluid through the power steering system. The booster assembly, sometimes known generically by the brand name Hydro-Boost, contains a valve which controls pump pressure while braking, a lever to control the position of the valve and a boost piston to provide the force to operate the master cylinder attached to the front of the booster. The unit has a reserve system designed to store pressurized fluid to provide at least 2 brake applications in the event of hydraulic supply system failure, such as a broken power steering belt. The brakes can also be applied unassisted in the event of system depletion.

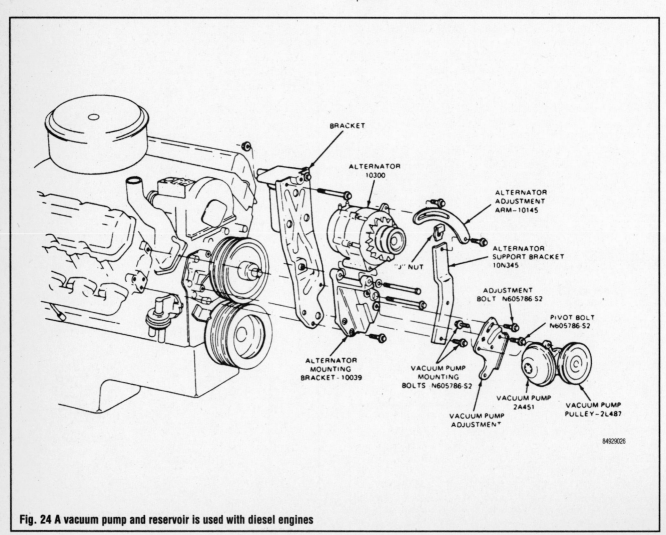

Fig. 24 A vacuum pump and reservoir is used with diesel engines

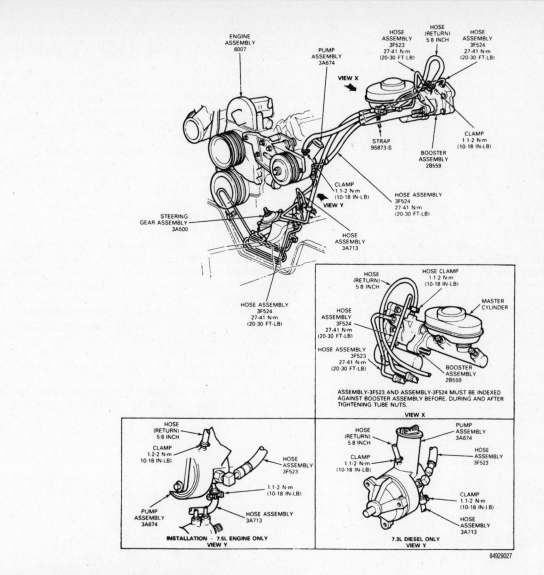

Fig. 25 A common hydraulic booster installation

Anti-Lock Brake Systems

GENERAL INFORMATION

The purpose of the Anti-lock Brake System (ABS) is to prevent wheel lock-up under hard braking conditions. This is especially critical on wet or slippery surfaces. ABS is desirable because a vehicle that is stopped without locking one or more wheels, can stop with more control and in a shorter distance than a vehicle with locked wheels.

Under normal braking conditions, the ABS system operates just like a standard system. When one or more wheels shows a tendency to lock during braking, the ABS computer detects this and puts the system into the anti-lock mode. In this mode, hydraulic pressure is modulated to each wheel, preventing any one wheel from locking. The system can hold or reduce pressure at each wheel as necessary, depending on the signal received by the computer.

The effect is sort of like pumping your brakes, although it's done hundreds of time faster. In fact, when driving an ABS vehicle on ice or snow, a driver must overcome the urge to pump the brake during a stop. Let the ABS system work. Pumping the pedal on an ABS equipped vehicle will defeat the system.

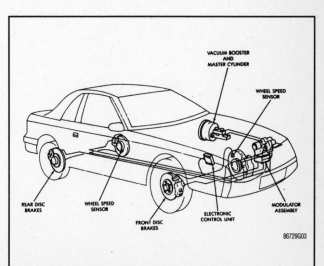

Fig. 26 A simplified drawing of what most 4-wheel anti-lock brake systems look like

Parking Brake Systems

GENERAL INFORMATION

Parking brakes are designed to hold your vehicle in position while the vehicle is at rest. Which means that, if you apply the parking brake fully, with the transmission in neutral, the vehicle shouldn't go anywhere on its own.

If, however, that is not the case, you'll probably have to make a parking brake adjustment or, possibly, replace a part in the parking brake system.

➡**For parking brake adjustments, see the Inspection and Adjustment section in this book.**

On the vast majority of vehicles, the parking brakes work on the rear wheels. Some imported cars have used cables which actuated the front brakes. And some trucks use transmission mounted brake assemblies, that lock the rear wheels, not at the wheel brakes, but at a transmission or driveshaft mounted brake assembly.

In the case of vehicles with rear drum brakes, the parking brake system utilizes one brake shoe on each wheel. In most cases, when you activate the parking brake pedal or lever, a cable is pulled, which in turn is connected to a device called an equalizer, which is connected to 2 cables, one each going to a rear wheel. Some lever type systems route both rear cables directly to the lever, eliminating the single lead cable and equalizer. Back at the rear wheels, the brake cable pulls on a lever that forces the rearmost brake shoe against the drum. Once the cable tension is released, a spring on the shoe returns it to its original position and a spring on the cable relaxes it.

With rear disc brakes, one of 2 systems is used.

Some vehicles incorporate the parking brake mechanism into the caliper at each rear wheel. In this type caliper, the cable pulls on a lever attached to the caliper that then rotates the caliper piston outward forcing the pads against the rotor.

The other method with rear disc brakes is essentially the same as a drum brake setup. The rotor incorporates a brake drum. A backing plate is fixed to the spindle or axle that carries a set of brake shoes. When the cable is pulled, these shoes expand against the brake drum-like inner surface of the rotor. And, like rear drum brakes, they retract via springs when the cable tension is released.

Just to complicate matters, there is a third type of parking brake system. It's used on some heavy-duty light trucks. In this system, a drum-type parking brake is attached to the rear of the transmission and the driveshaft. When the cable is pulled, expanding internal brake shoes lock the drum, thereby locking the driveshaft.

The parking brakes are applied, on most vehicles, in one of 3 ways:
   a. A foot-operated pedal
   b. A pull-up lever
   c. An underdash pull handle

Most modern cars and trucks have gone to the pull-up lever. Next most popular is the foot-operated pedal. An underdash handle is found mostly on older vehicles and some imports.

All 3 operate much in the same way. The lever or pedal incorporates a notched section. When the pedal is depressed, or the lever or handle is pulled, a spring-loaded pawl drops into the notches, holding the pedal or lever in whatever position you set it. To release the parking brakes, the pawl has to be disengaged.

On pedal-operated systems, this is done with either a release handle, which removes the pawl from the notches or by stepping on the pedal again, which retracts the pawl via a spring.

On the pull-lever type, the pawl is usually released by depressing a button on the end of the lever. On some systems, the release is performed by momentarily lifting the lever.

On the pull-handle type, the systems is released by turning the handle slightly so that the notches are turned away from the pawl, much like a caulk gun.

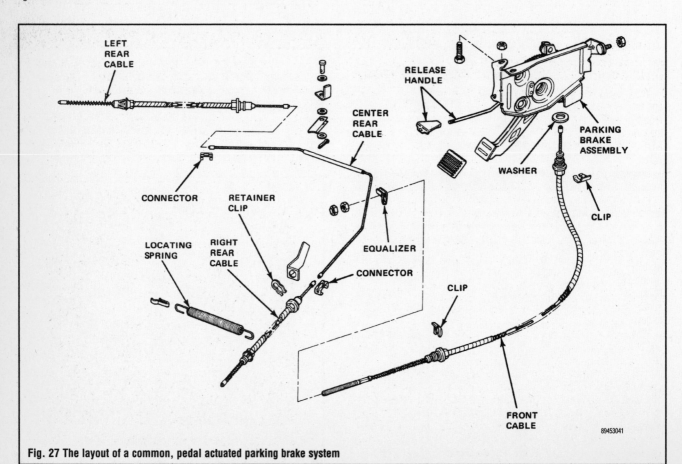

Fig. 27 The layout of a common, pedal actuated parking brake system

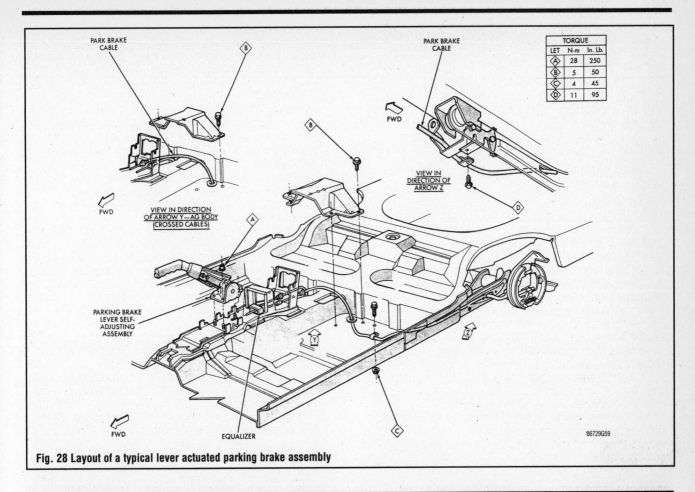

TORQUE		
LET	N·m	In. Lb.
A	28	250
B	5	50
C	4	45
D	11	95

Fig. 28 Layout of a typical lever actuated parking brake assembly

BRAKE SYSTEM MAINTENANCE (INSPECTION AND ADJUSTMENTS)

Inspection

You should inspect your brakes periodically, really. You check your oil and antifreeze regularly, right? You check your tire tread and air pressure regularly, right? You give a quick look at the belts and hoses now and then, right? Well, you should! You check all these things regularly. But, if any of these fail, at worst you'll get stuck in the rain, at night, on the Interstate.

Howvever, if your brakes should fail . . . the kids get the estate. Slightly more important, isn't it?

Inspecting the brake system isn't tough to do, so don't use that as an excuse. On vehicles with disc brakes, just remove the wheels and take a look. The brake pads can be seen, either through the top of the caliper or by looking at the side of the caliper. A good, safe limit is ⅛ inch. Some vehicles have brake pads equipped with a wear sensor. It's no so much a sensor as it is a curb feeler. It's a piece of metal attached to the brake pad that extends down the side of the pad to a point equal to the minimum brake thickness. When the pad wears to that point, the sensor starts scraping the surface of the rotor making a really annoying squeal. You really don't want to get to that point.

With drum brakes, it's a little tougher. You'll have to remove the wheels and brake drums. If the brake shoes are worn to within ⅛ inch of the metal backing plate, they need replacing.

If you find that brake shoes or pads must be replaced, take some time to check the drum or rotor before proceeding. The rotor can be checked for excessive run-out using a dial gauge (or it can be taken to a machine shop for measurement if you don't have one. Both drums and rotors are normally stamped with wear measurements. In the case of a drum, it shows the maximum wear diameter (beyond which a drum should be replaced). In the case of a rotor, a minimum thickness measurement should be supplied which tells you when it should be discarded.

Also, if, when inspecting either front or rear brakes, you notice any wetness, you have a problem that needs immediate attention. Calipers and wheel cylinders are hydraulically actuated devices. They are full of brake fluid that comes under pressure when the brakes are applied. Holding this fluid in are rubber seals. Seals wear out and leak over time. If you run out of brake fluid, you run out of brakes. Also, as fluid leaks out, air gets in. Air is bad for hydraulic brake systems. Air contains moisture that can contaminate the system. Air is compressible, causing a spongy pedal feeling,

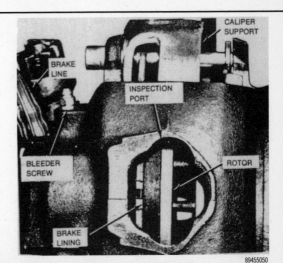

Fig. 29 On most vehicles, brake pad wear can be checked by peering through the caliper

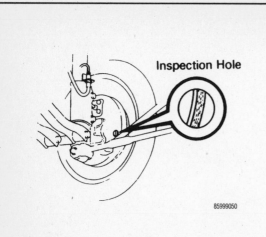

Fig. 30 If you are lucky, your drum brake vehicle might have an inspection hole . . .

reducing brake effectiveness. Service to correct the problem should be performed without delay!

While you're down there, you may as well inspect the hoses and pipes that carry the fluid. Hoses should be flexible and without cracks. Pipes should be rust-free or with a light rust coating, which is normal over time. If a hose has cracked rubber or a pipe has thick, scaly rust, it should be replaced. Down there, too, most vehicles have what's called a proportioning valve. It's usually located below the master cylinder and has the front and rear brakes pipes attached. Its job is to divide up braking action between the front and rear and it's subject to leaks just like any other brake part.

Lastly, the master cylinder. This is the easiest to check since you don't have to do any work, or even, in most cases, bend over. The cap should be in good condition and fit securely. No wetness should be present.

This inspection program should be done AT LEAST once a year. But, we recommend that you perform it more frequently. Every time the hood is open, you should glance at the brake fluid level. Every time the vehicle is raised (as during oil changes for example), you should inspect the hoses and lines. And every time a wheel is removed (to rotate tires or install seasonal tires), the pads and shoes should be checked for wear. It's cheap insurance and brakes are an integral part of safety maintenance.

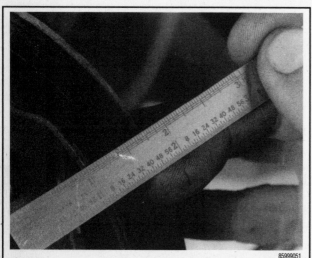

Fig. 31 . . . but it is more likely that you will have to remove the drums in order to measure brake shoe wear

Fig. 33 Drums and rotors normally have a wear limit machined into the surface to tell you when they must be replaced

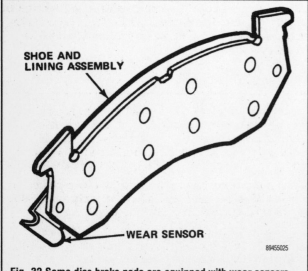

Fig. 32 Some disc brake pads are equipped with wear sensors

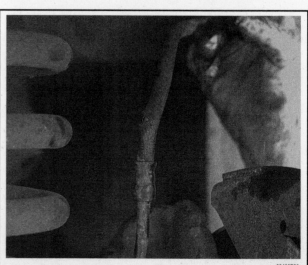

Fig. 34 This is an example of a damaged hose . . .

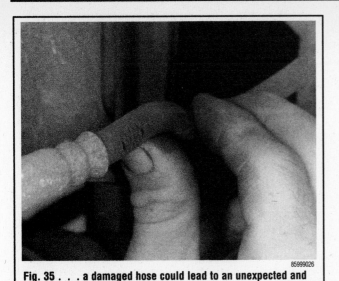

Fig. 35 . . . a damaged hose could lead to an unexpected and sudden brake failure, so check them often

Adjustments

BRAKE PEDAL

The brake pedal, on most modern vehicles, is mounted up under the instrument panel. The pedal pivots on a stud or rod. The top end of the pedal is connected to the master cylinder or power booster via a link or linkage. When you step on the bottom end, the pedal pivots, the linkage moves and the master cylinder and/or booster applies pressure to the fluid.

On most older vehicles, the pedal went straight through the floor to a pivot point on the frame. The pedal on these vehicles actuates a rod which depresses the master cylinder piston. Road fumes and dirt are kept out of the vehicle with rubber seals.

Many brake pedals can be adjusted for free-play. This is usually done at the pushrod or the stop light switch. This adjustment varies by manufacturer and model, however, it's generally about 1–5mm ($\frac{1}{16}$–$\frac{1}{8}$ in.). The accompanying illustration shows a typical adjustment sequence.

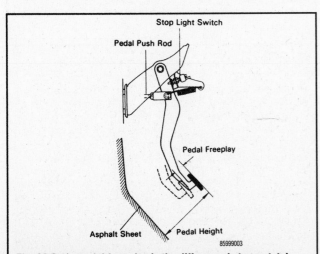

Fig. 36 Brake pedal free-play is the difference between total pedal height and the height at which resistance is felt (the pedal begins to actuate the brakes)

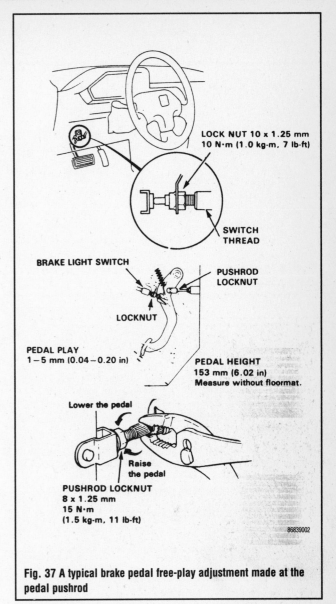

Fig. 37 A typical brake pedal free-play adjustment made at the pedal pushrod

➡In no case should the pedal go all the way to the floor. Also, there should be some, no matter how slight, movement, or free-play, with the pedal released. If the pedal goes all the way to the floor or has no free movement at all, there is a problem somewhere and the system should be troubleshot.

STOP LIGHT SWITCH

On most vehicles, the stop light switch is mounted on or near the pedal arm. The switch is an electro-mechanical device. That means that a mechanical motion allows an electric current to make a circuit.

When you depress the brake pedal, a plunger in the switch is depressed, connecting 2 contacts within the switch, completing a circuit, lighting the brake lights.

➡Some switches may have multiple electrical connections or even a vacuum connection that is used to cancel the cruise control when the brakes are applied.

If you're not sure whether the switch is bad or not, it can be easily checked with an ohmmeter. Continuity should be present at one plunger position and not at the other.

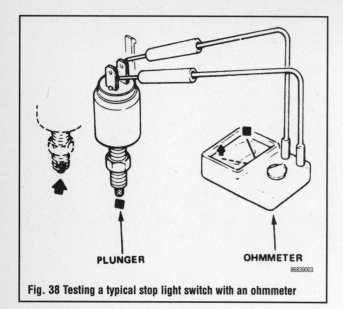

Fig. 38 Testing a typical stop light switch with an ohmmeter

Stop Light Switch

Some switches are not adjustable. This means that they are in the proper position when installed correctly.

On those switches which are adjustable, when you install them, they are either screwed or slid into proximity with the pedal arm contact point.

In most cases, the adjustment is made by positioning the switch so that the plunger just contacts the pedal arm, then moving it away slightly—usually about 1/32 in. (0.8mm).

➡**Many domestic vehicles use a switch which is fitted into a ratcheting clip. On these types, switch is seated in the clip, then the pedal is manually pulled upward to adjust the switch (you should listen for a clicking sound as the switch is adjusted by the pedal).**

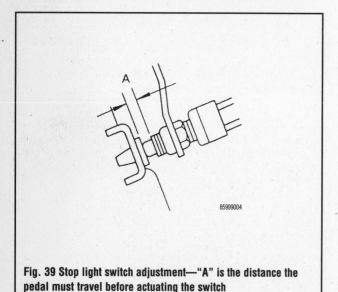

Fig. 39 Stop light switch adjustment—"A" is the distance the pedal must travel before actuating the switch

DISC BRAKES

Disc brakes are inherently self-adjusting. That means that you don't have to do anything routinely or at replacement. As the pads wear down, the piston(s) moves out to compensate.

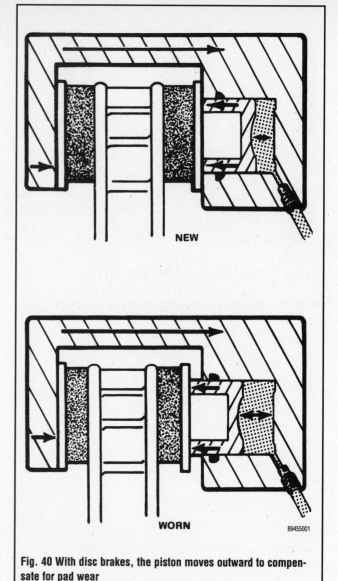

Fig. 40 With disc brakes, the piston moves outward to compensate for pad wear

DRUM BRAKES

Drum brakes on all modern vehicles are self-adjusting, however, when the shoes are replaced, a preliminary adjustment makes the job easier.

On most vehicles, the adjustment is made with an expanding adjuster that is a threaded sleeve/stud assembly. Turning the knurled nut or star-wheel expands or contracts the spring-loaded brake shoes. On most vehicles, this adjuster can be accessed without removing the drum, or, for that matter, the wheel.

Jack up the rear of the vehicle and support it safely on jackstands. Block the front wheels and release the parking brake. Put the transmission in neutral. All this allows the wheels to turn freely. Remove the rubber plug in the brake backing plate and insert a brake adjusting tool. If you're applying brake pressure, that is, expanding the brakes, just turn the star-wheel or knurled adjuster until the brake shoes lock the drum, meaning, you can't turn it. Then, back off the adjustment until the drum can JUST turn freely. Some manufacturers even say it's okay to have a SLIGHT amount of drag. If your vehicle has self-adjusters, you'll find that the adjuster can't be backed off. That's because the adjusting lever is holding it in place. You'll have to shove a thin punch or similar device in the hole

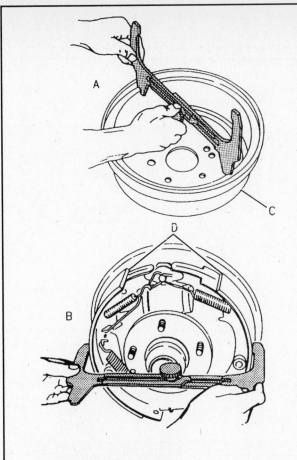

A SETTING TOOL TO DRUM
B SETTING BRAKE SHOES TO TOOL
C BRAKE DRUM
D BRAKE LININGS

87959003

Fig. 41 After a brake job and before installing the drum, check the inside diameter of the drum as well as the widest point of the installed shoes

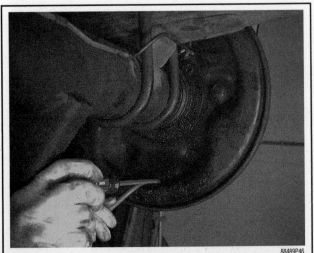

88489P46

Fig. 42 Backing off the drum brake adjustment while holding the adjusting lever

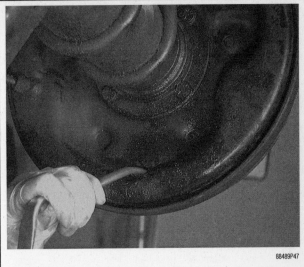

88489P47

Fig. 43 Adjusting the drum brakes using a brake spoon tool

with the brake adjusting tool. Just push slightly on the adjusting lever. That'll free the adjuster.

There are a few vehicle models that use cam-type adjusters. With these, a hex or square headed stud protrudes through the backing plate. Turning this stud rotates an eccentric cam that contacts the brake shoe. Turning it one way pushes the shoe outward; turning it the other way rotates the cam away from the shoe allowing the springs to pull the shoe away from the drum.

PARKING BRAKES

Vehicles with Rear Wheel Mounted Parking Brakes

Some parking brakes are self-adjusting. The following applies to most vehicles with adjustable parking brakes.

1. Release the parking brakes fully.
2. Raise and safely support the vehicle.
3. Adjust the rear brakes.
4. Loosen the adjusting nut(s) until there is slack in all the cables. On vehicles with a parking brake pedal and some lever-actuated types, a single cable from the pedal or lever connects with the rear cables via a device called an equalizer. The adjusting nut is located at this point. On some

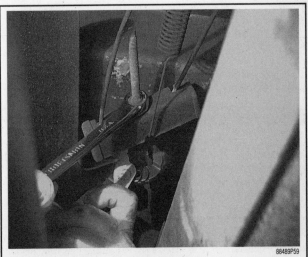

88489P59

Fig. 44 Most parking brakes are adjusted using jam and adjusting nuts on a threaded rod at the equalizer

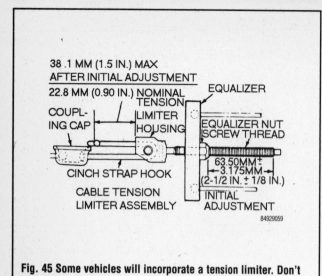

Fig. 45 Some vehicles will incorporate a tension limiter. Don't let this bother you. The adjustment will be the same

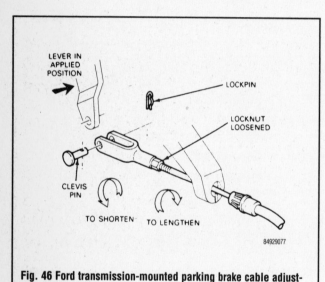

Fig. 46 Ford transmission-mounted parking brake cable adjusting points

lever-type systems, both rear cables go directly to the lever. There is an adjusting nut for each cable at the lever.

5. Rotate the rear wheels and tighten the cable adjusting nut(s) until there is a slight drag at the wheels.

6. Loosen the nut until all drag is eliminated.

7. Apply and release the parking brake several times. Make sure there is no drag at the wheels.

BRAKE RELATED SYSTEMS

There are times in brake service when a wheel bearing hub must be removed because it is an integral part of the brake disc or drum. Because non-sealed wheel bearings may require periodic service, inspection and adjustment when they are removed, you should become familiar with them during brake service.

Wheel Bearings

A lot of brake work involves removing the wheel bearings. Whenever this is done, the bearings should be repacked and must be adjusted. Also,

8. To check the operation, make sure the parking brake holds with the vehicle in gear.

One more item . . . on vehicles with rear disc brakes, wherein the parking brake is inside the drum-like rotor, an adjustment can be made. To adjust the parking brake shoes perform the following procedure.

a. Back off the cable adjuster locknut.

b. Raise and safely support the vehicle and remove the wheel. Remove the hole plug in the brake rotor.

c. Use an adjuster tool to turn the adjuster wheel to expand the brake shoes until the rotor will not turn.

d. Turn the adjuster until the rotor turns freely with a slight drag.

9. Once the parking brake shoes have been properly adjusted, you can adjust the cable mechanism.

Trucks with Transmission Mounted Parking Brakes

FORD TYPE

1. Place the transmission in gear.

2. Fully release the parking brake pedal.

3. Raise and safely support the vehicle.

4. Spray penetrating oil on the adjusting clevis, jam nut and threaded end of the cable.

5. Loosen the jam nut and remove the locking pin from the clevis pin.

6. Remove the clevis pin, clevis and jam nut from the cable.

7. Back off the clevis until there is slack in the cable.

8. Screw on the clevis until the pin can be inserted while the lever and cable are held tightly in the applied position. Then, remove the pin, let go of the cable and lever and turn the clevis 10 full turns counterclockwise (loosen).

9. Install the pin.

GENERAL MOTORS, INTERNATIONAL HARVESTER AND JEEP

1. Raise and support the vehicle safely.

2. Spray penetrating oil on the adjusting clevis, jam nut and threaded end of the cable.

3. Loosen the jam nut and remove the locking pin from the clevis pin.

4. Rotate the brake drum to align the access hole with the adjusting screw. If equipped with manual transmission the access hole is located at the bottom of the backing plate. If equipped with automatic transmission the access hole is located at the top of the shoe.

5. For first time adjustment it will be necessary to remove the driveshaft and the drum in order to remove the lanced area from the drum and clean out the metal shavings.

6. Adjust the screw until the drum cannot be rotated by hand. Back off the adjusting screw 10 notches, the drum should rotate freely.

7. Position the parking brake lever in the fully released position. Take up the slack in the cable to overcome spring tension.

8. Adjust the clevis of the pull rod to align with the hole in the relay lever. Install the clevis pin. Install a new cover in the drum access hole.

wheel bearings require periodic maintenance. A premium, high melting point grease must be used. Long fiber type greases must not be used. This service is recommended by most manufacturers every 30,000 miles or whenever the drums or rotors are resurfaced. Before handling the bearings, there are a few things that you should remember to do and not to do.

DO the following:

• Remove all outside dirt from the housing before exposing the bearing.

• Treat a used bearing as gently as you would a new one.

• Work with clean tools in clean surroundings.

• Use clean, dry gloves, or at least clean, dry hands.

• Clean solvents and flushing fluids are a must.
• Use clean paper when laying out the bearings to dry.
• Protect disassembled bearings from rust and dirt. Cover them up.
• Use clean, lint-free rags to wipe the bearings.
• Keep the bearings in oil-proof paper when they are to be stored or are not in use.
• Clean the inside of the housing before replacing the bearing.

Do NOT do the following:
• Do not work in dirty surroundings.
• Do not use dirty, chipped or damaged tools.
• Do not work on wooden work benches or use wooden mallets.
• Do not handle bearings with dirty or moist hands.
• Do not use gasoline for cleaning. Use a safe solvent.
• Do not spin dry bearings with compressed air. They will be damaged.
• Do not use cotton waste or dirty cloths to wipe bearings.
• Do not scratch or nick bearing surfaces.
• Do not allow the bearing to come in contact with dirt or rust at any time.

REMOVAL, REPACKING & INSTALLATION

2-Wheel Drive Vehicles

The following procedure applies to most non-drive wheel, tapered roller bearings (rear wheel bearings on front wheel drive vehicles and front wheel bearings on rear wheel drive vehicles). It does not apply to 4-wheel drive vehicles or vehicles with unitized bearings. Unitized bearings are sealed hub/bearing assemblies. With these assemblies, the bearings cannot be accessed. The hub/bearing assembly is replaced as a unit.

REMOVAL

1. Raise and support the front or rear end on jackstands.
2. Remove the wheel.
3. If you're working with disc brakes, remove the caliper from the disc and wire it to the underbody to prevent damage to the brake hose. If you have a rotor that's not part of the hub, remove it.
4. Remove the grease cap from the hub. Then, remove the cotter pin, nut lock, adjusting nut and flat washer from the spindle. Wiggle the hub to free the outer bearing. Remove the outer bearing from the hub.
5. Pull the hub assembly off the spindle and place it, outside up, on 2 wood blocks.
6. Drive out the inner bearing and grease seal from the hub. If the bearings are being reused, drive it out with a hammer handle. The wood will protect the bearing from damage.

Fig. 48 Pry the dust cap from the hub, taking care not to distort or damage its flange

Fig. 49 Once the bent ends are cut, grasp the cotter pin and pull or pry it free of the spindle . . .

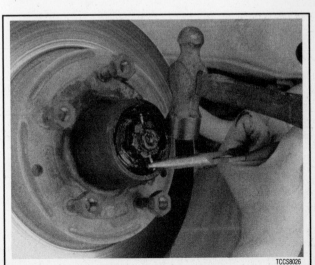

Fig. 50 . . . if difficulty is encountered, gently tap on the pliers with a hammer to help free the cotter pin

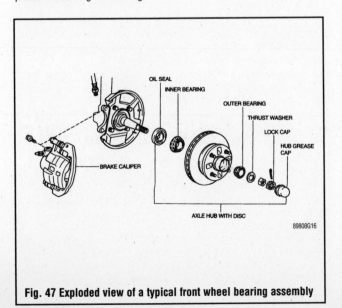

Fig. 47 Exploded view of a typical front wheel bearing assembly

Fig. 51 Loosen and remove the castellated nut from the spindle—some vehicles use a nut lock instead of a castellated nut

Fig. 52 Remove the washer from the spindle . . .

Fig. 53 . . . then with the nut and washer out of the way, the outer bearing may be removed from the hub

Fig. 54 Pull the hub and inner bearing assembly from the spindle

Fig. 55 Use a small prytool (or a seal puller if available) to remove the old inner bearing seal

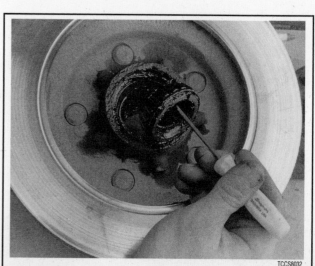

Fig. 56 With the seal removed, the inner bearing may be withdrawn from the hub

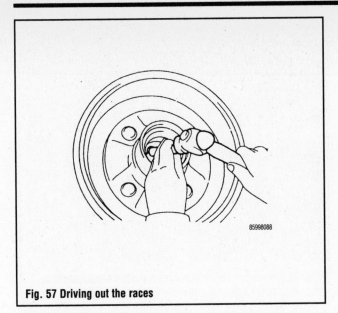

Fig. 57 Driving out the races

→If the bearings are being replaced, the bearing races should also be replaced since bearings and races are a matched set and establish a wear pattern. Never install new bearings in old races. Premature wear will result.

7. To remove the races, remove the old grease from the hub. Working from either side, place a long punch against the inner shoulder of the race. In some hubs, notches or slots are provided for this purpose. Drive out the race, hammering a various points around its circumference. When one is out, go to the other.

CLEANING AND INSPECTION

→Clean all parts in a non-flammable solvent and let them air dry. Only use lint-free rags to dry the bearings. Never spin-dry a bearing with compressed air, as this will damage the rollers.

1. Clean all grease from the inner and outer bearing cups with solvent. Inspect the races for pits, scratches, or excessive wear. If the races are damaged, remove them.

2. Clean the inner and outer cone and roller assemblies with solvent and shake them dry. If the cone and roller assemblies show excessive wear or damage, replace them with the bearing races as a unit.

3. Clean the spindle and the inside of the hub with solvent to thoroughly remove all old grease.

4. Covering the spindle with a clean cloth, brush all loose dirt and dust from the brake assembly. Remove the cloth carefully so as to not get dirt on the spindle.

→It is imperative that all old grease be removed from the bearings and surrounding surfaces before repacking. The new lithium-based grease is not compatible with the sodium base grease used in the past.

Bearings that show signs of heat discoloration, pitting, uneven wear, rust, corrosion or loose rollers, should be replaced. Bearing races should be shiny and smooth or replace them. Don't forget, never replace just the bearings or races. Bearings and races are a matched set. Replacing bearings without replacing the races will result in premature wear and bearing failure.

Check the spindle for signs of heat discoloration, pitting, uneven wear, rust, corrosion, etc. Some light yellowing is normal. If the spindles show signs of blue discoloration, it's a sign of overheating due to a lack of lubrication or overly tight bearings. Excessively blued spindles should be replaced. Light rust or corrosion should be removed. Excessively rusted or corroded spindles should be replaced.

REPACKING

→Don't mix different types of grease. For example, sodium based grease is not compatible with lithium based grease. Read the package labels and be careful not to mix types. If there is any doubt as to the type of grease used, completely clean the old grease from the bearing and hub before replacing.

Packing wheel bearings with grease is best accomplished by using a wheel bearing packer (available at most automotive parts stores).

1. If a wheel bearing packer is not available, the bearings may be packed by hand.

   a. Place a "healthy" glob of grease in the palm of one hand.

   b. Force the edge of the bearing into the grease so that the grease fills the space between the rollers and the bearing cage.

   c. Keep rotating the bearing while continuing to push the grease through.

   d. Continue until the grease is forced out the other side of the bearing.

2. Place the packed bearing on a clean surface and cover it until it is time for installation.

Fig. 58 Thoroughly pack the bearing with fresh, high temperature wheel-bearing grease before installation

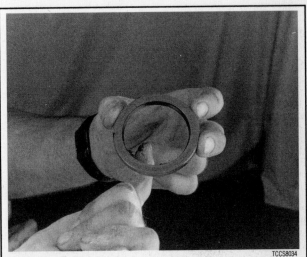

Fig. 59 Apply a thin coat of fresh grease to the new inner bearing seal lip

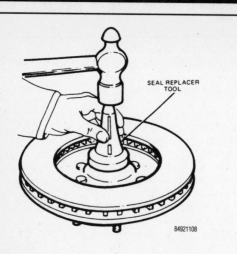

Fig. 60 If available, use a seal installer to drive the new seal into position. But if a driver is not available . . .

Fig. 62 Tighten the nut to specifications while gently spinning the wheel, then adjust the bearing

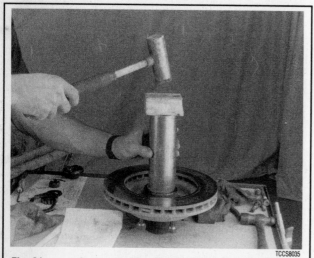

Fig. 61 . . . a large, smooth socket or pipe can be used to install the inner bearing seal to the hub

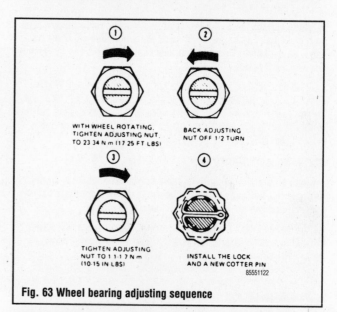

Fig. 63 Wheel bearing adjusting sequence

INSTALLATION

If the inner and/or outer bearing races were removed, install the replacement races in the hub. Sometimes it's hard to tell if the races are fully seated. One trick is to coat the installment area with a light coating of grease. As the races are driven in the grease will be squeezed out against the seating ridge. When the races are fully seated, a ring of grease will be noticed. Also, if you have a good ear for sound changes, you'll notice a distinct change in tone when the race contacts the seating ridge. The clinking will turn to a clunk or clank.

To install the races:

1. Coat the outside of the race with grease.
2. Position the race in the hub as evenly as possible.

➡There are drivers made for this purpose. If one isn't available, find a socket that's the same diameter as the race. If you don't have one of these, either, it is possible to install the race by hammering on the outside edge, evenly. Don't hammer directly on the race. Use something between the hammer and race such as a short, wide punch.

3. Drive the race into the hub until it's fully seated against the ridge. Now, do the other one.

Fig. 64 After the bearings are adjusted, install the dust cap by gently tapping on its flange

To install the inner bearing and seal:

➡**Always use a new seal.**

4. Coat the race with grease.

5. Place the greased inner bearing in the race.

6. Coat the outer edge of the new seal with grease. Some seals have a coating on the outer edge when new. These seals should not be coated with grease. The packaging should tell you. If not, just look at the edge. If it has the look and feel of sealer—green, red or blue coloring, or sticky—it has a sealer coating.

7. Place the seal, with the smooth side out, on the hub.

➡**Seal drivers should be used. If you don't have one, tap gently on the seal with a rubber or plastic mallet.**

8. Drive the seal into place. "Place" is, usually, flush with the end of the hub.

To install the hub and outer bearing:

9. Fill the hub cavity—the part between the bearings—with wheel bearing grease. The recess of the cavity should be filled flush. Don't overfill it.

10. Install the hub on the spindle. To prevent damage to the seal and spindle threads, keep the hub centered on the spindle.

11. Install the outer bearing in the hub race and the flat washer on the spindle. Install the adjusting nut.

➡**The following adjustment is for most vehicles. Yours may be different. If you're in doubt, check the appropriate Chilton manual for your vehicle.**

12. Adjust the wheel bearings by tightening the adjusting nut to 17–25 ft. lbs. (23–34 Nm) while rotating the wheel to seat the bearing. Then back off the adjusting nut ¼ to ½ turn (90–180°). Retighten the adjusting nut finger-tight.

13. Install the locknut so that the castellations are aligned with the cotter pin hole. Install the new cotter pin. It's best not to reuse a cotter pin. Bend the ends of the cotter pin around the castellations of the locknut to prevent interference with the grease cap.

14. Position the grease cap on the hub and tap it into place. Try to avoid denting it. You don't want it contacting the spindle.

4-Wheel Drive Trucks and Sport Utility Vehicles

The following procedure applies to most vehicles. If you're in doubt as to whether or not it applies to your vehicle, consult the appropriate Chilton manual.

REMOVAL

1. Raise the vehicle and install safety stands.

2. Remove the wheel.

3. Refer to the appropriate Chilton Manual and remove the locking hub assemblies.

4. On most vehicles, remove the outer locknut. This requires a socket made for that purpose, available at most auto parts stores. Then, remove the lock ring from the bearing adjusting nut. This can be done with your finger tips or a screwdriver. Use the locknut socket to remove the bearing adjusting nut.

On some vehicles, a self-locking adjusting nut is used. Remove the self-locking nut with a suitable hub nut wrench, applying inward pressure to disengage the adjusting nut locking splines, while turning it counterclockwise to remove it.

5. Remove the caliper and suspend it out of the way.

6. Slide the hub assembly off of the spindle. The outer wheel bearing will slide out as the hub is removed, so be prepared to catch it.

7. Lay the hub, outside up, on 2 wood blocks. Drive the inner bearing and grease seal out of the hub. If the bearings are being reused, you can do

Fig. 66 Loosening the outer locknut—On most vehicles this requires a special socket

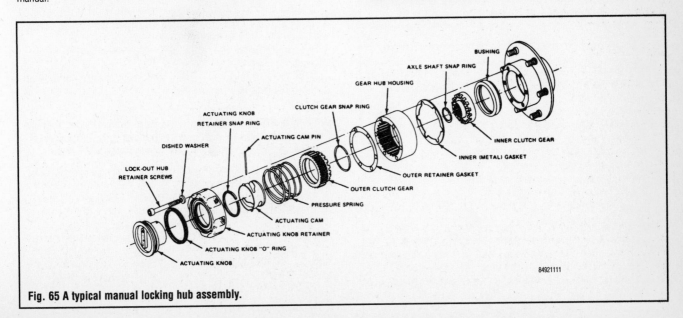

Fig. 65 A typical manual locking hub assembly.

Fig. 67 As you removed components, like this outer locknut, organize them for cleaning and inspection

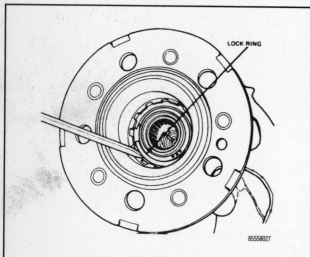

Fig. 68 Some models use a locking ring. Getting at it can be difficult. Try using a small pick to loosen it

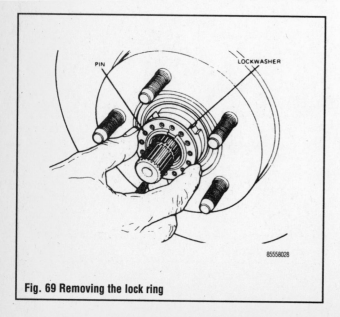

Fig. 69 Removing the lock ring

Fig. 70 On some models the hub and disc are removed from the spindle as an assembly

this with the end of a hammer handle. The wood will protect the bearing from damage.

➡️If the bearings are being replaced, the bearing races should also be replaced since bearings and races are a matched set and establish a wear pattern. Never install new bearings in old races. Premature wear will result.

8. To remove the races, remove the old grease from the hub. Working from either side, place a long punch against the inner shoulder of the race. In some hubs, notches or slots are provided for this purpose. Drive out the race, hammering at various points around its circumference. When one is out, go to the other.

CLEANING AND INSPECTION

➡️Clean all parts in a non-flammable solvent and let them air dry. Only use lint-free rags to dry the bearings. Never spin-dry a bearing with compressed air, as this will damage the rollers.

1. Clean all grease from the inner and outer bearing cups with solvent. Inspect the races for pits, scratches, or excessive wear. If the races are damaged, remove them.

2. Clean the inner and outer cone and roller assemblies with solvent and shake them dry. If the cone and roller assemblies show excessive wear or damage, replace them along with the bearing races as a unit.

3. Clean the spindle and the inside of the hub with solvent to thoroughly remove all old grease.

4. Covering the spindle with a clean cloth, brush all loose dirt and dust from the brake assembly. Remove the cloth carefully so as to not get dirt on the spindle.

➡️It is imperative that all old grease be removed from the bearings and surrounding surfaces before repacking. The new lithium-based grease is not compatible with the sodium base grease used in the past.

Bearings that show signs of heat discoloration, pitting, uneven wear, rust, corrosion or loose rollers, should be replaced. Bearing races should be shiny and smooth or replace them. Don't forget, never replace just the bearings or races. Bearings and races are a matched set. Replacing one without the other will result in premature wear and bearing failure.

Check the spindle for signs of heat discoloration, pitting, uneven wear, rust, corrosion, etc. Some light yellowing is normal. If the spindles show signs of blue discoloration, it's a sign of overheating due to a lack of lubrication or overly-tight bearings. Excessively blued spindles should be replaced. Light rust or corrosion should be removed. Excessively rusted or corroded spindles should be replaced.

REPACKING

➡️**Don't mix different types of grease. For example, sodium based grease is not compatible with lithium based grease. Read the package labels and be careful not to mix types. If there is any doubt as to the type of grease used, completely clean the old grease from the bearing and hub before replacing.**

Packing wheel bearings with grease is best accomplished by using a wheel bearing packer (available at most automotive parts stores).

1. If a wheel bearing packer is not available, the bearings may be packed by hand.
   a. Place a "healthy" glob of grease in the palm of one hand.
   b. Force the edge of the bearing into the grease so that the grease fills the space between the rollers and the bearing cage.
   c. Keep rotating the bearing while continuing to push the grease through.
   d. Continue until the grease is forced out the other side of the bearing.
2. Place the packed bearing on a clean surface and cover it until it is time for installation.

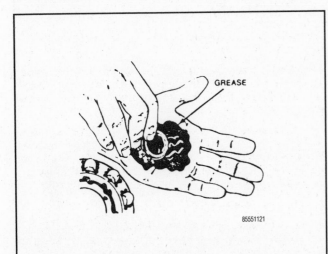

Fig. 71 Place a glob of grease in the palm of your hand and squish the bearing into it

INSTALLATION

If the inner and/or outer bearing races were removed, install the replacement races in the hub. Sometimes it's hard to tell if the races are fully seated. One trick is to coat the installment area with a light coating of grease. As the races are driven in the grease will be squeezed out against the seating ridge. When the races are fully seated, a ring of grease will be noticed. Also, if you have a good ear for sound changes, you'll notice a distinct change in tone when the race contacts the seating ridge. The clinking will turn to a clunk or clank.

To install the races:

1. Coat the outside of the race with grease.
2. Position the race in the hub as evenly as possible.

➡️**There are drivers made for this purpose. If one isn't available, find a socket that's the same diameter as the race. If you don't have one of these, either, it is possible to install the race by hammering on the outside edge, evenly. Don't hammer directly on the race. Use something between the hammer and race such as a short, wide punch.**

3. Drive the race into the hub until it's fully seated against the ridge. Now, do the other one.

To install the inner bearing and seal:

➡️**Always use a new seal.**

4. Coat the race with grease.
5. Place the greased inner bearing in the race.
6. Coat the outer edge of the new seal with grease. Some seals have a coating on the outer edge when new. These seals should not be coated with grease. The packaging should tell you. If not, just look at the edge. If it has the look and feel of sealer—green, red or blue coloring, or sticky—it has a sealer coating.
7. Place the seal, with the smooth side out, on the hub.

➡️**Seal drivers should be used. If you don't have one, tap gently on the seal with a rubber or plastic mallet.**

8. Drive the seal into place. "Place" is, usually, flush with the end of the hub.

To install the hub and outer bearing:

9. Fill the hub cavity—the part between the bearings—with wheel bearing grease. The recess of the cavity should be filled flush. Don't overfill it.

Fig. 72 Always replace the inner seal after removal

Fig. 73 Use as suitable driver tool (or a smooth socket/piece of pipe) to install the seal

10. Install the hub on the spindle. To prevent damage to the seal and spindle threads, keep the hub centered on the spindle.

11. Carefully position the hub assembly on the spindle.

12. Install the outer bearing cone and roller, and the adjusting nut.

13. On vehicles with a self-locking adjusting nut:

    a. Apply inward pressure on the hub nut wrench and tighten the adjusting nut to 70 ft. lbs. (95 Nm) while rotating the hub back and forth to seat the bearings.

    b. Apply inward pressure on the wrench and back off the nut about 90° then, re-tighten the nut to 15–20 ft. lbs. (20–27 Nm).

    c. Remove the wrench. End-play of the hub/rotor assembly should be 0 (zero) and the torque required to rotate the hub assembly should not exceed 20 inch lbs. (2.2 Nm).

14. On vehicles with manually adjusted bearings:

➡ **The adjusting nut has a small dowel on one side. This dowel faces outward to engage the locking ring.**

    a. Using the hub nut socket and a torque wrench, tighten the bearing adjusting nut to 50 ft. lbs. (68 Nm), while rotating the wheel back and forth to seat the bearings.

    b. Back off the adjusting nut approximately ¼ turn (90°).

    c. Install the lock ring by turning the nut to the nearest hole and inserting the dowel pin.

✸✸ WARNING

The dowel pin must seat in a lock ring hole for proper bearing adjustment and wheel retention!

    d. Install the outer lock nut and tighten to 50 ft. lbs. (70 Nm) for most light and medium duty trucks and 175 ft. lbs. (238 Nm) for most heavy duty trucks. Refer to the appropriate Chilton manual for your vehicle. Final end-play of the wheel on the spindle should be 0–0.004 in. (0–0.15mm).

15. Assemble the hub parts.

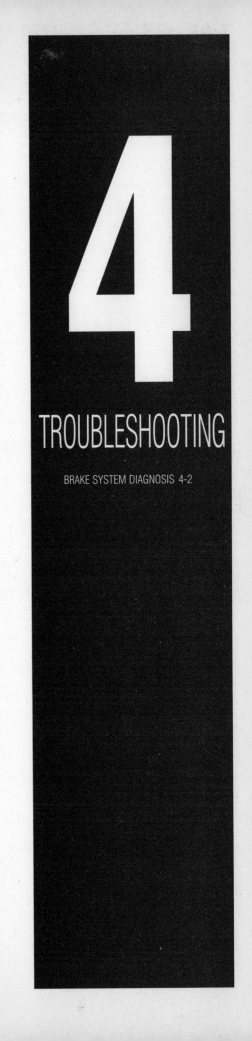

4
TROUBLESHOOTING

BRAKE SYSTEM DIAGNOSIS

General Information

Troubleshooting is a logical procedure, which means that if there is a problem, the cause of which is not immediately obvious, you'll have to figure out what's wrong in a step-by-step manner.

Often, basic do-it-yourselfer's rules are, "start with the easiest thing to fix first," or "start with the cheapest part first." Sound rules, but not necessarily always the best method. The best method is to start with what is most likely wrong and then proceed to the least likely. This way, you'll save time and money. It's not unusual to jump to an unfounded conclusion based on intuition or hope, and, if you do, you will probably end up replacing a wrong part and not fixing the problem.

The following text will attempt to provide you with a logical problem-by-problem troubleshooting guide. The symptom will be presented, with its possible causes listed in order of their probability (most likely first, and so on) and what to do about it.

➡**The following troubleshooting text applies to non-ABS systems, and ABS system components common to both ABS and non-ABS systems. A problem is that, generally, ABS system diagnosis requires a lot of special training, expensive diagnostic tools and, possibly, many hours of time. If you own an ABS-equipped vehicle and the following troubleshooting procedures don't help, have the problem diagnosed by a qualified service technician.**

Symptom Diagnosis

BRAKES DO NOT WORK

- No brake fluid or very low fluid level—If there's no fluid in the fluid reservoir, or a very low fluid level, and you occasionally check the fluid level, the brake system has a leak. Find the leak, fix it, flush and refill the system and bleed the brakes.
- Front and/or rear linings completely worn—If the linings are completely worn, replace them and have the rotors or drums machined.
- Drum brakes completely out of adjustment—If the drum brakes are that far out of adjustment and they are equipped with automatic adjusters, they are broken! Check the mechanism and determine the cause.
- Improperly attached pedal, booster or master cylinder—If the cause is pedal, booster or master cylinder mounting, try tightening the component's fasteners. Replace any broken mounting fasteners.
- Damaged rotors or drums—Yes, rotors and drums can crack. Usually it's due to rust, but it's possible that impact damage from road hazards could be the cause. It's also possible, but rare, that a defective caliper can put undue stress in one direction on a rotor, which can cause it to crack.

EXCESSIVE PEDAL TRAVEL OR SPONGY FEEL

- Low fluid level or air in the hydraulic system—If the fluid level is low and you occasionally check the fluid level, you have a leak. If there's air in the system, you have a leak. Either way, find the leak, fix it, flush and refill the system, then bleed the brakes.
- Drum brakes out of adjustment (manual adjusters) or automatic adjusters not working—If the drum brakes are that far out of adjustment and they are equipped with automatic adjusters, the adjusters are broken! Check the mechanism and determine the cause.
- Wheel bearings out of adjustment—If you suspect the wheel bearings, raise and support the vehicle on jackstands. Check for excessive wheel bearing play by pulling and pushing on the wheel. If there is excessive play, remove the bearings, check them for wear, clean and repack them, install and adjust them. If the wheel bearings or cage are worn, pitted, corroded, or cracked, install new bearings and races.
- Glazed, worn or damaged brake linings—Check the condition of the linings. If disc brake pads show these symptoms, the calipers are defective

and should either be rebuilt or replaced. If drum brake shoes show these symptoms, either they are over-adjusted or are not retracting properly. Check the self-adjusters, return springs and wheel cylinders for damage. Repair as needed.
- Drums out of round or excessively worn—Measure the inside diameter and inspect the inside surface. If they're still okay, have them machined, otherwise install new drum(s).
- Caliper mountings loose—Check and tighten the caliper mounting fasteners as necessary.
- Booster or master cylinder mountings loose—Check and tighten the mounting fasteners as necessary.

EXCESSIVE PEDAL EFFORT

- Overloaded vehicle—Unload it.
- Defective power booster—Check the booster with a vacuum pump, and check the booster vacuum hose for leaks. Repair or replace as necessary.
- Booster/pedal linkage binding—Check all pivot points for rust and corrosion. Clean and lubricate the pivot surfaces, or replace any worn linkage bushings with new ones as necessary.
- Linings worn, glazed or contaminated—Any lining that shows these symptoms should be replaced. Any lining that shows glazing indicates a problem with the applying mechanism (caliper or wheel cylinder); repair the problem as necessary. Any lining that is contaminated with brake fluid or oil indicates a leak. Find the leak, then repair it as necessary.
- Improperly installed pads or shoes—Pads and shoes can be installed backwards, inverted, or not secured correctly. Repair as necessary.
- Seized caliper or wheel cylinder pistons—Rebuild or replace the caliper/wheel cylinder as needed.
- Restricted pipes or hoses—Check the length of each brake line for kinks, pinches or other problems. If any flexible brake hose is kinked or pinched, reroute it to alleviate the problem (as long as it's not damaged in any other way). If a metal brake pipe is kinked, replace it with a new one.

BRAKES DRAG OR RELEASE SLOWLY

- Parking brake handle or pedal binding—Check the handle or pedal pivot and slide points for rust, corrosion or pinching. Clean and lubricate the pivot and sliding surfaces with multi-purpose grease.
- Parking brake cable binding—Check along the cable routings for rust, corrosion, pinching, kinking, missing return spring(s), etc. Correct the condition or replace the cable(s) as necessary.
- Parking brake cable out of adjustment—Adjust the cable tension as necessary.
- Wheel bearings out of adjustment—If you suspect the wheel bearings, raise and support the vehicle on jackstands. Check for excessive wheel bearing play by pulling and pushing on the wheel. If there is excessive play, remove the bearings, check them for wear, clean and repack them, install and adjust them. If the wheel bearings or cage are worn, pitted, corroded, or cracked, install new bearings and races.
- Worn or damaged master cylinder—The pistons can drag due to corrosion or fluid contamination. Rebuild or replace the master cylinder.
- Drum brakes out of adjustment—Adjust as necessary.
- Restricted pipes or hoses—Check the length of each brake line for kinks, pinches or other problems. If any flexible brake hose is kinked or pinched, reroute it to alleviate the problem (as long as it's not damaged in any other way). If a metal brake pipe is kinked, replace it with a new one.
- Seized caliper or wheel cylinder pistons—Rebuild or replace the component as needed.
- Brake light switch out of adjustment—With pedal-actuated switches, the switch itself can be out of adjustment, preventing the pedal from returning to the fully released position. Adjust the switch position as necessary.

SNAPPING OR CLICKING NOISE

- Cracked welds on the brake shoe webs—Replace the brake shoes.
- Brake shoes binding on the backing plate pads—Lubricate the backing plate pads with high temperature brake grease, or similar lubricant.
- Grooved brake drums—Machine or replace the drums as necessary.
- Backing plate pads worn—Install a new backing plate.
- Rust on inboard edges of the brake pad(s)—Clean or replace the pads.
- Loose or missing disc brake anti-rattle clips—Replace the clips.
- Riveted linings loose—Replace the linings.
- Defective caliper support spring or pins—Replace the parts as necessary.

SCRAPING OR GRINDING NOISE

- Worn-out linings, loose rivets or foreign material between the linings and drums or rotors—Replace the linings and refinish the drums or rotors as necessary.
- Brake shoes touching the drum face, or rotor-to-dust shield contact—Repair as necessary.
- Cracked drums or rotors—Replace the drum/rotor as necessary.

SQUEAK, SQUEAL OR CHATTER NOISE

With the Brakes Applied

- Worn-out linings, or worn or scored drums and rotors—Replace the linings, and refinish or replace the drums/rotors as necessary.
- Missing or damaged brake pad insulators, or anti-squeal springs or clips—Replace as necessary.
- Pads not fully seating on caliper—Clean rust or foreign material from the caliper as necessary.
- Glazed or contaminated linings—Replace the linings (pads or shoes).
- Lining rivets loose—Replace the linings (pads or shoes).
- Weak or damaged shoe return springs—Install new return springs.
- Weak or damaged shoe hold-down springs or pins—Install new parts, as necessary.
- Grooved backing plate pads—Replace the backing plates with new ones.

Without the Brakes Applied

- Brake pad wear indicator contacting the rotor—Install new brake pads.
- Excessive rotor runout—Refinish or replace the rotor.
- Loose wheel lug nuts or lug bolts—Tighten the lunettes/bolts.
- Wheel bearings out of adjustment—If you suspect the wheel bearings, raise and support the vehicle on jackstands. Check for excessive wheel bearing play by pulling and pushing on the wheel. If there is excessive play, remove the bearings, check them for wear, clean and repack them, install and adjust them. If the wheel bearings or cage are worn, pitted, corroded, or cracked, install new bearings and races.
- Brake linings adjusted too tightly—Readjust the linings.
- Weak or damaged shoe return springs—Install new return springs.
- Grooved backing plate pads—Replace the backing plates with new ones.
- Brake pads improperly positioned in caliper—Repair as required.

CLACKING, GROWLING OR RATTLING NOISE

Without the Brakes Applied

- Foreign material inside the drum(s)—Clean the drums and inspect the brakes.
- Loose wheel lunettes or lug bolts—Tighten the lunettes/bolts.
- Missing, loose or damaged brake pad anti-squeal spring or clips, or worn caliper support pins or springs—Replace as necessary.

- Wheel bearings out of adjustment—If you suspect the wheel bearings, raise and support the vehicle on jackstands. Check for excessive wheel bearing play by pulling and pushing on the wheel. If there is excessive play, remove the bearings, check them for wear, clean and repack them, install and adjust them. If the wheel bearings or cage are worn, pitted, corroded, or cracked, install new bearings and races.

GROANING NOISE OR ROUGH PEDAL FEEL

- Loose wheel lunettes/bolts—Tighten the lunettes/bolts.
- Wheel bearings worn, dry or out of adjustment—If you suspect the wheel bearings, raise and support the vehicle on jackstands. Check for excessive wheel bearing play by pulling and pushing on the wheel. If there is excessive play, remove the bearings, check them for wear, clean and repack them, install and adjust them. If the wheel bearings or cage are worn, pitted, corroded, or cracked, install new bearings and races.
- Loose or worn front suspension parts—Inspect, and repair or replace as necessary.
- Cracked or out-of-round drums, or excessive rotor runout—Replace as necessary.
- Caliper loose—Replace mounting parts or tighten the mounting bolts.
- Worn tires—Replace the tires.

INTERMITTENT LOSS OF PEDAL PRESSURE

- Worn, rusted or corroded master cylinder, calipers or wheel cylinders—Rebuild or replace the parts as necessary.
- Drum brakes out of adjustment or worn—Inspect, and adjust or replace as necessary.
- Cracked brake drum(s)—Install new brake drum(s).
- Improperly attached pedal, booster or master cylinder—If the cause is pedal, booster or master cylinder mounting, try tightening the component's fasteners. Replace any broken mounting fasteners.
- Loose caliper—Replace mounting parts or tighten the mounting bolts.

BRAKES PULL TO ONE SIDE

- Unequal tire pressures—Add or remove air from the applicable tires.
- Contaminated linings—Replace the linings.
- Loose caliper—Replace mounting parts or tighten the mounting bolts.
- Different lining material on either side—Replace the linings.
- Seized caliper or wheel cylinder pistons—Rebuild or replace as needed.
- Restricted pipes or hoses—Check the length of each brake line for kinks, pinches or other problems. If any flexible brake hose is kinked or pinched, reroute it to alleviate the problem (as long as it's not damaged in any other way). If a metal brake pipe is kinked, replace it with a new one.
- Drum brake adjustment uneven—Correct the adjustment.
- Wheel bearings worn, dry or out of adjustment—If you suspect the wheel bearings, raise and support the vehicle on jackstands. Check for excessive wheel bearing play by pulling and pushing on the wheel. If there is excessive play, remove the bearings, check them for wear, clean and repack them, install and adjust them. If the wheel bearings or cage are worn, pitted, corroded, or cracked, install new bearings and races.
- Linings worn on one side—Find the cause, correct it and replace the linings.
- If no fault is found in the brakes—Check the steering and suspension for worn, broken or missing parts.

PEDAL VIBRATION OR PULSATION

To isolate the problem, raise and safely support the front or rear end, depending on where the drive wheels are vehicle. Make sure the tires aren't contacting anything. On front wheel drive vehicles, support the control arms in a horizontal position. Start the engine and accelerate to an indicated speed of about 35 mph. Lightly apply the brakes. If no symptoms occur, the problem is at the other end of the vehicle.

- Loose wheel lugs—Check and tighten as necessary.
- Cracked rotors or drums—Replace as necessary.
- Excessive rotor runout or thickness variation—Refinish or replace the rotor(s) as necessary.
- Brake drums out-of-round—Refinish or replace the drum(s) as necessary.
- Loose caliper—Replace the mounting parts or tighten the mounting fasteners.
- Wheel bearings worn, dry or out of adjustment—If you suspect the wheel bearings, raise and support the vehicle on jackstands. Check for excessive wheel bearing play by pulling and pushing on the wheel. If there is excessive play, remove the bearings, check them for wear, clean and repack them, install and adjust them. If the wheel bearings or cage are worn, pitted, corroded, or cracked, install new bearings and races.
- Bent wheel(s)—Check and replace as necessary.
- Misaligned or damaged radial tire belt—Replace the tire(s).

BRAKES GRAB OR LOCK-UP WHEN APPLIED

- Tires severely under-inflated—Adjust the inflation pressures.
- Contaminated linings—Replace the linings.
- Brake booster over-reacting—Check the booster operation against a known good booster, or replace it.
- Defective proportioning valve—If just the rear brakes lock-up or grab at low pedal effort, this could be the problem.
- Loose caliper—Replace mounting parts or tighten the mounting bolts.
- Wheel bearings worn, dry or out of adjustment—If you suspect the wheel bearings, raise and support the vehicle on jackstands. Check for excessive wheel bearing play by pulling and pushing on the wheel. If there is excessive play, remove the bearings, check them for wear, clean and repack them, install and adjust them. If the wheel bearings or cage are worn, pitted, corroded, or cracked, install new bearings and races.
- Parking brake handle or pedal binding—Check the handle or pedal pivot and slide points for rust, corrosion or pinching. Clean and lubricate the pivot and slide surfaces, or replace the component as necessary.

- Parking brake cable binding—Check along the cable routings for rust, corrosion, pinching, kinking, missing return spring(s), etc. Correct the condition or replace the cable(s) as necessary.
- Parking brake cable out of adjustment—Adjust as necessary.

BRAKE WARNING LIGHT STAYS ON

- Low fluid level—Add brake fluid to the master cylinder reservoir.
- Shorted light circuit—Locate the short and repair it.
- Worn or damaged warning switch—Replace the switch.
- Worn or damaged master cylinder—Rebuild or replace the master cylinder.
- Fluid leak—Find the leak and correct the situation as necessary.
- Worn or damaged pressure differential valve—Replace the valve.

PARKING BRAKE DOES NOT HOLD

- Parking brake handle or pedal binding—Check the handle or pedal pivot and slide points for rust, corrosion or pinching. Clean and lubricate the pivot and slide surfaces, or replace the component as necessary.
- Parking brake cable binding—Check along the cable routings for rust, corrosion, pinching, kinking, missing return spring(s), etc. Correct the condition or replace the cable(s) as necessary.
- Parking brake cable out of adjustment—Adjust as necessary.

PARKING BRAKE DOESN'T FULLY RELEASE

- Parking brake handle or pedal binding—Check the handle or pedal pivot and slide points for rust, corrosion or pinching. Clean and lubricate the pivot and slide surfaces, or replace the component as necessary.
- Parking brake cable binding—Check along the cable routings for rust, corrosion, pinching, kinking, missing return spring(s), etc. Correct the condition or replace the cable(s) as necessary.
- Worn, weak or damaged rear brake parts—Check the springs and mounting pads, and replace them as necessary.

5

DISC BRAKE SERVICE

DISC BRAKE SERVICE

✳✳ CAUTION

Brake dust may contain asbestos. Asbestos is a known cancer-causing agent. Never use compressed air to clean brake surfaces! Never cause brake dust to become airborne! Always use a spray-type brake cleaner to clean all brake surfaces. It's a good idea to wear a dust mask when disassembling the brakes.

Instead of the traditional expanding brakes that press outward against a circular drum, disc brake systems utilize a disc (rotor) with brake pads positioned on either side of it. An easily-seen analogy is the hand brake arrangement on a bicycle. The pads squeeze onto the rim of the bike wheel, slowing its motion. Automobile disc brakes use the identical principle, but apply the braking effort to a separate disc instead of the wheel.

The disc (rotor) is a casting, usually equipped with cooling fins between the two braking surfaces. This enables air to circulate between the braking surfaces making them less sensitive to heat buildup and more resistant to fade. Dirt and water do not drastically affect braking action since contaminants are thrown off by the centrifugal action of the rotor or scraped off the by the pads. Also, the equal clamping action of the two brake pads tends to ensure uniform, straight line stops. Disc brakes are inherently self-adjusting. There are three general types of disc brake:

1. Sliding caliper.
2. Floating caliper.
3. Fixed caliper.

The fixed caliper design uses one or two pistons mounted on each side of the rotor (in each side of the caliper). The caliper is mounted rigidly and does not move.

The sliding and floating designs are quite similar. In fact, these two types are often lumped together. In both designs, the pad on the inside of the rotor is moved into contact with the rotor by hydraulic force. The caliper, which is not held in a fixed position, moves slightly, bringing the outside pad into contact with the rotor.

Floating calipers use threaded guide pins and bushings, or sleeves to allow the caliper to slide and apply the brake pads.

There are typically three methods of securing a sliding caliper to its mounting bracket: with a retaining pin, with a key and bolt, or with a wedge and pin. On calipers which use the retaining pin method, you will find pins driven into the slot between the caliper and the caliper mount. On calipers which use the bolt and key method, a key is used between the caliper and the mounting bracket to allow the caliper to slide. The key is held in position by a lockbolt. On calipers which use the pin and wedge method, a wedge, retained by a pin, is used between the caliper and the mounting bracket.

For pad removal purposes, fixed calipers are usually not removed, floating calipers are either removed or flipped (hinged up or down on one pin), and sliding calipers are removed.

✳✳ CAUTION

On models with air suspension, the air suspension must be turned OFF before raising the vehicle. Failure to do so may result in unexpected inflation or deflation of the air springs, which may result in shifting of the vehicle during service. Refer to your vehicle's owner's manual for more precautions concerning jacking.

➡On some vehicles with anti-lock brakes, the brake system must be depressurized before opening the hydraulic system. The ABS Chapter contains a description of brake system depressurization. Also, if the brake service being performed requires opening the hydraulic system, the system must be bled. Both depressurizing and bleeding are complicated procedures that may require special, expensive tools. If these tools are not available to you and/or you are not familiar with their use, do not attempt to perform procedure. If you are unsure as to whether your vehicle's ABS system requires depressurization, check your Chilton's Total Car Care manual, or contact your vehicle dealer's service shop.

Brake Calipers

REMOVAL & INSTALLATION

Calipers without Integral Parking Brake Mechanisms

SLIDING CALIPER

✳✳ CAUTION

Brake dust may contain asbestos! Asbestos is harmful to your health. Never use compressed air to clean any brake component. A filtering mask should be worn during any brake repair.

There are typically three methods of securing a sliding caliper to its mounting bracket: with a retaining pin, with a key and bolt, or with a wedge and pin. On calipers which use the retaining pin method, you will find pins driven into the slot between the caliper and the caliper mount. On calipers which use the bolt and key method, a key (small piece of metal) is used between the caliper and the mounting bracket to allow the caliper to slide. The key is held in position by a lockbolt. On calipers which use the pin and wedge method, a wedge, retained by a pin, is used between the caliper and the mounting bracket in much the same manner as with the key and bolt method.

1. Loosen the lug nuts on the applicable wheels.
2. If servicing the front brakes, apply the parking brake, block the rear wheels, then raise and safely support the front of the vehicle securely on jackstands.
3. If servicing the rear wheels, block the front wheels, then raise and safely support the rear of the vehicle securely on jackstands.
4. Remove the wheels.

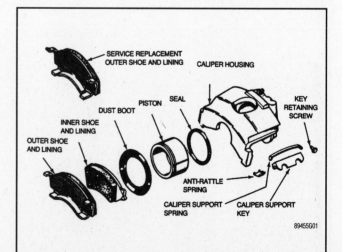

Fig. 1 Exploded view of a typical sliding caliper, showing the key and bolt (retaining screw)

Fig. 2 To remove a typical sliding caliper, remove the anti-rattle clips (if equipped)

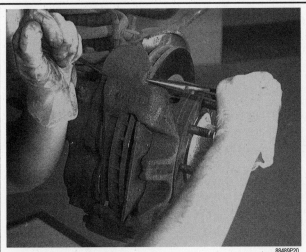

Fig. 3 Compress the upper pin tabs and pry on the inner end of the pin . . .

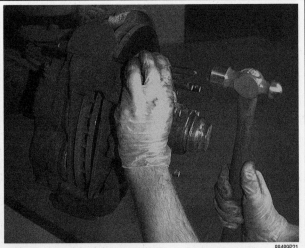

Fig. 4 . . . then use a hammer and punch to drive the pin out of the groove . . .

Fig. 5 . . . until it can be removed by hand

Fig. 6 Perform the same for the lower pin as well . . .

Fig. 7 . . . then pull the caliper off of the rotor and bracket

Fig. 8 Once the caliper is removed, the brake pads can be removed

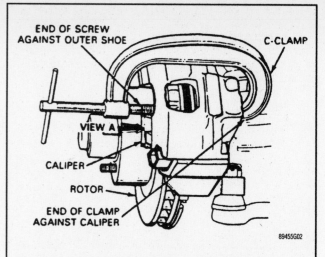

Fig. 10 Use a large C-clamp to seat the caliper piston, make sure that one end of the clamp is positioned against the outer shoe

✳✳ CAUTION

Any brake fluid that is removed from the system should be discarded. Also, do not allow any brake fluid to come in contact with a painted surface; it will damage the paint. Also, brake fluid contains polyglycol ethers and polyglycols. Avoid contact with the eyes and wash your hands thoroughly after handling brake fluid. If you do get brake fluid in your eyes, flush your eyes with clean, running water for 15 minutes. If eye irritation persists, or if you have taken brake fluid internally, IMMEDIATELY seek medical assistance.

5. Remove some brake fluid from the brake fluid reservoir. Use a clean suction pump, a turkey baster (not to be returned to the kitchen), or an absorbent pad to do so. Never reuse any brake fluid.

6. Place a drain pan under the work area. Clean the brake pad and rotor area with spray brake cleaner.

7. Disconnect any electrical brake pad wear sensor.

➡ **If servicing disc brakes equipped with an integral parking brake mechanism, please refer to the applicable procedure later in this section before seating the piston caliper with a C-clamp. Otherwise, you may damage your caliper.**

8. Using a C-clamp on the caliper, seat the piston into its bore. Position one end of the C-clamp on the backing surface of the outer brake pad and the other end against the inboard side of the caliper. Be sure not to compress only the caliper; it may crack, necessitating installation of a replacement caliper.

9. Remove any rattle clips or retaining clips from the caliper.

10. On calipers which use the pin method, remove the pin by squeezing the outboard end of the lower pin with a pair of pliers while prying out on the inboard end with a prybar. Once the pin retaining tabs are positioned in the caliper/bracket groove, use a punch and hammer to knock the lower pin the rest of the way out of the groove. Repeat this step for the upper pin.

11. Inspect the pins for damage, wear, and rust. Replace as needed in pairs.

12. On calipers which use the bolt and key method, remove the retaining bolt, then use a hammer and punch to drive the key out. (Be careful not to lose the caliper support spring, if equipped.) Check parts for wear and replace as necessary.

13. On calipers which use the wedge and pin method, remove the retaining pin from the guide plate, then use a punch and hammer to tap out the guide plate. Inspect parts for wear and replace as necessary.

14. If the caliper is going to be removed for overhaul or replacement, loosen the brake hose, lift off the caliper and remove the brake hose completely. Immediately plug the open end of the rubber brake hose to prevent

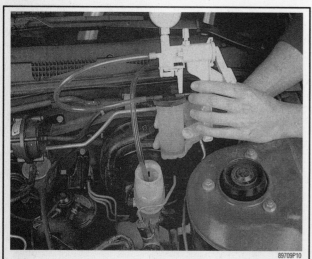

Fig. 9 A vacuum pump setup can be used to draw brake fluid from the reservoir

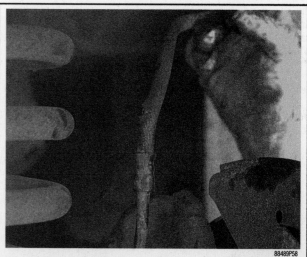

Fig. 11 When inspecting the flexible brake hoses, check for rips (as shown), tears and cracks

contamination of the brake fluid. If the brake hose was attached to the caliper via a banjo connection, be sure to remove and discard the two copper washers.

15. If the caliper does not require overhaul or replacement, prepare a length of wire (a coat hanger works well), cord, or a length of strong string to support the caliper. DO NOT let the caliper hang from the brake hose; it may be damaged.

16. Remove the caliper and suspend it from the wire.

17. If the brake pads came off the rotor with the caliper, remove them by prying the pads out of the caliper piston.

18. Inspect the caliper for fluid leakage, torn dust boots, or missing parts. Rebuild or replace the caliper if a problem is found.

19. Inspect the rubber brake hose for cracks or signs of rubbing against the body or steering components. Also, it is a good idea to replace them if they are over 10 years old to maintain proper brake operation.

20. Inspect metal lines for corrosion and kinks from road debris kicked up under the vehicle. If a problem is found, replace the line.

21. Inspect the rotor for non-machine grooves, heat stress cracks, glazing, minimum wear thickness, and disk runout. Replace the rotor or have it machined to repair the damage.

22. Inspect the brake pads for minimum thickness, loose rivets, or glazing. Install new brake pads if any such problems exist.

To install:

23. Clean the sliding surfaces of the caliper and mounting bracket with spray brake cleaner and a small wire brush, then lubricate them with high temperature brake grease.

24. If necessary, place the pad(s) back onto the caliper or mounting bracket.

25. If the brake hose was removed, reattach it to the caliper. If so equipped, use two new copper washers for the banjo fitting.

26. Install the caliper onto its mounting bracket.

27. For calipers which use the pin retaining method, use a hammer to tap the pins back into position, then install any anti-rattle clips.

28. For calipers which use the bolt and key method, use a prybar to lift the caliper up to create a gap into which the key and spring can slide. Tap the key and spring into position, then install the locking bolt and any anti-rattle clips. Tighten the locking bolt securely.

29. For calipers which use the wedge and pin method, slide the guide plates (wedge) between the gaps of the caliper and mounting bracket, then install the retaining pin. Tighten the retaining pin securely.

30. Reattach any electrical brake pad sensors.

✳✳ WARNING

Clean, high quality brake fluid is essential to the safe and proper operation of the brake system. You should always buy the highest quality brake fluid that is available. If the brake fluid becomes contaminated, drain and flush the system, then refill the master cylinder with new fluid. Never reuse any brake fluid. Any brake fluid that is removed from the system should be discarded. Also, do not allow any brake fluid to come in contact with a painted surface; it will damage the paint.

31. Bleed the brakes if a brake line was replaced, or the caliper was detached from a brake line.

32. Seat the brake pads, otherwise the vehicle may coast out of the work area and into traffic before the brakes become effective. It will take several pumps of the brake pedal to seat the pads against the rotor.

33. Check the brake fluid level in the reservoir and top off as needed.

34. Install the wheels and snug the lug nuts.

35. Lower the vehicle.

36. Tighten the lug nuts fully.

37. Road test the vehicle.

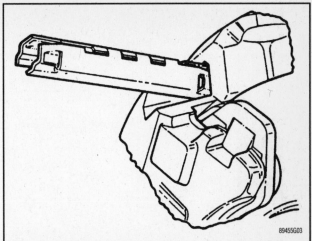

89455G03

Fig. 12 Install the caliper retaining pin by positioning it in the caliper/bracket groove and driving it in until properly seated (the retaining tabs on both ends should protrude from the groove)

89709P12

Fig. 13 With the vacuum pump setup it is possible for one person to bleed the brakes

FLOATING CALIPER

✳✳ CAUTION

Brake dust may contain asbestos! Asbestos is harmful to your health. Never use compressed air to clean any brake component. A filtering mask should be worn during any brake repair.

The floating style of caliper uses threaded guide pins and bushings, or sleeves to allow the caliper to slide and apply the brake pads.

1. Loosen the lug nuts on the applicable wheels.

2. If servicing the front brakes, apply the parking brake, block the rear wheels, then raise and safely support the front of the vehicle securely on jackstands.

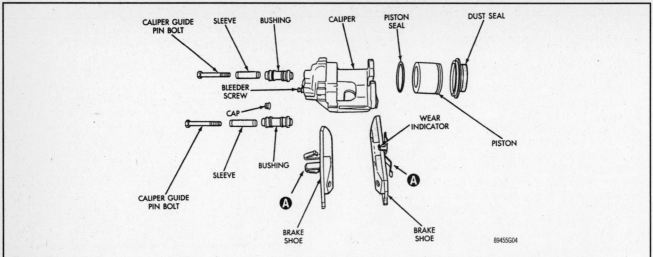

Fig. 14 Exploded view of a typical floating caliper—when installing the brake pads, ensure that the retaining clips (A) are properly engaged in the caliper

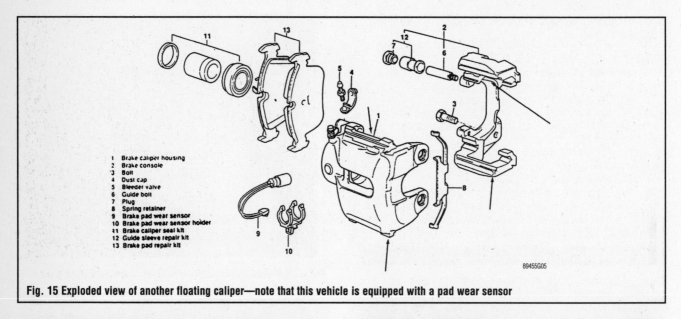

1 Brake caliper housing
2 Brake console
3 Bolt
4 Dust cap
5 Bleeder valve
6 Guide bolt
7 Plug
8 Spring retainer
9 Brake pad wear sensor
10 Brake pad wear sensor holder
11 Brake caliper seal kit
12 Guide sleeve repair kit
13 Brake pad repair kit

Fig. 15 Exploded view of another floating caliper—note that this vehicle is equipped with a pad wear sensor

Fig. 16 Some vehicles are equipped with brake pad wear sensors, indicated by the wire leading to the pad

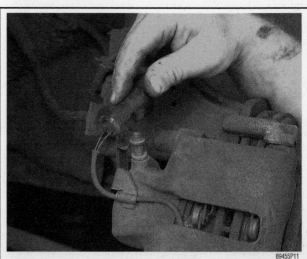

Fig. 17 To remove the caliper, disengage the sensor wire connector from its mounting clip (if equipped) . . .

Fig. 18 . . . then separate the two connector halves

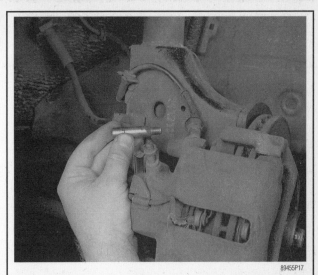

Fig. 21 . . . and remove the sliding pins from the caliper

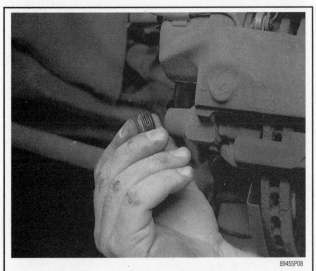

Fig. 19 If equipped, remove the sliding pin covers . . .

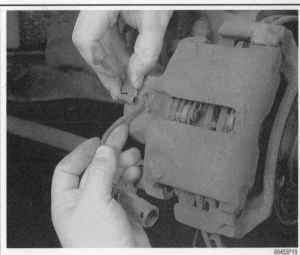

Fig. 22 If equipped, unfasten the sensor wire from its retaining clip . . .

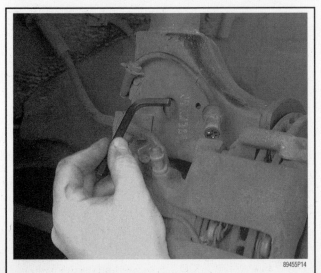

Fig. 20 . . . then loosen . . .

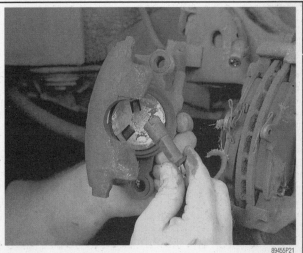

Fig. 23 . . . then lift the caliper up and off of the mounting bracket

3. If servicing the rear wheels, block the front wheels, then raise and safely support the rear of the vehicle securely on jackstands.

4. Remove the wheels.

✳✳ CAUTION

Any brake fluid that is removed from the system should be discarded. Also, brake fluid contains polyglycol ethers and polyglycols. Avoid contact with the eyes and wash your hands thoroughly after handling brake fluid. If you do get brake fluid in your eyes, flush your eyes with clean, running water for 15 minutes. If eye irritation persists, or if you have taken brake fluid internally, IMMEDIATELY seek medical assistance.

✳✳ WARNING

Clean, high quality brake fluid is essential to the safe and proper operation of the brake system. You should always buy the highest quality brake fluid that is available. If the brake fluid becomes contaminated, drain and flush the system, then refill the master cylinder with new fluid. Never reuse any brake fluid. Any brake fluid that is removed from the system should be discarded. Also, do not allow any brake fluid to come in contact with a painted surface; it will damage the paint.

5. Remove some brake fluid from the brake fluid reservoir. Use a clean suction pump, a turkey baster (not to be returned to the kitchen), or an absorbent pad to do so. Never reuse any brake fluid.

6. Place a drain pan under the work area. Clean the brake pad and rotor area with spray brake cleaner.

7. Disconnect any electrical brake pad wear sensor.

8. If an anti-rattle spring is used and is not part of the brake pad, it can usually be pried off or pulled out.

➡If servicing disc brakes equipped with an integral parking brake mechanism, please refer to the applicable procedure later in this section before seating the piston caliper with a C-clamp. Otherwise, you may damage your caliper.

9. Using a C-clamp on the caliper, seat the piston into its bore. Position one end of the C-clamp on the backing surface of the outer brake pad and the other end against the inboard side of the caliper. Be sure not to compress only the caliper; it may crack, necessitating installation of a replacement caliper.

10. Loosen and remove the guide pins from the caliper.

Fig. 25 A vacuum pump setup can be used to draw brake fluid from the reservoir

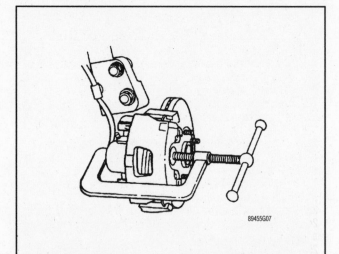
Fig. 26 Use a large C-clamp to seat the piston in its bore before removing the caliper

Fig. 24 Be sure to note the positions of any clips or springs on the caliper

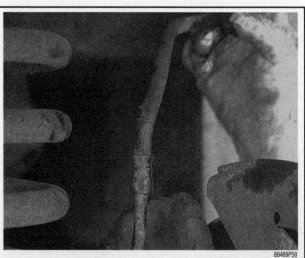
Fig. 27 When inspecting the flexible brake hoses, check for rips (as shown), tears and cracks

11. If the caliper is going to be removed for overhaul or replacement, loosen the brake hose, lift off the caliper and remove the brake hose completely. Immediately plug the open end of the rubber brake hose to prevent contamination of the brake fluid. If the brake hose was attached to the caliper via a banjo connection, be sure to remove and discard the two copper washers.

12. If the caliper does not require overhaul or replacement, prepare a length of wire (a coat hanger works well), cord, or a length of strong string to support the caliper. DO NOT let the caliper hang from the brake hose; it may be damaged.

13. Remove the caliper from the rotor and, if equipped, the mounting bracket.

➡ **The pads may or may not come off with the caliper; this is normal.**

14. If the brake pads stay on the caliper, they can usually be tapped off with a hammer, or pried out by hand or with prytool.

15. If the brake pads remain on the bracket, when applicable, they can be removed from the bracket by hand.

16. Inspect the caliper for fluid leakage, torn dust boot, or missing parts. Rebuild or replace if a problem is found.

17. Inspect the rubber brake hose for cracks or signs of rubbing against the body or steering components. Install a new rubber hose if any such conditions exist. Also, it is a good idea to replace them if over 10 years old to maintain proper brake operation.

18. Inspect the metal lines for corrosion and kinks from road debris kicked up under the vehicle. If a problem is found, replace the line.

19. Inspect the rotor for non-machine grooves, heat stress cracks, glazing, minimum wear thickness, and disk runout. Replace the rotor or have it machined to repair the damage.

20. Inspect the brake pads for minimum thickness, loose rivets, or glazing. If such a problem is found, new pads must be installed.

To install:

21. If equipped with a mounting bracket, clean the sliding surfaces of the caliper and mounting bracket with spray brake cleaner and a small wire brush, then lubricate them with high temperature brake grease.

22. If the brake hose was removed, reattach it to the caliper. If so equipped, use two new copper washers for the banjo fitting.

23. Transfer old pad hardware to the new pads, or install new hardware.

24. Clean and inspect the caliper guide pins, if they are okay then lubricate them with high temperature brake grease.

25. On caliper mounted pads, position the pads on the caliper, then install the caliper on the rotor.

26. On bracket mounted pads, install the pads on the mounting bracket. Install the caliper on the rotor.

27. Tighten the caliper guide pins securely, and replace any anti rattle clips.

28. Connect any electrical brake pad sensors.

✳✳ WARNING

Clean, high quality brake fluid is essential to the safe and proper operation of the brake system. You should always buy the highest quality brake fluid that is available. If the brake fluid becomes contaminated, drain and flush the system, then refill the master cylinder with new fluid. Never reuse any brake fluid. Any brake fluid that is removed from the system should be discarded. Also, do not allow any brake fluid to come in contact with a painted surface; it will damage the paint.

29. Bleed the brakes, if a brake line was replaced or the caliper was detached from a brake line.

30. Seat the brake pads, otherwise the vehicle may coast out of the work area and into traffic before the brakes become effective. It will take several pumps of the brake pedal to seat the pads against the rotor.

31. Check the brake fluid level in the reservoir and top off as needed.

32. Install the wheels and snug the lug nuts.

33. Lower the vehicle.

Fig. 28 With the vacuum pump setup it is possible for one person to bleed the brakes

34. Tighten the lug nuts fully.

35. Road test the vehicle.

FIXED CALIPER

✳✳ CAUTION

Brake dust may contain asbestos! Asbestos is harmful to your health. Never use compressed air to clean any brake component. A filtering mask should be worn during any brake repair.

The fixed type caliper is bolted to the steering knuckle. The brake pads on this style of caliper are typically held in place by one or two retaining pins. Some other pads use hold down clips. It may not be necessary to remove the brake pads in order to remove the caliper.

1. Loosen the lug nuts on the applicable wheels.

2. If servicing the front brakes, apply the parking brake, block the rear wheels, then raise and safely support the front of the vehicle securely on jackstands.

3. If servicing the rear wheels, block the front wheels, then raise and safely support the rear of the vehicle securely on jackstands.

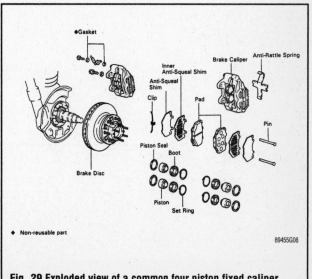

Fig. 29 Exploded view of a common four piston fixed caliper

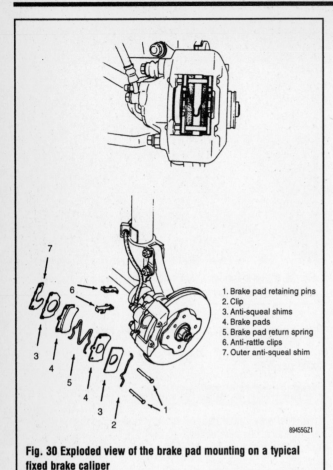

1. Brake pad retaining pins
2. Clip
3. Anti-squeal shims
4. Brake pads
5. Brake pad return spring
6. Anti-rattle clips
7. Outer anti-squeal shim

89455GZ1

Fig. 30 Exploded view of the brake pad mounting on a typical fixed brake caliper

✳✳ CAUTION

Any brake fluid that is removed from the system should be discarded. Also, do not allow any brake fluid to come in contact with a painted surface; it will damage the paint.

4. Remove the wheels.

✳✳ CAUTION

Brake fluid contains polyglycol ethers and polyglycols. Avoid contact with the eyes and wash your hands thoroughly after handling brake fluid. If you do get brake fluid in your eyes, flush your eyes with clean, running water for 15 minutes. If eye irritation persists, or if you have taken brake fluid internally, IMMEDIATELY seek medical assistance.

5. Remove some brake fluid from the brake fluid reservoir. Use a clean suction pump, a turkey baster (not to be returned to the kitchen), or an absorbent pad to do so. Never reuse any brake fluid.

6. Place a drain pan under the work area. Clean the brake pad and rotor area with spray brake cleaner.

7. If equipped, disconnect any electrical brake pad wear sensor.

8. Although not necessary for caliper removal, the brake pads can now be removed from the caliper.

9. Loosen the caliper mounting bolts.

10. If the caliper is going to be removed for overhaul or replacement purposes, loosen the brake hose, remove the caliper bolts, and disconnect the brake line.

11. If the caliper does not require overhaul or replacement (in other words, you only need to remove it for access to some other component), prepare a length of wire (coat hanger), cord, or a length of strong string from which the caliper can be hung. DO NOT let the caliper hang from the brake hose; it may be damaged and need to be replaced. Remove the caliper and hang it from the wire.

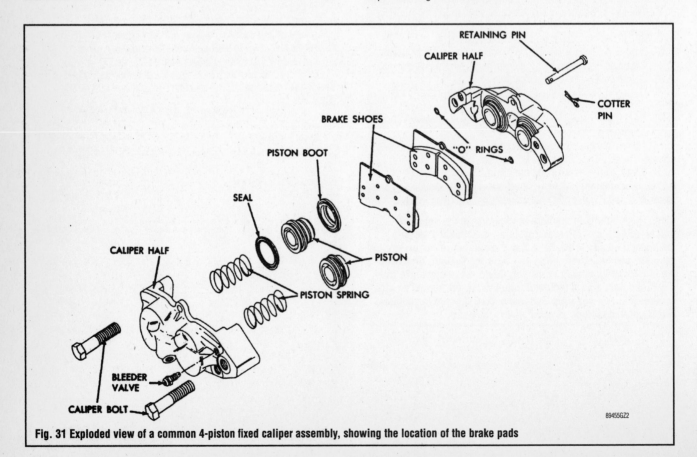

89455GZ2

Fig. 31 Exploded view of a common 4-piston fixed caliper assembly, showing the location of the brake pads

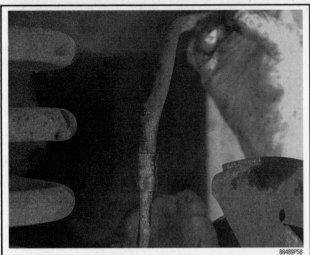

Fig. 32 When inspecting the flexible brake hoses, check for rips (as shown), tears and cracks

Fig. 33 With the vacuum pump setup it is possible for one person to bleed the brakes

12. Inspect the caliper for fluid leakage, torn dust boot, or missing parts. Rebuild or replace if a problem is found.

13. Inspect the rubber brake hose for cracks or signs of rubbing against the body or steering components. Install a new brake hose if any such damage is evident. Also, it is a good idea to replace them if over 10 years old to maintain proper brake operation.

14. Inspect the metal brake lines for corrosion and kinks from road debris kicked up under the vehicle. If a problem is found replace the line.

15. Inspect the rotor for non-machine grooves, heat stress cracks, glazing, minimum wear thickness, and disk runout. Replace the rotor or have it machined to repair the damage.

16. Inspect the brake pads for minimum thickness, loose rivets, or glazing. If any such problem is found, new pads must be installed.

To install:

17. Install the caliper and tighten bolts securely.

18. If the brake hose was removed, reattach it to the caliper. If so equipped, use two new copper washers for the banjo fitting.

19. If removed, install the brake pads.

20. Reconnect any electrical brake pad sensors.

⁘ WARNING

Clean, high quality brake fluid is essential to the safe and proper operation of the brake system. You should always buy the highest quality brake fluid that is available. If the brake fluid becomes contaminated, drain and flush the system, then refill the master cylinder with new fluid. Never reuse any brake fluid. Any brake fluid that is removed from the system should be discarded. Also, do not allow any brake fluid to come in contact with a painted surface; it will damage the paint.

21. Bleed the brakes, if a brake line was replaced or the caliper was detached from a brake line.

22. Seat the brake pads, otherwise the vehicle may coast out of the work area and into traffic before the brakes become effective. It will take several pumps of the brake pedal to seat the pads against the rotor.

23. Check the brake fluid level in the reservoir and top off as needed.

24. Install the wheels and snug the lug nuts.

25. Lower the vehicle.

26. Tighten the lug nuts fully.

27. Road test the vehicle.

Calipers with Integral Parking Brake Mechanisms

The procedure to remove or replace the caliper and/or pads on vehicles equipped with rear disc brakes designed with integral parking brake mechanisms is essentially the same as rear disc brake calipers without integral parking brakes. There are usually two major differences between these two rear disc brake caliper designs.

➡For the actual caliper removal and installation process, refer to the applicable procedure earlier in this section. Read the following two procedures, and perform them in conjunction with the caliper procedures.

REMOVING THE PARKING BRAKE CABLE

The first, and most obvious, difference is that, in one fashion or another, the parking brake cable is attached to the caliper. Before removing the caliper from the rotor, you must first disengage the parking brake cable from the caliper. To detach the parking brake cable from the caliper, perform the following:

➡This is a general procedure and may need slight alteration to apply fully to your specific vehicle. The most important thing to remember is to carefully inspect your caliper to identify the applicable parking brake cable components before disconnecting anything.

1. Loosen the lug nuts on the applicable wheels.

2. If servicing the front brakes, apply the parking brake, block the rear wheels, then raise and safely support the front of the vehicle securely on jackstands.

➡Some vehicles, in fact, are designed with front parking brake assemblies.

3. If servicing the rear brakes, block the front wheels, then raise and safely support the rear of the vehicle securely on jackstands.

4. Remove the wheels for easier access to the brake assembly.

5. Relieve the parking brake cable tension, as described in Section 3 of this manual.

6. Carefully inspect the parking brake cable mounting and attaching (to the caliper) points. Most parking brake cable conduits are retained to a mounting bracket either by a jam nut and locknut setup, or by a retaining clip. Either remove the jam and locknuts, or pull the retaining clip off of the bracket, then disengage the cable conduit from the mounting bracket. If your

vehicle utilizes jam and locknuts to secure the conduit onto the bracket, matchmark the nuts' locations on the cable conduit threads for reinstallation; if marking the threads is not possible, measure (and note the measurements) from the end of the cable conduit to the jam nut and to the locknut.

➡**With the conduit detached from its mounting bracket, there should be enough slack to disengage the parking brake cable end from the caliper lever, or similar linkage. On some models, there may be a cable end retaining fastener (clip, bolt, etc.), which must be removed before the cable can be detached from the caliper.**

7. Detach the parking brake cable end from the caliper lever, or linkage. Often, the cable end must be twisted up and around (or some similar manipulation) to disengage it from the caliper lever.

8. Remove the caliper, as described earlier in this section. Be sure to read the following procedure on seating the caliper piston before commencing with the caliper removal procedure.

To install:

9. After installing the brake caliper, as described earlier in this section, reattach the parking brake cable end to the caliper lever. If equipped, install the cable end securing fastener.

10. Position the cable conduit in the mounting bracket, then either install the retaining clip, or the jam and locknuts. If equipped with jam and locknuts, position the nuts on the cable conduit so that the nuts are positioned as before (using the marks on the threads or a ruler).

11. Adjust the parking brake cable tension, as described in Section 3.

12. Install the wheels and snug the lug nuts.

13. Lower the vehicle.

14. Tighten the lug nuts fully.

15. Depress the brake pedal a few times to ensure that the brake pads are fully seated.

❋❋ **CAUTION**

If you do not seat the pads before driving the vehicle, the first few times you apply the brake pedal the vehicle may not stop as anticipated; this could lead to an accident with a telephone pole or one of your neighbors' cars.

SEATING THE CALIPER PISTON

➡**Be sure to read this entirely before commencing with caliper service.**

The second difference is in how the caliper pistons should be seated into their bores.

Whereas most pistons on calipers which are not equipped with integral parking brake mechanisms can be seated by using a large C-clamp, this is USUALLY not the case with calipers designed with integral parking brake mechanisms. Most integral parking brake calipers apply parking brake pressure to the rotor as follows: when the parking brake is applied, the

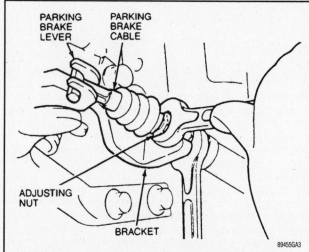

Fig. 35 If it is necessary to remove the parking brake cable, carefully inspect it to determine how it is attached and adjusted

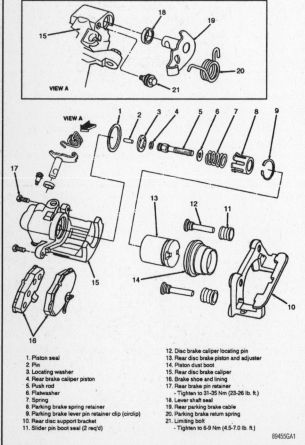

1. Piston seal
2. Pin
3. Locating washer
4. Rear brake caliper piston
5. Push rod
6. Flatwasher
7. Spring
8. Parking brake spring retainer
9. Parking brake lever pin retainer clip (circlip)
10. Rear disc support bracket
11. Slider pin boot seal (2 req'd)
12. Disc brake caliper locating pin
13. Rear disc brake piston and adjuster
14. Piston dust boot
15. Rear disc brake caliper
16. Brake shoe and lining
17. Rear brake pin retainer
   - Tighten to 31-35 Nm (23-26 lb. ft.)
18. Lever shaft seal
19. Rear parking brake cable
20. Parking brake return spring
21. Limiting bolt
   - Tighten to 6-9 Nm (4.5-7.0 lb. ft.)

Fig. 34 Exploded view of a typical rear brake caliper with integral parking brake—note the wedge-shaped notches on the face of the piston (13)

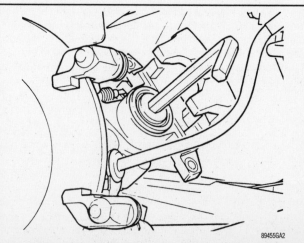

Fig. 36 With the proper tool in place, rotate the piston until it is fully seated into the caliper bore—note that this particular vehicle uses a normal hex key for this job

cable pulls on the caliper lever. The lever, in turn, applies a rotational (spinning) movement to the caliper piston. The piston is designed much like an ordinary screw, so that when a rotational movement is applied to the piston, it slowly presses in against the rotor. To prevent having to constantly adjust the parking brake cable tension as the brake pads slowly wear down, the internal parking brake mechanism is designed with a ratcheting apparatus, which automatically readjusts the parking brake tension.

Since the caliper is designed to protrude from its bore when turned, usually, it cannot be seated in its bore in a conventional manner (with a large C-clamp).

✳✳ WARNING

On most of these calipers, if you use a C-clamp, or similar method, to seat the piston in its bore, you will damage the caliper beyond use. A new caliper will have to be purchased.

To seat the piston in the caliper, spanner or other model-specific tool must be used to turn the piston back into its bore. However (and to complicate things), a few of the integral parking brake calipers utilize an internal cam and/or lever type device that applies parking brake pressure to the rotor by pushing the caliper piston outward rather than turning it. On these uncommon type of calipers, you use a C-clamp to seat the piston into the caliper bore; just like the non-integral parking brake calipers. Unfortunately, the only way to tell which style of caliper you have is to remove it and inspect it.

✳✳ WARNING

When removing a caliper equipped with an integral parking brake mechanism, DO NOT seat the pads with a C-clamp.

Once the caliper and pads are removed, examine the caliper piston to determine how the piston is to be seated back into the caliper bore. All pistons which are rotated into the caliper will have some type of notch, slot or hexagonal depression or protrusion on its face, to which a tool can be attached and rotational force applied. To determine in which direction the piston must be rotated, SLOWLY turn the piston in one direction, and watch the piston's movement. Ensure that the piston moves inward in the bore. If the piston moves outward, reverse the direction of rotation and fully seat the piston. If the piston does not seem to be moving in or out, apply slight inward pressure by hand and continue turning the piston. Some models may have an adjuster or lockbolt on the back of the caliper which must be loosened or removed in order for the piston to rotate in.

➡On some vehicles, namely some GM models, the pistons in the calipers on both sides of the vehicle must be turned in opposite directions. That means that, if the right-hand caliper piston must be turned clockwise, then the left-hand caliper piston must be turned counterclockwise (this is ONLY an example).

If the piston does not seem to move in or out while rotating, if it moves in while rotating it BOTH direction, or if there is no visible depressions or protrusions to which a tool could be attached, you may have a press-in style of caliper. Place an old brake pad against the piston face and install a C-clamp on the caliper. Slowly, and gently, press the piston into the caliper. If the piston does not move inward, DO NOT force it! Damage to the caliper can occur.

Once the caliper piston is fully seated in its bore, install the caliper (depending on its type: sliding, floating or fixed) as described earlier in this section.

OVERHAUL

➡Some vehicles may be equipped dual or 4-piston calipers. The procedure to overhaul the caliper is essentially the same with the exception of multiple pistons, O-rings and dust boots.

1. Remove the caliper from the vehicle and place on a clean workbench.

✳✳ CAUTION

NEVER place your fingers in front of the pistons in an attempt to catch or protect the pistons when applying compressed air. This could result in personal injury!

➡Depending upon the vehicle, there are two different ways to remove the piston from the caliper. Refer to the brake pad replacement procedure to make sure you have the correct procedure for your vehicle.

2. The first method is as follows:
   a. Stuff a shop towel or a block of wood into the caliper to catch the piston.
   b. Remove the caliper piston using compressed air applied into the caliper inlet hole. Inspect the piston for scoring, nicks, corrosion and/or worn or damaged chrome plating. The piston must be replaced if any of these conditions are found.

3. For the second method, you must rotate the piston to retract it from

Fig. 37 If removal is difficult, use compressed air to drive the piston out of the caliper, but keep your fingers clear

Fig. 38 Withdraw the piston from the caliper bore

Fig. 39 On some vehicles, you must remove the anti-rattle clip

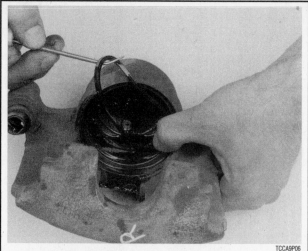

Fig. 42 Use extreme caution when removing the piston seal; DO NOT scratch the caliper bore

Fig. 40 Use a prytool to carefully pry around the edge of the boot . . .

Fig. 43 Use the proper size driving tool and a mallet to properly seal the boots in the caliper housing

Fig. 41 . . . then remove the boot from the caliper housing, taking care not to score or damage the bore

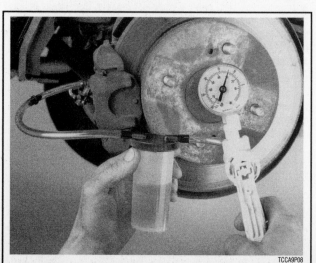

Fig. 44 There are tools, such as this Mighty-Vac, available to assist in proper brake system bleeding

the caliper. Refer to the procedure dealing with disc brake calipers equipped with integral parking brake mechanisms.

4. If equipped, remove the anti-rattle clip.

5. Use a prytool to remove the caliper boot, being careful not to scratch the housing bore.

6. Remove the piston seals from the groove in the caliper bore.

7. Carefully loosen the brake bleeder valve cap and valve from the caliper housing.

8. Inspect the caliper bores, pistons and mounting threads for scoring or excessive wear.

9. Use crocus cloth to polish out light corrosion from the piston and bore.

10. Clean all parts with denatured alcohol and dry with compressed air.

To assemble:

11. Lubricate and install the bleeder valve and cap.

12. Install the new seals into the caliper bore grooves, making sure they are not twisted.

13. Lubricate the piston bore.

14. Install the pistons and boots into the bores of the calipers and push to the bottom of the bores.

15. Use a suitable driving tool to seat the boots in the housing.

16. Install the caliper in the vehicle.

17. Install the wheel and tire assembly, then carefully lower the vehicle.

18. Properly bleed the brake system.

Brake Pads

REMOVAL & INSTALLATION

❋❋ CAUTION

Brake dust may contain asbestos! Asbestos is harmful to your health. Never use compressed air to clean any brake component. A filtering mask should be worn during any brake repair.

Brake pad replacement should always be performed on both front or rear wheels at the same time. Never replace pads on only one wheel. When servicing any brakes use only OEM or better quality pads and parts. When the caliper is removed some brake pads stay with the caliper, others remain on the caliper mounting bracket. Use new pad mounting hardware (springs, anti-rattle clips, or shims) whenever possible to make for a better repair.

Sliding and Floating Calipers

➥**On certain floating calipers it may be possible to remove one of the guide pins and pivot the caliper up or down to gain access to the brake pads. If you decide to do this, be sure that pivoting the caliper will not damage the flexible brake hose.**

1. Open the hood and locate the master brake cylinder fluid reservoir. Clean the area surrounding the reservoir cap, then remove the cap. Remove some of the brake fluid from the reservoir.

2. Loosen the lug nuts on the applicable wheels.

3. If servicing the front brakes, apply the parking brake, block the rear wheels, then raise and safely support the front of the vehicle securely on jackstands.

4. If servicing the rear wheels, block the front wheels, then raise and safely support the rear of the vehicle securely on jackstands.

5. Remove the wheels.

6. Disconnect any electrical brake pad wear sensors.

➥**It is not necessary, and actually discouraged, to detach the brake hose from the caliper during this procedure. If you decide to detach the hose, it will be necessary for you to bleed your brake system.**

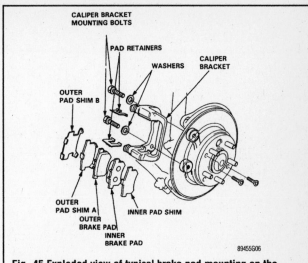

Fig. 45 Exploded view of typical brake pad mounting on the caliper bracket

Fig. 46 To remove the brake pads, first clean the brake master cylinder reservoir cap . . .

Fig. 47 . . . then remove it

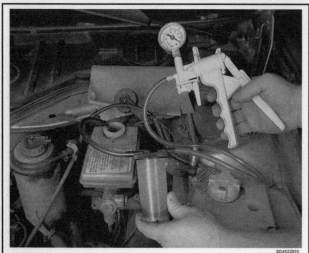

Fig. 48 Using a vacuum pump, or some other method, remove some of the brake fluid from the reservoir

Fig. 49 Remove the disc brake caliper from the rotor

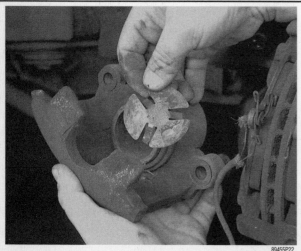

Fig. 50 Be sure to note the positions of any clips or springs on the caliper

Fig. 51 Remove the outboard pad from the mounting bracket . . .

Fig. 52 . . . then remove the inboard pad

Fig. 53 Clean the caliper and mounting bracket with spray brake solvent and a wire brush

Fig. 54 Apply a thin coat of high-temperature brake grease to the sliding surfaces of the bracket and caliper

Fig. 57 When installing the caliper and pads, make sure not to pinch the sensor wire (if equipped)

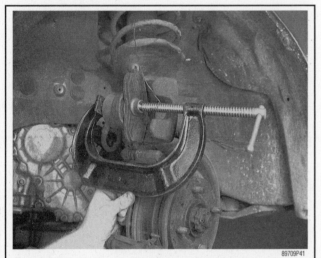

Fig. 55 A large C-clamp can be used to seat the piston in the caliper bore

Fig. 58 Clean the area around the reservoir to prevent contamination

Fig. 56 Install all of the springs and clips in their original positions

7. Remove and suspend the caliper with a piece of wire, cord or strong string. Make sure that it is not placing any stress on the brake hose.

8. For caliper bracket-mounted pads, perform the following:

    a. If present, remove any anti-squeal shims noting their positions.

    b. Also, remove any anti-rattle springs that may be present. If these springs don't provide good tension, then replace them.

    c. Remove the brake pads from the caliper bracket by lifting the pad out by hand or with a slight tap of a hammer to help.

9. For caliper mounted pads, perform the following:

    a. Some outer pads have tabs that are bent over the edge of the caliper, which hold the pads tight in the caliper. Straighten the tabs with pliers before trying to remove the brake pad from the caliper.

    b. Then, remove the outer brake pad by a slight tap to the back of the pad with a hammer.

    c. Other outer pads use a spring-clip to mount to the caliper. To remove this type of pad, press the pad towards the center of the caliper and slide it off. It maybe helpful to use a small prybar.

    d. Remove the inner pad by pulling it out of the piston.

To install:

10. Clean the caliper sliding area using a wire brush and spray brake cleaner.

11. Lubricate the sliding area of the caliper and the pins with high temperature brake grease.

12. Apply anti-squeal compound to the back side of both brake pads. Allow the compound to set-up according to the instructions on the package.

13. Install one of the old brake pads against the caliper piston, then use a large C-clamp to press the piston back into its bore.

14. Install any new hardware provided with the new pads.

15. For bracket-mounted pads, perform the following steps:

   a. Install the pads onto the caliper bracket. Some pads are marked for position.

   b. Make sure that the notches or ears of the brake pads are properly engaged on the bracket.

   c. Place the caliper over the pads and onto the caliper mounting bracket.

   d. Install the caliper mounting hardware and anti-rattle clips. Tighten the guide pins or lockbolt to the proper specification.

→It is a good idea to use some thread-locking compound (removable type) to the threaded fasteners of the caliper.

16. For caliper mounted pads, perform the following:

   a. Install the inner pad by pushing the retaining fingers of the pad into the piston of the caliper.

   b. If the outer pad has a spring-clip, slide the pad over the edge of the caliper into the caliper frame.

   c. If you have the bent-tab style outer brake pad, then test fit the pad; it should fit tight. If the tabs do not secure the pad snugly in the caliper, place the pad on a piece of wood and tap the tab with a hammer to adjust it. It may take a few tries to get it right.

   d. Place the caliper with the pads onto the rotor and, if equipped, caliper bracket.

   e. Install the caliper mounting hardware and anti-rattle clips. Tighten the guide pins or lockbolt to the proper specification.

→It is a good idea to use some thread-locking compound (removable type) on the threaded fasteners of the caliper.

17. Connect any electrical brake pad wear sensors.

18. Seat the brake pads, otherwise the vehicle may coast out of the work area and into traffic before the brakes become effective. It will take several pumps of the brake pedal to seat the pads against the rotor.

19. If a firm pedal is not achieved, it may be necessary to bleed the brakes.

20. Check the brake fluid level in the reservoir and top off as needed.

21. Install the wheels and snug the lug nuts.

22. Lower the vehicle.

23. Tighten the lug nuts fully.

24. Road test the vehicle.

Fixed Calipers

→It is not necessary to remove the caliper to replace the brake pads on a fixed caliper.

1. Loosen the lug nuts on the applicable wheels.

2. If servicing the front brakes, apply the parking brake, block the rear wheels, then raise and safely support the front of the vehicle securely on jackstands.

3. If servicing the rear wheels, block the front wheels, then raise and safely support the rear of the vehicle securely on jackstands.

4. Remove the wheels.

5. Disconnect any electrical brake pad ware sensors.

6. Remove the pad retaining pins by pulling out the spring-clip or cotter pin, then use a punch and hammer to drive the pin out. Pins without a spring-clip or cotter pin, may be equipped with a spring steel collar on the head of the pin. To remove this style pin, just drive the pin out with a punch and hammer.

7. On calipers with hold-down clips, remove the bolt that holds the clip down.

8. Remove the pads from the caliper with a pair of pliers.

9. To seat the pistons of a fixed caliper, use a piece of wood or a pry-bar with a rag wrapped around the end, then wedge it between the rotor and the piston and slide the piston into its seat.

→It is helpful to replace one pad at a time, to reduce the risk of a piston coming out of its bore, which would lead to its needing to be rebuilt.

10. Lubricate the sliding area of the caliper and the brake pads with high temperature brake grease.

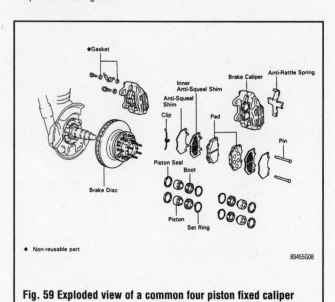

Fig. 59 Exploded view of a common four piston fixed caliper

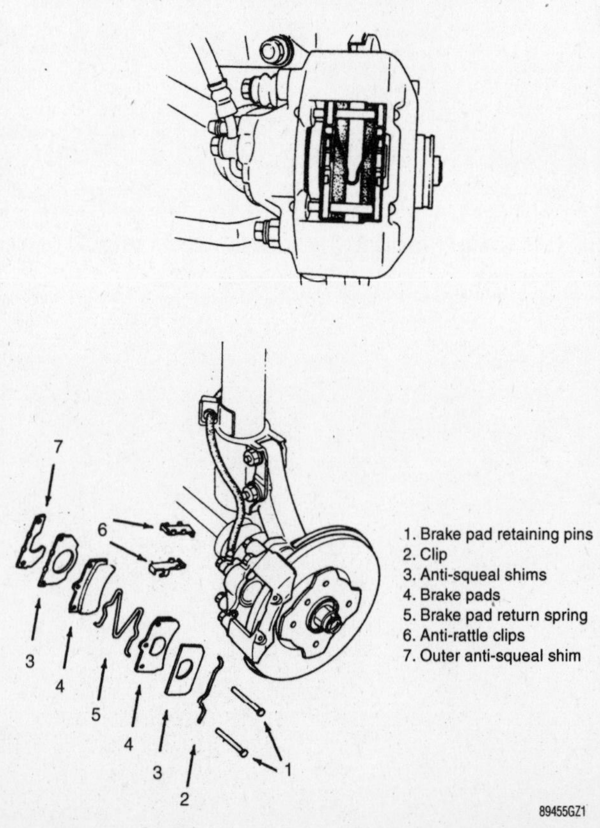

Fig. 60 Exploded view of the brake pad mounting on a typical fixed brake caliper

1. Brake pad retaining pins
2. Clip
3. Anti-squeal shims
4. Brake pads
5. Brake pad return spring
6. Anti-rattle clips
7. Outer anti-squeal shim

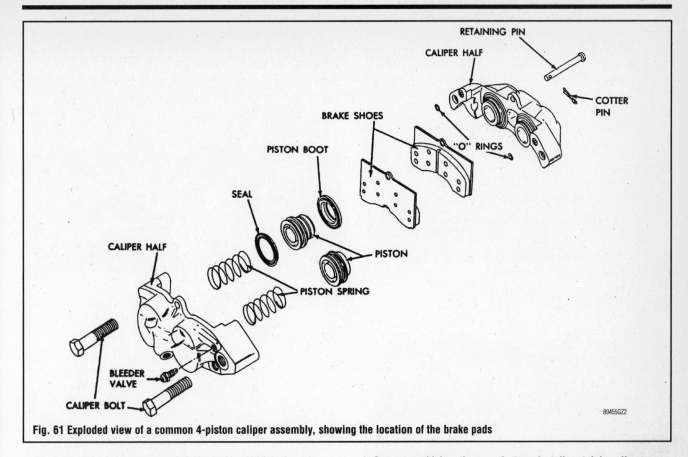

Fig. 61 Exploded view of a common 4-piston caliper assembly, showing the location of the brake pads

11. Apply anti-squeal compound to the back side of both brake pads. Allow the compound to set-up according to the instructions on the product.

12. Insert the new pads into the caliper .

13. If equipped, install the anti-rattle clip or retaining pin spring-clip or cotter pin. On pins with a spring steel collar, you must knock them in until seated against the shoulder in the caliper.

➡️**It is a good idea to use some thread-locking compound (removable type) to the threaded fasteners of the caliper.**

14. Connect any electrical brake pad wear sensors.

15. Seat the brake pads, otherwise the vehicle may coast out of the work area and into traffic before the brakes become effective. It will take several pumps of the brake pedal to seat the pads against the rotor.

➡️**If a firm pedal is not achieved, it may be necessary to bleed the brakes.**

16. Check the brake fluid level in the reservoir and top off as needed.
17. Install the wheels and snug the lug nuts.
18. Lower the vehicle.
19. Tighten the lug nuts fully.
20. Road test the vehicle.

Brake Rotors

REMOVAL & INSTALLATION

Rotors mount in one of 2 ways: either directly on the hub (held in place by the wheels or small fasteners), which are referred to as non-integral (they are not one piece with the hub), or are integral with the hub.

➡️**On some vehicles, the manufacturer installs retaining clips over one or two of the wheel lugs to hold the rotor in place during assembly. Although it is generally thought that these retainers are not necessary and may be discarded, it is a good idea to reinstall them anyway (better safe than sorry). Other manufacturers use one or two small machine screws to hold the rotor in place on the hub; these screws MUST be reinstalled.**

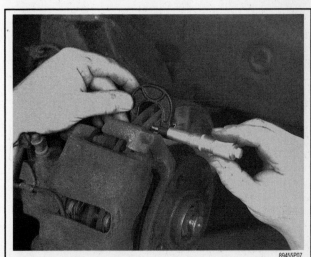

Fig. 62 Use a micrometer to measure the rotor thickness, and replace it if it is below specifications

Fig. 63 To remove the rotor, remove the disc brake caliper . . .

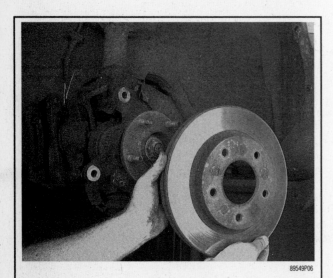

Fig. 64 . . . then pull the rotor off by hand

Fig. 65 If the rotor is equipped with holes and is difficult to remove, it can be loosened using two small bolts . . .

Fig. 66 . . . then removed by hand

Non-Integral Rotors

1. Loosen the lug nuts on the applicable wheels.
2. If servicing the front brakes, apply the parking brake, block the rear wheels, then raise and safely support the front of the vehicle securely on jackstands.
3. If servicing the rear brakes, block the front wheels, then raise and safely support the rear of the vehicle securely on jackstands.
4. Remove the wheels.
5. Clean the brake assembly thoroughly with spray brake cleaner.
6. Remove the caliper.
7. If any rotor retainers are present, remove them. The push-nut type of retainer is usually damaged during removal; discard the old ones and procure new ones.
8. Remove the rotor. On some vehicles, the rotor simply slides off the wheel studs. However, some rotors are pressed into place and must be removed by screwing bolts in the threaded holes provided, forcing the rotor off the hub. Other rotors, not equipped with the threaded holes for press-off bolts, may require the use of a puller to dislodge them from the hub.

➡The rotor may be rusted in place. Spray the area liberally with WD-40®, Liquid Wrench® or equivalent and tap the rotor loose.

To install:

➡New rotors come with an oily, rust-preventive coating on the braking surface. This coating can be removed with brake parts cleaner or most cleaners which are good for oil removal. Make sure that all traces of the coating are removed. Allow the rotor to dry before installation.

9. Position the rotor on the hub and install any retainers.
10. Install the caliper.
11. Install the wheels.
12. Lower the vehicle.
13. Seat the brake pads, otherwise the vehicle may coast out of the work area and into traffic before the brakes become effective. It will take several pumps of the brake pedal to seat the pads against the rotor.
14. Check the brake system for proper operation.

Integral Rotor/Hub Assemblies

EXCEPT 4WD TRUCK FRONT ROTORS—NON-SEALED HUB/BEARING ASSEMBLIES

1. Loosen the lug nuts on the applicable wheels.
2. If servicing the front brakes, apply the parking brake, block the rear wheels, then raise and safely support the front of the vehicle securely on jackstands.

Fig. 67 Pry loose the grease cap

Fig. 70 Removing the locking cap

Fig. 68 Removing the grease cap

Fig. 71 Removing the adjusting nut

Fig. 69 Removing the cotter pin

Fig. 72 Removing the outer bearing

88489P15

Fig. 73 Removing the hub/rotor assembly

3. If servicing the rear brakes, block the front wheels, then raise and safely support the rear of the vehicle securely on jackstands.

4. Remove the wheels.

5. Clean the brake assembly thoroughly with spray brake cleaner.

6. Remove the caliper and suspend it out of the way with wire.

7. Remove the hub grease cap.

8. Remove the cotter pin and wheel bearing nut locking cap. Discard the cotter pin.

9. Remove the wheel bearing nut.

➡**On some vehicles, a left-hand threaded nut is used on the right wheel spindle. Turn this locknut clockwise to loosen.**

10. Remove the brake rotor/hub, washer and bearings as an assembly. Be careful not to let the outer wheel bearing fall out of the hub during removal.

11. If the brake rotor is to be machined or replaced, remove the wheel bearings and grease seal.

To install:

➡**New rotors come with an oily, rust-preventive coating on the braking surface. This coating can be removed with brake parts cleaner or most cleaners which are good for oil removal. Make sure that all traces of the coating are removed. Allow the rotor to dry before installation.**

12. If removed, install the inner wheel bearing and a new grease seal.

13. Make sure the bearings and hub contain an adequate amount of clean wheel bearing grease.

14. Position the rotor/hub assembly on the spindle. Keep the hub centered on the spindle to prevent damage to the grease seal and spindle threads.

15. Install the outer wheel bearing, washer and wheel bearing nut.

16. Properly adjust the wheel bearing. On most vehicles (those with tapered roller bearing) this is done by tightening the adjusting nut until drag is felt on the bearing while rotating the rotor; then, back off the nut about ¼ turn (90°). The rotor/hub should turn freely with no end-play. If you are in any doubt about the proper adjustment procedure, refer to a Chilton manual for the procedure written for your vehicle.

➡**On some vehicles (those with ball bearings), the nut is not so much an adjuster as a locknut. Tighten this nut to the manufacturer's specifications.**

17. Install the wheel bearing nut cover and a new cotter pin.

18. Install the caliper.

19. Install the wheels and snug the lug nuts.

20. Lower the vehicle.

21. Tighten the lug nuts fully.

22. Seat the brake pads, otherwise the vehicle may coast out of the work area and into traffic before the brakes become effective. It will take several pumps of the brake pedal to seat the pads against the rotor.

23. Check the brake system for proper operation.

EXCEPT 4WD TRUCK FRONT ROTORS—SEALED HUB/BEARING ASSEMBLIES

These are unitized hubs that contain the bearing assembly. The hub/bearing unit is replaced as an assembly.

1. Loosen the lug nuts on the applicable wheels.

2. If servicing the front brakes, apply the parking brake, block the rear wheels, then raise and safely support the front of the vehicle securely on jackstands.

3. If servicing the rear brakes, block the front wheels, then raise and safely support the rear of the vehicle securely on jackstands.

4. Remove the wheels.

5. Clean the brake assembly thoroughly with spray brake cleaner.

6. Remove the caliper and suspend it out of the way with wire.

7. On models so equipped, disconnect the ABS sensor wire.

8. Working through the hole provided in the rotor, or working from behind the rotor, remove the hub retaining bolts or nuts.

9. Remove the hub assembly.

To install:

➡**New rotors come with an oily, rust-preventive coating on the braking surface. This coating can be removed with brake parts cleaner or most cleaners which are good for oil removal. Make sure that all traces of the coating are removed. Allow the rotor to dry before installation.**

10. Clean the mounting surfaces of the hub and spindle.

11. Install the hub assembly and tighten the bolts/nuts securely.

12. Connect the ABS wire on models so equipped.

13. Install the caliper.

14. Install the wheels and snug the lug nuts.

15. Lower the vehicle.

16. Tighten the lug nuts fully.

17. Seat the brake pads, otherwise the vehicle may coast out of the work area and into traffic before the brakes become effective. It will take several pumps of the brake pedal to seat the pads against the rotor.

18. Check the brake system for proper operation.

4WD TRUCK FRONT ROTORS

The following procedure applies to most vehicles. If you're in doubt as to whether or not it applies to your vehicle, consult the appropriate Chilton manual for your vehicle.

1. Loosen the lug nuts on the front wheels.

2. Apply the parking brake, block the rear wheels, then raise and safely support the front of the vehicle securely on jackstands.

3. Remove the wheels.

4. Refer to the appropriate Chilton Manual for your vehicle and remove the locking hub assemblies.

5. On most vehicles, remove the outer locknut. This requires a socket made expressly for that purpose, available at many auto parts stores. Then, remove the lockring from the bearing adjusting nut. This can be done with your finger tips or a prytool. Use the locknut socket to remove the bearing adjusting nut.

On some vehicles, a self-locking adjusting nut is used. Remove the self-locking nut with a hub nut wrench, applying inward pressure to disengage the adjusting nut locking splines, while turning it counterclockwise to remove it.

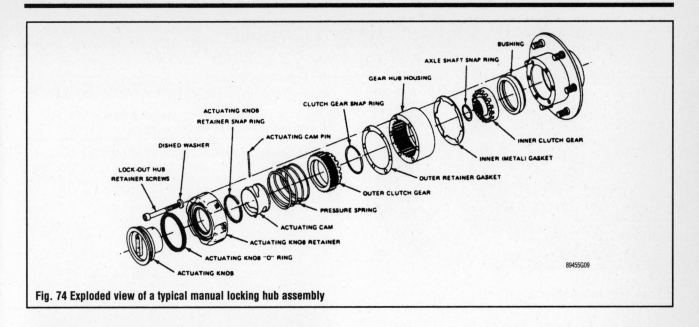

Fig. 74 Exploded view of a typical manual locking hub assembly

Fig. 75 Loosening the outer locknut

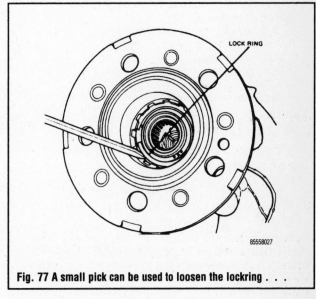

Fig. 77 A small pick can be used to loosen the lockring . . .

Fig. 76 Removing the outer locknut

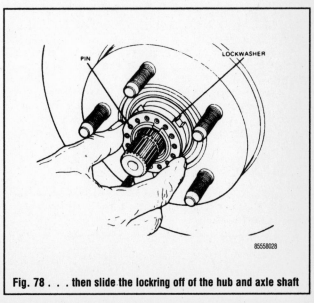

Fig. 78 . . . then slide the lockring off of the hub and axle shaft

88281P24

Fig. 79 Slide the hub off the spindle

6. Remove the caliper and suspend it out of the way.

7. Slide the hub assembly off of the spindle. The outer wheel bearing will slide out as the hub is removed, so be prepared to catch it.

To install:

✳✳ WARNING

Install the hub on the spindle. To prevent damage to the seal and spindle threads, keep the hub centered on the spindle.

8. Carefully position the hub assembly on the spindle.

9. Install the outer bearing cone and roller, and the adjusting nut. Refer to the model-specific Chilton manual for the proper wheel bearing adjustment procedure for your particular vehicle.

10. Reassemble the hub parts.

11. Install the caliper(s).

12. Install the wheels and snug the lug nuts.

13. Lower the vehicle.

14. Tighten the lug nuts fully.

15. Seat the brake pads, otherwise the vehicle may coast out of the work area and into traffic before the brakes become effective. It will take several pumps of the brake pedal to seat the pads against the rotor.

16. Check the brake system for proper operation.

6

DRUM BRAKE SERVICE

DRUM BRAKE SERVICE 6-2

DRUM BRAKE SERVICE

Brake Drums

→Most vehicles have rubber plugs in the backing plates that are removed to access the brake adjusters. However, some vehicles are built with what are called knock-out plugs. These are areas in the backing plate that are made to be knocked out with a hammer and punch. Once the drum is off, the knock-out plug is removed and a rubber plug used in its place.

REMOVAL & INSTALLATION

Brake drums are either separate components or an integral part of the hub assembly. Non-integral brake drums are held onto the axle flange or hub by the wheel and lug nuts; once the wheel is removed, the brake drum can be pulled off of the axle flange. Integral (with the hub assembly) brake drums are combined with the bearing hub to comprise one piece, which means that the wheel bearings must be disturbed (loosened or removed) in one way or another to remove the drum/hub assembly.

✳ WARNING

If the drum is excessively difficult to remove, loosen the brake pads by adjusting their position with a brake "spoon." Access for adjusting the brake pads is often gained through a small hole in the backing plate. If a brake drum is forced off of an axle flange without loosening the brake pads, damage can occur to the brake or axle components.

Non-integral drums (those that are not part of the hub) are usually fairly easy to remove. There are always exceptions to the rule, however. There are drums that are retained to the hub with one or two small bolts. Some drums can be drawn off of the hub by installing two small bolts into threaded holes in the drum; as these bolts are tightened, they slowly press the drum off of the hub. Occasionally a drum is difficult to remove because it binds on the hub flange; these must be worked off by prying gently between the drum and backing plate while applying penetrating oil to the drum/flange contact point. Some older vehicles have a drum assembly that fits over splines on the end of the axle shaft. Others just rust in place. If this occurs, just spray the area around each lug stud and the hub flange with a penetrant such as WD-40®, Liquid Wrench® or equivalent. Let the stuff work for a while, then try pulling or prying the drum off.

Non-Integral Drums

✳ CAUTION

It is always a good idea to wear eye protection when working on brake components, especially drum brakes. Drum brakes often use powerful springs which could cause severe eye injury if they accidentally break.

FREE-MOUNTED TYPE

✳ CAUTION

Brake shoes may contain asbestos, which is a known cancer-causing agent. As soon as the drum is removed, generously spray the entire brake assembly with brake parts cleaner. Let it dry before proceeding. It's a good idea to wear a filter mask when doing brake work.

Fig. 2 To remove the rear brake drum, first safely raise the rear of the vehicle and remove the wheel . . .

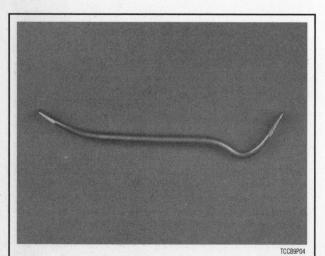

Fig. 1 A brake prytool, known often as a "spoon", can be used to back off the shoe adjustment to allow drum removal

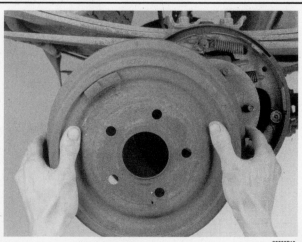

Fig. 3 . . . then grasp hold of the drum and pull it from the axle flange and brake shoes

➡**Some vehicles are built with retainers threaded over 2 or more lug studs to hold the drum in place during assembly. Although these retainers may not be necessary (according to the manufacturer), it may be a good idea to reinstall new retainers anyhow.**

1. Loosen the lug nuts on the applicable wheels.
2. Raise and safely support the vehicle on jackstands.
3. Remove the wheels.
4. If necessary, remove and discard the retainers holding the drum to the hub.
5. If applicable, back off the parking brake adjustment.
6. Back off the brake adjustment until the wheels rotate freely, as follows:

a. On vehicles with a starwheel-type adjuster: Remove the plug on the backing plate then insert a thin prytool and a brake "spoon" (a brake adjusting tool) into the slot. Hold the adjuster lever away from the adjuster wheel with the thin prytool and back of the adjuster wheel with the brake spoon.

b. On vehicles with an expanding-type adjuster, remove the plug and rotate the adjuster screw (usually in an upward motion).

c. On vehicles with ratcheting-type adjusters, remove the plug and insert a thin punch in the hole until it contacts the adjuster assembly pivot. Apply side pressure on this pivot point to allow the adjuster quadrant to ratchet and release the brake adjustment.

d. Some vehicles, notably with manual adjusters, use adjusting cams. On these vehicles, the cam can be turned back from behind the backing plate.

➡**It is helpful to prevent pinched or smashed fingers by wearing heavy gloves when handling a rusty, and often heavy, brake drum.**

7. Grasp the drum and pull it off the hub.

➡**On some vehicles, the drum won't come off even with the shoes completely backed off. This is due to the drum binding on the hub boss. The safest way to remove the drum when this happens, is to spray the binding point with lubricant and to carefully pry between the hub and backing plate. Use a small prybar and pry at various points while rotating the drum. It helps to occasionally tap the hub with a deadblow, or brass mallet.**

8. Spray the brake shoe assembly thoroughly with brake parts cleaner and let it dry. Similarly, spray the inside of the drum.
9. Inspect the drum for wear and/or damage, such as deep grooves, excessive thinness, cracks, etc. Machine or replace the drum as necessary. When machining, observe the maximum diameter specification. The maximum machining diameter is stamped into the drum. If the drum braking surface shows signs of blue discoloration, overheating is indicated. If the bluing is extensive the drum must be replaced. Extensive bluing indicates a weakening of the metal.

To install:

➡**New brake drums come with an oily, rust-preventive coating on the braking surface. This coating can be removed with brake parts cleaner or most cleaners which are good for oil removal. Make sure that all traces of the coating are removed. Allow the drum to dry before installation.**

10. If a new brake drum is being installed, remove the protective coating from the inner braking surface.
11. Adjust the brake shoes to just smaller than the inside diameter of the brake drum.
12. Slide the brake drum onto the hub. Make sure that the brake shoes are not dragging on the brake drum. Install new brake drum retainers.
13. Install the wheels and tighten the lug nuts in a star pattern until tight.
14. Adjust the brakes shoes, as described in Section 3 of this manual.
15. Adjust the parking brake.
16. Install the rubber plug in the access hole.
17. Lower the vehicle. To activate the adjusters, some vehicles require you to make several quick pulls on the parking brake lever. On most, however, several short back-ups, about 10 ft. (3m) each, should do it.
18. Road test the vehicle and check for proper brake operation.

FORCE-FIT TYPE

✳✳✳ CAUTION

Brake shoes may contain asbestos, which is a known cancer-causing agent. As soon as the drum is removed, generously spray the entire brake assembly with brake parts cleaner. Let it dry before proceeding. It's a good idea to wear a filter mask when doing brake work.

1. Loosen the lug nuts on the applicable wheels.
2. Raise and safely support the vehicle on jackstands.
3. Remove the wheels.
4. If necessary, remove and discard the retainers holding the drum to the hub.
5. If applicable, back off the parking brake adjustment.
6. Back off the brake adjustment until the wheels rotate freely, as follows:

a. On vehicles with a starwheel-type adjuster: Remove the plug on the backing plate then insert a thin prytool and a brake "spoon" (a brake adjusting tool) into the slot. Hold the adjuster lever away from the adjuster wheel with the thin prytool and back of the adjuster wheel with the brake spoon.

b. On vehicles with an expanding-type adjuster, remove the plug and rotate the adjuster screw (usually in an upward motion).

c. On vehicles with ratcheting-type adjusters, remove the plug and insert a thin punch in the hole until it contacts the adjuster assembly pivot. Apply side pressure on this pivot point to allow the adjuster quadrant to ratchet and release the brake adjustment.

d. Some vehicles, notably with manual adjusters, use adjusting cams. On these vehicles, the cam can be turned back from behind the backing plate.

7. Thread the proper size bolts into the holes provided in the drum until each contacts the hub. Turn the bolts evenly, a little at a time, until the drum slides free.
8. Grasp the drum and remove it from the axle flange or hub assembly. Remove the forcing bolts.
9. Spray the brake assembly thoroughly with brake parts cleaner and let it dry. Similarly, spray the inside of the drum.
10. Inspect the drum for wear and/or damage, such as deep grooves, excessive thinness, cracks, etc. Machine or replace the drum as necessary. When machining, observe the maximum diameter specification. The maximum machining diameter is stamped into the drum. If the drum braking surface shows signs of blue discoloration, overheating is indicated. If the bluing is extensive the drum must be replaced. Extensive bluing indicates a weakening of the metal.

88279P13

Fig. 4 If equipped with threaded holes, it is possible to press the drum off of the hub using bolts, as shown

To install:

➡New brake drums come with an oily, rust-preventive coating on the braking surface. This coating can be removed with brake parts cleaner or most cleaners which are good for oil removal. Make sure that all traces of the coating are removed. Allow the drum to dry before installation.

11. If a new brake drum is being installed, remove the protective coating from the inner braking surface.

12. Adjust the brake shoes to match the inside diameter of the brake drum.

13. Slide the brake drum onto the hub. Install 2 wheel lug nuts and tighten them, forcing the drum into place on the hub. Remove the lug nuts, then, if equipped, install new drum retainers.

14. Install the wheels.

15. Adjust the brake shoes, as described in Section 3 of this manual.

16. Adjust the parking brake.

17. Install the rubber plug in the access hole.

18. Lower the vehicle. To activate the adjusters, some vehicles require you to make several quick pulls on the parking brake lever. On most, however, several short back-ups, about 10 ft. (3m) each, should do it.

19. Road test the vehicle and check for proper brake operation.

BOLTED-IN-PLACE TYPE

> ❋❋ **CAUTION**
>
> Brake shoes may contain asbestos, which is a known cancer-causing agent. As soon as the drum is removed, generously spray the entire brake assembly with brake parts cleaner. Let it dry before proceeding. It's a good idea to wear a filter mask when doing brake work.

1. Loosen the lug nuts on the applicable wheels.
2. Raise and safely support the vehicle on jackstands.
3. Remove the wheels.
4. If applicable, back off the parking brake adjustment.
5. Back off the brake adjustment until the wheels rotate freely, as follows:

   a. On vehicles with a starwheel-type adjuster: Remove the plug on the backing plate then insert a thin prytool and a brake "spoon" (a brake adjusting tool) into the slot. Hold the adjuster lever away from the adjuster wheel with the thin prytool and back of the adjuster wheel with the brake spoon.

   b. On vehicles with an expanding-type adjuster, remove the plug and rotate the adjuster screw (usually in an upward motion).

   c. On vehicles with ratcheting-type adjusters, remove the plug and insert a thin punch in the hole until it contacts the adjuster assembly pivot. Apply side pressure on this pivot point to allow the adjuster quadrant to ratchet and release the brake adjustment.

   d. Some vehicles, notably with manual adjusters, use adjusting cams. On these vehicles, the cam can be turned back from behind the backing plate.

6. Remove the drum-to-hub attaching bolts.

7. Grasp the drum and remove it from the axle flange or hub assembly.

8. Spray the brake assembly thoroughly with brake parts cleaner and let it dry. Similarly, spray the inside of the drum.

➡On some vehicles, the drum won't come off even with the shoes completely backed off. This is due to the drum binding on the hub boss. The safest way to remove the drum when this happens, is to spray the binding point with lubricant and pry, carefully between the hub and backing plate. Use a small prybar and pry at various points while rotating the drum. It helps to occasionally rap the hub with a deadblow, or brass mallet.

9. Inspect the drum for wear and/or damage, such as deep grooves, excessive thinness, cracks, etc. Machine or replace the drum as necessary. When machining, observe the maximum diameter specification. The maxi-

mum machining diameter is stamped into the drum. If the drum braking surface shows signs of blue discoloration, overheating is indicated. If the bluing is extensive the drum must be replaced. Extensive bluing indicates a weakening of the metal.

To install:

➡New brake drums come with an oily, rust-preventive coating on the braking surface. This coating can be removed with brake parts cleaner or most cleaners which are good for oil removal. Make sure that all traces of the coating are removed. Allow the drum to dry before installation.

10. If a new brake drum is being installed, remove the protective coating from the inner braking surface.

11. Adjust the brake shoes to match the inside diameter of the brake drum.

12. Slide the brake drum onto the hub. Make sure that the brake shoes are not dragging on the brake drum.

13. Install the drum-to-hub attaching bolts and tighten them securely.

14. Install the wheels.

15. Adjust the brakes as follows:

   a. Adjust the brake shoes so that you can feel a slight drag on, or hear a scraping noise coming from the wheel when you spin it.

   b. Back the shoes off just until the drag is no longer felt, or the rasping noise is no longer heard.

16. Adjust the parking brake.

17. Install the rubber plug in the access hole.

18. Lower the vehicle. To activate the adjusters, some vehicles require you to make several quick pulls on the parking brake lever. On most, however, several short back-ups, about 10 ft. (3m) each, should do it.

19. Road test the vehicle and check for proper brake operation.

Integral Drum/Hub Assemblies

> ❋❋ **CAUTION**
>
> It is always a good idea to wear eye protection when working on brake components, especially drum brakes. Drum brakes often use powerful springs which could cause severe eye injury if they accidentally break.

EXCEPT 4WD TRUCK FRONT DRUM/HUB ASSEMBLIES

> ❋❋ **CAUTION**
>
> Brake shoes may contain asbestos, which is a known cancer-causing agent. As soon as the drum is removed, generously spray the entire brake assembly with brake parts cleaner. Let it dry before proceeding. It's a good idea to wear a filter mask when doing brake work.

Some Rear Wheel Drive (RWD) front drums and some Front Wheel Drive (FWD) rear drums are designed with the bearing hub as an integral assembly with the drum.

1. Raise and safely support the vehicle on jackstands.
2. Remove the wheels.
3. If applicable, back off the parking brake adjustment.
4. Back off the brake adjustment until the wheels rotate freely.

   a. On vehicles with a starwheel-type adjuster: Remove the plug on the backing plate then insert a thin prytool and a brake "spoon" (a brake adjusting tool) into the slot. Hold the adjuster lever away from the adjuster wheel with the thin prytool and back of the adjuster wheel with the brake spoon.

   b. On vehicles with an expanding-type adjuster, remove the plug and rotate the adjuster screw (usually in an upward motion).

   c. On vehicles with ratcheting-type adjusters, remove the plug and insert a thin punch in the hole until it contacts the adjuster assembly pivot. Apply side pressure on this pivot point to allow the adjuster quadrant to ratchet and release the brake adjustment.

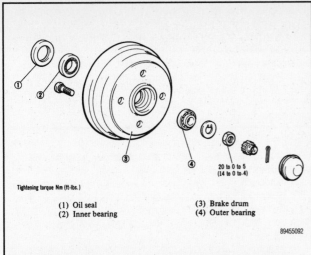

Tightening torque Nm (ft-lbs.)

(1) Oil seal
(2) Inner bearing
(3) Brake drum
(4) Outer bearing

20 to 0 to 5
(14 to 0 to 4)

89455092

Fig. 5 Exploded view of a typical integral drum/hub assembly, showing the placement of the inner and outer wheel bearings

d. Some vehicles, notably with manual adjusters, use adjusting cams. On these vehicles, the cam can be turned back from behind the backing plate.

5. Remove the hub grease cap.

6. Remove the cotter pin and wheel bearing adjusting nut cover. Discard the cotter pin.

7. Remove the wheel bearing nut.

※ WARNING

On some vehicles, a left-hand threaded nut is used on the right wheel spindle. Turn this locknut clockwise to loosen, otherwise damage to the spindle threads will occur.

8. Remove the brake drum, washer and bearings as an assembly. Be careful not to let the outer wheel bearing fall out of the hub during removal.

9. Spray the brake assembly thoroughly with brake parts cleaner and let it dry. Similarly, spray the inside of the drum.

10. Remove the brake drum/hub assembly. Inspect the drum for wear and/or damage. Machine or replace as necessary. When machining, observe the maximum diameter specification. The maximum machining diameter is stamped into the drum. If the drum braking surface shows signs of blue discoloration, overheating is indicated. If the bluing is extensive the drum/hub assembly must be replaced. Extensive bluing indicates a weakening of the metal.

➡**If the brake drum is to be machined or replaced, remove the inner wheel bearing and grease seal.**

To install:

➡**New brake drums come with an oily, rust-preventive coating on the braking surface. This coating can be removed with brake parts cleaner or most cleaners which are good for oil removal. Make sure that all traces of the coating are removed. Allow the drum to dry before installation.**

11. If a new brake drum is being installed, remove the protective coating from the inner braking surface.

12. If removed, install the inner wheel bearing and a new grease seal.

13. Make sure the bearings and hub contain an adequate amount of clean wheel bearing grease.

14. Adjust the distance between the brake shoes to match the inner diameter of the brake drum.

15. Position the brake drum on the spindle. Keep the drum centered

on the spindle to prevent damage to the grease seal and spindle threads.

16. Install the outer wheel bearing, washer and wheel bearing nut.

17. Properly adjust the wheel bearing. On most vehicles (those with tapered roller bearing) this is done by tightening the adjusting nut until drag is felt on the bearing while rotating the drum, then back off the nut about ¼ turn (90°). The drum/hub should turn freely with no end-play. On some vehicles (those with ball bearings), the nut is not so much an adjuster as a locknut. Tighten this nut to the manufacturer's specifications.

➡**If you are at all in doubt as to the proper procedure, check the Chilton manual written specifically for your vehicle.**

18. Install the wheel bearing nut cover and a new cotter pin.

19. Install the hub grease cap.

20. Install the wheels.

21. Adjust the brake shoes, as described in Section 3 of this manual.

22. Adjust the parking brake.

23. Install the rubber plug in the access hole.

24. Lower the vehicle. To activate the adjusters, some vehicles require you to make several quick pulls on the parking brake lever. On most, however, several short back-ups, about 10 ft. (3m) each, should do it.

25. Road test the vehicle and check for proper brake operation.

4WD TRUCK FRONT DRUM/HUB ASSEMBLIES

※ CAUTION

Brake shoes may contain asbestos, which is a known cancer-causing agent. As soon as the drum is removed, generously spray the entire brake assembly with brake parts cleaner. Let it dry before proceeding. It's a good idea to wear a filter mask when doing brake work.

1. These vehicles may be equipped with locking hubs. If so, the hub mechanism will have to be disassembled to gain access to the bearing assembly. Once access is gained, the locknut, locking ring and adjusting nut are removed and the hub/drum assembly can be slid off the axle shaft.

2. Spray the brake assembly thoroughly with brake parts cleaner and let it dry. Similarly, spray the inside of the drum.

3. Inspect the drum for wear and/or damage. Machine or replace as necessary. When machining, observe the maximum diameter specification. The maximum machining diameter is stamped into the drum. If the drum braking surface shows signs of blue discoloration, overheating is indicated. If the bluing is extensive the drum/hub assembly must be replaced. Extensive bluing indicates a weakening of the metal.

➡**New brake drums come with an oily, rust-preventive coating on the braking surface. This coating can be removed with brake parts cleaner or most cleaners which are good for oil removal. Make sure that all traces of the coating are removed. Allow the drum to dry before installation.**

4. If no locking hub is present, simply remove the grease cap and locknut and washer assembly, then slide the hub/drum assembly from the axle shaft.

5. For installation, refer to the Section 3 for adjustment of the bearing assembly.

Full Floating Axle Drums

※ CAUTION

It is always a good idea to wear eye protection when working on brake components, especially drum brakes. Drum brakes often use powerful springs which could cause severe eye injury if they accidentally break.

NON-SPLINED TYPE

✳ CAUTION

Brake shoes may contain asbestos, which is a known cancer-causing agent. As soon as the drum is removed, generously spray the entire brake assembly with brake parts cleaner. Let it dry before proceeding. It's a good idea to wear a filter mask when doing brake work.

To remove the drums from full floating rear axles, the axle shaft will have to be removed. The bearing housing protruding through the center of the wheel can readily identify full floating rear axles.

1. Loosen the lug nuts on the applicable wheels.
2. If servicing the front brakes, apply the parking brake, block the rear wheels, then raise and safely support the front of the vehicle securely on jackstands.
3. If servicing the rear brakes, block the front wheels, then raise and safely support the rear of the vehicle securely on jackstands.
4. Remove the wheels.
5. If applicable, back off the parking brake adjustment.
6. Back off the brake adjustment until the wheels rotate freely.
    a. On vehicles with a starwheel-type adjuster: Remove the plug on the backing plate then insert a thin prytool and a brake "spoon" (a brake adjusting tool) into the slot. Hold the adjuster lever away from the adjuster wheel with the thin prytool and back of the adjuster wheel with the brake spoon.
    b. On vehicles with an expanding-type adjuster, remove the plug and rotate the adjuster screw (usually in an upward motion).
    c. On vehicles with ratcheting-type adjusters, remove the plug and insert a thin punch in the hole until it contacts the adjuster assembly pivot. Apply side pressure on this pivot point to allow the adjuster quadrant to ratchet and release the brake adjustment.
    d. Some vehicles, notably with manual adjusters, use adjusting cams. On these vehicles, the cam can be turned back from behind the backing plate.
7. Remove the axle shaft.
8. Remove the retaining ring, key and axle shaft nut.
9. Remove the hub and drum.
10. Spray the brake assembly thoroughly with brake parts cleaner and let it dry. Similarly, spray the inside of the drum.
11. Inspect the drum for wear and/or damage. Machine or replace as necessary. When machining, observe the maximum diameter specification. The maximum machining diameter is stamped into the drum. If the drum braking surface shows signs of blue discoloration, overheating is indicated. If the bluing is extensive the drum assembly must be replaced. Extensive bluing indicates a weakening of the metal.

To install:

➡**New brake drums come with an oily, rust-preventive coating on the braking surface. This coating can be removed with brake parts cleaner or most cleaners which are good for oil removal. Make sure that all traces of the coating are removed. Allow the drum to dry before installation.**

12. If a new brake drum is being installed, remove the protective coating from the inner braking surface.
13. Install the hub and drum to the tube.
14. Install the axle shaft nut and tighten it to the manufacturer's specification. Refer to the Chilton manual written specifically for your vehicle.
15. Install the key and retaining ring.
16. Install the axle shaft and wheel.
17. Adjust the brake shoes, as described in Section 3 of this manual.
18. Adjust the parking brake.
19. Install the rubber plug in the access hole.
20. Lower the vehicle. To activate the adjusters, some vehicles require you to make several quick pulls on the parking brake lever. On most, however, several short back-ups, about 10 ft. (3m) each, should do it.
21. Road test the vehicle and check for proper brake operation.

SPLINED TYPE

✳ CAUTION

Brake shoes may contain asbestos, which is a known cancer-causing agent. As soon as the drum is removed, generously spray the entire brake assembly with brake parts cleaner. Let it dry before proceeding. It's a good idea to wear a filter mask when doing brake work.

Splines are raised ridges on a shaft or in a bore. The axle shaft on these vehicles has splines cast into the end which mesh with corresponding splines cast into the center hole of the drum. A large, 3-jawed puller is necessary for this job.

1. Loosen the lug nuts on the applicable wheels.
2. If servicing the front brakes, apply the parking brake, block the rear wheels, then raise and safely support the front of the vehicle securely on jackstands.
3. If servicing the rear brakes, block the front wheels, then raise and safely support the rear of the vehicle securely on jackstands.
4. Remove the wheels.
5. If applicable, back off the parking brake adjustment.
6. Back off the brake adjustment until the wheels rotate freely.
    a. On vehicles with a starwheel-type adjuster: Remove the plug on the backing plate then insert a thin prytool and a brake "spoon" (a brake adjusting tool) into the slot. Hold the adjuster lever away from the adjuster wheel with the thin prytool and back of the adjuster wheel with the brake spoon.
    b. On vehicles with an expanding-type adjuster, remove the plug and rotate the adjuster screw (usually in an upward motion).
    c. On vehicles with ratcheting-type adjusters, remove the plug and insert a thin punch in the hole until it contacts the adjuster assembly pivot. Apply side pressure on this pivot point to allow the adjuster quadrant to ratchet and release the brake adjustment.
    d. Some vehicles, notably with manual adjusters, use adjusting cams. On these vehicles, the cam can be turned back from behind the backing plate.
7. Remove the axle shaft nut.

➡**Some of these nuts may be left-hand threads. That is, you turn them right to loosen.**

8. Grasp the drum and try pulling it off the shaft. If it comes off, great! If not, place the puller screw on the end of the shaft, with the jaws evenly spaced around the drum rim. Slowly tighten the puller screw until the drum slide free. It may be helpful to spray the splines with a penetrant such as WD-40®, Liquid Wrench® or equivalent.
9. Remove the brake drum.
10. Spray the brake assembly thoroughly with brake parts cleaner and let it dry. Similarly, spray the inside of the drum.
11. Inspect the drum for wear and/or damage. Machine or replace as necessary. When machining, observe the maximum diameter specification. The maximum machining diameter is stamped into the drum. If the drum braking surface shows signs of blue discoloration, overheating is indicated. If the bluing is extensive the drum must be replaced. Extensive bluing indicates a weakening of the metal.

To install:

➡**New brake drums come with an oily, rust-preventive coating on the braking surface. This coating can be removed with brake parts cleaner or most cleaners which are good for oil removal. Make sure that all traces of the coating are removed. Allow the drum to dry before installation.**

12. If a new brake drum is being installed, remove the protective coating from the inner braking surface.
13. Adjust the brake shoes to match the inside diameter of the brake drum.
14. Slide the brake drum onto the shaft splines as far as you can by hand.

15. Install the axle shaft nut and tighten it until the drum seats completely. Tighten the nut to specification. Check the Chilton manual written specifically for your vehicle for the proper procedure.

16. Install the wheels.

17. Adjust the brakes as follows:

a. Adjust the brake shoes so that you can feel a slight drag on, or hear a scraping noise coming from the wheel when you spin it.

b. Back the shoes off just until the drag is no longer felt, or the rasping noise is no longer heard.

18. Adjust the parking brake.

19. Install the rubber plug in the access hole.

20. Lower the vehicle. To activate the adjusters, some vehicles require you to make several quick pulls on the parking brake lever. On most, however, several short back-ups, about 10 ft. (3m) each, should do it.

21. Road test the vehicle and check for proper brake operation.

Brake Shoes

Most vehicles use a 2-shoe leading/trailing, internal expanding type of drum brake with automatic self-adjuster mechanisms. The automatic self-adjuster mechanisms can take several forms, but the overwhelming majority utilize the starwheel-type, located between the bottom ends of the two shoes, or the ratcheting type, located directly below the wheel cylinder. When the ratcheting type of adjuster is used, the lower ends of the brake shoes usually rest on an anchor plate.

➡**On some vehicles, notably those with unitized rear hubs, and some vehicles with full-floating axles, not only does the brake drum have to be removed, but the hub assembly must be removed as well.**

✳ CAUTION

Brake shoes must always be replaced as an axle set. That is, do not just replace the shoes on one side of the vehicle. Replace them on both sides. Replacing shoes on only one side will result in poor braking performance. Besides, if the shoes wore out on one side faster than the other side, there is a malfunction in the brake system. Inspect the brake system, and, if necessary, repair the problem before proceeding.

On older cars and trucks, drum brakes were used on all 4 wheels. The only difference between the front and rear brakes is the presence of the parking brake assembly.

There are often a lot of springs, washers and clips involved with drum brakes. Usually these components are contained in brake hardware kits available at your local auto parts store. Purchase the kit and replace these parts whenever you replace the shoes. You should never reuse these parts.

✳ CAUTION

Used brake components, especially springs, are worn out from repeated normal use, do not work as well as new parts, and are subject to failure. A worn spring or retainer may break and fall inside the drum causing damage to the shoes, drums and other parts, and possibly even causing the wheel to lock up (a very dangerous situation). Decide for yourself, but considering the risk to you and anyone riding in your vehicle it is cheap insurance to buy a new parts kit.

➡**It is not a good idea to disassemble the brakes on both sides at the same time. There are a lot of parts involved which must be replaced in a certain way. Work on one side at a time, only. If you become confused as to the particular position of the various brake parts during the brake shoe replacement, refer to the other side. Remember, however, the other side is a mirror image (everything is reversed).**

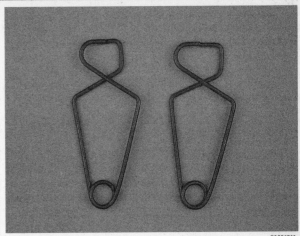

TCCB9P02

Fig. 6 Spring clamp tools, such as those shown, can hold the wheel cylinder pistons in while servicing the shoes

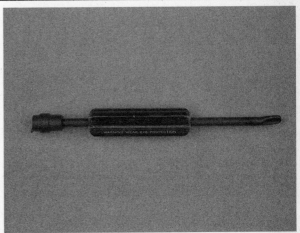

TCCB9P05

Fig. 7 There are several varieties of spring removal and installation tools available, such as this straight one . . .

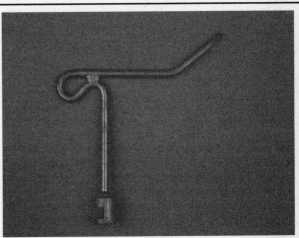

TCCB9P01

Fig. 8 . . . and this curved one—The shape of this tool is designed to provide more leverage during use

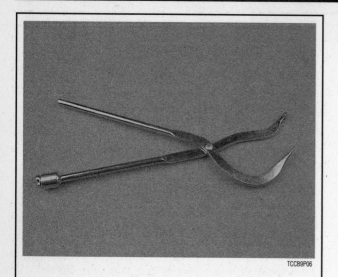

TCCB9P06

Fig. 9 This spring tool combines three different tools into one

While the brake shoes are off, pull back slightly on the wheel cylinder rubber caps. If any brake fluid leakage is evident, replace the defective wheel cylinder.

There is a tool that is, essentially, a large spring clamp used to make sure that the wheel cylinder pistons do not pop out while the shoes are removed. This occurrence is unlikely, but it's cheap insurance to use the tool.

Speaking of tools, brake work can often be frustrating because of the various springs and cables, which are often difficult to remove and install. Most of the work can be accomplished without the use of special tools, however brake tools are not expensive, can be purchased at most auto parts stores, and reduce the risk of personal injury and component damage. Also, brake tools can make the job a lot easier and quicker.

✳✳ CAUTION

Since you'll be working around heavy-duty springs, the use of safety glasses is STRONGLY recommended!

REMOVAL & INSTALLATION

✳✳ CAUTION

Brake shoes may contain asbestos, which is a known cancer-causing agent. As soon as the drum is removed, generously spray the entire brake assembly with brake parts cleaner. Let it dry before proceeding. It's a good idea to wear a filter mask when doing brake work.

Models with Dual Return Springs and Starwheel-type Adjuster

✳✳ CAUTION

It is always a good idea to wear eye protection when working on brake components, especially drum brakes. Drum brakes often use powerful springs which could cause severe eye injury if they accidentally break.

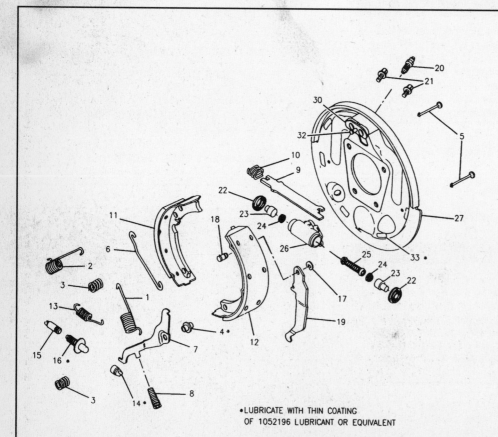

1	RETURN SPRING
2	RETURN SPRING
3	HOLD DOWN SPRING
4	BEARING SLEEVE
5	HOLD−DOWN PIN
6	ACTUATOR LINK
7	ACTUATOR LEVER
8	LEVER RETURN SPRING
9	PARKING BRAKE STRUT
10	STRUT SPRING
11	PRIMARY SHOE AND LINING
12	SECONDARY SHOE AND LINING
13	ADJUSTING SCREW SPRING
14	SOCKET
15	PIVOT NUT
16	ADJUSTING SCREW
17	RETAINING RING
18	PIN
19	PARKING BRAKE LEVER
20	BLEEDER VALVE
21	BOLT
22	BOOT
23	PISTON
24	SEAL
25	SPRING ASSEMBLY
26	WHEEL CYLINDER
27	BACKING PLATE
30	SHOE RETAINER
32	ANCHOR PIN
33	SHOE PADS (6 PLACES)

•LUBRICATE WITH THIN COATING OF 1052196 LUBRICANT OR EQUIVALENT

87959042

Fig. 10 Exploded view of the most common GM rear drum brake setup

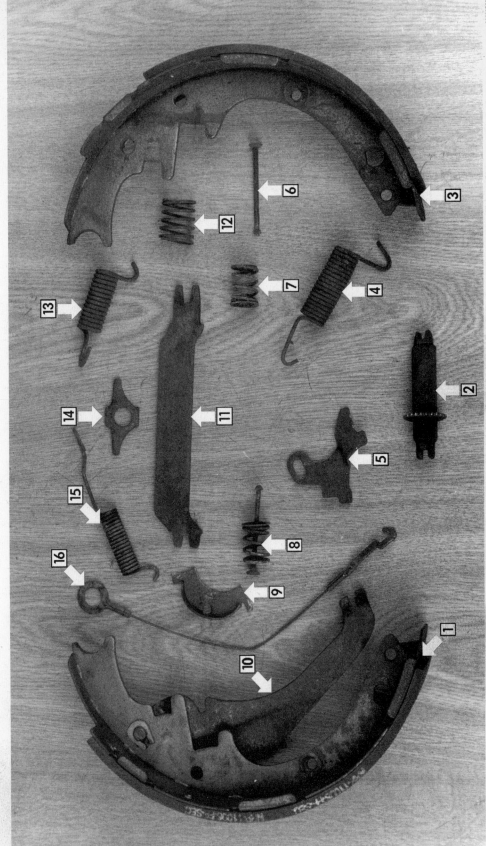

REAR DRUM BRAKE COMPONENTS

1. Secondary shoe
2. Adjusting screw assembly
3. Primary shoe
4. Adjuster spring
5. Adjuster lever
6. Hold-down pin

7. Hold-down spring
8. Hold-down assembly
9. Adjuster cable guide
10. Parking brake lever
11. Parking brake link
12. Link spring

13. Primary shoe return spring
14. Anchor pin plate
15. Secondary shoe return spring
16. Adjuster cable

Fig. 11 Typical dual return spring drum brake setup component identification

1. Loosen the lug nuts on the applicable wheels.

2. If servicing the front brakes, apply the parking brake, block the rear wheels, then raise and safely support the front of the vehicle securely on jackstands.

3. If servicing the rear brakes, block the front wheels, then raise and safely support the rear of the vehicle securely on jackstands.

4. Remove the wheels.

5. Remove the brake drum.

6. Spray the brake assembly thoroughly with brake parts cleaner and let it dry. Similarly, spray the inside of the drum.

7. Inspect the drum for wear and/or damage. Machine or replace as necessary. When machining, observe the maximum diameter specification. The maximum machining diameter is stamped into the drum. If the drum braking surface shows signs of blue discoloration, overheating is indicated. If the bluing is extensive the drum/hub assembly must be replaced. Extensive bluing indicates a weakening of the metal.

➡Note the location of all springs and clips for proper assembly. If you own an instant camera, it may be a good idea to take a picture of your brake assembly with the brake drum removed. This will make reassembly much easier.

Fig. 14 A specially-designed brake tool can make disconnecting the upper return springs much easier

Fig. 12 Clean the brake shoe assemblies with a liquid cleaning solution, NEVER with compressed air

Fig. 15 Detach the upper return springs first from the anchor bolt, then from the brake shoes . . .

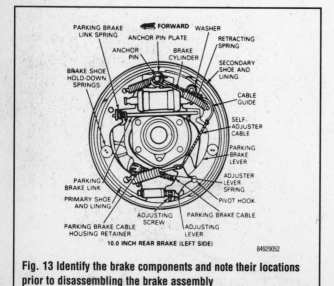

Fig. 13 Identify the brake components and note their locations prior to disassembling the brake assembly

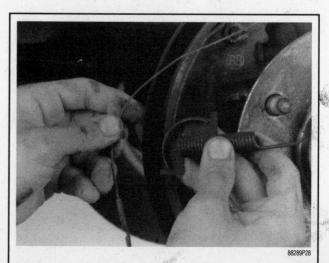

Fig. 16 . . . then remove the adjusting cable from the guide (if equipped), and the guide from the brake shoe

Fig. 17 Remove the anchor block plate . . .

Fig. 20 . . . then detach the parking brake cable from the lever

8. Completely retract the adjuster by rotating the starwheel to relieve tension on the lower spring.

9. Remove the starwheel assembly and adjuster lever from between the two brake shoes.

10. Using a brake spring tool, remove the 2 upper return springs.

11. Remove the adjuster cable and cable guide.

12. Remove the anchor block plate.

13. Using a hold-down spring tool or pliers, while holding the back of the spring mounting pin with one hand, press inward on the hold-down spring plate, turn it slightly to align the notches and pin ears, then remove the hold-down spring assembly with your other hand. Remove the other hold-down spring in the same manner.

14. Lift the shoes off the pins and remove the pins from the backing plate.

15. Remove the parking brake link.

16. Pull back on the parking brake cable spring and twist the cable out of the parking brake lever.

17. The parking brake lever is held onto the rear shoe with a horseshoe clip. Spread the clip and remove the lever and washer.

Fig. 18 . . . then remove the hold-down springs, retainers and pins from both shoes

Fig. 19 Lift the brake shoes off of the backing plate . . .

Fig. 21 Another way to remove the shoes for a dual spring setup is to pull the adjuster cable toward the shoe . . .

Fig. 22 . . . and disconnect the pivot hook from the adjusting lever. Wind the starwheel all the way in

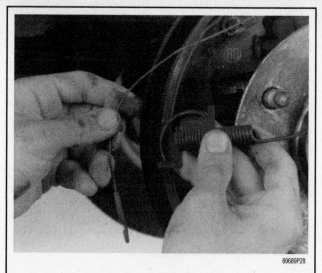

Fig. 25 Next, using a brake spring removal tool . . .

Fig. 23 Disconnect the adjuster lever return spring from the lever . . .

Fig. 26 . . . disconnect the primary brake shoe return spring from the anchor pin

Fig. 24 . . . and remove the spring and the lever

Fig. 27 Repeat the procedure and remove the secondary return spring, adjuster cable and its guide

89689P31

Fig. 28 Also remove the anchor pin plate

89689P34

Fig. 31 . . . and release to remove the hold-down spring. Pull the nail out from the backing plate

89689P32

Fig. 29 Pull the bottoms of the shoes apart and remove the adjuster screw assembly

89689P35

Fig. 32 Remove the primary (front) brake shoe from the backing plate . . .

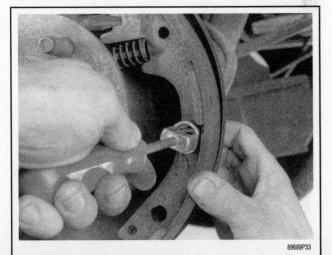

89689P33

Fig. 30 Press in the hold-down springs while holding in on the nail from behind, then turn the cup 90° . . .

89689P36

Fig. 33 . . . and the parking brake strut as well

Fig. 34 Remove the secondary shoe hold-down, pull the shoe out then press up on the cable spring . . .

Fig. 35 . . . and disconnect the parking brake cable from its lever by pulling it from the slot

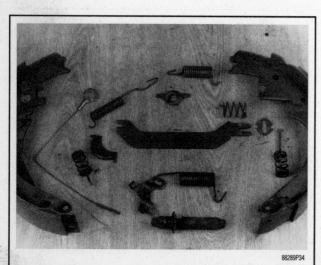

Fig. 36 It's a good idea to arrange all the parts in their approximate installed positions on a clean work surface

To install:

18. Thoroughly clean and dry the backing plate and starwheel assembly.

19. Lubricate the backing plate bosses, anchor plate surfaces, and starwheel threads and contact points with silicone grease. High-temperature wheel bearing grease or synthetic brake grease also work well for this application.

⁂ CAUTION

When applying lubricant to the backing plate and other components, do not use' so much grease that it may get spread onto the new brake shoes' friction material; this can adversely affect the performance of the new brake shoes and, therefore, increase vehicle stopping distance.

20. Insert the parking brake lever pivot stud through the applicable hole in the rear shoe, then install a new wave washer and horseshoe clip. Squeeze the clip ends until the clip cannot be pulled from the lever pivot stud.

21. Connect the parking brake cable to the lever.

22. Position the rear shoe assembly on the backing plate and install the hold-down pin and spring assembly.

23. Install the front shoe and secure it with the hold-down spring assembly.

24. Position the parking brake link and spring between the front shoe and parking brake lever.

Fig. 37 Thoroughly clean the backing plate, then be sure to lubricate the brake shoe bosses on the backing plate

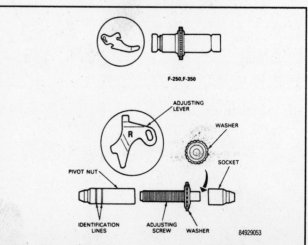

Fig. 38 Exploded view of a typical starwheel adjuster mechanism—the adjusting levers may be stamped for left side and right side applications

25. Position the adjuster cable on the anchor plate pin, install the cable guide and lay the cable across the guide.

✳✳ CAUTION

Be careful! Wear safety glasses during the next few steps, because they involve stretching heavy-duty springs. Getting hurt is very possible, even if you are careful.

26. Make sure that the notch in the upper end of the shoe is engaging the wheel cylinder piston or piston pin.
27. Position the rear shoe return spring into the guide and shoe hole, and, using a brake spring tool, stretch the spring onto the anchor plate pin. Make sure that the cable guide remained in place.
28. Position the front shoe return spring in its hole in the shoe.
29. Make sure that the parking brake link is properly positioned and that the upper end of the shoe will enter the wheel cylinder or engage the wheel cylinder piston.
30. Using the spring tool, stretch the spring into position on the anchor plate pin.

➡**If the shoe doesn't properly engage the link or wheel cylinder piston, try again by removing the spring.**

31. Position the adjuster lever in its hole in the rear shoe and hook the cable to it.
32. Position the lower spring in its hole in the front shoe. Now comes the hard part. Clamp a pair of locking pliers, like Vise Grips® on the spring and stretch it to engage the hole in the adjuster lever. Make sure that the cable stays in place on the guide.
33. Check that the shoes are evenly positioned on the backing plate.
34. Turn the starwheel to spread the shoes to the point at which the drum can be installed with very slight drag.
35. Install the drum and adjust the starwheel until the drum can't be turned. Then, back off the adjustment until the drum can just be turned without drag.
36. Install the wheels, lower the vehicle and check brake action. A firm pedal should be felt.
37. To activate the adjusters, some vehicles require you to make several quick pulls on the parking brake lever. On most, however, several short back-ups, about 10 ft. (3m) each, should do it.

Models with a Single Upper Shoe-to-Shoe Return Spring

✳✳ CAUTION

It is always a good idea to wear eye protection when working on brake components, especially drum brakes. Drum brakes often use powerful springs which could cause severe eye injury if they accidentally break. Also, Brake shoes may contain asbestos, which is a known cancer-causing agent. As soon as the drum is removed, generously spray the entire brake assembly with brake parts cleaner. Let it dry before proceeding. It's a good idea to wear a filter mask when doing brake work.

WITH LOWER ANCHOR PLATE

1. Loosen the lug nuts on the applicable wheels.
2. If servicing the front brakes, apply the parking brake, block the rear wheels, then raise and safely support the front of the vehicle securely on jackstands.
3. If servicing the rear brakes, block the front wheels, then raise and safely support the rear of the vehicle securely on jackstands.
4. Remove the wheels.
5. Remove the brake drum.
Spray the brake assembly thoroughly with brake parts cleaner and let it dry. Similarly, spray the inside of the drum.
Inspect the drum for wear and/or damage. Machine or replace as necessary. When machining, observe the maximum diameter specification. The

Fig. 39 Remove the brake drum for access to the brake components

Fig. 40 Pliers can be used to disengage the hold-down spring retainer by rotating it until aligned with the pin tabs . . .

Fig. 41 . . . then remove the retainer, spring and pin from the shoe and backing plate

88279P17

Fig. 42 Use a pair of needlenose pliers, or similar tool, to detach the upper return spring from both shoes . . .

88279P18

Fig. 43 . . . then remove the brake shoes from the backing plate . . .

88279P19

Fig. 44 . . . and detach the parking brake cable from the applicable brake shoe

maximum machining diameter is stamped into the drum. If the drum braking surface shows signs of blue discoloration, overheating is indicated. If the bluing is extensive the drum/hub assembly must be replaced. Extensive bluing indicates a weakening of the metal.

➡Note the location of all springs and clips for proper assembly. If you own an instant camera, to make installation easier it may be a good idea to take a picture of your brake assembly with the brake drum removed.

6. Remove the shoe-to-lever spring and remove the adjuster lever.
7. Remove the auto-adjuster assembly.
8. Remove the retainer spring.
9. Using a hold-down spring tool or pliers, while holding the back of the spring mounting pin with one hand, press inward on the hold-down spring plate, turn it slightly to align the notches and pin ears, then remove the hold-down spring assemblies with your other hand.
10. Remove the shoe-to-shoe spring.
11. Remove the brake shoes from the backing plate.
12. Using a flat-tipped tool, pry open the parking brake lever retaining clip. Remove the clip and washer from the pin on the shoe assembly and remove the shoe from the lever assembly.

➡On some vehicles, the parking brake actuating lever is permanently attached to the trailing brake shoe assembly. Do not attempt to remove it from the original brake shoe assembly or reuse the original actuating lever on a replacement brake shoe assembly. All replacement brake shoe assemblies for these vehicles must come with the actuating lever as part of the trailing brake shoe assembly.

To install:
13. Thoroughly clean all parts.
14. On vehicles with the ratcheting upper mounted adjuster, clean and inspect the brake support plate and the automatic adjuster mechanism. Be sure the quadrant (toothed part) of the adjuster is free to rotate throughout its entire tooth contact range and is free to slide the full length of its mounting slot. Check the knurled pin. It should be securely attached to the adjuster mechanism and its teeth should be in good condition. If the adjuster is worn or damaged, replace it. If the adjuster is serviceable, lubricate lightly with high-temperature grease between the strut and the quadrant.

✳✳ CAUTION

The trailing brake shoe assemblies used on the rear brakes of these vehicles are different for the left and right side of the vehicle. Care must be taken to ensure the brake shoes are properly installed in their correct side of the vehicle. Otherwise the brakes will probably malfunction, thereby creating a very dangerous condition. When the trailing shoes are properly installed on their correct side of the vehicle, the park brake actuating lever will be positioned under the brake shoe web.

15. Thoroughly clean and dry the backing plate. Lubricate the backing plate at the brake shoe contact points. Also, lubricate backing plate bosses, anchor pin, and parking brake actuating mechanism with silicone grease. High-temperature wheel bearing grease or synthetic brake grease also work well for this application.
16. Install the parking brake lever assembly on the lever pin. Install the wave washer and a new retaining clip. Use pliers, or the like, to install the retainer on the pin. If removed, connect the parking brake lever to the parking brake cable and verify that the cable is properly routed.
17. Clean and lubricate the adjuster assembly. Make sure the nut-adjuster is drawn all the way to the stop, but the nut must NOT lock firmly at the end of the assembly.
18. Install the brake shoes on the backing plate with the hold-down springs, washers and pins.
19. Install the shoe-to-shoe spring.
20. Install the retainer spring.
21. Install the auto-adjuster assembly and install the adjuster lever and the shoe-to-lever spring.

22. Pre-adjust the shoes so the drum slides on with a light drag and install the brake drum.

23. Adjust the brake shoes, as described in Section 3 of this manual.

24. Install the rear wheels.

25. To activate the adjusters, some vehicles require you to make several quick pulls on the parking brake lever. On most, however, several short back-ups, about 10 ft. (3m) each, should do it.

26. Adjust the parking brake cable.

27. Lower the vehicle and check for proper brake operation.

WITH LOWER STARWHEEL-TYPE ADJUSTER

1. Loosen the lug nuts on the applicable wheels.

2. If servicing the front brakes, apply the parking brake, block the rear wheels, then raise and safely support the front of the vehicle securely on jackstands.

3. If servicing the rear brakes, block the front wheels, then raise and safely support the rear of the vehicle securely on jackstands.

4. Remove the wheels.

5. Remove the drums.

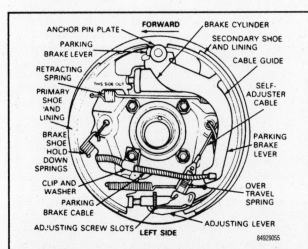

Fig. 45 Identification of the typical components used on drum brakes which use dual return springs and a lower starwheel-type adjuster

Fig. 46 Remove the brake drum from the rear axle

Fig. 47 Remove the parking brake lever retaining nut which is located behind the backing plate

Fig. 48 Disconnect the adjusting cable from the anchor pin, guide and lever

6. Spray the brake assembly thoroughly with brake parts cleaner and let it dry. Similarly, spray the inside of the drum.

7. Inspect the drum for wear and/or damage. Machine or replace as necessary. When machining, observe the maximum diameter specification. The maximum machining diameter is stamped into the drum. If the drum braking surface shows signs of blue discoloration, overheating is indicated. If the bluing is extensive the drum/hub assembly must be replaced. Extensive bluing indicates a weakening of the metal.

➡Note the location of all springs and clips for proper assembly. If you own an instant camera, to make installation easier it may be a good idea to take a picture of your brake assembly with the brake drum removed.

8. Remove the parking brake lever assembly from the backing plate.

9. Remove the adjusting cable assembly from the anchor pin, cable guide and adjusting lever.

10. Remove the brake shoe retracting springs.

11. Remove the brake shoe hold-down spring from each shoe.

12. Remove the brake shoes and adjusting screw assembly.

13. Disassemble the adjusting screw assembly.

Fig. 49 Slide the parking brake lever out from its mounting

Fig. 50 Disconnect the parking brake cable from the lever

Fig. 51 Use an appropriate tool to disconnect the return springs from their retaining holes

Fig. 52 Disengage the hold-down springs from the retaining clips on the backing plate

Fig. 53 Back off the adjusting screw and remove it from the brake assembly

Fig. 54 Spread the shoes apart and remove them from the backing plate

→It's a good idea to arrange all the parts in the approximate installed positions as a guide for reassembly.

To install:

14. Clean the ledge pads on the backing plate. Apply a light coat of silicone grease to the ledge pads (where the brake shoes rub the backing plate). High-temperature wheel bearing grease or synthetic brake grease (designed specifically for this) also work well. Also, apply grease to the adjusting screw assembly and the hold-down and retracting spring contacts on the brake shoes.

15. Install the upper retracting spring on the primary and secondary shoes, then position the shoe assembly on the backing plate with the wheel cylinder pistons engaged with the shoes.

16. Install the brake shoe hold-down springs.

17. Install the brake shoe adjustment screw assembly so that the slot in the head of the adjusting screw is toward the primary (leading) shoe, along with the lower retracting spring, adjusting lever spring, adjusting lever assembly and connect the adjusting cable to the adjusting lever. Position the cable in the cable guide and install the cable anchor fitting on the anchor pin.

18. Install the adjusting screw assemblies in the same locations from which they were removed.

✳✳ CAUTION

Interchanging the brake shoe adjusting screws from one side of the vehicle to the other will cause the brake shoes to retract rather than expand each time the automatic adjusting mechanism is operated; this will create an extremely dangerous condition when driving the vehicle. To prevent incorrect installation, the socket end of each adjusting screw is usually stamped with an R or an L to indicate their installation on the right or left side of the vehicle. In some cases, the adjusting pivot nuts can be distinguished by the number of lines machined around the body of the nut. Two lines indicate a nut which should be installed on the right side of the vehicle; one line indicates a nut that must be installed on the left side of the vehicle.

19. Install the parking brake assembly in the anchor pin and secure with the retaining nut behind the backing plate.

20. Adjust the brakes before installing the brake drums and wheels. Install the brake drums and wheels.

21. To activate the adjusters, some vehicles require you to make several

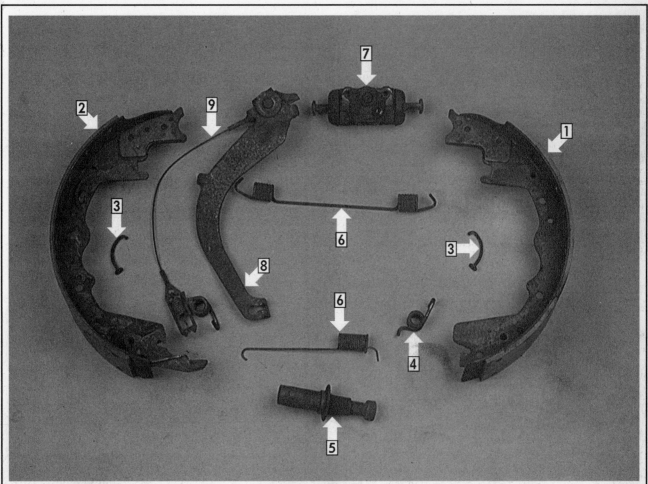

1. Front brake shoe	4. Shoe hold-down spring	7. Wheel cylinder
2. Rear brake shoe	5. Adjuster	8. Parking brake lever
3. Hold-down pin	6. Return spring	9. Parking brake adjuster cable

88489P44

Fig. 55 It is a good idea to lay the brake parts out in their positions on a clean work surface as they are removed

Fig. 56 Connecting the lower retracting spring can often be difficult—be careful and have patience

Fig. 57 This is how everything should look after assembly

quick pulls on the parking brake lever. On most, however, several short back-ups, about 10 ft. (3m) each, should do it.

22. Lower the vehicle and road test the brakes. New brakes may pull to one side or the other before they are seated. Continued pulling or erratic braking should not occur.

Models with a Single U-Shaped Return Spring

✻✻ CAUTION

It is always a good idea to wear eye protection when working on brake components, especially drum brakes. Drum brakes often use powerful springs which could cause severe eye injury if they accidentally break. Also, brake shoes may contain asbestos, which is a known cancer-causing agent. As soon as the drum is removed, generously spray the entire brake assembly with brake parts cleaner. Let it dry before proceeding. It's a good idea to wear a filter mask when doing brake work.

1. Loosen the lug nuts on the applicable wheels.
2. If servicing the front brakes, apply the parking brake, block the rear wheels, then raise and safely support the front of the vehicle securely on jackstands.
3. If servicing the rear brakes, block the front wheels, then raise and safely support the rear of the vehicle securely on jackstands.
4. Remove the wheels.
5. Remove the brake drum.
6. Spray the brake assembly thoroughly with brake parts cleaner and let it dry. Similarly, spray the inside of the drum.
7. Inspect the drum for wear and/or damage. Machine or replace as necessary. When machining, observe the maximum diameter specification. The maximum machining diameter is stamped into the drum. If the drum braking surface shows signs of blue discoloration, overheating is indicated. If the bluing is extensive the drum/hub assembly must be replaced. Extensive bluing indicates a weakening of the metal.

➡Note the location of all springs and clips for proper assembly. If you own an instant camera, to make installation easier it may be a good idea to take a picture of your brake assembly with the brake drum removed.

8. Remove the return spring clip from the lower anchor block.
9. Squeeze the upper ends of the return spring slightly and remove it from the shoes.

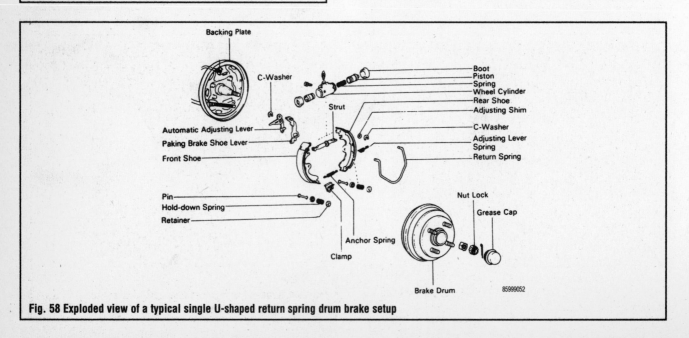

Fig. 58 Exploded view of a typical single U-shaped return spring drum brake setup

Fig. 59 Before removing any parts, make a note of their positions

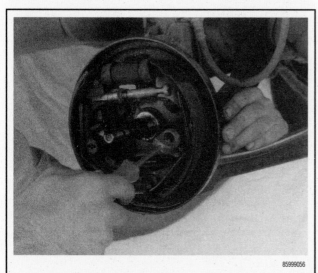

Fig. 60 Depress and rotate the hold-down spring retainer . . .

Fig. 61 . . . then remove the spring, retainer and pin from the backing plate and shoes

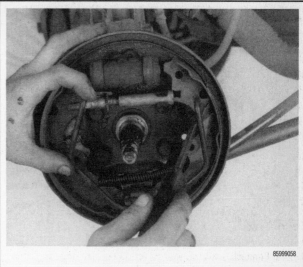

Fig. 62 Remove the return spring from both brake shoes . . .

Fig. 63 . . . then separate the shoes from the backing plate

Fig. 64 A large pair of pliers can be used to disconnect the parking brake cable from the lever

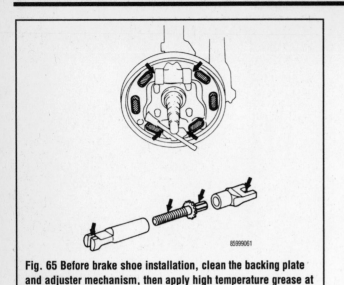

Fig. 65 Before brake shoe installation, clean the backing plate and adjuster mechanism, then apply high temperature grease at these points (arrows)

10. Using a hold-down spring tool or pliers, remove the hold-down springs. While holding the back of the spring mounting pin with one hand, press inward on the hold-down spring plate, turn it slightly to align the notches and pin ears, then remove the hold-down spring assemblies with your other hand.

11. Lift the shoes off of the pins, then remove the pins from the backing plate.

12. Remove the shoes and adjuster as an assembly.

13. Pull back on the parking brake cable spring and twist the cable out of the parking brake lever.

14. The parking brake lever is held onto the rear shoe with a horseshoe clip. Spread the clip and detach the lever and washer from the shoe.

To install:

15. Thoroughly clean and dry the backing plate assembly.

16. Lubricate the backing plate bosses, anchor plate surfaces, and all contact points with silicone grease. High-temperature wheel bearing grease or synthetic brake grease (designed specifically for this) also work well.

17. Lubricate the parking brake lever pivot stud, then insert the pivot stud through the applicable hole in the rear shoe, then install a new wave washer and horseshoe clip. Squeeze the clip ends until the clip cannot be pulled from the lever pivot stud.

18. Connect the parking brake cable to the lever.

19. Position the front and rear shoe assemblies and adjuster on the backing plate, then install the hold-down pin and spring assemblies.

20. Position the return spring in the shoes, rotate it down into position on the anchor block, and install the retaining clip.

21. Turn the strut adjusting screw to spread the shoes to the point at which the drum can just be installed without drag.

22. Install the drum.

23. Adjust the brake shoes, as described in Section 3 of this manual.

24. Install the wheels, lower the vehicle and check brake action. A firm pedal should be felt.

25. To activate the adjusters, some vehicles require you to make several quick pulls on the parking brake lever. On most, however, several short back-ups, about 10 ft. (3m) each, should do it.

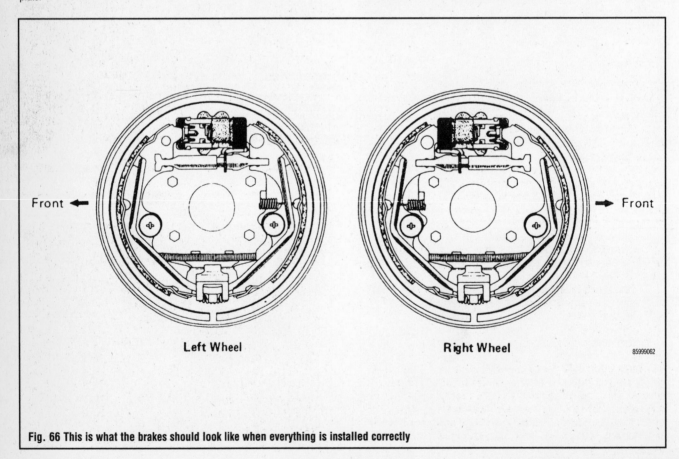

Front ← Left Wheel   Right Wheel → Front

Fig. 66 This is what the brakes should look like when everything is installed correctly

Wheel Cylinders

REMOVAL & INSTALLATION

Wheel cylinders are held in place on the backing plate with either bolts or spring clips. A first glance, this looks like a fairly easy job, and it can be. However, a lot can go wrong. If the wheel cylinder has been there a long time, the bolts or clips can be rusted in place. Worse, the brake line flare nut may be rusted in place. The flats on the nut are easily rounded off. Also, the flare nut can be rusted to the line, meaning the line will twist when the nut is turned. So, before starting, it's best to thoroughly soak the area with penetrating oil where the brake line threads into the wheel cylinder. Also, apply penetrating oil to the mounting bolts or clips.

If you run into problems, here are some general tips:
• Use a flare nut wrench on the flare nuts. Sounds logical, doesn't it? Flare nut wrenches are designed to reduce the possibility of rounding-off.
• Use a box end wrench, or, if room permits, a socket on the bolts. The better grip of a box end wrench or socket will help prevent rounding off the bolt head(s).
• If you round off a bolt head, you'll have to try using Vise-Grips® (or equivalent), one of those wrenches designed for rounded-off bolts (space permitting), a nut splitter (again, space permitting), or grind off the bolt head.
• If the brake line won't budge, you fear kinking or twisting the line, or you rounded off the flare nut, try this: remove the wheel cylinder bolts or clips and pull the wheel cylinder, line attached, away from the backing plate. Usually, there is enough play in the brake line. Hold the flare nut with Vise-Grips® or equivalent, and try turning the wheel cylinder. The wheel cylinder gives you greater mechanical advantage than the flare nut. If nothing works, disconnect the line at the junction box. You'll have to purchase a new line.

Bolt-on Type

❊❊ CAUTION

It is always a good idea to wear eye protection when working on brake components, especially drum brakes. Drum brakes often use powerful springs which could cause severe eye injury if they accidentally break. Also, brake shoes may contain asbestos, which is a known cancer-causing agent. As soon as the drum is removed, generously spray the entire brake assembly with brake parts cleaner. Let it dry before proceeding. It's a good idea to wear a filter mask when doing brake work.

1. Loosen the lug nuts on the applicable wheels.
2. If servicing the front brakes, apply the parking brake, block the rear wheels, then raise and safely support the front of the vehicle securely on jackstands.
3. If servicing the rear brakes, block the front wheels, then raise and safely support the rear of the vehicle securely on jackstands.
4. Remove the wheels.
5. Remove the drum.
6. Remove the brake shoes.

➡On some vehicles, it may be possible to just remove the return springs and pull the shoes apart far enough for wheel cylinder removal. We do not recommend this for two reasons: wheel cylinder removal involves spilling some brake fluid—brake fluid can contaminate brake shoe friction material—and leaving the brake shoes on the backing plate can reduce working space and interfere with the job.

7. Loosen the brake fluid line fitting, then separate the line from the wheel cylinder.

Fig. 67 Use a flare nut wrench to loosen the brake line fitting from the inboard side of the wheel cylinder

Fig. 68 When the brake line is disconnected there will be some fluid leakage—plug the line to avoid contamination

Fig. 69 Remove the wheel cylinder retaining bolts, then separate the cylinder from the backing plate

✷✷ CAUTION

Plug the line immediately to prevent contamination of the brake fluid, because brake fluid absorbs water from the atmosphere very quickly. Water reduces the effectiveness of brake fluid, leading to increased brake fade.

  8. Remove the wheel cylinder bolts, and separate the cylinder from the backing plate.

To install:

  9. Clean the backing plate thoroughly.

  10. Apply a very thin coating of RTV silicone sealer to the cylinder mounting surface. This will aid in keeping moisture and dirt out of the brakes.

  11. Position the cylinder on the backing plate, then install the retaining bolts.

  12. Reattach the brake line to the wheel cylinder.

  13. Install the brake shoes.

  14. Install the drum.

  15. Bleed the brake system.

  16. Adjust the brake shoes, as described in Section 3 of this manual.

  17. Install the wheels and snug the lug nuts.

  18. Lower the vehicle.

  19. Tighten the lug nuts on the wheels fully.

Spring Clip Type

✷✷ CAUTION

It is always a good idea to wear eye protection when working on brake components, especially drum brakes. Drum brakes often use powerful springs which could cause severe eye injury if they accidentally break. Also, brake shoes may contain asbestos, which is a known cancer-causing agent. As soon as the drum is removed, generously spray the entire brake assembly with brake parts cleaner. Let it dry before proceeding. It's a good idea to wear a filter mask when doing brake work.

  1. Loosen the lug nuts on the applicable wheels.

  2. If servicing the front brakes, apply the parking brake, block the rear wheels, then raise and safely support the front of the vehicle securely on jackstands.

  3. If servicing the rear brakes, block the front wheels, then raise and safely support the rear of the vehicle securely on jackstands.

  4. Remove the wheels.

  5. Remove the brake drum.

  6. Remove the brake shoes.

➡On some vehicles, it may be possible to just remove the return springs and pull the shoes apart far enough for wheel cylinder removal. We do not recommend this for two reasons: wheel cylinder removal involves spilling some brake fluid—brake fluid can contaminate brake shoe friction material—and leaving the brake shoes on the backing plate can reduce working space and interfere with the job.

  7. Disconnect and cap the brake line at the wheel cylinder.

✷✷ CAUTION

Plug the line immediately to prevent contamination of the brake fluid, because brake fluid absorbs water from the atmosphere very quickly. Water reduces the effectiveness of brake fluid, leading to increased brake fade.

  8. Using two awls, release the spring clip securing the wheel cylinder to the backing plate.

  9. Remove the wheel cylinder from the vehicle.

➡On some GM vehicles it may be necessary to remove the bleeder screw from the wheel cylinder to remove it from the backing plate.

To install:

  10. If you are installing a new wheel cylinder, remove the bleeder screw from the wheel cylinder, then position the cylinder in the backing plate. Removing the bleeder screw will keep it out of harm's way when installing the retaining clip.

  11. Hold the wheel cylinder in place with a small prybar, and, using a socket (usually 1⅛ in. on domestic vehicles) on the end of an extension, push the spring clip into place. Make sure both spring clip ears are seated correctly.

  12. Connect the brake line to the wheel cylinder.

  13. Install the bleeder screw and temporarily tighten it.

  14. Install the brake shoes.

  15. Install the brake drum.

  16. Bleed the brake system.

  17. Adjust the brake shoes, as described in Section 3 of this manual.

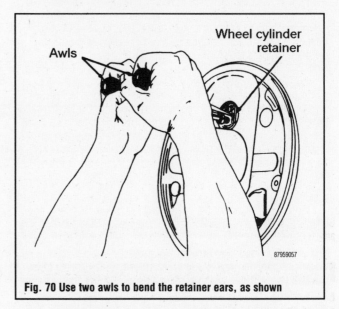

Fig. 70 Use two awls to bend the retainer ears, as shown

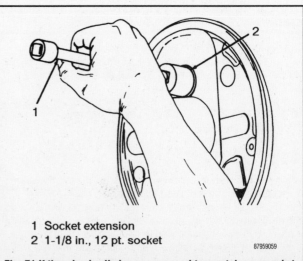

1 Socket extension
2 1-1/8 in., 12 pt. socket

Fig. 71 If the wheel cylinder uses a round type retainer, a socket and extension can be used to seat the retainer

18. Install the wheels and snug the lug nuts.
19. Lower the vehicle.
20. Tighten the lug nuts on the wheels fully.

OVERHAUL

Wheel cylinders can be overhauled, although most people do not bother. Replacing the wheel cylinder is much easier and requires no special tools or experience. If the cost difference between a rebuilding kit and new cylinder is not great, it's much safer to install the new cylinder.

If you decide to overhaul your wheel cylinder(s), you will need a wheel cylinder hone and a rebuild parts kit.

➡**It is possible to rebuild the wheel cylinder while still in place on the backing plate. There is no good reason to do so other than that, for some reason, you can't remove the cylinder. If you choose to do this, it is of the UTMOST importance that all material be flushed out of the bore before installing new parts. We DO NOT recommend rebuilding a wheel cylinder while it is installed on the backing plate.**

1. Remove the old wheel cylinder.
2. Thoroughly clean the outside of the unit with brake parts cleaner.
3. Place the cylinder on a clean work surface.
4. Remove the boots, then use a finger to push the pistons, cups and spring out of the bore.
5. Inspect the inner bore surface. If it is not badly pitted, rusted or scored, it can be rebuilt.
6. Remove the bleeder screw.
7. Install a wheel cylinder hone into a low-speed drill, and coat the inside of the cylinder with clean brake fluid.
8. Make several passes through the cylinder bore with the hone, never stopping in one place or passing completely through the bore.
9. Remove just enough material to establish a clean, crosshatched inner surface.
10. Thoroughly clean the wheel cylinder bore with alcohol and let it dry. Blow out all passages with compressed air, including the bleeder screw area.
11. Coat the bore with clean brake fluid.

✳✳ WARNING

Be sure to use all of the replacement parts which come with the rebuild kit you purchased, otherwise the rebuilt wheel cylinder may not function properly.

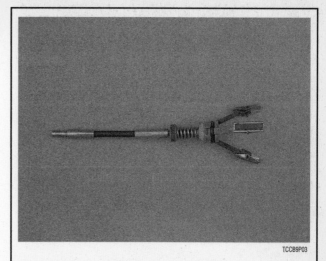
TCCB9P03
Fig. 73 A wheel cylinder hone is used to polish the inside of the bore, thereby removing any scratches or nicks

TCCA9P13
Fig. 74 To disassemble the wheel cylinder, first remove the outer boots . . .

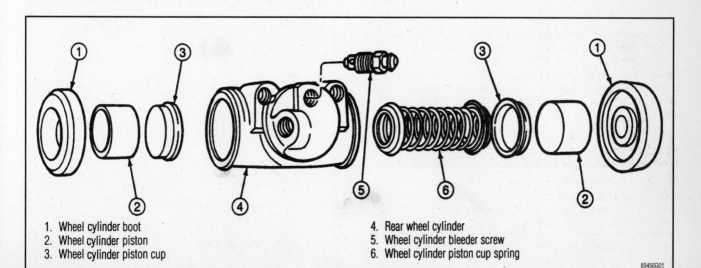

1. Wheel cylinder boot
2. Wheel cylinder piston
3. Wheel cylinder piston cup
4. Rear wheel cylinder
5. Wheel cylinder bleeder screw
6. Wheel cylinder piston cup spring

89456G01

Fig. 72 Exploded view of a typical wheel cylinder

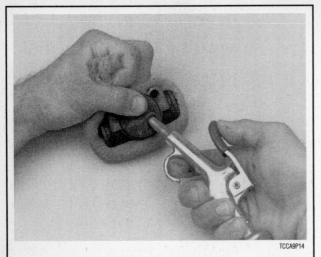

Fig. 75 . . . then carefully apply compressed air to the bleeder valve hole to extract the pistons and seals

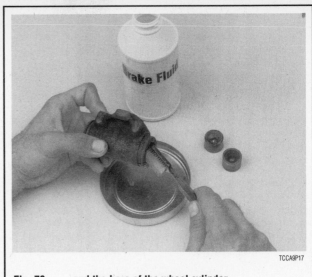

Fig. 78 . . . and the bore of the wheel cylinder

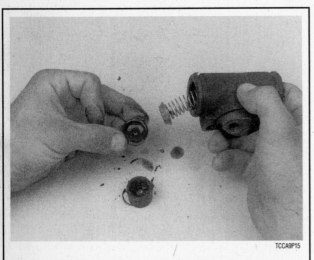

Fig. 76 Remove the pistons, cup seals and spring from the cylinder

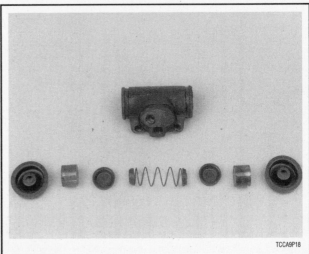

Fig. 79 Once cleaned and inspected, the wheel cylinder is ready for assembly

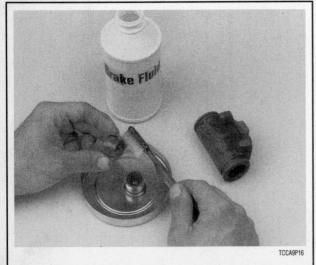

Fig. 77 Use brake fluid and a soft brush to clean the pistons . . .

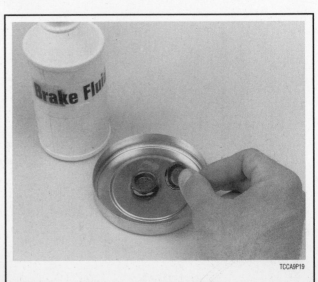

Fig. 80 Lubricate the cup seals with brake fluid . . .

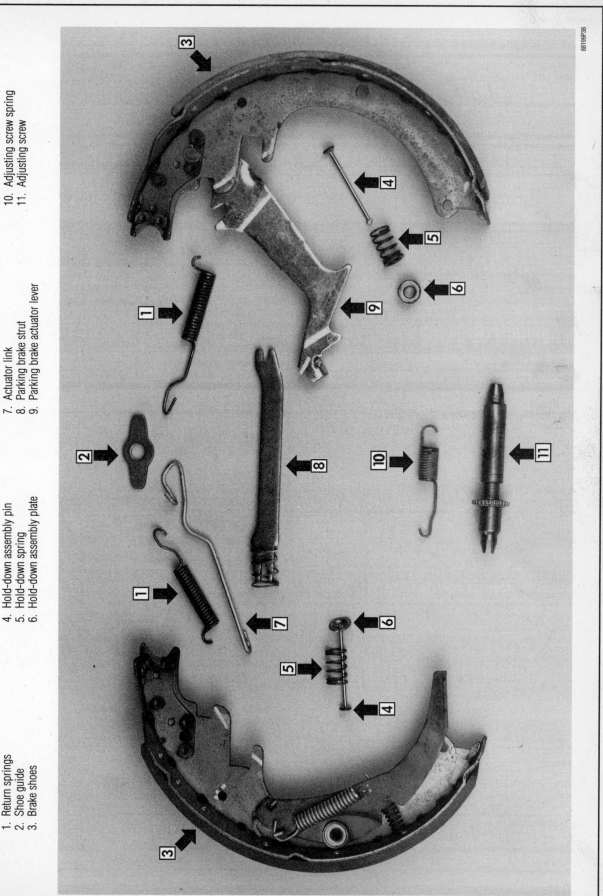

TYPICAL DRUM BRAKE COMPONENTS

1. Return springs
2. Shoe guide
3. Brake shoes
4. Hold-down assembly pin
5. Hold-down spring
6. Hold-down assembly plate
7. Actuator link
8. Parking brake strut
9. Parking brake actuator lever
10. Adjusting screw spring
11. Adjusting screw

8819P36

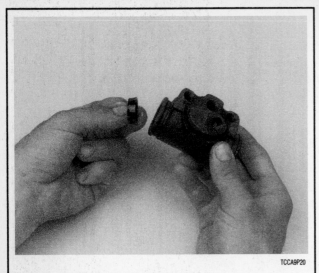

TCCA9P20

Fig. 81 . . . then install the spring and cup seals in the bore

TCCA9P22

Fig. 83 Finally, install the boots over the wheel cylinder piston ends

12. Coat all replacement parts with clean brake fluid.

13. Install a cup and piston in one side, place the spring into the other side, followed by the other cup and piston. Push the pistons in until both are within the bore.

14. Install the end caps.

15. Loosely install the bleeder screw.

16. Install the rebuilt wheel cylinder.

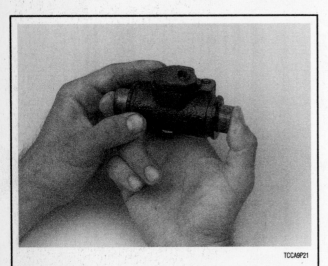

TCCA9P21

Fig. 82 Lightly lubricate the pistons, then insert them into the wheel cylinder bore

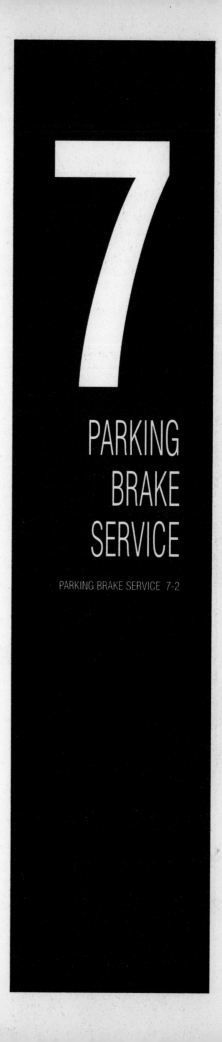

7

PARKING BRAKE SERVICE

PARKING BRAKE SERVICE

Parking Brake Levers and Handles

REMOVAL & INSTALLATION

Pull-Up Lever Type

Almost all pull-up levers are mounted in the center console or on the floor, between the front seats. Some, however, can be found on the left side of the driver's seat.

1. If necessary for access, remove the console, as follows:

a. Before removing any of the console fasteners, inspect the entire console to locate all of the mounting fasteners and ascertain what type of fastener is used.

Most center floor consoles are retained to the dashboard and floor brackets with either screws (Phillips, Torx®, and standard are the most common) or plastic fasteners. To disengage the plastic fasteners, usually you must pry out the center pin of the fastener, then pull the entire fastener out of the console. Be careful, however, because some manufacturers (Suzuki, for example) utilize fasteners for which the center pin must be pressed **IN**, not out. One way to tell whether the center pin of the fastener should be pried out, rather than pressed in, is whether the pin is designed with a large head (much like an ordinary nail). If so designed, the head on the pin should prevent the pin from being pressed in.

b. Often, the shifter handle and/or trim panel may need to be removed before the center console can be removed from the vehicle. Most shifter handles are retained either by a setscrew, or a large retaining nut (hidden beneath the handle's button). However, some handles may be secured to the shifter shaft with a retaining clip, or similar fas-

tener. Inspect the handle before trying to separate it from the shaft to verify the retaining method.

To remove the handle trim plate(s), usually held in place by screws, remove the retaining fasteners. If no screws or other fasteners are visible, the trim plate may simply "snap" into the hole in the console. Using a plastic or wooden tool, gently pry the plate up and out of the console.

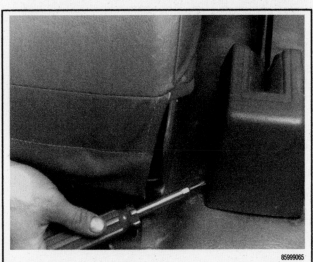

Fig. 2 To replace the parking brake lever or cable, the first step is to remove the console for access

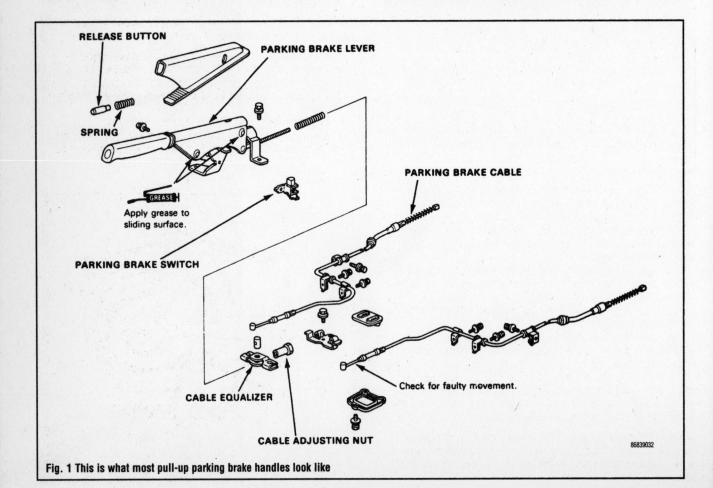

Fig. 1 This is what most pull-up parking brake handles look like

Fig. 3 You will have to disconnect the cable from the lever in either case—on this vehicle, that involves loosening the locknut

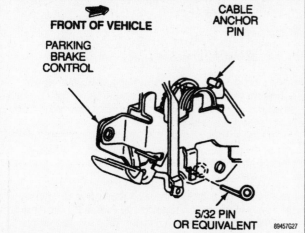

Fig. 4 With the parking brake released, insert the pin into the brake control assembly as shown to lock the cable tension spring

c. Lift the console up and off of the vehicle's floor, then, if necessary, disengage any electrical wiring harness connectors from the console. Remove the console from the vehicle.

2. For vehicles not equipped with an automatic parking brake cable tensioner, release the parking brake cable tension. Generally, this can be accomplished as follows:

a. Locate the parking brake equalizer (rear cable and front cable junction), usually under the mid-section of the vehicle or at the parking brake lever itself.

b. Block the front wheels, then raise and safely support the rear of the vehicle securely on jackstands.

c. Grip the cable threaded rod to prevent it from spinning, then loosen the equalizer nut until the rear cables can be disengaged from the equalizer bracket.

3. However, some vehicles (namely most 1993 and newer Ford models) are equipped with auto-tensioning parking brake mechanisms. These models do not use a threaded rod at the equalizer. In order to remove any of these cables or components, the following procedure must be followed:

➡️**If your vehicle is equipped with an automatic tension adjuster mechanism, and it is not manufactured by Ford, it may be a good idea to refer to the model-specific Chilton Total Car Care for your vehicle.**

a. Place the parking brake cable control in the released position.

b. Have an assistant pull on the intermediate brake cable while you insert a 5/32 in. (4mm) diameter steel pin (or drill bit) into the hole provided in the parking brake control assembly.

4. Detach the front parking brake cable from the lever assembly.

5. Unbolt the lever assembly from the floor, and detach any electrical connections. Lift the lever assembly up and disconnect the cables.

To install:

6. Install the parking brake in the vehicle, reattach any wiring harness connectors, then install and tighten the mounting fasteners.

7. Reattach the cable top the lever assembly.

8. Adjust the parking brake cable tension. For vehicles not equipped with an auto-tensioning mechanism, perform the following:

a. Position the parking brake lever 3–5 clicks above the fully depressed position.

b. Grip the threaded rod to prevent it from spinning and tighten the equalizer nut until the rear wheels will no longer spin.

c. Release parking brake and check for rear wheel drag. The cables should be tight enough to provide full application of the rear brake shoes when the parking brake lever is positioned 3–5 clicks above the fully released position, yet loose enough to ensure complete release of the brake shoes when the lever is in the released position.

9. For vehicles equipped with the Ford automatic tensioner, release the cable tension, pull out the lock pin from the control assembly.

10. If necessary, lower the vehicle.

11. If your vehicle is equipped with an auto-tensioner mechanism, withdraw the 5/32 in. (4mm) diameter steel pin (or drill bit) from the hole provided in the parking brake control assembly.

12. If necessary, install the console in the vehicle. Ensure that all wiring harness connectors are properly reattached, and that all mounting fasteners are properly engaged.

FORD AUTO-TENSIONER RESETTING

➡️**This procedure is only applicable if you own a vehicle equipped with the Ford auto-tensioner mechanism**

In the event that one of the cables has broken or the cable tension release procedure was not followed, perform the following procedures:

1. Remove the parking brake control lever assembly.

2. Engage the coil spring to the tab on the adjusting wheel in the control assembly.

3. Ensure the control assembly is in the released position.

4. Slip a spare front parking brake (or remove your existing one) cable around the pulley and insert the cable end into the pivot hole in the ratchet plate.

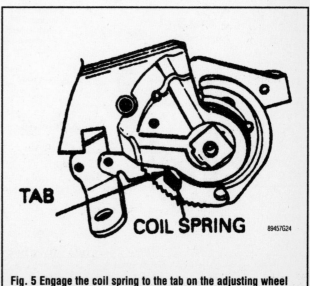

Fig. 5 Engage the coil spring to the tab on the adjusting wheel

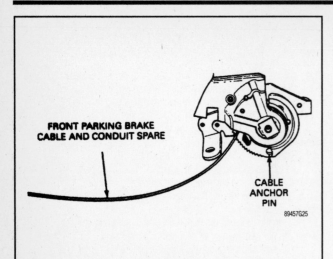

Fig. 6 Slip the front parking brake cable around the pulley and insert the cable end to the ratchet plate

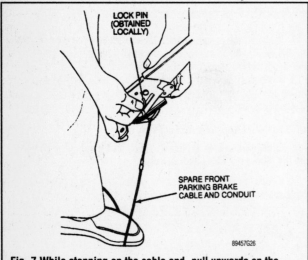

Fig. 7 While stepping on the cable end, pull upwards on the control assembly then install the lock pin when the holes align

5. Position the free end of the parking brake cable on the floor and either step on it or clamp it in a vise.

6. Pull on the control assembly, holding the mounting bracket tightly against the body of the control, until the cable tension rotates the cable track assembly so that the (lock pin) 5⁄32 in. (4mm) diameter steel pin (or drill bit) can be fully seated through the plate.

7. Insert the lock pin so that the assembly is in the "cable released" position.

8. Install the parking brake control lever.

Pull-Handle Type

Usually the handle assembly bolts to the underside of the instrument panel.

1. Remove the mounting fasteners.
2. Loosen the cable tension, then detach the cable from the handle.
3. If necessary, detach any electrical connectors.
4. Remove the handle assembly from the vehicle.

To install:

5. Reattach any wiring harness connectors to the handle assembly, then reconnect the parking brake cable.
6. Position the handle assembly beneath the instrument cluster and install the mounting fasteners.
7. Refer to Section 3 to adjust the parking brake cable(s) tension.
8. Check parking brake operation.

Foot Pedal Type

These are generally the most difficult type of parking brake mechanism to remove.

1. For vehicles not equipped with the Ford auto-tensioner parking brake assembly, back off the cable adjustment. See Section 3 of this manual for the adjustment procedure. If there are any return springs on the cable mechanism, disconnect them at this time.

2. For vehicles equipped with auto-tensioning parking brake mechanisms (namely most 1993 and newer Ford models), the following procedure must be followed to detach any of the parking brake cables from the control assembly:

➡**If your vehicle is equipped with an automatic tension adjuster mechanism, and it is not manufactured by Ford, it may be a good idea to refer to the model-specific Chilton Total Car Care for your vehicle.**

a. Place the parking brake cable control in the released position.
b. Have an assistant pull on the intermediate brake cable while you

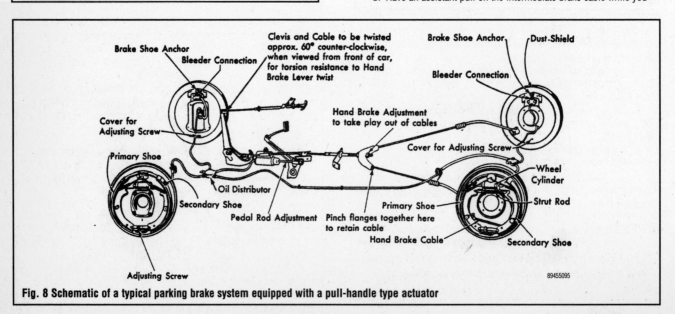

Fig. 8 Schematic of a typical parking brake system equipped with a pull-handle type actuator

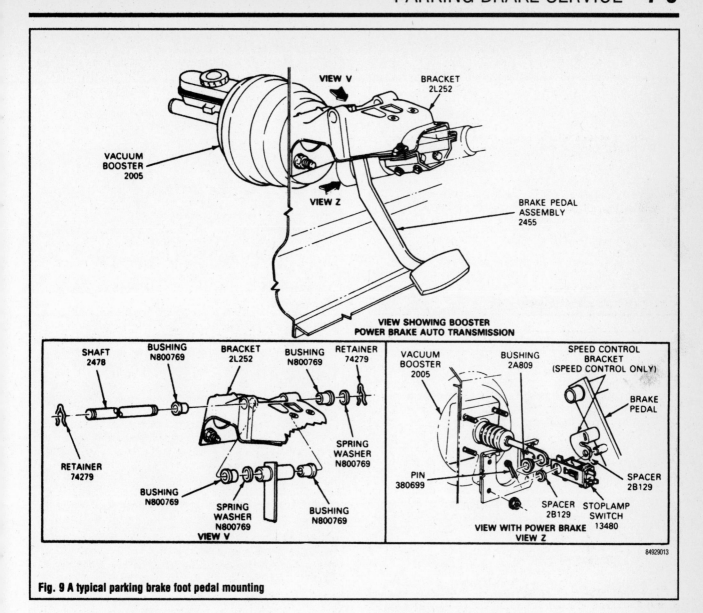

VIEW V

BRACKET
2L252

VACUUM
BOOSTER
2005

VIEW Z

BRAKE PEDAL
ASSEMBLY
2455

**VIEW SHOWING BOOSTER
POWER BRAKE AUTO TRANSMISSION**

SHAFT
2478

BUSHING
N800769

BRACKET
2L252

BUSHING
N800769

RETAINER
74279

VACUUM
BOOSTER
2005

BUSHING
2A809

SPEED CONTROL
BRACKET
(SPEED CONTROL ONLY)

BRAKE
PEDAL

RETAINER
74279

SPRING
WASHER
N800769

PIN
380699

SPACER
2B129

BUSHING
N800769

SPRING
WASHER
N800769

BUSHING
N800769

SPACER
2B129

STOPLAMP
SWITCH
13480

VIEW V

**VIEW WITH POWER BRAKE
VIEW Z**

84929013

Fig. 9 A typical parking brake foot pedal mounting

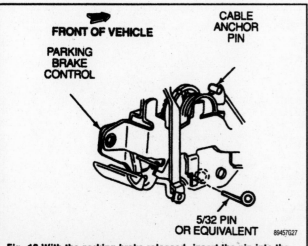

FRONT OF VEHICLE

CABLE
ANCHOR
PIN

PARKING
BRAKE
CONTROL

5/32 PIN
OR EQUIVALENT

89457G27

Fig. 10 With the parking brake released, insert the pin into the brake control assembly as shown to lock the cable tension spring

insert a ⁵⁄₃₂ in. (4mm) diameter steel pin (or drill bit) into the hole provided in the parking brake control assembly.

3. Disengage any electrical connectors attached to the mechanism. Most connectors are snap-types with some incorporating a locking tab. Be careful not to break the tab.

4. At this point, check the cable attachment. On some installations, it's impossible to get at the cable with the assembly in place. If, however, you can get at it, pull up on the cable and disconnect it from the unit. Removing the cable makes it that much easier to remove the unit.

➡ **On a few vehicles, the system uses a vacuum-release mechanism; disconnect it. If you are at all in doubt as to how to disconnect the vacuum unit, refer to the model-specific Chilton Total Car Care for your vehicle**

5. Now, remove the unit. The assembly attaches, in most cases, to the firewall. On a few vehicles, it attaches to the underside of the dash, usually to a mounting bracket. On some vehicles, it attaches to both the firewall and under-dash.

6. Remove the mounting bolts or nuts. On firewall-mounted types, the nuts may be in the engine compartment. Lower the unit from under the dash and out of the vehicle.

To install:

7. On firewall-mounted types, replace any sealer to keep the weather and fumes out of the passenger's compartment.

8. Position the unit under the instrument panel and reattach the cable.

9. Hold the unit in place and install the nuts and/or bolts. It may be helpful to have an assistant hold the unit for those vehicles with the attaching nuts in the engine compartment.

10. If equipped, connect the vacuum unit.

11. Reattach any wiring harness connectors.

12. For vehicles not equipped with the Ford auto-tensioner mechanism, refer to Section 3 and adjust the cable(s).

13. For vehicles equipped with the Ford automatic tensioner, release the cable tension, pull out the lock pin from the control assembly.

14. Check the parking brake operation.

FORD AUTO-TENSIONER RESETTING

For Ford auto-tensioner resetting, please refer to the same procedure earlier in this section.

Parking Brake Cables

REMOVAL & INSTALLATION

Wheel-Mounted Parking Brakes

Depending on what system it uses, your vehicle could have anywhere from 1 to 5 cables. Most common, however would be the 3-cable setup, common to pedal and pull-handle types, and the 2-cable setup, common to the pull-up lever type.

Single cable setups are common to the driveshaft-mounted parking brake assembly, while 5-cable setups are common to trucks with long wheel bases.

The 3- and 5-cable setups all use a single cable that connects the pedal or handle to an equalizer. The equalizer is a device that connects the front cable to the cables going to the rear wheels. It also functions as an adjustment point and distributes the pulling forces equally between the wheels.

The 2-cable setup uses cables that run from the pull-up lever, directly to each wheel.

We'll give you several illustrations of common parking brake cable routings on popular vehicles. Yours is probably similar to one of these. If you're in doubt, raise and safely support your vehicle on jackstands. With a droplight, trace you cable routings. The cable(s) may disappear into frame rails

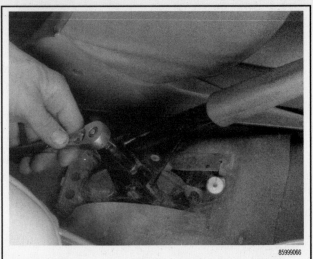

Fig. 12 However, on some vehicles adjustment takes place at the hand lever

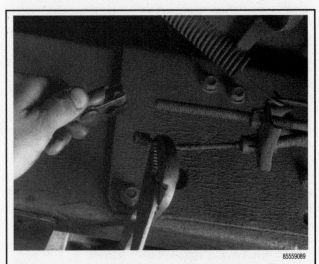

Fig. 13 Most rear cables must be removed from an equalizer assembly

Fig. 11 To start removal, back off the adjuster to loosen the cable—on most models a threaded adjuster is found under the vehicle

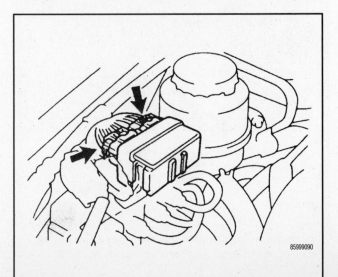

Fig. 14 This type uses a return spring on the equalizer

or body panels. You'll have to follow them on your own; it can get fairly complicated on some vehicles.

FRONT CABLE

1. Back off the cable adjustment completely and remove the cable from the equalizer or driveshaft brake assembly lever.
2. Unhook the cable at the pedal or handle. It may be necessary to remove the pedal or lever assembly to disconnect the cable.
3. Pull the cable from the vehicle, some cases the firewall. It may be necessary to remove any sealing grommets.
4. Installation is the reverse of removal. Repair any sealer that was dislodged from the firewall or replace the grommet.

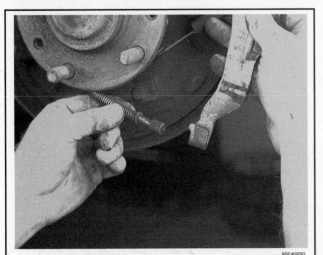
Fig. 15 The next step in rear cable replacement is to disconnect the cable end from the brake mechanism

Fig. 16 Though some can be disconnected by hand, a pair of pliers will give you better leverage

REAR CABLES

Depending on your vehicle, this could be relatively easy, or, depending how the cables are routed, very time consuming, involving removal of interior trim, seats and trunk lining. Refer to the model-specific Chilton manual written for your vehicle.

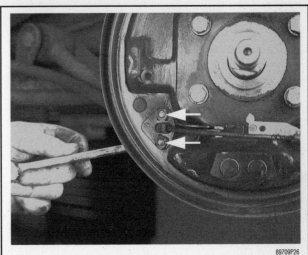
Fig. 17 The last step is to free the cable from the vehicle—some cables are bolted in place . . .

Fig. 18 . . . unbolt the cable flange and remove the assembly from the vehicle

1. Raise and safely support the rear of the vehicle on jackstands.
2. As needed, remove the rear wheels.
3. Back off on the adjustment at the lever or equalizer, and disconnect the cables at that point.
4. On vehicles with rear disc brakes, disconnect the cables at each lever at the calipers or backing plates.
5. On vehicles with rear drum brakes, perform the following:
   a. Remove the brake drums.
   b. If it makes the job easier, remove the brake shoes.

➡Although it is not always necessary, in most cases removing the brake shoes will make cable removal a much, much easier task. Do yourself a favor and remove the shoes at the first sign of difficulty, it will be much better than struggling for 10 or 15 minutes and then deciding to remove them anyway.

   c. Disconnect the cable end from the parking brake lever.
   d. On most vehicles, the cable sheath is retained at the backing plate by expanding tangs. Depress the tangs at the backing plate. A

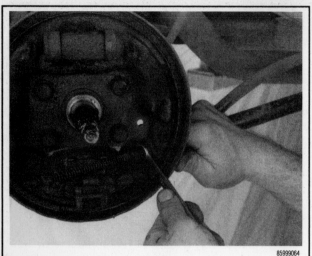

Fig. 19 On cables with retaining tangs, a box end wrench can be very helpful to depress all of the tangs at once

tip: to make that job easier, take a spiral type hose clamp and place it around the tangs. Tighten the clamp until the tangs clear the opening. Pull the cable out of the backing plate. On some vehicles, the cable is retained by a clamp, in which case the clamp is simply unbolted.

6. On all systems, remove the cables from all the retaining clips, springs and grommets, then pull them out of the vehicle.

7. Installation is the reverse of removal.

Parking Brake Cable Routing

We have provided a sampling of parking brake cables for many of the most popular production vehicles. If your specific vehicle is not shown, find a similar model or another model from the same manufacturer to use as a guide.

1. Front parking brake cable and conduit
2. Parking brake control
3. Parking brake rear cable and conduit (LH)
4. Parking brake rear cable and conduit (RH)
5. Parking brake cable bracket (rear)
6. Parking brake equalizer cable spring
7. Parking brake cable bracket (front)
8. Parking brake release handle
9. Bolt, parking brake control-to-cowl side

A. Parking brake front cable and conduit, before inserting into ratchet plate pivot hole
B. Parking brake front cable and conduit, after inserting into ratchet plate pivot hole
C. Parking brake front cable and conduit, installed
D. 4mm (5/32-Inch) steel pin or equivalent size drill bit

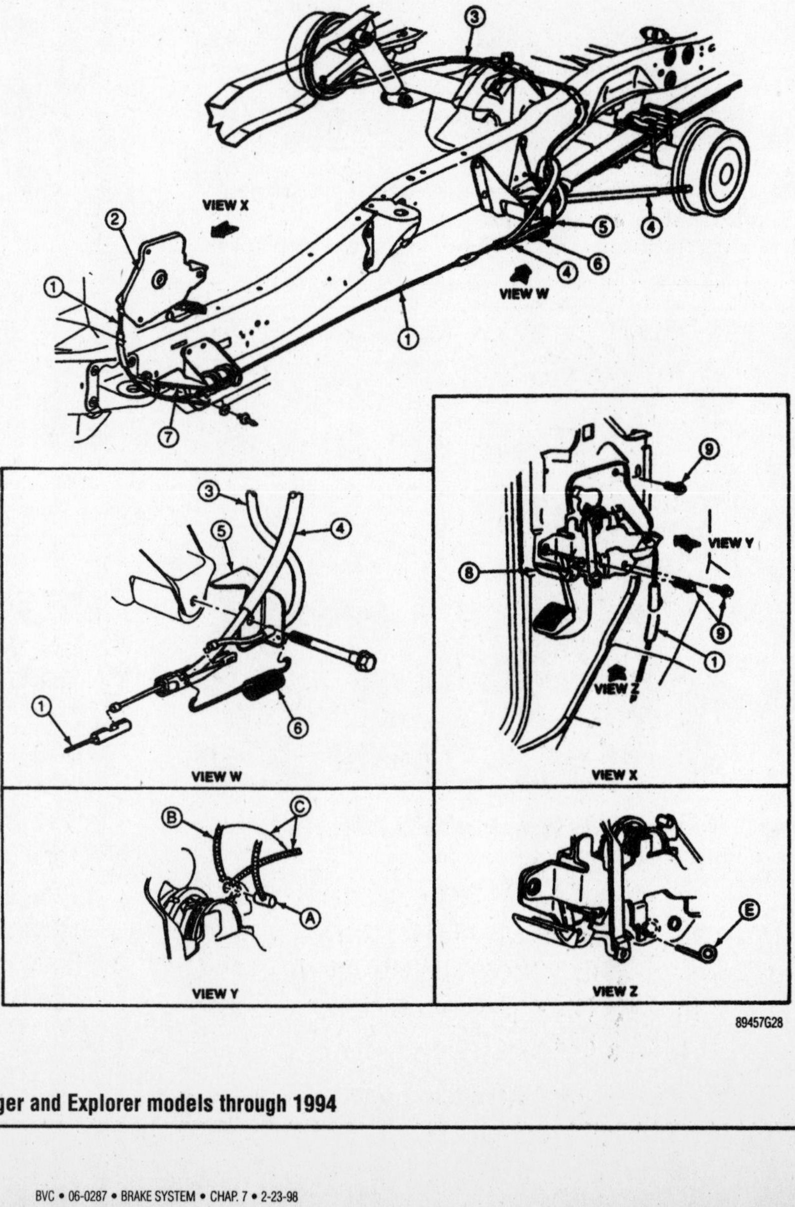

VIEW X
VIEW W
VIEW W
VIEW X
VIEW Y
VIEW Z

Fig. 20 Typical parking brake cable routing for Ranger and Explorer models through 1994

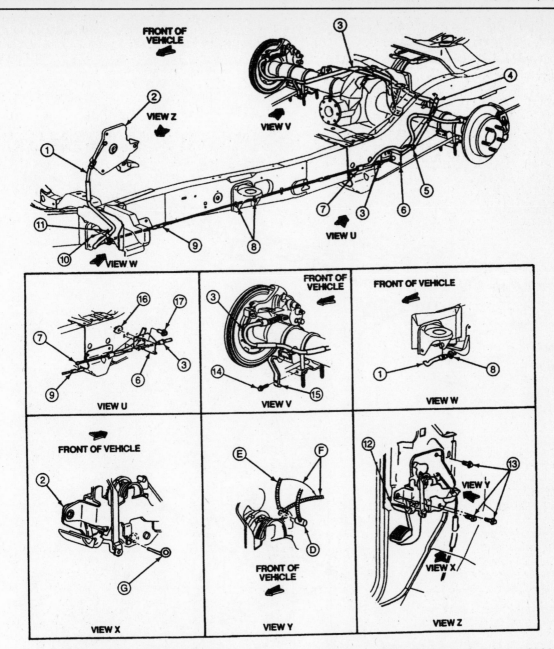

1. Front parking brake cable and conduit
2. Parking brake control
3. Parking brake rear cable and conduit (RH)
4. Rear parking brake cable retainer
5. Parking brake cable insulator
6. Parking brake cable bracket
7. Parking brake rear cable and conduit (LH)
8. Grommet
9. Parking brake intermediate cable
10. Bolt, front parking brake cable clamp
11. Clamp, front parking brake cable and conduit
12. Parking brake release handle
13. Bolt, parking brake control-to-cowl side
14. Bolt, parking brake cable retainer clip
15. Parking brake cable retainer clip
16. Nut
17. Bolt, parking brake cable bracket-to-frame
D. Parking brake front cable and conduit before inserting into ratchet plate pivot hole
E. Parking brake front cable and conduit after inserting into ratchet plate pivot hole
F. Parking brake front cable and conduit, installed
G. 4mm (5/32-Inch) steel pin or equivalent size drill bit

89457G29

Fig. 21 Typical parking brake cable routing for 1995 and later Explorer and Mountaineer models

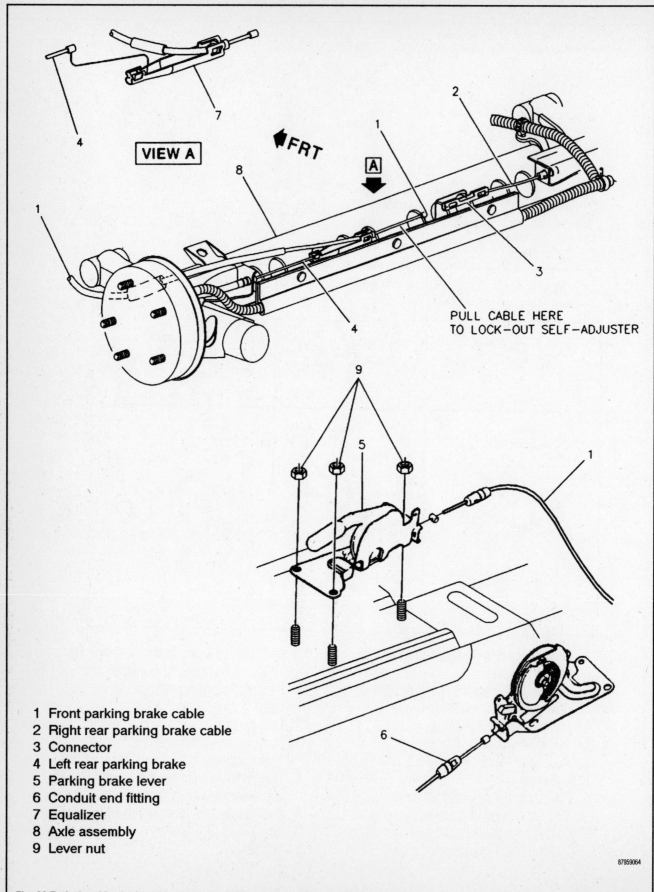

VIEW A

FRT

PULL CABLE HERE
TO LOCK-OUT SELF-ADJUSTER

1 Front parking brake cable
2 Right rear parking brake cable
3 Connector
4 Left rear parking brake
5 Parking brake lever
6 Conduit end fitting
7 Equalizer
8 Axle assembly
9 Lever nut

87959064

Fig. 22 Typical parking brake cable routing for 1995 and newer Chevrolet Cavalier models

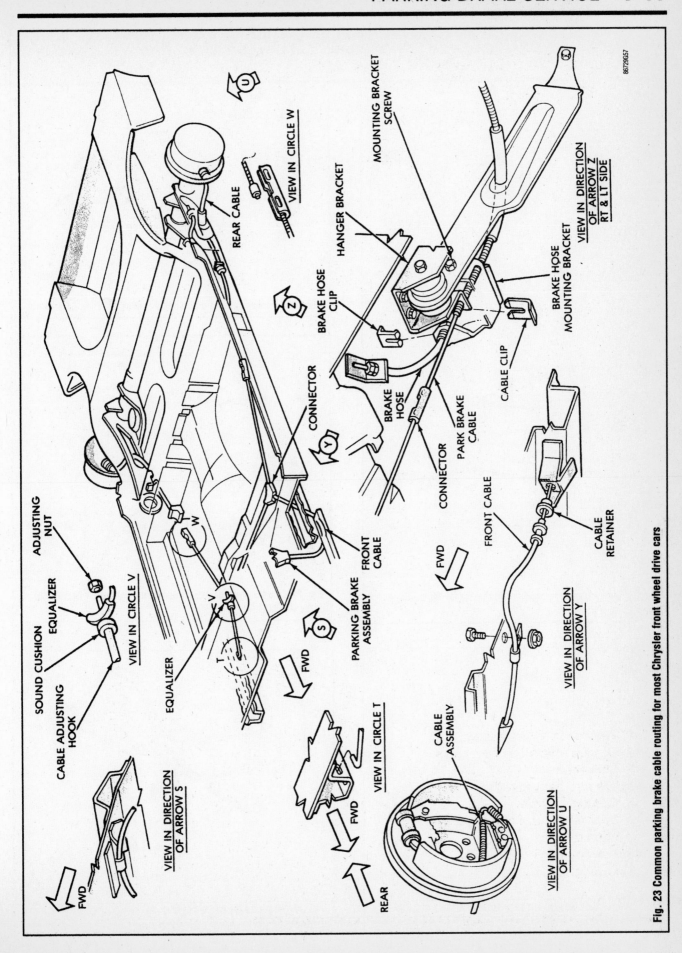

Fig. 23 Common parking brake cable routing for most Chrysler front wheel drive cars

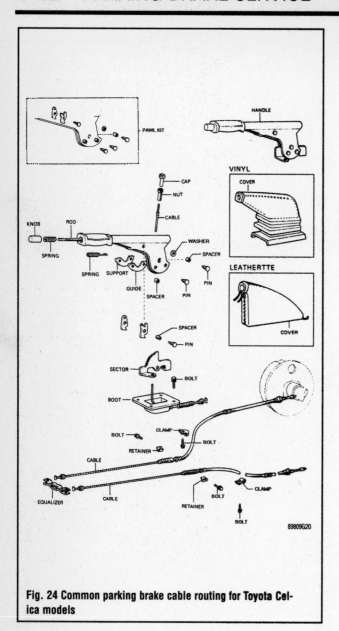

Fig. 24 Common parking brake cable routing for Toyota Celica models

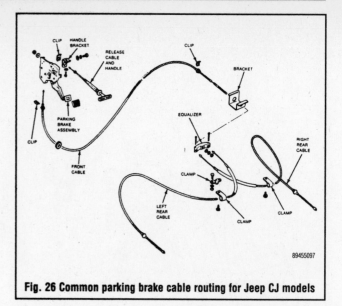

Fig. 26 Common parking brake cable routing for Jeep CJ models

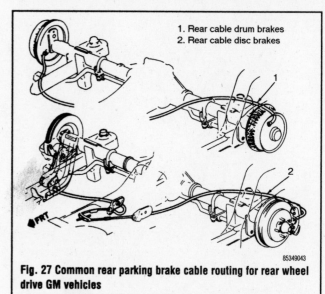

1. Rear cable drum brakes
2. Rear cable disc brakes

Fig. 27 Common rear parking brake cable routing for rear wheel drive GM vehicles

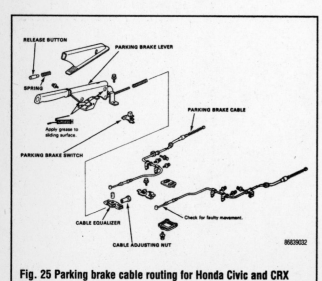

Fig. 25 Parking brake cable routing for Honda Civic and CRX models

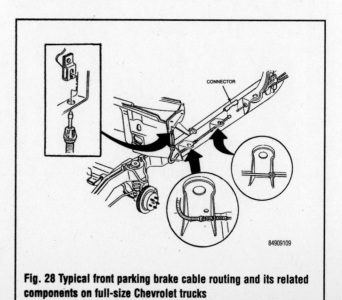

Fig. 28 Typical front parking brake cable routing and its related components on full-size Chevrolet trucks

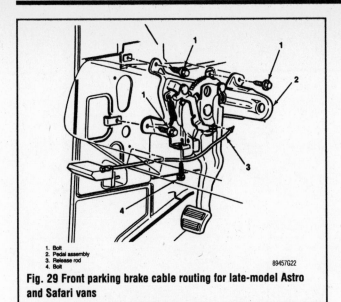

1. Bolt
2. Pedal assembly
3. Release rod
4. Bolt

89457G22

Fig. 29 Front parking brake cable routing for late-model Astro and Safari vans

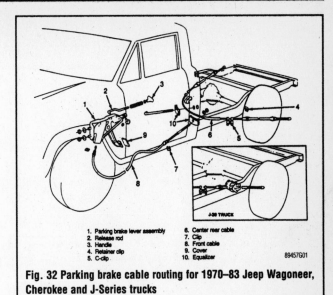

1. Parking brake lever assembly
2. Release rod
3. Handle
4. Retainer clip
5. C-clip
6. Center rear cable
7. Clip
8. Front cable
9. Cover
10. Equalizer

89457G01

Fig. 32 Parking brake cable routing for 1970–83 Jeep Wagoneer, Cherokee and J-Series trucks

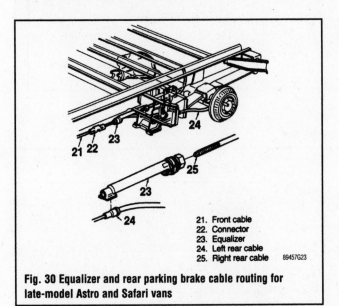

21. Front cable
22. Connector
23. Equalizer
24. Left rear cable
25. Right rear cable

89457G23

Fig. 30 Equalizer and rear parking brake cable routing for late-model Astro and Safari vans

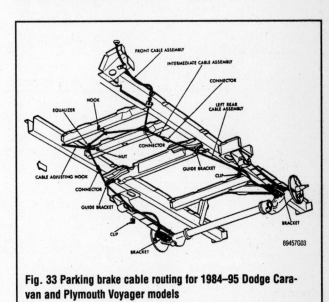

89457G03

Fig. 33 Parking brake cable routing for 1984–95 Dodge Caravan and Plymouth Voyager models

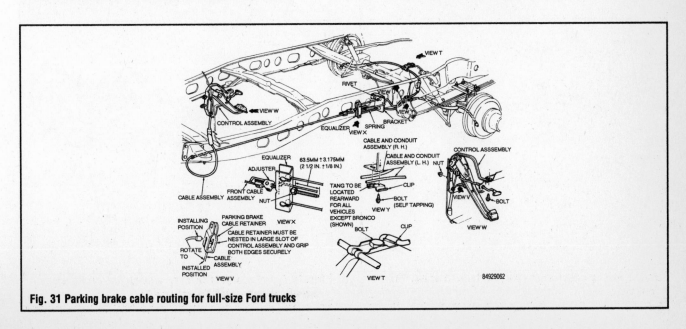

84929062

Fig. 31 Parking brake cable routing for full-size Ford trucks

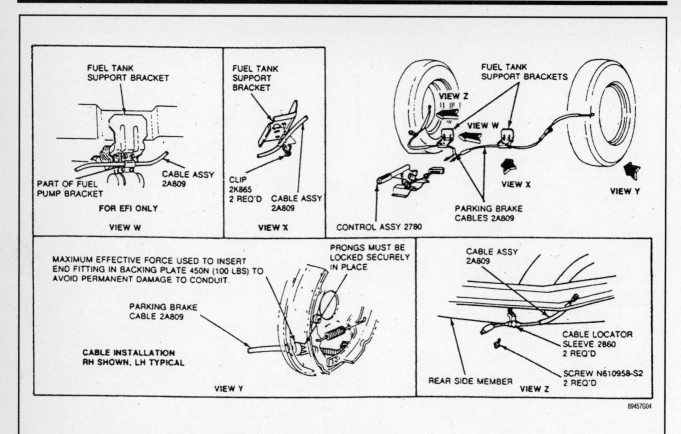

Fig. 34 Parking brake cable routing for 1986–90 Ford Escort/Mercury Lynx vehicles

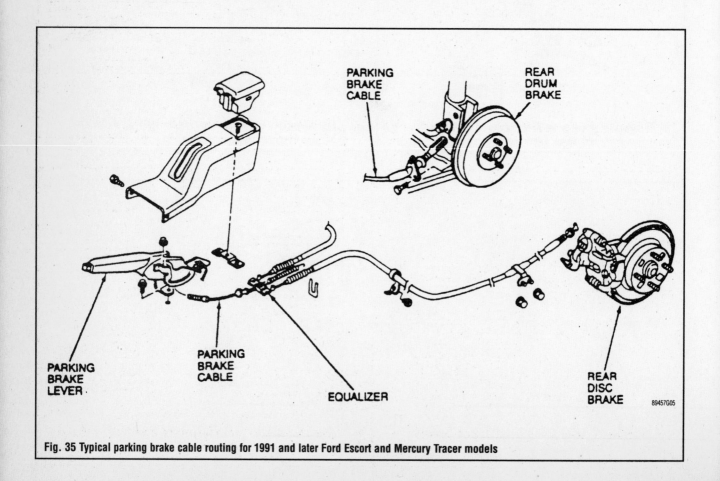

Fig. 35 Typical parking brake cable routing for 1991 and later Ford Escort and Mercury Tracer models

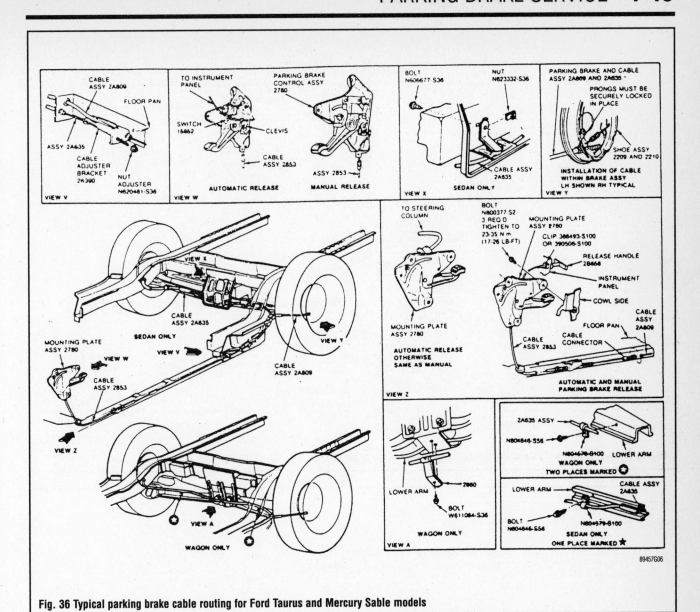

Fig. 36 Typical parking brake cable routing for Ford Taurus and Mercury Sable models

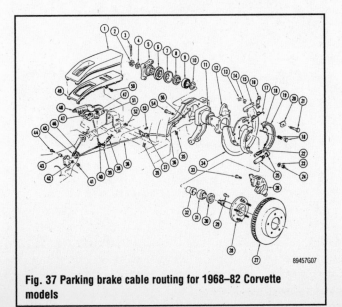

Fig. 37 Parking brake cable routing for 1968–82 Corvette models

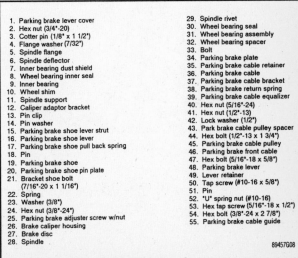

1. Parking brake lever cover
2. Hex nut (3/4"-20)
3. Cotter pin (1/8" x 1 1/2")
4. Flange washer (7/32")
5. Spindle flange
6. Spindle deflector
7. Inner bearing dust shield
8. Wheel bearing inner seal
9. Inner bearing
10. Wheel shim
11. Spindle support
12. Caliper adaptor bracket
13. Pin clip
14. Pin washer
15. Parking brake shoe lever strut
16. Parking brake shoe lever
17. Parking brake shoe pull back spring
18. Pin
19. Parking brake shoe
20. Parking brake shoe pin plate
21. Bracket shoe bolt
   (7/16"-20 x 1 1/16")
22. Spring
23. Washer (3/8")
24. Hex nut (3/8"-24)
25. Parking brake adjuster screw w/nut
26. Brake caliper housing
27. Brake disc
28. Spindle
29. Spindle rivet
30. Wheel bearing seal
31. Wheel bearing assembly
32. Wheel bearing spacer
33. Bolt
34. Parking brake plate
35. Parking brake cable retainer
36. Parking brake cable
37. Parking brake cable bracket
38. Parking brake return spring
39. Parking brake cable equalizer
40. Hex nut (5/16"-24)
41. Hex nut (1/2"-13)
42. Lock washer (1/2")
43. Park brake cable pulley spacer
44. Hex bolt (1/2"-13 x 1 3/4")
45. Parking brake cable pulley
46. Parking brake front cable
47. Hex bolt (5/16"-18 x 5/8")
48. Parking brake lever
49. Lever retainer
50. Tap screw (#10-16 x 5/8")
51. Pin
52. *U* spring nut (#10-16)
53. Hex tap screw (5/16"-18 x 1/2")
54. Hex bolt (3/8"-24 x 2 7/8")
55. Parking brake cable guide

Fig. 38 Component list for the parking brake cable routing for 1968–82 Corvette models

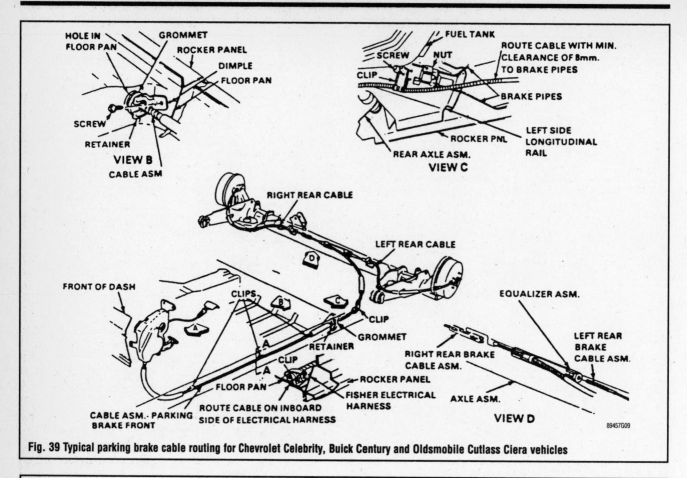

Fig. 39 Typical parking brake cable routing for Chevrolet Celebrity, Buick Century and Oldsmobile Cutlass Ciera vehicles

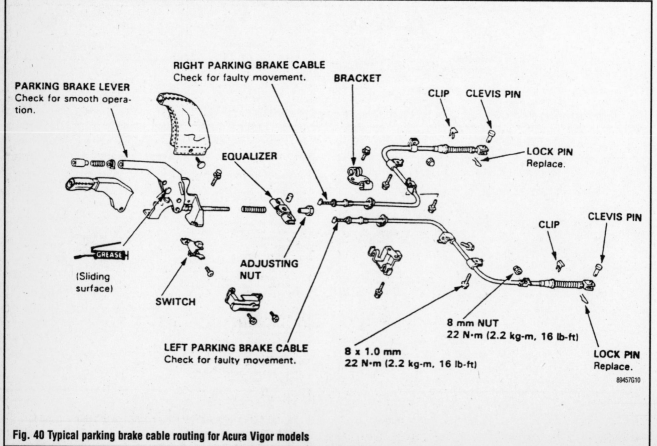

Fig. 40 Typical parking brake cable routing for Acura Vigor models

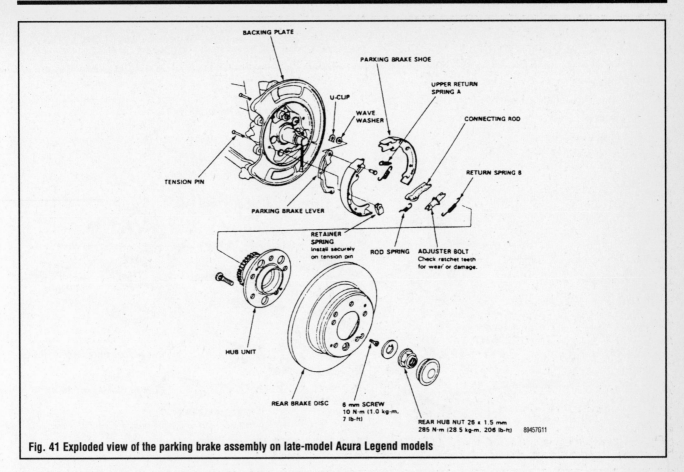

Fig. 41 Exploded view of the parking brake assembly on late-model Acura Legend models

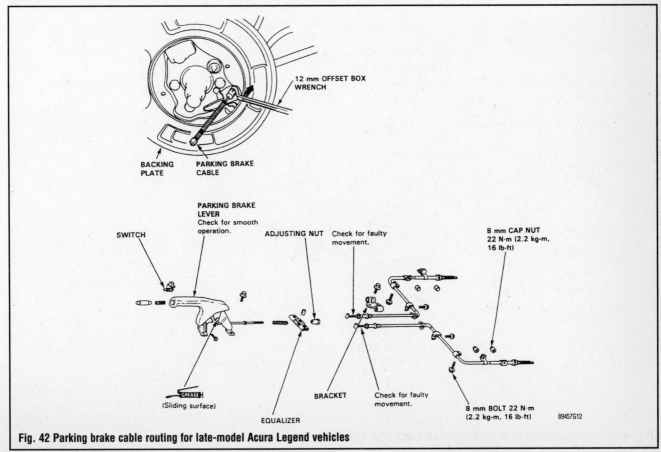

Fig. 42 Parking brake cable routing for late-model Acura Legend vehicles

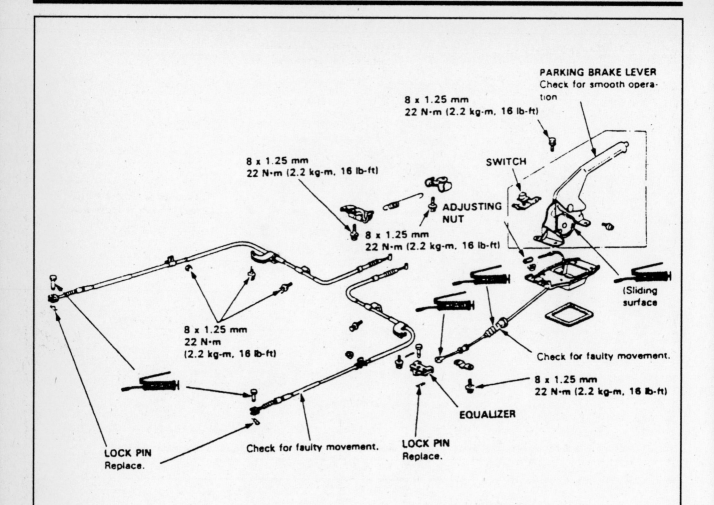

PARKING BRAKE LEVER
Check for smooth operation

8 x 1.25 mm
22 N·m (2.2 kg·m, 16 lb-ft)

SWITCH

8 x 1.25 mm
22 N·m (2.2 kg·m, 16 lb-ft)

ADJUSTING NUT

8 x 1.25 mm
22 N·m (2.2 kg·m, 16 lb-ft)

(Sliding surface)

8 x 1.25 mm
22 N·m (2.2 kg·m, 16 lb-ft)

Check for faulty movement.

8 x 1.25 mm
22 N·m (2.2 kg·m, 16 lb-ft)

LOCK PIN
Replace.

Check for faulty movement.

LOCK PIN
Replace.

EQUALIZER

NOTE: To disconnect the parking brake:
1. Pull out lock pin.
2. Remove clevis pin.
3. Remove clip.

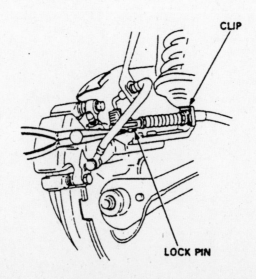

CLIP

LOCK PIN

89457G13

Fig. 43 Parking brake cable routing for 1986–90 Acura Legend models

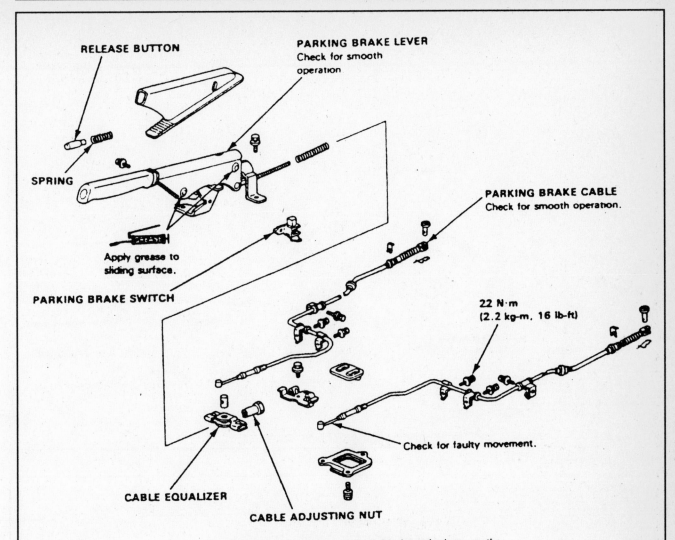

RELEASE BUTTON

PARKING BRAKE LEVER
Check for smooth operation

SPRING

Apply grease to sliding surface.

PARKING BRAKE SWITCH

PARKING BRAKE CABLE
Check for smooth operation.

22 N·m
(2.2 kg-m, 16 lb-ft)

CABLE EQUALIZER

CABLE ADJUSTING NUT

Check for faulty movement.

Disconnect the parking brake cable from the lever on the caliper by removing the lock pin.

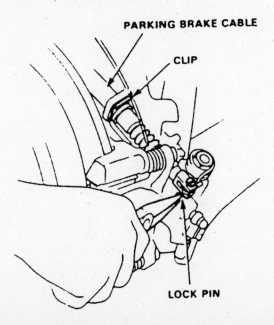

PARKING BRAKE CABLE

CLIP

LOCK PIN

Fig. 44 Parking brake cable routing for 1990–93 Acura Integra vehicles

89457G14

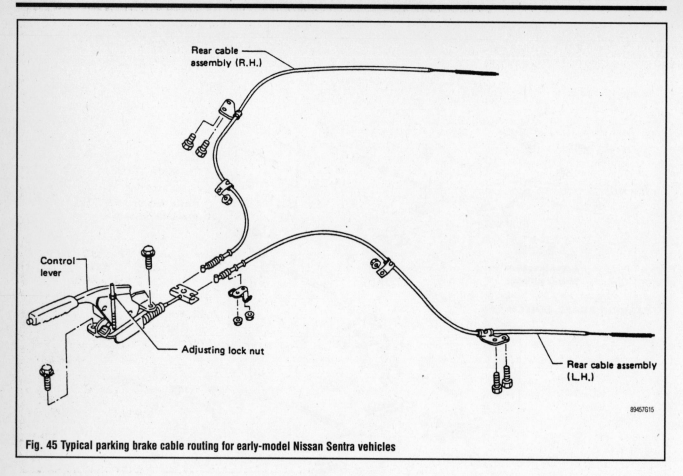

Fig. 45 Typical parking brake cable routing for early-model Nissan Sentra vehicles

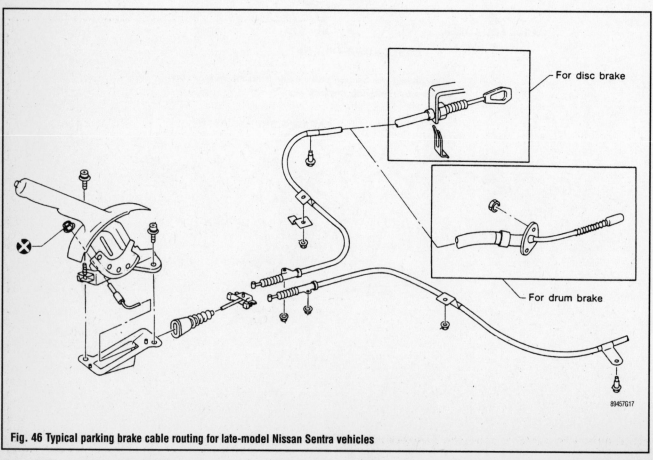

Fig. 46 Typical parking brake cable routing for late-model Nissan Sentra vehicles

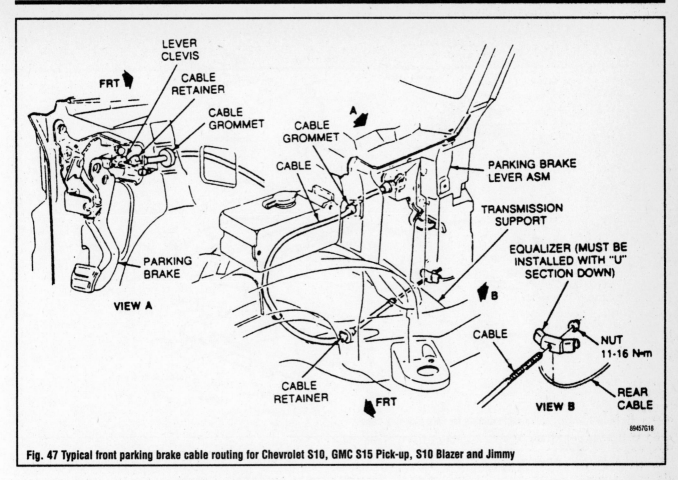

Fig. 47 Typical front parking brake cable routing for Chevrolet S10, GMC S15 Pick-up, S10 Blazer and Jimmy

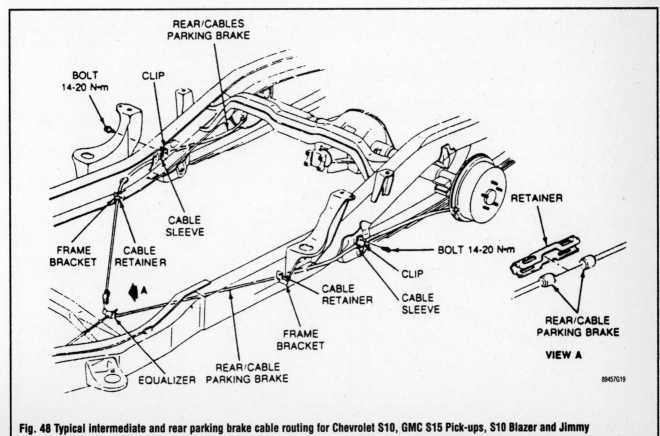

Fig. 48 Typical intermediate and rear parking brake cable routing for Chevrolet S10, GMC S15 Pick-ups, S10 Blazer and Jimmy

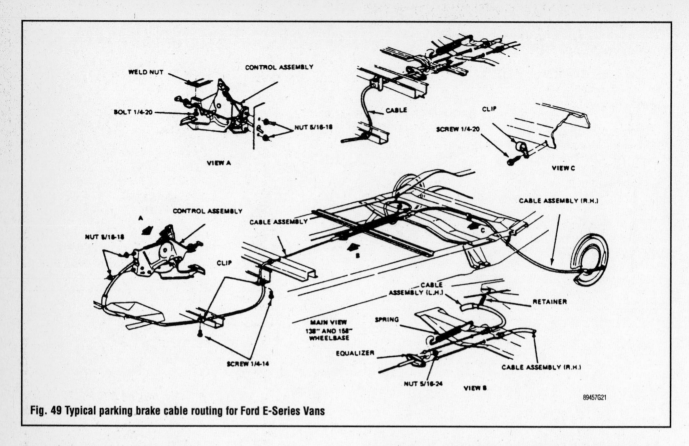

Fig. 49 Typical parking brake cable routing for Ford E-Series Vans

Transmission-Mounted Parking Brakes

F SUPER-DUTY AND F-350 MODELS

1. Place the transmission in gear.
2. Fully release the parking brake pedal.
3. Raise and safely support the vehicle on jackstands.
4. Disconnect the speedometer cable from the transmission.
5. Spray penetrating oil on the adjusting clevis, jam nut and threaded end of the cable.
6. Loosen the jam nut and remove the locking pin from the clevis pin.
7. Remove the clevis pin, clevis and jam nut from the cable.
8. Remove the cable from the bracket on the case.

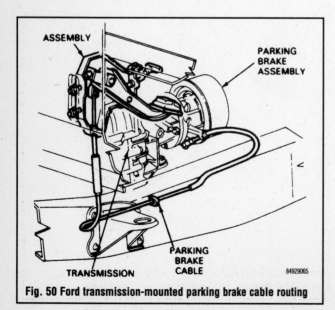

Fig. 50 Ford transmission-mounted parking brake cable routing

➡The unit is filled with Ford Type H automatic transmission fluid.

To install:

9. Assemble the cable components. Thread the clevis on until the pin can be inserted while the lever and cable are held tightly in the applied position. Then, remove the pin, let go of the cable and lever, and turn the clevis 10 full turns counterclockwise (loosen).
10. Install the pin.
11. Reattach the speedometer cable to the transmission.
12. Lower the vehicle.

GENERAL MOTORS, INTERNATIONAL HARVESTER AND JEEP

1. Raise and support the vehicle safely on jackstands.
2. Spray penetrating oil on the adjusting clevis, jam nut and threaded end of the cable.
3. Loosen the jam nut and remove the locking pin from the clevis pin.
4. Remove the clevis pin, clevis and jam nut from the cable.
5. Remove the cable from the bracket on the case.

To install:

6. Assemble the cable components.
7. Rotate the brake drum to align the access hole with the adjusting screw. If equipped with a manual transmission, the access hole is located at the bottom of the backing plate. If equipped with an automatic transmission, the access hole is located at the top of the shoe.
8. For first time adjustment it will be necessary to remove the driveshaft and the drum in order to remove the lanced area from the drum and clean out the metal shavings.
9. Adjust the screw until the drum cannot be rotated by hand. Back off the adjusting screw 10 notches; the drum should rotate freely.
10. Position the parking brake lever in the fully released position. Take up the slack in the cable to overcome spring tension.
11. Adjust the clevis of the pull rod to align with the hole in the relay lever. Install the clevis pin. Install a new cover in the drum access hole.

Parking Brake Shoes

Separate parking brake shoes are used on some vehicles with rear disc brakes and on vehicles with a transmission-mounted parking brake.

REMOVAL & INSTALLATION

With Rear Disc Brakes

There are several varieties of design with these units. The following procedure is general and applies to most vehicles so equipped. If this procedure does not seem to apply to your vehicle, refer to the model-specific Chilton Total Car Care manual which covers your model.

Most vehicles incorporate a drum-type surface inside the rear rotors. A backing plate is used, on which 2 drum brake-type shoes are mounted with springs and clips.

1. Loosen the lug nuts on the rear wheels.
2. Block the front wheels, then raise and safely support the rear of the vehicle securely on jackstands.
3. Remove the wheels.
4. Remove the calipers and rotors. Don't disconnect the flexible rubber

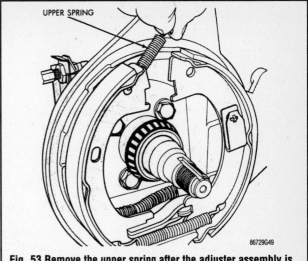

Fig. 53 Remove the upper spring after the adjuster assembly is removed . . .

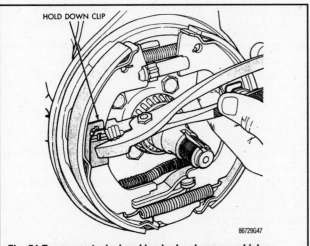

Fig. 51 To remove typical parking brake shoes on vehicles equipped with rear disc brakes, use a pair of pliers to disengage the hold-down clip, then . . .

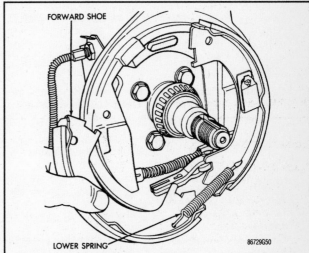

Fig. 54 . . . then remove the forward shoe and detach the lower spring from the rear shoe

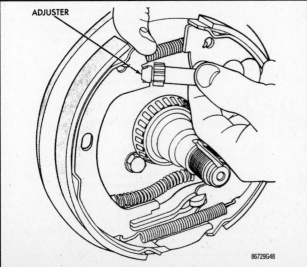

Fig. 52 . . . remove the adjuster from between the brake shoes

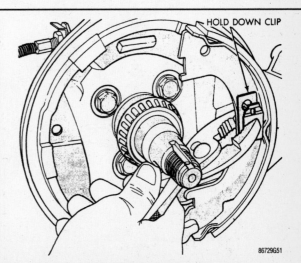

Fig. 55 Use the pliers to remove the hold-down clip from the rear shoe, then remove the shoe

brake hoses from the calipers; suspend the calipers with a length of wire so that they do not hang on the rubber hoses.

5. Clean the brake assembly with a commercially-available spray brake cleaner.

6. Remove the return spring(s) and hold-down springs.

7. Lift the shoes off the backing plate, and remove the adjuster mechanism.

8. Disconnect the parking brake cable or cable lever.

To install:

9. Clean, then lubricate the brake shoe/backing plate sliding points with synthetic brake grease, high-temperature wheel bearing grease or silicone grease.

10. Clean, then lubricate the adjuster mechanism threads. Assemble the mechanism and completely screw it in.

11. Position the shoes on the backing plate and install the hold-down springs.

12. Install the adjuster and cable or lever.

13. Install the return springs.

14. Expand the adjuster until the rotor just fits over the shoes without drag.

15. Install the wheels.

With Transmission-Mounted Parking Brake

The disassembly of some of these units, particularly the fluid-filled type, requires expensive special tools and a degree of skill beyond the average do-it-yourselfer. For these reasons, we suggest that you take your vehicle to a qualified service technician.

For some, however, the unit is a simple design, very similar in layout to a conventional drum brake setup. The following procedure is general and applies to most mechanical units.

➡**The driveshaft yoke is retained by a nut. The tightening torque for this nut can be very high, depending on the manufacturer. Sometimes, the torque can be as much a 300 ft. lbs. (408 Nm).**

1. Raise and safely support the vehicle on jackstands.

2. Matchmark the driveshaft-to-yoke position for reassembly and remove it. Driveshafts are a balanced unit at assembly and installation in the same place may help prevent driveline vibration.

3. Apply the parking brake tightly. On vehicles equipped with automatic transmission, place the transmission in **PARK**.

4. Using the appropriate size socket and a breaker bar, remove the nut

attaching the drive yoke; it may be very tight. It may help to spray the nut and shaft with a penetrant, such as WD-40® or Liquid Wrench®.

5. Slide the drive yoke from the unit.

➡**It may be necessary to hold the drive yoke with a device such as a large pipe wrench. There are tools designed for this purpose, which make the job a lot easier.**

6. Release the parking brake.

7. Disconnect the actuating linkage from the parking brake assembly.

8. Remove the parking brake drum.

9. Thoroughly clean the shoe and drum assemblies with spray brake cleaner.

10. On most of these vehicles, the brake shoes are held in place with conventional hold-down springs. A dual return spring system is used with the springs connecting both shoes at either end. Remove the hold-down springs and lift the shoes off the backing plate.

To install:

11. Thoroughly clean the backing plate, and coat the backing plate-to-brake shoe contact surfaces with synthetic brake grease, high-temperature wheel bearing grease, or silicone grease.

✸✸✸ CAUTION

NEVER apply grease, or any other lubricant, to the friction surface of a brake pad or shoe! Ensure that only a thin layer of grease is applied to the backing plate, so that excess grease does not spread to the shoe/pad friction surface.

12. Inspect the drum braking surface for signs of scoring, rust, cracking or heat bluing. Minor problems may be able to be remedied by machining the drum.

13. Mount the shoes on the backing plate and install the hold-down springs.

14. Install the return springs, then install the drum.

15. Reattach, then adjust the parking brake linkage.

16. Install the yoke and retaining nut. If necessary, refer to the Chilton Total Car Care written specifically for your vehicle for the proper nut torque figure. On some vehicles, the nut may not be reusable. A new one must be used.

17. Install the driveshaft, aligning the matchmarks.

18. Check parking brake operation.

19. Lower the vehicle.

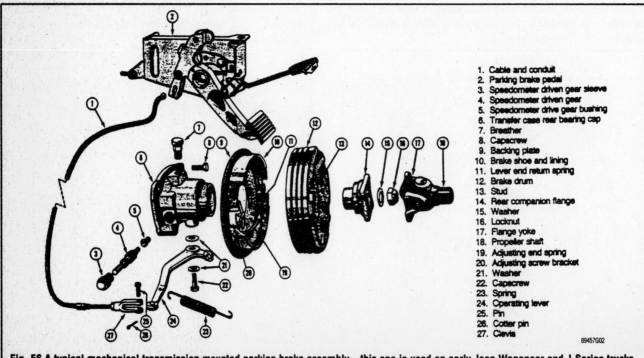

1. Cable and conduit
2. Parking brake pedal
3. Speedometer driven gear sleeve
4. Speedometer driven gear
5. Speedometer drive gear bushing
6. Transfer case rear bearing cap
7. Breather
8. Capscrew
9. Backing plate
10. Brake shoe and lining
11. Lever end return spring
12. Brake drum
13. Stud
14. Rear companion flange
15. Washer
16. Locknut
17. Flange yoke
18. Propeller shaft
19. Adjusting end spring
20. Adjusting screw bracket
21. Washer
22. Capscrew
23. Spring
24. Operating lever
25. Pin
26. Cotter pin
27. Clevis

89457G02

Fig. 56 A typical mechanical transmission mounted parking brake assembly—this one is used on early Jeep Wagoneer and J-Series trucks

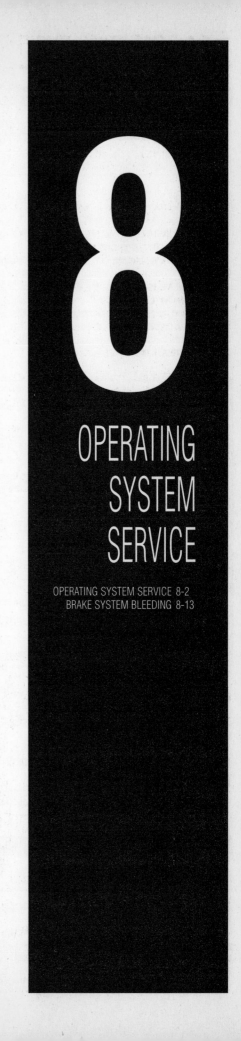

8

OPERATING
SYSTEM
SERVICE

OPERATING SYSTEM SERVICE

Brake Pedal

REMOVAL & INSTALLATION

Hanging Type

1. Disconnect the stop light switch wiring.
2. Remove the switch.
3. Disconnect any return springs.
4. Disconnect the linkage from the pedal. This usually involves removing a clip or retaining pin and sliding the linkage off the pedal arm stud.
5. Remove the nut, bolt or clip that retains the pedal to the rod or stud on which it pivots. On vehicles with manual transmission, the brake and clutch pedals may mount on the same pivot rod. On some of these vehicles, both pedals will be disengaged when the mounting bolt is removed.
6. Installation is the reverse of removal. Lubricate the pivot and linkage points with chassis lube.

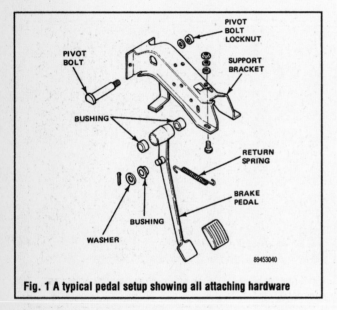

Fig. 1 A typical pedal setup showing all attaching hardware

Through-the-Floor Type

1. Working under the vehicle, disconnect the stop light switch wires.
2. Disconnect the pedal arm from the pushrod or link.
3. Remove the nut, bolt or clip retaining the pedal pivot point to the frame or bracket.
4. Slide the pedal off the pivot and pull it up through the floor.
5. Installation is the reverse of removal. Lubricate all pivot and linkage points with chassis lube.

Stop Light Switch

REMOVAL & INSTALLATION

1. Check under the dash at the pedal mounting bracket to locate the switch assembly.

➡The switch is either mounted to a bracket so that pedal movement will actuate the switch plunger, or in some cases, it may be mounted to the pedal itself.

2. Disconnect the wiring and, if equipped, the vacuum line(s) from the switch.
3. Check the switch for fasteners (nuts, screws or retaining c-clips). If present remove the fasteners from the switch.

➡There are a variety of ways that stop light switches are secured. Some are bolted in place using threaded retainers. Others may be fastened using a C-clip or cotter pin. And many domestic vehicles use a switch which ratchets into a plastic clip.

4. Remove the clip, nuts or screws attaching the switch to the pedal or mounting bracket.

➡With some switches, the clip stays in place. The switch is slid off or out of the clip.

5. Remove the switch.
6. Installation is the reverse of removal. Some switches are adjustable. The adjustment is made either by screwing or sliding the switch toward or away from the plunger contact point.

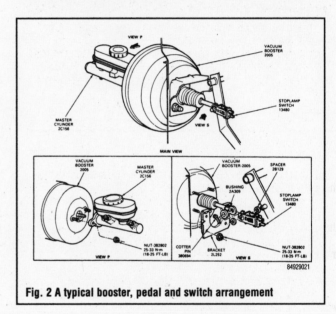

Fig. 2 A typical booster, pedal and switch arrangement

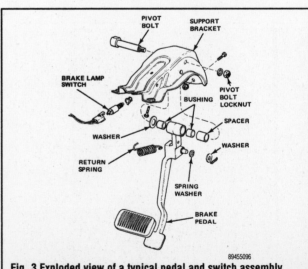

Fig. 3 Exploded view of a typical pedal and switch assembly (this switch is mounted to a retaining clip)

Brake Hoses and Pipes

Brake fluid gets from the master cylinder to the calipers and wheel cylinders through steel brake pipes and flexible brake hoses. On some vehicles, a single brake line can be a combination hose and pipe. Usually, however, hoses and pipes are separate. These lines do require replacement over time or when damaged. The average useful life of a hose is about 5 years. After this time the rubber outer cover will start to deteriorate and crack. The causes can vary, ranging from heat and cold to flexing and road hazards such as salt and oil. Don't overlook them!

HYDRAULIC BRAKE LINE CHECK

The hydraulic brake lines should be inspected at least whenever the brake pads or shoes are replaced. It's good practice to check the brake hoses whenever you have removed a wheel.

Brake hoses should be flexible and not cracked. Brake pipes will show some signs of rust over a period of years. If the rust becomes scaly, it's time to replace the pipe.

✳ CAUTION

Copper tubing should never be used in the brake system. Use only SAE J526 or J527 steel tubing.

When installing a new section of brake hose or pipe, flush clean brake fluid or denatured alcohol through it to remove any dirt or foreign material from the line.

REPLACEMENT

Brake Hoses

1. Raise the end of the vehicle that contains the hose to be replaced, then support the vehicle safely using jackstands.
2. If necessary, remove the wheel for easier access to the hose.
3. Disconnect the hose from the wheel cylinder, caliper or axle and plug the opening to avoid excessive fluid loss or contamination.
4. Disconnect the hose from the brake pipe and plug the openings to avoid excessive fluid loss or contamination.
   To install:
5. Install the brake hose to the brake pipe and tighten securely.
6. If installing a front brake hose, make sure the hose is routed properly, with the loop to the rear of the vehicle.

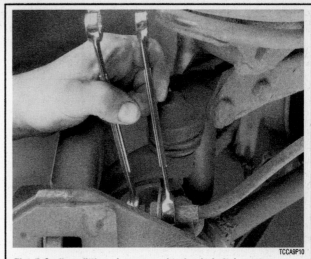
TCCA9P10
Fig. 5 On flare fittings (as opposed to banjo bolts) use two wrenches to loosen the fitting

TCCA9P11
Fig. 6 Any gaskets/crush washers should be replaced with new ones during installation

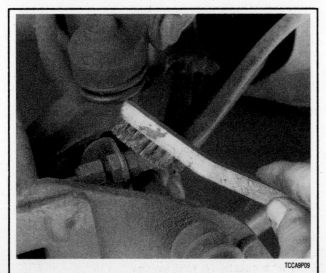
TCCA9P09
Fig. 4 Use a brush to clean the fittings of any debris

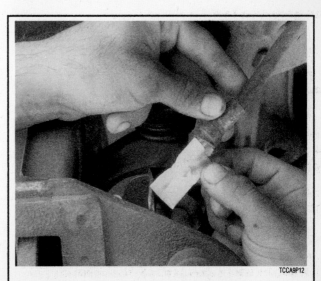
TCCA9P12
Fig. 7 Tape or plug the line to prevent contamination

Fig. 8 This is a typical hose-to-bracket retaining clip

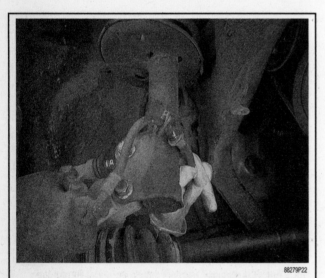

Fig. 9 Many vehicles route the hoses through brackets

Fig. 10 Most vehicles attach the brake line to some convenient point near the caliper, usually the strut, control arm or backing plate

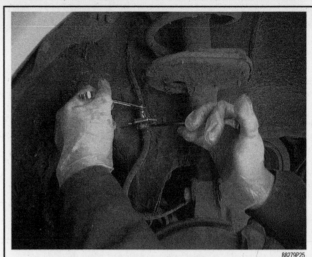

Fig. 11 Loosening a brake hose union using 2 wrenches (note that it is best to use line or flare nut wrenches)

Fig. 12 Separating the brake lines. Plug the openings to prevent contamination and fluid loss

7. When installing a hose with a banjo-fitting, be sure to use NEW washers.
8. Properly bleed the brake system, then check the connections for leaks.
9. Remove the jackstands and carefully lower the vehicle.

Brake Pipes

There are 2 options available when replacing a brake pipe. The first, and most preferable, is to replace the entire pipe using a pipe of similar length which is already equipped with machined flared ends. These pipes are available at auto parts stores and usually require only a minimum of bending in order to properly fit then to the vehicle. The second option is to bend and flare the entire replacement pipe using the appropriate tools.

Buying a pipe with machined flares is usually preferable because of the time and effort saved, not to mention the cost of special tools if you don't already have them. Also, machined flares are usually of a much higher quality than those produced by hand flaring tools or kits. A poorly made flare can leak and/or crack causing a loss of braking action.

✳✳ CAUTION

Double-flare brake pipes; never install a new pipe with only a single flare.

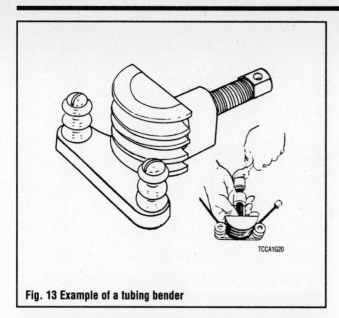

Fig. 13 Example of a tubing bender

Fig. 14 Disconnecting the pipe at the wheel cylinder

1. Raise the end of the vehicle that contains the pipe to be replaced, then support the vehicle safely using jackstands.

2. Remove the components necessary for access to the brake pipe that is being replaced.

3. Disconnect the fittings at each end of the pipe, and then plug the openings to prevent excessive fluid loss or contamination.

4. Trace the pipe from one end to the other and disconnect the pipe from any retaining clips, then remove the pipe from the vehicle.

To install:

5. Try to obtain a replacement pipe that is the same length as the pipe that was removed. If the pipe is longer, you will have to do some fancy bending to get it to fit. We don't recommend that.

6. Use a suitable tubing bender to make the necessary bends in the pipe. Work slowly and carefully; try to make the bends look as close as possible to those on the pipe being replaced.

➥When bending the brake pipe, be careful not to kink or crack the pipe. If the brake pipe becomes kinked or cracked, it must be replaced.

7. Before installing the brake pipe, flush it with brake cleaner or alcohol to remove any dirt or foreign material.

8. Install the pipe into the vehicle. Be sure to attach the pipe to the retaining clips, as necessary. Make sure the replacement brake pipe does not contact any components that could rub the pipe and cause a leak.

9. Connect the brake pipe fittings. Pipe fittings are usually tightened to 15–18 ft. lbs. (20–24 Nm). Tightening pipe fittings requires a crow's foot adapter for your torque wrench (and some math to make sure the wrench setting is correct). If you don't have one of these, just tighten the fitting securely.

10. Properly bleed the brake system and check for leaks.

11. Install any removed components, then remove the supports and carefully lower the vehicle.

BRAKE PIPE FLARING

⁂ CAUTION

Use only brake pipe tubing approved for automotive use; never use copper tubing.

Using a Split-Die Flaring Tool

1. Use a tubing cutter to cut the required length of line.
2. Square the end with a file and chamfer the end.
3. Place the tube in the proper size die hole and position it so that it is flush with the die face. Lock the line with the wing nut.

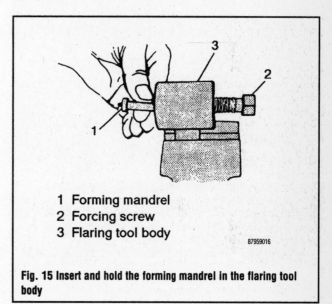

1 Forming mandrel
2 Forcing screw
3 Flaring tool body

Fig. 15 Insert and hold the forming mandrel in the flaring tool body

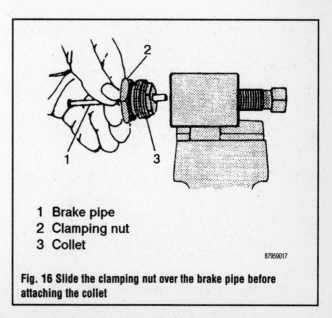

1 Brake pipe
2 Clamping nut
3 Collet

Fig. 16 Slide the clamping nut over the brake pipe before attaching the collet

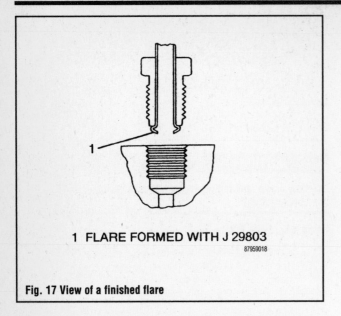

1 FLARE FORMED WITH J 29803

87959018

Fig. 17 View of a finished flare

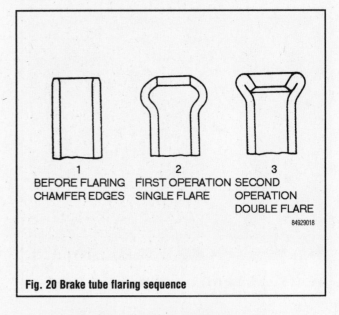

HYDRAULIC BRAKE
LINE TUBING

86729G45

Fig. 19 It is very important to cut the tubing on a 90° angle. It helps ensure an even flaring of the tube

4. The punches included with most tools are marked to identify the sequence of flaring. Such marks are usually OP.1 and OP. 2 or something similar.

5. Slide the OP.1 punch into position and tighten the screw to form a single flare.

6. Remove the screw and position the OP.2 punch. Tighten the screw to form the double flare.

7. Remove the punch and release the line from the die.

8. Inspect the finished flare for cracks or uneven flare form. If the flare is not perfect, cut it off and re-flare the end.

Using a Flaring Bar Tool

1. Use a tubing cutter to cut the required length of line.

2. Square the end with a file and chamfer the end.

3. Insert the tube into the proper size hole in the bar, until the end of the tube sticks out as far as the thickness of the adapter above the bar, or, depending on the tool, even with the bar face.

4. Fit the adapter onto the tube and slide the bar into the yoke. Lock the bar in position with the tube beneath the yoke screw.

5. Tighten the yoke screw and form the single flare.

6. Release the yoke screw and remove the adapter.

7. Install the second adapter and form the double flare.

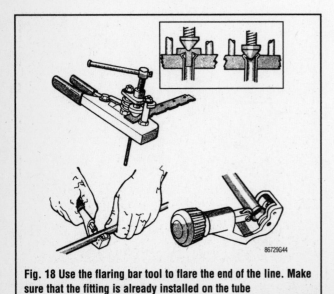

86729G44

Fig. 18 Use the flaring bar tool to flare the end of the line. Make sure that the fitting is already installed on the tube

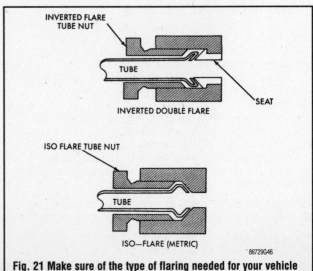

Fig. 20 Brake tube flaring sequence

INVERTED FLARE
TUBE NUT

TUBE

INVERTED DOUBLE FLARE

SEAT

ISO FLARE TUBE NUT

TUBE

ISO—FLARE (METRIC)

86729G46

Fig. 21 Make sure of the type of flaring needed for your vehicle before acquiring the tool

8. Release the screw and remove the tube. Inspect the finished flare for cracks or uneven flare form. If the flare is not perfect, cut it off and re-flare the end.

Master Cylinder

➡The following procedures apply to non-ABS systems and ABS system master cylinders that are separate from other ABS system components. ABS systems with integral master cylinder components often require a great many special tools and specialized knowledge to be successfully worked on by most do-it-yourselfers. To determine if the master cylinder on your ABS equipped vehicle can be serviced at home, check a Chilton Total Car Care manual for your vehicle.

REMOVAL & INSTALLATION

With Power Assisted Brakes

1. Disconnect the negative battery cable.
2. Apply the brake pedal several times to exhaust all vacuum in the system.

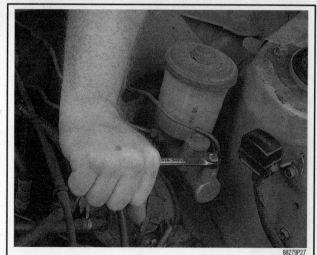

Fig. 24 Use an open-end wrench (a line wrench is preferable) to loosen the brake pipe fittings . . .

Fig. 22 Disconnect any electrical connectors at . . .

Fig. 25 . . .the disconnect the pipes from the master cylinder assembly

Fig. 23 . . . or near the master cylinder

Fig. 26 Loosen the master cylinder retainers . . .

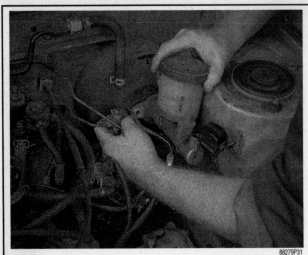

Fig. 27 . . . then slide the master cylinder assembly from the mount

Fig. 28 Most master cylinders are secured to the brake booster using 2 retaining nuts

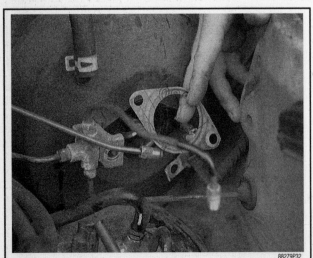

Fig. 29 Some vehicles have gaskets between the master cylinder and booster

3. Disconnect any electrical connectors from any switches mounted in the master cylinder.

4. Place absorbent rags under the points at which the brake pipes connect to the master cylinder.

5. Remove the brake lines from the primary and secondary outlet ports of the master cylinder. Cap or plug the lines to prevent fluid loss and contamination.

6. Remove the fasteners retaining the master cylinder to the power brake booster.

➡Most master cylinder assemblies are secured to mounting studs on the brake booster using retaining nuts. However some master cylinders are bolted in place.

7. Slide the master cylinder forward and remove it from the vehicle.

⁕⁕⁕ WARNING

Many manufacturers have power booster pushrods that can be removed. DON'T do it! Don't dislodge the pushrod. Behind the pushrod, on many of these vehicles, is what is called a reaction disc. It is a buffer between the booster power cylinder and the pushrod. If this reaction disc becomes dislodged, it can't be put back into place.

To install:

8. Transfer any switches from the old master cylinder to the new master cylinder.

9. Bench bleed the new master cylinder. Refer to the procedure in this Section.

10. Some manufacturers, particularly Ford, Mitsubishi and Toyota, have adjustable pushrods in the power booster. Before installing the master cylinder onto these power brake boosters, check the brake booster pushrod length by fabricating a gauge block that when set against the brake booster will determine if the pushrod needs to be lengthened or shortened. An accompanying illustration shows you how to make this gauge block. Cardboard works just fine. The pushrod should protrude out of the brake booster a set distance, in most cases, 0.980–0.995 inch (24.89–25.27 mm). The pushrod is adjusted by turning the adjustment screw on the end of the pushrod. For the exact specification, check the Chilton Total Car Care manual written specifically for your vehicle.

11. Position the brake master cylinder on power brake booster.

12. Install retaining nuts or bolts and tighten securely.

13. Install both the primary and secondary brake lines at the master cylinder.

14. When both brake lines are installed, tighten them securely.

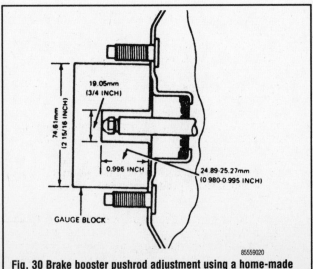

Fig. 30 Brake booster pushrod adjustment using a home-made gauge

15. Connect any electrical connectors.
16. Fill the master cylinder with the proper brake fluid.
17. Bleed the brake system. Top off the master cylinder when complete.
18. Connect the negative battery cable.
19. Road test the vehicle and check for proper brake system operation.

With Non-Power Brakes

➤**Many older vehicles have the master cylinder mounted on the frame rail, under the floor. The procedure is the same; the location is different.**

1. Disconnect the master cylinder pushrod from the brake pedal linkage. This connection can be either inside the passenger compartment or inside the engine compartment. The connection is usually by way of a rod fitting over a stud on the pedal arm, retained by washers and a cotter pin or clip.
2. Place absorbent rags under the points at which the brake pipes connect to the master cylinder.
3. Remove the brake lines from the primary and secondary outlet ports of the master cylinder. Cap or plug the lines to prevent fluid loss and contamination.
4. Remove fasteners retaining the master cylinder to the firewall.
5. Slide the master cylinder forward and remove it from the vehicle.

To install:

6. Bench bleed the new master cylinder. Refer to the procedure in this Section.
7. Place the brake master cylinder onto firewall.
8. Install fasteners and tighten them securely.
9. Install both the primary and secondary brake lines at the master cylinder.
10. When both brake lines are installed, tighten them securely.
11. Fill the master cylinder with the proper brake fluid.
12. Bleed the brake system. Top off the master cylinder when complete.
13. Road test the vehicle and check for proper brake system operation.

OVERHAUL

➤**Not all master cylinders can be overhauled. In general, the older, cast iron master cylinders can all be rebuilt. Newer master cylinders, however are made of aluminum or composite metals or plastic. Most of these newer types cannot be rebuilt. If you're unsure, check with your local parts store. They can look it up in their parts information.**

1. Remove the master cylinder from the vehicle.
2. Drain the excess fluid from the reservoir.
3. Thoroughly clean the master cylinder with brake cleaner or alcohol.
4. Clamp the cylinder in a soft-jawed vise.
5. If your unit has a removable reservoir, remove the reservoir attaching screw or pin, if equipped.
6. Carefully pry the reservoir from the master cylinder using a side-to-side motion.
7. Remove and discard the reservoir seals from the master cylinder.
8. Push the primary piston into the master cylinder and remove the snapring.
9. Remove the primary piston.
10. Push the secondary piston into the master cylinder and remove the stop screw from the outer casing, if equipped.
11. Tap the open end of the cylinder lightly on a work surface to help dislodge the pistons, then remove the secondary piston from the cylinder body.

➤**If the secondary piston does not readily come out, apply low level air pressure to the secondary outlet port to assist in removal.**

To assemble:

12. Thoroughly wash the parts in clean denatured alcohol and dry with unlubricated compressed air.
13. Lubricate the parts with clean brake fluid.
14. Install new seals on the primary and secondary pistons.
15. Install the secondary piston assembly.

Fig. 31 Removing the snapring

Fig. 32 Removing the outer cup

Fig. 33 Removing the stop bolt

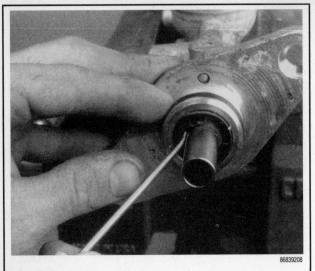

Fig. 34 Removing the inner cup

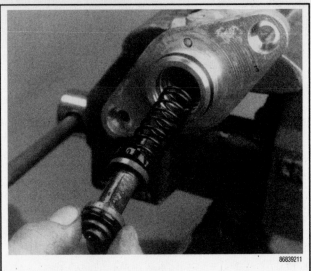

Fig. 37 Removing the primary piston

Fig. 35 Removing the inner snapring

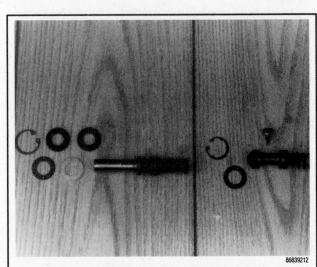

Fig. 38 Arrange all parts as they are removed in order to help assure proper assembly

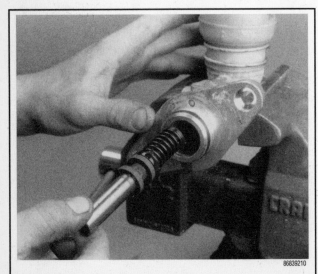

Fig. 36 Removing the secondary piston

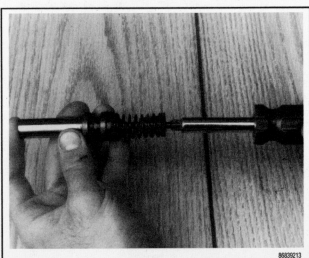

Fig. 39 In some master cylinders, the piston components are secured with a screw

Fig. 40 Coat all parts with clean brake fluid as lubrication prior to installation

➡️**To prevent damage to the lip seals, ease the seal into the master cylinder bore while slowly rotating and pushing.**

16. Push the secondary piston in until it bottoms out and install the stop screw, if equipped. Tighten the screw.
17. Push the primary piston in and install the snapring.
18. Install new reservoir seals on the cylinder.
19. Install the reservoir on the master cylinder.
20. Turn the assembly upside down and press down on the master cylinder with hand pressure and install the screw.

Hydraulic Control Valves

On most vehicles, the proportioning valve is mounted in the system, below the master cylinder. Usually it's found on the frame rail or firewall. On some vehicles, however, the proportioning valve part is integral with the master cylinder and is replaced with it. The following procedure refers to combination valves mounted apart from the master cylinder. Combination valves are almost never serviceable and must be replaced if defective.

REMOVAL & INSTALLATION

1. If necessary, raise and safely support the front end on jackstands.
2. Have a number of plugs ready to cap the brake lines. Place a drip pan under the valve and carefully disconnect and cap all the brake lines connected to it.
3. Remove the bolt(s), nuts or clips retaining the valve. Remove the valve.
4. Installation is the reverse of removal. Securely tighten, but don't overtighten, the brake lines.
5. Bleed the entire brake system.

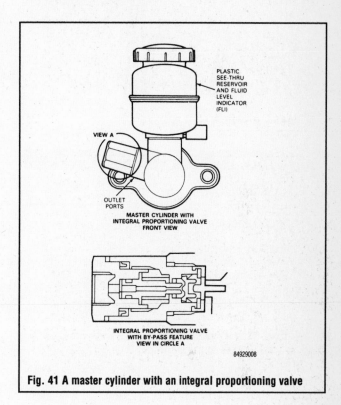

Fig. 41 A master cylinder with an integral proportioning valve

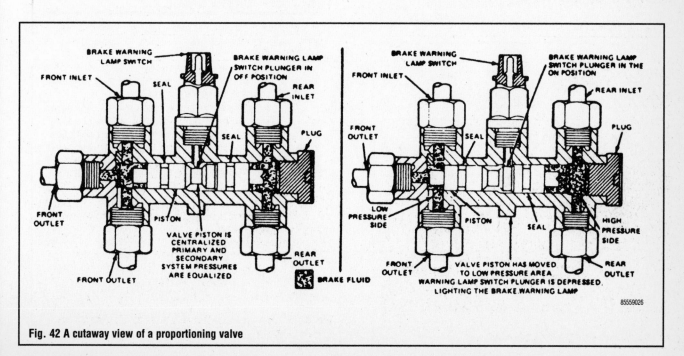

Fig. 42 A cutaway view of a proportioning valve

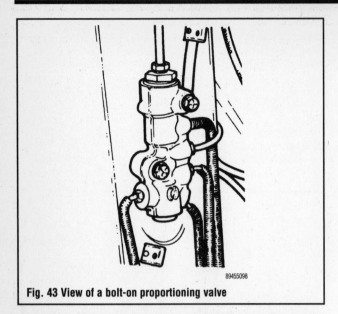

Fig. 43 View of a bolt-on proportioning valve

Power Boosters

REMOVAL & INSTALLATION

Vacuum-Type Boosters

Most vehicles use vacuum-type power boosters.

1. If necessary, disconnect the brake light switch wires.
2. Support the master cylinder from below, with a prop of some kind.
3. Loosen the clamp and remove the booster vacuum hose.
4. If necessary, remove any retaining clips from the booster studs.

➡It is, usually, not necessary to disconnect the brake lines, but be careful not to stress and damage them.

5. Remove the master cylinder from the booster. Position it as far aside as the lines will allow. Keep it supported.
6. Working inside the vehicle below the instrument panel, disconnect the booster valve operating rod from the brake pedal assembly.
7. Remove the booster bracket-to-dash panel attaching nuts.

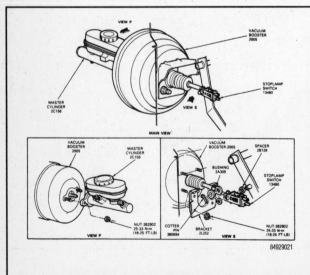

Fig. 44 A common brake vacuum booster mounting

8. Remove the booster and bracket assembly from the dash panel, sliding the valve operating rod out from the engine side of the dash panel.

To install:

9. Usually, there is some kind of gasket between the booster and firewall. If it's okay-looking, just leave it. If it's worn or broken, replace it. You can make one from gasket material available at most auto parts stores.
10. Mount the booster and bracket assembly on the dash panel by sliding the valve operating rod in through the hole in the dash panel, and installing the attaching nuts. Tighten the fasteners securely.
11. Connect the manifold vacuum hose to the booster.
12. Install the master cylinder. Tighten the fasteners securely.
13. Install any clips on the studs.
14. If disconnected, connect the stop light switch wires.
15. Working inside the vehicle below the instrument panel, connect the pushrod and stoplight switch.

Hydraulic Boosters

Some vehicles use hydraulically activated boosters commonly called Hydro-boost.

❋❋ CAUTION

Do not depress the brake pedal with the master cylinder removed!

1. Remove the master cylinder from the booster unit. It is, usually, not necessary to disconnect the brake lines. Position the master cylinder as far out of the way as the lines will allow and support it to keep the lines from kinking.
2. Disconnect the hydraulic lines from the booster unit.
3. Disconnect the pushrod from the brake pedal.
4. Remove the booster mounting nuts and lift the booster from the firewall.

❋❋ CAUTION

The booster should never be carried by the accumulator. The accumulator normally contains high pressure gas, usually nitrogen, and can be dangerous if mishandled! If the accumulator is to be disposed of, do not expose it to fire or other forms of incineration! Gas pressure can be relieved by drilling a 1/16 in. (1.5mm) hole in the end of the accumulator can. Always wear safety goggles during the drilling!

5. Installation is the reverse of removal. Tighten the booster mounting nuts and master cylinder nuts securely; connect the hydraulic lines, refill and bleed the booster as follows:

a. Fill the pump reservoir with a suitable fluid (usually an ATF like Dexron®II, Dexron® III or Mercon®). Refer to your owner's manual or a Chilton Total Car Care for recommendations.

b. Disable the ignition system. On vehicles with distributors and external coils, remove the coil-to-distributor wire. On vehicles with internal distributor coils or distributorless ignition systems, check the Chilton manual for written specifically for your vehicle (it may require unplugging a coil pack, removing a fuse or disconnecting the ignition module wiring). Crank the engine for several seconds.

c. Check the fluid level and refill, if necessary.

d. Connect the ignition system and start the engine.

e. With the engine running, turn the steering wheel lock-to-lock twice. Shut off the engine.

f. Depress the brake pedal several times to discharge the accumulator.

g. Start the engine and repeat the steering wheel turning.

h. If foam appears in the reservoir, allow the foam to dissipate.

i. Repeat the steering wheel turning as often as necessary to expel all air from the system.

➡The system is, in effect, self-bleeding and normal vehicle operation will expel any further trapped air.

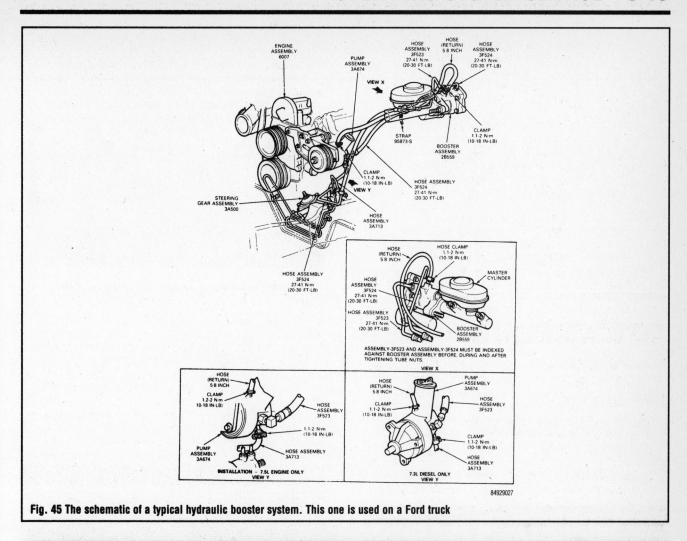

Fig. 45 The schematic of a typical hydraulic booster system. This one is used on a Ford truck

BRAKE SYSTEM BLEEDING

☼ CAUTION

Always wear eye protection when bleeding the brakes!

The hydraulic brake system must be bled any time any of the lines is disconnected or any time air enters the system. If a point in the system, such as a wheel cylinder or caliper brake line is the only point which was opened, the bleeder screws down stream in the hydraulic system are the only ones which must be bled. If however, the master cylinder fittings are opened or if the reservoir level drops sufficiently that air is drawn into the system, air must be bled from the entire hydraulic system. If the brake pedal feels spongy upon application, and goes almost to the floor but regains height when pumped, air has entered the system. It must be bled out. If no fittings were recently opened for service, check for leaks that would have allowed the entry of air and repair them before attempting to bleed the system.

As a general rule, once the master cylinder (and the brake pressure modulator valve or combination valve on ABS systems) is bled, the remainder of the hydraulic system should be bled in the proper sequence.

The hydraulic system can be bled in one of two ways: manual bleeding and bleeding using a pressure bleeder. Most of us use the manual bleeding method. But, we'll describe both ways here.

Bleeding Tools

There are special tools available at most auto parts stores which attempt to make one-person bleeding possible. If you have no one to help you

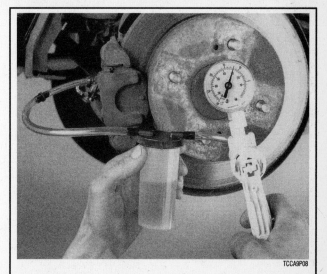

Fig. 46 A vacuum pump is a fast and efficient bleeding aid

bleed your brakes, you might want to try one of these devices. The two most popular are the check valve type and the vacuum pump type.

The check valve method is just what it sounds like. You get two lengths of hose, some adapter nipples and a small container. One end of one hose goes on the caliper or wheel cylinder nipple and the other end on the up side of a one-way check valve. The other length of hose connects to the down side of the check valve, then, into the container, which must be partially filled with clean brake fluid. When you depress the brake pedal, fluid and air pass through the check valve but not back up. This method requires a lot of jumping in and out of the vehicle.

The vacuum pump device connects a partially filled container to the caliper or wheel cylinder nipple at one side and a hand-operated vacuum pump on the other side. When you actuate the pump, vacuum draws fluid and air out of the brake system and into the container. The advantage of this is that you don't have to run back and forth between the passenger compartment and wheel. The disadvantage is the small size of the container and the awkwardness of having to pump with one hand, hold the container somehow and open and close the bleeder screw. Three hands would be nice.

There is one, additional way, which can work very well on basic systems (non-ABS, without complicated control valves). The gravity bleed method. In this method, the bleeder screws are simply left open and brake fluid is allowed to run out under atmospheric pressure. This means you can't have the bottom end of the clear tube in brake fluid and you can't have the master cylinder capped. The disadvantages are that moisture can enter the system and the master cylinder must be repeatedly checked, but it does work well on the appropriate vehicle.

Lastly, there is always one vehicle that has a problem system. Air simply won't give up! You just can't seem to get it all out. If that's the case, check a couple of things first. Using a trouble light, trace the system from front to back, checking all connections. See if there is any leakage. If your calipers are old, try rapping on them with a hammer when you open the bleeder. In older calipers, tiny air bubbles can lodge on interior passage walls. Also, the spongy pedal feel may not be air at all. It's possible that one or both seals inside the master cylinder may be worn, allowing fluid to pass back and forth. This condition gives the same pedal feel as air. If that's the case, repair or replace the master cylinder. If all else fails, try pressure bleeding. Air can't escape a pressure bleeder.

Non-ABS System Bleeding

MANUAL BLEEDING

Master Cylinder

If the unit is removed from the vehicle, there are 2 ways to "bench-bleed" a master cylinder.

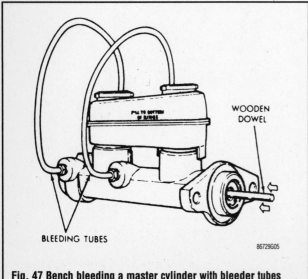

Fig. 47 Bench bleeding a master cylinder with bleeder tubes

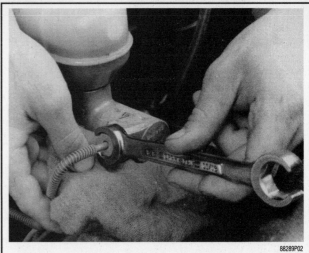

Fig. 48 Bleeding the master cylinder by cracking open the fittings

One is with a large, clear plastic syringe made for the purpose. They are usually available at auto parts stores. In this procedure, the master cylinder is clamped in a soft-jawed vise and filled with fluid. The outlet ports are capped or plugged. Then, uncap each port, place the syringe securely in the outlet port and draw fluid into the syringe until no air is left in the master cylinder, capping the ports when done.

The other is with 2 lengths of hose or pipe (to use as bleeder tubes). Plastic hoses, made for the purpose, are available at most auto parts stores. These hoses have threaded ends for attachment to the outlet ports. Otherwise, you'll have to make your own bleeder pipes from 2 lengths of brake pipe equipped with threaded ends. Try to get the plastic ones. In this procedure, clamp the master cylinder in a soft-jawed vise. Connect the pieces of brake pipe or the plastic hoses to the outlet fittings, bend them until the free end is the master cylinder reservoir. Fill the reservoir with fresh DOT 3 or equivalent, brake fluid from a closed container, completely covering the tube ends. Pump the piston slowly until no more air bubbles appear in the reservoir. Remove the tubes, refill the brake master cylinder and securely install caps or plugs in the ports.

If the brake master cylinder is on the vehicle, place a large, absorbent rag under the fittings. Open the brake lines slightly with the flare nut wrench while pressure is applied to the brake pedal by a helper inside the vehicle. Be sure to tighten the line before the brake pedal is released. Repeat the process with both lines until no air bubbles come out.

In both cases, the rest of the brake system must be bled to assure that all trapped has been removed and that the system will operate properly.

Calipers and Wheel Cylinders

We recommend that the brake system be bled using the jar and tube method. We know some people just let the fluid spray all over the place from the nipple. This is not only unprofessional, but it's messy and potentially dangerous. Brake fluid damages paint, concrete, your clothes, your skin and, most importantly, your eyes.

➡**Hydraulic brake systems must be totally flushed if the fluid becomes contaminated with water, dirt or other corrosive chemicals. Also, many manufacturers recommend that the system be flushed routinely, every 2 years or so. To flush, bleed the entire system until all fluid has been replaced and the new brake fluid runs clear.**

The hydraulic system on vehicles with a split system—a 2-chambered master cylinder—can be split either into front/rear or diagonally. That is, one front and one rear on each system. If you are in doubt as to the zoning of your vehicle's system, you can check the brake lines. Follow them to each wheel and see which are paired. If you are still in doubt, check the Chilton manual written especially for your vehicle.

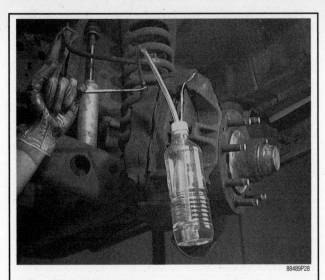

Fig. 49 Bleeding the calipers

Fig. 50 Bleeding the wheel cylinders

➡️If, during the bleeding procedure, you can't get a good flow of fluid from the front brakes, the problem is with the metering part of the combination valve. Check the valve and you'll see a small stem sticking out of one end. You'll have to fabricate a little clip to hold the stem out as far as it will go. This will allow a full flow to the front brakes. Also, when using this clip on vehicles with power brakes, try bleeding with the engine running. The greater pressure allowed by the power booster will aid in purging the system.

1. Fill the brake master cylinder with the fluid recommended for your vehicle. Check the level often during the procedure. Never let the master cylinder go dry or the procedure will have to be performed over again.
2. Raise and support the vehicle safely on jackstands.
3. If necessary for better access, remove the wheels.
4. On vehicles with a single chamber system or dual chambered systems split front/rear, you can bleed the system in the following order:
- Right rear
- Left rear
- Right front
- Left front
5. On vehicles with a dual chambered system split diagonally, the usual bleeding order is:

- Right rear
- Left front
- Left rear
- Right front

If you are in doubt, check the Chilton Total Car Care manual written specifically for your vehicle.

6. Find a wrench, a box wrench if possible, of the right size for the bleeder screw and place it on the nipple of the first cylinder to be bled.
7. Connect a clear, vinyl tube to the bleeder nipple. Place the other end of the tube in a clear glass jar of at least 8 ounce capacity. The jar should be about ½ full of clean brake fluid. Submerge the end of the tube.
8. Have an assistant, neighbor, wife, husband or kid, pump the brake pedal, then hold it down. Slowly open the bleeder screw. When the pedal reaches the floor, close the bleeder and have the helper slowly release the pedal. Wait 15 seconds, then repeat the procedure until no more air comes out of the bleeder.
9. Repeat the procedure on the remaining calipers or wheel cylinders in the appropriate order.
10. If the brake pedal has a spongy feel, the brake system must be bled again to remove air still trapped in the system.
11. Install the bleeder caps to keep dirt out.
12. If removed for access, install the wheels.
13. Lower the vehicle.
14. Road test the vehicle and check for proper brake system operation.

PRESSURE BLEEDING

A pressure bleeder is a device that uses compressed air and a series of adapters to forcibly expel air from the hydraulic system. When using a pressure bleeder, always follow the manufacturer's instructions. What we've given you here are general instructions.

When using pressure bleeding equipment, it's best to use a bladder-type bleeder tank. In this type of bleeder, the brake fluid is separated from the air by a rubber diaphragm. The bleeder tank must contain enough brake fluid to complete the bleeding operation and should be charged with only 10–30 psi. Never exceed 50 psi.

1. Clean all dirt from the master cylinder fluid reservoir filler cap. Important: The reservoir must be at least ¾-full during the bleeding procedure. Fill the reservoir as necessary. Use only clean, fresh brake fluid from a sealed container. Fill to the MAX level line on the reservoir.
2. Install the bleeder adapter tool on the master cylinder and attach the hose from the bleeder tank to the fitting on the adapter. Follow the manufacturer's instructions when installing and connecting the master cylinder adapter.
3. Open the valve on the bleeder tank.

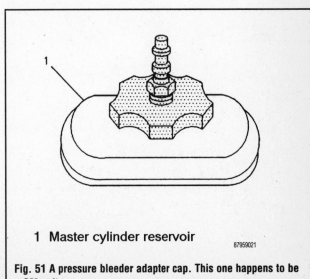

1 Master cylinder reservoir

Fig. 51 A pressure bleeder adapter cap. This one happens to be a GM unit

Master Cylinder

1. If the master cylinder is known or suspected to contain air, it must be bled before the wheel cylinders or calipers. Place a large, absorbent rag under the pipe fittings. Beginning at the front of the master cylinder, alternately loosen and tighten the brake line flare nuts. Allow the fluid to flow for several seconds before tightening the flare nut. Repeat this operation several times to make sure all air has been removed from the master cylinder.

Calipers and Wheel Cylinders

Pressure system bleeding must be performed in the correct order. Refer to the manual bleeding procedure for proper bleeding sequences.

1. Raise and safely support the vehicle on jackstands.
2. Remove the protective bleeder screw cap from the caliper or wheel cylinder and clean the nipple.
3. Place a wrench, preferably a box wrench, on the bleeder screw.
4. Attach a length of clear vinyl hose onto the bleeder nipple. The hose must fit tightly around the bleeder screw.
5. Submerge the free end of the hose in a large (about 16 ounce) clean glass jar about half filled with clean brake fluid.
6. Loosen the bleeder screw approximately ¾ of a turn. When the fluid entering the jar is completely free of bubbles, tighten the bleeder screw.
7. Remove the bleeder hose and attach the protective screw cap.
8. Repeat the bleeding procedure at each brake.
9. Close the valve at the bleeder tank, disconnect the hose from the master cylinder adapter and remove the master cylinder adapter.
10. Check the fluid level in the remote reservoir, refilling with clean, fresh brake fluid, as necessary.
11. Check the brake pedal feel. If spongy, repeat the bleeding process and/or look for defective system components.

ABS System Bleeding

There are 2 potential problems with attempting to bleed an ABS system. The first is that many use control valves and pressure modulators which might trap air if they are not opened and closed during the procedure using a scan tool. The second potential problem is that some ABS systems operate under extremely high pressure (making bleeding dangerous at worst or messy at best).

With this said, there are still many systems which can be bled with common tools. Many of the control valves have pressure relief knobs at one end of the valve which can be help open using a small tool (or pair of locking pliers). And, just about all systems can be bled at the wheels provided that the openings are capped immediately during service. The caps keep enough fluid in the lines to prevent air from working its way back to the control or modulator valves.

Before starting, remember that many manufacturers require the use of special scan tools to bleed any part of the system other than the caliper or wheel cylinders. Some manufacturers recommend the scan tool be used when bleeding any part of the system on some of their models. All manufacturers recommend the use of pressure bleeding equipment for ABS systems, especially when bleeding the rear brakes even though manual bleeding can be done successfully, in most cases. If you are in doubt, check the Chilton Total Car Care manual written specifically for your vehicle to determine if your system can be bled successfully without special tools.

If you decide to attempt bleeding the calipers or wheel cylinders, and you are sure that any residual high pressure is depleted, use the same procedure for bleeding as described for non-ABS systems. During the bleeding procedure, wait 10–15 seconds after closing the bleeder screw before reopening it each time. This is recommended by most manufacturers due to the number of valved components in the system.

Once the procedure is complete, start the engine and allow it to run for 15–30 seconds. Depress the brake pedal. The ABS light should not be **ON**. If the light is **ON**, there is a system problem, probably air still trapped somewhere. At this point, you can try the bleeding procedure again or have the vehicle towed to a dealer or repair shop for system bleeding.

As in all bleeding procedures, DO NOT attempt to move the vehicle unless a firm brake pedal feel has been obtained.

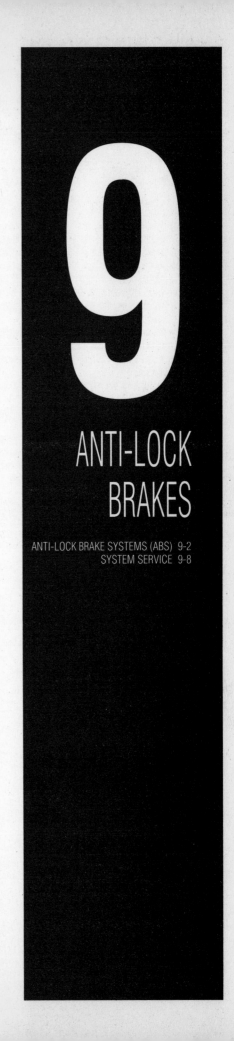

9

ANTI-LOCK
BRAKES

ANTI-LOCK BRAKE SYSTEMS (ABS)

Operation

Under normal braking conditions, the ABS system operates just like a standard system. When one or more wheels shows a tendency to lock during braking, the ABS computer detects this and puts the system into the anti-lock mode. In this mode, hydraulic pressure is modulated to each wheel, preventing any one wheel from locking. Depending on the vehicle manufacturer's system, the ABS unit can build, hold or reduce pressure at each wheel as necessary, depending on the signal received by the computer.

The effect is similar to pumping your brakes, although the ABS system performs this function hundreds of times faster than you can pump your brake pedal. In fact, when driving an ABS vehicle on ice or snow, a driver must overcome the urge to pump the brake during a stop; let the ABS system do the work. Pumping the pedal on an ABS equipped vehicle will defeat the system.

All this is accomplished by a sophisticated system of electronic and hydraulic components that differ from conventional vacuum-boosted hydraulic systems. As a result, there are a few differences that can be noticed by the driver.

The first, and most commonly noticed, difference is reduced pedal travel. The pedal feel will also be noticeably different. With the vehicle at rest, the pedal may feel springy or spongy. This causes a problem in diagnosing some defects, such as air in the hydraulic system.

Another common characteristic is the clicking or clacking noise heard during ABS application on slippery surfaces. This noise is an audible sign that the system is working. A pulsation in the pedal may be felt at this time. This is perfectly normal, but, for diagnostic purposes, it does hide a possibly warped rotor.

ABS systems are most commonly one of two styles. Most modern vehicles are equipped with what's called 4-wheel ABS. In this system, there is a sensor at each wheel and all 4 wheels fall under the control of the ABS computer. Older vehicles are more likely to be equipped with some version of Rear wheel Anti-lock Brake System (RABS), which controls the braking action of just the rear wheels. Most often, this type of ABS is found on light duty 2-wheel drive trucks and some 4-wheel drive vehicles.

Components

As may be expected, different vehicle manufacturers use different systems. Not every vehicle is equipped with the same components as every other. In fact, the components used in an ABS system can vary among models from the same manufacturer. Also, as technology develops, ABS systems may become simpler or more complicated, resulting in different system configurations. Therefore, the components described here are common to most vehicles. Some models may use all of the component described, whereas some models only use some of the components. Most components will be common to all models, such as speed sensors. If necessary, refer to the Chilton model-specific manual for your vehicle to determine with which components your vehicle is equipped.

Most systems are of a design known as the integral system. Others are, by definition, non-integral. The principal difference is in construction. The non-integral system is found mainly in earlier ABS-equipped vehicles. A conventional master cylinder/power booster actuated system is used, to which an ABS computer and controlling devices are added. The non-integral system is called this, because the master cylinder and ABS control valves are not designed as one integral unit.

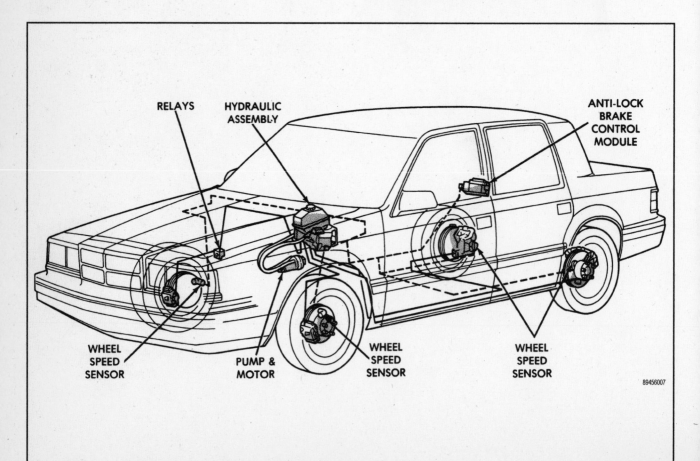

Fig. 1 View of a typical 4-wheel, integral Anti-lock Brake System (ABS)

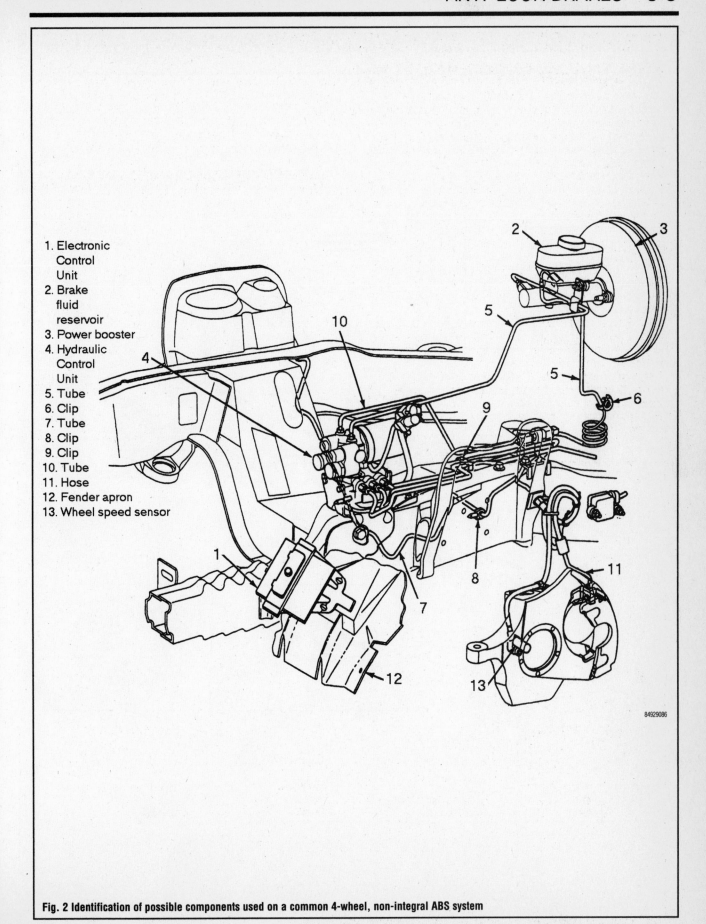

1. Electronic Control Unit
2. Brake fluid reservoir
3. Power booster
4. Hydraulic Control Unit
5. Tube
6. Clip
7. Tube
8. Clip
9. Clip
10. Tube
11. Hose
12. Fender apron
13. Wheel speed sensor

84929086

Fig. 2 Identification of possible components used on a common 4-wheel, non-integral ABS system

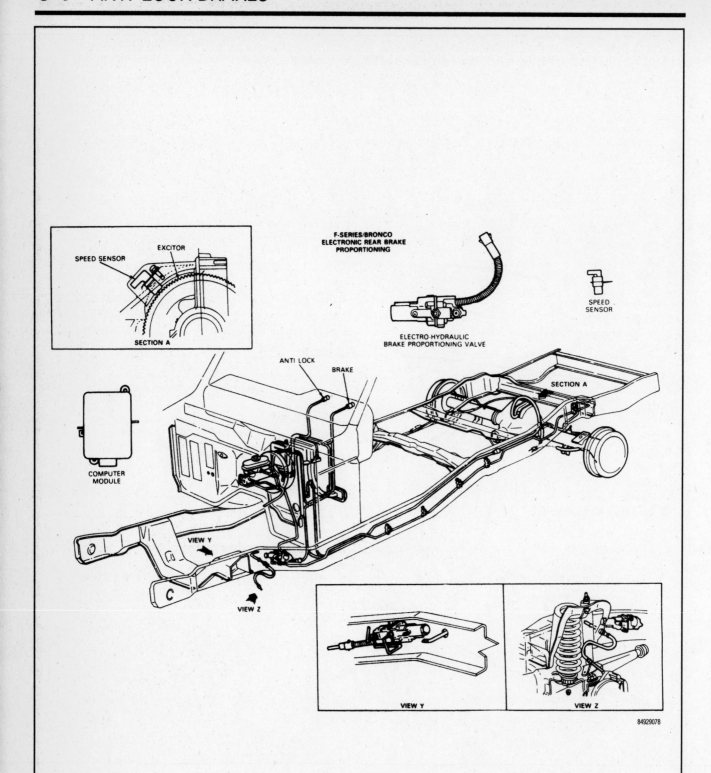

Fig. 3 Typical Rear wheel Anti-lock Brake System (RABS) component identification

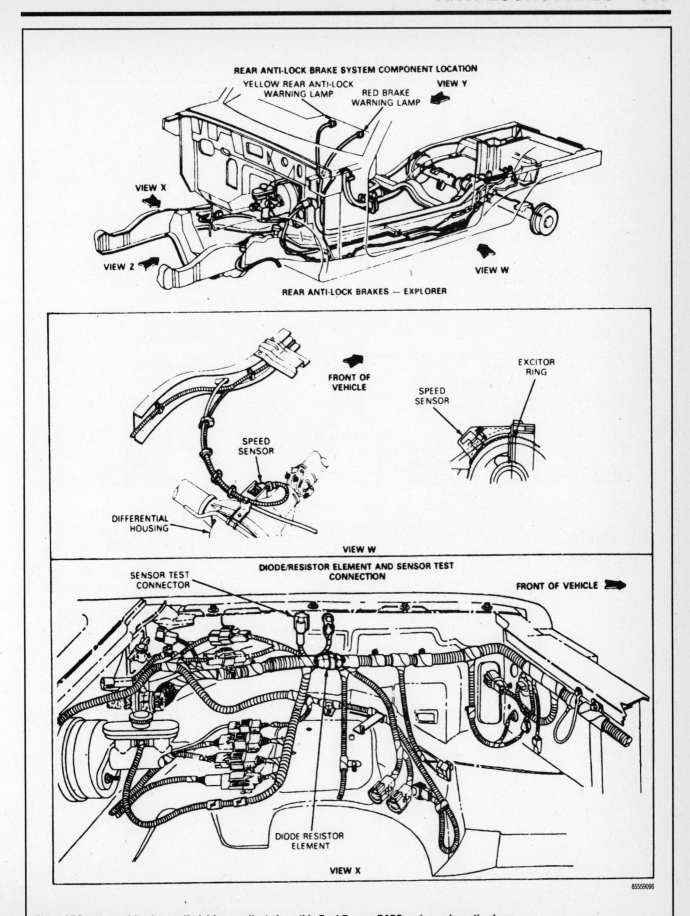

REAR ANTI-LOCK BRAKE SYSTEM COMPONENT LOCATION

YELLOW REAR ANTI-LOCK WARNING LAMP

RED BRAKE WARNING LAMP

VIEW Y

VIEW X

VIEW Z

VIEW W

REAR ANTI-LOCK BRAKES — EXPLORER

FRONT OF VEHICLE

SPEED SENSOR

EXCITOR RING

SPEED SENSOR

DIFFERENTIAL HOUSING

VIEW W

DIODE/RESISTOR ELEMENT AND SENSOR TEST CONNECTION

SENSOR TEST CONNECTOR

FRONT OF VEHICLE

DIODE RESISTOR ELEMENT

VIEW X

85559096

Fig. 4 ABS system wiring is usually fairly complicated, as this Ford Ranger RABS system schematic shows

The integral system incorporates the functions of master cylinder, booster and ABS controlling units into a single assembly, thus termed "integral."

On most vehicles, none of the ABS system components are serviceable and are repaired by replacement only. On integral systems, where components are part of one larger unit, they are not individually removable from the one unit; the entire unit must be replaced if any one part fails.

The many components of an ABS system will vary slightly by manufacturer. In general, however, they are typically the same from one vehicle to another. The following is a brief overview of system components:

Wheel Speed Sensors

A wheel speed sensor is a small electromagnetic device that is mounted at each controlled wheel. It is mounted near a toothed ring that rotates with the wheel. Magnetic induction occurs as each tooth passes the sensor, thereby sending a signal to the ABS computer. This signal tells the computer exactly what each wheel is doing under braking.

One exception to the sensor location occurs on some light trucks, especially those with Rear Anti-lock Brake System (RABS). On these trucks, the toothed ring is located in the differential, next to the ring gear. The sensor is usually screwed into, or bolted onto, the differential housing.

Hydraulic Assembly

In an integral ABS system, the hydraulic assembly is the central component of the system. This assembly combines the power booster, master cylinder, brake fluid reservoir, hydraulic accumulator and all of the controlling valves into one large unit. Generally, none of the individual parts of the hydraulic assembly (such as one of the control valves) is serviceable; the entire unit must be replaced.

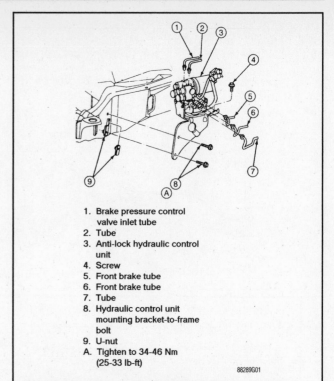

1. Brake pressure control valve inlet tube
2. Tube
3. Anti-lock hydraulic control unit
4. Screw
5. Front brake tube
6. Front brake tube
7. Tube
8. Hydraulic control unit mounting bracket-to-frame bolt
9. U-nut
A. Tighten to 34-46 Nm (25-33 lb-ft)

88289G01

Fig. 6 Exploded view of a typical RABS hydraulic assembly mounting

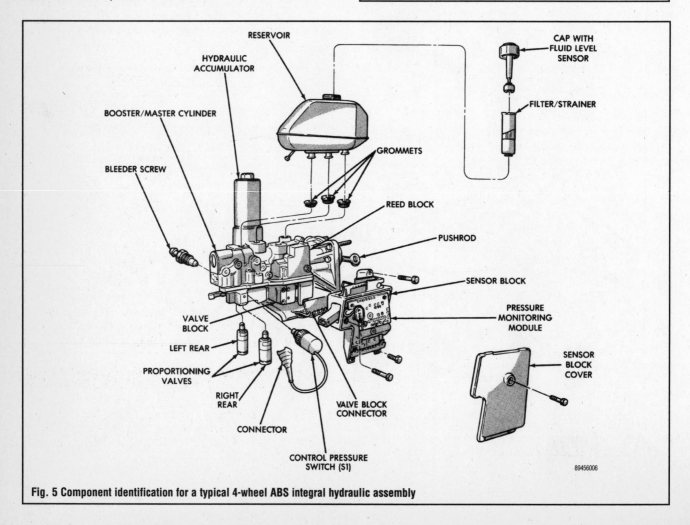

89456006

Fig. 5 Component identification for a typical 4-wheel ABS integral hydraulic assembly

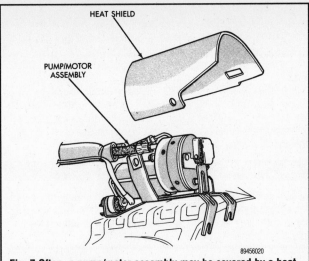

Fig. 7 Often, a pump/motor assembly may be covered by a heat shield (as shown)

BOOSTER/MASTER CYLINDER

Some systems use a hydraulic assembly equipped with a booster/master cylinder unit. If so equipped, boost is provided by an electro-hydraulic pump that pressurizes the fluid and supplies the pressurized fluid to the accumulator. The pump, itself, can be mounted anywhere in the engine compartment or surrounding area, depending on the vehicle. Hoses connect the pump to the accumulator. Booster pressure is controlled by a spool valve that opens in response to brake pedal pressure.

The master cylinder portion of the unit functions in much the same way as a conventional, non-ABS master cylinder. A split system is employed, preventing complete system loss in the event of a leak in either part. Most systems include internal switches that provide master cylinder piston travel information to the ABS computer. This lets the computer know if the master cylinder is functioning correctly.

HYDRAULIC ACCUMULATOR

This device is used to store brake fluid at high pressure, allowing pressurized fluid to be available during all braking actions. Most accumulators are designed as a sliding piston configuration, using precharged nitrogen gas. In most systems, the gas is pressurized at 500–800 psi (3450–5500 kPa). During system operation, the pressure can increase to 2000–2600 psi (13,800–18,000 kPa), which is one reason ABS system service can be dangerous and is best left to a trained professional technician.

VALVE BLOCK

This section contains the proportioning valves and replenishing valve. The proportioning valves control the brake pressure applied to each wheel and their positions are controlled by the computer. The replenishing valve controls pedal height by redirecting fluid from the booster circuit to the master cylinder.

SENSOR BLOCK

This unit can be called the central processing unit, because all electrical communication between the computer and system components goes through this block.

Modulator

In a non-integral system, this unit contains solenoid operated proportioning valves. The proportioning valves control the brake pressure applied to each wheel, and their positions are controlled by the computer.

Pressure Monitoring Module

In some systems, this module controls pump operation by grounding the pump relay coil in response to accumulator pressure. The unit contains two switches. If the switches don't read the same pressure in each circuit, or if total circuit pressure is low, the brake warning light will be turned ON as well as the ABS warning light. The ABS system will be disabled. Normal, non-ABS system function will be unaffected.

Fluid Level Sensor

This unit is located in the reservoir or cap and monitors the brake fluid level via a float and switch. When the fluid level is low, a signal is sent to the computer. The brake warning light will turn ON, and the ABS system will be disabled, turning on the ABS warning lamp. Normal, non-ABS system function will be unaffected.

Electronic Control Module

This is the ABS control computer. It has several different names, depending on the manufacturer: Electronic Control Unit (ECU), Anti-lock Brake Control Module (ABCM), Brake Control Module (BCM)—you get the idea. It is a small computer and can be located anywhere from the firewall to the trunk, again depending on the manufacturer. The computer monitors all functions of the ABS system.

The control computer's primary functions are to detect wheel lock-up, control the brake system in the anti-lock mode, monitor the system for proper operation and store fault codes for display during ABS diagnosis.

The computer continuously monitors the system. If any wheel indicates an impending lock-up, the computer controls the appropriate proportioning valve to modulate brake pressure in the system, thereby preventing lock-up.

If any other system fault is detected, the computer can disable the anti-lock feature of the brake system, to allow normal, non-ABS braking operation. When this happens, the brake warning lamp and/or ABS warning lamp will be illuminated.

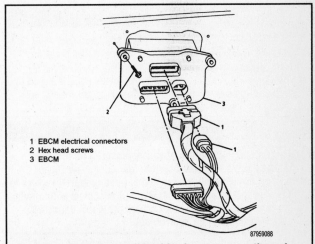

1 EBCM electrical connectors
2 Hex head screws
3 EBCM

Fig. 8 This shows the possible wiring harness connections of a common Electronic Brake Control Module (EBCM)—this particular EBCM was used on some General Motors through 1994

Precautions

• Do not use rubber hoses or other parts not specifically designed for the ABS system used by your vehicle. When using repair kits, replace all parts included in the kit. Partial or incorrect repair may lead to functional problems and require the replacement of components. NEVER fabricate your own replacement parts!

• Lubricate rubber parts with clean, fresh brake fluid to ease assembly. Do not use lubricated shop air to clean parts; damage to rubber components may result.

• Use only specified brake fluid from an unopened container.

• If any hydraulic component or line is removed or replaced, it may be necessary to bleed the entire system. This is always true when any upper end component (master cylinder, accumulator, control unit, etc.) is opened. It is also true when any lower end component (caliper or wheel cylinder) is opened and too much brake fluid has been lost; this does not happen often. If simply servicing a brake caliper, wheel cylinder, etc. and the line was adequately plugged after it was disconnected, the entire system will not need bleeding; only the component which was serviced. However, when in doubt, play it safe and bleed the entire system.

• A clean repair area is essential. Always clean the reservoir and cap thoroughly before removing the cap. The slightest amount of dirt in the fluid may plug an orifice and impair system function. Perform repairs after components have been thoroughly cleaned; use only denatured alcohol to clean components. Do not allow ABS components to come into contact with any substance containing mineral oil; this includes used shoprags.

• The anti-lock control unit is a microprocessor similar to other computer units in the vehicle. Ensure that the ignition switch is **OFF** before removing or installing controller wiring harnesses. Avoid static electricity discharge at or near the controller.

• If any arc welding is to be done on the vehicle, the control unit should be unplugged before welding operations begin.

SYSTEM SERVICE

Many ABS system component replacement procedures require special skills and training, as well as expensive special tools. This work is best left to a qualified professional. However, one component, the wheel speed sensor, is relatively easy to replace and requires no special tools or skills. It is, also, a component that operates in a harsh environment and often is damaged.

Wheel Speed Sensor

With 4-wheel ABS, each wheel has its own wheel speed sensor that sends a small AC signal to the control module. Correct ABS operation depends on accurate wheel speed signals. The vehicle's wheels and tires must all be the same size and type in order to generate accurate signals. If there is a variation between wheel and tire sizes, inaccurate wheel speed signals will be produced.

❉❉ CAUTION

It is very critical that the wheel speed sensor(s) be installed correctly to ensure continued system operation. The sensor cables must be installed, routed and clipped properly. Failure to install the sensor(s) properly could result in contact with moving parts or over-extension of sensor cables. This will cause ABS component failure and an open circuit.

REMOVAL & INSTALLATION

Front Wheel Speed Sensor

1. Disconnect the negative battery cable.
2. Loosen the lug nuts on the front wheel(s).
3. Apply the parking brake, block the rear wheels, then raise and safely support the front of the vehicle securely on jackstands.
4. Remove the front wheel(s) of the wheel speed sensor(s) requiring removal.
5. Remove the speed sensor cable from the routing bracket.
6. Remove any speed sensor wiring harness sealing grommet retainer/routing brackets.
7. Disconnect the speed sensor cable from the vehicle wiring harness.

ABS Depressurizing

Some ABS systems store the brake fluid at high pressures, which must be released before any service is attempted. Check the Chilton model-specific manual written for your vehicle if you aren't sure whether this applies to you.

On these systems, the hydraulic accumulator contains brake fluid and nitrogen gas at extremely high pressures. Certain other system components may also contain brake fluid at high pressure. It is mandatory that the system pressure is relieved before disconnecting any hoses, lines or fittings, otherwise personal injury may result.

❉❉ CAUTION

On ABS systems designed to store brake fluid at high pressures, it is necessary to depressurize the system before disconnecting any hoses, lines or fittings. Otherwise, personal injury may result.

On most vehicles, ABS pressure can be depleted simply by pumping the brake pedal 20–30 times with the ignition switch **OFF**.

On some systems, particularly some GM systems, pressure should be bled using a specific, expensive scan tool. For this reason, we recommend that when in doubt, all ABS system service be referred to a professional, qualified technician.

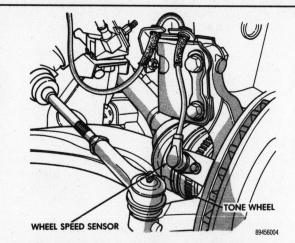

Fig. 9 The ABS wheel sensor is almost always positioned directly adjacent to the tone (toothed) wheel, which produces the fluctuating voltage signals in the sensor

➡ The sensor will be mounted on the knuckle, adapter or bracket near the toothed ring at the wheel.

8. Remove the speed sensor retaining bolt(s).
9. Remove the speed sensor.
10. If the speed sensor can't be removed due to corrosion, remove the brake caliper from the brake rotor and support it using a strong piece of wire. This will provide you with better access. On vehicles with knuckle-mounted sensors, remove the brake rotor from the vehicle and insert a pin punch through the hole on the front part of the steering knuckle for the sensor head locating pin. Tap the locating pin for the wheel speed sensor out of the steering knuckle.
11. Carefully inspect the toothed ring for broken or missing teeth, which can cause erratic sensor signals.

To install:
12. If equipped, install all sensor cable sealing grommets.
13. Install and tighten any routing bracket mounting bolts.

14. Install the speed sensor cable routing bracket. Be sure the sensor cable is routed correctly.

15. With knuckle-mounted sensors, apply a light coating of multi-purpose grease, or equivalent, to the locating pin of the speed sensor, then install the speed sensor head onto the steering knuckle.

16. Install the sensor head mounting bolt(s).

17. Reattach the wheel speed sensor wiring connector to the vehicle wiring harness.

18. Install the front wheel(s).

19. Lower the vehicle.

20. Reconnect the negative battery cable.

21. Test drive the vehicle to check for proper operation of the base and anti-lock brake systems.

Rear Wheel Speed Sensor

MULTIPLE REAR SENSOR SYSTEM—INDEPENDENT TYPE

1. Disconnect the negative battery cable.

2. Loosen the lug nuts on the rear wheels.

3. Block the front wheels, then raise and safely support the rear of the vehicle securely on jackstands.

4. Remove the applicable wheel(s).

5. Disengage the speed sensor cable electrical connector from the vehicle wiring harness.

6. Remove the rear wheel(s) of the wheel speed sensor(s) requiring removal.

7. Remove any speed sensor routing clips.

8. On vehicles with drum brakes, remove the speed sensor from the rear brake support plate. On vehicles with disc brakes, remove the sensor from the adapter bracket.

9. Carefully inspect the toothed ring for broken or missing teeth, which can cause erratic sensor signals.

To install:

10. Install the wheel speed sensor and tighten the bolt(s).

11. Install all speed sensor cable routing clips.

12. Install any speed sensor sealing grommets.

13. Install the wheel(s).

14. Lower the vehicle.

15. Reattach the sensor cable connector to the vehicle wiring harness.

16. Reconnect the negative battery cable.

17. Test drive the vehicle to check for proper operation of the base and anti-lock brake systems.

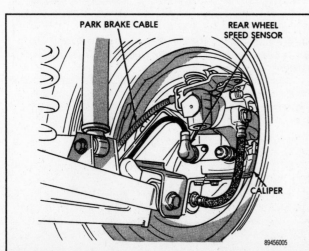

Fig. 10 Speed sensors used on rear wheels with disc brakes are usually secured either by a retaining bolt (as shown), or are directly threaded into the bracket

MULTIPLE REAR SENSOR SYSTEM—INTEGRAL SENSOR/HUB TYPE

Some vehicles have the sensors as an integral part of the hub/bearing assembly. With this type, the entire hub/bearing assembly must be replaced if the sensor fails. This system is most often found on GM vehicles.

1. Disconnect the negative battery cable.

2. Loosen the lug nuts on the rear wheel(s).

3. Block the front wheels, then raise and safely support the rear of the vehicle securely on jackstands.

4. Remove the applicable wheel(s).

5. Remove the brake drum.

6. Remove the bolts and nuts attaching the rear wheel bearing and speed sensor assembly.

7. Remove the wheel bearing and speed sensor assembly, then disengage the wiring harness connector from the speed sensor.

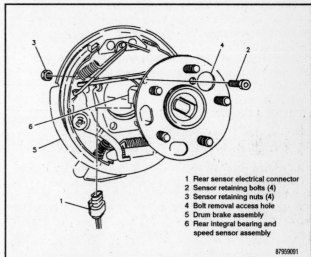

1 Rear sensor electrical connector
2 Sensor retaining bolts (4)
3 Sensor retaining nuts (4)
4 Bolt removal access hole
5 Drum brake assembly
6 Rear integral bearing and speed sensor assembly

Fig. 11 Some vehicles are equipped with one-piece speed sensor/wheel hub assemblies, like this GM unit

---

❄ **WARNING**

The brake assembly will be held in place by the brake pipe connection at this point. Use care not to bump or exert force on the brake assembly, or damage can occur to the brake pipe.

To install:

8. Reattach the wiring harness connector to the wheel speed sensor.

9. Install the wheel bearing and speed sensor assembly into place.

10. Install the mounting bolts and nuts.

11. Install the brake drum.

12. Install the wheel(s), then lower the vehicle.

13. Connect the negative battery cable.

14. Road test the vehicle and verify proper operation.

SINGLE REAR SENSOR SYSTEM

➡This procedure applies to models equipped with a single, differential mounted sensor.

1. Disconnect the negative battery cable.

2. If undervehicle clearance is needed for access to the sensor, block the front wheels, then raise and safely support the rear of the vehicle securely on jackstands.

3. Detach the sensor connector from the wiring harness.

4. Remove the sensor hold-down bolt or unscrew the sensor (depending on the individual sensor), then remove the sensor from the differential housing.

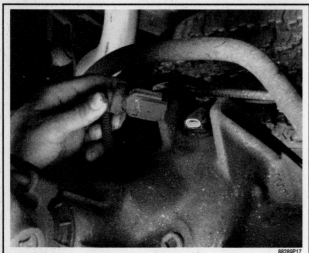

Fig. 12 To remove a common single rear speed sensor, first detach the wiring harness connector from it . . .

Fig. 14 Pull the sensor out of the differential housing—sure to install a new O-ring on the sensor before installing it

Fig. 13 . . . then loosen the RABS speed sensor hold-down bolt

To install:

5. Thoroughly clean the mounting surfaces. Make sure no dirt falls into the axle. Clean the magnetized sensor pole piece; metal particles can cause sensor problems. If equipped, install a new O-ring on the sensor.

6. If applicable, coat the new O-ring with clean engine oil.

7. Position the new sensor in the differential housing. It should slide into place easily. Correct installation will provide the proper sensor-to-ring gap.

8. Screw the sensor into place and tighten it securely, or insert the sensor and tighten the hold-down bolt.

9. Reattach the sensor connector to the wiring harness.

10. Connect the negative battery cable.

11. Test drive the vehicle to check for proper operation of the base and ABS systems.

ABS Trouble Codes

The on-board computer system receives input from sensors all over the vehicle. The sensors signal the operating condition of every controlled component from the engine on down to the wheels.

Part of this overall system is the brake system. When any fault or problem in the brake system is detected by a sensor, a signal is sent to the computer and recorded in its memory in the form of a trouble code. The trouble codes can be accessed, in most cases, through the use of an electronic device known as a scan tool. Each ABS equipped vehicle has a connector designed to receive the scan tools wiring harness plug(s).

Scan tool are relatively expensive devices. If you plan to use one on a regular basis to diagnose problems with your vehicle, they may be worth the price.

Vehicle computer systems vary from manufacturer-to-manufacturer and from model-to-model. For more information regarding the use of scan tools, see the Chilton manual written specifically for your vehicle.

10

BRAKE SPECIFICATIONS

BRAKE SPECIFICATIONS

The accompanying charts supply the most used brake specifications and torque values for most popular, modern vehicles. The charts were compiled from the most up-to-date information which was available at the time of this book's publication. If your vehicle is not listed, check the appropriate Chilton Manual for your vehicle.

PASSENGER CARS

Vehicle	Brake Shoe	Brake Drum		Brake Pad	Brake Rotor				Caliper			Wheel
	O.E. Minimum Lining Thickness	Diameter		O.E. Minimum Lining Thickness	Min. Thickness		Variation From Paral-lelism	Runout TIR	D E S I G N	Mounting Bolts Torque (ft. lbs.)	Bridge, Pin or Key Bolts Torque (ft. lbs)	Lugs or Nuts Torque (ft. lbs.)
Year / Make / Model		Standard Size	Machine To		Machine To	Discard At						
ACURA												
97-90 Integra: Front	—	—	—	.060	.750	—	.0006	.004	73	56④	24	80
Rear	—	—	—	.060	.310	—	.0006	.004	46	28	16	80
89-86 Integra: Front	—	—	—	.120	.670	—	.0006	.004	73	53	33	80
Rear	—	—	—	.063	.310	—	.0006	.006	46	28	17	80
95-93 Legend: Sedan Front	—	—	—	.060	.830	—	.0006	.004	73	80	36	80
Coupe Front	—	—	—	.060	1.02	—	.0006	.004	73	80	36	80
Rear	—	—	—	.060	.300	—	.0006	.004	73	28	17	80
92-91 Legend: Coupe & Sedan Front	—	—	—	.060	.830	—	.0006	.004	73	80	36	80
Rear	—	—	—	.060	.300	—	.0006	.006	73	28	17	80
90-86 Legend: Coupe & Sedan Front	—	—	—	.120①	.750	—	.0006	.004	73	56	24	80
Rear	—	—	—	.060	.310	—	.0006	.004③	46	28	20②	80
97 NSX: Front	—	—	—	.060	1.020	—	.0006	.004	95	80	36	80
Rear	—	—	—	.060	.830	—	.0006	.004	96	80	36	80
96-91 NSX: Front	—	—	—	.060	1.020	—	.0006	.004	95	80	36	80
Rear	—	—	—	.060	.750	—	.0006	.004	96	80	36	80
94-92 Vigor: Front	—	—	—	.060	.830	—	.0006	.004	73	80	36	80
Rear	—	—	—	.060	.310	—	.0006	.004	73	28	17	80
97 2.2 CL: Front	—	—	—	.060	—	.830	.0006	.004	73	—	54	80
Rear	—	—	—	.060	—	.310	.0006	.004	46	28	18	80
97 3.0 CL: Front	—	—	—	.060	—	.830	.0006	.004	73	—	54	80
Rear	—	—	—	.060	—	.310	.0006	.004	46	28	18	80
97-95 2.5 TL: Front	—	—	—	.060	—	.830	.0006	.004	73	80	36	80
Rear	—	—	—	.060	—	.300	.0006	.004	46	28	17	80
97-96 3.2 TL: Front	—	—	—	.060	—	.830	.0006	.004	73	80	36	80
Rear	—	—	—	.060	—	.300	.0006	.004	46	28	17	80
97-96 3.5 RL: Front	—	—	—	.060	—	.830	.0006	.004	73	80	36	80
Rear	—	—	—	.060	—	.300	.0006	.006	46	28	17	80

①Sedan shown; Coupe .060". ②1990-89 16 ft/lbs. ③1990-89 .006". ④1990-91 shown; 1992-96 use 80 ft/lbs.

AMERICAN MOTORS												
83-82 Concord, Spirit, SX-4:	.030	9.000	9.060	.030③	.815	.810	.0005	.003	1	85	30	75
83-82 Concord Wagon:	.030	10.000	10.060	.030③	.815	.810	.0005	.003	1	85	30	75
81 Concord, Spirit, SX-4:	.030	9.000	9.060	.030③	.815	.810	.0005	.003	1	80	15	75
81 Concord Wagon, Eagle Wagon:	.030	10.000	10.060	.030③	.815	.810	.0005	.003①	1	80	15	75
80-78 Concord, Eagle, AMX:	.030	10.000	10.060	.062	.815	.810	.0005	.003①	1	80	15	75
88-82 Eagle:	.030	10.000	10.060	.030③	.815	.810	.0005	.004	1	100	30	75
80-78 Gremlin, Spirit: L4 eng.	.030	9.000	9.060	.062	.815	.810	.0005	.003	1	80	15	75
L6 eng.	.030	10.000	10.060	.062	.815	.810	.0005	.003①	1	80	15	75
77 Gremlin, Hornet:	.030	10.000	10.060	.062	.815	.810	.0005	.003	1	80-90	15-18	75-90
76-75 Gremlin, Hornet: L6 eng.	.030	9.000	9.060	.062	1.130	1.120	.0005	.003	1	80	15	75
V8 eng.	.030	10.000	10.060	.062	1.130	1.120	.0005	.003	1	80	15	75
74-72 Gremlin, Hornet, Javelin:												
L6 eng. w/drum brakes	.030	9.000	9.060	—	—	—	—	—	—	—	—	75
L6 eng. w/disc brakes	.030	9.000	9.060	.062	—	.940	.0005	.005	2	80	—	75
L6 eng. w/disc brakes (72)	.030	10.000	10.060	.062	—	.940	.0005	.005	2	80	—	75
V8 eng. w/drum brakes	.030	10.000	10.060	—	—	—	—	—	—	—	—	75
V8 eng. w/disc brakes	.030	10.000	10.060	.062	—	.940	.0005	.005	2	80	—	75
78 Matador:	.030	10.000	10.060	.062	—	1.120	.0005	.003	1	80	15	75
77 Matador:	.030	10.000	10.060	.062	—	1.120	.0005	.003	1	80-90	15-18	75-90
76-75 Matador:	.030	10.000	10.060	.062	1.130	1.120	.0005	.003	1	80	15	75
74-72 Matador, Ambassador:	.030	10.000	10.060	.062	—	.940	.0005	.005	2	80	—	75
80-78 Pacer:	.030	10.000	10.060	.062	.815	.810	.0005	.003①	1	80	15	75
77 Pacer:	.030	10.000	10.060	.062	.815	.810	.0005	.003	1	80-90	15-18	75-90
76-75 Pacer: Front w/drum brakes	.030	10.000	10.060	—	—	—	—	—	—	—	—	60-90
Rear w/drum brakes	.030	9.000	9.060	—	—	—	—	—	—	—	—	75
w/disc brakes	.030	9.000	9.060	.062	—	1.120	.0005	.003	1	80	15	60-90

①Eagle .004". ②1972 12 in/lbs. ③.030" over rivet head; if bonded lining use .062".

89450C00

PASSENGER CARS

Year / Make / Model	Brake Shoe O.E. Minimum Lining Thickness	Brake Drum Diameter Standard Size	Brake Drum Diameter Machine To	Brake Pad O.E. Minimum Lining Thickness	Brake Rotor Min. Thickness Machine To	Brake Rotor Min. Thickness Discard At	Brake Rotor variation From Parallelism	Brake Rotor Runout TIR	Caliper DESIGN	Caliper Mounting Bolts Torque (ft. lbs.)	Caliper Bridge, Pin or Key Bolts Torque (ft. lbs)	Wheel Lugs or Nuts Torque (ft. lbs.)
AUDI												
97-92 100, 100 Quattro, A6, A6 Quattro: Front	—	—	—	.079	—	.906	—	—	51	92	18	81
Rear	—	—	—	.079	—	.315	—	—	77	48	26	81
91-89 100: Front	—	—	—	.078	.807	.787	.0008	.002	51⑦	52	18⑧	81
Rear	—	—	—	.276⑥	.335	.315	.0008	.002	77	48	25	81
91-89 100 Quattro: Front	—	—	—	.078	.945	.905	.0008	.001	76	92	26	81
Rear	—	—	—	.276⑥	.335	.315	.0008	.002	77	50	25	81
91-89 200: Front	—	—	—	.078	.945	.905	.0008	.001	76	92	26	81
Rear	—	—	—	.276⑥	.335	.315	.0008	.002	77	48	25	81
91-89 200 Quattro:												
Front w/single piston	—	—	—	.078	.945	.905	.0008	.001	51	92	—	81
Front w/dual piston	—	—	—	.078	.945	.905	.0008	.001	76	92	26	81
Rear	—	—	—	.276⑥	.335	.315	.0008	.002	77	50	25	81
87-85 4000, Coupe GT:	.097	—	7.894	.079	.728	.709	.0003	.001	31	52	25	80
84-80 4000, Coupe:	.097	—	7.894	.079	.413	.394	—	.002	37	50④	25	65
87-84 4000 Quattro: Front	—	—	—	.079	.728	.709	.0003	.001	61	52	25	80
Rear	—	—	—	.079	.335	.315	.0008	.002	33	47	25	80
88-81 5000:	.098	9.055	9.075	.079	.807	.787	.0008	.002	37	52③	18	80
80-78 5000:	.098	9.055	9.094	.078	.807	.787	.0008	.004	39	83	—	80
88-80 5000 Turbo, 5000 Turbo Quattro, 5000 Quattro:												
Front w/single piston	—	—	—	.079	.807	.787	.0008	.002	31⑤	52③	25	80
w/dual piston	—	—	—	.079	.984	.905	.0008	.001	76	92	26	80
Rear w/Girling	—	—	—	.079	.335	.315	.0008	.002	33	47	25	80
w/Teves	—	—	—	.276⑥	.335	.315	.0004	.001	77	50	18	80
95-88 80, 90: Front	—	—	—	.078	.807	.787	.0008	.002	51⑦	92	18⑧	81
Rear	—	—	—	.078	.334	.315	.0008	.002	77	48	25	81
95-88 80 Quattro, 90 Quattro: Front	—	—	—	.078	.807	.787	.0008	.002	51⑦	92	18⑧	81
Rear	—	—	—	.078	.334	.315	.0008	.002	33	48	18	81
79-78 Fox:	.097	7.870	7.900	.078	.413	.393	—	.002	37	43	25	65
77-73 Fox:	.097	7.870	7.900	.078	.413	.393	—	.004	39	43	—	65
91-90 Quattro Coupe: Front	—	—	—	.078	.945	.905	.0008	.001	76	92	26	81
Rear	—	—	—	.078	.335	.315	.0008	.002	33	48	25	81
85-83 Quattro Turbo Coupe: Front	—	—	—	.079	.807	.787	.0008	.002	31②	83	25	80
Rear	—	—	—	.079	.335	.315	.0008	.002	33	47	25	80
97-96 A4: Front	—	—	—	.080	—	.906	—	—	51⑪	92	18⑨	89
Rear	—	—	—	.080	—	.315	—	—	77	70⑩	22	89
95-92 S4, S6: Front	—	—	—	.079	—	.906	—	—	51	184	18	81
Rear	—	—	—	.079	—	.709	—	—	77	48	26	81
94-90 V8 Quattro: Front	—	—	—	.080	.945	.905	.0008	.001	51	92	—	81
Rear	—	—	—	.080	.728	.710	.0003	.001	77	48	26	81

①Seat brg. while turning wheel. Back off nut until thrust washer can be moved slightly by screwdriver w/finger pressure. Lock. (Quattro models non adjustable)   ②1985 use ill. 61.
③1988-84 shown; 1983-80 83 ft/lbs.   ④w/standard bolt, 1980-81 & early 1982 36 ft/lbs.   ⑤1988-85 use ill. 61.   ⑥Measurement of lining & metal.   ⑦Teves shown; Girling use ill. 61.
⑧Teves shown; Girling 25 ft/lbs.   ⑨Teves ATE caliper shown. With Lucas caliper use 22 ft/lbs.   ⑩FWD (ribbed bolt) shown. AWD (socket-head cap screw) 44 ft/lbs.
⑪Teves ATE shown. With Lucas use #61.

Year / Make / Model	Brake Shoe O.E. Minimum Lining Thickness	Brake Drum Diameter Standard Size	Brake Drum Diameter Machine To	Brake Pad O.E. Minimum Lining Thickness	Brake Rotor Min. Thickness Machine To	Brake Rotor Min. Thickness Discard At	Brake Rotor variation From Parallelism	Brake Rotor Runout TIR	Caliper DESIGN	Caliper Mounting Bolts Torque (ft. lbs.)	Caliper Bridge, Pin or Key Bolts Torque (ft. lbs)	Wheel Lugs or Nuts Torque (ft. lbs.)
BMW												
76-72 2002:	.120	9.060	9.100	.080	.354	—	.0008	.008	16	58-69	16-19	59-65
74-72 2002tii:	.120	9.060	9.100	.080	.459	—	.0008	.008	16	58-69	33-40	59-65
97 318i, 318is, 328i, 328is, Z3:												
w/solid rotor	—	—	—	.118	.409	—	.00078	—	—	—	—	—
w/vented rotor	—	—	—	.118	.803	—	.00078	—	—	—	—	—
w/solid rear disc brakes	—	—	—	.118	.331	—	.00078	—	—	—	—	—
96-93 318i: Front	—	—	—	.079	.409	.394	.0008	.008	6	63-79	22-25	65-79
Rear	—	—	—	.079	.331	.315	.0008	.008	6	43-48	22-25	65-79
92-91 318i: Front	—	—	—	.079	.437	.421	.0008	.008	6	63-79	22-25	65-79
Rear	—	—	—	.079	.331	.315	.0008	.008	6	43-48	22-25	65-79

89450C01

PASSENGER CARS

Vehicle Year / Make / Model	Brake Shoe O.E. Minimum Lining Thickness	Brake Drum Diameter Standard Size	Brake Drum Diameter Machine To	Brake Pad O.E. Minimum Lining Thickness	Brake Rotor Min. Thickness Machine To	Brake Rotor Min. Thickness Discard At	Brake Rotor Variation From Parallelism	Brake Rotor Runout TIR	Design	Caliper Mounting Bolts Torque (ft. lbs.)	Caliper Bridge, Pin or Key Bolts Torque (ft. lbs)	Wheel Lugs or Nuts Torque (ft. lbs.)
BMW												
91-88 318is, 325i, 325is, 325ix: Front	—	—	—	.079	.803	.787	.0008	.008	6	63-79	22-25	65-79
Rear	—	—	—	.079	.331	.315	.0008	.008	6	43-48	22-25	65-79
85-84 318i	.060	—	9.035	.080	.437	.421	.0008	.008	6	63-79	22-25	65-79
83-82 320i: w/ATE	.118	9.842	9.882	.118	.803	.787	.0008	.008	17	58-69	—	59-65
w/Girling Caliper	.118	9.842	9.882	.118	.480	.461	.0008	.008	14	58-69	—	59-65
81-77 320i	.118	9.842	9.882	.118	.803	.787	.0008	.008	17	58-69	—	59-65
95-92 325i, 325is: Front	—	—	—	.079	.803	—	.0008	.008	6	63-79	22-25	65-79
Rear	—	—	—	.079	.331	.315	.0008	.008	6	43-48	22-25	65-79
88-84 325e, 325es: Front	—	—	—	.080	.803	.787	.0008	.008	6	63-79	22-25	65-79
Rear	—	—	—	.080	.331	.315	.0008	.008	6	43-48	22-25	65-79
86-85 524td: Front	—	—	—	.079	.409	.394	.0008	.008	6	80-89	22-25	65-79
Rear	—	—	—	.079	.331	.315	.0008	.008	6	43-48	22-25	65-79
97 528i: Front	—	—	—	.118	.803	—	.00078	—	—	—	—	—
Rear	—	—	—	.118	.331	—	.00078	—	—	—	—	—
95-83 525i, 528e, 533i, 535i, 535is: Front	—	—	—	.080	.803	.787	.0008	.008	6	80-89	22-25	65-79
Rear	—	—	—	.080	.331	.315	.0008	.008	6	43-48	22-25	65-79
82 528e: Front	—	—	—	.138	.803	—	.0008	.008	6	89	14-18	72-80
Rear	—	—	—	.138	.331	—	.0008	.008	6	43-48	14-18	72-80
81-79 528i: Front	—	—	—	.080	.846	.827	.0008	.008	16	—	—	59-65
Rear	—	—	—	.080	.354	.335	.0008	.008	17	—	—	59-65
78-77 530i: Front	—	—	—	.080	.480	.461	.0008	.008	16	58-69	33-40	59-65
Rear	—	—	—	.080	.354	.335	.0008	.008	17	44-48	16-19	59-65
97 540i: Front	—	—	—	.118	.803	—	.00078	—	—	—	—	—
Rear	—	—	—	.118	.724	—	.00078	—	—	—	—	—
79-77 630CSi: Front	—	—	—	.080	.846	.827	.0008	.008	16	58-69	—	59-65
Rear	—	—	—	.080	.728	.709	.0008	.008	17	44-48	—	59-65
89-83 633CSi, 635CSi: Front	—	—	—	.079	.921	.906	.0008	.008	6	80-89	22-25	65-79
Rear	—	—	—	.079	.331	.315	.0008	.008	6	43-48	22-25	65-79
82-79 633CSi: Front	—	—	—	.080	.846	.827	.0008	.008	16	—	—	59-65
Rear	—	—	—	.080	.728	.709	.0008	.008	17	—	—	59-65
92-83 733i, 735i, 735iL, L7: Front	—	—	—	.080	1.039	1.024	.0008	.008	16	80-89	22-25	65-79
Rear	—	—	—	.080	.409	.394	.0008	.008	6	43-48	22-25	65-79
82-78 733i: Front	—	—	—	.080	.846	.827	.0008	.006	16	59-70	—	60-66
Rear	—	—	—	.080	.374	.354	.0008	.006	17	44-49	—	60-66
97 740i, 740iL: Front	—	—	—	.118	1.118	—	.00078	—	—	—	—	—
Rear	—	—	—	.118	.409	—	.00078	—	—	—	—	—
97 750iL: Front	—	—	—	.118	1.197	—	.00078	—	—	—	—	—
Rear	—	—	—	.118	.724	—	.00078	—	—	—	—	—
97 840Ci, 850Ci: Front	—	—	—	.118	1.118	—	.00078	—	—	—	—	—
Rear	—	—	—	.118	.409	—	.00078	—	—	—	—	—
96-88 740i, 740iL, 750iL, 850i, 850Ci: Front	—	—	—	.079	1.118	1.102	.0008	.008	6	80-89	22-25	65-79
Rear	—	—	—	.079	.724	.709	.0008	.008	6	43-48	22-25	65-79
97 M3: Front	—	—	—	.118	1.118	—	.00078	—	—	—	—	—
Rear	—	—	—	.118	.724	—	.00078	—	—	—	—	—
91-90 M3: Front	—	—	—	.079	.921	.906	.0008	.008	6	63-79	22-25	65-79
Rear	—	—	—	.079	.331	.315	.0008	.008	6	43-48	22-25	65-79
89-88 M3: Front	—	—	—	.079	.921	.906	.0008	.008	6	63-79	22-25	65-79
Rear	—	—	—	.079	.409	.394	.0008	.008	6	43-48	22-25	65-79
87 M3: Front	—	—	—	.079	.921	.906	.0008	.008	6	63-79	22-25	65-79
Rear	—	—	—	.079	.409	.394	.0008	.008	6	43-48	22-25	65-79
93-90 M5: Front	—	—	—	.079	①	1.039	.0008	.008	6	80-89	22-25	65-79
Rear	—	—	—	.079	.724	.709	.0008	.008	6	43-48	22-25	65-79
89-87 M5: Front	—	—	—	.079	1.118	1.102	.0008	.008	6	80-89	22-25	65-79
Rear	—	—	—	.079	.331	.315	.0008	.008	6	43-48	22-25	65-79
89-87 M6: Front	—	—	—	.079	1.118	1.102	.0008	.008	6	80-89	22-25	65-79
Rear	—	—	—	.079	.331	.315	.0008	.008	6	43-48	22-25	65-79

①Do not machine. ②1992-87 Not Adjustable. ③Keep nut stationary and tighten bearing cover two full turns. ④Loosen castle nut and retighten a maximum of 24 ft/lbs.

89450C02

PASSENGER CARS

Year / Make / Model	Brake Shoe O.E. Minimum Lining Thickness	Brake Drum Diameter Standard Size	Brake Drum Diameter Machine To	Brake Pad O.E. Minimum Lining Thickness	Brake Rotor Min. Thickness Machine To	Brake Rotor Min. Thickness Discard At	Brake Rotor Variation From Parallelism	Brake Rotor Runout TIR	DESIGN	Caliper Mounting Bolts Torque (ft. lbs.)	Caliper Bridge, Pin or Key Bolts Torque (ft. lbs)	Wheel Lugs or Nuts Torque (ft. lbs.)
BUICK												
97 Century: exc. rear disc brakes	④	8.863	8.880	.040	1.250	1.210	—	.003	83	148	80	100
w/ rear disc brakes	—	—	—	.060	.410	.350	—	.003	111	81	20	100
96-95 Century:	③	8.863	8.880	.030	.972	.957	.0005	.002	40	38	—	100
94-88 Century: w/H.D.	③	8.863	8.880	.030	.972	.957	.0005	.002	40	38	—	100
exc. H.D.	③	8.863	8.880	.030	.830	.815	.0005	.002	40	38	—	100
87-86 Century: w/H.D.	③	8.863	8.877	.030	.972	.957	.0005	.004	40	38	—	100
exc. H.D.	③	8.863	8.877	.030	.830	.815	.0005	.004	40	38	—	100
85 Century: w/H.D.	③	8.863	8.880	.030	.972	.957	.0005	.004	40	38	—	100
exc. H.D.	③	8.863	8.880	.030	.830	.815	.0005	.004	40	38	—	100
84 Century: w/H.D.	③	8.863	8.883	.030	.972	.957	.0005	.004	40	28	—	100
exc. H.D.	③	8.863	8.883	.030	.830	.815	.0005	.004	40	28	—	100
83-82 Century:	③	7.879	7.899	.030	.830	.815	.0005	.002	40	28	—	100
81-79 Century, Regal, LeSabre:	③	9.500	9.560	.030	.980	.965	.0005	.004	4	—	35	80⑤
78-77 Century, Regal, LeSabre:	③	9.500	9.560	.030	.980	.965	.0005	.004	4	—	35	80④
75 Century, Regal:	③	9.500	9.560	.030	.980	.965	.0005	.004	4	—	35	70
74-73 Century, Regal:	③	9.500	9.560	.030	.980	.965	.0005	.004	4	—	35	65-70
90-83 Electra, Estate Wagon: (RWD)	③	11.000	11.060	.030	.980	.965	.0005	.004	4	—	28②	100
82-79 Electra, Estate Wagon:	③	11.000	11.060	.030	.980	.965	.0005	.004	4	—	35	100
78-77 Electra, Estate Wagon, Riviera:	③	11.000	11.060	.030	.980	.965	.0005	.004	4	—	35	80④
76-75 Electra, Custom, LeSabre, Estate Wagon, Riviera:	③	12.000	12.060	.030	1.230	1.215	.0005	.005	4	—	30-40	90
74-72 Electra, Custom, LeSabre, Centurion, Riviera, Wildcat:	③	11.000	11.060	.030	1.230	1.215	.0005	.005	4	—	30-40	75
74-73 Estate Wagon:	③	12.000	12.060	.030	1.230	1.215	.0005	.005	4	—	30-40	75
97 LeSabre:	.030	8.863	8.880	.030	1.224	1.209	.0005	.002	50	38	—	100
96-92 LeSabre: (FWD)	.030	8.860	8.880	.030	1.224	1.209	.0005	.003	50	38	—	100
91 LeSabre: (FWD)	③	8.860	8.880	.030	.972	.957	.0005	.004	62	38	—	100
90-83 LeSabre, Electra: (FWD)	③	8.858	8.880	.030	.972	.957	.0005	.002⑥	4①	—	28②	100
97 Park Avenue: Front	—	—	—	.030⑪	1.224	1.209	.0005	.003	90	137	63	100
Rear	—	—	—	.030⑪	.423	.374	.0005	.003	73	137	38	100
96-92 Park Avenue:	.030	8.860	8.880	.030	1.224	1.209	.0005	.003	50	38	—	100
91 Park Avenue:	③	8.860	8.880	.030	—	1.200	.0005	.004	62	38	—	100
97 Regal: exc. rear disc brakes	④	8.863	8.880	.040	1.250	1.210	—	.003	83	148	80	100
w/rear disc brakes	—	—	—	.060	.410	.350	—	.003	111	81	20	100
96 Regal: Front	—	—	—	.030	.972	.956	.0005	.003	83	148	80	100
Rear	—	—	—	.030	.385	.370	.0005	.003	111	81	20	100
95-94 Regal: Front	—	—	—	.030	.987⑪	.972⑪	.0005	.003	83	148	80	100
Rear	—	—	—	.030	.385	.370	.0005	.003	111	—	20	100
93-92 Regal: Front	—	—	—	.030	.987	.972	.0005	.003	83	148	80	100⑧
Rear	—	—	—	.030	.444	.429	.0005	.003	84	92	—	100⑧
91-88 Regal: (FWD) Front	—	—	—	.030	.984	.972	.0005	.003⑨	83	79	—	100⑧
Rear	—	—	—	.030	.441	.429	.0005	.003⑨	84	92	—	100⑧
87-83 Regal, LeSabre: (RWD)	③	9.500	9.560	.030	.980	.965	.0005	.004	4	—	28②	80⑤
82 Regal, LeSabre:	③	9.500	9.560	.030	.980	.965	.0005	.004	4	—	35	80⑤
97-95 Riviera: Front	—	—	—	.030	1.224	1.209	.0005	.003	90	38	—	100
Rear	—	—	—	.030	.423	.374	.0005	.003	73	—	20	100
93-92 Riviera: Front	—	—	—	.030	1.250	1.209	.0005	.002	40	38	—	100
Rear	—	—	—	.030	.423	.374	.0005	.002	73	81	20	100
91-86 Riviera, Reatta: Front	—	—	—	.030	.971	.956	.0005	.004	71	83	63	100
Rear	—	—	—	.030	.444	.429	.0005	.003	72	83	63	100

①1990-85 use ill. 62. ②1990-85 38 ft/lbs. ③.030" over rivet head; if bonded lining use .062". ④w/½" stud 100 ft/lbs. ⑤w/Aluminum wheels LeSabre 90 ft/lbs., Regal 100 ft/lbs. ⑥1990-84 .004". ⑦1993 shown, 1992-91 .004". ⑧Exc. 1993-90: 103 ft/lbs. ⑨1993 shown, 1992-88 .004" ⑩Backoff to "just loose". Handtighten. Loosen to next slot in nut to fit cotter pin. ⑪For late 1995 vehicles, see 1996 front rotor specifications. Refer to discard specification on rotor if needed.

89450C03

PASSENGER CARS

Vehicle Year / Make / Model	Brake Shoe O.E. Minimum Lining Thickness	Brake Drum Diameter Standard Size	Machine To	Brake Pad O.E. Minimum Lining Thickness	Brake Rotor Min. Thickness Machine To	Discard At	Variation From Parallelism	Runout TIR	Caliper DESIGN	Mounting Bolts Torque (ft. lbs.)	Bridge, Pin or Key Bolts Torque (ft. lbs)	Wheel Lugs or Nuts Torque (ft. lbs.)
BUICK												
85-83 Riviera: exc. rear disc brakes	③	9.500	9.560	.030	.980	.965	.0005	.004	4	—	28②	100
w/rear disc brakes	—	—	—	.030	.980	.965	.0005	.004	41	32	30	100
82-79 Riviera: exc. rear disc brakes	③	9.500	9.560	.030	.980	.965	.0005	.004	4	—	35	100
w/rear disc brakes	—	—	—	.030	.980	.965	.0005	.004	41	32	30	100
96-94 Roadmaster:	.030	11.000	11.060	.030	.980	.965	.0005	.004	4	—	38	100
w/rear disc brakes	—	—	—	.030	.735	.728	.0005	.004	95	74	23	100
93-91 Roadmaster:	.030	11.000	11.060	.030	.980	.965	.0005	.003⑦	71	38	—	100
89-82 Skyhawk: vented rotor (89-82)	③	7.880	7.899	.030③	.830	.815	.0005	.002⑥	40①	—	28②	100
solid rotor (82)	③	7.880	7.899	.030③	.444	.429	.0005	.002	40	—	28	100
80-76 Skyhawk:	③	9.500	9.560	.030	.830	.815	.0005	.005	15	—	—	80
75 Skyhawk:	③	9.000	9.060	.030	.455	.440	.0005	.005	15	—	35	70
97-93 Skylark:	③	7.874	7.899	.030	.751	.736	.0005	.003	62	38	—	100
92-91 Skylark:	③	7.879	7.899	.030	.751	.736	.0005	.003	62	38	—	100
90-80 Skylark, Regal: (FWD)	③	7.880	7.899	.030	.830	.815	.0005	.002⑥	40①	—	28②	100
79-77 Skylark:	③	9.500	9.560	.030	.980	.965	.0005	.004	4	—	35	80
76-75 Skylark, Apollo:	③	9.500	9.560	.030	.980	.965	.0005	.004	4	—	35	70
72 Skylark, Gran Sport, GS, Sports Wagon:	③	9.500	9.560	.030	.980	.965	.0005	.004	4	—	35	65-70④

①1990-85 use ill. 62.　②1990-85 38 ft/lbs.　③.030" over rivet head; if bonded lining use .062".　④w/½" stud 100 ft/lbs.　⑤w/Aluminum wheels LeSabre 90 ft/lbs., Regal 100 ft/lbs.
⑥1990-84 .004".　⑦1993 shown, 1992-91 .004".　⑧Exc. 1993-90: 103 ft/lbs.　⑨1993 shown, 1992-88 .004"　⑩Backoff to "just loose". Handtighten. Loosen to next slot in nut to fit cotter pin.　⑪For late 1995 vehicles, see 1996 front rotor specifications. Refer to discard specification on rotor if needed.

Vehicle Year / Make / Model	Brake Shoe O.E. Minimum Lining Thickness	Brake Drum Diameter Standard Size	Machine To	Brake Pad O.E. Minimum Lining Thickness	Brake Rotor Min. Thickness Machine To	Discard At	Variation From Parallelism	Runout TIR	Caliper DESIGN	Mounting Bolts Torque (ft. lbs.)	Bridge, Pin or Key Bolts Torque (ft. lbs)	Wheel Lugs or Nuts Torque (ft. lbs.)
CADILLAC												
93 Allante: Front	—	—	—	.030	1.224	1.209	.0005	.002	40	77	—	100
Rear	—	—	—	.030	.423	.374	.0005	.002	72	81	20	100
92-87 Allante: Front	—	—	—	.030	.971	.956	.0005	.004	71	83	63	100
Rear	—	—	—	.030	.444	.429	.0005	.003	72	83	63	100
97 Catera: Front	—	—	—	.030	1.043	.984	.0005	.004	58	⑦	22	80
Rear	—	—	—	.030	.433	.393	.0005	.004	—	59	—	80
96-93 Fleetwood Brougham: (RWD)	①	11.000	11.060	.030	.980	.965	.0005	.004	4	—	38	100
92-82 Brougham, Fleetwood, Deville: (RWD)	①	11.000	11.060	.030	.972	.957	.0005	.004	4	—	28④	100
81-79 Brougham, Fleetwood, Deville, Seville: (RWD)	①	11.000	11.060	.062	.980	.965	.0005	.004	4	—	30	100
w/rear disc brakes (79)	—	—	—	.062	.980	.965	.0005	.004	41	34	30	100
78-77 Brougham, Seville: Front	—	—	—	.062	.980	.965	.0005	.005	4	—	30	100
Rear	—	—	—	.062	.910	.905	.0005	.003	41	35	30	100
78-77 DeVille:	①	11.000	11.060	.062	.980	.965	.0005	.005	4	—	30	100
76 Seville:	①	11.000	11.060	.062	.980	.965	.0005	.005	4	—	30	80
76-74 Calais, Deville, Brougham, Fleetwood 75, Commercial Ch.:	①	12.000	12.060	.062	1.220	1.215	.0005	.005	4	U60-L80	30-40	100②
73-72 Calais, Deville, Fleetwood 60, Fleetwood 75, Commercial Ch.:	①	12.000	12.060	.062	1.220	1.215	.0007	.005	4	U60-L80	30	130
88-82 Cimarron:	①	7.880	7.899	.030	.830	.815	.0005	.002③	40⑤	—	28④	100
97 Commercial Chassis: (FWD)												
Front	—	—	—	.030	1.224	1.209	.0005	.002	67	137	63	100
Rear	—	—	—	.030	.389	.374	.0005	.002	73	81	20	100
96-94 Commercial Chassis: (FWD)												
Front	—	—	—	.030	1.224	1.209	.0005	.002	90	—	38	100
Rear	—	—	—	.030	.389	.374	.0005	.002	73	81	20	100
93-91 Commercial Chassis: (FWD)	①	8.860	8.880	.030	1.224	1.209	.0005	.004	62	—	38	100
90-86 Commercial Chassis: (FWD)	①	7.880	7.899	.030⑥	.972	.965	.0005	.004	62	—	38	100

①.030" over rivet head; if bonded lining use .062".　②1975-74 130 ft/lbs.　④1992-85 38 ft/lbs.　⑥Inner Pad shown; outer .062" (thickness over steel)　⑦70 ft/lbs. plus 37 degrees.

89450C04

PASSENGER CARS

Year / Make / Model	Brake Shoe O.E. Minimum Lining Thickness	Brake Drum Diameter Standard Size	Brake Drum Machine To	Brake Pad O.E. Minimum Lining Thickness	Brake Rotor Min. Thickness Machine To	Brake Rotor Discard At	Brake Rotor Variation From Parallelism	Brake Rotor Runout TIR	Caliper DESIGN	Caliper Mounting Bolts Torque (ft. lbs.)	Caliper Bridge, Pin or Key Bolts Torque (ft lbs)	Wheel Lugs or Nuts Torque (ft. lbs.)
CADILLAC												
97 Eldorado, Seville: Front	—	—	—	.030	1.224	1.209	.0005	.002	67	137	63	100
Rear	—	—	—	.030	.389	.374	.0005	.002	73	81	20	100
96-92 Eldorado, Seville: Front	—	—	—	.030	1.224	1.209	.0005	.002	90	38	—	100
Rear	—	—	—	.030	.389	.374	.0005	.002	73	81	20	100
91-86 Eldorado, Seville: Front	—	—	—	.030	.971	.956	.0005	.004	71	83	63	100
Rear	—	—	—	.030	.444	.429	.0005	.003	72	83	63	100
85-82 Eldorado, Seville: Front	—	—	—	.030	.980	.965	.0005	.004	4	—	28④	100
Rear	—	—	—	.030	.980	.965	.0005	.004	41	35	38	100
81-79 Eldorado, Seville: Front	—	—	—	.062	.980	.965	.0005	.004	4	—	30	100
Rear	—	—	—	.062	.980	.965	.0005	.004	41	35	30	100
78-77 Eldorado: Front	—	—	—	.062	—	1.170	.0005	.008	4	—	30	130
Rear	—	—	—	.062	—	1.170	.0005	.008	41	35	30	130
76 Eldorado: Front	—	—	—	.062	1.205	1.190	.0005	.008	4	—	30	130
Rear	—	—	—	.062	1.205	1.190	.0005	.008	41	35	30	130
75-72 Eldorado:	①	11.000	11.060	.062	1.205	1.190	.0005	.008	4	35	30	130
97 DeVille, Concours: (FWD) Front	—	—	—	.030	1.224	1.209	.0005	.002	67	137	63	100
Rear	—	—	—	.030	.389	.374	.0005	.002	73	81	20	100
96-94 DeVille, Concours: (FWD) Front	—	—	—	.030	1.224	1.209	.0005	.002	90	—	38	100
Rear	—	—	—	.030	.389	.374	.0005	.002	73	81	20	100
93-91 Fleetwood, DeVille: (FWD)	①	8.860	8.880	.030	1.224	1.209	.0005	.004	62	38	—	100
90-86 Fleetwood, Deville: (FWD)	①	8.863	8.917	.030	.972	.965	.0005	.004	62	—	38	100
85 Fleetwood, Deville: (FWD)	①	8.858	8.880	.030	.972	.957	.0005	.004	62	—	35	100
85-77 Fleetwood Limo, Comm. Ch.: (RWD)	①	12.000	12.060	.062	1.230	1.215	.0005	.004	4	—	30	100

①.030" over rivet head; if bonded lining use .062". ③1988-84 .004". ④1992-85 38 ft/lbs.

Year / Make / Model	Brake Shoe O.E. Minimum Lining Thickness	Brake Drum Diameter Standard Size	Brake Drum Machine To	Brake Pad O.E. Minimum Lining Thickness	Brake Rotor Min. Thickness Machine To	Brake Rotor Discard At	Brake Rotor Variation From Parallelism	Brake Rotor Runout TIR	Caliper DESIGN	Caliper Mounting Bolts Torque (ft. lbs.)	Caliper Bridge, Pin or Key Bolts Torque (ft lbs)	Wheel Lugs or Nuts Torque (ft. lbs.)
CHEVROLET												
96-93 Beretta, Corsica:	④	7.874	7.899	.030	.751	.736	.0005	.003	40	—	38	100
92 Beretta, Corsica:	④	7.880	7.889	.030	.751	.736	.0005	.003	40	—	38	100
91-87 Beretta, Corsica:	④	7.880	7.899	.030	.830	.815	.0005	.004	62	—	38	100
97-93 Camaro:	.030	9.500	9.560	.030	1.250	1.209	.0005	.005	40	—	38	100
w/rear disc brakes	—	—	—	.030	.733	.724	.0005	.006	86	74	27	100
92-89 Camaro: exc. H.D.	④	9.500	9.560	.030	.980	.965	.0005	.005	4	—	37	81
H.D. Front	—	—	—	.030	.980	.965	.0005	.005	85	137	—	81
H.D. Rear	—	—	—	.030	.744	.724	.0005	.005	86	70	⑧	81
88-86 Camaro: w/rear drum brakes	④	9.500	9.560	.030	.980	.965	.0005	.005	4	—	38	80
w/rear disc brakes	—	—	—	.030	.986	.956	.0005	.005	41	—	38	80
85-82 Camaro: w/rear drum brakes	④	9.500	9.560	.030	.980	.965	.0005	.004	4	—	21-35	80⑥
w/rear disc brakes	—	—	—	.030	.980	.965	.0005	.004	41	—	30-45	80⑥
81-79 Camaro, Nova, Malibu, Monte Carlo:	④	9.500	9.560	.030	.980	.965	.0005	.004	4	—	35	80⑥
78-77 Camaro, Nova:	④	9.500	9.560	.030④	.980	.965	.0005	.004	4	—	35	80⑥
76-73 Camaro, Chevelle, Monte Carlo:	④	9.500	9.560	.030④	.980	.965	.0005	.005	4	—	35	70
72 Camaro, Chevelle:	④	9.500	9.560	.030④	.980	.965	.0005	.005	4	—	35	70
96-94 Caprice, Impala:	④	9.500	9.560	.030	.980	.965	.0005	.004	4	—	38	100
w/11" rear drum brakes	④	11.000	11.060	.030	.980	.965	.0005	.004	4	—	38	100
w/rear disc brakes	—	—	—	.030	.735	.728	.0005	.004	95	74	23	100
93-79 Caprice, Impala:	④	9.500	9.560	.030	.980	.965	.0005	.004	4	—	35③	80
w/11" rear drum brakes	④	11.000	11.060	.030	.980	.965	.0005	.004⑨	4	—	35③	100

①1991-85 use ill. 62. ②1991-84 .004". ③1992-85 38 ft/lbs. ④.030" over rivet head; if bonded lining use .062". ⑤1995-90 166 ft/lbs.
⑥Aluminum wheels; 1986-84 Corvette 80 ft/lbs., Camaro 105 ft/lbs., others 90ft/lbs. ⑧Hex bolt 26 ft/lbs.; allen bolt 16 ft/lbs. ⑨1993 use .003".
⑭Backoff to "just loose". Handtighten. Loosen to next slot in nut to fit cotter pin.

89450C05

PASSENGER CARS

Vehicle Year / Make / Model	Brake Shoe O.E. Minimum Lining Thickness	Brake Drum Diameter Standard Size	Brake Drum Machine To	Brake Pad O.E. Minimum Lining Thickness	Brake Rotor Min. Thickness Machine To	Brake Rotor Discard At	Brake Rotor Variation From Parallelism	Brake Rotor Runout TIR	DESIGN	Caliper Mounting Bolts Torque (ft. lbs.)	Caliper Bridge, Pin or Key Bolts Torque (ft. lbs)	Wheel Lugs or Nuts Torque (ft. lbs.)
CHEVROLET												
78 Caprice, Impala: exc. wagon	[4]	9.500	9.560	.030	.980	.965	.0005	.004	4	—	35	80[6]
wagon	[4]	11.000	11.060	.030	.980	.965	.0005	.004	4	—	35	100
77 Caprice, Impala: exc. wagon	[4]	9.500	9.560	.030	.980	.965	.0005	.005	4	—	35	80
wagon	[4]	11.000	11.060	.030	.980	.965	.0005	.005	4	—	35	100
76-72 Caprice, Impala, Bel Air:	[4]	11.000	11.060	.030[4]	1.230	1.215	.0005	.005	4	—	35	80
97-93 Cavalier:	.030	7.874	7.889	.030	.751	.736	.0005	.003	40	—	38	100
92 Cavalier:	.030	7.880	7.889	.030	.751	.736	.0005	.003	40	—	38	100
91-82 Cavalier: vented rotor (91-82)	[4]	7.880	7.899	.030	.830	.815	.0005	.002[2]	40[1]	—	28[3]	100
solid rotor (82)	[4]	7.880	7.899	.030	.444	.429	.0005	.002	40	—	28	100
90-87 Celebrity: H.D. Front	—	—	—	.030	.972	.957	.0005	.003	88	74	74	100
exc. H.D. Front	—	—	—	.030	.830	.815	.0005	.004	40	38	—	100
Rear coupe/sedan	[4]	8.863	8.877	—	—	—	—	—	—	—	—	100
Rear wagon	[4]	8.863	8.877	—	—	—	—	—	—	—	—	100
w/rear disc brakes	—	—	—	.030	.702	.681	.0005	.003	88	74	74	100
86-85 Celebrity: w/ H.D.	[4]	8.863	8.877	.030	.972	.957	.0005	.004	40	38	—	100
exc. H.D.	[4]	8.863	8.877	.030	.830	.815	.0005	.004	40	38	—	100
84-82 Celebrity:	[4]	7.879	7.899	.030	.830	.815	.0005	.002	40	28	—	100
87-86 Chevette:	[4]	7.880	7.899	.030	.404	.374	.0005	.005	50	70	30-45	80
85-84 Chevette:	[4]	7.874	7.899	.030	.430	.374	.0005	.005	50	—	21-25	70
83 Chevette:	[4]	7.874	7.899	.030	.390	.374	.0005	.005	50	—	21-25	70
82-78 Chevette:	[4]	7.874	7.899	.030	.390	.374	.0005	.005	20	70	28	70
77 Chevette:	[4]	7.880	7.899	.030	.456	.441	.0005	.005	20	70	28	70
76 Chevette:	[4]	7.870	7.899	.030	.448	.433	.0005	.005	20	70	28	70
85-80 Citation:	[4]	7.880	7.899	.030	.830	.815	.0005	.002[2]	40	—	28[3]	103
97 Corvette: Front	—	—	—	.030	1.200	1.200	.0005	.003	—	160	23	100
Rear	—	—	—	.030	.965	.965	.0005	.003	—	160	23	100
96-88 Corvette: Front exc. H.D.	—	—	—	.030	.744	.724	.0005	.006	85	137[5]	—	100
Front H.D.	—	—	—	.030	1.059	1.039	.0005	.006	85	137[5]	—	100
Rear exc. H.D.	—	—	—	.030	.744	.724	.0005	.006	86	70	[8]	100
Rear H.D.	—	—	—	.030	1.059	1.039	.0005	.006	86	70	[8]	100
87-84 Corvette: Front	—	—	—	.062	.724	—	.0005	.006	61	70[7]	30-34	100[6]
Rear	—	—	—	.062	.724	—	.0005	.006	61	44[7]	30-34	100[6]
82-77 Corvette: Front	—	—	—	.030[4]	1.230	1.215	.0005	.005	13	70	130	70[6]
Rear	—	—	—	.030[4]	1.230	1.215	.0005	.005	13	70	60	70[6]
76-72 Corvette: Front	—	—	—	.030[4]	1.230	1.215	.0005	.005	13	75	130	75
Rear	—	—	—	.030[4]	1.230	1.215	.0005	.005	13	75	50	75
97 Lumina, Monte Carlo:												
exc. rear disc brakes	.030	8.863	8.880	.303	.987	.972	.0005	.003	83	148	80	100
w/rear disc brakes	—	—	—	.030	.385	.370	.0005	.003	111	81	20	100
96 Lumina, Monte Carlo:												
exc. rear disc brakes	.030	8.863	8.880	.030	.972	.956	.0005	.003	83	148	80	100
w/rear disc brakes	—	—	—	.030	.385	.370	.0005	.003	111	81	20	100
95 Lumina, Monte Carlo:												
exc. rear disc brakes	.030	8.863	8.880	.030	.987[16]	.972[16]	.0005	.003	83	148	80	100
w/rear disc brakes	—	—	—	.030	.385	.370	.0005	.003	111	—	20	100
94-92 Lumina: Front	—	—	—	.030	.987	.972	.0005	.003	83	148	80	100[7]
Rear	—	—	—	.030	.444	.429	.0005	.003	84	92	—	100[15]
91-90 Lumina: Front	—	—	—	.030	.984	.972	.0005	.003[2]	83	79	—	103[3]
Rear	—	—	—	.030	.441	.429	.0005	.003[2]	84	92	—	103[3]
97 Malibu:	.030	8.863	8.880	.030	.987	.972	.0005	.0025	83	85	38	100
88-82 Malibu, Monte Carlo:	[4]	9.500	9.560	.030	.980	.965	.0005	.004	4	—	35[3]	80[6]
78-77 Malibu, Monte Carlo, Chevelle:	[4]	11.000	11.060	.030	.980	.965	.0005	.005	4	—	35	80
80-76 Monza:	[4]	9.500	9.560	.030	.830	.815	.0005	.005	15	—	—	80[8]

[3]1992-85 38 ft/lbs. [4].030" over rivet head; if bonded lining use .062". [6]Aluminum wheels; 1986-84 Corvette 80 ft/lbs., Camaro 105 ft/lbs., others 90ft/lbs.
[7]1987-85 front 133 ft/lbs.; rear 70 ft/lbs. [9]1990 92 ft/lbs. [10]Measurement of lining & metal. [11]w/Aluminum wheels 87 ft/lbs. [12]1993 shown, 1992-90 .004".
[15]Exc. 1993-92: 103 ft/lbs. [16]For late 1995 vehicles, refer to 1996 front rotor specifications. Refer to discard specification on rotor if needed.

89450C06

PASSENGER CARS

Vehicle Year / Make / Model	Brake Shoe O.E. Minimum Lining Thickness	Brake Drum Diameter Standard Size	Brake Drum Diameter Machine To	Brake Pad O.E. Minimum Lining Thickness	Brake Rotor Min. Thickness Machine To	Brake Rotor Min. Thickness Discard At	Brake Rotor Variation From Parallelism	Brake Rotor Runout TIR	DESIGN	Caliper Mounting Bolts Torque (ft. lbs.)	Caliper Bridge, Pin or Key Bolts Torque (ft. lbs)	Wheel Lugs or Nuts Torque (ft. lbs.)
CHEVROLET												
75 Monza:	④	9.000	9.060	.030	.455	.440	.0005	.005	15	—	—	65
88-85 Nova:	.039	7.874	7.913	.039	—	.492	—	.0059	65	65	18	76
w/rear disc brakes	—	—	—	.039	—	.315	—	.0059	70	34	14	76
76-72 Nova:	④	9.500	9.560	.030④	.980	.965	.0005	.005	4	—	35	70
88-85 Spectrum: exc. Turbo	.031	7.090	7.140	.039	—	.378	—	.0059	57	40	36	65⑪
w/Turbo	.039	7.090	7.140	.039	—	.650	—	.0059	47	40	36	65⑪
88-85 Sprint:	.110⑧	7.090	7.160	.315	—	.315	—	.0028	66	17-26	—	29-50
77-76 Vega:	④	9.500	9.560	.030	.455	.440	.0005	.005	15	—	—	80⑤
75-72 Vega:	④	9.000	9.060	.030	.455	.440	.0005	.005	15	—	—	65

③1992-85 38 ft/lbs. ④.030" over rivet head; if bonded lining use .062". ⑤Aluminum wheels; 1986-84 Corvette 80 ft/lbs., Camaro 105 ft/lbs., others 90ft/lbs.
⑦1990 92 ft/lbs. ⑧Measurement of lining & metal. ⑨w/Aluminum wheels 87 ft/lbs. ⑩1993 shown, 1992-90 .004". ⑪Exc. 1993-92: 103 ft/lbs.
⑧For late 1995 vehicles, refer to 1996 front rotor specifications. Refer to discard specification on rotor if needed.

Vehicle Year / Make / Model	Brake Shoe O.E. Min. Lining Thk.	Brake Drum Standard Size	Brake Drum Machine To	Brake Pad O.E. Min. Lining Thk.	Rotor Machine To	Rotor Discard At	Variation From Parallelism	Runout TIR	DESIGN	Mounting Bolts	Bridge Pin/Key Bolts	Lugs/Nuts
CHRYSLER CORP. — Chrysler, Dodge, Eagle, Plymouth												
95-90 Acclaim, Spirit:	.030	8.661	8.691	.030	.912	.882	.0005	.005	6	130-190	⑧	95
w/rear disc brakes				.281	.439	.409	.0005	.005	90	—	16	95
89 Acclaim, Spirit:	.030	8.661	8.691	.030	.865	.803	.0005	.005	6	130-190	⑧	95
89-83 Aries, Reliant, Lancer, LeBaron, 400, 600:												
w/7 7/8" rear brakes	.030	7.874	7.904	.030	.912	.882	.0005	.004①	⑥	130-190	⑧	80④
w/8 21/32" rear brakes	.030	8.661	8.691	.030	.912	.882	.0005	.004①	⑥	130-190	⑧	80④
82 Aries, Reliant, LeBaron, 400:	.030	7.870	7.900	.030	.912	.882	.0005	.004	6	70-100	18-22	85
81 Aries, Reliant:	.030	7.870	7.900	.030	.912	.882	.0005	.004	6	70-100	18-22	85
80-76 Arrow: w/rear drum brakes	.040	9.000	9.050	.040	—	.450	—	.006	34	51-65	—	51-58⑭
w/rear disc brakes	—	—	—	.040	—	.330	—	.006	27	29-36	—	51-58⑭
81-78 Aspen, Volare:	.030	10.000	10.060	.030	.970	.940	.0005	.005③	5	95-125	15-20	85
77-76 Aspen, Volare: exc. wagon	.030	10.000	10.060	.030	.970	.940	.0005	.004	5	95-125	25-35	85
wagon	.030	11.000	11.060	.030	.970	.940	.0005	.004	5	95-125	15	85
97-96 Avenger, Sebring Coupe:	.039	—	9.000	.080	—	.881	.0006	.0031	101	65	54	87-101
w/rear disc brakes (solid)	—	—	—	.080	—	.330	.0006	.0031	101	36-43	—	87-101
w/rear disc brakes (vented)	—	—	—	.080	—	.724	.0006	.0031	101	36-43	—	87-101
95 Avenger, Sebring Coupe: Front	.039	—	9.000	.080	—	.881	.0006	.0031	101	65	54	65-80
Rear w/disc brakes	—	—	—	.080	—	.330	.0006	.0031	101	36-43	—	65-80
97-96 Sebring Convertible:	—	—	—	—	.873	.843	.0005	.005	6	—	16	100
97-95 Breeze, Cirrus, Stratus:	—	7.874	—	—	.873	.843	.0005	.005	6	—	16	95
83-78 Challenger: w/rear drum brakes	.040	9.000	9.050	.040	—	.430	—	.006	34	51-65	—	51-58⑭
w/rear disc brakes	—	—	—	.040	—	.330	—	.006	27	29-36	—	51-58⑭
82-79 Champ: (FWD)	.040	7.100	7.150	.040	—	.450	—	.006	18	43-58	—	51-58⑭
74-73 Charger, Coronet, Challenger, Belvedere, Satellite, Barracuda: w/front disc brakes	.030	10.000	10.060	.030	.970	.940	.0005	.004	⑤	75-100	25-35	65
72 Charger, Coronet, Crestwood, SE, Super Bee, Belvedere, Satelite, GTX, Regent, Road Runner, Sebring, Barracuda, Challenger:												
w/front disc brakes	.030	10.000	10.060	.030	.970	.940	.0005	.0025	5	75-100	30-35	65
w/10" drum brakes	.030	10.000	10.060	—	—	—	—	—	—	—	—	65
w/11" drum brakes	.030	11.000	11.060	—	—	—	—	—	—	—	—	65
96-95 Eagle Summit: Coupe Std.	.040	7.100	7.200	.080	—	.450	.0006	.0028	69	65	36②	65-80
Coupe Opt'l	.040	8.000	8.100	.080	—	.650	.0006	.0028	69	65	36②	65-80
Sedan	.040	8.000	8.100	.080	—	.650	.0006	.0028	69	65	36②	65-80
Sedan w/rear disc brakes	—	—	—	.080	—	.330	.0006	.0031	70	36-43	20	65-80
94 Colt, Eagle Summit: Coupe w/1.5L engine	.040	7.100	7.200	.080	—	.450	.0006	.0028	69	65	36②	65-80

①1991-87 .005". ③1982-80 .004". ④1993-84 95 ft/lbs. ⑤Use ill. 2 or 5. ⑥Use ill. 6 or 8. ⑧K.H. 25-35 ft/lbs.; ATE 18-26 ft/lbs. ⑭w/Aluminum wheels; 58-72 ft/lbs.
②Upper shown; lower 61-69 ft/lbs.

89450C07

PASSENGER CARS

Vehicle Year / Make / Model	Brake Shoe O.E. Minimum Lining Thickness	Brake Drum Diameter Standard Size	Brake Drum Machine To	Brake Pad O.E. Minimum Lining Thickness	Brake Rotor Min. Thickness Machine To	Brake Rotor Discard At	Variation From Parallelism	Runout TIR	DESIGN	Caliper Mounting Bolts Torque (ft. lbs.)	Caliper Bridge, Pin or Key Bolts Torque (ft. lbs)	Wheel Lugs or Nuts Torque (ft. lbs.)
CHRYSLER CORP. — Chrysler, Dodge, Eagle, Plymouth												
Coupe w/1.8L engine	.040	7.100	7.200	.080	—	.650	.0006	.0028	69	65	36②	65-80
Sedan	.040	8.000	8.100	.080	—	.650	.0006	.0028	69	65	36②	65-80
Sedan w/rear disc brakes				.080	—	.330	—	.0031	70	36-43	20	65-80
93 Colt, Eagle Summit: Coupe	.040	7.100	7.200	.080	—	.449	—	.0031	69	58-72	27-36	65-80
Sedan	.040	8.000	8.100	.080	—	.646	—	.0031	69	58-72	27-36	65-80
w/rear disc brakes	—			.080	—	.331	—	.0031	70	36-43	20	65-80
92-91 Colt, Eagle Summit: Hatchback	.040	7.100	7.200	.080	—	.449	—	.006	69	58-72	27-36	65-80
Sedan	.040	7.100	7.200	.080	—	.646	—	.006	69	58-72	27-36	65-80
90-89 Colt, Eagle Summit:												
exc. rear disc brakes	.040	7.100	7.200	.080	—	.449	—	.006	69	58-72	16-23	65-80
w/rear disc brakes Front	—	—	—	.080	—	.882	—	.006	69	58-72	16-23	65-80
w/rear disc brakes Rear	—	—	—	.080	—	.331	—	.006	70	36-43	16-23	65-80
88 Colt: exc. Turbo	.040	7.100	7.200	.080	—	.450	—	.006	69	58-72	16-23	65-80
Turbo	.040	7.100	7.200	.080	—	.645	—	.006	69	58-72	16-23	65-80
87-85 Colt: exc. Turbo	.040	7.100	7.150	.040	—	.450	—	.006	69	58-72	16-23	50-57⑯
87-84 Colt: Turbo	.040	7.100	7.150	.040	—	.645	—	.006	69	58-72⑮	16-23	51-58⑭
84-79 Colt: (FWD) exc. Turbo	.040	7.100	7.150	.040	—	.450	—	.006	18	43-58	58-69	51-58⑭
80-78 Colt: (RWD) exc. Wagon	.040	9.000	9.050	.080	—	.450	—	.006	18	51-65⑰	—	51-58
77-73 Colt:	.040	9.000	9.050	.080	—	.450	—	.006	18	51-65⑰	—	51-58⑭
72 Colt:	.040	9.000	9.050	.080	—	.374	—	.006	14	30-36	—	51-58⑭
96-95 Eagle Summit SW:												
w/8" drum brakes	.040	8.000	8.100	.080	—	.882	.0006	.0028	69	65	54	65-80
w/9" drum brakes	.040	9.000	9.100	.080	—	.882	.0006	.0028	69	65	54	65-80
w/rear disc brakes	—	—	—	.080	—	.331	.0006	.0031	69	36-43	32	65-80
94-92 Colt Vista, Eagle Summit SW:												
w/8" drum brakes	.040	8.000	8.071	.080	—	.882	.0006	.003	69	65	54	65-80
w/9" drum brakes	.040	9.000	9.079	.080	—	.882	.0006	.003	69	65	54	65-80
w/rear disc brakes	—	—	—	.080	—	.331	.0006	.003	69	40	32	65-80
91-89 Colt Vista, Eagle Vista: (4x2)	.040	8.000	8.100	.080	—	.650	—	.006	69	56-72	16-23	50-57⑯
(4x4)	.040	9.000	9.100	.080	—	.880	—	.004	69	56-72	16-23	50-57⑯
88 Colt Vista: (4x2)	.040	8.000	8.100	.080	—	.650	—	.006	69	58-72	16-23	50-57⑯
(4x4)	.040	9.000	9.100	.080	—	.880	—	.006	69	58-72	16-23	50-57⑯
87-84 Colt Vista: (4x2)	.040	8.000	8.150	.040	—	.650	—	.006	69	58-72	16-23	50-57⑯
(4x4)	.040	9.000	9.078	.040	—	.880	—	.004	69	58-72	16-23	50-57⑯
90-89 Colt Wagon: (4x2)	.040	8.000	8.100	.080	—	.449	—	.006	69	58-72	16-23	65-80
(4x4)	.040	8.000	8.100	.080	—	.646	—	.006	69	58-72	16-23	65-80
88 Colt Wagon:	.040	8.000	8.100	.080	—	.450	—	.006	69	58-72	16-23	65-80
80-78 Colt Wagon: w/rear drum brakes	.040	9.000	9.050	.040	—	.330	—	.006	34	51-65	—	51-58⑭
w/rear disc brakes	—	—	—	.040	—	.330	—	.006	27	29-36	—	51-58⑭
97-93 Concorde, Intrepid, Vision:	.030	8.661	8.691	.030	—	.882	.0005	.003	6		16	95
w/rear disc brakes				.030	—	.409	.0005	.003	90	—	16	95
89-88 Conquest: Front	—	—	—	.080	—	.880	—	.006	57	58-72	61-69	65-80
Rear	—	—	—	.080	—	.650	—	.006	56	29-36	36-43	65-80
87-84 Conquest: Front	—	—	—	.040	—	.880	—	.006	57	58-72	61-69	50-57⑯
Rear	—	—	—	.040	—	.650	—	.006	56	29-36	36-43	50-57⑯
83-82 Cordoba, Mirada:	.030	10.000	10.060	.125	.970	.940	.0005	.004	5	95-125	15-20	85
w/11" rear brakes	.030	11.000	11.060	.125	.970	.940	.0005	.004	5	95-125	15-20	85
81-78 Cordoba, Mirada:	.030	10.000	10.060	.030	.970	.940	.0005	.005③	5	95-125	15-20	85
w/11" rear brakes	.030	11.000	11.060	.030	.970	.940	.0005	.005③	5	95-125	15-20	85
77-76 Cordoba, Charger SE:	.030	11.000	11.060	.030	.970	.940	.0005	.004	⑥	95-125	25-40	85
75 Cordoba, Charger:	.030	10.000	10.060	.030	.970	.940	.0005	.004	2	95-125	25-35	70
76-75 Dart, Valiant: w/disc brakes	.030	10.000	10.060	—	—	—	.0005	.004	5	95-125	15	70
w/front drum brakes Front	.030	10.000	10.060	—	—	—	—	—	—	—	—	70
Rear	.030	9.000	9.060	—	—	—	—	—	—	—	—	70

①1991-87 .005". ②.030" over rivet head; if bonded lining use .062". ③1982-80 .004". ⑤Use ill. 2 or 5. ⑥Use ill. 6 or 8. ⑦1975-65 ft/lbs. ⑧K.H. 25-35 ft/lbs.; ATE 18-26 ft/lbs. ⑬1984 shown; 1987-85 Not Adjustable. ⑭w/Aluminum wheels; 58-72 ft/lbs. ⑮1984 43-58 ft/lbs. ⑯w/Aluminum wheels 65-80 ft/lbs. ⑰Caliper to adapter shown; adapter to caliper 29-36 ft/lbs.

PASSENGER CARS

Vehicle Year / Make / Model	Brake Shoe O.E. Minimum Lining Thickness	Brake Drum Diameter Standard Size	Brake Drum Diameter Machine To	Brake Pad O.E. Minimum Lining Thickness	Brake Rotor Min. Thickness Machine To	Brake Rotor Min. Thickness Discard At	Brake Rotor Variation From Parallelism	Brake Rotor Runout TIR	Design	Caliper Mounting Bolts Torque (ft. lbs.)	Caliper Bridge, Pin or Key Bolts Torque (ft. lbs)	Wheel Lugs or Nuts Torque (ft. lbs.)
CHRYSLER CORP. — Chrysler, Dodge, Eagle, Plymouth												
74-73 Dart, Valiant: w/disc brakes	.030	10.000	10.060	.030	.970	.940	.0005	.004	⑤	75-100	25-35	65
w/front drum brakes Front	.030	10.000	10.060	—	—	—	—	—	—	—	—	65
Rear	.030	9.000	9.060	—	—	—	—	—	—	—	—	65
72 Dart, Valiant, GT, GTS, Swinger, Demon, Duster, Scamp, Signet: w/disc brakes	.030	10.000	10.060	.030	.790	.780	.0005	.0025	9	50-80	70-80	55
w/10" drum brakes	.030	10.000	10.060	—	—	—	—	—	—	—	—	55
w/9" drum brakes	.030	9.000	9.060	—	—	—	—	—	—	—	—	55
93-89 Daytona:	—	—	—	.030	.912	.882	.0005	.005	6	130-190	25-35	95
Rear w/solid rotor	—	—	—	.030	.439	.409	.0005	.005	90	130-190	25-35	95
Rear w/vented rotor	—	—	—	.030	.827	.797	.0005	.003	90	130-190	25-35	95
88 Daytona:	.030	8.661	8.691	.030	.912	.882	.0005	.005	⑥	130-190	18-26	95
w/rear disc brakes	—	—	—	.030	.321	.291	.0005	.005	90	130-190	18-26	95
87-84 Daytona, Laser: (FWD) exc. rear disc brakes	.030	8.661	8.691	.030	.912	.882	.0005	.004①	⑥	130-190	⑥	95
w/rear disc brakes	—	—	—	.030	.321	.291	.0005	.005	74	130-190	18-26	95
93-92 Dynasty, New Yorker, Imperial, Fifth Ave.:	.030	8.661	8.691	.030	.912	.882	.0005	.005	6	130-190	25-35	95
w/rear disc brakes	—	—	—	.030	.439	.409	.0005	.005	90	130-190	25-35	95
91-89 Dynasty, New Yorker, Imperial, Fifth Ave.:	.030	8.661	8.691	.030	.912	.882	.0005	.005	6	130-190	25-35	95
w/rear disc brakes	—	—	—	.030	.369	.339	.0005	.003	91	130-190	25-35	95
88 Dynasty, New Yorker:	.030	8.661	8.691	.030	.912	.882	.0005	.005	⑥	130-190	⑥	95
w/rear disc brakes	—	—	—	.030	.321	.291	.0005	.003	91	130-190	18-26	95
88 Eagle:	.030	10.000	10.060	.030②	.815	.810	.0005	.004	1	100	30	75
78 Fury, Monaco:	.030	10.000	10.060	.030	.970	.940	.0005	.004	5	95-125	25-40	85
w/11" rear brakes	.030	11.000	11.060	.030	.970	.940	.0005	.004	5	95-125	25-40	85
77-76 Fury, Monaco, Coronet:	.030	11.000	11.060	.030	.970	.940	.0005	.004	⑤	95-125	25-40	85
75 Fury, Monaco, Coronet: exc. wagon	.030	10.000	10.060	.030	.970	.940	.0005	.004	2	95-125	25-35	70
wagon	.030	11.000	11.060	.030	.970	.940	.0005	.004	2	95-125	25-35	70
74-72 Fury, Monaco, Polara, Newport, New Yorker, Town & Country, V.I.P.:	.030	11.000	11.060	.030	1.195	1.180	.0005	.004	5	75-100	25-35	65
89-82 Gran Fury, Diplomat, Fifth Ave., Newport, New Yorker, Imperial, Caravelle: (RWD)	.030	10.000	10.060	.125	.970	.940	.0005	.004	5	95-125	15-20	85
w/11" rear brakes	.030	11.000	11.060	.125	.970	.940	.0005	.004	5	95-125	15-20	85
81-78 Gran Fury, Diplomat, LeBaron, St: Regis, Magnum, Newport, New Yorker, Imperial:	.030	10.000	10.060	.030	.970	.940	.0005	.005③	5	95-125	15-20	85
w/11" rear brakes	.030	11.000	11.060	.030	.970	.940	.0005	.005③	5	95-125	15-20	85
77-75 Gran Fury, Royal Monaco, New Yorker, Newport, Town & Country:	.030	11.000	11.060	.030	1.195	1.180	.0005	.004	5	95-125	25-35	85⑦
75-74 Imperial: Front	—	—	—	.030	1.195	1.180	.0005	.004	5	95-125	25-35	85
Rear	—	—	—	.030	.970	.940	.0005	.004	5	95-125	25-35	85
73-72 Imperial:	.030	11.000	11.060	.030	1.195	1.180	.0005	.0025	5	75-100	30-35	65
97 Talon:	.039	—	9.100	.080	—	.880	.0006	.0024	69⑧	54	—	87-101
w/rear disc brakes	—	—	—	.080	—	.330		.0031	101	54	—	87-101
96 Talon:	.039	—	9.100	.080	—	.882	.0006	.0031	69⑧	65	54	87-101
w/ rear disc brakes	—	—	—	.080	—	.330	—	.0031	101	36-43	54	87-101
95 Talon: Front	—	—	—	.080	—	.882	.0006	.0031	69⑧	65	54	65-80
Rear (Solid)	—	—	—	.080	—	.330	—	.0031	101	36-43	54	65-80
Rear (Vented)	—	—	—	.080	—	.724	—	.0031	101	36-43	54	65-80

①1991-87 .005". ②.030" over rivet head; if bonded lining use .062". ③1982-80 .004". ⑤Use ill. 2 or 5. ⑥Use ill. 6 or 8. ⑦1975-65 ft/lbs. ⑧K.H. 25-35 ft/lbs.; ATE 18-26 ft/lbs. ⑧AWD Turbo use ill. #81.

89450C09

PASSENGER CARS

Year / Make / Model	Brake Shoe O.E. Minimum Lining Thickness	Brake Drum Diameter Standard Size	Brake Drum Diameter Machine To	Brake Pad O.E. Minimum Lining Thickness	Brake Rotor Min. Thickness Machine To	Brake Rotor Min. Thickness Discard At	Brake Rotor Variation From Parallelism	Brake Rotor Runout TIR	DESIGN	Caliper Mounting Bolts Torque (ft. lbs.)	Caliper Bridge, Pin or Key Bolts Torque (ft. lbs)	Wheel Lugs or Nuts Torque (ft. lbs.)
CHRYSLER CORP. — Chrysler, Dodge, Eagle, Plymouth												
94-90 Laser, Talon: Front	—	—	—	.080	.912	.882	—	.003	69	58-72	⑫	87-101
Rear	—	—	—	.080	.360	.331	—	.003	70	36-43	16-23	87-101
94-87 Lebaron:	.030	8.661	8.691	.281	.912	.882	.0005	.005	6	130-190	25-35	95
Rear w/solid rotor				.281	.439	.409	.0005	.005	90	130-190	25-35	95
Rear w/vented rotor				.281	.827	.797	.0005	.003	90	130-190	25-35	95
89-88 Medallion:	.098	9.000	9.030	.256	⑨	.697	—	.002	51	48	18	67
92-91 Monaco, Premier:	.132	8.858	8.917	.160	—	.890	.0005	.003	51	70	15-22	63⑪
w/rear disc brakes	—			.062	—	.374	.0005	.003	93	70	15-22	63⑪
90-88 Monaco, Premier:	.132	8.858	8.917	.236	⑨	.807	—	.003	51	70	18	63⑪
97-95 Neon: exc. rear disc brakes	—	7.874	—	—	.754	.724	.0005	.005	6	—	16	95
w/rear disc brakes	—	—	—	.281⑲	—	—	.0005	.005	90	—	16	95
97-94 New Yorker, LHS: Front	—	—	—	.030	—	.882	.0005	.003	6	—	16	95
Rear	—	—	—	.030	—	.409	.0005	.003	90	—	16	95
88 New Yorker Turbo, Town & Country SW, Caravelle:	.030	8.661	8.691	.030	.912	.882	.0005	.005	⑥	130-190	⑧	95
87-83 New Yorker Turbo, Town & Country SW, Caravelle:												
(FWD) exc. rear disc brakes	.030	8.661	8.691	.030	.912	.882	.0005	.004①	⑧	130-190	⑧	80④
w/rear disc brakes	—	—	—	.030	.321	.291	.0005	.005	74	130-190	18-26	95
90-83 Omni, Charger, Horizon, Turismo:	.030	7.874	7.904	.030	.461	.431	.0005	.004①	6	130-190	⑧	80④
82-78 Omni, Horizon:	.030	7.870	7.900	.030	.461	.431	.0005	.005③	8	70-100	25-40	85
83-78 Sapporo: w/rear drum brakes	.040	9.000	9.050	.040	—	.430	—	.006	34	51-65	—	51-58⑭
w/rear disc brakes	—	—	—	.040	—	.330	—	.006	27	29-36	—	51-58⑭
94-89 Shadow, Sundance:												
w/7 7/8" rear brakes	.030	7.874	7.904	.030	.912	.882	.0005	.005①	⑥	130-190	⑧	80④
88-86 Shadow, Sundance:												
w/7 7/8" rear brakes	.030	7.874	7.904	.030	.912	.882	.0005	.004①	⑥	130-190	⑧	80④
w/8 21/32" rear brakes	.030	8.661	8.691	.030	.912	.882	.0005	.004①	⑥	130-190	⑧	80④
96-91 Stealth: (FWD) Front	—	—	—	.080	—	.880	—	.004②	81	65	54	87-101
(FWD) Rear	—	—	—	.080	—	.650	—	.0031	47	36-43	20	87-101
(AWD) Front	—	—	—	.080	—	1.120	—	.004	16	65	—	87-101
(AWD) Rear	—	—	—	.080	—	.720	—	.0031	47	36-43	32	87-101
91-89 TC Maserati:	—	—	—	.030	.912	.882	.0005	.005	6	130-190	18-26	95
w/rear disc brakes	—	—	—	.030	.321	.291	.0005	.005	74	130-190	18-26	95
95-92 Viper: Front	—	—	—	.100	1.227	1.197	.0005	.003	107	85	—	90
Rear	—	—	—	.100	.833	.803	.0005	.003	NA	—	24㉑	90

①1991-87 .005". ③1982-80 .004". ④1993-84 95 ft/lbs. ⑥Use ill. 6 or 8. ⑧K.H. 25-35 ft/lbs.; ATE 18-26 ft/lbs. ⑨Machining not recommended.
⑪Steel wheel shown; Aluminum 95 ft/lbs. ⑫Steel wheel shown; Aluminum 90 ft/lbs. ⑯16-23 ft/lbs. to 4/30/89, 46-62 ft/lbs. from 5/1/89. ⑭w/Aluminum wheels; 58-72 ft/lbs.
⑧AWD Turbo use ill. #81. ⑲Measurement of lining and backing plate. ㉑Allen head bolt shown; hex head bolt 38 ft/lbs. ㉒1993-91 shown; 1995-94 use .0028.

Year / Make / Model	Brake Shoe O.E. Minimum Lining Thickness	Brake Drum Diameter Standard Size	Brake Drum Diameter Machine To	Brake Pad O.E. Minimum Lining Thickness	Brake Rotor Min. Thickness Machine To	Brake Rotor Min. Thickness Discard At	Brake Rotor Variation From Parallelism	Brake Rotor Runout TIR	DESIGN	Caliper Mounting Bolts Torque (ft. lbs.)	Caliper Bridge, Pin or Key Bolts Torque (ft. lbs)	Wheel Lugs or Nuts Torque (ft. lbs.)
DAIHATSU												
92-91 Charade: 1.0 eng.	.039	7.087	7.126	.120	—	.390	—	.004	58	—	23-30	65-87
1.3 eng.	.039	7.874	7.913	.120	—	.670	—	.004	58	—	23-30	65-87
89-88 Charade:	.040	7.090	7.126	.120	—	.390	—	.003	58	—	23-30	65-87
FIAT												
82-75 124, 2000: Front	—	—	—	.080	.368	.354	—	.006	22	59	—	65
Rear	—	—	—	.080	.372	.354	—	.006	27	55	—	65
74-72 124: Front	—	—	—	.080	.368	.354	—	.006	22	36	—	51
Rear	—	—	—	.080	.372	.354	—	.006	27	40	—	51
79-73 128:	.060	7.300	7.332	.080	.368	.354	.002	.006	22	36	—	51
78-75 131:	.181	9.000	9.030	.060	.368	.354	.002	.006	22	50	—	65
81-79 Brava:	.181	9.000	9.030	.060	—	.386	.002	.004	22	50	—	65
82-79 Strada:	.060	7.293	7.336	.060	.368	.350	—	.006	33	—	—	65
82-74 X 1/9: Front	—	—	—	.080	.368	.354	.002	.006	43	36	—	51
Rear	—	—	—	.080	.368	.354	.002	.006	27	36	—	51

89450C10

PASSENGER CARS

Vehicle Year / Make / Model	Brake Shoe O.E. Minimum Lining Thickness	Brake Drum Diameter Standard Size	Brake Drum Machine To	Brake Pad O.E. Minimum Lining Thickness	Brake Rotor Min. Thickness Machine To	Brake Rotor Min. Thickness Discard At	Brake Rotor Variation From Parallelism	Brake Rotor Runout TIR	DESIGN	Caliper Mounting Bolts Torque (ft. lbs.)	Caliper Bridge, Pin or Key Bolts Torque (ft. lbs)	Wheel Lugs or Nuts Torque (ft. lbs.)
FORD MOTOR CO. — Ford, Lincoln, Mercury												
97-94 Aspire:												
w\automatic transmission	.040	7.870	7.930	.080	.817	.780	.0009	.004	102	29-36	—	65-87
w\manual transmission	.040	7.870	7.930	.080	.660	.630	.0009	.004	102	29-36	—	65-87
94-91 Capri: Front	—	—	—	.120	.660	.630	.0004	.004	10	—	29-36	67-88
Rear	—	—	—	.120	.380	.350	.0004	.004	70	—	29-36	67-88
77-76 Capri:	.030	9.000	9.050	.100	.460	.450	.0004	.002	14	45-50	—	50-55
74-72 Capri:	.030	9.000	9.050	.100	—	⑨	—	.0035	14	40-50	—	50-55
97-95 Continental: Front	—	—	—	.125	—	.974	.0004	.003	45	84	25	85-105
Rear	—	—	—	.123	—	.502	.0004	.001⑮	99	64-87	23-25	85-105
94-93 Continental: Front	—	—	—	.040	—	.974	.00027	.003	44	65-85	16-24	85-105
Rear	—	—	—	.123	—	.500	.0004	.0014	99	64-88	23-26	85-105
92 Continental: Front	—	—	—	.125	—	.974	.0005	.003	44	—	18-25	85-104
Rear	—	—	—	.123	—	.900	.0005	.003	99	45-65	23-26	85-104
91 Continental: Front	—	—	—	.125	—	.970	.0004	.002	44	—	18-25	85-105
Rear	—	—	—	.123	—	.900	.0005	.003	99	45-65	23-26	85-105
90-88 Continental: Front	—	—	—	.125	—	.970	.0004	.002	44	—	18-25	80-105
Rear	—	—	—	.125	—	.974	.0005	.002	99	80-100	23-26	80-105
87-84 Continental: Front	—	—	—	.125	—	.972	.0005	.003	10	—	40-60	80-105
Rear	—	—	—	.125	—	.895	.0005	.004	99	80-110	29-37	80-105
83-82 Continental: Front	—	—	—	.125	—	.972	.0005	.003	10	—	40-60	80-105
Rear	—	—	—	.125	—	.895	.0005	.004	11	80-110	29-37	80-105
81-80 Continental: w/10" rear brakes	.030	10.000	10.060	.125	—	.972	.0005	.003	10	—	40-60	80-105
w/11" rear brakes	.030	11.030	11.090	.125	—	.972	.0005	.003	10	—	40-60	80-105
79-73 Continental: w/10" rear brakes	.030	10.000	10.090	.125	—	1.120	.0005	.003	1	90-120	12-16	80-105
w/11" rear brakes	.030	11.030	11.090	.125	—	1.120	.0005	.003	1	90-120	12-16	80-105
72 Continental:	.030	11.030	11.090	.030	1.135	1.120	.0007	.003	24	U125-L105	25-35	70-115
97-95 Contour, Mystique:												
exc. rear disc brakes	㊚	8.000	8.040	.125	—	.870	.0006	.006	10	88	20	62
w/rear disc brakes	—	—	—	.125	—	.710	.0006	.006	—	43	30	62
97-96 Cougar, Thunderbird:	.030	9.800	9.860	.125	—	.974	.0004	.003	44	95	60	85-105
w/rear disc brakes	—	—	—	.125	—	.657	.0003	.002	99	72-97	23-26	85-105
95-93 Cougar, Thunderbird:	.030	9.800	9.860	.125	—	.974	.0004	.003	44	95	65	85-105
w/rear disc brakes	—	—	—	.123	—	.657	.0003	.002	99	64-88	23-26	85-105
92 Cougar, Thunderbird:	.030	9.800	9.860	.125	—	.974	.0005	.003	44	—	19-25	85-105
w/rear disc brakes	—	—	—	.123	—	.900	.0005	.003	99	45-65	23-26	80-105
91-90 Cougar, Thunderbird:	.030	9.800	9.860	.125	—	.935	.0005	.003	10	—	19-25	80-105
w/rear disc brakes	—	—	—	.123	—	.900	.0005	.003	99	45-65	23-26	80-105
89 Cougar, Thunderbird:	.030	9.800	9.860	.125	—	.935	.0005	.003	10	—	19-25	80-105
w/rear disc brakes	—	—	—	.123	—	.895	.0005	.003	99	80-100	18-24	80-105
88-87 Cougar, Thunderbird: exc. Turbo												
w/9" rear brakes	.030	9.000	9.060	.125	—	.810	.0005④	.003	10	—	30-40	80-105
w/10" rear brakes	.030	10.000	10.060	.125	—	.810	.0005④	.003	10	—	30-40	80-105
w/Turbo	.030	9.000	9.060	.125	—	.972	.0005	.003	10	80-110	40-60	80-105
w/rear disc brakes	—	—	—	.125	—	.895	.0005	.003	64	80-110	29-37	80-105
86-83 Cougar, Thunderbird, XR-7:												
w/9" rear brakes	.030	9.000	9.060	.125	—	.810	.0005⑤	.003	10	—	30-40	80-105
w/10" rear brakes	.030	10.000	10.060	.125	—	.810	.0005④	.003	10	—	30-40	80-105
82-81 Cougar, Thunderbird, XR-7:												
w/9" rear brakes	.030	9.000	9.060	.125	-–	.810	.0005	.003	10	—	30-40	80-105
w/10" rear brakes	.030	10.000	10.060	.125	—	.810	.0005	.003	10	—	30-40	80-105
80 Cougar, Thunderbird:	.030	9.000	9.060	.125	—	.810	.0005	.003	10	—	30-40	80-105
79 Cougar, Thunderbird, LTD II:	.030	11.030	11.090	.125	—	1.120	.0005	.003	1	90-120	12-16	80-105
78-77 Cougar, Thunderbird, LTD II:	.030	11.030	11.090	.125	—	1.120	.0005	.003	1	90-120	12-16	70-115
76-74 Cougar, w/10" rear brakes	.030	10.000	10.060	.030	—	1.120	.0005	.003	1	90-120	12-16	70-115
w/11" rear brakes	.030	11.030	11.090	.030	—	1.120	.0005	.003	1	90-120	12-16	70-115
73-72 Cougar, Mustang:	.030	10.000	10.060	.030	.890	.875	.0007	.002	23	U125-L65	25-35	70-115

②.030" over rivet head; if bonded lining use .062".   ④1993-86 .0003" w/Aluminum wheels; 1985-84 LTD., Marquis .0003".   ⑤1988-84 Escort, Lynx, EXP .004".
⑥1988-84 Escort, Lynx, EXP; 1987 Taurus, Sable .002".   ⑦See O.E. Manual   ⑨Machining not recommended.   ㊚.0313" rivet head; if bonded lining use use .125"   ⑮1997 use .004".

89450C11

PASSENGER CARS

Vehicle Year / Make / Model	Brake Shoe O.E. Minimum Lining Thickness	Brake Drum Diameter Standard Size	Brake Drum Diameter Machine To	Brake Pad O.E. Minimum Lining Thickness	Brake Rotor Min. Thickness Machine To	Brake Rotor Min. Thickness Discard At	Brake Rotor Variation From Parallelism	Brake Rotor Runout TIR	Caliper Design	Caliper Mounting Bolts Torque (ft. lbs.)	Caliper Bridge, Pin or Key Bolts Torque (ft. lbs)	Wheel Lugs or Nuts Torque (ft. lbs.)
FORD MOTOR CO. — Ford, Lincoln, Mercury												
97-96 Crown Victoria, Grand Marquis: Front	—	—	—	.125	—	.974	.00035	.0016	10	125-170	21-26	85-105
Rear	—	—	—	.125	—	.511	.0004	.002	98	40-50	16-20	85-105
95 Crown Victoria, Grand Marquis: Front	—	—	—	.125	—	.974	.00035	.003	10	125-170	18-26	85-105
Rear	—	—	—	.125	—	.440	.0005	.003	98	20-40	22-30	85-105
94-92 Crown Victoria, Grand Marquis: Front	—	—	—	.125	—	.974	.0005	.003	10	—	45-65	85-105
Rear	—	—	—	.125	—	.440	.0005	.003	98	—	19-26	85-105
91 Crown Victoria, Grand Marquis: w/10" rear brakes	.030②	10.000	10.060	.125	—	.972	.0005	.003	10	—	45-64	85-105
w/11" rear brakes	.030②	11.030	11.090	.125	—	.972	.0005	.003	10	—	45-64	85-105
90-83 Crown Victoria, Grand Marquis: w/11" rear brakes	.030	11.030	11.090	.125	—	.972	.0005	.003	10	—	40-60	80-105
w/10" rear brakes	.030	10.000	10.060	.125	—	.972	.0005	.003	10	—	40-60	80-105
78-74 Custom, Country Sedan, Country Squire, Galaxie, LTD, Colony Park, Marquis: exc. rear disc brakes	.030	11.030	11.090	.125	—	1.120	.0005	.003	1	90-120	12-16	70-115
w/rear disc brakes	—	—	—	.030	—	.895	.0005	.004	11	90-120	12-16	70-115
73 Custom, Country Sedan, Country Squire, Galaxie, LTD, Colony Park, Marquis:	.030	11.030	11.090	.125	—	1.120	.0005	.003	1	90-120	—	70-115
72 Custom, Country Sedan, Country Squire, Galaxie, LTD, Colony Park, Marquis:	.030	11.030	11.090	.030	1.135	1.120	.0007	.003	24	U125-L105	25-35	70-115
97-93 Escort, Tracer:	.040	7.870	7.910	.080	.820	.790	—	.004	82	29-36	—	65-87
w/rear disc brakes	—	—	—	.040	.310	.280	.001	.004	94	—	33-43	65-87
92-91 Escort, Tracer:	.040	9.000	9.040	.080	.820	.790	—	.004	82	29-36	—	65-87
w/rear disc brakes	—	—	—	.040	.310	.280	—	.004	94	—	33-43	65-87
90-89 Escort: w/7" rear brakes	.030②	7.090	7.149	.125	—	.882	.0005	.003	44	—	18-25	80-105
w/8" rear brakes	.030②	8.000	8.060	.125	—	.882	.0005	.003	44	—	18-25	80-105
88-81 Escort, EXP, Lynx, LN7: w/7" rear brakes	.030②	7.090	7.149	.125	—	.882	.0005⑤	.003⑥	44	—	18-25	80-105
w/8" rear brakes	.030②	8.000	8.060	.125	—	.882	.0005⑤	.003⑥	44	—	18-25	80-105
86-83 Fairmont, Zephyr, LTD, Marquis: w/9" rear brakes	.030	9.000	9.060	.125	—	.810	.005④	.003	10	—	30-40	80-105
w/10" rear brakes	.030	10.000	10.060	.125	—	.810	.005④	.003	10	—	30-40	80-105
82-79 Fairmont, Zephyr: w/9" rear brakes	.030	9.000	9.060	.125	—	.810	.0005	.003	10	—	30-40	80-105
w/10" rear brakes	.030	10.000	10.060	.125	—	.810	.0005	.003	10	—	30-40	80-105
78 Fairmont, Zephyr: exc. Wagon	.030	9.000	9.060	.125	—	.810	.0005	.003	10	—	30-40	70-115
Wagon	.030	10.000	10.060	.125	—	.810	.0005	.003	10	—	30-40	70-115
93-88 Festiva:	.040	6.690	6.750	.120	.463	.433	.0006	.003	82	29-36	—	65-87
80-78 Fiesta:	.060	7.000	—	.060	—	.340	—	.006	22	38-45	—	63-85
82-81 Granada: w/9" rear brakes	.030	9.000	9.060	.125	—	.810	.0005	.003	10	—	30-40	80-105
w/10" rear brakes	.030	10.000	10.060	.125	—	.810	.0005	.003	10	—	30-40	80-105
80-79 Granada, Monarch:	.030	10.000	10.060	.125	—	.810	.0005	.003	1	U105-L65	12-16	80-105
78-77 Granada, Monarch:	.030	10.000	10.060	.125	—	.810	.0005	.003	1	U105-L65	12-16	70-115
76-75 Granada, Monarch: exc. rear disc brakes	.030	10.000	10.060	.125	—	.810	.0005	.003	1	U105-L65	12-16	70-115
w/rear disc brakes	—	—	—	.125	—	.895	.0005	.003	11	90-120	12-16	70-115
97-96 Mark VIII: Front	—	—	—	.125	—	.974	.00035	.002	45	87	23-25	85-105
Rear	—	—	—	.125	—	.657	.00035	.002	99	72-97	23-26	85-105

②.030" over rivet head; if bonded lining use .062".   ④1993-86 .0003" w/Aluminum wheels; 1985-84 LTD., Marquis .0003".   ⑤1988-84 Escort, Lynx, EXP .004".
⑥1988-84 Escort, Lynx, EXP; 1987 Taurus, Sable .002".   ⑧.0313" rivet head; if bonded lining use use .125"

89450C12

PASSENGER CARS

Vehicle Year / Make / Model	Brake Shoe O.E. Minimum Lining Thickness	Brake Drum Diameter Standard Size	Brake Drum Machine To	Brake Pad O.E. Minimum Lining Thickness	Brake Rotor Min. Thickness Machine To	Brake Rotor Discard At	Brake Rotor Variation From Parallelism	Brake Rotor Runout TIR	Caliper DESIGN	Caliper Mounting Bolts Torque (ft. lbs.)	Caliper Bridge, Pin or Key Bolts Torque (ft. lbs)	Wheel Lugs or Nuts Torque (ft. lbs.)
FORD MOTOR CO. — Ford, Lincoln, Mercury												
95-93 Mark VIII: Front	—	—	—	.125	—	.974	.00035	.003	45	65-88③	16-24	85-105
Rear	—	—	—	.125	—	.657	.00035	.002	99	64-88	23-26	85-105
92-91 Mark VII: Front	—	—	—	.125	—	.972	.0005	.003	10	—	45-65	85-105
Rear	—	—	—	.123	—	.890	.0005	.002	99	44-60	23-36	85-105
90-88 Mark VII: Front	—	—	—	.125	—	.972	.0005	.003	10	—	45-65	80-105
Rear	—	—	—	.125	—	.895	.0005	.004	99	80-110	29-37	80-105
87-84 Mark VII: Front	—	—	—	.125	—	.972	.0005	.003	10	—	40-60	80-105
Rear	—	—	—	.125	—	.895	.0005	.004	99	80-110	29-37	80-105
83-80 Mark VI: w/10" rear brakes	.030	10.000	10.060	.125	—	.972	.0005	.003	10	—	40-60	80-105
w/11" rear brakes	.030	11.000	11.090	.125	—	.972	.0005	.003	10	—	40-60	80-105
79-77 Mark V: exc. rear disc brakes	.030	11.030	11.090	.125	—	1.120	.00025	.003	1	90-120	12-16	80-105
w/rear disc brakes	—	—	—	.125	—	.895	.0004	.004	11	90-120	12-16	80-105
77-73 Mark IV: exc. rear disc brakes	.030	11.030	11.090	.125	—	1.120	.00025	.003	1	90-120	12-16	70-115
w/rear disc brakes	—	—	—	.125	—	.895	.0004	.004	11	90-120	12-16	70-115
72 Mark IV:	.030	11.030	11.090	.030	1.135	1.120	.0007	.003	24	U125-L105	25-35	70-115
78-77 Maverick, Comet:	.030	10.000	10.060	.125	—	.810	.0005	.003	1	U105-L65	12-16	70-115
76-75 Maverick, Comet:	.030	10.000	10.060	.125	—	.810	.0005	.003	1	U105-L65	12-16	70-115
74 Maverick, Comet:	.030	10.000	10.060	.125	—	.810	.0005	.003	1	U105-L65	12-16	70-115
73-72 Maverick, Comet:												
w/9" drum brakes	.030	9.000	9.060	—	—	—	—	—	—	—	—	70-115
w/10" drum brakes	.030	10.000	10.060	—	—	—	—	—	—	—	—	70-115
97-96 Mustang: exc. Cobra Front	—	—	—	.125	—	.970	.0004	.001	92	95	64	85-105
Cobra Front	—	—	—	.125	—	1.040	.0004	.001	85	95	—	85-105
exc. Cobra Rear	—	—	—	.125	—	.500	.0003	.002	99	64-88	23-26	85-105
Cobra Rear	—	—	—	.125	—	.660	.0003	.002	99	64-88	23-26	85-105
95-94 Mustang: exc. Cobra Front	—	—	—	.040	—	.970	.0004	.001	92	95	65	85-105
Cobra Front	—	—	—	.040	—	1.040	.0004	.001	85	95	—	85-105
exc. Cobra Rear	—	—	—	.125	—	.500	.0003	.002	99	64-88	30-35	85-105
Cobra Rear	—	—	—	.125	—	.660	.0003	.002	99	64-83	30-35	85-105
93-89 Mustang: exc. 5.0L eng.	.030②	9.000	9.060	.125	—	.810	.0005④	.003	10	—	45-65	85-105
w/5.0L eng.	.030②	9.000	9.060	.125	—	.972	.0005④	.003	10	—	45-65	85-105
88-87 Mustang: exc. 5.0L eng.												
w/9" rear brakes	.030	9.000	9.060	.125	—	.810	.0005④	.003	10	—	30-40	80-105
w/10" rear brakes	.030	10.000	10.060	.125	—	.810	.0005④	.003	10	—	30-40	80-105
w/5.0L eng.												
exc. rear disc brakes	.030	10.000	10.060	.125	—	.972	.0005	.003	10	—	40-60	80-105
w/rear disc brakes	—	—	—	.125	—	.895	.0005	.003	64	80-110	29-37	80-105
86-83 Mustang, Capri: exc. 5.0L eng. or SVO												
w/9" rear brakes	.030	9.000	9.060	.125	—	.810	.0005④	.003	10	—	30-40	80-105
w/10" rear brakes	.030	10.000	10.060	.125	—	.810	.0005④	.003	10	—	30-40	80-105
86-83 Mustang: w/5.0L eng. or SVO												
exc. rear disc brakes	.030	10.000	10.060	.125	—	.972	.0005	.003	10	—	40-60	80-105
w/rear disc brakes	—	—	—	.125	—	.895	.0005	.004	99	80-110	29-37	80-105
82-79 Mustang, Capri:												
w/9" rear brakes	.030	9.000	9.060	.125	—	.810	.0005	.003	10	—	30-40	80-105
w/10" rear brakes	.030	10.000	10.060	.125	—	.810	.0005	.003	10	—	30-40	80-105
80-77 Pinto, Bobcat, Mustang II:	.030	9.000	9.060	.030	—	.810	.0005	.003	1	U105-L65	12-16	80-105
76-75 Pinto, Bobcat, Mustang II:	.030	9.000	9.060	.030	—	.810	.0005	.003	1	U105-L65	12-16	70-115
74 Pinto, Mustang II:	.030	9.000	9.060	.030	—	.875	.0005	.002	1	U105-L65	12-16	70-115
73-72 Pinto:	.030	9.000	9.060	.030	.700	.685	.0007	.003	21	U105-L65	—	70-115
97-93 Probe:	.040	9.000	9.060	.040	.890	.860	.001	.004	58	58-74	33-36	65-87
w/rear disc brakes				.040	.345	.315	.001	.004	70	33-49	25-29	65-87
92-89 Probe:	.040	9.000	9.060	.120	.890	.860	.001	.004⑧	58	58-72	23-30	65-87
w/rear disc brakes	—	—	—	.040	.345	.315	.001	.004⑧	70	33-49	12-17	65-87

②.030" over rivet head; if bonded lining use .062".   ④1993-86 .0003" w/Aluminum wheels; 1985-84 LTD., Marquis .0003".   ⑥1988-84 Escort, Lynx, EXP; 1987 Taurus, Sable .002".
⑧1989 .003".   ②1995-93 use .500".   ③1995 use 88 ft/lbs.   ⑨.0313" rivet head; if bonded lining use use .125"

89450C13

PASSENGER CARS

Vehicle	Brake Shoe	Brake Drum		Brake Pad	Brake Rotor					Caliper			Wheel
	O.E. Minimum Lining Thickness	Diameter		O.E. Minimum Lining Thickness	Min. Thickness		Variation From Paral-lelism	Runout TIR	D E S I G N	Mounting Bolts Torque (ft. lbs.)	Bridge, Pin or Key Bolts Torque (ft. lbs)	Lugs or Nuts Torque (ft. lbs.)
Year / Make / Model		Standard Size	Machine To		Machine To	Discard At							
FORD MOTOR CO. — Ford, Lincoln, Mercury													
97-96 Taurus, Sable: Sedan	⑩	8.858	8.918	.125	—	.974	.0004	.0024	44	85	23-28	85-105
Wagon	⑩	9.842	9.902	.125	—	.974	.0004	.0024	44	85	23-28	85-105
SHO	—	—	—	.060	—	.974	.0004	.0024	44	85	23-28	85-105
w/rear disc brakes	—	—	—	.125	—	.500	.0004	.0004	99	64-88	23-26	85-105
95-90 Taurus, Sable: Sedan	.030	8.858	8.918	.040	—	.974	.0004	.003	44	85	23-28	85-105
Wagon	.030	9.842	9.902	.040	—	.974	.0004	.003	44	85	23-28	85-105
w/rear disc brakes	—	—	—	.123	—	.900②	.0004	.002	99	45-65	23-26	85-105
89-88 Taurus, Sable: Sedan	.030	8.858	8.918	.125	—	.974	.0005	.003	44	—	18-25	80-105
Wagon	.030	9.842	9.902	.125	—	.974	.0005	.003	44	—	18-25	80-105
87-86 Taurus, Sable: Sedan	.030	8.858	8.918	.125	—	.896	.0005	.003⑥	44	—	18-25	80-105
Wagon	.030	9.842	9.902	.125	—	.896	.0005	.003⑥	44	—	18-25	80-105
94-91 Tempo, Topaz:	.060	8.060	8.120	.125	—	.882	.0005	.003	44	—	18-25	85-105
90-89 Tempo, Topaz:	.030②	8.000	8.060	.125	—	.882	.0005	.003	44	—	18-25	80-105
88-84 Tempo, Topaz:	.030②	8.000	8.060	.125	—	.882	.0005	.003	44	—	18-25	80-105
76-73 Thunderbird:	.030	11.030	11.090	.125	—	1.120	.00025	.003	1	90-120	12-16	70-115
72 Thunderbird:	.030	11.030	11.090	.030	1.135	1.120	.0007	.003	24	U125-L105	25-35	70-115
76-74 Torino, Montego:												
w/10" rear brakes	.030	10.000	10.060	.030	—	1.120	.0005	.003	1	90-120	12-16	70-115
w/11" rear brakes	.030	11.030	11.090	.030	—	1.120	.0005	.003	1	90-120	12-16	70-115
73-72 Torino, Montego:	.030	10.000	10.060	.030	—	1.120	.0005	.003	1	90-120	25-35	70-115
97-96 Town Car: Front	—	—	—	.125	—	.974	.00035	.009	10	125-170	21-26	85-105
Rear	—	—	—	.125	—	.511	.0004	.002	98	40-50	16-20	85-105
95 Town Car: Front	—	—	—	.125	—	.974	.00035	.003	10	125-170	18-26	85-105
Rear	—	—	—	.125	—	.440	.0005	.003	98	20-40	22-30	85-105
94-91 Town Car: Front	—	—	—	.125	—	.974	.0005	.003	10	—	45-65	85-105
Rear	—	—	—	.125	—	.440	.0005	.003	98	—	19-26	85-105
90-83 Town Car: w/10" rear brakes	.030	10.000	10.060	.125	—	.972	.0005	.003	10	—	40-60	80-105
w/11" rear brakes	.030	11.030	11.090	.125	—	.972	.0005	.003	10	—	40-60	80-105
82-79 Town Car, LTD, Marquis:												
w/10" rear brakes	.030	10.000	10.060	.125	—	.972	.0005	.003	10	—	40-60	80-105
w/11" rear brakes	.030	11.030	11.090	.125	—	.972	.0005	.003	10	—	40-60	80-105
89-88 Tracer: exc. rear disc brakes	.040	7.870	7.910	.120	.660	.630	—	.003	82	20-36	—	65-87
w/rear disc brakes	—	—	—	.120	.380	.350	—	.003	70	29-36	—	65-87
80-79 Versailles:												
exc. rear disc brakes	.030	10.000	10.060	.125	—	.810	.0005	.003	1	U105-L65	12-16	80-105
w/rear disc brakes	—	—	—	.125	—	.895	.0005	.004	11	90-120	12-16	80-105
78-77 Versailles:	.030	10.000	10.060	.125	—	.810	.0005	.003	1	U105-L65	12-16	70-115

②.030" over rivet head; if bonded lining use .062".　④1993-86 .0003" w/Aluminum wheels; 1985-84 LTD., Marquis .0003".　⑥1988-84 Escort, Lynx, EXP; 1987 Taurus, Sable .002".
⑧1989 .003".　②1995-93 use .500".　③1995 use 88 ft/lbs.　⑩.0313" rivet head; if bonded lining use use .125"

GEO

97-95 Metro: Front	—	—	—	.040	—	.590	.0005	.004	—	22	—	44
96-95 Metro: 2 door Rear	.040	7.09	7.16	—	—	—	—	—	—	—	—	44
4 door Rear	.040	7.87	7.95	—	—	—	—	—	—	—	—	44
94-92 Metro:	.039	7.090	7.160	.120	—	.315	.0005	.004	66	—	22	44
91 Metro: Hardtop	.110②	7.090	7.160	.315	—	.315	.0008	.0061	66	63	22	44
Convertible	.110②	7.090	7.160	.320	—	.630	—	—	89	63	20	44
90-89 Metro:	.110②	7.090	7.160	.315	—	.315	.0008	.004	66	—	22	44
97-93 Prizm:	.039	7.874	7.913	.039	—	.787	.0005	.0035	65	65	25	76
92-89 Prizm: Front	.039	7.874	7.913	.030	—	.669	.0005	.0035	65	65	18	76
Rear w/disc brakes	—	—	—	.039	—	.315	—	.0039	70	34	14	76
89 Spectrum: exc. Turbo	.039	7.090	7.140	.039	—	.378	—	.0059	57	40	36	65①
Turbo	.039	7.090	7.140	.039	—	.650	—	.0059	47	40	36	65①
93-90 Storm:	.039	7.870	7.930	.039	—	.811	.0005	.0059	57	76	36	87

①w/Aluminum wheels 87 ft/lbs.　②Measurement of lining & metal.

89450C14

PASSENGER CARS

Vehicle	Brake Shoe	Brake Drum		Brake Pad	Brake Rotor				Caliper			Wheel
		Diameter			Min. Thickness				D E S I G N		Bridge, Pin or Key	Lugs or
Year / Make / Model	O.E. Minimum Lining Thickness	Standard Size	Machine To	O.E. Minimum Lining Thickness	Machine To	Discard At	Variation From Parallelism	Runout TIR		Mounting Bolts Torque (ft. lbs.)	Bolts Torque (ft. lbs)	Nuts Torque (ft. lbs.)
HONDA												
97-94 Accord: exc. SW and V6	.080	8.661	8.701	.063	—	.827	.0006	.004	89	80	54	80
SW and V6	.080	8.661	8.701	.063	—	.910	.0006	.004	89	80	54	80
w/rear disc brakes	—	—	—	.063	—	.315	.0006	.004	46	28	17	80
93-90 Accord: exc. Wagon	.080	8.661	8.701	.063	.827	—	.0006	.004	89	80	36⑤	80
Wagon	.080	8.661	8.701	.063	.910	—	.0006	.004	89	80	36⑤	80
w/rear disc brakes	—	—	—	.063	.315	—	.0006	.004	46	28	17	80
89 Accord: exc. Fuel Inj.	.080	7.870	7.910	.120	.670	—	.0006	.004	73	53	33	80
w/Fuel Inj.	.080	7.870	7.910	.120	.750	—	.0006	.004	89	56	24	80
w/rear disc brakes	—	—	—	.060	.310	—	.0006	.006	46	28	17	80
88 Accord: exc. Fuel Inj.	.080	7.870	7.910	.120	.670	—	.0006	.006	73	53	33	80
w/Fuel Inj.	.080	7.870	7.910	.060	.750	—	.0006	.006	89	56	24	80
87-86 Accord:	.080	7.870	7.910	.120	.670	—	.0006	.006	73	53	33②	80
85-84 Accord:	.080	7.870	7.910	.059	.670	—	.0006	.006	30	56	20	80
83-82 Accord:	.079	7.870	7.910	.063	.600	—	.0006	.006	37	56	20	80
81-79 Accord:	.079	7.080	7.130	.063	.413	—	.0006	.006	22	56	—	58
78-76 Accord:	.079	7.080	7.130	.063	.449	.437	.0006	.006	22	58-65	—	50-65
91-90 Civic CRX: DX	.080	7.090	7.130	.120	.750	—	.0006	.004	69	53	20	80
HF	.080	7.090	7.130	.120	.590	—	.0006	.004	69	53	17	80
Si	.080	7.090	7.130	.120	.670	—	.0006	.004	59	53	36	80
w/rear disc brakes	—	—	—	.120	.310	—	.0006	.006	46	28	16	80
89 Civic CRX: w/DX, Si	.080	7.090	7.130	.120	.670	—	.0006	.004	69	53	U25-L20	80
w/HF	.080	7.090	7.130	.120	.590	—	.0006	.004	69	53	U25-L20	80
88 Civic CRX: w/DX, Si	.080	7.090	7.130	.120	.670	—	.0006	.006	69	53	U40-L33	80
w/HF	.080	7.090	7.130	.120	.590	—	.0006	.006	69	53	U40-L33	80
87-84 Civic CRX: w/1300 HF	.080	7.090	7.130	.120	.350	—	.0006	.004	37	56	①	80
w/1500 exc. HF	.080	7.090	7.130	.120	.590	—	.0006	.004	30	56	①	80
97-93 Civic del Sol:	.080	7.090	7.130	.060	.750	—	.0006	.004	69	80	24④	80
w/rear disc brakes	—	—	—	.060	.315	—	.0006	.004	106	28	17	80
97-92 Civic Hatchback, Civic Sedan, Civic Coupe:	.080	7.090	7.130	.060	.750	—	.0006	.004	69	80	24④	80
w/H.D. rear drum brakes	.080	7.870	7.910	.060	.750	—	.0006	.004	69	80	24④	80
w/rear disc brakes	—	—	—	.060	.310	—	.0006	.004	106	28	17	80
91-90 Civic Hatchback, Civic Sedan:	.080	7.087	7.126	.120	.750	—	.0006	.004	69	53-56	24-25	80
89 Civic Hatchback, Civic Sedan:	.080	7.090	7.130	.120	.670	—	.0006	.004	69	53	U25-L20	80
88 Civic Hatchback, Civic Sedan:	.080	7.090	7.130	.120	.669	—	.0006	.004	69	53	U40-L33	80
87-84 Civic Hatchback: w/1300	.080	7.090	7.130	.120	.390	—	.0006	.004	37	56	①	80
w/1500	.080	7.090	7.130	.120	.590	—	.0006	.004	37	56	①	80
83 Civic Hatchback: w/1300 4 SPD	.079	7.090	7.130	.063	.350	—	.0006	.006	37	56	20	58
w/1300 5 SPD	.079	7.090	7.130	.063	.390	—	.0006	.006	37	56	20	58
w/1500	.079	7.090	7.130	.063	.590	—	.0006	.006	37	56	20	58
82 Civic Hatchback: w/1300 4 SPD	.079	7.090	7.130	.063	.350	—	.0006	.006	37	56	20	58
exc. 1300 4 SPD	.079	7.090	7.130	.063	.390	—	.0006	.006	37	56	20	58
81-80 Civic Hatchback, Civic CVCC:	.079	7.090	7.130	.063	.350	—	.0006	.006	37	56	20	58
79-75 Civic Hatchback, Civic CVCC:	.079	7.080	7.130	.063	.354	.343	.0006	.006	38	36-43	—	51-65
74-73 Civic Hatchback:	.079	7.080	7.130	.063	.354	.343	.0006	.006	38	36-43	—	51-65
87-84 Civic Sedan:	.080	7.090	7.130	.120	.590	—	.0006	.004	37	56	①	80
83 Civic Sedan:	.079	7.090	7.130	.063	.590	—	.0006	.006	37	56	20	58
82-81 Civic Sedan:	.079	7.090	7.130	.063	.390	—	.0006	.006	37	56	20	58
91-90 Civic Wagon, Wagovan: (4x2)	.080	7.874	7.913	.120	.750	—	.0006	.004	69	56	U25-L20	80
(4x4)	.080	7.874	7.913	.120	.670	—	.0006	.004	73	56	36	80
89 Civic Wagon, Wagovan: (4x2)	.080	7.870	7.910	.060	.669	—	.0006	.004	69	53	U25-L20	80
(4x4)	.080	7.870	7.910	.120	.669	—	.0006	.004	73	53	36	80
88 Civic Wagon, Wagovan: (4x2)	.080	7.870	7.910	.080	.669	—	.0006	.006	66	53	U40-L33	80
(4x4)	.080	7.870	7.910	.120	.669	—	.0006	.006	73	53	36	80
87-84 Civic Wagon:	.080	7.870	7.910	.120	.590	—	.0006	.004	30	56	①	80

①Upper pin 14 ft/lbs.; lower pin 13 ft/lbs.   ②Lower bolt only.   ③1988 .004".   ④Nissin caliper shown; with Akebono caliper use 25 ft/lbs. on upper pin and 20 ft/lbs. on the lower pin.
⑤Nissin shown; w/Akebono caliper 54 ft/lbs.

89450C15

PASSENGER CARS

Vehicle Year / Make / Model	Brake Shoe O.E. Minimum Lining Thickness	Brake Drum Diameter Standard Size	Brake Drum Machine To	Brake Pad O.E. Minimum Lining Thickness	Brake Rotor Min. Thickness Machine To	Brake Rotor Discard At	Brake Rotor Variation From Parallelism	Brake Rotor Runout TIR	DESIGN	Caliper Mounting Bolts Torque (ft. lbs.)	Caliper Bridge, Pin or Key Bolts Torque (ft. lbs)	Wheel Lugs or Nuts Torque (ft. lbs.)
HONDA												
83-80 Civic Wagon	.079	7.870	7.910	.063	.390	—	.0006	.006	22	56	—	58
79-76 Civic Wagon	.079	7.870	7.910	.063	.449	.437	.0006	.006	18	63	63	51-65
97 CR-V	.080	8.660	8.700	.060	.830	—	.0006	.004	89	83	36	80
97-92 Prelude: Front	—	—	—	.060	.830	—	.0006	.004	89	80	36	80
Rear	—	—	—	.060	.315	—	.0006	.004	46	28	17	80
91 Prelude: Front	—	—	—	.060	.750	—	.0006	.004	89	56	24	80
Rear	—	—	—	.060	.310	—	.0006	.006	46	28	17	80
90-88 Prelude: Front exc. Fuel Inj.	—	—	—	.120	.670	—	.0006	.004	73	56	36	80
w/Fuel Inj.	—	—	—	.120	.750	—	.0006	.004	89	56	24	80
Rear	—	—	—	.080	.310	—	.0006	.006③	46	28	16	80
87-86 Prelude: Front exc. Fuel Inj.	—	—	—	.118	.670	—	.0006	.004	30	56	①	79
Rear	—	—	—	.063	.310	—	.0006	.006	46	28	22	79
Front w/Fuel Inj.	—	—	—	.120	.670	—	.0006	.006	73	53	33	79
Rear	—	—	—	.063	.310	—	.0006	.006	46	28	17	79
85-84 Prelude: Front	—	—	—	.120	.670	—	.0006	.004	30	56	①	79
Rear	—	—	—	.060	.310	—	.0006	.004	33	28	22	79
83 Prelude	.080	7.870	7.910	.120	.670	—	.0006	.006	30	56	①	80
82-79 Prelude	.079	7.080	7.130	.063	.413	—	.0006	.006	37	56	13	80

①Upper pin 14 ft/lbs.; lower pin 13 ft/lbs. ②Lower bolt only. ③1988 .004". ④Nissin caliper shown; with Akebono caliper use 25 ft/lbs. on upper pin and 20 ft/lbs. on the lower pin. ⑤Nissin shown; w/Akebono caliper 54 ft/lbs.

Vehicle Year / Make / Model	Brake Shoe O.E. Min. Lining Thickness	Brake Drum Standard Size	Brake Drum Machine To	Brake Pad O.E. Min. Lining Thickness	Brake Rotor Machine To	Brake Rotor Discard At	Brake Rotor Variation	Brake Rotor Runout TIR	DESIGN	Caliper Mounting Bolts	Caliper Bridge, Pin or Key Bolts	Wheel Lugs or Nuts
HYUNDAI												
97-95 Accent	.039	7.090	7.165	.039	—	.670	—	.002	37	48-55	U30-L20	65-80
97-96 Elantra	.059	8.000	8.079	.079	—	.787	—	.002	37	44-63	U30-L20	65-80
w/rear disc brakes	—	—	—	.031	—	—	—	—	101	—	16-23	65-80
95-92 Elantra	.059	8.000	8.079	.079	—	.787	—	.006⑤	37	47-60	U30-L20	65-80
94-91 Excel	.039	7.087	7.165	.039	—	.669	—	.006	69	48-55	U30-L20	65-80
90 Excel	.039	7.100	7.165	.039	—	.670	—	.006	69	47-54	U28-L19	65-80
89 Excel	.040	7.100	7.200	.040	—	.450	—	.006	69	47-54	U28-L19	50-58③
88 Excel: w/solid rotor	.040	7.100	7.200	.040	—	.450	—	.006	18	43-58	58-69	51-58③
w/vented rotor	.040	7.100	7.200	.040	—	.670	—	.006	69	47-54	U29-L20	51-58③
87-85 Excel	.040	7.086	7.165	.040	—	.450	—	.006	18	43-58	58-69	50-58③
87-86 Pony Sedan	.039	7.992	④	.079	—	.449	—	.006	18	58	63	51-58
85-83 Pony Sedan	.039	7.992	④	.079	—	.449	—	.006	18	58-73	58-69	50-58
95-91 Scoupe	.039⑥	7.100	7.165	.039	—	.669	—	.006⑤	69	48-55	U28-L20	65-80
97 Sonata:												
exc. rear disc brakes (V6)	.059	9.000	9.080	.079	—	.787	—	.0024	37	51-63	16-24	65-80
exc. rear disc brakes (4 cyl.)	.031	8.858	8.936	.079	—	.787	—	.0024	37	51-63	16-24	65-80
w/rear disc brakes	—	—	—	.079	—	.413	—	—	101	—	16-23	65-80
96-95 Sonata:												
exc. rear disc brakes (V6)	.059	9.000	9.080	.079	—	.787	—	.004	37	51-63	16-24	65-80
exc. rear disc brakes (4 cyl.)	.031	8.858	8.936	.079	—	.787	—	.004	37	51-63	16-24	65-80
w/rear disc brakes	—	—	—	.079	—	.413	—	—	101	—	16-23	65-80
93-91 Sonata	.031	8.858	8.936	.079	—	.797	—	.004	37	51-63	16-24	65-80
w/rear disc brakes	—	—	—	.031	—	.413	—	.005	59	—	18-25	65-80
90 Sonata	.039	9.000	9.079	.079	—	.787	—	.004	37	50-61	31-35①	60-80
w/rear disc brakes	—	—	—	.031	—	.413	—	.005	59	—	18-25	60-80
89 Sonata	.059	9.000	9.079	.079	—	.787	—	.004	37	50-61	16-23	60-80
87 Stellar	.040	9.000	9.079	.040	—	.669	—	.004	69	51	U29-L20	54②
86-85 Stellar	.060	9.000	—	.060	—	.450	—	.002	17	45-55	15-18	50-58
97 Tiburon: exc. rear disc brakes	.059	8.000	8.079	.079	—	.787	—	.002	37	44-63	U30-L20	65-80
	—	—	—	.031	—	.413	—	—	101	—	16-23	65-80

①Bendix shown; Mando 16-23 ft/lbs. ②w/Aluminum wheels 65 ft/lbs. ③w/Aluminum wheels 58-72 ft/lbs. ④Machining specification is not available; discard at 8.071". ⑤1995 use .002". ⑥1995-93 use .031".

89450C16

PASSENGER CARS

Year / Make / Model	Brake Shoe O.E. Minimum Lining Thickness	Brake Drum Diameter Standard Size	Brake Drum Diameter Machine To	Brake Pad O.E. Minimum Lining Thickness	Brake Rotor Min. Thickness Machine To	Brake Rotor Min. Thickness Discard At	Brake Rotor Variation From Parallelism	Brake Rotor Runout TIR	DESIGN	Caliper Mounting Bolts Torque (ft. lbs.)	Caliper Bridge, Pin or Key Bolts Torque (ft. lbs)	Wheel Lugs or Nuts Torque (ft. lbs.)
INFINITI												
96-91 G20: Front	—	—	—	.079	—	.787	.0004②	.0028	71	53-72	16-23	72-87
Rear	—	—	—	.079①	—	.310	.0008	.0028	46	25-31③	16-23	72-87
97-96 I30: Front	—	—	—	.079	—	.787	.0004	.0031	71	53-72	16-23	72-87
Rear	—	—	—	.059	—	.315	.0008	.0059	46	16-23	16-23	72-87
97-93 J30: Front	—	—	—	.079	—	1.024	.0004	.0028	76	53-72	16-23	72-87
Rear	—	—	—	.079	—	.551	.0008	.0059	71	28-38	23-30	72-87
92-90 M30: Front	—	—	—	.079	—	.787	—	.0028	71	53-72	16-23	72-87
Rear	—	—	—	.079	—	.354	—	.0028	71	28-38	23-30	72-87
97-90 Q45: Front	—	—	—	.079	—	1.024	.0004	.0028	76	53-72④	61-69	72-87
Rear	—	—	—	.079	—	.315⑤	.0008	.0028	71	28-38	23-30	72-87

①1991-93 shown. 1994-96 use .059". ②1992-96 shown, 1991 use .0008". ③1991 shown, 1992-96 use 28-38 ft/lbs. ④1990-94 shown, 1995-96 use 87-101 ft/lbs. ⑤1997 .551

Year / Make / Model	Brake Shoe O.E. Minimum Lining Thickness	Brake Drum Diameter Standard Size	Brake Drum Diameter Machine To	Brake Pad O.E. Minimum Lining Thickness	Brake Rotor Min. Thickness Machine To	Brake Rotor Min. Thickness Discard At	Brake Rotor Variation From Parallelism	Brake Rotor Runout TIR	DESIGN	Caliper Mounting Bolts Torque (ft. lbs.)	Caliper Bridge, Pin or Key Bolts Torque (ft. lbs)	Wheel Lugs or Nuts Torque (ft. lbs.)
ISUZU												
89-88 I-Mark: exc. Turbo or DOHC eng.	.040	7.090	7.140	.040	—	.378	—	.005	57	40	36	65③
w/Turbo or DOHC eng.	.040	7.090	7.140	.040	—	.650	—	.005	58	40	27	65③
87-85 I-Mark:	.039	7.090	7.140	.039	—	.378	—	.006	54	40	36	60①
84-81 I-Mark:	.039	9.000	9.040	.067	.354	.338	—	.006	49	36	—	50①
92-90 Impulse: Front	—	—	—	.039	—	.810	.0005	.0059	57	72	36	87
Rear	—	—	—	.039	—	.299	.0005	.0059	97	72	32	87
89-85 Impulse: Front	—	—	—	.040	.668	.654	.0006	.005	58	36	27	87
Rear	—	—	—	.040	.668	.654	.0006	.005	47	36	15	87
84-83 Impulse: Front	—	—	—	.125	.706	.654	.0012	.005	47	35-38	25-28	80-94
Rear	—	—	—	.125	.706	.654	.0012	.005	47	35-38	13-16	80-94
93-91 Stylus: w/rear drum brakes	.039	7.870	7.929	.039	—	.653	.0005	.0059	57	72	36	87
w/rear disc brakes	—	—	—	.039	—	.810	.0005	.0059	97	72	32	87

①w/Aluminum wheels 90 ft/lbs. ②Radial pull in pounds at lug nut. ③w/Aluminum wheels 86 ft/lbs.

Year / Make / Model	Brake Shoe O.E. Minimum Lining Thickness	Brake Drum Diameter Standard Size	Brake Drum Diameter Machine To	Brake Pad O.E. Minimum Lining Thickness	Brake Rotor Min. Thickness Machine To	Brake Rotor Min. Thickness Discard At	Brake Rotor Variation From Parallelism	Brake Rotor Runout TIR	DESIGN	Caliper Mounting Bolts Torque (ft. lbs.)	Caliper Bridge, Pin or Key Bolts Torque (ft. lbs)	Wheel Lugs or Nuts Torque (ft. lbs.)
JAGUAR												
97-95 XJ6, XJS, XJ12, XJR, Vanden Plas: Front	—	—	—	—	—	1.063	.0005	.004	—	89-118	18-26	40-50③
Rear	—	—	—	—	—	.728	.0005	.004	—	40-49	18-26	40-50③
94-88 XJ6, XJ12: Front	—	—	—	.125	—	②	.0005	.004	61	74-94①	23-26	48-62③
Rear	—	—	—	.125	—	②	.0005	.004	61	74-94①	23-26	48-62③
87-75 XJ6, Vanden Plas: Front	—	—	—	.125	—	②	—	.006	16	55	—	40-60
Rear	—	—	—	.125	—	.450	—	.004	53	49-55	—	40-60
74-72 XJ6: Front	—	—	—	.125	—	.450	—	.006	80	55	—	40-60
Rear	—	—	—	.125	—	.450	—	.004	53	49-55	—	40-60
94-76 XJS, Saloons: Front	—	—	—	.125	—	②	—	.006	16	50-60	—	40-60③
Rear w/overdrive	—	—	—	.125	—	②	—	.004	53	49-55	—	40-60③
Rear exc. Overdrive	—	—	—	.125	—	.450	—	.004	53	49-55	—	40-60③
79-78 XJ12: Front	—	—	—	.125	—	②	—	.004	16	50-60	—	45
Rear	—	—	—	.125	—	.450	—	.004	53	49-55	—	45
77-72 XJ12, V12: Front	—	—	—	.125	—	②	—	.004	80	50-60	—	40-60
Rear	—	—	—	.125	—	.450	—	.004	53	49-55	—	40-60

①To link shown; to hub carrier 40-45 ft/lbs. ②Minimum thickness is stamped on rotor. ③w/Alloy wheels 65-75 ft/lbs. ④Wheel brg. end play should not exceed .003".

Year / Make / Model	Brake Shoe O.E. Minimum Lining Thickness	Brake Drum Diameter Standard Size	Brake Drum Diameter Machine To	Brake Pad O.E. Minimum Lining Thickness	Brake Rotor Min. Thickness Machine To	Brake Rotor Min. Thickness Discard At	Brake Rotor Variation From Parallelism	Brake Rotor Runout TIR	DESIGN	Caliper Mounting Bolts Torque (ft. lbs.)	Caliper Bridge, Pin or Key Bolts Torque (ft. lbs)	Wheel Lugs or Nuts Torque (ft. lbs.)
KIA												
97-95 Sephia: Front	.040	7.870	7.910	.080	—	.710	—	.004	—	33-50	15-21	65-87
w/rear disc brakes	—	—	—	.080	—	.320	—	.004	—	18-24	—	65-87
94 Sephia:	.040	7.870	7.910	.080	—	.710	—	.004	—	—	15-21	65-87

89450C17

PASSENGER CARS

Vehicle Year / Make / Model	Brake Shoe O.E. Minimum Lining Thickness	Brake Drum Diameter Standard Size	Brake Drum Diameter Machine To	Brake Pad O.E. Minimum Lining Thickness	Brake Rotor Min. Thickness Machine To	Brake Rotor Min. Thickness Discard At	Brake Rotor Variation From Parallelism	Brake Rotor Runout TIR	DESIGN N	Caliper Mounting Bolts Torque (ft. lbs.)	Caliper Bridge, Pin or Key Bolts Torque (ft. lbs)	Wheel Lugs or Nuts Torque (ft. lbs.)
LEXUS												
91-90 ES250: Front	—	—	—	.039	—	.945	—	.0028	65	79	29	76
Rear	—	—	—	.039	—	.354	—	.0054	66	34	14	76
97-92 ES300: Front	—	—	—	.039	—	1.024	—	.002	66①	79	25	76
Rear	—	—	—	.039	—	.354	—	.0059	66	34	14	76
97-93 GS300: Front	—	—	—	.039	—	1.181	—	.002	103	87	25	76
Rear	—	—	—	.039	—	.591	—	.002	102	77	25	76
97 LS400: Front	—	—	—	.039	—	1.024	—	.002	110	87	—	76
Rear	—	—	—	.039	—	.591	—	.002	105	77	25	76
96-95 LS400: Front	—	—	—	.118	—	1.024	—	.002	110	87	—	76
Rear	—	—	—	.098	—	.591	—	.002	105	77	25	76
94-93 LS400: Front	—	—	—	.039	—	1.181	—	.002	81	87	25	76
Rear	—	—	—	.039	—	.591	—	.002	105	77	25	76
92-91 LS400: Front	—	—	—	.039	—	1.024	—	.002	81	87	25	76
Rear	—	—	—	.039	—	.591	—	.002	105	77	25	76
90 LS400: Front	—	—	—	.039	—	.906	—	.002	65	87	25	76
Rear	—	—	—	.039	—	.591	—	.002	66	77	25	76
97-92 SC300: Front	—	—	—	.039	—	1.024	—	.002	103	87	25	76
Rear	—	—	—	.039	—	.591	—	.002	105	77	25	76
97-92 SC400: Front	—	—	—	.039	—	1.181	—	.002	103	87	25	76
Rear	—	—	—	.039	—	.591	—	.002	105	77	25	76

①For 1994-96 use ill. #81.

Vehicle Year / Make / Model	Brake Shoe O.E. Minimum Lining Thickness	Brake Drum Diameter Standard Size	Brake Drum Diameter Machine To	Brake Pad O.E. Minimum Lining Thickness	Brake Rotor Min. Thickness Machine To	Brake Rotor Min. Thickness Discard At	Brake Rotor Variation From Parallelism	Brake Rotor Runout TIR	DESIGN N	Caliper Mounting Bolts Torque (ft. lbs.)	Caliper Bridge, Pin or Key Bolts Torque (ft. lbs)	Wheel Lugs or Nuts Torque (ft. lbs.)
MAZDA												
97-95 Protege: exc. rear disc brakes	.039	7.874	7.933	.039	.819	.787	—	.002	58	—	29-36	65-87
w/rear disc brakes	—	—	—	.039	.307	.276	—	.002	70	34-44	33-44	65-87
94-92 323, Protege:	.040	7.870	7.910	.080	—	.790	—	.004	82	29-36	—	65-87
w/rear disc brakes	—	—	—	.040	—	.310	—	.004	70	33-43	26-28	65-87
91-90 323, Protege:	.040	9.000	9.040	.080	—	.790	—	.004	82	29-36	—	65-87
w/rear disc brakes	—	—	—	.040	—	.280	—	.004	70	33-43	—	65-87
89-88 323 Hatchback, 323 Sedan:	.040	7.870	7.910	.080	—	.630	—	.004	82	36-43③	—	65-87
w/rear disc brakes	—	—	—	.040	—	.310	—	.004	70	12-17	—	65-87
87-86 323 Hatchback, 323 Sedan:	.040	7.870	7.910	.118	—	.630	—	.003	82	29-36	—	65-87
w/rear disc brakes	—	—	—	.040	—	.350	—	.003	70	12-17	—	65-87
88-87 323 Wagon:	.040	9.000	9.040	.118②	—	.630	—	.004	66	29-36	—	65-87
97-96 626, MX-6:	.040	9.000	9.059	.080	.900	.870	—	.002	58	58-75	33-36	65-87
w/rear disc brakes	—	—	—	.040	.350	.310	—	.002	70	34-49	26-28	65-87
95-93 626, MX-6:	.040	9.000	9.059	.080	—	.870	—	.004	58	58-74	33-36	65-87
w/rear disc brakes	—	—	—	.040	—	.310	—	.004	70	33-49	25-29	65-87
92-88 626, MX-6:	.040	9.000	9.060	.080	—	.870	—	.004	58	58-72	23-30	65-87
w/rear disc brakes	—	—	—	.040	—	.310	—	.004	70	33-49	12-17	65-87
87-86 626:	.040	7.870	7.910	.118	—	.710	—	.004	58	①	—	65-87
w/rear disc brakes	—	—	—	.040	—	.350	—	.004	70	①	—	65-87
85 626: w/gas eng.	.040	7.870	7.910	.118	—	.470	—	.004	58	①	—	65-87
w/diesel eng.	.040	7.870	7.910	.118	—	.710	—	.004	58	①	—	65-87
84-83 626:	.040	7.874	7.913	.040	—	.490	—	.004	58	①	—	65-80
82-79 626:	.040	9.000	9.040	.040	—	.472	—	.004	37	33-40	—	65-80
77-74 808:	.040	7.874	7.914	.256④	—	.394	—	.004	18	—	—	65-72
73-72 808:	.040	7.874	7.914	.256④	—	.394	—	.003	18	—	—	65
95-92 929: Front	—	—	—	.040	—	.870	—	.004	54	75-87	46-62	65-87
Rear	—	—	—	.040	—	.630	—	.004	66	33-50	28-36	65-87
91-90 929: Front	—	—	—	.080	—	.790	—	.004	54	58-86	61-69	65-87
Rear	—	—	—	.080	—	.630	—	.004	66	33-50	12-17	65-87
89-88 929: Front	—	—	—	.080	—	.790	—	.004	54	58-86	61-69	65-87
Rear	—	—	—	.080	—	.310	—	.004	66	33-50	12-17	65-87
78-76 Cosmo: Front	—	—	—	.276④	—	.669	—	.004	35	40-47	—	65-72
Rear	—	—	—	.276④	—	.354	—	.004	35	40-47	—	65-72

①Upper bolt 11-18 ft/lbs.; lower bolt 15-22 ft/lbs.   ②1988 .080".   ③1989 29-36 ft/lbs.   ④Measurement of lining & metal.   ⑤Radial pull in pounds at lug nut.

PASSENGER CARS

Year / Make / Model	Brake Shoe O.E. Minimum Lining Thickness	Brake Drum Diameter Standard Size	Brake Drum Machine To	Brake Pad O.E. Minimum Lining Thickness	Brake Rotor Min. Thickness Machine To	Brake Rotor Discard At	Variation From Parallelism	Runout TIR	DESIGN	Caliper Mounting Bolts Torque (ft. lbs.)	Bridge, Pin or Key Bolts Torque (ft. lbs.)	Wheel Lugs or Nuts Torque (ft. lbs.)
MAZDA												
85 GLC Hatchback, GLC Sedan:	.040	7.090	7.130	.118	—	.390	—	.004	57	33-40	—	65-87
84-81 GLC Hatchback, GLC Sedan:	.040	7.090	7.130	.040	—	.393	—	.004	35	33-40	—	65-80
80-77 GLC Hatchback, GLC SEdan:	.040	7.874	7.914	.040	—	.472	—	.003	35	33-40	—	65-80
83-81 GLC Wagon:	.040	7.874	7.913	.040	—	.472	—	.003	35	33-40	—	65-80
97-95 Miata, MX-5: Front	—	—	—	.040	.740	.710	—	.002	54	36-51	58-65	65-87
Rear	—	—	—	.040	.330	.310	—	.002	70	34-49	U35-L27	65-87
94 Miata MX-5: Front	—	—	—	.040	—	.710	—	.004	54	36-51	58-65	65-87
Rear	—	—	—	.040	—	.310	—	.004	70	34-49	U35-L27	65-87
93-91 Miata MX-5: Front	—	—	—	.040	—	.630	—	.004	54	36-51	58-65	65-87
Rear	—	—	—	.040	—	.280	—	.004	70	36-51	25-29	65-87
90 Miata MX-5: Front	—	—	—	.040	—	.630	—	.004	54	36-51	33-40	65-87
Rear	—	—	—	.080	—	.280	—	.004	70	—	33-43	65-87
97-96 Millenia: Front	—	—	—	.080	1.055	1.024	—	.002	112	76-101	47-62	65-87
Rear	—	—	—	.080	.330	.295	—	.002	66	37-50	—	65-87
95 Millenia: Front	—	—	—	.080	—	1.024	—	.004	112	76-101	47-62	65-87
Rear	—	—	—	.080	—	.295	—	.004	66	37-50	—	65-87
95 MX-3:	.040	7.874	7.913	.080	.818	.787	—	.002	102	29-36	—	65-87
w/rear disc brakes	—	—	—	.040	.331	.315	—	.002	103	33-45	12-17	65-87
94 MX-3:	.040	7.870	7.910	.080	—	.790	—	.004	102	29-36	—	65-87
w/rear disc brakes	—	—	—	.040	—	.310	—	.004	103	33-45	12-17	65-87
93-92 MX-3:	.040	7.870	7.910	.080	—	.790	—	.004	102	—	29-36	65-87
w/rear disc brakes	—	—	—	.040	—	.310	—	.004	103	33-45	33-45	65-87
73-72 RX-2:	.040	7.874	7.914	.276④	—	.433	—	.003	18	—	—	65
77-75 RX-3:	.040	7.874	7.914	.276④	—	.394	—	.004	18	—	—	65-72
73-72 RX-3:	.040	7.874	7.914	.256④	—	.394	—	.003	18	—	—	65
78-74 RX-4:	.040	9.000	9.040	.276④	—	.433	—	.004	35	36-40	—	65-72
95-93 RX-7: Front	—	—	—	.040	—	.790	—	.004	16	58-72	—	66-86
Rear	—	—	—	.040	—	.710	—	.004	70	34-49	47-62	66-86
91-89 RX-7: Front Std.	—	—	—	.080	—	.790	—	.004	32	58-72	23-30	65-87
Front H.D.	—	—	—	.080	—	.790	—	.004	16	58-72	—	65-87
Rear Std.	—	—	—	.040	—	.310	—	.004	70	33-40	12-17	65-87
Rear H.D.	—	—	—	.040	—	.710	—	.004	70	33-40	12-17	65-87
88-86 RX-7: Front w/14" Wheels	—	—	—	.040	—	.790	—	.004	32	58-72	23-30	65-87
Front w/15" Wheels	—	—	—	.118	—	.790	—	.004	16	58-72	—	65-87
Rear w/14" Wheels	—	—	—	.040	—	.310	—	.004	70	33-40	22-30	65-87
Rear w/15" Wheels	—	—	—	.040	—	.710	—	.004	70	33-40	22-30②	65-87
85-80 RX-7:	.040	7.874	7.914	.040	—	.670	—	.004	32	—	—	65-80
w/rear solid rotor	—	—	—	.040	—	.354	—	.004	32	—	22-30	65-80
w/rear vented rotor	—	—	—	.040	—	.787	—	.004	32	—	22-30	65-80
79 RX-7:	.040	7.874	7.914	.040	—	.670	—	.004	35	33-40	—	65-80

①Upper bolt 11-18 ft/lbs.; lower bolt 15-22 ft/lbs. ②1988 .080". ③1989 29-36 ft/lbs. ④Measurement of lining & metal. ⑤Radial pull in pounds at lug nut.

Year / Make / Model	Brake Shoe O.E. Minimum Lining Thickness	Brake Drum Diameter Standard Size	Brake Drum Machine To	Brake Pad O.E. Minimum Lining Thickness	Brake Rotor Min. Thickness Machine To	Brake Rotor Discard At	Variation From Parallelism	Runout TIR	DESIGN	Caliper Mounting Bolts Torque (ft. lbs.)	Bridge, Pin or Key Bolts Torque (ft. lbs.)	Wheel Lugs or Nuts Torque (ft. lbs.)
MERCEDES BENZ												
93-86 190E: 2.3, 2.3-16, 2.6 Front	—	—	—	.138	.787	.764	—	.004	—	85	26	81
2.3, 2.3-16, 2.6 Rear	—	—	—	.138	.300	.287	—	.005	14	37	—	81
90-84 190D,E: Front	—	—	—	.138	.374	.354	—	.005	—	85	26	81
Rear	—	—	—	.079	.300	.287	—	.005	—	37	—	81
97-94 C220, C230, C36, C280, E300 Diesel: Front	—	—	—	.078	.787	.764	—	.005	—	85	—	81
Rear	—	—	—	.078	.300	.287	—	.005	—	32	—	81
93-86 260E, 300CE,TE,DT,E,TDT,D: Front	—	—	—	.079	.787	.764	—	.004	—	—	—	81
Rear	—	—	—	.079	.300	.287	—	.005	—	—	—	81

89450C19

PASSENGER CARS

Vehicle Year / Make / Model	Brake Shoe O.E. Minimum Lining Thickness	Brake Drum Diameter Standard Size	Brake Drum Diameter Machine To	Brake Pad O.E. Minimum Lining Thickness	Brake Rotor Min. Thickness Machine To	Brake Rotor Min. Thickness Discard At	Brake Rotor Variation From Parallelism	Brake Rotor Runout TIR	DESIGN	Caliper Mounting Bolts Torque (ft. lbs.)	Caliper Bridge, Pin or Key Bolts Torque (ft. lbs)	Wheel Lugs or Nuts Torque (ft. lbs.)
MERCEDES BENZ												
91-81 300 SD,SE,SEL, 300 SDL Turbo Diesel, 350 SD,SDL, 380 SE,SEC,SEL, 420 SEL, 500 SEC,SEL, 560 SEC,SEL:												
Front Fixed Caliper 60mm	—	—	—	.079	.787	.764	—	.004	14	85	—	81
Fixed Caliper 57mm	—	—	—	.079	1.024	1.000	—	.004	14	85	—	81
Floating Caliper	—	—	—	.138	.787	.764	—	.004	37	85	26	81
Rear	—	—	—	.079	.339	.327	—	.005	14	66	—	81
95-94 E320 Exc. Wagon: Front	—	—	—	.078	.906	.882	—	.005	—	85	—	81
Rear	—	—	—	.078	.300	.287	—	.005	—	37	—	81
95-94 E320 Wagon: Front	—	—	—	.078	.906	.882	—	.005	—	85	—	81
Rear	—	—	—	.078	.697	.685	—	.005	—	37	—	81
97-94 S320, S350 Turbo Diesel:												
Front 2 Piston Caliper	—	—	—	.078	1.023	1.000	—	.003	—	132	—	81
Front 4 Piston Caliper	—	—	—	.078	1.102	1.079	—	.003	—	132	—	81
Rear	—	—	—	.078	.413	.385	—	.004	—	85	—	81
97-94 SL320, SL500: Front	—	—	—	.078	1.026	1.000	—	.005	—	85	—	81
Rear	—	—	—	.078	.300	.287	—	.005	—	37	—	81
93-90 300SL, 500SL: Front	—	—	—	.079	1.024	1.000	—	.005	14	85	—	81
Rear	—	—	—	.079	.300	.287	—	.004	14	37	—	81
95-93 E420, 400E: Front	—	—	—	.078	.906	.882	—	.005	14	85	—	81
Rear	—	—	—	.078	.866	.843	—	.005	16	—	—	81
92 400E: Front	—	—	—	.078	.787	.764	—	.005	14	85	—	81
Rear	—	—	—	.078	.866	.843	—	.005	16	—	—	81
97-94 S420, S500, S600:												
Front 2 Piston Caliper	—	—	—	.078	1.023	1.000	—	.003	—	132	—	81
Front 4 Piston Caliper	—	—	—	.078	1.102	1.079	—	.003	—	132	—	81
Rear	—	—	—	.078	.787	.764	—	.004	—	85	—	81
94-93 E500, 500E: Front (As of 2/93)	—	—	—	.078	1.122	1.102	—	.003	—	85	—	81
Rear	—	—	—	.078	.866	.843	—	.005	—	37	—	81
93-92 500E: Front (To 1/93)	—	—	—	.079	1.024	1.000	—	.005	14	85	—	81
Rear	—	—	—	.079	.866	.842	—	.006	16	—	—	81
97-94 SL600: Front	—	—	—	.078	1.122	1.102	—	.003	—	85	—	81
Rear	—	—	—	.078	.787	.764	—	.004	—	37	—	81
89-86 560SL: Front	—	—	—	.079	.787	.764	—	.004	16	85	—	81
Rear	—	—	—	.079	.338	.327	—	.005	14	66	—	81
85-73 380SL,SLC, 450SL,SLC: Front	—	—	—	.079	—	.811①	—	.005	14	85	—	81
Rear	—	—	—	.079	—	.327	—	.005	14	66	—	81
85-77 230, 240D, 300D,CD,TD, 280E,CE: Front	—	—	—	.079	—	.417	—	.005	14	85	—	81
Rear	—	—	—	.079	—	.327	—	.005	14	66	—	81
80 280SE, 300SD, 450SEL: Front	—	—	—	.079	—	.764	—	.005	14	85	—	81
Rear	—	—	—	.079	—	.327	—	.005	14	66	—	81
79-73 280S,SE, 300SD, 450SE,SEL, 6.9: Front	—	—	—	.079	—	.787	—	.005	14	85	—	81
Rear	—	—	—	.079	—	.327	—	.005	14	85	—	81
76-72 220,D, 220/8, 230, 240D, 250,C, 280,C, 300D: Front	—	—	—	.079	—	.432②	—	.005	14	85	—	81
Rear	—	—	—	.079	—	.327	—	.005	14	66	—	81
73-72 280,SE,SEL, 300SEL: Front	—	—	—	.079	—	.431③	—	.005	14	85	—	81
Rear	—	—	—	.079	—	.327	—	.005	14	66	—	81
72 600: Front	—	—	—	.354	—	.725	—	—	14	—	—	125
Rear	—	—	—	.079	—	.570	—	—	14	—	—	125

①w/57mm caliper piston shown; w/60mm caliper piston up to 3/80 .787" from 3/80 .763". ②w/57mm caliper piston shown; w/60mm caliper piston .417". ③1st version shown; 2nd version .700".

89450C20

PASSENGER CARS

Vehicle	Brake Shoe	Brake Drum		Brake Pad	Brake Rotor				Caliper			Wheel
	O.E. Minimum Lining Thickness	Diameter		O.E. Minimum Lining Thickness	Min. Thickness		Variation From Parallelism	Runout TIR	DESIGN	Mounting Bolts Torque (ft. lbs.)	Bridge, Pin or Key Bolts Torque (ft. lbs)	Lugs or Nuts Torque (ft. lbs.)
Year / Make / Model		Standard Size	Machine To		Machine To	Discard At						
MERKUR												
90-88 Scorpio: Front	—	—	—	.140	—	.900	.0003	.003[2]	44	37-48	—	52-73
Rear	—	—	—	.150	—	.350	.0003	.003[2]	68	37-48	23-26	52-73
89-85 XR4Ti:	.040	10.000	10.060	.060	.927	.897	.0006[1]	.002	44	43-44	18-23	55-70

① 1987 .0004".   ② 1990 .002"

Vehicle	Brake Shoe	Brake Drum		Brake Pad	Brake Rotor				Caliper			Wheel
MITSUBISHI												
97-91 3000GT: (FWD) Front	—	—	—	.080	—	.880	—	.0028[11]	81	65	54	87-101
(FWD) Rear	—	—	—	.080	—	.650	—	.0031	69	36-43	20	87-101
(AWD) Front	—	—	—	.080	—	1.120	—	.004	16	65	—	87-101
(AWD) Rear	—	—	—	.080	—	.720	—	.0031	69	36-43	32	87-101
88 Cordia, Tredia: exc. Turbo	.040	8.000	8.100	.080	—	.650	—	.006	69	58-72	16-23	65-80
w/Turbo	.040	8.000	8.100	.080	—	.880	—	.006	69	58-72	16-23	65-80
87-84 Cordia, Tredia:	.040	8.000	8.050	.040	—	.650	—	.006	60	58-72	16-23	50-57[5]
83 Cordia, Tredia:	.040	8.000	8.050	.040	—	.450	—	.006	58	58-72	16-23	50-57[5]
97 Diamante: Front	—	—	—	.080	—	.880	.0006	.0031	81	65	54	65-80
Rear	—	—	—	.080	—	.330	—	.002	69	36-43	20	65-80
96-92 Diamante: Front	—	—	—	.080	—	.880	.0006	.0028	81	65	54	65-80
exc. Wagon Rear	—	—	—	.080	—	.650	.0006	.0031	69	36-43	20	65-80
Wagon Rear	—	—	—	.080	—	.720	.0006	.0031	69	36-43	20	65-80
97-96 Eclipse, Spyder: Front	.039	—	9.100	.080	—	.882	.0006	.0031	69[10]	65	54	87-101
Rear	—	—	—	.080	—	.330	—	.0031	101	36-43	54	87-101
95 Eclipse: Front	.039	—	8.070	.080	—	.882	.0006	.0031	69[10]	—	54	65-80
FWD w/rear disc brakes	—	—	—	.080	—	.330	—	.0031	101	—	54	65-80
AWD w/rear disc brakes	—	—	—	.080	—	.724	—	.0031	101	—	54	65-80
94-90 Eclipse: Front	—	—	—	.080	—	.882	—	.003	69	58-72	16-23[9]	87-101
Rear	—	—	—	.080	—	.331	—	.003	70	36-43	16-23	87-101
97 Galant:	.040	8.976	9.000	.080	—	.880	.0006	.003	101	65	54	65-80
96-94 Galant:	.040	8.976	9.078	.080	—	.882	.0006	.003	101	65	54	65-80
w/rear disc brakes	—	—	—	.080	—	.331	.0006	.003	101	36-43	54	65-80
93-89 Galant: w/rear drum brakes	.040	8.000	8.100	.080	—	.882	—	.003	69[2]	58-72	16-23[1]	65-80
w/rear disc brakes	—	—	—	.080	—	.331	—	.003	70	36-43	16-23	65-80
90-88 Galant Sigma: Front	—	—	—	.079	—	.882	—	.004	73	58-72	U33-L27	65-80
Rear	—	—	—	.079	—	.646	—	.004	73	36-43	16-23	65-80
87 Galant: w/rear drum brakes	.040	8.000	8.050	.080	—	.880	—	.004	69	58-72	16-23	65-80
w/rear disc brakes	—	—	—	.040	—	.330	—	.012	70	36-43	16-23	65-80
86-85 Galant: w/rear drum brakes	.040	8.000	8.050	.040	—	.880	—	.006	69	58-72	16-23	50-57[3]
w/rear disc brakes	—	—	—	.040	—	.330	—	.006	70	36-43	16-23	50-57[3]
97 Mirage:	.039	8.000	8.100	.080	—	.650	.0006	.0024	69	67-81	U36-L65	65-80
96-93 Mirage: w/solid rotor	.040	7.100	7.200	.080	—	.449	—	.0028	69	65	U36-L65	65-80
97-93 Mirage: w/vented rotor	.040	8.000	8.100	.080	—	.646	—	.0028	69	65	U36-L65	65-80
w/rear disc brakes	—	—	—	.080	—	.331	—	.0031	70	36-43	20	65-80
92-91 Mirage: w/solid rotor	.040	7.100	7.200	.080	—	.449	—	.006	71	58-72	U39-L65	65-80
w/vented rotor	.040	7.100	7.200	.080	—	.646	—	.006	69	58-72	27-36	65-80
w/rear disc brakes Front	—	—	—	.080	—	.882	—	.006	69	58-72	46-62	65-80
Rear	—	—	—	.080	—	.331	—	.006	70	36-43	16-23	65-80
90 Mirage: exc. disc brakes	.040	7.100	7.200	.080	—	.449	—	.006	69	58-72	16-23	65-80
Front w/rear disc brakes	—	—	—	.080	—	.882	—	.006	71	58-72	23-30[7]	65-80
Rear	—	—	—	.080	—	.331	—	.006	70	58-72	16-23	65-80
89 Mirage: exc. rear disc brakes	.040	7.100	7.200	.080	—	.449	—	.006	69	58-72	16-23	65-80
Front w/rear disc brakes	—	—	—	.080	—	.882	—	.006	69	58-72	16-23	65-80
Rear	—	—	—	.080	—	.331	—	.006	70	36-43	16-23	65-80
88-85 Mirage: exc. Turbo	.040	7.100	7.150	.040[4]	—	.450	—	.006	69	58-72	16-23	50-57[3]
w/Turbo	.040	7.100	7.150	.040	—	.650	—	.006	69	58-72	16-23	50-57[3]
94-90 Precis:	.040	7.087	7.165	.040	—	.670	—	.006	71	47-54	U29-L20	65-80

① 1993-91 46-62 ft/lbs.   ② Turbo use ill. 81.   ③ w/Aluminum wheels 66-81 ft/lbs.   ④ 1989-88 .080".   ⑤ w/Aluminum wheels 57-72 ft/lbs.   ⑥ w/Aluminum wheels 58-72 ft/lbs.
⑦ 1.5L eng. shown; 1.6L eng. 46-62 ft/lbs.   ⑧ w/Aluminum wheels; 1989-84 65-80 ft/lbs.; 1983 57-72 ft/lbs.   ⑨ Vehicles built up to 04/89 shown; from 5/89 46-62 ft/lbs.
⑩ AWD Turbo use ill. #81.   ⑪ 1992-97 shown; 1991 use .004".

89450C21

PASSENGER CARS

Vehicle Year / Make / Model	Brake Shoe O.E. Minimum Lining Thickness	Brake Drum Diameter Standard Size	Machine To	Brake Pad O.E. Minimum Lining Thickness	Brake Rotor Min. Thickness Machine To	Discard At	Variation From Parallelism	Runout TIR	DESIGN	Caliper Mounting Bolts Torque (ft. lbs.)	Bridge, Pin or Key Bolts Torque (ft. lbs)	Wheel Lugs or Nuts Torque (ft. lbs.)
MITSUBISHI												
89-88 Precis: w/solid rotor	.040	7.100	7.200	.040	—	.450	—	.006	18	43-58	58-69	50-57⑥
w/vented rotor	.040	7.100	7.200	.040	—	.670	—	.006	69	47-54	U29-L20	50-57⑥
89-83 Starion: Front	—	—	—	.040④	—	.880	—	.006	57	58-72	61-69	50-57⑧
Rear	—	—	—	.040④	—	.650	—	.006	56	29-36	36-43	50-57⑧

④1989-88 .080". ⑥w/Aluminum wheels 58-72 ft/lbs. ⑧w/Aluminum wheels; 1989-84 65-80 ft/lbs.; 1983 57-72 ft/lbs.

Vehicle Year / Make / Model	Brake Shoe O.E. Minimum Lining Thickness	Brake Drum Diameter Standard Size	Machine To	Brake Pad O.E. Minimum Lining Thickness	Brake Rotor Min. Thickness Machine To	Discard At	Variation From Parallelism	Runout TIR	DESIGN	Caliper Mounting Bolts Torque (ft. lbs.)	Bridge, Pin or Key Bolts Torque (ft. lbs)	Wheel Lugs or Nuts Torque (ft. lbs.)
NISSAN (DATSUN)												
97-95 200SX:	.059	7.090	7.130	.079	—	.630	.0008	.0028	30	40-47	16-23	72-87
w/rear disc brakes	—	—	—	.059	—	.236	.0008	.0028	46	—	16-23	72-87
88-87 200SX: Front w/4 cyl. eng.	—	—	—	.079	—	.630	—	.0028	37	53-72	12-15	87-108
Front w/6 cyl. eng.	—	—	—	.079	—	.787	—	.0028	37	53-72	16-23	87-108
Rear	—	—	—	.079	—	.354	—	.0028	46	28-38	16-23	87-108
86-84 200SX: w/rear drum brakes	.059	9.000	9.055	.079	—	.630	.0012	.0028	36	53-72	23-30	58-72
w/rear disc brakes	—	—	—	.079	—	.354	.0012	.0028	46	28-38	16-23	58-72
83 200SX: Front	—	—	—	.079	—	.413	.0012	.0024	36	53-72	12-15	58-72
Rear	—	—	—	.079	—	.354	.0012	.0028	46	28-38	16-23	58-72
82 200SX: Front	—	—	—	.079	—	.413	.0012	.005	36	53-72	12-15	58-72
Rear	—	—	—	.079	—	.339	.0012	.006	46	28-38	16-23	58-72
81 200SX: Front	—	—	—	.079	—	.413	.0028	.005	36	53-72	12-15	58-72
Rear	—	—	—	.063	—	.339	.0028	.006	42	28-38	—	58-72
80 200SX: Front	—	—	—	.079	—	.413	.0028	.005	36	53-72	12-15	58-72
Rear	—	—	—	.079	—	.339	.0028	.006	42	28-38	—	58-72
79 200SX:	.059	9.000	9.055	.060	—	.331	.0012	.005	38	53-72	—	58-65
78-77 200SX:	.059	9.000	9.055	.063	—	.331	—	.005	38	53-72	—	58-65
82-79 210:	.059	8.000	8.050	.063	—	.331	.0012	.005	38	53-72	—	58-72
97 240SX: Front	—	—	—	.079	—	.787	.0004	.0028	37	53-72	16-23	73-86
Rear	—	—	—	.079	—	.310	.0008	.0028	46	28-38	16-23	73-86
96-95 240SX: Front	—	—	—	.079	—	.709	.0004	.0028	37	53-72	16-23	73-86
Rear	—	—	—	.079	—	.315	.0008	.0028	46	28-38	16-23	73-86
94-89 240SX: exc. ABS Front	—	—	—	.079	—	.709	—	.0028	37	53-72	16-23	72-87
w/ABS Front	—	—	—	.079	—	.787	—	.0028	37	53-72	16-23	72-87
Rear	—	—	—	.079	—	.315	—	.0028	46	28-38	16-23	72-87
83-82 280ZX: Front	—	—	—	.080	—	.709	.0012	.004③	37	53-72	16-23	58-72
Rear	—	—	—	.080	—	.339	.0012	.006③	46	28-38	16-23	58-72
81-79 280ZX: Front	—	—	—	.080	—	.709	.0012	.004	37	53-72	16-23	58-72
Rear	—	—	—	.080	—	.339	.0012	.006	42	28-38	—	58-72
78-72 280Z, 260Z, 240Z:	.059	9.000	9.055	.080	.423	.413	.0015	.004	14	53-72	—	58-65
96-95 300ZX: Front	—	—	—	.079	—	1.102	.0004	.0020	79	72-87	—	72-87
Rear	—	—	—	.079	—	.630	—	.0028	53	28-38	—	72-87
94-91 300ZX: Front	—	—	—	.079	—	1.102	—	.0028	79	72-87	—	72-87
Rear	—	—	—	.079	—	.630	—	.0028	53	28-38	—	72-87
90 300ZX: Front	—	—	—	.079	—	.945	—	.0028	79	53-72	—	72-87
Rear	—	—	—	.079	—	.630	—	.0028	53	28-38	—	72-87
89-87 300ZX: Front w/Turbo	—	—	—	.079	—	.945	—	.0028	76	53-72	16-23	72-87
Front exc. Turbo	—	—	—	.079	—	.787	—	.0028	37	53-72	16-23	72-87
Rear	—	—	—	.079	—	.709	—	.0028	46	28-38	23-30④	72-87
86-84 300ZX: Front	—	—	—	.080	—	.787	—	.0028	37	53-72	16-23	58-72
Rear	—	—	—	.080	—	.354	—	.0028	46	53-72②	16-23	58-72
82-79 310:	.059	8.000	8.050	.079	—	.339	.0012	.005	38	40-47	—	58-72
81-78 510:	.059	9.000	9.055	.080	—	.331	.0012	.005	36	53-72	12-15	58-65
73-72 510:	.059	9.000	9.055	.040	—	.331	.0012	.005	26	53-72	—	58-65
76-75 610:	.059	9.000	9.055	.063	—	.331	—	.005	38	53-72	—	58-65

②1986-85 28-38 ft/lbs. ③1983 .0028". ④1989 16-23 ft/lbs. ⑤1988-87 72-87 ft/lbs.

89450C22

PASSENGER CARS

Year / Make / Model	Brake Shoe O.E. Minimum Lining Thickness	Brake Drum Diameter Standard Size	Brake Drum Diameter Machine To	Brake Pad O.E. Minimum Lining Thickness	Brake Rotor Min. Thickness Machine To	Brake Rotor Min. Thickness Discard At	Brake Rotor Variation From Parallelism	Brake Rotor Runout TIR	Caliper DESIGN	Caliper Mounting Bolts Torque (ft. lbs.)	Caliper Bridge, Pin or Key Bolts Torque (ft. lbs)	Wheel Lugs or Nuts Torque (ft. lbs.)
NISSAN (DATSUN)												
74-73 610:	.059	9.000	9.055	.040	—	.331	.0012	.005	26	53-72	—	58-65
77-76 710:	.059	9.000	9.055	.063	—	.331	.0012	.005	26	12-15	—	58-65
75-73 710:	.059	9.000	9.055	.063	.341	.331	.0012	.005	26	53-72	—	58-65
88-85 810 Maxima: Front	—	—	—	.079	—	.787	—	.0028	30	53-72	16-23	58-72⑤
Rear	—	—	—	.079	—	.354	—	.0028	46	28-38	16-23	58-72⑤
84-83 810 Maxima:	.059	9.000	9.055	.079	—	.630	.0012	.0028	30	53-72	12-15	58-72
w/rear disc brakes	—	—	—	.079	—	.354	.0012	.0028	46	28-38	16-23	58-72
82 810 Maxima:	.059	9.000	9.055	.079	—	.630	.0012	.006	30	53-72	12-15	58-72
w/rear disc brakes	—	—	—	.079	—	.339	.0012	.006	46	28-38	16-23	58-72
81 810:	.059	9.000	9.055	.079	—	.630	.0028	.006	30	53-72	12-15	58-72
w/rear disc brakes	—	—	—	.079	—	.339	.0028	.006	42	28-38	—	58-72
80-77 810:	.059	9.000	9.055	.080	—	.413	.0012	.006	36	53-72	12-15	58-65
73-72 1200:	.059	8.000	8.051	.063	—	.331	.0015	.005	38	33-41	—	60
97-93 Altima:	.059	9.000	9.060	.079	—	.787	.0004	.0028	30	53-72	16-23	72-87
w/rear disc brakes	—	—	—	.059	—	.315	.0008	.0028	46	28-38	16-23	72-87
78-74 B210:	.059	8.000	8.050	.063	—	.331	.0012	.005	38	53-72	—	58-72
78-76 F10:	.039	8.000	8.051	.063	—	.339	—	.006	38	40-47	—	58-65
97 Maxima: Front	—	—	—	.079	—	.787	.0004	.0031	30	53-72	16-23	72-87
Rear	—	—	—	.059	—	.310	.0008	.0059	46	16-23	16-23	72-87
96-95 Maxima: Front	—	—	—	.079	—	.787	.0004	.0031	30	53-72	16-23	72-87
Rear	—	—	—	.059	—	.315	.0008	.0059	46	16-23	16-23	72-87
94-92 Maxima:	.059	9.000	9.060	.079	—	.787	—	.0028	30	53-72	16-23	72-87
w/rear disc brakes	—	—	—	.079	—	.315	—	.0028	46	28-38	16-23	72-87
91-90 Maxima:	.059	9.000	9.060	.079	—	.787	—	.0028	30	53-72	16-23	72-87
w/rear disc brakes	—	—	—	.079	—	.354	—	.0028	46	28-38	16-23	72-87
89 Maxima:	.059	9.000	9.060	.079	—	.787	—	.0028	30	53-72	16-23	72-87
w/rear disc brakes	—	—	—	.079	—	.315	—	.0028	46	28-38	16-23	72-87
90-87 Pulsar NX: exc. SE	.059	8.000	8.050	.079	—	.394	—	.0028	30	40-47	16-23	72-87
SE	.059	8.000	8.050	.079	—	.630	—	.0028	45	40-47	23-30	72-87
86 Pulsar NX:	.059	8.000	8.050	.079	—	.433	.0012	.0028	30	40-47	16-23	58-72
85 Pulsar NX:	.059	8.000	8.050	.079	—	.394	.0012	.0028	30	40-47	23-30	58-72
84-83 Pulsar NX:	.059	7.090	7.130	.080	—	.394	.0012	.0028	30	40-47	16-23	72-87
97-95 Sentra:	.059	7.090	7.130	.079	—	.630	.0008	.0028	30	40-47	16-23	72-87
w/rear disc brakes	—	—	—	.059	—	.236	.0008	.0028	46	—	16-23	72-87
94-91 Sentra, NX Coupe: Front exc. SE	—	—	—	.079	—	.630	.0004	.0028	30	40-47	16-23	72-87
Front SE	—	—	—	.079	—	.945	.0008	.0028	45	40-47	16-23	72-87
w/rear drum brakes	.059	7.090	7.130	—	—	—	—	—	—	—	—	72-87
w/rear disc brakes	—	—	—	.079	—	.236	.0004	.0028	70	28-38	16-23	72-87
90-88 Sentra: (4x2) exc. Wagon	.059	8.000	8.050	.079	—	.394	—	.0028	30	40-47	16-23	72-87
Wagon	.059	8.000	8.050	.079	—	.630	—	.0028	45	40-47	16-23	72-87
(4x4)	.059	9.000	9.050	.079	—	.630	—	.0028	45	40-47	16-23	72-87
87 Sentra: w/gas eng.	.059	8.000	8.050	.079	—	.394	—	.0028	30	40-47	16-23	72-87
w/diesel eng.	.059	8.000	8.050	.079	—	.630	—	.0028	45	40-47	16-23	72-87
86-85 Sentra: w/gas eng. (1986)	.059	8.000	8.050	.079	—	.433	.0012	.0028	30	40-47	16-23	58-72
w/gas eng. (1985)	.059	8.000	8.050	.079	—	.394	.0012	.0028	30	40-47	16-23	58-72
w/diesel eng.	.059	8.000	8.050	.079	—	.630	.0012	.0028	45	40-47	23-30	58-72
84-83 Sentra: w/gas eng.	.059	7.090	7.130	.080	—	.394	.0012	.0028	30	40-47	16-23	58-72
w/diesel eng.	.059	8.000	8.050	.080	—	.630	.0012	.0028	45	53-72	23-30	58-72
92-91 Stanza:	.059	9.000	9.060	.079	—	.787	—	.0028	30	53-72	16-23	72-87
w/rear disc brakes	—	—	—	.079	—	.354	—	.0028	46	28-38	16-23	72-87
90 Stanza:	.059	9.000	9.060	.079	—	.787	—	.0028	30	53-72	23-30	72-87
w/rear disc brakes	—	—	—	.079	—	.354	—	.0028	46	28-38	16-23	72-87
89-88 Stanza:	.059	9.000	9.060	.079	—	.787	—	.0028	30	53-72	16-23	72-87

③1983 .0028".   ⑤1988-87 72-87 ft/lbs.

89450C23

PASSENGER CARS

Vehicle Year / Make / Model	Brake Shoe O.E. Minimum Lining Thickness	Brake Drum Diameter Standard Size	Brake Drum Machine To	Brake Pad O.E. Minimum Lining Thickness	Brake Rotor Min. Thickness Machine To	Brake Rotor Discard At	Variation From Paral-lelism	Runout TIR	DESIGN	Caliper Mounting Bolts Torque (ft. lbs.)	Bridge, Pin or Key Bolts Torque (ft. lbs)	Wheel Lugs or Nuts Torque (ft. lbs.)
NISSAN (DATSUN)												
87 Stanza: exc. Wagon	.059	10.240	10.300	.079	—	.787	—	.0028	37	53-72	16-23	72-87
86-84 Stanza: exc. Wagon	.059	8.000	8.050	.080	—	.630	.0008	.0028	45	53-72	23-30	58-72
83-82 Stanza:	.059	8.000	8.050	.080	—	.630	.0012	.006③	45	53-72	23-30	58-72
88-86 Stanza Wagon: (4x2)	.059	9.000	9.060	.079	—	.787	.0012	.0028	37	53-72	16-23	58-72⑤
(4x4)	.059	10.240	10.300	.079	—	.787	.0012	.0028	37	53-72	16-23	58-72⑤

③1983 .0028". ⑤1988-87 72-87 ft/lbs.

Vehicle Year / Make / Model	Brake Shoe O.E. Min Lining	Std Size	Machine To	Pad O.E. Min Lining	Rotor Machine To	Discard At	Variation	Runout TIR	DESIGN	Mounting Bolts	Bridge/Pin/Key Bolts	Wheel Lugs/Nuts
OLDSMOBILE												
96-92 98:	.030	8.860	8.880	.030	1.224	1.209	.0005	.003	50	—	38	100
91 98:	②	8.860	8.880	.030	1.224	1.209	.0005	.004	62	—	38	100
97-93 Achieva:	.030	7.874	7.899	.030	.751	.736	.0005	.003	62	38	—	100
92 Achieva:	.030	7.879	7.899	.030	.751	.736	.0005	.003	62	38	—	100
97-95 Aurora: Front	—	—	—	.030	1.224	1.209	.0005	.003	90	38	—	100
Rear	—	—	—	.030	.423	.374	.0005	.003	73	—	20	100
91 Calais:	②	7.879	7.899	.030	.751	.736	.0005	.003	62	—	38	100
90-80 Calais, Omega:	②	7.880	7.899	.030	.830	.815	.0005	.002④	40①	—	28⑤	100
96-95 Ciera, Cruiser:	②	8.863	8.880	.030	.972	.957	.0005	.002	40	38	—	100
94-88 Ciera, Cruiser: Front H.D.	—	—	—	.030	.972	.957	.0005	.002	40	38	—	100
Front exc. H.D.	—	—	—	.030	.830	.815	.0005	.002	40	38	—	100
Rear	②	8.863	8.880	—	—	—	—	—	—	—	—	100
87-86 Ciera: H.D.	②	8.863	8.877	.030	.972	.957	.0005	.004	40	38	—	100
exc. H.D.	②	8.863	8.877	.030	.830	.815	.0005	.004	40	38	—	100
85 Ciera: H.D.	②	8.863	8.877	.030	.972	.957	.0005	.004	40	38	—	100
exc. H.D.	②	8.863	8.877	.030	.830	.815	.0005	.004	40	38	—	100
84 Ciera: H.D.	②	8.863	8.883	.030	.972	.957	.0005	.004	40	28	—	100
exc. H.D.	②	8.863	8.883	.030	.830	.815	.0005	.004	40	28	—	100
83-82 Ciera:	②	7.879	7.899	.030	.830	.815	.0005	.002	40	28	—	100
91-78 Custom Cruiser, Delta 88, 98: (Delta 88 w/403) (RWD)	②	11.000	11.060	.030	.980	.965	.0005	.004	4	—	35⑤	100
77 Custom Cruiser, Delta 88, 98: (Delta 88 w/403) (RWD)	②	11.000	11.060	.030	.980	.965	.0005	.005	4	—	40	100
97 Cutlass Supreme: exc. rear disc brakes	.030	8.863	8.880	.030	.987	.972	—	.003	83	148	80	100
w/ rear disc brakes	—	—	—	.030	.385	.370	.0005	.003	111	81	20	100
97 Cutlass: (FWD)	.030	8.863	8.880	.030	.987	.972	.0005	.0025	83	85	38	100
96 Cutlass: (FWD) Front	—	—	—	.030	.972	.956	.0005	.003	83	148	80	100
Rear	—	—	—	.030	.385	.370	.0005	.003	111	81	20	100
95-94 Cutlass: (FWD) Front	—	—	—	.030	.987⑧	.972⑧	.0005	.003	83	148	80	100
Rear	—	—	—	.030	.385	.370	.0005	.003	111	—	20	100
93-92 Cutlass: (FWD) Front	—	—	—	.030	.987	.972	.0005	.003	83	148	80	100⑥
Rear	—	—	—	.030	.444	.429	.0005	.003	84	92	—	100⑥
91-88 Cutlass: (FWD) Front	—	—	—	.030	.987	.972	.0005	.003⑦	83	148	79	100⑥
Rear	—	—	—	.030	.444	.429	.0005	.003⑦	84	—	92	100⑥
77-76 Cutlass:	②	11.000	11.060	.030	.980	.965	.0005	.004	4	—	40	80
75-72 Cutlass, Omega: exc. Vista Cruiser	②	9.500	9.560	.062	.980	.965	.0005	.004	4	—	40	80
97 88, 88LS, LSS, Regency:	.030	8.863	8.880	.030	1.224	1.209	.0005	.002	50	38	—	100
96-92 Delta 88, 88:	.030	8.863	8.880	.030	1.224	1.209	.0005	.003	50	—	38	100
91 Delta 88:	②	8.860	8.880	.030	.972	.957	.0005	.004	62	—	38	100
90-83 Delta 88, 98: (FWD)	②	8.858	8.880	.030	.972	.957	.0005	.002④	4①	—	28⑤	100
88-82 Delta 88, Cutlass: (RWD)	②	9.500	9.560	.030	.980	.965	.0005	.004	4	—	35⑤	100③
81-78 Delta 88, Cutlass: (RWD) (Delta 88 w/o 403 eng.)	②	9.500	9.560	.030	.980	.965	.0005	.004	4	—	35	80

①1992-85 use ill. 62. ②.030" over rivet head; if bonded lining use .062". ③Delta 88 w/⁷/₁₆ stud, 1983 Cutlass; 80 ft/lbs. ④1990-84 .004". ⑤1991-85 38 ft/lbs. ⑥Exc. 1993-90: 103 ft/lbs. ⑦1993 shown, 1992-88 .004" ⑧Late 1995 vehicles use 1996 front rotor specifications. Refer to discard specification on rotor if needed.

89450C24

PASSENGER CARS

Vehicle Year / Make / Model	Brake Shoe O.E. Minimum Lining Thickness	Brake Drum Diameter Standard Size	Brake Drum Diameter Machine To	Brake Pad O.E. Minimum Lining Thickness	Brake Rotor Min. Thickness Machine To	Brake Rotor Min. Thickness Discard At	Brake Rotor Variation From Parallelism	Brake Rotor Runout TIR	Caliper DESIGN	Caliper Mounting Bolts Torque (ft. lbs.)	Caliper Bridge, Pin or Key Bolts Torque (ft. lbs)	Wheel Lugs or Nuts Torque (ft. lbs.)
OLDSMOBILE												
77 Delta 88: (RWD) (w/o 403 eng.)	②	9.500	9.560	.030	.980	.965	.0005	.004	4	—	40	80
76-72 Delta 88, 98: exc. Wagon & H.D. Pkg.	②	11.000	11.060	.062	1.230	1.215	.0005	.005	4	—	40	80
76-72 Delta 88: Wagon & H.D. Pkg.	②	12.000	12.060	.062	1.230	1.215	.0005	.005	4	—	40	80
88-82 Firenza: vented rotor (88-82)	②	7.880	7.899	.030	.830	.815	.0005	.002④	40①	—	28⑤	100
solid rotor (82)	②	7.880	7.899	.030	.444	.429	.0005	.002	40	—	28	100
79-78 Omega: w/5 Speed	②	11.000	11.060	.030	.980	.965	.0005	.005	4	—	35	80
w/o 5 Speed	②	9.500	9.560	.030	.980	.965	.0005	.005	4	—	35	80
77-76 Omega: w/5 Speed	②	11.000	11.060	.030	.980	.965	.0005	.004	4	—	40	80
w/o 5 Speed	②	9.500	9.560	.030	.980	.965	.0005	.004	4	—	40	80
80-76 Starfire:	②	9.500	9.560	.062	.830	.815	.0005	.005	15	—	—	80
75 Starfire:	②	9.000	9.060	.062	.455	.440	.0005	.005	15	—	40	80
92 Toronado, Trofeo: Front	—	—	—	.030	1.250	1.209	.0005	.002	50	77	—	100
Rear	—	—	—	.030	.423	.374	.0005	.002	84	77	—	100
91-86 Toronado, Trofeo: Front	—	—	—	.030	.971	.956	.0005	.004	71	83	63	100
Rear	—	—	—	.030	.444	.429	.0005	.003	72	83	63	100
85-79 Toronado:	②	9.500	9.560	.030	.980	.965	.0005	.004	4	—	35	100
w/rear disc brakes	—	—	—	.030	.980	.965	.0005	.004	41	32	30	100
78-72 Toronado:	②	11.000	11.060	.062	1.185	1.170	.0005	.002	4	—	35-40	130
75-72 Vista Cruiser:	②	11.000	11.060	.062	.980	.965	.0005	.004	4	—	40	80

①1992-85 use ill. 62. ②.030" over rivet head; if bonded lining use .062". ④1990-84 .004". ⑤1991-85 38 ft/lbs.

Vehicle Year / Make / Model	Brake Shoe O.E. Minimum Lining Thickness	Brake Drum Diameter Standard Size	Brake Drum Diameter Machine To	Brake Pad O.E. Minimum Lining Thickness	Brake Rotor Min. Thickness Machine To	Brake Rotor Min. Thickness Discard At	Brake Rotor Variation From Parallelism	Brake Rotor Runout TIR	Caliper DESIGN	Caliper Mounting Bolts Torque (ft. lbs.)	Caliper Bridge, Pin or Key Bolts Torque (ft. lbs)	Wheel Lugs or Nuts Torque (ft. lbs.)
OPEL												
79-76 Coupe, Sedan:	.040	9.000	9.040	.067	—	.339	.0006	.006	14	36	—	50
75 Manta, 1900 Wagon:	.040	9.000	9.040	.067	—	.465	.0004	.004	17	72	—	65
74-72 1900 Coupe, 1900 Sedan, 1900 Wagon, Manta, GT:	.030	9.060	9.090	.067	.404	.394	.0006	.006	17	72	—	65

Vehicle Year / Make / Model	Brake Shoe O.E. Minimum Lining Thickness	Brake Drum Diameter Standard Size	Brake Drum Diameter Machine To	Brake Pad O.E. Minimum Lining Thickness	Brake Rotor Min. Thickness Machine To	Brake Rotor Min. Thickness Discard At	Brake Rotor Variation From Parallelism	Brake Rotor Runout TIR	Caliper DESIGN	Caliper Mounting Bolts Torque (ft. lbs.)	Caliper Bridge, Pin or Key Bolts Torque (ft. lbs)	Wheel Lugs or Nuts Torque (ft. lbs.)
PEUGEOT												
92-89 405: Front	—	—	—	—	—	.728	.0008	.003	—	—	26	—
Rear	—	—	—	—	—	.315	.0008	.003	—	—	26	—
83-80 504: Front	—	—	—	—	.443	.423	.0008	.003	—	—	—	50-60
w/10 in. drum Rear	—	10.039	10.079	—	—	—	—	—	—	—	—	50-60
w/11 in. drum Rear	—	11.023	11.063	—	—	—	—	—	—	—	—	50-60
w/10 mm caliper Rear	—	—	—	—	.354	.335	.0008	.003	—	—	—	50-60
w/12 mm caliper Rear	—	—	—	—	.433	.413	.0008	.003	—	—	—	50-60
91-80 505: w/solid rotors	—	—	10.098	—	—	.443	.0008	.003	—	—	—	50-60
91-85 505: w/vented rotors	—	—	—	—	—	.709	.0008	.003	—	—	—	50-60
91-80 505: w/rear disc brakes	—	—	—	—	—	.315	.0008	.003	—	—	—	50-60
84-82 604: Front	—	—	—	—	—	.709	.0008	.003	—	—	—	50-60
Rear	—	—	—	—	—	.394	.0008	.019	—	—	—	50-60

Vehicle Year / Make / Model	Brake Shoe O.E. Minimum Lining Thickness	Brake Drum Diameter Standard Size	Brake Drum Diameter Machine To	Brake Pad O.E. Minimum Lining Thickness	Brake Rotor Min. Thickness Machine To	Brake Rotor Min. Thickness Discard At	Brake Rotor Variation From Parallelism	Brake Rotor Runout TIR	Caliper DESIGN	Caliper Mounting Bolts Torque (ft. lbs.)	Caliper Bridge, Pin or Key Bolts Torque (ft. lbs)	Wheel Lugs or Nuts Torque (ft. lbs.)
PONTIAC												
91-89 6000: Front w/H.D.	—	—	—	.030	.972	.957	.0005	.004	40	38	—	100
exc. H.D.				.030	.830	.815	.0005	.004	40	38	—	100
Rear coupe/sedan	④	8.863	8.880	—	—	—	—	—	—	—	—	100
wagon	④	8.863	8.880	—	—	—	—	—	—	—	—	100
w/rear disc brakes	—	—	—	.030	.702	.681	.0005	.003	88	74	74	100
88-87 6000: Front w/H.D.	—	—	—	.030	.972	.957	.0005	.004	40	38	—	Nuts
exc. H.D.				.030	.830	.815	.0005	.004	40	38	—	100
Rear coupe/sedan	④	8.863	8.880	—	—	—	—	—	—	—	—	100
Wagon	④	8.863	8.880	—	—	—	—	—	—	—	—	100
w/rear disc brakes	—	—	—	.030	.444	.429	.0005	.004	63	30-45	—	100
86-85 6000: exc. H.D.	④	8.863	8.880	.030	.830	.815	.0005	.004	40	38	—	100

④.030" over rivet head; if bonded lining use .062".

89450C25

PASSENGER CARS

| Vehicle | Brake Shoe | Brake Drum | | Brake Pad | Brake Rotor | | | | D E S I G N | Caliper | | Wheel |
| | O.E. Minimum Lining Thickness | Diameter | | O.E. Minimum Lining Thickness | Min. Thickness | | Variation From Parallelism | Runout TIR | | Mounting Bolts Torque (ft. lbs.) | Bridge, Pin or Key Bolts Torque (ft. lbs) | Lugs or Nuts Torque (ft. lbs.) |
Year / Make / Model		Standard Size	Machine To		Machine To	Discard At						
PONTIAC												
86 6000: w/H.D.	④	8.863	8.880	.030	.978	.931	.0005	.004	40	38	—	100
85 6000: w/H.D.	④	8.863	8.880	.030	.972	.957	.0005	.004	40	38	—	100
84 6000: w/H.D.	④	8.863	8.883	.030	.972	.957	.0005	.004	40	28	—	100
exc. H.D.	④	8.863	8.883	.030	.830	.815	.0005	.004	40	28	—	100
83-82 6000:	④	7.879	7.899	.030	.830	.815	.0005	.002	40	28	—	100
97-92 Bonneville:	.030	8.860	8.880	.030	1.224	1.209	.0005	.003	50	38	—	100
91-87 Bonneville:	④	8.860	8.880	.030	.972	.957	.0005	.004	62	—	38	100
89-77 Bonneville, Catalina, LeMans, Grand Prix, Grand Am, Parisienne, Safari:												
(RWD) w/9.5" rear brakes	④	9.500	9.560	.030	.980	.965	.0005	.004	4	—	35⑧	80①
(RWD) w/11" rear brakes	④	11.000	11.060	.030	.980	.965	.0005	.004	4	—	35⑧	80⑤
76-72 Bonneville, Catalina, Gran Ville: exc. Wagon	.125	11.000	11.060	.125	1.230	1.215	.0005	.004	4	—	35	75
Wagon, Grand Safari	.125	12.000	12.060	.125	1.230	1.215	.0005	.004	4	—	35	75
88 Fiero: Front	—	—	—	.030	.702	.681	.0005	.003	87	74	74	100
Rear	—	—	—	.030	.702	.681	.0005	.003	88	74	74	100
87-84 Fiero: Front	—	—	—	.062	.386	.374	.0005	.004	62	21-35	—	80⑥
Rear	—	—	—	.062	.440	.430	.0005	.004	63	21-35	—	80⑥
97-93 Firebird:	.030	9.500	9.560	.030	1.250	1.209	.0005	.005	40	—	38	100
w/rear disc brakes	—	—	—	.030	.733	.724	.0005	.006	86	74	27	100
92-89 Firebird: exc. H.D.	④	9.500	9.560	.030	.980	.965	.0005	.005	4	—	37	81⑫
H.D. Front	—	—	—	.030	.980	.965	.0005	.005	85	137	—	81⑫
H.D. Rear	—	—	—	.030	.744	.724	.0005	.005	86	70	⑨	81⑫
88-86 Firebird: w/rear drum brakes	④	9.500	9.560	.030	.980	.965	.0005	.005	4	—	38	80⑥
w/rear disc brakes	—	—	—	.030	.986	.956	.0005	.005	41	—	38	80⑥
85-82 Firebird: w/rear drum brakes	④	9.500	9.560	.030	.980	.965	.0005	.004	4	—	21-35	80⑥
w/rear disc brakes	—	—	—	.030	.980	.965	.0005	.004	41	—	30-45	80⑥
81-77 Firebird, Ventura, Phoenix:	④	9.500	9.560	.030	.980	.965	.0005	.004	4	—	35	80
w/rear disc (81-79)	—	—	—	.030	.921	.905	.0005	.004	41	—	30	80
88-85 Firefly:	.110	7.090	7.160	.315	—	.315	—	.0028	66	17-26	—	29-50
97-93 Grand Am: (FWD)	④	7.874	7.899	.030	.751	.736	.0005	.003	62	38	—	100
92-91 Grand Am: (FWD)	④	7.879	7.899	.030	.751	.736	.0005	.003	62	38	—	100
90-80 Grand Am, Phoenix: (FWD)	④	7.880	7.899	.030	.830	.815	.0005	.002⑦	40③	—	35⑧	100
97 Grand Prix: exc. rear disc brakes	④	8.863	8.880	.040	1.250	1.210	—	.003	83	148	80	100
w/ rear disc brakes	—	—	—	.060	.410	.350	—	.003	111	81	20	100
96 Grand Prix: (FWD) Front	—	—	—	.030	.972	.956	.0005	.003	83	148	80	100
Rear	—	—	—	.030	.385	.370	.0005	.003	111	81	20	100
95-94 Grand Prix: (FWD) Front	—	—	—	.030	.987⑮	.972⑮	.0005	.003	83	148	80	100
Rear	—	—	—	.030	.385	.370	.0005	.003	111	—	20	100
93-92 Grand Prix: (FWD) Front	—	—	—	.030	.987	.972	.0005	.003	83	80	—	100⑭
Rear	—	—	—	.030	.444	.429	.0005	.003	84	92	—	100⑭
91-89 Grand Prix: (FWD) Front	—	—	—	.030	.984	.972	.0005	.003⑬	83	79	—	100
Rear	—	—	—	.030	.441	.429	.0005	.003⑬	84	92	—	100
88 Grand Prix: (FWD) Front	—	—	—	.030	1.019	.972	.0005	.003	83	79	—	100
Rear	—	—	—	.030	.441	.429	.0005	.003	84	92	—	100
93-88 LeMans: w/9" solid rotor	.030	7.870	7.900	.030	.420	.380	.0004	.004	87	70	—	66
w/9" vented rotor	.030	7.870	7.900	.030	.669	.646	.0004	.004	87	70	—	66
w/10" vented rotor	.030	7.870	7.900	.030	.870	.830	.0004	.004	87	70	—	66
76-74 LeMans, Firebird, Grand Prix, Ventura: exc. Wagon	.125	9.500	9.560	.125	.980	.965	.0005	.004	4	—	35	70
Wagon	.125	11.000	11.060	.125	.980	.965	.0005	.004	4	—	35	70

①1989-87 100 ft.lbs. ③1991-85 use ill. 62. ④.030" over rivet head; if bonded lining use .062". ⑤½" stud 100 ft.lbs. ⑥w/Aluminum wheels 105 ft.lbs. ⑦1991-84 .004".
⑧1991-85 38 ft.lbs. ⑨Hex bolt 26 ft.lbs.; allen bolt 16 ft.lbs. ⑫1992 use 100 ft.lbs.
⑬1993 shown, 1992-89 .004" ⑭Exc. 1993-90: 103 ft.lbs. ⑮Late 1995 vehicles use 1996 front rotor specifications. Refer to discard specification on rotor if needed.

89450C26

PASSENGER CARS

Vehicle Year / Make / Model	Brake Shoe O.E. Minimum Lining Thickness	Brake Drum Diameter Standard Size	Machine To	Brake Pad O.E. Minimum Lining Thickness	Brake Rotor Min. Thickness Machine To	Discard At	Variation From Parallelism	Runout TIR	DESIGN	Caliper Mounting Bolts Torque (ft. lbs.)	Bridge, Pin or Key Bolts Torque (ft. lbs)	Wheel Lugs or Nuts Torque (ft. lbs.)
PONTIAC												
73-72 LeMans, Firebird, Grand Prix:	.125	9.500	9.560	.125	.980	.965	.0005	.004	4	—	35	70
97-93 Sunbird, Sunfire:	.030	7.874	7.899	.030	.751	.736	.0005	.003	62	38	—	100
92 Sunbird, J2000:	.030	7.880	7.900	.030	.751	.736	.0005	.003	62	38	—	100
91-82 Sunbird, J2000:												
vented rotor (91-82)	④	7.880	7.899	.030	.830	.815	.0005	.002⑦	40③	—	28⑧	100
solid rotor (82)	④	7.880	7.899	.030	.444	.429	.0005	.002	40	—	28	100
80-76 Sunbird, Astre:	④	9.500	9.560	.030	.830	.815	.0005	.004	15	—	35	80
89-85 Sunburst: exc. Turbo	.039	7.090	7.140	.039	—	.378	—	.0059	57	40	36	65⑪
Turbo	.039	7.090	7.140	.039	—	.650	—	.0059	47	40	36	65⑪
87-86 T1000:	④	7.880	7.899	.030	.404	.374	.0005	.005	50	70	21-35②	80
85-83 T1000:	④	7.874	7.899	.030	.390	.374	.0005	.005	50	—	21-25	70
82-81 T1000:	④	7.874	7.899	.030	.390	.374	.0005	.005	20	70	28	70
73-72 Ventura:	.125	9.500	9.560	.125	—	.980	.0005	.004	4	—	35	70

②1987 30-45 ft/lbs.   ③1991-85 use ill. 62.   ④.030" over rivet head; if bonded lining use .062".   ⑦1991-84 .004".   ⑧1991-85 38 ft/lbs.   ⑪Steel wheel shown; Aluminum 87 ft/lbs.
⑬1993 shown, 1992-89 .004"   ⑭Exc. 1993-90: 103 ft/lbs.   ⑮Late 1995 vehicles use 1996 front rotor specifications. Refer to discard specification on rotor if needed.

Vehicle Year / Make / Model	Brake Shoe O.E. Minimum Lining Thickness	Brake Drum Diameter Standard Size	Machine To	Brake Pad O.E. Minimum Lining Thickness	Brake Rotor Min. Thickness Machine To	Discard At	Variation From Parallelism	Runout TIR	DESIGN	Caliper Mounting Bolts Torque (ft. lbs.)	Bridge, Pin or Key Bolts Torque (ft. lbs)	Wheel Lugs or Nuts Torque (ft. lbs.)
PORSCHE												
97-95 911: Front	—	—	—	.079	1.205	1.181	.0007	.002	75	63	—	96
Rear (exc. 4S)	—	—	—	.079	.890	.866	.0007	.002	75	63	—	96
Rear (4S)	—	—	—	.079	1.047	1.024	.0007	.002	75	63	—	96
94-90 911: Front	—	—	—	.079	1.047	1.024③	.0007	.002	75	62	—	96
Front	—	—	—	.079	1.205	1.181③	.0007	.002	75	63	—	96
Rear	—	—	—	.079	.890	.866③	.0007	.002	75	62	—	96
Rear	—	—	—	.079	1.047	1.024③	.0007	.002	75	62	—	96
94-91 911 Turbo: Front	—	—	—	.079	1.200	1.180	.0007	.004	78	62	—	95
Rear	—	—	—	.079	1.050	1.020	.0007	.004	79	62	—	95
89-84 911: exc. Turbo & Turbo Look												
Front	—	—	—	.079	.890	.866	.0002	.004	17	51	—	94
Rear	—	—	—	.079	.890	.866	.0002	.004	17	43	—	94
Turbo & Turbo Look Front	—	—	—	.079	1.200	1.180	.0002	.004	75	51	—	94
Rear	—	—	—	.079	1.050	1.020	.0002	.004	75	43	—	94
83-78 911: Front	—	—	—	.079	.750	.728	.0002	.004	17	51	24	94
Rear	—	—	—	.079	.732	.709	.0002	.004	17	43	13	94
77-72 911: Front	—	—	—	.079	.732	.709	.0002	.008	17	51	24	94
Rear	—	—	—	.079	.732	.709	.0002	.008	17	43	13	94
76-72 914: Front	—	—	—	.080	.394	.375	.0008	.008	17	62	16	94
Rear	—	—	—	.080	.351	.335	.0008	.008	14	50	16	94
76-72 914, 916: Front	—	—	—	.080	.732	.709	.0008	.008	17	62	25	94
Rear	—	—	—	.080	.374	.354	.0008	.008	14	50	16	94
88-86 924S: Front	—	—	—	.079	.751	.728	.0007	.003	39	63	—	94
Rear	—	—	—	.079	.751	.728	.0007	.003	39	63	—	94
82-80 924: Turbo Front	—	—	—	.079	.751	.728	.0007	.003	39	60	—	94
Turbo Rear	—	—	—	.079	.755	.732	.0007	.003	39	60	—	94
82-77 924: exc. Turbo	.098	9.055	9.094	.079	.472	.453	—	—	39	60	—	80②
95-86 928S, 928S-4, 928GT, 928GTS:												
Front	—	—	—	.079	1.205	1.181	.0007	.004	78	63	—	94
Rear	—	—	—	.079	.890	.866	.0007	.004	79	63	—	94
85-82 928, 928S: Front	—	—	—	.079	1.228	1.205	.0002	.004	74	61	11-14	94
Rear	—	—	—	.079	.756	.732	.0002	.004	74	61	11-14	94
81-78 928: Front	—	—	—	.079	.756	.732	.0002	.004	39	61	—	94
Rear	—	—	—	.079	.756	.732	.0002	.004	39	61	—	94
90 944: Turbo S Front	—	—	—	.079	1.205	1.180	.0007	.004	75	63	—	96
Turbo S Rear	—	—	—	.079	.890	.866	.0007	.004	75	63	—	96
91-90 944 S2: Front	—	—	—	.079	1.047	1.024	.0007	.004	75	63	—	96
Rear	—	—	—	.079	.890	.866	.0007	.004	75	63	—	96

②w/Aluminum wheels 94 ft/lbs.   ③Refer to individual rotor for discard dimension.

89450C27

PASSENGER CARS

Vehicle	Brake Shoe	Brake Drum		Brake Pad	Brake Rotor				Caliper			Wheel
		Diameter			Min. Thickness		Variation From Paral-lelism		DESIGN		Bridge, Pin or Key	
Year / Make / Model	O.E. Minimum Lining Thickness	Standard Size	Machine To	O.E. Minimum Lining Thickness	Machine To	Discard At		Runout TIR		Mounting Bolts Torque (ft. lbs.)	Bolts Torque (ft. lbs.)	Lugs or Nuts Torque (ft. lbs.)
PORSCHE												
90-83 944: exc. Turbo Front	—	—	—	.079	.752	.728	.0002	.004	39	63	—	96
exc. Turbo Rear	—	—	—	.079	.756	.732	.0002	.004	39	63	—	96
90-86 944: Turbo Front	—	—	—	.079	1.047	1.024	.0002	.004	75	63	—	96
Turbo Rear	—	—	—	.079	.890	.866	.0002	.004	75	63	—	96
95-94 968: Front	—	—	—	.079	1.050	1.020	.0007	.004	78	63	—	96
w/sport suspension Front	—	—	—	.079	1.200	1.180	.0007	.004	78	63	—	96
Rear	—	—	—	.079	.890	.866	.0007	.004	79	63	—	96

①Seat brg. while turning wheel. Back off nut until thrust washer can be moved slightly by screwdriver w/finger pressure. Lock.　②w/Aluminum wheels 94 ft/lbs.
③Refer to individual rotor for discard dimension.

Vehicle	O.E. Min Lining	Std Size	Machine To	O.E. Min Lining	Machine To	Discard At	Variation	Runout TIR	Design	Mounting Bolts	Bridge Bolts	Wheel
RENAULT												
86-84 18i Sportwagon:	.188②	9.000	9.040	.359②	—	.709	—	.003	31	48	26	59
83-80 18i:	.020	8.996	9.035	.276②	—	.433	—	.003	29	74	42	59
87-83 Alliance, Encore:	.020	8.000	8.060	.276②	—	.433	—	.003	51	74	26	52-66
85-80 Fuego: exc. Turbo	.020	8.996	9.035	.276②	—	.433	—	.003	29	74	42	59
84-82 Fuego: Turbo	.020	8.996	9.035	.276②	—	.709	—	.003	29	74	42	59
80-74 Gordini:	.203②	9.000	9.035	.276②	—	.354	.0004	.008	43	—	—	45-60
87 GTA:	.020	8.000	8.060	.276②	—	.750	—	.003	51	74	26	52-66
84-76 LeCar: (5 Series)	.203②	7.096	7.136	.275②	—	.354	—	.004	43	50	—	40-45
89-88 Medallion:	.098	9.000	9.030	.256	①	.697	—	.002	51	48	18	67

①Machining not recommended.　②Measurement of lining & metal.　③.001"-.002" end play.

Vehicle	O.E. Min Lining	Std Size	Machine To	O.E. Min Lining	Machine To	Discard At	Variation	Runout TIR	Design	Mounting Bolts	Bridge Bolts	Wheel
SAAB												
97 900: Front	—	—	—	.200	—	.910	.0006	.003	—	81	21	88
Rear	—	—	—	.200	—	.310	.0006	.003	—	59	—	88
96-94 900, 900 S, 900 Turbo: Front	—	—	—	.200	.890	.870	.0006	.003	61	78	19	74①
Rear	—	—	—	.200	.330	.310	.0006	.003	74	59	—	74①
93-88 900, 900 S, 900 Turbo: Front	—	—	—	.040	.870	.850	.0006	.003	61	52-82	22-26	80-90
Rear	—	—	—	.040	.320	.300	.0006	.003	74	30-40	18-22	80-90
87-86 900: Turbo 16 Valve Front	—	—	—	.040	.744	.709	.0006	.003	28	81-96	—	65-80
Rear	—	—	—	.040	.374	—	.0006	.003	17	52-66	—	65-80
87-79 900: exc. Turbo 16 Valve												
Front	—	—	—	.040	.461	—	.0006	.004	28	81-96	—	65-80
Rear	—	—	—	.040	.374	—	.0006	.004	17	52-66	—	65-80
97-88 9000 Turbo: Front	—	—	—	.160	.925	.905	.0006	.003	61	62	21	89
Rear	—	—	—	.160	.315	.295	.0006	.003	74	35	21	89
87 9000 Turbo: Front	—	—	—	.040	.890	.850	.0006	.003	61	52-82	—	80-90
Rear	—	—	—	.040	.325	.300	.0006	.004	74	52-66	—	80-90
97-90 9000 S, 9000 CS, 9000 CD:												
Front	—	—	—	.160	.925	.905	.0006	.003	61	62	21	89
Rear	—	—	—	.160	.315	.295	.0006	.003	74	35	21	89
89-87 9000 S: Front	—	—	—	.040	.890	.850	.0006	.003	61	52-82	—	80-90
Rear	—	—	—	.040	.325	.300	.0006	.004	74	52-66	—	80-90
87-86 9000: Front	—	—	—	.039	.787	.768	.0006	.003	61	52-82	—	76-90
Rear	—	—	—	.039	.295	.276	.0006	.003	74	52-67	—	76-90
78-75 99: Front	—	—	—	.080	.461	—	.0006	.004	28	—	—	65-80
Rear	—	—	—	.080	.374	—	.0006	.004	17	—	—	65-80
74-70 99: Front	—	—	—	.080	.374	—	.0006	.004	17	—	—	65-80
Rear	—	—	—	.080	.374	—	.0006	.004	17	—	—	65-80

①Steel wheels shown; w/aluminum wheels use 87 ft/lbs.

Vehicle	O.E. Min Lining	Std Size	Machine To	O.E. Min Lining	Machine To	Discard At	Variation	Runout TIR	Design	Mounting Bolts	Bridge Bolts	Wheel
SATURN												
97-91 SC, SC1, SC2, SL, SL1, SL2, SW1, SW2: w/rear drum brakes	.040	7.870	7.900	.080	.633	.625	.0005	.0024	73	81	27	103
w/rear disc brakes	—	—	—	.080	.370	.350	.0005	.0024	99	63	27	103

89450C28

PASSENGER CARS

Year / Make / Model	Brake Shoe O.E. Minimum Lining Thickness	Brake Drum Diameter Standard Size	Brake Drum Diameter Machine To	Brake Pad O.E. Minimum Lining Thickness	Brake Rotor Min. Thickness Machine To	Brake Rotor Min. Thickness Discard At	Brake Rotor Variation From Parallelism	Brake Rotor Runout TIR	Caliper DESIGN	Caliper Mounting Bolts Torque (ft. lbs.)	Caliper Bridge, Pin or Key Bolts Torque (ft. lbs)	Wheel Lugs or Nuts Torque (ft. lbs.)
STERLING												
91-87 825: Front	—	—	—	.322①	—	.748	.0006	.003	61	53	24	80
Rear	—	—	—	.283①	—	.314	.0006	.003	68	55	24	80

①Measurement of lining & metal.

Year / Make / Model	Brake Shoe O.E. Minimum Lining Thickness	Brake Drum Diameter Standard Size	Brake Drum Diameter Machine To	Brake Pad O.E. Minimum Lining Thickness	Brake Rotor Min. Thickness Machine To	Brake Rotor Min. Thickness Discard At	Brake Rotor Variation From Parallelism	Brake Rotor Runout TIR	Caliper DESIGN	Caliper Mounting Bolts Torque (ft. lbs.)	Caliper Bridge, Pin or Key Bolts Torque (ft. lbs)	Wheel Lugs or Nuts Torque (ft. lbs.)
SUBARU												
86-85 DL, GL:	.060	7.090	7.170	.295②	—	.630	—	.004	48	36-51	④	58-72
w/rear disc brakes	—	—	—	.256②	—	.335	—	.004	61	34-43	16-23	58-72
84-83 DL, GL: w/solid rotor	.060	7.090	7.120	.295②	—	.394	—	.004	48	36-51	12-17	58-72
w/vented rotor	.060	7.090	7.120	.295②	—	.610	—	.004	48	36-51	12-17	58-72
82-80 DL, GL:	.060	7.090	7.120	.295②	—	.394	—	.004	48	36-51	33-54	58-72
79-75 DL, GL:	.060	7.090	7.120	.060	—	.330	—	.006	27	36-51	—	58-72
74-72 DL, GL Coupe:	.060	7.090	7.120	.060	—	.330	—	.006	27	36-51	—	40-54
74-72 DL, GL Sedan, Wagon: Front	.060	9.000	9.040	—	—	—	—	—	—	—	—	40-54
Rear	.060	7.090	7.120	—	—	—	—	—	—	—	—	40-54
96-93 Impreza: w/13" rotor Front	—	—	—	.295	—	.630	—	.003	108	58	27	58-72
w/14" rotor Front	—	—	—	.259	—	.870	—	.003	108	58	27	58-72
w/rear drum brakes Rear	.059	9.000	9.079	—	—	—	—	—	—	—	—	—
w/rear disc brakes Rear	—	—	—	.256	—	.335	—	.004	109	—	15	58-72
94-89 Justy: w/12" Wheels	.067	7.090	7.170	.295②	—	.610	—	.006	30	38-48	16-23	58-72
w/13" Wheels	.067	7.090	7.170	.315②	—	.610	—	.006	47	38-48	⑤	58-72
88-87 Justy:	.067	7.090	7.170	.295②	—	.610	—	.006	30	38-48	16-22	58-72
97-95 Legacy:	.059	9.000	9.080	.295②	—	.866	—	.003	73	52-65	26-32	58-72
w/rear disc brakes	—	—	—	.256②	—	.335	—	.004	60	34-42	⑦	58-72
94-90 Legacy: Front	—	—	—	.295②	—	.870	.0006	.004	73	51-65	④	58-72
Rear	—	—	—	.256②	—	.335	.0006	.004	60	34-43	⑥	58-72
94-87 Loyale:	.060	7.090	7.170	.295②	—	.630	—	.004	48	36-51	④	58-72
w/rear disc brakes	—	—	—	.256②	—	.335	—	.004	61	34-43	16-23	58-72
97-92 SVX: Front	—	—	—	.295②	—	1.020	—	.004	76	25-33	25-33	72-86
Rear	—	—	—	.256②	—	.335	—	.004	71	16-23	12-17	72-86
91-85 XT:	.060	7.090	7.170	.295②	—	.630	—	.004	48	36-51	④	58-72
w/rear disc brakes	—	—	—	.256②	—	.335	—	.004	61	34-43	16-23	58-72
91-88 XT6: Front	—	—	—	.295②	—	.787	—	.004	48	36-51	④	58-72
Rear	—	—	—	.315②	—	.335	—	.004	61	34-43	16-23	58-72

①4x2 shown; 4x4 Not Adjustable. ②Measurement of lining & metal. ③Radial pull in pounds at lug nut. ④Upper bolt 33-40 ft./lbs.; lower bolt 23-30 ft./lbs.
⑤Upper bolt 25-33 ft/lbs.; lower bolt 16-23 ft/lbs. ⑥Upper bolt 12-17 ft/lbs.; lower bolt 16-23 ft/lbs. ⑦Lower bolt 11-17 ft/lbs. Upper bolt 16-23 ft/lbs.

Year / Make / Model	Brake Shoe O.E. Minimum Lining Thickness	Brake Drum Diameter Standard Size	Brake Drum Diameter Machine To	Brake Pad O.E. Minimum Lining Thickness	Brake Rotor Min. Thickness Machine To	Brake Rotor Min. Thickness Discard At	Brake Rotor Variation From Parallelism	Brake Rotor Runout TIR	Caliper DESIGN	Caliper Mounting Bolts Torque (ft. lbs.)	Caliper Bridge, Pin or Key Bolts Torque (ft. lbs)	Wheel Lugs or Nuts Torque (ft. lbs.)
SUZUKI												
97-95 Esteem:	.040	7.874	7.950	.040	—	.710	—	.0039	30	62	16	62
97-95 Swift:	.040	7.09	7.13	.040	—	.590	.0005	.004	30	22	—	37-58
94-93 Swift GA, Swift GS: Hatchback	.110①	7.090	7.160	.315①	—	.590	—	.004	30	51-72	16-23	36-50
Sedan	.110①	7.870	7.950	.315①	—	.590	—	.004	30	51-72	16-23	36-50
92-89 Swift GLX:	.110①	7.090	7.160	.315①	—	.590	—	.004	30	51-72	16-23	36-50
94-89 Swift GT, Swift GTI: Front	—	—	—	.315①	—	.650	—	.004	30	51-72	16-23	36-50
Rear	—	—	—	.236①	—	.315	—	.004	68	29-43	16-23	36-50

①Measurement of lining & metal.

Year / Make / Model	Brake Shoe O.E. Minimum Lining Thickness	Brake Drum Diameter Standard Size	Brake Drum Diameter Machine To	Brake Pad O.E. Minimum Lining Thickness	Brake Rotor Min. Thickness Machine To	Brake Rotor Min. Thickness Discard At	Brake Rotor Variation From Parallelism	Brake Rotor Runout TIR	Caliper DESIGN	Caliper Mounting Bolts Torque (ft. lbs.)	Caliper Bridge, Pin or Key Bolts Torque (ft. lbs)	Wheel Lugs or Nuts Torque (ft. lbs.)
TOYOTA												
97-95 Avalon: Front	—	—	—	.039	—	1.024	—	.002	65⑥	79	25	76
Rear	—	—	—	.039	—	.315	—	.0059	105	34	25	76
97-92 Camry: w/rear drum brakes	.039	9.000	9.079	.039	—	1.024	—	.002	65⑥	79	25	76
w/rear disc brakes	—	—	—	.039	—	.354	—	.0059	65	34	14	76
91-88 Camry: w/rear drum brakes	.040	9.000	9.079	.040	—	.945	—	.003	65	79	29	76
w/rear disc brakes	—	—	—	.040	—	.354	—	.006	65	34	14	76

⑥Dual piston caliper ill. 81.

89450C29

PASSENGER CARS

Vehicle	Brake Shoe	Brake Drum		Brake Pad	Brake Rotor				D E S I G N	Caliper		Wheel
	O.E. Minimum Lining Thickness	Diameter		O.E. Minimum Lining Thickness	Min. Thickness		Variation From Parallelism	Runout TIR		Mounting Bolts Torque (ft. lbs.)	Bridge, Pin or Key Bolts Torque (ft. lbs)	Lugs or Nuts Torque (ft. lbs.)
Year / Make / Model		Standard Size	Machine To		Machine To	Discard At						
TOYOTA												
87 Camry:	.040	9.000	9.079	.040	—	.827	—	.005	65	79	29	76
86-83 Camry:	.040	7.874	7.913	.040	—	.827	—	.006	65	65	18	76
97-96 Celica: Front w/1.8L	.039	7.874	7.913	.039	—	.906	—	.002	65	79	25	76
Front w/2.2L	—	—	—	.039	—	1.024	—	.002	65	79	25	76
Rear w/disc brakes	—	—	—	.039	—	.314	—	.0059	32	34	14⑩	76
95-94 Celica: Front w/1.8L	.039	7.874	7.913	.039	—	.906	—	.002	65	69⑪	25	76
Front w/2.2L	—	—	—	.039	—	1.024	—	.002	65	79	25	76
Rear w/disc brakes	—	—	—	.039	—	.354	—	.0059	32	34	14⑩	76
93-92 Celica: w/rear drum brakes	.039	7.874	7.913	.039	—	.906	—	.0028	65	79	29	76
w/rear disc brakes	—	—	—	.039	—	.354	—	.0059	32	34	14	76
91-90 Celica: w/rear drum brakes	.040	7.874	7.913	.040	—	.787	—	.003	65	79	18①	76
w/All-Trac Turbo (Front)	—	—	—	.040	—	.906	—	.003	65	79	29	76
w/rear disc brakes	—	—	—	.040	—	.354	—	.006	32	34	14	76
89-88 Celica: (4x2) exc. ABS	.040	7.874	7.913	.040	—	.827	—	.003②	65	69	18	76
(4x2)w/ABS Front	—	—	—	.040	—	.945	—	.003②	65	69	18	76
(4x2)w/ABS Rear	—	—	—	.040	—	.354	—	.006	32	34	14	76
(4x4) Front	—	—	—	.040	—	.945	—	.003②	81	73	27	76
(4x4) Rear	—	—	—	.040	—	.354	—	.006	32	34	14	76
87-86 Celica: w/rear drum brakes	.040	7.874	7.913	.040	—	.827	—	.006	65	69	18	76
w/rear disc brakes	—	—	—	.040	—	.354	—	.006	32	34	14	76
85-82 Celica: w/rear drum brakes	.040	9.000	9.040	.118	—	.750	—	.006	47	59-75	12-17	66-86
w/rear disc brakes	—	—	—	.118	—	.670	—	.006	7	29-39	—	66-86
81 Celica:	.040	9.000	9.040	.118	—	.450	—	.006	22	40-54	—	65-86
80-77 Celica:	.040	9.000	9.040	.040	—	.450	—	.006	22	40-54	—	65-86
76 Celica:	.040	9.000	9.040	.040	—	.350	—	.006	22	48	—	65-86
75-72 Celica:	.040	9.000	9.040	.040	—	.350	—	.006	22	48	—	70-75
97-93 Corolla:	.039	7.874	7.913	.039	—	.787	—	.002	65	65	25	76
92 Corolla:	.039	7.874	7.913	.039	—	.669	—	.0035	65	65	18	76
91-90 Corolla: Front SOHC eng.	.040	7.874	7.913	.040	—	.669	—	.003	65	65	18	76
Front DOHC eng.	.040	7.874	7.913	.040	—	.827	—	.003	65	65	18	76
Rear	—	—	—	.040	—	.315	—	.004	70	34	20	76
89-88 Corolla FX, Corolla FX16:												
w/rear drum brakes	.040	7.874	7.913	.040	—	.669⑤	—	.004	65	65	18	76
w/rear disc brakes	—	—	—	.040	—	.315	—	.004②	70	34	U20-L14	76
87 Corolla FX16: Front	—	—	—	.040	—	.669	—	.005	65	65	18	76
Rear	—	—	—	.040	—	.315	—	.005	70	34	14	76
87-84 Corolla: exc. Coupe, FX16	.040	7.874	7.913	.040	—	.492	—	.006	65	65	18	76
Coupe w/front disc brakes	.040	9.000	9.079	.040	—	.669	—	.006	66	47	14	76
Coupe w/rear disc brakes	—	—	—	.040	—	.354	—	.006	70	47④	14	76
83-80 Corolla:	.040	9.000	9.040	.040	—	.453	—	.006	18	40-54	58-68	66-86
79-75 Corolla 1200:	.040	7.874	7.914	.040	—	.350	—	.006	18	30-40	—	58-69
74-72 Corolla 1200:	.040	7.874	7.914	.040	.360	.350	—	.006	22	40-54	—	65-86
79-75 Corolla 1600:	.040	9.000	9.040	.040	—	.350	—	.006	22	40-54	—	66-86
74-72 Corolla 1600:	.040	9.000	9.040	.040	—	.350	—	.006	22	48	—	70-75
82-75 Corona:	.040	9.000	9.040	.040	—	.450	—	.006	14	67-87⑧	—	65-86
74 Corona: Deluxe	.040	9.000	9.040	.040	—	.450	—	.006	14	67-87⑧	—	65-86
Standard	.040	9.000	9.040	.040	—	.350	—	.006	22	53	—	65-86
73-72 Corona:	.040	9.010	9.050	.040	—	.350	—	.006	22	53	—	65-86
76-73 Corona Mark II:	.040	9.000	9.040	.040	—	.450	—	.006	14	67-87	—	65-94
73-72 Corona Mark II:	.040	9.000	9.040	.040	—	.450	—	.006	14	67-87	—	65-86
92-89 Cressida: Front	—	—	—	.040	—	.827	—	.003	54	67	65	76
Rear	—	—	—	.040	—	.669	—	.005	54	34	18	76
88-85 Cressida: w/rear drum brakes	.040	9.000	9.040	.040	—	.830	—	.006	54	67-86	62-68	66-86
w/rear disc brakes	—	—	—	.040	—	.670	—	.006	54	34	18	76
84-83 Cressida: w/rear drum brakes	.040	9.000	9.040	.040	—	.830	—	.006	54	67-86	62-68	66-86
w/rear disc brakes	—	—	—	.040	—	.670	—	.006	55	29-39	37-43	66-86

①13" wheels shown; 14" & 15" wheels 29 ft/lbs. ②1988 .006". ③Radial pull in pounds at lug nut. ④1987 34 ft/lbs. ⑤FX, FX16, DOHC eng. shown; SOHC eng. .492".
⑥Dual piston caliper ill. 81. ⑦Dual piston caliper 25 ft/lbs. ⑧14" wheel shown; 13" wheel 51-65 ft/lbs. ⑨1995 shown; 1994-93 use .003. ⑩Lower shown; upper use 19 ft/lbs.
⑪1994 shown; 1995 use 79 ft/lbs.

89450C30

PASSENGER CARS

Vehicle — Year / Make / Model	Brake Shoe — O.E. Minimum Lining Thickness	Brake Drum — Diameter Standard Size	Brake Drum — Diameter Machine To	Brake Pad — O.E. Minimum Lining Thickness	Brake Rotor — Min. Thickness Machine To	Brake Rotor — Min. Thickness Discard At	Brake Rotor — Variation From Parallelism	Brake Rotor — Runout TIR	Caliper — Design	Caliper — Mounting Bolts Torque (ft. lbs.)	Caliper — Bridge, Pin or Key Bolts Torque (ft. lbs.)	Wheel — Lugs or Nuts Torque (ft. lbs.)
TOYOTA												
82-81 Cressida:	.040	9.000	9.040	.040	—	.669	—	.006	54	68-86	62-68	65-86
80-78 Cressida:	.040	9.000	9.040	.040	—	.450	—	.006	14	67-87	—	65-86
95-93 MR2: Front exc. Turbo	—	—	—	.039	—	.945	—	.002[9]	32	65	18	76
Front w/Turbo	—	—	—	.039	—	1.102	—	.002[9]	81	65	25	76
Rear exc. Turbo	—	—	—	.039	—	.591	—	.004	70	43	14	76
Rear w/Turbo	—	—	—	.039	—	.827	—	.004	70	43	14	76
92-91 MR2: Front	—	—	—	.040	—	.945	—	.003	32[6]	65	18[7]	76
Rear	—	—	—	.040	—	.591	—	.004	70	43	14	76
89-87 MR2: Front	—	—	—	.118	—	.827	—	.005	32	65	18	76
Rear	—	—	—	.040	—	.354	—	.005	70	43	14	76
86-85 MR2: Front	—	—	—	.040	—	.670	—	.006	32	65	18	76
Rear	—	—	—	.040	—	.354	—	.006	70	43	14	76
97-96 Paseo:	.039	7.087	7.126	.039	—	.630	—	.002	65	65	18	76
95-92 Paseo:	.039	7.087	7.126	.039	—	.669	—	.0035	65	65	18	76
84-81 Starlet:	.040	7.870	7.910	.040	—	.354	—	.006	7	29-54	11-15	66-86
97-94 Supra: Front Non-Turbo	—	—	—	.039	—	1.181	—	.002	103	87	25	76
Front Turbo	—	—	—	.039	—	1.102	—	.002	110	87	—	76
Rear Non-Turbo	—	—	—	.039	—	.591	—	.002	105	77	25	76
Rear Turbo	—	—	—	.039	—	.591	—	.002	113	77	—	76
92-86 Supra: Front	—	—	—	.040	—	.827	—	.005	47	77	27	76
Rear	—	—	—	.040	—	.669	—	.005	7	34	14	76
86-82 Supra: Front	—	—	—	.118	—	.750	—	.006	47	59-75	12-17	66-86
Rear	—	—	—	.118	—	.669	—	.006	7	30-39	12-17	66-86
81-79 Supra: Front	—	—	—	.118	—	.450	—	.006	22	40-54	—	65-86
Rear	—	—	—	.040	—	.354	—	.006	27	29-39	—	66-86
97 Tercel:	.039	7.087	7.126	.039	—	.630	—	.0028	65	65	18	76
96 Tercel:	.039	7.087	7.126	.039	—	.669	—	.0028	65	65	18	76
95-91 Tercel:	.040	7.087	7.126	.040	—	.669	—	.0035	65	65	18	76
90-85 Tercel: Sedan	.040	7.087	7.126	.040	—	.394	—	.006	65	65	18	76
Wagon	.040	7.874	7.913	.040	—	.394	—	.006	65	65	18	66-86
84-83 Tercel: (4x2)	.040	7.087	7.126	.040	—	.394	—	.006	65	65	18	66-86
(4x4)	.040	7.874	7.913	.040	—	.394	—	.006	7	33-39	11-15	66-86
82-80 Tercel:	.040	7.087	—	.040	—	.354	—	.006				

①13" wheels shown; 14" & 15" wheels 29 ft/lbs. ②1988 .006". ③Radial pull in pounds at lug nut. ④1987 34 ft/lbs. ⑤FX, FX16, DOHC eng. shown; SOHC eng. .492". ⑥Dual piston caliper ill. 81. ⑦Dual piston caliper 25 ft/lbs. ⑧14" wheel shown; 13" wheel 51-65 ft/lbs. ⑨1995 shown; 1994-93 use .003. ⑩Lower shown; upper use 19 ft/lbs. ⑪1994 shown; 1995 use 79 ft/lbs.

Vehicle — Year / Make / Model	Brake Shoe	Std Size	Machine To	Brake Pad	Machine To	Discard At	Variation	Runout TIR	Design	Mounting	Bridge/Pin	Wheel
VOLKSWAGEN												
74-72 411, 412: Sedan	.100	9.768	9.803	.080	—	.393	.0008	.004	17	58-65	—	94
78-72 Beetle: Front	.100	9.059	9.068	—	—	—	—	—	—	—	—	87-94
Rear	.100	9.055	9.094	—	—	—	—	—	—	—	—	87-94
92-87 Cabriolet:	.098	7.087	7.106	.276[4]	—	.709	—	.002	67	51	18	87
95-90 Corrado: Front	—	—	—	.276[4]	—	.787	.0004	.001	61	92	26	81
Rear	—	—	—	.276[4]	—	.315	—	.002	68	48	26	81
81-78 Dasher:	[2]	7.850	7.900	.080	.413	.393	—	.004	[3]	43[5]	25	87
77 Dasher:	[2]	7.850	7.900	.080	.413	.393	.0008	.004	[3]	43	—	87
76-74 Dasher:	[2]	7.850	7.900	.080	.433	.413	—	.004	[3]	43	—	87
91-87 Fox: exc. Wagon	.098	7.087	7.106	.276[4]	—	.393	—	.002	8	48	30	87
Wagon	.098	7.874	7.894	.276[4]	—	.393	—	.002	8	48	30	87
97-93 Golf III, GTI, Jetta III, Cabrio: exc. Plus Suspension	.098	7.874	7.913	.276[4]	—	.394	—	—	—	—	18	81
w/Plus Suspension										92	26	81
Front exc. 6 cyl.	—	—	—	.276[4]	—	.709	—					

①Seat brg. while turning wheel. Back off nut until thrust washer can be moved slightly by screwdriver w/finger pressure. Lock. ②.098" riveted; .059" bonded. ③Ill. 38 or 39. ④Measurement of lining & metal. ⑤w/self locking bolt 50 ft/lbs. ⑥Use ill. 67 from 2/84. ⑦4 cylinder: Not Adj., 6 cyl.: w/car on the ground, tighten to 66 ft. lbs. plus 45 degrees.

89450C31

PASSENGER CARS

Year / Make / Model	Brake Shoe O.E. Minimum Lining Thickness	Brake Drum Diameter Standard Size	Brake Drum Diameter Machine To	Brake Pad O.E. Minimum Lining Thickness	Brake Rotor Min. Thickness Machine To	Brake Rotor Min. Thickness Discard At	Brake Rotor Variation From Parallelism	Brake Rotor Runout TIR	Caliper DESIGN	Caliper Mounting Bolts Torque (ft. lbs.)	Caliper Bridge, Pin or Key Bolts Torque (ft. lbs)	Wheel Lugs or Nuts Torque (ft. lbs.)
VOLKSWAGEN												
Front w/6 cyl.	—	—	—	.276④	—	.787	—	—	—	92	26	81
Rear	—	—	—	.276④	—	.315	—	—	68	41	26	81
92-85 Golf, GTI, Jetta: exc. ABS												
w/solid front rotor	.098	7.087	7.106	.276④	—	.393	—	.002	67	51	18	87
exc. ABS w/vented front rotor	.098	7.087	7.106	.276④	—	.709	—	.002	67	51	18	87
w/rear disc brakes	—	—	—	.276④	—	.315	—	.002	68	48	26	87
92-89 Jetta: w/ABS Front	—	—	—	.276④	—	.709	.0004	.001	61	92	26	87
w/ABS Rear	—	—	—	.276④	—	.315	—	.002	68	48	26	87
74-73 Karman Ghia:	.100	9.055	9.094	.080	—	.335	.0008	.004	17	58-65	—	94
72 Karman Ghia:	.100	9.055	9.094	.080	—	.335	.0008	.008	17	58-65	—	108
97-90 Passat: Front	—	—	—	.276④	—	.709	.0004	.001	61	92	26	87
Rear	—	—	—	.276④	—	.315	—	.002	68	48	26	87
88-82 Quantum: w/4 cyl. eng.	.098	7.874	7.894	.276④	.413	.393	—	.002	8⑥	50	30	87
w/5 cyl. eng.	.098	7.874	7.894	.276④	—	.709	.0009	.002	8⑥	52	26	87
88-85 Quantum Syncro: Front	—	—	—	.276④	—	.709	.0009	.002	67	52	26	87
Rear	—	—	—	.276④	—	.315	—	.002	68	48	26	87
86-85 Rabbit: Conv.	.098	7.086	7.150	.250④	.413	.393	—	.002	67	50	30	87
84-83 Rabbit GTI	.098	7.086	7.150	.375④	.728	.709	—	.002	8	50	30	87
84-82 Rabbit, Jetta, Scirocco:	.098	7.086	7.105	.250④	.413	.393	—	.002	8⑥	50	30	87
81-80 Rabbit, Jetta, Scirocco:												
w/Girling Caliper	②	7.086	7.105	.080	.413	.393	—	.004	38	36	—	87
w/Kelsey-Hayes Caliper	②	7.086	7.105	.080	.413	.393	—	.004	8	36⑤	30	87
79-77 Rabbit: w/drum brakes Front	.040	9.059	9.079	—	—	—	—	—	—	—	—	87
w/drum brakes Rear	②	7.086	7.105	—	—	—	—	—	—	—	—	87
79-75 Rabbit, Scirocco:												
w/Girling Caliper	②	7.086	7.105	.080	.452	.413	—	.004	38	36	—	87
w/ATE Caliper	②	7.086	7.105	.080	.452	.413	—	.004	39	43	—	87
89-86 Scirocco: Front exc. 16 V eng.	.098	7.087	7.106	.276④	—	.709	—	.002	67	51	18	87
Front w/16 V eng.	—	—	—	.276④	—	.709	—	.002	61	52	26	87
Rear	—	—	—	.276④	—	.315	—	.002	68	48	26	87
85 Scirocco:	.098	7.086	7.150	.250④	.413	.393	—	.002	67	50	30	87
73-72 Squareback, Fastback:	.100	9.768	9.803	.080	—	.393	.0008	.008	17	56-65	—	94
79-72 Super Beetle: Front	.100	9.768	9.803	—	—	—	—	—	—	—	—	87-94
Rear	.100	9.055	9.094	—	—	—	—	—	—	—	—	87-94

①Seat brg. while turning wheel. Back off nut until thrust washer can be moved slightly by screwdriver w/finger pressure. Lock. ②.098" riveted; .059" bonded. ③Ill. 38 or 39.
④Measurement of lining & metal. ⑤w/self locking bolt 50 ft/lbs. ⑥Use ill. 67 from 2/84. ⑦4 cylinder: Not Adj., 6 cyl.: w/car on the ground, tighten to 66 ft. lbs. plus 45 degrees.

Year / Make / Model	Brake Shoe O.E. Minimum Lining Thickness	Brake Drum Diameter Standard Size	Brake Drum Diameter Machine To	Brake Pad O.E. Minimum Lining Thickness	Brake Rotor Min. Thickness Machine To	Brake Rotor Min. Thickness Discard At	Brake Rotor Variation From Parallelism	Brake Rotor Runout TIR	Caliper DESIGN	Caliper Mounting Bolts Torque (ft. lbs.)	Caliper Bridge, Pin or Key Bolts Torque (ft. lbs)	Wheel Lugs or Nuts Torque (ft. lbs.)
VOLVO												
74-72 140: Front	—	—	—	.062	.457	—	.0012	.004	16	65-70	—	70-100
Rear w/Girling	—	—	—	.062	.331	—	.0012	.006	14	45-50	—	70-100
Rear w/ATE	—	—	—	.062	.331	—	.0012	.006	17	45-50	—	70-100
75-72 160: Front	—	—	—	.062	.900	—	.0012	.004	16	65-70	—	70-95
Rear w/Girling	—	—	—	.062	.331	—	.0012	.006	14	38-47	—	70-95
Rear w/ATE	—	—	—	.062	.331	—	.0012	.006	17	38-47	—	70-95
73-72 1800: Sport Coupe Front	—	—	—	.062	—	.520	.0012	.006	16	65-70	—	70-100
Rear	—	—	—	.062	—	.331	.0012	.006	17	45-80	—	70-100
93-88 240: Front Solid Disc	—	—	—	.120	.500	—	—	.004	16	75	—	85
Front Vented: ATE	—	—	—	.120	.898	—	—	.004	16	75	—	85
Front Girling	—	—	—	.120	.803	—	—	.004	16	75	—	85
Rear	—	—	—	.120	.330	—	—	.004	14	43	—	85
87-75 240: Front w/ATE: vented disc	—	—	—	.062	.897	—	.0008	.004	16	65-70	—	70-95
Front w/Girling: vented disc	—	—	—	.062	.818	—	.0008	.004	16	65-70	—	70-95
Front Solid disc	—	—	—	.062	.519	—	.0008	.004	16	65-70	—	70-95
Rear w/ATE	—	—	—	.062	.331	—	.0008	.004	14	38-46	—	70-95

89450C32

PASSENGER CARS

Vehicle Year / Make / Model	Brake Shoe O.E. Minimum Lining Thickness	Brake Drum Diameter Standard Size	Brake Drum Machine To	Brake Pad O.E. Minimum Lining Thickness	Brake Rotor Min. Thickness Machine To	Brake Rotor Discard At	Variation From Parallelism	Runout TIR	DESIGN	Caliper Mounting Bolts Torque (ft. lbs.)	Caliper Bridge, Pin or Key Bolts Torque (ft. lbs)	Wheel Lugs or Nuts Torque (ft. lbs.)
VOLVO												
Rear w/Girling	—	—	—	.062	.331	—	.0008	.004	17	38-46	—	70-95
82-76 260: Front w/vented disc brakes	—	—	—	.062	.818	—	.0008	.004	16	65-72	—	72-94
Front w/solid disc brakes	—	—	—	.062	.519	—	.0008	.004	16	65-72	—	72-94
Rear w/ATE	—	—	—	.062	.331	—	.0008	.004	14	38-46	—	72-94
Rear w/Girling	—	—	—	.062	.331	—	.0008	.004	17	38-46	—	72-94
92-88 740: Front Solid disc	—	—	—	.120	—	.433	—	.002	76	74	25	65
Front Vented disc	—	—	—	.120	—	.787	—	.002	76	74	25	65
Front Vented H.D.	—	—	—	.120	—	.910	—	—	76	74	25	65
Rear Standard	—	—	—	.078	—	.330	—	.004	14	43	—	65
Rear w/Multi-Link	—	—	—	.078	—	.314	—	.003	14	43	—	65
87-82 740, 760, 780:												
Front w/solid disc brakes	—	—	—	.118	—	.433	—	.003	52	74	①	63
Front w/vented disc brakes	—	—	—	.118	—	.788	—	.003	52	74	①	63
Rear	—	—	—	.078	—	.330	—	.004	53	43	—	63
91-88 760, 780: Front	—	—	—	.120	—	.788	—	.002	76	74	25	65
Rear	—	—	—	.078	—	.314	—	.003	31	43	25	65
97-93 850: Front	—	—	—	.120	.937	.905	.0003	.001	76	74	22	81
Rear	—	—	—	.078	.350	.330	.0003	.002	14	37	22	81
97-91 940, 960:												
Front w/solid disc brakes	—	—	—	.120	—	.433	—	.002	76	74	25	65
Front w/vented disc brakes	—	—	—	.120	—	.788	.0003	.001	76	74	22	65
Front w/H.D. vented disc	—	—	—	.120	—	.910	.0003	.001	76	74	22	65
Rear w/Multi-Link	—	—	—	.078	—	.314	.0003	.002	14	44	22	65
Rear Standard	—	—	—	.078	—	.330	.0005	.002	14	44	—	65
YUGO												
92-86 Cabrio, GV, GVL, GVX:	.059	7.293	7.336	.059	.368	.354	—	.006	22	35	—	64

①Upper pin 19 ft/lbs.; lower pin 25 ft/lbs.

89450C33

LIGHT TRUCKS

Vehicle Year / Make / Model	Brake Shoe O.E. Minimum Lining Thickness	Brake Drum Diameter Standard Size	Brake Drum Diameter Machine To	Brake Pad O.E. Minimum Lining Thickness	Brake Rotor Min. Thickness Machine To	Brake Rotor Min. Thickness Discard At	Brake Rotor Variation From Parallelism	Brake Rotor Runout TIR	DESIGN	Caliper Mounting Bolts Torque (ft. lbs.)	Caliper Bridge, Pin or Key Bolts Torque (ft. lbs)	Wheel Lugs or Nuts Torque (ft. lbs.)
ACURA TRUCK												
97-96 SLX: Front	—	—	—	.039	.983	.969	.0004	.005	73	115	54	87
Rear	—	—	—	.039	.668	.654	.0004	.005	57	76	32	87

① Radial pull in pounds at lugnut.

Vehicle Year / Make / Model	Brake Shoe O.E. Minimum Lining Thickness	Brake Drum Diameter Standard Size	Brake Drum Diameter Machine To	Brake Pad O.E. Minimum Lining Thickness	Brake Rotor Min. Thickness Machine To	Brake Rotor Min. Thickness Discard At	Brake Rotor Variation From Parallelism	Brake Rotor Runout TIR	DESIGN	Caliper Mounting Bolts Torque (ft. lbs.)	Caliper Bridge, Pin or Key Bolts Torque (ft. lbs)	Wheel Lugs or Nuts Torque (ft. lbs.)
CHRYSLER CORP. TRUCK — Chrysler, Dodge, Plymouth												
82-79 Arrow Pickup:	.040	9.500	9.550	.040	—	.720	—	.006	34	51-65	—	51-58
85-76 B100, B150, PB100, PB150:												
w/10" rear brakes	.030	10.000	10.060	.030	1.210	1.180	.0005	.004	5	95-125	14-22	85-125
w/11" rear brakes	.030	11.000	11.060	.030	1.210	1.180	.0005	.004	5	95-125	14-22	85-125
75-73 B100, PB100: w/10" rear brakes	.030	10.000	10.060	.030	1.210	1.180	.0005	.004	5	75-100	17	65-85
w/11" rear brakes	.030	11.000	11.060	.030	1.210	1.180	.0005	.004	5	75-100	17	65-85
72 B100: w/10" rear brakes	.030	10.000	10.060	.030	1.210	1.180	.0005	.004	(5)	75-100	17	65-85
w/11" rear brakes	.030	11.000	11.060	.030	1.210	1.180	.0005	.004	(5)	75-100	17	65-85
97-86 B150, B250:	.030	11.000	11.060	.125(9)	1.210	1.180	.0005	.004	5	95-125	14-22	85-110
83-78 B200, B250, PB200, PB250:	.030	10.000	10.060	.030	1.210	1.180	.0005	.004	5	95-125	14-22	85-125
77-76 B200, PB200:	.030	11.000	11.060	.030	1.210	1.180	.0005	.004	5	75-100	17	65-85
75-73 B200, PB200:	.030	11.000	11.060	.030	1.210	1.180	.0005	.004	5	75-100	17	65-85
72 B200: w/10" rear brakes	.030	10.000	10.060	.030	1.210	1.180	.0005	.004	(5)	75-100	17	65-85
w/11" rear brakes	.030	11.000	11.060	.030	1.210	1.180	.0005	.004	(5)	75-100	17	65-85
85-84 B250, PB250:	.030	11.000	11.060	.030	1.210	1.180	.0005	.004	5	95-125	14-22	85-125
85-79 B300, B350, CB300, CB350, PB300, PB350: w/3,600lb. F.A.	.030	12.000	12.060	.030	1.210	1.180	.0005	.004	4	95-125②	14-22	85-125
w/4,000lb. F.A.	.030	12.000	12.060	.030	1.160	1.130	.0005	.004	5	95-125②	14-22	175-225
78-76 B300, CB300, PB300:	.030	12.000	12.060	.030	1.160	1.130	.0005	.004	5	95-125②	14-22	85-125④
75-73 B300, CB300, PB300:	.030	12.000	12.060	.030	1.160	1.130	.0005	.004	5	140-180	17	65-85④
72 B300, CB300:	.030	12.000	12.060	.030	1.160	1.130	.0005	.004	(5)	140-180	17	65-85④
97-87 B350: w/3,600lb. F.A.	.030	12.000	12.060	.125(9)	1.210	1.180	.0005	.004	5	95-125②	14-22	85-110
w/4,000lb. F.A.	.030	12.000	12.060	.125(9)	1.155	1.125	.0005	.004	5	95-125②	14-22	⑥
86 B350: w/3,600lb. F.A.	.030	12.000	12.060	.125(9)	1.210	1.180	.0005	.004	5	95-125②	15	85-110
w/4,000lb. F.A.	.030	12.000	12.060	.125(9)	1.155	1.125	.0005	.004	5	95-125②	15	⑥
97 Caravan, Voyager:												
exc. rear disc brakes	—	9.842	9.902	.313⑦	—	.881	.0005	.003	6	—	30	95
w/rear disc brakes	—	—	—	—	—	.409	.0005	.003	—	—	—	95
96 Caravan, Voyager:	—	9.842	9.902	.313⑦	—	.881	.0005	.003	6	—	30	95
95-91 Caravan, Voyager: (FWD)	.030	9.000	9.060	.030	.912	.882	.0005	.005	8	130-190	25-35	95
(AWD)	.030	11.000	11.060	.030	.912	.882	.0005	.005	8	130-190	25-35	95
90-84 Caravan, Mini Ram Van, Voyager:	.030	9.000	9.060	.030⑦	.833	.803	.0005	.005	8	130-190	25-35	95
83-75 D100, D150: exc. w/9 1/4" rear axle	.030	10.000	10.060	.030	1.220	1.190	.0005	.004	5	110③	17	105
76-75 D100: w/9 1/4" rear axle	.030	11.000	11.060	.030	1.220	1.190	.0005	.004	5	100	17	105
74-73 D100: exc. w/11" front brakes	.030	10.000	10.060	.030	1.220	1.190	.0005	.004	5	100	17	65-85
73-72 D100: w/11" front brakes	.030	11.000	11.060	—	—	—	—	—	—	—	—	65-85
72 D100:	.030	10.000	10.060	.030	—	1.180	.0005	.0025	2	75-100	30-35	70-90
93-90 D150:	.030	11.000	11.060	.030	1.220	1.190	.0005	.004	5	110	17	105
89-84 D150:	.030	11.000	11.060	.030	1.220	1.190	.0005	.004	5	110	17	105
93-90 D200, D250: w/3,300lb. F.A.	.030	12.000	12.060	.030	1.220	1.190	.0005	.004	5	110	17	105
93-90 D200, D250, D300, D350: w/4,000lb. F.A.	.030	12.000	12.060	.030	1.220	1.190	.0005	.004	5	160	17	105①
89-81 D200, D250: w/3,300lb. F.A.	.030	12.000	12.060	.030	1.220	1.190	.001	.005	5	110	17	105
89-79 D200, D250, D300, D350: w/4,000lb. F.A.	.030	12.000	12.060	.030	1.160	1.130	.001	.005	5	160	17	105①

②5/8" bolt 140-180 ft/lbs. ③1980-75 100 ft/lbs. ④w/dual rear wheels 1978-76 300-350 ft/lbs.; 1975-72 (F)125-175 ft/lbs., (R)300-350 ft/lbs. ⑤Use ill. 2 or 5.
⑥w/cone type nut 175-225 ft/lbs.; w/flanged 300-350 ft/lbs. ⑦.030" over rivet head; if bonded lining use .062". ⑨Combined shoe & lining thickness .3125".
⑦Measurement of lining and metal.

89450C34

LIGHT TRUCKS

Vehicle Year / Make / Model	Brake Shoe O.E. Minimum Lining Thickness	Brake Drum Diameter Standard Size	Brake Drum Machine To	Brake Pad O.E. Minimum Lining Thickness	Brake Rotor Min. Thickness Machine To	Brake Rotor Min. Thickness Discard At	Brake Rotor Variation From Parallelism	Brake Rotor Runout TIR	Design	Caliper Mounting Bolts Torque (ft. lbs.)	Caliper Bridge, Pin or Key Bolts Torque (ft. lbs.)	Wheel Lugs or Nuts Torque (ft. lbs.)
CHRYSLER CORP. TRUCK — Chrysler, Dodge, Plymouth												
80-79 D200:												
w/3,300lb. F.A. over 6,200lbs. GVW ...	.030	12.000	12.060	.030	1.220	1.190	.001	.005	5	100	17	105
w/3,300lb. F.A. 6,200lbs. GVW ...	.030	12.120	12.180	.030	1.220	1.190	.001	.005	5	100	17	105
78-75 D200: w/6600lbs. GVW ...	.030	12.120	12.180	.030	1.160	1.130	.0005	.004	5	100	17	105
78-75 D200, D300: over 6,000lbs. GVW ...	.030	12.000	12.060	.030	1.160	1.130	.0005	.004	5	160	17	105①
74 D200: w/6,000lbs. GVW ...	.030	12.120	12.180	.030	1.160	1.130	.0005	.004	5	100	17	65-85
74 D200, D300: over 6,000lbs. GVW ...	.030	12.000	12.060	.030	1.160	1.130	.0005	.004	5	160	17	68-85①
73 D200: w/6,000lbs. GVW ...	.030	12.120	12.180	.030	—	1.125	.0005	.004	5	100	17	70-90
w/12.57" rotor diameter ...	.030	12.000	12.060	.030	—	1.180	.0005	.004	5	100	17	70-90
w/12.82" rotor diameter ...	.030	12.000	12.060	.030	—	1.125	.0005	.004	5	100	17	70-90
72 D200: w/6,000lbs. GVW ...	.030	12.120	12.180	.030	—	1.125	.0005	.0025	2	75-100	30-35	70-90
w/12.57" rotor diameter ...	.030	12.000	12.060	.030	—	1.180	.0005	.0025	2	75-100	30-35	70-90
w/12.82" rotor diameter ...	.030	12.000	12.060	.030	—	1.125	.0005	.0025	5	75-100	30-35	70-90
73-72 D300: ...	.030	12.000	12.060	—	—	—	—	—	—	—	—	70-90①
97 Dakota: w/9" rear brakes ...	.030⑦	9.000	9.060	—	—	⑯	.0005	.004	8	—	22	85-110
w/10" rear brakes ...	.030⑦	10.000	10.060	—	—	⑯	.0005	.004	8	—	22	85-110
96-91 Dakota: (4x2) w/9" rear brakes ...	.030⑦	9.000	9.060	.250	—	.890	.0005	.004	8	—	18-26	85⑬
(4x2) w/10" rear brakes ...	.030⑦	10.000	10.060	.250	—	.890	.0005	.004	8	—	18-26	85⑬
(4x4) w/9" rear brakes ...	.030⑦	9.000	9.060	.250	—	.890	.0005	.004	51	—	18-26	85⑬
(4x4) w/10" rear brakes ...	.030⑦	10.000	10.060	.250	—	.890	.0005	.004	51	—	18-26	85⑬
90-87 Dakota: (4x2) w/9" rear brakes ...	.030⑦	9.000	9.060	.250	.841	.811	.0005	.004	8	—	18-26	85
(4x2) w/10" rear brakes ...	.030⑦	10.000	10.060	.250	.841	.811	.0005	.004	8	—	18-26	85
(4x4) w/9" rear brakes ...	.030⑦	9.000	9.060	.250	.841	.811	.0005	.004	51	—	18-26	85
(4x4) w/10" rear brakes ...	.030⑦	10.000	10.060	.250	.841	.811	.0005	.004	51	—	18-26	85
89-88 Raider: ...	.040	10.000	10.079	.079	—	.803	—	.0059	69	58-72	U33-L27	72-87
87 Raider: ...	.040	10.000	10.079	.040	—	.724	—	.0059	34	58-72	—	72-87
97-94 Ram 1500: 2WD ...	.188⑭	11.000	11.060	.188⑭	—	⑯	.001	.005	62	—	38	80-110
4WD ...	.188⑭	11.000	11.060	.188⑭	—	⑯	.001	.005	62	—	38	80-110
97-94 Ram 2500, Ram 3500: 2WD ...	.188⑭	13.000	13.060	.188⑭	—	⑯	.001	.005	62	—	38	120-150⑮
4WD ...	.188⑭	13.000	13.060	.188⑭	—	⑯	.001	.005	62	—	38	120-150⑮
93-87 Ram 50: (4x2) ...	.040	10.000	10.079	.080	—	.803	—	.0059	69	58-72	U33-L27	87-101
(4X4) ...	.040	10.000	10.079	.080	—	.803	—	.0059	69	58-72	U33-L27	87-101
86-83 Ram 50: w/9 ½" rear brakes ...	.040	9.500	9.570	.040	—	.720	—	.006	34	51-65	—	51-57
W/10" rear brakes ...	.040	10.000	10.070	.040	—	.720	—	.006	34	51-65②	—	51-57
82-79 D 50, Ram 50: ...	.040	9.500	9.550	.040	—	.720	—	.006	34	51-65	—	51-58
93-90 Ramcharger: (4x2) ...	.030	11.000	11.060	.030	1.220	1.190	.0005	.004	5	110	17	105
(4x4) ...	.030	11.000	11.060	.030	1.220	1.190	.0005	.004	5	150	17	105
89-84 Ramcharger: (4x2) ...	.030	11.000	11.060	.030	1.220	1.190	.0005	.004	5	110	17	105
(4x4) ...	.030	11.000	11.060	.030	1.220	1.190	.001	.005	5	150	17	105
83-79 Ramcharger: (4x2) ...	.030	10.000	10.060	.030	1.220	1.190	.0005	.004	5	110	17	105
(4x4) ...	.030	10.000	10.060	.030	1.220	1.190	.001	.005	5	150	17	105
78-74 Ramcharger: (4x2) ...	.030	11.000	11.060	.030	1.220	1.190	.0005	.004	5	95	17	85-125
(4x4) ...	.030	11.000	11.060	.030	1.220	1.190	.0005	.004	5	95	17	85-125
84-83 Rampage, Scamp: ...	.030	7.874	7.904	.030	.461	.431	.0005	.004	8	130-190	25-35	80⑧
82 Rampage: ...	.030	7.780	7.900	.030	.461	.431	.0005	.004	8	70-100	25-40	85
97 Town & Country:												
exc. rear disc brakes ...	—	9.842	9.902	.313⑦	—	.881	.0005	.003	6	—	30	95
w/ rear disc brakes ...	—	—	—	—	—	.409	.0005	.003	—	—	95	95
96 Town & Country: ...	—	9.842	9.902	.313⑦	—	.881	.0005	.003	6	—	30	95
95-91 Town & Country Van: (FWD) ...	.030	9.000	9.060	.030	.912	.882	.0005	.005	8	130-190	25-35	95
(AWD) ...	.030	11.000	11.060	.030	.912	.882	.0005	.005	8	130-190	25-35	95
90 Town & Country Van: ...	.030	9.000	9.060	.030⑦	.833	.803	.0005	.005	8	130-190	25-35	95

①w/⅝" wheel stud 200 ft/lbs.; 1974 175-225 ft/lbs.; 1973-72 125-175 ft/lbs. w/dual rear whls. 325 ft/lbs.   ⑦.030" over rivet head; if bonded lining use .062".   ⑧1984 95 ft/lbs.   ⑭4 WD.
⑫2 WD.   ②1986-85 4 WD 58-72 ft/lbs.   ⑬1991 shown; 1996-92 use 95 ft/lbs.   ⑭Bonded lining shown; if riveted lining use .063" over rivet head.
⑮8-lug single wheel shown; 8-lug dual wheel use 130-160 ft/lbs.   ⑯Refer to marking on rotor for discard dimension.   ⑦Measurement of lining and metal.

89450C35

LIGHT TRUCKS

Year / Make / Model	Brake Shoe O.E. Minimum Lining Thickness	Brake Drum Diameter Standard Size	Brake Drum Diameter Machine To	Brake Pad O.E. Minimum Lining Thickness	Brake Rotor Min. Thickness Machine To	Brake Rotor Min. Thickness Discard At	Brake Rotor Variation From Parallelism	Brake Rotor Runout TIR	DESIGN	Caliper Mounting Bolts Torque (ft. lbs.)	Caliper Bridge, Pin or Key Bolts Torque (ft. lbs)	Wheel Lugs or Nuts Torque (ft. lbs.)
CHRYSLER CORP. TRUCK — Chrysler, Dodge, Plymouth												
83-79 W100, W150:	.030	10.000	10.060	.030	1.220	1.190	.001	.005	5	150	17	105
78-77 W100:	.030	11.000	11.060	.030	1.220	1.190	.0005	.004	5	100	17	105
76-75 W100:	.030	11.000	11.060	.030	1.220	1.190	.0005	.004	5	100	17	105
74-72 W100:	.030	11.000	11.060	—	—	—	—	—	—	—	—	70-90
93-90 W150:	.030	11.000	11.060	.030	1.220	1.190	.0005	.004	5	150	17	105
89-84 W150:	.030	11.000	11.060	.030	1.220	1.190	.001	.005	5	150	17	105
93-90 W200, W250: exc. w/Spicer 60	.030	12.000	12.060	.030	1.220	1.190	.001	.005	5	150	17	105
93-79 W200, W250, W300, W350: w/Spicer 60	.030	12.000	12.060	.030	1.160	1.130	.001	.005	21	160	15	105①
89-79 W200, W250: exc. w/Spicer 60	.030	12.000	12.060	.030	1.160	1.130	.001	.005	5	150	17	105
78-75 W200: exc. w/Spicer 60	.030	12.000	12.060	.030	1.160	1.130	.0005	.004	5	100	17	105
78-75 W200, W300: w/Spicer 60	.030	12.000	12.060	.030	1.160	1.130	.0005	.004	21	160	15	105
74-72 W200: Front	.030	12.120	12.180	—	—	—	—	—	—	—	—	—
Rear	.030	12.000	12.060	—	—	—	—	—	—	—	—	—
74-72 W200, W300: w/4,500lb. F.A.	.030	12.000	12.060	—	—	—	—	—	—	—	—	—

①w/⅝" wheel stud 200 ft/lbs.; 1974 175-225 ft/lbs.; 1973-72 125-175 ft/lbs. w/dual rear whls. 325 ft/lbs.

Year / Make / Model	Brake Shoe O.E. Minimum Lining Thickness	Brake Drum Diameter Standard Size	Brake Drum Diameter Machine To	Brake Pad O.E. Minimum Lining Thickness	Brake Rotor Min. Thickness Machine To	Brake Rotor Min. Thickness Discard At	Brake Rotor Variation From Parallelism	Brake Rotor Runout TIR	DESIGN	Caliper Mounting Bolts Torque (ft. lbs.)	Caliper Bridge, Pin or Key Bolts Torque (ft. lbs)	Wheel Lugs or Nuts Torque (ft. lbs.)
DAIHATSU TRUCK												
92-90 Rocky:	.039	10.000	10.060	.060	—	.450	—	.0059	30	50-65	23-30	65-87

Year / Make / Model	Brake Shoe O.E. Minimum Lining Thickness	Brake Drum Diameter Standard Size	Brake Drum Diameter Machine To	Brake Pad O.E. Minimum Lining Thickness	Brake Rotor Min. Thickness Machine To	Brake Rotor Min. Thickness Discard At	Brake Rotor Variation From Parallelism	Brake Rotor Runout TIR	DESIGN	Caliper Mounting Bolts Torque (ft. lbs.)	Caliper Bridge, Pin or Key Bolts Torque (ft. lbs)	Wheel Lugs or Nuts Torque (ft. lbs.)
FORD MOTOR CO. TRUCK												
97-86 Aerostar: w/9" rear brakes	.030①	9.000	9.060	.030	—	.810	.001②	.003	59	—	—	85-115
w/10" rear brakes	.030①	10.000	10.060	.030	—	.810	.001②	.003	59	—	—	85-115
96-95 Bronco: exc. integral rotor	①	11.031	11.091	.030	—	.963	.0007	.005	1	—	22-26	100
w/integral rotor	①	11.031	11.091	.030	—	.963	.0005	.003	1	—	22-26	100
94 Bronco: exc. integral rotor	.030	11.031	11.091	.030	—	.960	.0007	.005	1	—	—	100
w/integral rotor	.030	11.031	11.091	.030	—	.960	.0005	.003	1	—	—	100
93-90 Bronco: w/integral rotor	.030	11.031	11.091	.030	—	1.120	.0005	.003	1	—	—	100
exc. integral rotor	.030	11.031	11.091	.030	—	1.120	.0007	.005	1	—	—	100
89-88 Bronco: w/integral rotor	.030	11.031	11.091	.030	—	1.120	.0005	.003	1	—	—	100⑥
exc. integral rotor	.030	11.031	11.091	.030	—	1.120	.0007	.003⑨	1	—	—	100⑥
87-86 Bronco: w/integral rotor	.030	11.031	11.091	.030	—	1.120	.0005	.003	1	—	—	100⑥
exc. integral rotor	.030	11.031	11.091	.030	—	1.120	.0007⑧	.003⑨	1	—	—	100⑥
85-81 Bronco:	.030	11.031	11.091	.030	—	1.120	.0007	.003	1	74-102	12-20	90
80-76 Bronco:	.030	11.031	11.091	.030	—	1.120	.0007	.003	1	50-60	12-20	90
75-72 Bronco: w/10" brakes	.030	10.000	10.060	—	—	—	—	—	—	—	—	90
w/11" brakes	.030	11.000	11.060	—	—	—	—	—	—	—	—	90
82-79 Courier:	.039	10.236	10.244	.276⑧	.433	—	.0005	.004	35	—	—	58-65
78-77 Courier:	.039	10.236	10.244	.314⑧	.433	—	.0005	.004	35	—	—	58-65
76-74 Courier:	.039	10.236	10.244	—	—	—	—	—	—	—	—	58-65⑮
73-72 Courier:	.039	10.236	10.244	—	—	—	—	—	—	—	—	85
97 E150:	.080	11.030	—	.031	—	.960	.0004	.0025	1	—	22-26	100
96-94 E150:	①	11.031	11.091	.031	—	.963	.0005	.003	1	—	22-26	100
93-90 E150: (4x2)	.030	11.031	11.091	.030	—	1.120	.0005	.003	1	—	—	100
89-86 E150, F150: (4x2)	.030	11.031	11.091	.030	—	1.120	.0005⑦	.003	1	—	—	100⑥
85-77 E100, E150, F100, F150: w/4,600-4,900lbs. GVW	.030	10.000	10.060	.030	—	.810	.0005	.003	1	—	12-20	90
	.030	11.031	11.091	.030	—	1.120	.0007	.003	1	—	12-20	90
76-75 E100, E150, F100, F150:	.030	11.031	11.091	.030	—	1.120	.0007	.003	1	—	12-20	90

①.030" over rivet head; if bonded lining use .062". ⑦1986 .0007". ②1993-91 .002". ⑧w/manual locking hubs shown; w/auto. locking hubs 50 ft/lbs., 372-468 in/lbs.
⑧Measurement of lining & metal. ⑮1974 85 ft/lbs. ⑥Manual locking hubs shown; w/auto. locking hubs, backoff inner locknut, torq to 30-40 ft/lbs. backoff 90 deg.
⑦Manual locking hubs shown; w/auto. locking hubs see O.E. Manual. ⑧See O.E. Manual.

89450C36

LIGHT TRUCKS

Year / Make / Model	Brake Shoe O.E. Minimum Lining Thickness	Brake Drum Diameter Standard Size	Brake Drum Machine To	Brake Pad O.E. Minimum Lining Thickness	Brake Rotor Min. Thickness Machine To	Brake Rotor Discard At	Brake Rotor Variation From Parallelism	Brake Rotor Runout TIR	DESIGN	Caliper Mounting Bolts Torque (ft. lbs.)	Caliper Bridge, Pin or Key Bolts Torque (ft. lbs)	Wheel Lugs or Nuts Torque (ft. lbs.)
FORD MOTOR CO. TRUCK												
74-72 E100, F100: w/10" brakes	.030	10.000	10.060	—	—	—	—	—	—	—	—	90
w/11" brakes	.030	11.031	11.091	.030	—	1.120	.0003	.003	1	—	12-20	90
97 E250:	.080	12.000	—	.031	—	1.100	.0005	.003	19	—	16-30	100
96-95 E250:	①	12.000	12.060	.031	—	1.102	.0005	.003	19	141-191	22-26	140
97 E350:	.080	12.125	—	.031	—	1.100	.0005	.003	19	—	16-30	100
96-95 E350:	①	12.125	12.185	.031	—	1.102	.0005	.003	19	141-191	22-26	140
97-96 E-Super Duty: Front	—	—	—	.030	—	1.102	.0005	.003	—	—	—	140
Rear	—	—	—	.030	—	1.430	.001	.008	—	74-100	—	140
94-90 E250, E350, F250, F350:												
(4x2) w/single rear wheels	.030	12.000	12.060	.030	—	1.180	.0007	.003	19	—	—	140
(4x2) w/dual rear wheels	.030	12.000	12.060	.030	—	1.180	.001	.005	19	—	—	140
89-86 E250, E350, F250, F350:												
(4x2) w/single rear wheels	.030	12.000	12.060	.030	—	1.180	.0007	.003	19	—	—	140
(4x2) w/dual rear wheels	.030	12.000	12.060	.030	—	1.180	.001	.003⑨	19	—	—	140
85-78 E250, E350, F250, F350: 6,900lbs. GVW H.D.	.030	12.000	12.060	.030	—	1.180	.0007	.003	19	74-102	12-20②	90③
77 E250, E350, F250, F350: 6,900lbs. GVW H.D.	.030	12.000	12.060	.030	—	1.214	.0007	.003	19	74-102	12-20②	90③
76 E250, E350, F250, F350:												
w/12" rear brakes	.030	12.000	12.060	.030	—	1.180	.0007	.003	19	74-102	12-20②	90③
w/12 ⅛" rear brakes	.030	12.125	12.185	.030	—	1.180	.0007	.003	19	74-102	12-20②	90③
75 E250, E350:	.030	12.000	12.060	.030	—	.940	.001	.003	23	55-72	17-23②	90③
74-72 E250:	.030	11.031	11.091	—	—	—	—	—	—	—	—	90
74-72 E350:	.030	12.000	12.060	—	—	—	—	—	—	—	—	135③
97-95 F-Super Duty: Front	—	—	—	.030	—	1.430	.001	.008	19	—	—	140
Rear	—	—	—	.030	—	1.430	.001	.008	19	—	—	140
94-90 F-Super Duty: Front	—	—	—	.030	—	1.430	.001	.008	19	—	—	140
Rear	—	—	—	.030	—	1.430	.001	.008	19	—	—	140
89-88 F-Super Duty: Front	—	—	—	.030	—	1.430	.001	.008	19	—	—	140
Rear	—	—	—	.030	—	1.430	.001	.008	19	—	—	140
97 F150: (4x2)	.030	11.000	11.120	.125	—	.972	—	—	1	125-169	21-26	83-112
(4x4)	.030	11.000	11.120	.125	—	1.090	—	—	1	125-169	21-26	83-112
w/rear disc brakes	—	—	—	.125	—	.472	.0005	.003	1	—	20	83-112
96-95 F150: (4x2)	①	11.031	11.091	.030	—	.963	.0005	.003	1	—	22-26	100
(4x4) exc. integral rotor	①	11.031	11.091	.030	—	.963	.0007	.005	1	—	22-26	100
(4x4) w/integral rotor	①	11.031	11.091	.030	—	.963	.0005	.003	1	—	22-26	100
94 F150: (4X2)	.030	11.031	11.091	.030	—	.960	.0005	.003	1	—	—	100
(4x4) exc. integral rotor	.030	11.031	11.091	.030	—	.960	.0007	.005	1	—	—	100
(4x4) w/integral rotor	.030	11.031	11.091	.030	—	.960	.0005	.003	1	—	—	100
93-90 F150: (4x2)	.030	11.031	11.091	.030	—	1.120	.0005	.003	1	—	—	100
(4x4) w/integral rotor	.030	11.031	11.091	.030	—	1.120	.0005	.003	1	—	—	100
(4x4) exc. integral rotor	.030	11.031	11.091	.030	—	1.120	.0007	.005	1	—	—	100
89-88 F150: (4x4) w/integral rotor	.030	11.031	11.091	.030	—	1.120	.0005	.003	1	—	—	100⑥
(4x4) exc. integral rotor	.030	11.031	11.091	.030	—	1.120	.0007	.003⑨	1	—	—	100⑥
87-86 F150: (4x4) w/integral rotor	.030	11.031	11.091	.030	—	1.120	.0005	.003	1	—	—	100⑥
(4x4) exc. integral rotor	.030	11.031	11.091	.030	—	1.120	.0007⑧	.003⑨	1	—	—	100⑥
85-81 F100, F150, F200: (4x4) w/Dana 44IFS F.A.	.030	11.031	11.091	.030	—	1.120	.0007	.003	1	74-102	12-20	90
80-76 F100, F150: (4x4)	.030	11.031	11.091	.030	—	1.120	.0007	.003	1	50-60	12-20	90
75-72 F100: (4x4) Front	.030	11.000	11.060	—	—	—	—	—	—	—	—	90
(4x4) Rear	.030	11.031·	11.091	—	—	—	—	—	—	—	—	90

①.030" over rivet head; if bonded lining use .062".   ②Caliper bridge bolt 155-185 ft/lbs.   ④1991-90: 90 degrees.
③E350,F350 w/single rear wheels; 1985 140 ft/lbs.; 1984-78.145 ft/lbs.; 1977-72 135 ft/lbs. W/dual rear wheels; 1985-78 220 ft/lbs.; 1977-72 210 ft/lbs.
⑤1986: 45 degrees.   ⑥1986 90 ft/lbs.   ⑧1986 .001".   ⑨1 piece rotor .003"; 2 piece .005".   ⑩w/manual locking hubs shown; w/auto. locking hubs 50 ft/lbs., 372-468 in/lbs.
⑭Manual locking hubs shown; w/auto. locking hubs, backoff inner locknut, torq to 30-40 ft/lbs. backoff 90 deg.   ⑦Manual locking hubs shown; w/auto. locking hubs see O.E. Manual.
⑯See O.E. Manual

89450C37

LIGHT TRUCKS

Vehicle Year / Make / Model	Brake Shoe O.E. Minimum Lining Thickness	Brake Drum Diameter Standard Size	Brake Drum Diameter Machine To	Brake Pad O.E. Minimum Lining Thickness	Brake Rotor Min. Thickness Machine To	Brake Rotor Min. Thickness Discard At	Brake Rotor Variation From Parallelism	Brake Rotor Runout TIR	DESIGN	Caliper Mounting Bolts Torque (ft. lbs.)	Caliper Bridge, Pin or Key Bolts Torque (ft. lbs)	Wheel Lugs or Nuts Torque (ft. lbs.)
FORD MOTOR CO. TRUCK												
97 F250, Expedition: (4x2)	.031	12.000	12.090	.125	—	1.090	—	—	1	125-169	21-26	83-112
(4x4)	.031	12.000	12.090	.125	—	1.090	—	—	1	125-169	21-26	83-112
w/rear disc brakes	—	—	—	.125	—	.472	.005	.003	1			83-112
97 F250HD: (4x2)	①	12.000	12.060	.030	—	1.102	.0005	.003	19	141-191	22-26	140
(4x4)	①	12.000	12.060	.030	—	1.122	.001	.005	19	141-191	22-26	140
96-95 F250: (4x2)	①	12.000	12.060	.030	—	1.102	.0005	.003	19	141-191	22-26	140
(4x4)	①	12.000	12.060	.030	—	1.122	.001	.005	19	141-191	22-26	140
97-95 F350:												
(4x2) exc. int. rotor, dual rr. whl.	①	12.125	12.185	.030	—	1.102	.001	.001	19	141-191	22-26	140
(4x2) w/int. rotor, sing. rr whl.	①	12.000	12.060	.030	—	1.102	.0005	.003	19	141-191	22-26	140
(4x4)	①	12.000⑩	12.060⑩	.030	—	1.122	.001	.005	19	141-191	22-26	140
94-86 F250, F350:												
(4X4) w/Dana 44IFS axle	.030	12.000	12.060	.030	—	1.180	.001	.005	19	—	—	140
(4x4) exc. Dana 44IFS axle	.030	12.000	12.060	.030	—	1.180	.001	.005	19	—	—	140
85-83 F250, F350:												
(4X4) exc.Dana 44IFS F.A.	.030	12.000	12.060	.030	—	1.180	.0007	.003	19	74-102	12-20②	100③
85-77 F250: 6,900lbs. GVW std.	.030	12.000	12.060	.030	—	1.120	.0007	.003	1	—	12-20	90
82-81 F250, F350: (4X4)	.030	12.000	12.060	.030	—	1.180	.0007	.003	19	74-102	12-20②	90
(4x4)	.030	12.000	12.060	.030	—	1.180	.0007	.003	19	74-102	12-20②	90③
80-76 F250, F350: (4x4)	.030	12.000	12.060	.030	—	1.180	.0007	.003	19	74-102	12-20②	90③
76-75 F250: 6,900lbs. GVW												
Std. w/12" rear brakes	.030	12.000	12.060	.030	—	1.120	.0007	.003	1	—	12-20	90
w/12 ⅛" rear brakes	.030	12.125	12.185	.030	—	1.120	.0007	.003	1	—	12-20	90
75-72 F250, F350: w/12" rear brakes	.030	12.000	12.060	.030	—	.940	.001	.003	23	55-72	17-23②	90③
w/12 ⅛" rear brakes	.030	12.125	12.185	.030	—	.940	.001	.003	23	55-72	17-23②	90③
75-72 F250: (4x4) Front	.030	12.125	12.185	—	—	—	—	—	—	—	—	90
(4x4) Rear	.030	12.000	12.060	—	—	—	—	—	—	—	—	90
74-73 F250: 6,900lbs. GVW												
Std. w/12" rear brakes	.030	12.000	12.060	.030	—	1.120	.0007	.003	1	—	12-20	90
w/12 ⅛" rear brakes	.030	12.125	12.185	.030	—	1.120	.0007	.003	1	—	12-20	90
72 F250: std. w/12" brakes	.030	12.000	12.060	—	—	—	—	—	—	—	—	90
w/12 ⅛" brakes	.030	12.125	12.185	—	—	—	—	—	—	—	—	90
75-72 F350: (4X4)	.030	12.000	12.060	.030	—	.940	.001	.003	23	55-72	17-23⑤	135③
97-95 Ranger:												
(4x2) w/9" rear brakes	.030①	9.000	9.060	.030①	.993	.964	.002	.003	—	73-97	23-26	85-115
(4x2) w/10" rear brakes	.030①	10.000	10.060	.030①	.993	.964	.002	.003	—	73-97	23-26	85-115
(4x4) w/9" rear brakes	.030①	9.000	9.060	.030①	.993	.964	.002	.003	—	73-97	23-26	85-115
(4x4) w/10" rear brakes	.030①	10.000	10.060	.030①	.993	.964	.002	.003	—	73-97	23-26	85-115
97 Explorer: 4x2 Front	—	—	—	.125	—	.964	.0005	.003	—	125-170	21-26	100
4x2 Rear	—	—	—	.125	—	.409	.0005	.003	—	—	20	100
4x4 Front	—	—	—	.125	—	.810	.0005	.003	—	125-170	21-26	100
4x4 Rear	—	—	—	.125	—	.409	.0005	.003	—	—	20	100
96-95 Explorer: Front	—	—	—	.030①	.993	.964	.002	.003	—	73-97	23-26	85-115
Rear	—	—	—	.125	—	.409	.0005	.003	—	—	20	100
94-91 Ranger, Explorer:												
(4x2) w/9" rear brakes	.030	9.000	9.060	.030	—	.810	.002	.003	59	—	—	100
(4x2) w/10" rear brakes	.030	10.000	10.060	.030	—	.810	.002	.003	59	—	—	100
(4x4) w/9" rear brakes	.030	9.000	9.060	.030	—	.810	.002	.003	59	—	—	100
(4x4) w/10" rear brakes	.030	10.000	10.060	.030	—	.810	.002	.003	59	—	—	100
90-83 Ranger, Bronco II:												
(4x2) w/9" rear brakes	.030	9.000	9.060	.030	—	.810	.001⑪	.003	59	—	32-47⑩	85-115
(4x2) w/10" rear brakes	.030	10.000	10.060	.030	—	.810	.001⑪	.003	59	—	32-47⑩	85-115
(4x4) w/9" rear brakes	.030	9.000	9.060	.030	—	.810	.001⑪	.003	59	—	—	85-115
(4x4) w/10" rear brakes	.030	10.000	10.060	.030	—	.810	.001⑪	.003	59	—	—	85-115

①.030" over rivet head; if bonded lining use .062". ②Caliper bridge bolt 155-185 ft/lbs.
③E350,F350 w/single rear wheels; 1985 140 ft/lbs.; 1984-78 145 ft/lbs.; 1977-72 135 ft/lbs. W/dual rear wheels; 1985-78 220 ft/lbs.; 1977-72 210 ft/lbs. ⑩1983 only. ⑪1987 .0005".
⑤1974 85 ft/lbs. ⑩12" drum shown, w/12.125" drum use 12.185" for machine to figure.

89450C38

LIGHT TRUCKS

Vehicle Year / Make / Model	Brake Shoe O.E. Minimum Lining Thickness	Brake Drum Diameter Standard Size	Brake Drum Machine To	Brake Pad O.E. Minimum Lining Thickness	Brake Rotor Min. Thickness Machine To	Brake Rotor Discard At	Brake Rotor Variation From Parallelism	Brake Rotor Runout TIR	Design	Caliper Mounting Bolts Torque (ft. lbs.)	Caliper Bridge, Pin or Key Bolts Torque (ft. lbs)	Wheel Lugs or Nuts Torque (ft. lbs)
FORD MOTOR CO. TRUCK												
97-95 Windstar:	.059	9.840	9.900	.125	—	.974	.0003	.003	44	84	25	83-113
w/rear disc brakes	—	—	—	.125	—	.409	.0005	.003	—	11-14	—	99
GENERAL MOTORS TRUCK — Chevrolet, GMC												
97-85 Astro, Safari Van:												
w/1.04" rotor	.030	9.500	9.560	.030	.980	.965	.0005	.004	4	—	30-45	90-100
w/1.25" rotor	.030	9.500	9.560	.030	1.230	1.215	.0005	.004	4	—	30-45	90-100
97 Blazer, Jimmy, Pickup, Sonoma, (S/T Series): w/1.03" rotor	.030	9.500	9.560	.030	.980	.965	.0003	.003	4	—	37	95
w/1.14" rotor	—	—	—	.030	1.130	1.080	.0003	.003	4	81	77	95
w/rear disc brakes	—	—	—	.030	.735	.728	.0005	.004	—	52	23	95
96-92 Blazer, Jimmy, Pickup, Sonoma: S/T Series	.030	9.500	9.560	.030	.980	.965	.0005	.003	4	—	37	95
91-88 Blazer, Jimmy, Pickup: (S/T Series)	.062	9.500	9.560	.030	.980	.965	.0005	.004	4	—	37	73⑤
87-83 Blazer, Jimmy, Pickup: (S/T Series)	.062	9.500	9.560	.030	.980	.965	.0005	.004	4	—	21-37	80⑩
97-96 Tahoe, Yukon:	.030	10.000	10.050	.030	1.230	1.215	.0005	.003	4	—	38	140
95-92 Blazer, Tahoe, Yukon: C/K Series	.030	10.000	10.051	.030	1.230	1.215	.0005	.003	62	—	38	120
91-88 Blazer, Jimmy: (Full Size)	.030	11.150	11.210	.030	1.230	1.215	.0005	.004	4	—	35	88⑤
87-83 Blazer, Jimmy: (Full Size)	.062	11.150	11.210	.030	1.230	1.215	.0005	.004	4	—	21-35	70-90⑨
82-76 Blazer, Jimmy: (4x2)	.062	11.150	11.210	.030	1.230	1.215	.0005	.004	4	—	35	75-100
(4x4)	.062	11.150	11.210	.030	1.230	1.215	.0005	.004	4	—	35	70-90
75-74 Blazer, Jimmy: (4x2)	.030	11.000	11.060	.030	1.230	1.215	.0005	.005	4	—	35	75-100
(4x4) w/11" rear brakes	.030	11.000	11.060	.030	1.230	1.215	.0005	.005	4	—	35	70-90
(4x4) w/11 ⅛" rear brakes	.030	11.150	11.210	.030	1.230	1.215	.0005	.005	4	—	35	70-90
73-72 Blazer, Jimmy: (4x2)	.030	11.000	11.060	.030	1.230	1.215	.0005	.005	4	—	35	65-90
(4x4)	.030	11.000	11.060	.030	1.230	1.215	.0005	.005	4	—	35	55-75
91-88 C10, C15, K10, K15:												
w/1.0" rotor	.142	10.000	10.051	.030	.980	.965	.0005	.004	62	—	28	90-105
w/1.25" rotor	.142	10.000	10.051	.030	1.230	1.215	.0005	.004	62	—	28	90-105
87-76 C10, C15, R10, R15, Suburban R10, Suburban R15: w/1.0" rotor												
w/11" rear brakes	.062	11.000	11.060	.030	.980	.965	.0005	.004	4	—	35	75-100
w/11 ⅛" rear brakes	.062	11.150	11.210	.030	.980	.965	.0005	.004	4	—	35	75-100
w/1.25" rotor												
w/11" rear brakes	.062	11.000	11.060	.030	1.230	1.215	.0005	.004	4	—	35	75-100
w/11 ⅛" rear brakes	.062	11.150	11.210	.030	1.230	1.215	.0005	.004	4	—	35	75-100
75-74 C10, C15, Suburban C10, Suburban C15:												
w/11" rear brakes	.030	11.000	11.060	.030	1.230	1.215	.0005	.005	4	—	35	75-100
w/11 ⅛" rear brakes	.030	11.050	11.210	.030	1.230	1.215	.0005	.005	4	—	35	75-100
73-72 C10, C15, Suburban C10, Suburban C15:	.030	11.000	11.060	.030	1.230	1.215	.0005	.005	4	—	35	65-90

⑤Steel wheel shown; Aluminum wheels 90 ft/lbs.   ⑥w/Auto hub shown; w/Manual hub 531 in/lbs.   ⑨Blazer, Jimmy, K,V 10/15 w/Aluminum wheels 100 ft/lbs.; K,V 20/25 90-120 ft/lbs.
⑩1987 90 ft/lbs.; 1986-83 4x2 std. shown; 4x2 & 4x4 w/½" bolt 100 ft/lbs.   ⑪4x2 only; 4x4 non adjustable.

89450C39

LIGHT TRUCKS

Year / Make / Model	Brake Shoe O.E. Minimum Lining Thickness	Brake Drum Diameter Standard Size	Brake Drum Diameter Machine To	Brake Pad O.E. Minimum Lining Thickness	Brake Rotor Min. Thickness Machine To	Brake Rotor Discard At	Brake Rotor Variation From Parallelism	Brake Rotor Runout TIR	Caliper DESIGN	Caliper Mounting Bolts Torque (ft. lbs.)	Caliper Bridge, Pin or Key Bolts Torque (ft. lbs)	Wheel Lugs or Nuts Torque (ft. lbs.)
GENERAL MOTORS TRUCK — Chevrolet, GMC												
97-96 1500 C/K Pickup:	.030	10.000	10.050	.030	1.230	1.215	.0005	.003	4	—	38	140
	.030	11.150	11.210	—	—	—	—	—	—	—	—	—
	.030	13.000	13.060	—	—	—	—	—	—	—	—	—
95-92 1500 C/K Pickup: w/1.0" rotor	.030	10.000	10.051	.030	.980	.965	.0005	.003	62	—	38	120
w/1.25" rotor	.030	10.000	10.051	.030	1.230	1.215	.0005	.003	62	—	38	120
97-96 2500,3500 C/K Pickup: (Exc. C3500 HD)												
w/1.25", 1.26" rotor	.030	11.150	11.210	.030	1.230	1.215	.0005	.003	4	—	38	140
w/1.50" rotor	.030	13.000	13.060	.030	1.480	1.465	.0005	.003	4	—	38	140
97-96 C3500 HD:												
Front	—	—	—	.030	1.382	1.366	.001	.010	—	210	15	177
Rear	—	—	—	.030	1.382	1.366	.001	.010	—	78	15	177
95-92 2500 C/K Pickup:	.030	11.150	11.210	.030	1.230	1.215	.0005	.003	4	—	38	120
95-92 3500 C/K Pickup: w/1.54" rotor	.030	13.000	13.060	.030	1.480	1.465	.0005	.003	4	—	38	120
w/1.26" rotor	.030	13.000	13.060	.030	1.230	1.215	.0005	.003	4	—	38	120
95-92 3500 C/K:												
Chassis Cab Front	—	—	—	.030	1.480	1.465	.0005	.003	20	—	15	140④
Rear	—	—	—	.030	1.480	1.465	.0005	.003	20	—	15	140④
97-96 1500 Suburban:	.030	11.150	11.210	.030	1.230	1.215	.0005	.003	4	—	38	140
2500 Suburban:	.030	13.000	13.060	.030	1.230	1.215	.0005	.003	4	—	38	140
95-92 1500 Suburban, 2500 Suburban:												
w/1.25" rotor	.030	11.150	11.210	.030	1.230	1.215	.0005	.003	62	—	38	120
w/1.26" rotor	.030	13.000	13.060	.030	1.230	1.215	.0005	.003	62	—	38	120
91-88 C20, C25, C30, C35, K20, K25, K30, K35:												
w/11 ⅛" rear brakes	.142	11.150	11.210	.030	1.230	1.215	.0005	.004	62	—	28	90-105
w/13" rear brakes	.142	13.000	13.060	.030	1.230	1.215	.0005	.004	62	—	28	90-105③
87-76 C20, C25, C30, C35, R20, R25, R30, R35, Suburban R20, Suburban R25:												
under 8,600 lbs. GVW w/11 ⅛" rear brakes	.062	11.150	11.210	.030	1.230	1.215	.0005	.004	4	—	35	90-120⑦
under 8,600 lbs. GVW w/13" rear brakes	.062	13.000	13.060	.030	1.230	1.215	.0005	.004	4	—	35	90-120⑦
75-74 C20, C25, C30, C35, Suburban C20, Suburban C25:												
w/11 ⅛" rear brakes	.030	11.150	11.210	.030	1.230	1.215	.0005	.005	4	—	35	90-120⑦
w/13" rear brakes	.030	13.000	13.060	.030	1.230	1.215	.0005	.005	4	—	35	90-120⑦
73-72 C20, C25:												
w/11 ⅛" rear brakes	.030	11.150	11.210	.030	1.230	1.215	.0005	.005	4	—	35	90-120
W/12" rear brakes	.030	12.000	12.060	.030	1.230	1.215	.0005	.005	4	—	35	90-120
w/13" rear brakes	.030	13.000	13.060	.030	1.230	1.215	.0005	.005	4	—	35	90-120
87-76 C30, C35, G30, G35, R30, R35:												
over 8,600lbs. GVW	.062	13.000	13.060	.030	1.480	1.465	.0005	.004	1	—	10-15	90-120⑧
75-74 C30, C35, G30, G35:												
over 8,600lbs. GVW	.030	13.000	13.060	.030	1.480	1.465	.0005	.005	1	—	15	90-120
73-72 C30, C35, G30, G35:												
w/13" rear brakes	.030	13.000	13.060	.030	1.230	1.215	.0005	.005	4	—	35	90-120
w/15" rear brakes	.030	15.000	15.060	.030	1.230	1.215	.0005	.005	4	—	35	90-120

①.030" over rivet head; if bonded lining use .062". ③Single rear wheels shown; Dual rear wheels 125 ft/lbs. ④Single steel rear wheels shown; Aluminum wheels 90ft/lbs.; Dual rear wheels 140 ft/lbs. ⑤w/Auto hub shown; w/Manual hub 531 in/lbs. ⑦G 20/25, K,V 10/15 75-100 ft/lbs. ⑧w/8 bolt whl. 110-140 ft/lbs.; w/10 bolt whl. 130-200 ft/lbs. ⑨Blazer, Jimmy, K,V 10/15 w/Aluminum wheels 100 ft/lbs.; K,V 20/25 90-120 ft/lbs. ⑩4x2 only; 4x4 non adjustable. ⑬Single rear wheels shown; w/dual rear wheels 140 ft/lbs. ⑭w/dual 8 lug wheels shown; w/dual 10 lug wheels 175 ft/lbs.

89450C40

LIGHT TRUCKS

Vehicle Year / Make / Model	Brake Shoe O.E. Minimum Lining Thickness	Brake Drum Diameter Standard Size	Brake Drum Machine To	Brake Pad O.E. Minimum Lining Thickness	Brake Rotor Min. Thickness Machine To	Brake Rotor Min. Thickness Discard At	Brake Rotor Variation From Parallelism	Brake Rotor Runout TIR	Design	Caliper Mounting Bolts Torque (ft. lbs.)	Caliper Bridge, Pin or Key Bolts Torque (ft lbs)	Wheel Lugs or Nuts Torque (ft. lbs.)
GENERAL MOTORS TRUCK — Chevrolet, GMC												
88-82 El Camino:	①	9.500	9.560	.030	.980	.965	.0005	.004	4	—	35	80
81-79 El Camino:	①	9.500	9.560	.030	.980	.965	.0005	.004	4	—	35	80
78 El Camino:	①	11.000	11.060	.030	.980	.965	.0005	.004	4	—	35	80
77 El Camino:	①	11.000	11.060	.030	.980	.965	.0005	.005	4	—	35	80
76-73 El Camino:	①	9.500	9.560	.030①	.980	.965	.0005	.005	4	—	35	70
72 El Camino:	①	9.500	9.560	.030①	.980	.965	.0005	.005	4	—	35	70
97-92 G10, G15, G20, G25:	.030	11.150	11.210	.030	1.230	1.215	.0005	.004	4	—	38	100
97-92 G30, G35: exc. Chassis Cab	.030	13.000	13.060	.030	1.230	1.215	.0005	.004	4	—	38	120③
Chassis Cab	.030	13.000	13.060	.030	1.480	1.465	.0005	.004	1	—	15	120③
91-88 G10, G15: w/11" rear brakes	.030	11.000	11.060	.030	1.230	1.215	.0005	.004	4	—	35	100
w/11 1/8" rear brakes	.030	11.150	11.210	.030	1.230	1.215	.0005	.004	4	—	35	100
87-76 G10, G15: w/1.0" rotor												
w/11" rear brakes	.062	11.000	11.060	.030	.980	.965	.0005	.004	4	—	35	75-100
w/11 1/8" rear brakes	.062	11.150	11.210	.030	.980	.965	.0005	.004	4	—	35	75-100
w/1.25" rotor												
w/11" rear brakes	.062	11.000	11.060	.030	1.230	1.215	.0005	.004	4	—	35	75-100
w/11 1/8" rear brakes	.062	11.150	11.210	.030	1.230	1.215	.0005	.004	4	—	35	75-100
75-74 G10, G15: w/11" rear brakes	.030	11.000	11.060	.030	1.230	1.215	.0005	.005	4	—	35	75-100
w/11 1/8" rear brakes	.030	11.050	11.210	.030	1.230	1.215	.0005	.005	4	—	35	75-100
73-72 G10, G15:	.030	11.000	11.060	.030	1.230	1.215	.0005	.005	4	—	35	65-90
91-88 G20, G25:	.030	11.150	11.210	.030	1.230	1.215	.0005	.004	4	—	35	100
87-76 G20, G25, G30, G35:												
under 8,600 lbs. GVW w/11 1/8" rear brakes	.062	11.150	11.210	.030	1.230	1.215	.0005	.004	4	—	35	90-120⑦
under 8,600 lbs. GVW w/13" rear brakes	.062	13.000	13.060	.030	1.230	1.215	.0005	.004	4	—	35	90-120⑦
75-74 G20, G25, G30, G35:												
w/11 1/8" rear brakes	.030	11.150	11.210	.030	1.230	1.215	.0005	.005	4	—	35	90-120⑦
w/13" rear brakes	.030	13.000	13.060	.030	1.230	1.215	.0005	.005	4	—	35	90-120⑦
73-72 G20, G25:	.030	11.000	11.060	.030	1.230	1.215	.0005	.005	4	—	35	75-100
91-88 G30, G35: w/1.28" rotor	.030	13.000	13.060	.030	1.230	1.215	.0005	.004	4	—	35	120④
w/1.54" rotor	.030	13.000	13.060	.030	1.480	1.465	.0005	.004	4	—	35	120④
87-76 K10, K15, K20, K25, V10, V15, V20, V25, Suburban:												
w/11 1/8" rear brakes	.062	11.150	11.210	.030	1.230	1.215	.0005	.004	4	—	35	70-90⑨
w/13" rear brakes	.062	13.000	13.060	.030	1.230	1.215	.0005	.004	4	—	35	70-90⑨
75-74 K10, K15, K25:												
w/11" rear brakes	.030	11.000	11.060	.030	1.230	1.215	.0005	.005	4	—	35	90-120⑦
w/11 1/8" rear brakes	.030	11.150	11.210	.030	1.230	1.215	.0005	.005	4	—	35	90-120⑦
W/13" rear brakes	.030	13.000	13.060	.030	1.230	1.215	.0005	.005	4	—	35	90-120⑦
73-72 K10, K15, K20, K25:												
w/11" rear brakes	.030	11.000	11.060	.030	1.230	1.215	.0005	.005	4	—	35	55-75
w/11 1/8" rear brakes	.030	11.150	11.210	.030	1.230	1.215	.0005	.005	4	—	35	55-75
w/13" rear brakes	.030	13.000	13.060	.030	1.230	1.215	.0005	.005	4	—	35	55-75
87-77 K30, K35, V30, V35:	.062	13.000	13.060	.030	1.480	1.465	.0005	.004	4	—	35	90-120⑧
96-93 Lumina APV, Lumina Minivan:	.030	8.863	8.877	.030	1.224	1.209	.0005	.002	62	—	38	100
92-90 Lumina APV:	①	8.863	8.877	.030	.972	.957	.0005	.004	62	—	38	100

①.030" over rivet head; if bonded lining use .062".   ③Single rear wheels shown; Dual rear wheels 125 ft/lbs.   ④Single steel rear wheels shown: Aluminum wheels 90ft/lbs.; Dual rear wheels 140 ft/lbs.   ⑤w/Auto hub shown; w/Manual hub 531 in/lbs.   ⑦G 20/25, K,V 10/15 75-100 ft/lbs.   ⑧w/8 bolt whl. 110-140 ft/lbs.; w/10 bolt whl. 130-200 ft/lbs.   ⑨Blazer, Jimmy, K,V 10/15 w/Aluminum wheels 100 ft/lbs.; K,V 20/25 90-120 ft/lbs.   ⑩4x2 only; 4x4 non adjustable.   ⑬Single rear wheels shown; w/dual rear wheels 140 ft/lbs.   ⑭w/dual 8 lug wheels shown; w/dual 10 lug wheels 175 ft/lbs.

89450C41

LIGHT TRUCKS

Vehicle	Brake Shoe	Brake Drum		Brake Pad	Brake Rotor				Design	Caliper		Wheel
	O.E. Minimum Lining Thickness	Diameter		O.E. Minimum Lining Thickness	Min. Thickness		Variation From Parallelism	Runout TIR		Mounting Bolts Torque (ft. lbs.)	Bridge, Pin or Key Bolts Torque (ft. lbs)	Lugs or Nuts Torque (ft. lbs.)
Year / Make / Model		Standard Size	Machine To		Machine To	Discard At						
GENERAL MOTORS TRUCK — Chevrolet, GMC												
82-81 LUV Pickup	.059	10.000	10.059	.236	.668	.653	.003	.005	47	64	15	65
80-76 LUV Pickup	.059	10.000	10.059	.236	.668	.653	.003	.005	22	64	—	65
75-72 LUV Pickup	.059	10.000	10.059	—	—	—	—	—	—	—	—	65
91-88 R10, R15, Suburban R10, Suburban R15	.030	11.150	11.210	.030	1.230	1.215	.0005	.004	4	—	35	100
91-88 R20, R25, R30, R35, Suburban R20, Suburban R25:												
w/1.28" rotor	.030	13.000	13.060	.030	1.230	1.215	.0005	.004	4	—	35	120④
w/1.54" rotor	.030	13.000	13.060	.030	1.480	1.465	.0005	.004	4	—	35	120④
91-88 V10, V15, Suburban V10, Suburban V15	.030	11.150	11.210	.030	1.230	1.215	.0005	.004	4	—	35	88②
91-88 V20, V25, V30, V35, Suburban V20, Suburban V25:												
w/1.28" rotor	.030	13.000	13.060	.030	1.230	1.215	.0005	.004	4	—	35	120④
w/1.54" rotor	.030	13.000	13.060	.030	1.480	1.465	.0005	.004	4	—	35	120④
97 Venture	—	8.863	8.880	.030	1.250	1.210	.0005	.003	—	137	63	100

①.030" over rivet head; if bonded lining use .062". ②Steel wheel shown; Aluminum wheel 100 ft/lbs. ③Single steel rear wheels shown; Aluminum wheels 90ft/lbs.;Dual rear wheels 140 ft/lbs.
④w/Auto hub shown; w/Manual hub 531 in/lbs. ⑤w/8 bolt whl. 110-140 ft/lbs.; w/10 bolt whl. 130-200 ft/lbs. ⑥4x2 only; 4x4 non adjustable.

Vehicle	Brake Shoe	Brake Drum		Brake Pad	Brake Rotor				Design	Caliper		Wheel
GEO TRUCK												
97-96 Tracker:												
Two Door	.120	8.660	8.740	.100	—	.315	.0005	.006	30	65	20	70
Four Door	.120	10.000	10.078	.100	—	.590	.0005	.006	30	65	20	70
95-91 Tracker	.039	8.660	8.740	.030	.345	.315	.0005	.006	30	65	—	70
90-89 Tracker	.039	8.660	8.740	.030	.345	.315	.0005	.006	30	51-72	16-23	48
HONDA TRUCK												
97-95 Odyssey: Front	—	—	—	.063	—	.830	.0006	.004	89	80	36	80
Rear	—	—	—	.063	—	.300	.0006	.004	89	28	17	80
97-96 Passport	.039	10.000	10.059	.039	.983	.969	.0004	.005	73	115	54	66①
w/rear disc brakes	—	—	—	.039	.668	.654	.0004	.005	73	76	32	66①
95-94 Passport: w/2.6L eng. Front	—	—	—	.039	.826	.811	.0006	.005	73	115	24	66①
w/3.2L eng. Front	—	—	—	.039	.983	.969	.0004	.005	73	115	54	66①
Rear	—	—	—	.039	.668	.654	.0004	.005	73	77	32	66①

①Steel wheels shown, w/aluminium wheels use 87 ft/lbs. ②Radial pull in pounds at lug nut.

Vehicle	Brake Shoe	Brake Drum		Brake Pad	Brake Rotor				Design	Caliper		Wheel
HYUNDAI TRUCK												
87-86 Pony Pickup	.039	7.992	①	.060	—	.449	—	.006	17	58	63	51-58
85-83 Pony Pickup	.098	7.992	①	.060	—	.314	—	.004	17	58-73	58-69	50-58

①Machining specification is not available; discard at 8.071".

Vehicle	Brake Shoe	Brake Drum		Brake Pad	Brake Rotor				Design	Caliper		Wheel
INFINITI TRUCK												
97 Qx4	.059	11.610	11.670	.079	—	1.024	.0006	.004	76	53-72	24-31	87-108

Vehicle	Brake Shoe	Brake Drum		Brake Pad	Brake Rotor				Design	Caliper		Wheel
ISUZU TRUCK												
95-94 Amigo: w/rear drum brakes	.039	10.000	10.059	.039	.985	.970	.0004	.005	73	103-126	54	65②
w/rear disc brakes	—	—	—	.039	.669	.654	.0004	.005	56	77	32	65②
93-90 Amigo: w/rear drum brakes	.039	10.000	10.059	.039	.826	.811	.0006	.005	73	103-126	20-27	65②
w/rear disc brakes	—	—	—	.039	.432	.417	.0006	.005	56	69-84	12-17	65②
97-96 Hombre	.030	9.500	9.560	.030	.980	.965	.0005	.003	4	—	37	95
97-96 Oasis: Front	—	—	—	.063	—	.830	.0006	.004	89	80	36	80
Rear	—	—	—	.063	—	.300	.0006	.004	89	28	17	80

①4x2 shown; 4x4 4.5 lbs. ②w/Aluminum wheels 86 ft/lbs. ③w/Aluminum wheels 90 ft/lbs. ④Radial pull in pounds at lug nut. ⑤4x2 shown; 4x4 3.3 lbs.
⑥w/Aluminum wheels 80-94 ft/lbs.

89450C42

LIGHT TRUCKS

Vehicle Year / Make / Model	Brake Shoe O.E. Minimum Lining Thickness	Brake Drum Diameter Standard Size	Machine To	Brake Pad O.E. Minimum Lining Thickness	Brake Rotor Min. Thickness Machine To	Discard At	Variation From Parallelism	Runout TIR	DESIGN	Caliper Mounting Bolts Torque (ft. lbs.)	Bridge, Pin or Key Bolts Torque (ft. lbs)	Wheel Lugs or Nuts Torque (ft. lbs)
ISUZU TRUCK												
95-88 Pickup: w/rear drum brakes	.039	10.000	10.059	.039	.826	.811	.0006	.005	73	103-126	20-27	65②
w/rear disc brakes	—	—	—	.039	.432	.417	.0006	.005	56	69-84	12-17	65②
87-84 Pickup:	.039	10.000	10.039	.039	.658	.654	.0012	.005	47	62-65	22-25	58-80③
83-81 Pickup:	.039	10.000	10.039	.039	.453	.437	.003	.005	47	64	15	65
97-96 Rodeo:	.039	10.000	10.059	.039	.983	.969	.0004	.005	73	115	54	66②
w/rear disc brakes	—	—	—	.039	.668	.654	.0004	.005	73	76	32	66②
95-93 Rodeo: w/2.6L eng.	.039	10.000	10.059	.039	.826	.811	.0006	.005	73	115	24	66②
w/3.2L eng. Front	—	—	—	.039	.983	.969	.0004	.005	73	115	54	66②
Rear	—	—	—	.039	.668	.654	.0004	.005	73	77	32	66②
92-91 Rodeo:	.039	10.000	10.059	.039	.826	.811	.0006	.005	73	115	24	66②
97-92 Trooper: Front	—	—	—	.039	.983	.969	.0004	.005	73	115	54	87
Rear	—	—	—	.039	.668	.654	.0004	.005	57	77	32	87
91-88 Trooper II: Front	—	—	—	.039	.826	.811	.0006	.005	73	103-126	20-27	58-87⑥
Rear	—	—	—	.039	.432	.417	.0006	.005	56	69-84	12-17	58-87⑥
87 Trooper II:	.039	10.000	10.039	.039	.826	.811	.0006	.005	58	103-126	20-27	58-87⑥
86-84 Trooper II:	.039	10.000	10.039	.039	.668	.654	.0012	.005	47	62-65	22-25	58-80③

①4x2 shown; 4x4 4.5 lbs.   ②w/Aluminum wheels 86 ft/lbs.   ③w/Aluminum wheels 90 ft/lbs.   ④Radial pull in pounds at lug nut.   ⑤4x2 shown; 4x4 3.3 lbs.
⑥w/Aluminum wheels 80-94 ft/lbs.

Vehicle Year / Make / Model	Brake Shoe O.E. Min Lining	Drum Std Size	Machine To	Brake Pad O.E. Min Lining	Rotor Machine To	Discard At	Variation From Parallelism	Runout TIR	DESIGN	Mounting Bolts Torque	Bridge, Pin or Key Bolts Torque	Lugs or Nuts Torque
JEEP TRUCK												
97-94 Cherokee: Front	—	—	—	.030	—	.890	.0005	.005	51	—	7-15	95
Rear w/9" drum	.030	9.000	9.060									
Rear w/10" drum	.030	10.000	10.060									
93-91 Cherokee: (4x2)	①	9.000	9.050	.030	—	.866	.0005	.005	8	77	25-35	88
(4X4)	①	9.000	9.050	.030	—	.890	.0005	.005	51	—	7-15	88
90 Cherokee: (4x2)	①	9.000	9.050	.030	—	.860	.0005	.005	8	77	25-35	75
(4x4)	①	9.000	9.050	.030	—	.890	.0005	.005	51	—	7-15	75
89-84 Cherokee, Wagoneer: (Sportwagons)	.030	10.000	10.060	.030	—	.815	—	.004	1	77	25-35	75
89-82 Cherokee, Wagoneer: (Full Size)	①	11.000	11.060	.062	—	1.215	.001	.005	4	35	30	75
81-78 Cherokee, Wagoneer:	①	11.000	11.060	.062	—	1.215	.001	.005	4	35	—	75
77-76 Cherokee, Wagoneer:	①	11.000	11.060	.062	—	1.215	.0005	.005	4	—	15	75
75-74 Cherokee, Wagoneer:	.030	11.000	11.060	.062	1.230	1.215	.003	.005	4	—	15	75
86-82 CJ, Scrambler:	①	10.000	10.060	.062	—	.815	.001	.005	1	—	30	75
81-79 CJ:	①	10.000	10.060	.062	—	.815	.001	.005	1	—	15	75
78-77 CJ:	①	11.000	11.060	.062	—	1.120	.001②	.005	1	—	15	75
76-72 CJ:	.030	11.000	11.060	—								75
92-90 Comanche: (4x2) w/9" rear brakes	①	9.000	9.050	.030	—	.860	.0005	.005	8	77	25-35	75
(4x2) w/10" rear brakes	①	10.000	10.060	.030	—	.860	.0005	.005	8	77	25-35	75
92-91 Comanche: (4x4) w/9" rear brakes	①	9.000	9.050	.030	—	.890	.0005	.005	51	—	7-15	75
(4x4) w/10" rear brakes	①	10.000	10.060	.030	—	.890	.0005	.005	51	—	7-15	75
90 Comanche: (4x4) w/9" rear brakes	①	9.000	9.050	.030	—	.890	.0005	.005	51	—	7-15	75
(4x4) w/10" rear brakes	①	10.000	10.060	.030	—	.890	.0005	.005	51	—	7-15	75
89-84 Comanche:	.030	10.000	10.060	.030	—	.815	—	.004	1	77	25-35	75
97-94 Grand Cherokee:	.030	10.000	10.060	.030	—	.890	.0005	.005	51	—	7-15	95
w/rear disc brakes	—	—	—	.030	—	.374	.001	.005	51	—	7-15	95
93 Grand Cherokee, Grand Wagoneer:	.030	10.000	10.060	.030	—	.890	.0005	.005	51	—	7-15	88
91-90 Grand Wagoneer:	①	11.000	11.060	.030	—	1.215	.0005	.005	4	77	35	75
89-82 J10 Pickup:	①	11.000	11.060	.062	—	1.215	.001	.005	4	35	30	75
81-78 J10 Pickup:	①	11.000	11.060	.062	—	1.215	.001	.005	4	35	—	75

①.030" over rivet head; if bonded lining use .062".   ②1977 .0005".   ③While rotating wheel, tighten nut until wheel binds.   ④J20 (8400 GVW) 130 ft/lbs.
⑤Torque hub bolts to 75 ft/lbs.; torque hub nut to 175 ft/lbs.

89450C43

LIGHT TRUCKS

Year / Make / Model	Brake Shoe O.E. Minimum Lining Thickness	Brake Drum Diameter Standard Size	Brake Drum Machine To	Brake Pad O.E. Minimum Lining Thickness	Brake Rotor Min. Thickness Machine To	Brake Rotor Discard At	Brake Rotor Variation From Parallelism	Brake Rotor Runout TIR	DESIGN	Caliper Mounting Bolts Torque (ft. lbs.)	Caliper Bridge, Pin or Key Bolts Torque (ft. lbs)	Wheel Lugs or Nuts Torque (ft. lbs.)
JEEP TRUCK												
77-76 J10 Pickup:	①	11.000	11.060	.062	—	1.215	.0005	.005	4	—	15	75
75-74 J10 Pickup:	.030	11.000	11.060	.062	1.230	1.215	.003	.005	4	—	15	75
87-82 J20 Pickup:	①	12.000	12.060	.062	—	1.215	.001	.005	4	35	30	75④
81-78 J20 Pickup:	①	12.000	12.060	.062	—	1.215	.001	.005	4	35	—	75④
77-76 J20 Pickup:	①	12.000	12.060	.062	—	1.215	.0005	.005	4	—	15	75④
75-74 J20 Pickup:	.030	12.000	12.060	.062	1.230	1.215	.003	.005	4	—	15	75④
97 Wrangler:	①	9.000	9.060	①	—	—	.0005	.004	51	—	11	95
96-92 Wrangler:	.030	9.000	9.060	.030	—	.890	.0005	.005	51	—	7-15	95
91 Wrangler:	①	9.000	9.050	.030	—	.890	.0005	.005	51	—	7-15	75
90 Wrangler:	①	9.000	9.050	.030	—	.890	.0005	.005	51	—	7-15	75
89-87 Wrangler:	.030	10.000	10.060	.030	—	.815	—	.004	1	77	25-35	75
73-72 Wagoneer, Pickup: w/11" brakes	.030	11.000	11.060	—	—	—	—	—	—	—	—	75
w/12" brakes	.030	12.000	12.060	—	—	—	—	—	—	—	—	75
73-72 Camper: 8,000lbs. GVW	.030	12.125	12.185	—	—	—	—	—	—	—	—	75

①.030" over rivet head; if bonded lining use .062". ②1977 .0005". ③While rotating wheel, tighten nut until wheel binds. ④J20 (8400 GVW) 130 ft/lbs.
⑤Torque hub bolts to 75 ft/lbs.; torque hub nut to 175 ft/lbs.

Year / Make / Model	Brake Shoe O.E. Minimum Lining Thickness	Brake Drum Diameter Standard Size	Brake Drum Machine To	Brake Pad O.E. Minimum Lining Thickness	Brake Rotor Min. Thickness Machine To	Brake Rotor Discard At	Brake Rotor Variation From Parallelism	Brake Rotor Runout TIR	DESIGN	Caliper Mounting Bolts Torque (ft. lbs.)	Caliper Bridge, Pin or Key Bolts Torque (ft. lbs)	Wheel Lugs or Nuts Torque (ft. lbs.)
KIA TRUCK												
97-95 Sportage:	.060	—	9.890	.080	—	.880	—	.004	—	72	17	73

①Adjust bearing preload until radial pull at lugnut is 10 in/lbs.

Year / Make / Model	Brake Shoe O.E. Minimum Lining Thickness	Brake Drum Diameter Standard Size	Brake Drum Machine To	Brake Pad O.E. Minimum Lining Thickness	Brake Rotor Min. Thickness Machine To	Brake Rotor Discard At	Brake Rotor Variation From Parallelism	Brake Rotor Runout TIR	DESIGN	Caliper Mounting Bolts Torque (ft. lbs.)	Caliper Bridge, Pin or Key Bolts Torque (ft. lbs)	Wheel Lugs or Nuts Torque (ft. lbs.)
LEXUS TRUCK												
97-96 LX450: Front	—	—	—	.039	—	1.181	—	.0059	16	90	—	76
Rear	—	—	—	.039	—	.630	—	.0059	65	76	65	76

①See O.E. Manual.

Year / Make / Model	Brake Shoe O.E. Minimum Lining Thickness	Brake Drum Diameter Standard Size	Brake Drum Machine To	Brake Pad O.E. Minimum Lining Thickness	Brake Rotor Min. Thickness Machine To	Brake Rotor Discard At	Brake Rotor Variation From Parallelism	Brake Rotor Runout TIR	DESIGN	Caliper Mounting Bolts Torque (ft. lbs.)	Caliper Bridge, Pin or Key Bolts Torque (ft. lbs)	Wheel Lugs or Nuts Torque (ft. lbs.)
MAZDA TRUCK												
97-95 B2300, B3000, B4000:												
(4x2) w/9" rear brakes	.030④	9.000	9.030	.120	—	.810	—	.003	—	73-97	23-26	85-115
(4x2) w/10" rear brakes	.030④	10.000	10.030	.120	—	.810	—	.003	—	73-97	23-26	85-115
(4x4) w/9" rear brakes	.030④	9.000	9.030	.120	—	.810	—	.003	—	73-97	23-26	85-115
(4x4) w/10" rear brakes	.030④	10.000	10.030	.120	—	.810	—	.003	—	73-97	23-26	85-115
94 B2300 Pickup, B3000 Pickup, B4000 Pickup: (4x2)	.030	9.000	9.030	.120	—	.810	—	.003	59	—	—	85-114
(4x4)	.030	10.000	10.030	.120	—	.810	—	.003	59	—	—	85-114
93-87 B2200 Pickup, B2600 Pickup: (4x2)	.040	10.240	10.300	.118	—	.710	—	.006	73	65-80	23-30	65-87③
(4x4)	.040	10.240	10.300	.118	—	.790	—	.006	73	65-80	23-30	65-87③
87-86 B2000 Pickup:	.040	10.240	10.310	.118	—	.710	—	.002	37	65-80	23-30	87-108
84 B2200 Pickup:	.040	10.236	10.275	.040	—	.748	—	.004	35	40-47	—	58-65
84 B2200 Pickup:	.040	10.236	10.275	.040	—	.433	—	.004	35	40-47	—	58-65
83-82 B2200 Pickup:	.040	10.236	10.275	.276①	—	.748	—	.004	35	40-47	—	58-65
83-77 B1800 Pickup, B2000 Pickup:	.040	10.236	10.275	.276①	—	.433	—	.004	35	40-47	—	58-65
76-72 B1600 Pickup:	.040	10.236	10.275	—	—	—	—	—	—	—	—	58-65
77-74 Pickup: Rotary eng.	.040	10.236	10.275	.276①	—	.433	—	.004	35	—	—	58-65
97-96 MPV: Front	—	—	—	.080	1.060	1.024	—	.002	100	66-79	62-68	65-87
Rear	—	—	—	.040	.660	.630	—	.002	101	37-50	28-36	65-87
95-94 MPV: 2WD Front	—	—	—	.080	—	1.100	—	.004	100	65-80	61-69	65-87
4WD Front	—	—	—	.080	—	1.020	—	.004	100	65-80	61-69	65-87
w/rear disc brakes	—	—	—	.080	—	.630	—	.004	101	37-50	28-36	65-87
93-92 MPV: 2WD	.040	10.240	10.300	.080	—	1.100	—	.004	100	65-80	61-69	65-87
4WD	.040	10.240	10.300	.080	—	1.020	—	.004	100	65-80	61-69	65-87
91-89 MPV:	.040	10.240	10.300	.080	—	.870	—	.004	54	65-80	61-69	65-87
94-91 Navajo: w/9" rear brakes	.030	9.000	9.060	.062	—	.810	.002	.003	59	—	—	100
w/10" rear brakes	.030	10.000	10.060	.062	—	.810	.002	.003	59	—	—	100

①Measurement of lining & metal. ②Radial pull in pounds at lug nut. ③Styled wheel 87-108 ft/lbs. ④.030" over rivet head; if bonded lining use .062".

89450C44

LIGHT TRUCKS

Vehicle	Brake Shoe	Brake Drum		Brake Pad	Brake Rotor				Caliper			Wheel
	O.E. Minimum Lining Thickness	Diameter		O.E. Minimum Lining Thickness	Min. Thickness		Variation From Paral- lelism	Runout TIR	D E S I G N	Mounting Bolts Torque (ft. lbs.)	Bridge, Pin or Key Bolts Torque (ft. lbs)	Lugs or Nuts Torque (ft. lbs.)
Year / Make / Model		Standard Size	Machine To		Machine To	Discard At						
MERCURY TRUCK												
97	Mountaineer: 4x2 Front	—	—	—	.125	—	.964	.0005	.003	—	125-170	21-26	100
	4x2 Rear	—	—	—	.125	—	.409	.0005	.003	—	—	20	100
	4x4 Front	—	—	—	.125	—	.810	.0005	.003	—	125-170	21-26	100
	4x4 Rear	—	—	—	.125	—	.409	.0005	.003	—	—	20	100
97-93	Villager:	.059	9.840	9.900	.080	.974	.945	.0004	.0028	30	—	18-25	72-87
MITSUBISHI TRUCK												
96-92	Expo, Expo LRV:												
	w/8" drum brakes	.040	8.071	8.100	.080		.880	.0006	.0031	73	65	54	65-80
	w/9" drum brakes	.040	9.079	9.100	.080		.880	.0006	.0031	73	65	54	65-80
	w/rear disc brakes	—	—	—	.080		.330	—	.0031	73	36-43	32	65-80
97-92	Montero: Front	—	—	—	.079		.882⑤	.0006	.004	100	65	54	72-87⑥
	Rear	—	—	—	.079		.646		.003	101	65	32	72-87⑥
91-88	Montero:	.040	10.000	10.079	.079		.803	—	.006	73	58-72	U33-L27	72-87
87	Montero:	.040	10.000	10.040	.040		.724	—	.006	34	58-72	—	72-87
86-83	Montero:	.040	10.000	10.040	.040		.720	—	.006	34	51-65④	—	72-87③
97	Montero Sport:	.040	10.630	10.710	.080		.881	—	.002	100	65	55	⑦
	w/rear disc brakes	—	—	—	.080		.646		.003	—	94	32	⑦
96-87	Pickup: (4x2)	.040	10.000	10.079	.080		.803	—	.006	34	58-72	U33-L27	87-101
94-87	Pickup: (4x4)	.040	10.000	10.079	.080		.803	—	.006	34	58-72	U33-L27	87-101
86-83	Pickup: w/9 ½" rear brakes	.040	9.500	9.550	.040		.720	—	.006	34	51-65	—	51-57
	w/10" rear brakes	.040	10.000	10.070	.040		.720	—	.006	34	51-65④	—	51-57
90-87	Van:	.040	10.000	10.080	.079		.803	—	.006	73	59-74	U28-L34	87-101

①2 WD ③1983 50-57 ft/lbs. ④1986-85 58-72 ft/lbs. ⑤3.0L engine figure shown; w/3.5L use 1.00". ⑥1992 shown; 1997-93 use 87-101 ft/lbs.
⑦Steel wheels: 87-101 ft/lbs., Aluminum wheels: 73-86 ft/lbs.

NAVISTAR — INTERNATIONAL TRUCK

80-72	Scout II:	.030	11.000	11.060	.125	—	1.120	.0005	.005	1	—	12-18	70-90
75-74	Travel All 100/150: (½ Ton)	.030	11.000	11.060	.125	—	1.120	.0005	.005	1	—	12-18	70-90
75-74	Travel All 200: (¾ Ton)	.030	12.000	12.060	.125	—	1.120	.0005	.005	1	—	12-18	70-90

NISSAN (DATSUN) TRUCK

79-78	620 Pickup:	.059	10.000	10.055	.080	—	.413	.0015	.006	36	53-72	12-15	58-72
77-72	620 Pickup:	.059	10.000	10.055	—	—	—	—	—	—	—	—	58-65
86-84	720 Pickup: w/single wheel	.059	10.000	10.060	.080	—	.787	.0012②	.0028	37	53-72	16-23	87-108
	w/dual wheels	.059	8.660	8.720	.080	—	.787	.0012②	.0028	37	53-72	16-23	87-108④
83-82	720 Pickup:	.059	10.000	10.055	.080	—	.413	.0012	.006	36	53-72	12-15	87-108
81	720 Pickup:	.059	10.000	10.055	.080	—	.413	.0028	.006	36	53-72	12-15	87-108
80	720 Pickup:	.059	10.000	10.055	.080	—	.413	.0028	.006	36	53-72	12-15	58-72
90	Axxess: w/9" rear brakes	.059	9.000	9.060	.079	—	.787	—	.0028	37	53-72	16-23	72-87
	w/10" rear brakes	.059	10.240	10.300	.079	—	.787	—	.0028	37	53-72	16-23	72-87
97	D21 Pickup: 4x2	.059	10.240	10.300	.079	—	.787	.0008	.0028	37	53-72	24-31	87-108
	(4x4)	.059	11.610	11.670	.079	—	.945	.0008	.0028	76	53-72	16-23	87-108
96-86	D21 Pickup:												
	(4x2) w/4 cyl. gas eng.	.059	10.240	10.300	.079	—	.787	—	.0028	37	53-72	16-23	87-108
	(4x2) exc. 4 cyl. gas eng.												
	w/8.66" rear brakes	.059	8.660	8.720	.079	—	.945	—	.0028	76	53-72	16-23	87-108
	w/10" rear brakes	.059	10.000	10.060	.079	—	.945	—	.0028	76	53-72	16-23	87-108
	w/10.24" rear brakes	.059	10.240	10.300	.079	—	.945	—	.0028	76	53-72	16-23	87-108
	(4x4) w/10.24" rear brakes	.059	10.240	10.300	.079	—	.945	—	.0028	76	53-72	16-23	87-108
	(4x4) w/11.61" rear brakes	.059	11.610	11.670	.079	—	.945	—	.0028	76	53-72	16-23	87-108
97-96	Pathfinder:	.059	11.610	11.670	.079	—	1.024	.0006	.004	76	53-72	24-31	87-100

①4x2 shown; 4x4 58-72 ft/lbs., 5-10 in/lbs., 15-30 . ②1986-85 .0008". ③2 WD only; 4 WD 58-72 ft/lbs.—loosen— 15-30 .
④Front shown; rear 1984 159-188 ft/lbs.; 1985 exc. Aluminum wheels 166-203 ft/lbs., Aluminum wheels 58-72 ft/lbs. ⑤4x2 shown; 4x4 Not Adjustable. ⑥1994-90 shown; 1995 use 40-47 ft/lbs.

89450C45

LIGHT TRUCKS

Year / Make / Model	Brake Shoe O.E. Minimum Lining Thickness	Brake Drum Diameter Standard Size	Brake Drum Diameter Machine To	Brake Pad O.E. Minimum Lining Thickness	Brake Rotor Min. Thickness Machine To	Brake Rotor Min. Thickness Discard At	Brake Rotor Variation From Parallelism	Brake Rotor Runout TIR	DESIGN	Caliper Mounting Bolts Torque (ft. lbs.)	Caliper Bridge, Pin or Key Bolts Torque (ft. lbs)	Wheel Lugs or Nuts Torque (ft. lbs.)
NISSAN (DATSUN) TRUCK												
95-90 Pathfinder: Front	—	—	—	.079	—	.945	—	.0028	76	53-72	16-23	87-108
Rear w/10.24" rear brakes	.059	10.240	10.300	—	—	—	—	—	—	—	—	87-108
Rear w/11.61" rear brakes	.059	11.610	11.670	—	—	—	—	—	—	—	—	87-108
Rear w/rear disc brakes	—	—	—	.079	—	.630	—	.0028	30	28-38⑥	16-23	87-108
89-87 Pathfinder: w/rear drum brakes	.059	10.000	10.060	.079	—	.945	—	.0028	76	53-72	16-23	87-108
w/rear disc brakes	—	—	—	.079	—	.630	—	.0028	30	28-38	23-30	87-108
97-93 Quest:	.079	9.840	9.900	.079	—	.945	.0004	.0028	30	—	18-25	72-87
88-87 Vanette:	.059	10.240	10.300	.079	—	.945	—	.0028	76	80-108	16-23	72-87

①4x2 shown; 4x4 58-72 ft/lbs., 5-10 in/lbs., 15-30 . ②1986-85 .0008". ②2 WD only; 4 WD 58-72 ft/lbs.—loosen— 15-30 .
④Front shown; rear 1984 159-188 ft/lbs.; 1985 exc. Aluminum wheels 166-203 ft/lbs., Aluminum wheels 58-72 ft/lbs. ⑤4x2 shown; 4x4 Not Adjustable.
⑥1994-90 shown; 1995 use 40-47 ft/lbs.

Year / Make / Model	Brake Shoe O.E. Minimum Lining Thickness	Brake Drum Diameter Standard Size	Brake Drum Diameter Machine To	Brake Pad O.E. Minimum Lining Thickness	Brake Rotor Min. Thickness Machine To	Brake Rotor Min. Thickness Discard At	Brake Rotor Variation From Parallelism	Brake Rotor Runout TIR	DESIGN	Caliper Mounting Bolts Torque (ft. lbs.)	Caliper Bridge, Pin or Key Bolts Torque (ft. lbs)	Wheel Lugs or Nuts Torque (ft. lbs.)
OLDSMOBILE TRUCK												
97 Bravada: Front	—	—	—	.030	1.130	1.080	.0003	.003	4	81	77	95
Rear	—	—	—	.030	.735	.728	.0005	.004	—	52	23	95
96 Bravada:	.030	9.500	9.560	.030	.980	.965	.0005	.004	62	-	37	95
94-91 Bravada:	①	9.500	9.560	.030	.980	.965	.0005	.004	62	—	37	90②
97 Silhouette:	—	8.863	8.880	.030	1.250	1.210	.0005	.003	—	137	63	100
96-93 Silhouette APV:	.030	8.863	8.877	.030	1.224	1.209	.0005	.002	62	—	38	100
92-90 Silhouette APV:	①	8.863	8.877	.030	.972	.957	.0005	.004	62	—	38	100

①.030" over rivet head; if bonded lining use .062". ②1992-91 shown; 1994-93 use 95 ft/lbs.

Year / Make / Model	Brake Shoe O.E. Minimum Lining Thickness	Brake Drum Diameter Standard Size	Brake Drum Diameter Machine To	Brake Pad O.E. Minimum Lining Thickness	Brake Rotor Min. Thickness Machine To	Brake Rotor Min. Thickness Discard At	Brake Rotor Variation From Parallelism	Brake Rotor Runout TIR	DESIGN	Caliper Mounting Bolts Torque (ft. lbs.)	Caliper Bridge, Pin or Key Bolts Torque (ft. lbs)	Wheel Lugs or Nuts Torque (ft. lbs.)
PONTIAC TRUCK												
97 Trans Sport:	—	8.863	8.880	.030	1.250	1.210	.0005	.003	—	137	63	100
96-93 Trans Sport APV:	.030	8.863	8.877	.030	1.224	1.209	.0005	.002	62	—	38	100
92-90 Trans Sport APV:	①	8.863	8.877	.030	.972	.957	.0005	.004	62	—	38	100

①.030" over rivet head; if bonded lining use .062".

Year / Make / Model	Brake Shoe O.E. Minimum Lining Thickness	Brake Drum Diameter Standard Size	Brake Drum Diameter Machine To	Brake Pad O.E. Minimum Lining Thickness	Brake Rotor Min. Thickness Machine To	Brake Rotor Min. Thickness Discard At	Brake Rotor Variation From Parallelism	Brake Rotor Runout TIR	DESIGN	Caliper Mounting Bolts Torque (ft. lbs.)	Caliper Bridge, Pin or Key Bolts Torque (ft. lbs)	Wheel Lugs or Nuts Torque (ft. lbs.)
SUBARU TRUCK												
86-85 Brat:	.060	7.090	7.170	.295②	—	.630	—	.004	48	36-51	④	58-72
w/rear disc brakes	—	—	—	.256②	—	.335	—	.004	61	34-43	16-23	58-72
84-83 Brat: w/solid rotor	.060	7.090	7.120	.295②	—	.394	—	.004	48	36-51	12-17	58-72
w/vented rotor	.060	7.090	7.120	.295②	—	.610	—	.004	48	36-51	12-17	58-72
82-80 Brat:	.060	7.090	7.120	.295②	—	.394	—	.004	48	36-51	33-54	58-72
79-77 Brat:	.060	7.090	7.120	.060	—	.330	—	.006	27	36-51	—	58-72

①4x2 shown; 4x4 Not Adjustable. ②Measurement of lining & metal. ③Radial pull in pounds at lug nut. ④Upper bolt 33-40 ft/lbs.; lower bolt 23-30 ft/lbs.

Year / Make / Model	Brake Shoe O.E. Minimum Lining Thickness	Brake Drum Diameter Standard Size	Brake Drum Diameter Machine To	Brake Pad O.E. Minimum Lining Thickness	Brake Rotor Min. Thickness Machine To	Brake Rotor Min. Thickness Discard At	Brake Rotor Variation From Parallelism	Brake Rotor Runout TIR	DESIGN	Caliper Mounting Bolts Torque (ft. lbs.)	Caliper Bridge, Pin or Key Bolts Torque (ft. lbs)	Wheel Lugs or Nuts Torque (ft. lbs.)
SUZUKI TRUCK												
95-86 Samurai:	.120①	8.660	8.740	.236①	—	.334	—	.006	44	51-72	18-21	36-57
96 Sidekick Sport :	.040	10.000	10.070	.275①	—	.787	—	.006	54	62	U42-L37	69
96 Sidekick: 2 Door	.040	8.660	8.740	.240①	—	.315	—	.006	30	62	20	69
4 Door	.040	10.000	10.070	.295①	—	.590	—	.006	30	62	20	69
95-89 Sidekick: 2 Door	.120①	8.660	8.740	.315①	—	.315	—	.006	30	51-72	16-23	58-80
95-92 Sidekick: 4 Door	.120①	10.000	10.070	.315①	—	.591	—	.006	30	51-72	16-23	58-80
96 X-90:	.040	8.660	8.740	.240①	—	.315	—	.006	30	62	20	69

①Measurement of lining & metal.

89450C46

LIGHT TRUCKS

Vehicle	Brake Shoe	Brake Drum		Brake Pad	Brake Rotor				D E S I G N	Caliper		Wheel
	O.E. Minimum Lining Thickness	Diameter		O.E. Minimum Lining Thickness	Min. Thickness		Variation From Parallelism	Runout TIR		Mounting Bolts Torque (ft. lbs.)	Bridge, Pin or Key Bolts Torque (ft. lbs)	Lugs or Nuts Torque (ft. lbs.)
Year / Make / Model		Standard Size	Machine To		Machine To	Discard At						
TOYOTA TRUCK												
97-96 4 Runner:	.039	11.614	11.693	.039	—	.787	—	.0028	110	90	—	83
95-92 4 Runner:	.039	11.614	11.693	.039	—	.906	—	.0035	16	90	—	101
91-89 4 Runner:	.040	11.614	11.693	.040	—	.709	—	.003	16	90	—	101
88-87 4 Runner:	.040	11.614	11.693	.040	—	.748	—	.006	16	90	—	76
86 4 Runner:	.060	11.614	11.654	.040	—	.748	—	.006	16	90	—	76
85-84 4 Runner:	.040	10.000	10.060	.040	—	.453	—	.006	16	55-75	—	76
97-95 Land Cruiser: Front	—	—	—	.039	—	1.181	—	.006	16	90	—	109⑧
Rear	—	—	—	.039	—	.630	—	.006	65	76	65	109⑧
94-93 Land Cruiser:	.060	11.614	11.693	.157	—	1.181	—	.006	16	90	—	116
w\rear disc brakes	—	—	—	.039	—	.630	—	.006	65	76	65	116
92-91 Land Cruiser:	.060	11.614	11.693	.157	—	.906	—	.006	16	90	—	116
90-89 Land Cruiser:	.060	11.614	11.693	.157	—	.748	—	.006	16	90	—	116
88-85 Land Cruiser:	.060	11.614	11.693	.040	—	.748	—	.006	16	90	—	101
84-75 Land Cruiser:	.060	11.610	11.650	.040	—	.748	—	.005	16	52-76	—	66-86
74-72 Land Cruiser:	.060	11.400	11.440	—	—	—	—	—	—	—	—	65-87
95 Pickup (4x2):	.039	10.000	10.079	.039	—	.787	—	.0035	54	80	65	101
94-89 Pickup: (4x2) ½ Ton	.039	10.000	10.079	.039	—	.787	—	.003	54	80	65	101
1 Ton exc. H.D. brakes	.039	10.000	10.079	.039	—	.906	—	.003	65	80	24	101④
1 Ton w/H.D. brakes	.039	10.000	10.079	.039	—	1.102	—	.005	65	80	24	101④
88-85 Pickup: (4x2) ½ Ton	.040	10.000	10.060	.040	—	.827	—	.006	54	80	65	76
1 Ton H.D.	.040	10.000	10.060	.040	—	.945	—	.006	65	80⑤	29	76⑥
84 Pickup: (4x2)	.040	10.000	10.060	.040	—	.827	—	.006	54	73-86	62-68	76
83-75 Pickup: (4x2)	.040	10.000	10.060	.040	—	.453	—	.006	14	68-86	—	66-86
83-79 Cab & Chassis: (4x2)	.040	10.000	10.060	.040	—	.748	—	.006	5	80-126	29-39	66-86
74-72 Pickup: (4x2) w/10" brakes	.040	10.000	10.060	—	—	—	—	—	—	—	—	65-87
72 Pickup: (4x2) w/9" brakes	.040	9.000	9.060	—	—	—	—	—	—	—	—	65-87
95-89 Pickup: (4x4) ½ Ton	.039	11.614	11.693	.039	—	.709	—	.003	16	90	—	101
88-87 Pickup: (4x4)	.040	11.614	11.693	.040	—	.748	—	.006	16	90	—	76
86 Pickup: (4x4)	.060	11.614	11.654	.040	—	.748	—	.006	16	90	—	76
85-84 Pickup: (4x4)	.040	10.000	10.060	.040	—	.453	—	.006	16	55-75	—	76
83-79 Pickup: (4x4)	.040	10.000	10.060	.040	—	.453	—	.006	16	55-75	—	66-86
97 Previa:	.039	10.000	10.079	.039	—	.787	—	.0028	65	65	27	76
w/rear disc brakes	—	—	—	.039	—	.650	—	.0039	65	65	18	76
96 Previa:	—	—	—	—	—	—	—	—	—	—	—	—
Front w/single piston caliper	.039	10.000	10.079	.039	—	.787	—	.0028	65	65	27	76
Front w/dual piston caliper	—	—	—	.039	—	.906	—	.0028	81	65	27	76
Rear w/disc brakes	—	—	—	.039	—	.630	—	.0039	65	65	18	76
95 Previa:												
Front w/single piston caliper	.039	10.000	10.079	.039	—	.787	—	.0028	65	65	27	76
Front w/dual piston caliper	—	—	—	.039	—	.906	—	.0028	81	65	27	76
Rear w/disc brakes	—	—	—	.039	—	.669	—	.0039	65	65	18	76
94-92 Previa: w/rear drum brakes	.039	10.000	10.079	.039	—	.906	—	.0028	65	65	27	76
w/rear disc brakes Front	—	—	—	.039	—	.787	—	.0028	65	65	27	76
Rear	—	—	—	.039	—	.669	—	.0039	65	65	18	76
91 Previa: w/rear drum brakes	.040	10.000	10.080	.040	—	.827	—	.003	65	65	27	76
w/rear disc brakes	—	—	—	.040	—	.669	—	.004	65	65	18	76
97-96 RAV4:	.039	9.000	9.079	.039	—	.630	—	.002	66	79	20⑨	76
97-96 Tacoma (4x2):	.039	10.000	10.079	.039	—	.787	—	.0028	65	80	65	83
97-96 Tacoma (4x4):	.039	11.614	11.693	.039	—	.787	—	.0028	16	90	—	83
97-96 T100 Pickup: (4x2) ½ ton	.039	11.614	11.693	.039	—	.906	—	.0028	65	80	27	76
(4x2) 1 ton	.039	11.614	11.693	.039	—	.906	—	.0028	65	80	29	76
95-93 T100 Pickup: (4x2) ½ Ton	.039	11.614	11.693	.039	—	.906	—	.0028	65	80	26	76
(4x2) 1 Ton	.039	11.614	11.693	.039	—	.906	—	.0035	65	80	29	76
97-93 T100 Pickup: (4x4)	.039	11.614	11.693	.039	—	.906	—	.0028	16	90	—	76
88-87 Van: (4x2)	.040	10.000	10.079	.040	—	.748	—	.006	66	77	14	76
(4x4)	.040	10.000	10.079	.118	—	.945	—	.006	81	61	27	76
86-84 Van:	.040	10.000	10.060	.040	—	.748	—	.006	66	61	14	76

①Radial pull in pounds at lug nut.   ②Torque locknut to 33 ft/lbs., brg. preload; 2.2-3.6 ft/lbs.   ③1991-87 w/dual rear wheels 0.9-2.2 ft/lbs.   ④w/dual rear wheels; rear wheels 170 ft/lbs.
⑤1987 90 ft/lbs.   ⑥1988-87 w/dual wheels; rear wheels 140 ft/lbs.   ⑦See O.E. Manual.   ⑧Steel wheels shown; w/aluminum wheels use 76 ft/lbs.   ⑨1997 22 ft/lbs.

89450C47

LIGHT TRUCKS

Vehicle	Brake Shoe	Brake Drum		Brake Pad	Brake Rotor				Caliper			Wheel
		Diameter			Min. Thickness					Bridge, Pin or Key		
Year / Make / Model	O.E. Minimum Lining Thickness	Standard Size	Machine To	O.E. Minimum Lining Thickness	Machine To	Discard At	Variation From Parallelism	Runout TIR	D E S I G N	Mounting Bolts Torque (ft. lbs.)	Bolts Torque (ft. lbs)	Lugs or Nuts Torque (ft. lbs.)
VOLKSWAGEN TRUCK												
94-93 Euro Van :	.040	—	10.610	.080	—	.787	—	—	—	199	⑥	118
91-86 Vanagon:	.098	9.921	9.960	.079	—	.512	—	.004	61	26	—	133
85-80 Vanagon:	.098	9.921	9.960	.078	.452	.433	—	.004	⑤	115	—	133
79-77 Van, Bus, Wagon, Transporter, Kombi:	.098	9.921	9.960	.080	.492	.453	.0008	.004	⑤	123	—	94
76-73 Van, Bus, Wagon, Transporter, Kombi:	.100	9.921	9.960	.080	—	.472	.0008	.004	⑤	116	—	94
72 Van, Bus, Wagon, Transporter, Kombi:	.100	9.921	9.960	.080	.482	.472	.0008	.004	17	72	—	94
84-82 Rabbit Pickup:	.098	7.874	7.894	.250④	.413	.393	—	.002	8	50	30	87
81-80 Rabbit Pickup: w/Kelsey-Hayes Caliper	②	7.086	7.105	.080	.413	.393	—	.004	8	36③	30	87

①Seat brg. while turning wheel, back off nut until thrust washer can be moved slightly by screwdriver w/finger pressure, lock. ②.098" riveted; .059" bonded. ③w/self locking bolt 50 ft/lbs.
④Measurement of lining & metal. ⑤Use ill. 14 or 17. ⑥Caliper to bridge bolts 66 ft/lbs. Guide bolt nuts 52 ft/lbs. See O.E. Manual for installation notes.

89450C48

CALIPER EXPLODED VIEWS

The following exploded views represent most of the calipers used in cars and lights trucks at the time of this book's publication. Refer to the design column of the Brake Specifications charts located in this section in order to identify the appropriate type of caliper used on your vehicle.

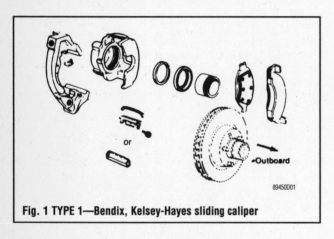

Fig. 1 TYPE 1—Bendix, Kelsey-Hayes sliding caliper

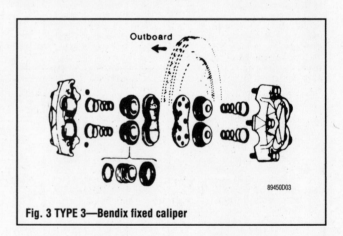

Fig. 3 TYPE 3—Bendix fixed caliper

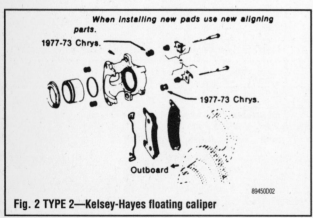

Fig. 2 TYPE 2—Kelsey-Hayes floating caliper

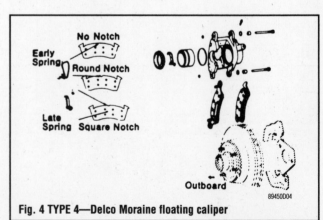

Fig. 4 TYPE 4—Delco Moraine floating caliper

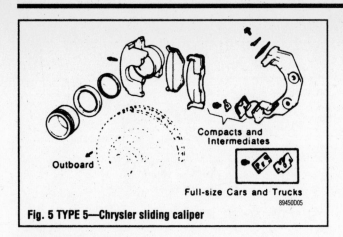

Fig. 5 TYPE 5—Chrysler sliding caliper

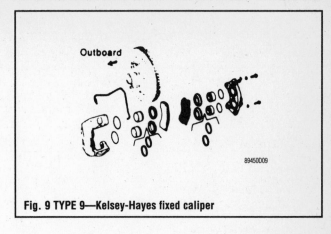

Fig. 9 TYPE 9—Kelsey-Hayes fixed caliper

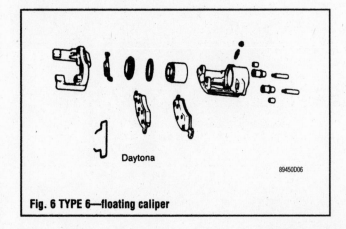

Fig. 6 TYPE 6—floating caliper

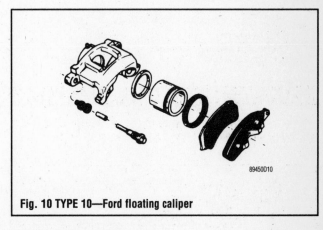

Fig. 10 TYPE 10—Ford floating caliper

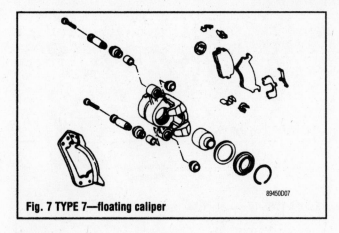

Fig. 7 TYPE 7—floating caliper

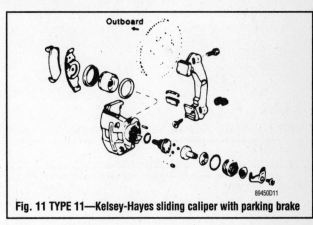

Fig. 11 TYPE 11—Kelsey-Hayes sliding caliper with parking brake

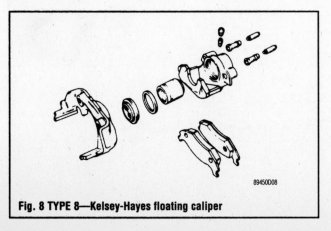

Fig. 8 TYPE 8—Kelsey-Hayes floating caliper

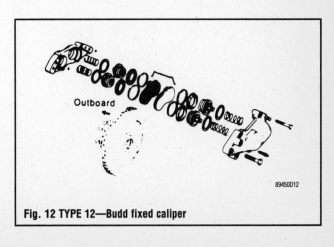

Fig. 12 TYPE 12—Budd fixed caliper

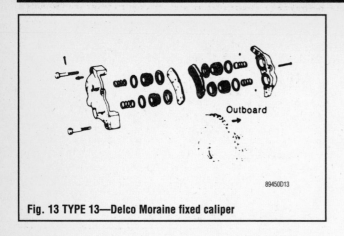

Fig. 13 TYPE 13—Delco Moraine fixed caliper

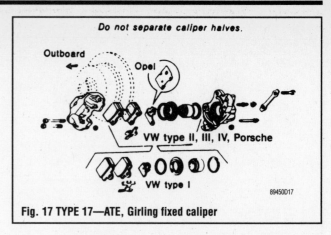

Fig. 17 TYPE 17—ATE, Girling fixed caliper

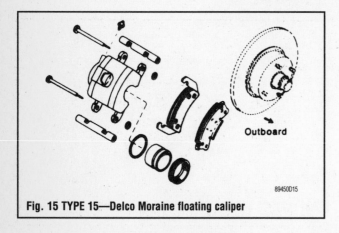

Fig. 14 TYPE 14—Bendix, Girling, Sumitoma, Teves fixed caliper

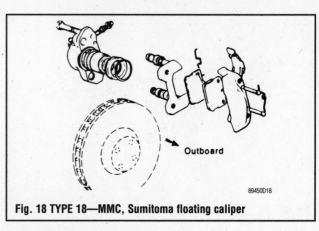

Fig. 18 TYPE 18—MMC, Sumitoma floating caliper

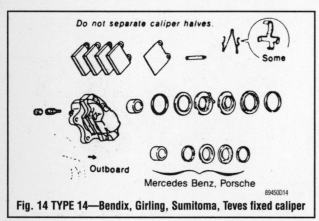

Fig. 15 TYPE 15—Delco Moraine floating caliper

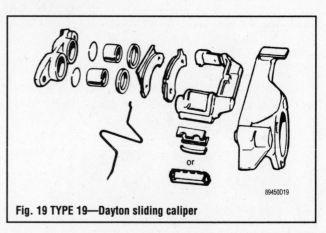

Fig. 19 TYPE 19—Dayton sliding caliper

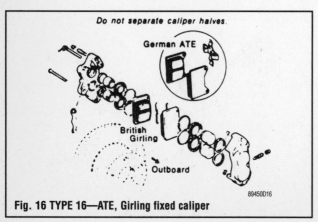

Fig. 16 TYPE 16—ATE, Girling fixed caliper

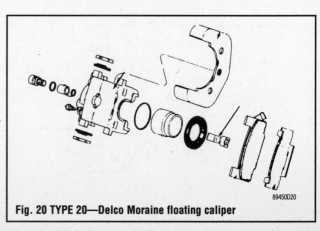

Fig. 20 TYPE 20—Delco Moraine floating caliper

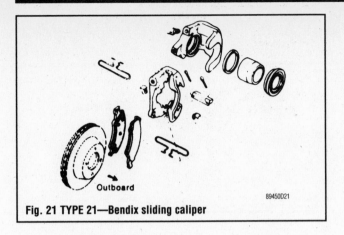

Fig. 21 TYPE 21—Bendix sliding caliper

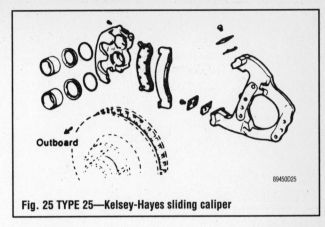

Fig. 25 TYPE 25—Kelsey-Hayes sliding caliper

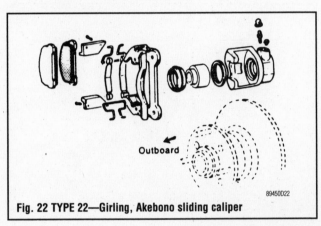

Fig. 22 TYPE 22—Girling, Akebono sliding caliper

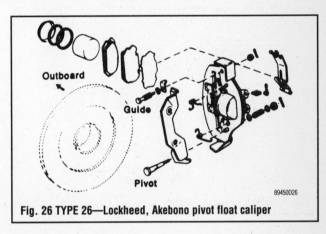

Fig. 26 TYPE 26—Lockheed, Akebono pivot float caliper

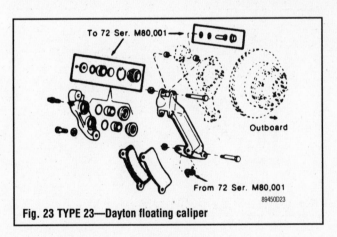

Fig. 23 TYPE 23—Dayton floating caliper

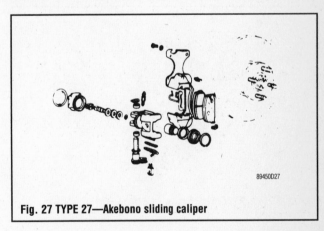

Fig. 27 TYPE 27—Akebono sliding caliper

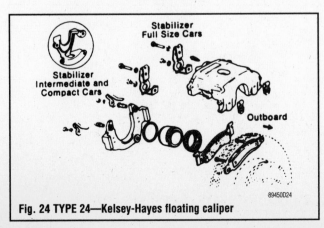

Fig. 24 TYPE 24—Kelsey-Hayes floating caliper

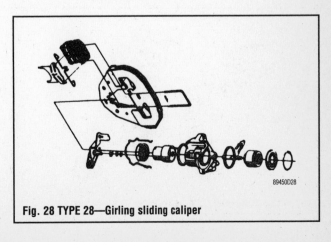

Fig. 28 TYPE 28—Girling sliding caliper

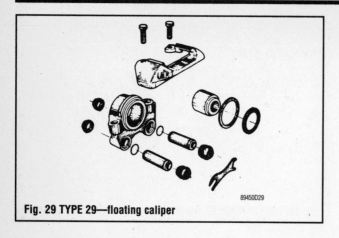

Fig. 29 TYPE 29—floating caliper

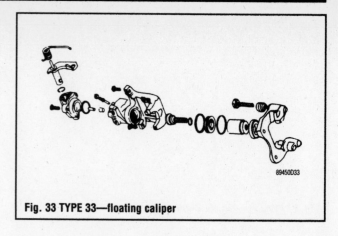

Fig. 33 TYPE 33—floating caliper

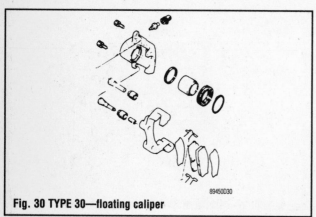

Fig. 30 TYPE 30—floating caliper

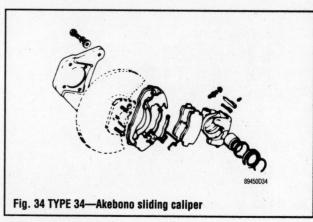

Fig. 34 TYPE 34—Akebono sliding caliper

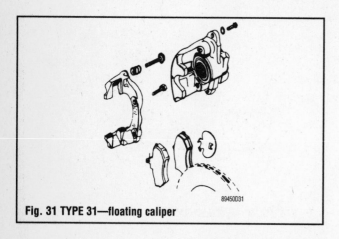

Fig. 31 TYPE 31—floating caliper

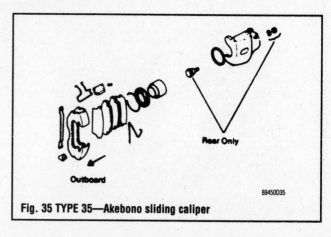

Fig. 35 TYPE 35—Akebono sliding caliper

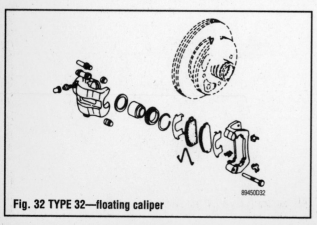

Fig. 32 TYPE 32—floating caliper

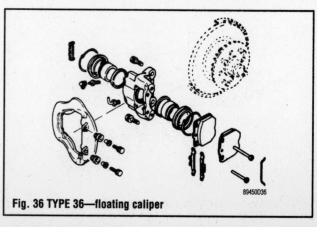

Fig. 36 TYPE 36—floating caliper

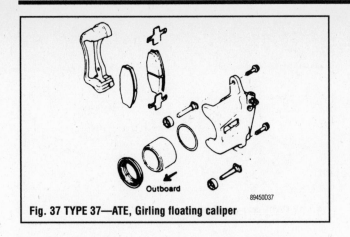

Fig. 37 TYPE 37—ATE, Girling floating caliper

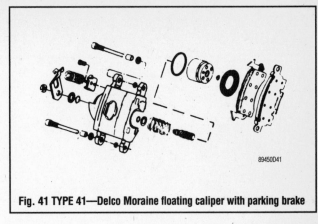

Fig. 41 TYPE 41—Delco Moraine floating caliper with parking brake

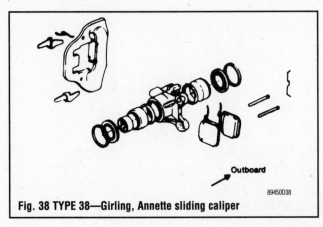

Fig. 38 TYPE 38—Girling, Annette sliding caliper

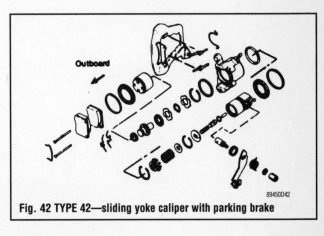

Fig. 42 TYPE 42—sliding yoke caliper with parking brake

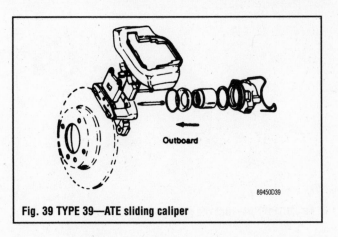

Fig. 39 TYPE 39—ATE sliding caliper

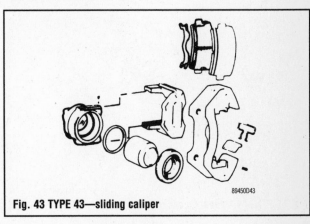

Fig. 43 TYPE 43—sliding caliper

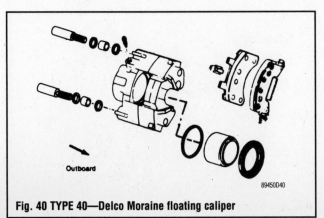

Fig. 40 TYPE 40—Delco Moraine floating caliper

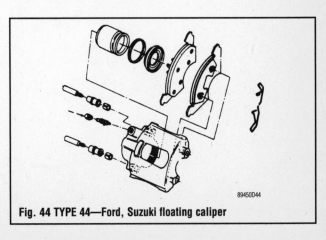

Fig. 44 TYPE 44—Ford, Suzuki floating caliper

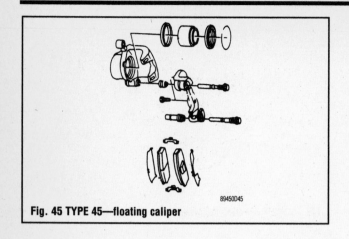

Fig. 45 TYPE 45—floating caliper

89450D45

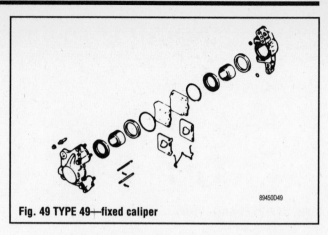

Fig. 49 TYPE 49—fixed caliper

89450D49

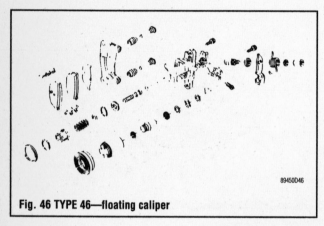

Fig. 46 TYPE 46—floating caliper

89450D46

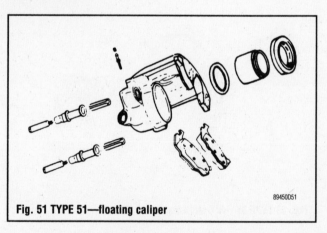

Fig. 50 TYPE 50—floating caliper

89450D50

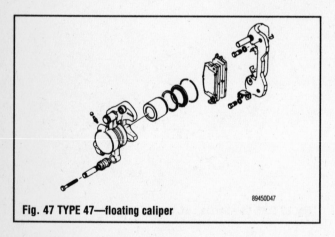

Fig. 47 TYPE 47—floating caliper

89450D47

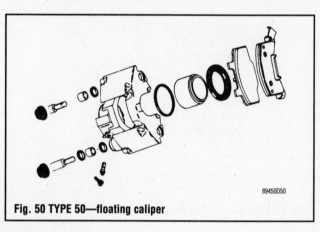

Fig. 51 TYPE 51—floating caliper

89450D51

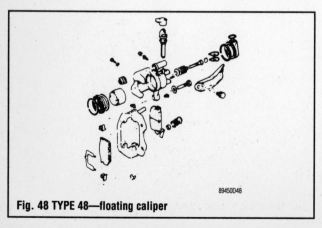

Fig. 48 TYPE 48—floating caliper

89450D48

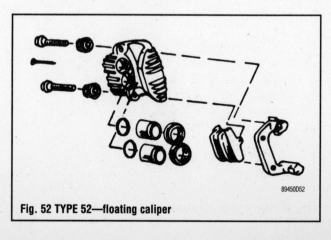

Fig. 52 TYPE 52—floating caliper

89450D52

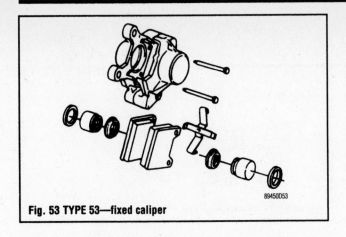

Fig. 53 TYPE 53—fixed caliper

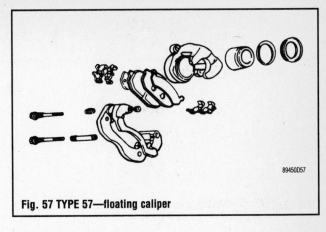

Fig. 57 TYPE 57—floating caliper

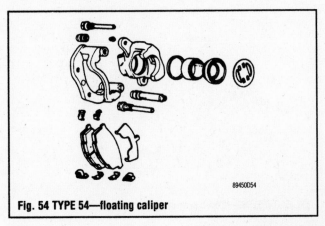

Fig. 54 TYPE 54—floating caliper

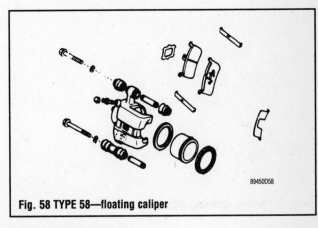

Fig. 58 TYPE 58—floating caliper

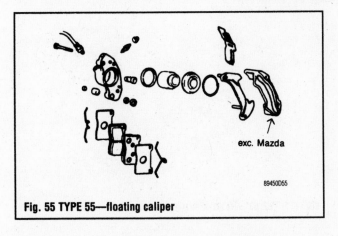

exc. Mazda

Fig. 55 TYPE 55—floating caliper

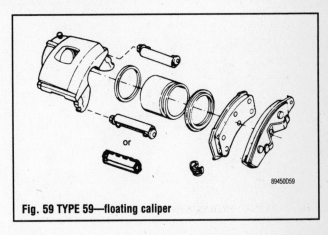

or

Fig. 59 TYPE 59—floating caliper

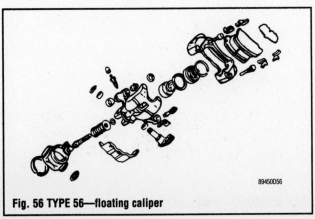

Fig. 56 TYPE 56—floating caliper

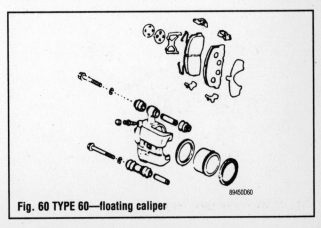

Fig. 60 TYPE 60—floating caliper

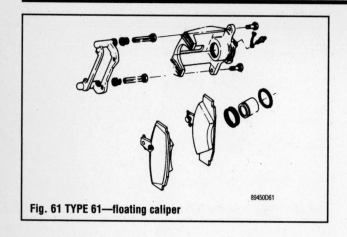

Fig. 61 TYPE 61—floating caliper

89450D61

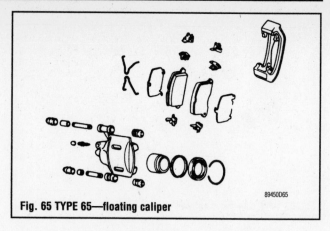

Fig. 65 TYPE 65—floating caliper

89450D65

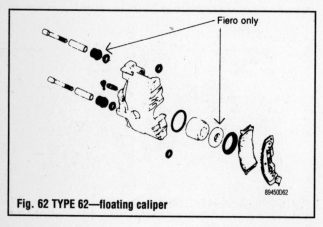

Fig. 62 TYPE 62—floating caliper

Fiero only

89450D62

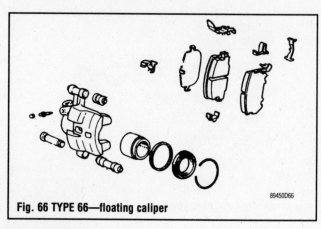

Fig. 66 TYPE 66—floating caliper

89450D66

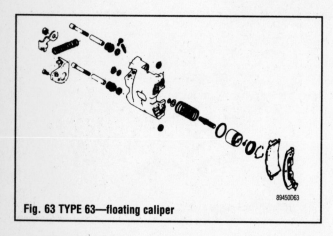

Fig. 63 TYPE 63—floating caliper

89450D63

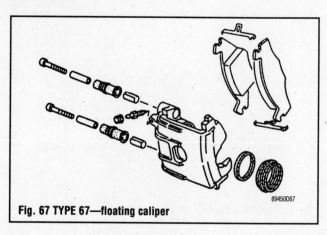

Fig. 67 TYPE 67—floating caliper

89450D67

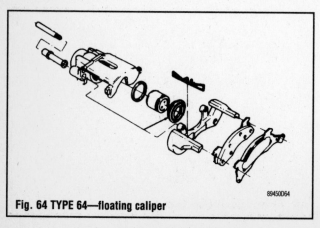

Fig. 64 TYPE 64—floating caliper

89450D64

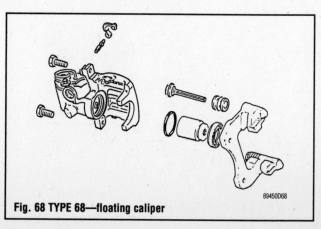

Fig. 68 TYPE 68—floating caliper

89450D68

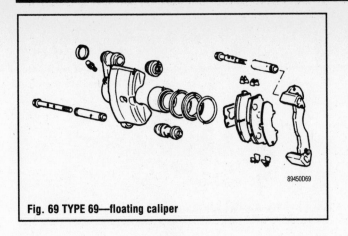

Fig. 69 TYPE 69—floating caliper

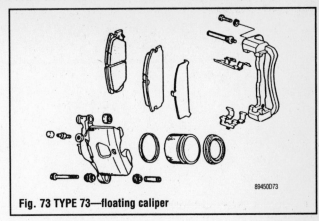

Fig. 73 TYPE 73—floating caliper

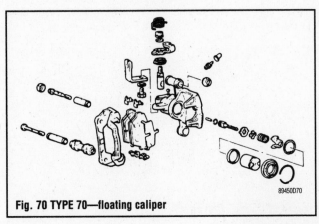

Fig. 70 TYPE 70—floating caliper

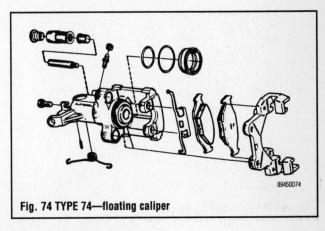

Fig. 74 TYPE 74—floating caliper

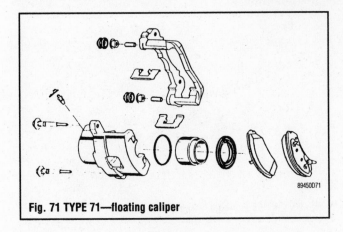

Fig. 71 TYPE 71—floating caliper

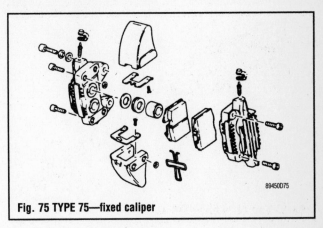

Fig. 75 TYPE 75—fixed caliper

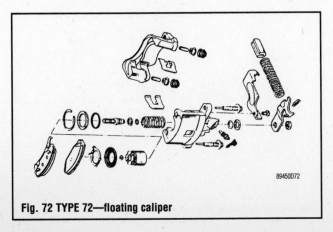

Fig. 72 TYPE 72—floating caliper

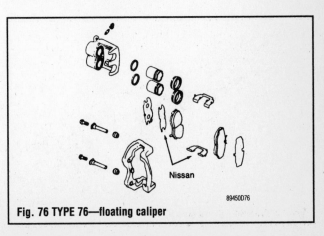

Fig. 76 TYPE 76—floating caliper

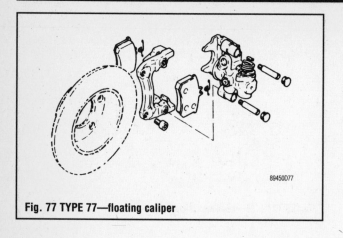

Fig. 77 TYPE 77—floating caliper

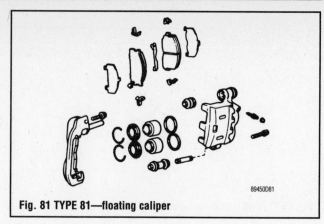

Fig. 81 TYPE 81—floating caliper

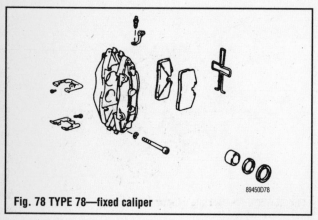

Fig. 78 TYPE 78—fixed caliper

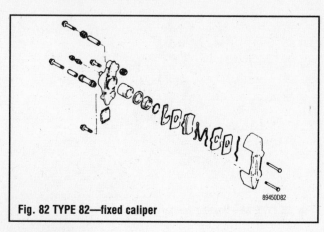

Fig. 82 TYPE 82—fixed caliper

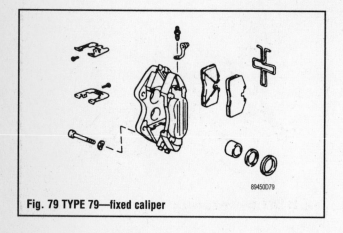

Fig. 79 TYPE 79—fixed caliper

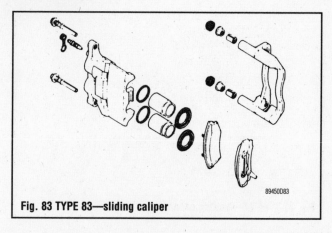

Fig. 83 TYPE 83—sliding caliper

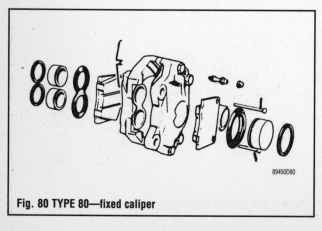

Fig. 80 TYPE 80—fixed caliper

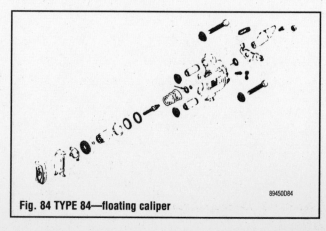

Fig. 84 TYPE 84—floating caliper

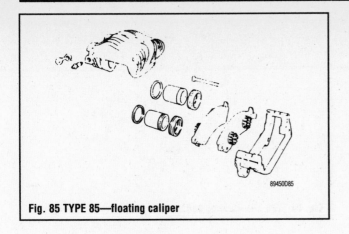

Fig. 85 TYPE 85—floating caliper

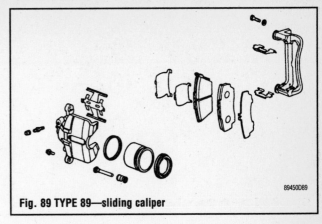

Fig. 89 TYPE 89—sliding caliper

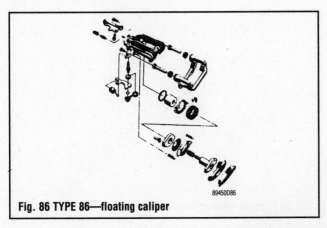

Fig. 86 TYPE 86—floating caliper

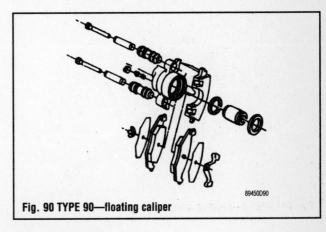

Fig. 90 TYPE 90—floating caliper

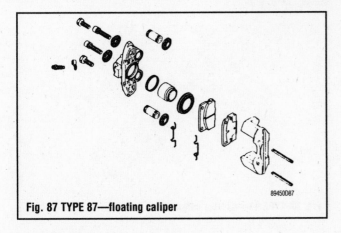

Fig. 87 TYPE 87—floating caliper

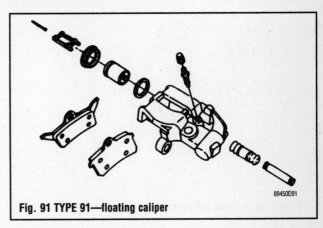

Fig. 91 TYPE 91—floating caliper

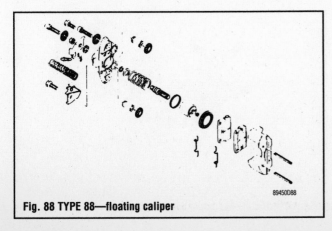

Fig. 88 TYPE 88—floating caliper

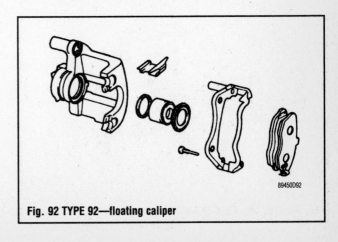

Fig. 92 TYPE 92—floating caliper

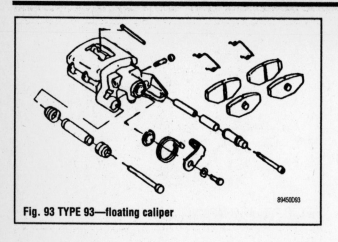

Fig. 93 TYPE 93—floating caliper

89450D93

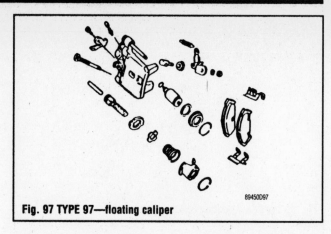

Fig. 97 TYPE 97—floating caliper

89450D97

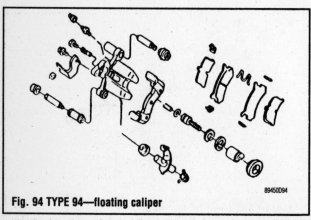

Fig. 94 TYPE 94—floating caliper

89450D94

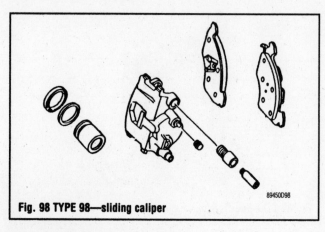

Fig. 98 TYPE 98—sliding caliper

89450D98

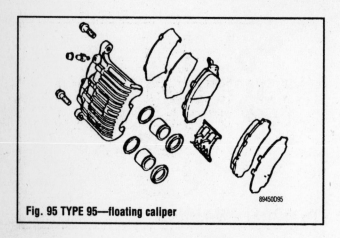

Fig. 95 TYPE 95—floating caliper

89450D95

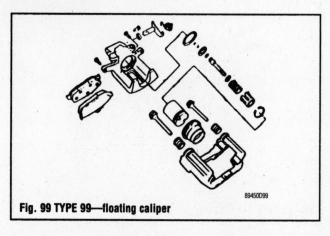

Fig. 99 TYPE 99—floating caliper

89450D99

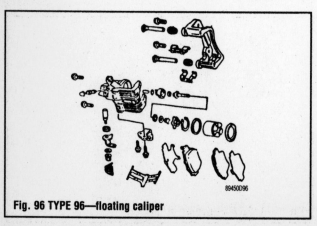

Fig. 96 TYPE 96—floating caliper

89450D96

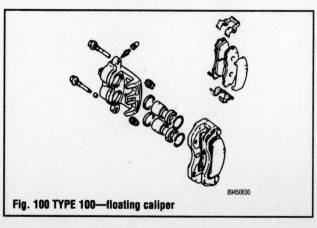

Fig. 100 TYPE 100—floating caliper

89450E00

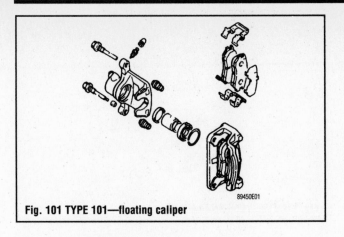

Fig. 101 TYPE 101—floating caliper

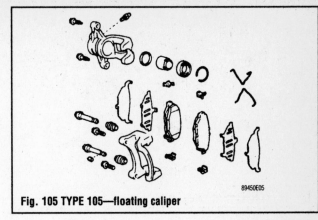

Fig. 105 TYPE 105—floating caliper

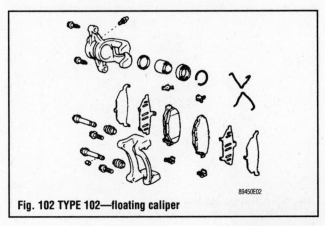

Fig. 102 TYPE 102—floating caliper

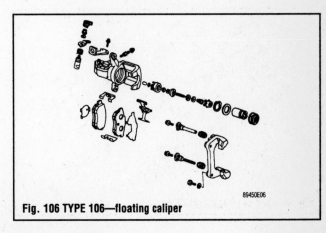

Fig. 106 TYPE 106—floating caliper

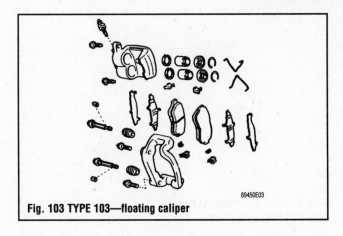

Fig. 103 TYPE 103—floating caliper

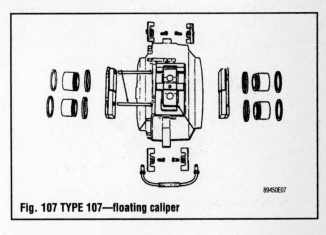

Fig. 107 TYPE 107—floating caliper

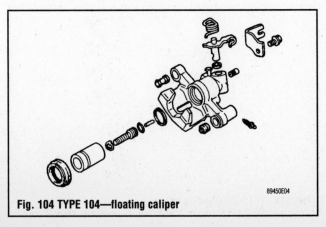

Fig. 104 TYPE 104—floating caliper

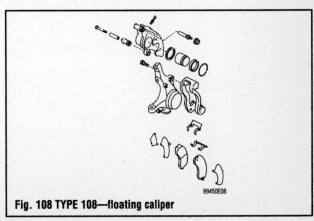

Fig. 108 TYPE 108—floating caliper

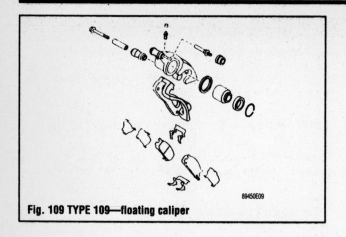

Fig. 109 TYPE 109—floating caliper

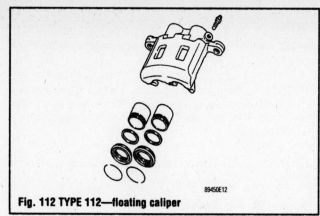

Fig. 112 TYPE 112—floating caliper

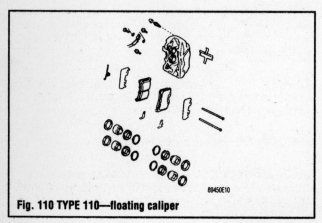

Fig. 110 TYPE 110—floating caliper

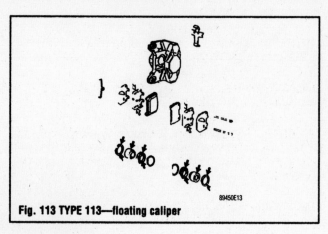

Fig. 113 TYPE 113—floating caliper

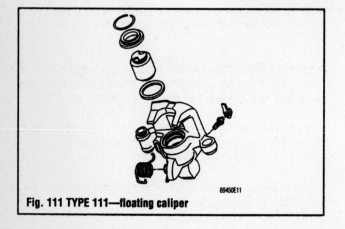

Fig. 111 TYPE 111—floating caliper

GLOSSARY

AIR/FUEL RATIO: The ratio of air-to-gasoline by weight in the fuel mixture drawn into the engine.

AIR INJECTION: One method of reducing harmful exhaust emissions by injecting air into each of the exhaust ports of an engine. The fresh air entering the hot exhaust manifold causes any remaining fuel to be burned before it can exit the tailpipe.

ALTERNATOR: A device used for converting mechanical energy into electrical energy.

AMMETER: An instrument, calibrated in amperes, used to measure the flow of an electrical current in a circuit. Ammeters are always connected in series with the circuit being tested.

AMPERE: The rate of flow of electrical current present when one volt of electrical pressure is applied against one ohm of electrical resistance.

ANALOG COMPUTER: Any microprocessor that uses similar (analogous) electrical signals to make its calculations.

ARMATURE: A laminated, soft iron core wrapped by a wire that converts electrical energy to mechanical energy as in a motor or relay. When rotated in a magnetic field, it changes mechanical energy into electrical energy as in a generator.

ATMOSPHERIC PRESSURE: The pressure on the Earth's surface caused by the weight of the air in the atmosphere. At sea level, this pressure is 14.7 psi at 32°F (101 kPa at 0°C).

ATOMIZATION: The breaking down of a liquid into a fine mist that can be suspended in air.

AXIAL PLAY: Movement parallel to a shaft or bearing bore.

BACKFIRE: The sudden combustion of gases in the intake or exhaust system that results in a loud explosion.

BACKLASH: The clearance or play between two parts, such as meshed gears.

BACKPRESSURE: Restrictions in the exhaust system that slow the exit of exhaust gases from the combustion chamber.

BAKELITE: A heat resistant, plastic insulator material commonly used in printed circuit boards and transistorized components.

BALL BEARING: A bearing made up of hardened inner and outer races between which hardened steel balls roll.

BALLAST RESISTOR: A resistor in the primary ignition circuit that lowers voltage after the engine is started to reduce wear on ignition components.

BEARING: A friction reducing, supportive device usually located between a stationary part and a moving part.

BIMETAL TEMPERATURE SENSOR: Any sensor or switch made of two dissimilar types of metal that bend when heated or cooled due to the different expansion rates of the alloys. These types of sensors usually function as an on/off switch.

BLOWBY: Combustion gases, composed of water vapor and unburned fuel, that leak past the piston rings into the crankcase during normal engine operation. These gases are removed by the PCV system to prevent the buildup of harmful acids in the crankcase.

BRAKE PAD: A brake shoe and lining assembly used with disc brakes.

BRAKE SHOE: The backing for the brake lining. The term is, however, usually applied to the assembly of the brake backing and lining.

BUSHING: A liner, usually removable, for a bearing; an anti-friction liner used in place of a bearing.

CALIPER: A hydraulically activated device in a disc brake system, which is mounted straddling the brake rotor (disc). The caliper contains at least one piston and two brake pads. Hydraulic pressure on the piston(s) forces the pads against the rotor.

CAMSHAFT: A shaft in the engine on which are the lobes (cams) which operate the valves. The camshaft is driven by the crankshaft, via a belt, chain or gears, at one half the crankshaft speed.

CAPACITOR: A device which stores an electrical charge.

CARBON MONOXIDE (CO): A colorless, odorless gas given off as a normal byproduct of combustion. It is poisonous and extremely dangerous in confined areas, building up slowly to toxic levels without warning if adequate ventilation is not available.

CARBURETOR: A device, usually mounted on the intake manifold of an engine, which mixes the air and fuel in the proper proportion to allow even combustion.

CATALYTIC CONVERTER: A device installed in the exhaust system, like a muffler, that converts harmful byproducts of combustion into carbon dioxide and water vapor by means of a heat-producing chemical reaction.

CENTRIFUGAL ADVANCE: A mechanical method of advancing the spark timing by using flyweights in the distributor that react to centrifugal force generated by the distributor shaft rotation.

CHECK VALVE: Any one-way valve installed to permit the flow of air, fuel or vacuum in one direction only.

CHOKE: A device, usually a moveable valve, placed in the intake path of a carburetor to restrict the flow of air.

CIRCUIT: Any unbroken path through which an electrical current can flow. Also used to describe fuel flow in some instances.

CIRCUIT BREAKER: A switch which protects an electrical circuit from overload by opening the circuit when the current flow exceeds a predetermined level. Some circuit breakers must be reset manually, while most reset automatically.

COIL (IGNITION): A transformer in the ignition circuit which steps up the voltage provided to the spark plugs.

COMBINATION MANIFOLD: An assembly which includes both the intake and exhaust manifolds in one casting.

COMBINATION VALVE: A device used in some fuel systems that routes fuel vapors to a charcoal storage canister instead of venting them into the atmosphere. The valve relieves fuel tank pressure and allows fresh air into the tank as the fuel level drops to prevent a vapor lock situation.

COMPRESSION RATIO: The comparison of the total volume of the cylinder and combustion chamber with the piston at BDC and the piston at TDC.

CONDENSER: 1. An electrical device which acts to store an electrical charge, preventing voltage surges. 2. A radiator-like device in the air conditioning system in which refrigerant gas condenses into a liquid, giving off heat.

CONDUCTOR: Any material through which an electrical current can be transmitted easily.

CONTINUITY: Continuous or complete circuit. Can be checked with an ohmmeter.

COUNTERSHAFT: An intermediate shaft which is rotated by a mainshaft and transmits, in turn, that rotation to a working part.

CRANKCASE: The lower part of an engine in which the crankshaft and related parts operate.

CRANKSHAFT: The main driving shaft of an engine which receives reciprocating motion from the pistons and converts it to rotary motion.

CYLINDER: In an engine, the round hole in the engine block in which the piston(s) ride.

CYLINDER BLOCK: The main structural member of an engine in which is found the cylinders, crankshaft and other principal parts.

CYLINDER HEAD: The detachable portion of the engine, usually fastened to the top of the cylinder block and containing all or most of the combustion chambers. On overhead valve engines, it contains the valves and their operating parts. On overhead cam engines, it contains the camshaft as well.

DEAD CENTER: The extreme top or bottom of the piston stroke.

DETONATION: An unwanted explosion of the air/fuel mixture in the combustion chamber caused by excess heat and compression, advanced timing, or an overly lean mixture. Also referred to as "ping".

DIAPHRAGM: A thin, flexible wall separating two cavities, such as in a vacuum advance unit.

DIESELING: A condition in which hot spots in the combustion chamber cause the engine to run on after the key is turned off.

DIFFERENTIAL: A geared assembly which allows the transmission of motion between drive axles, giving one axle the ability to turn faster than the other.

DIODE: An electrical device that will allow current to flow in one direction only.

DISC BRAKE: A hydraulic braking assembly consisting of a brake disc, or rotor, mounted on an axle, and a caliper assembly containing, usually two brake pads which are activated by hydraulic pressure. The pads are forced against the sides of the disc, creating friction which slows the vehicle.

DISTRIBUTOR: A mechanically driven device on an engine which is responsible for electrically firing the spark plug at a predetermined point of the piston stroke.

DOWEL PIN: A pin, inserted in mating holes in two different parts allowing those parts to maintain a fixed relationship.

DRUM BRAKE: A braking system which consists of two brake shoes and one or two wheel cylinders, mounted on a fixed backing plate, and a brake drum, mounted on an axle, which revolves around the assembly.

DWELL: The rate, measured in degrees of shaft rotation, at which an electrical circuit cycles on and off.

ELECTRONIC CONTROL UNIT (ECU): Ignition module, module, amplifier or igniter. See Module for definition.

ELECTRONIC IGNITION: A system in which the timing and firing of the spark plugs is controlled by an electronic control unit, usually called a module. These systems have no points or condenser.

END-PLAY: The measured amount of axial movement in a shaft.

ENGINE: A device that converts heat into mechanical energy.

EXHAUST MANIFOLD: A set of cast passages or pipes which conduct exhaust gases from the engine.

FEELER GAUGE: A blade, usually metal, or precisely predetermined thickness, used to measure the clearance between two parts.

FIRING ORDER: The order in which combustion occurs in the cylinders of an engine. Also the order in which spark is distributed to the plugs by the distributor.

FLOODING: The presence of too much fuel in the intake manifold and combustion chamber which prevents the air/fuel mixture from firing, thereby causing a no-start situation.

FLYWHEEL: A disc shaped part bolted to the rear end of the crankshaft. Around the outer perimeter is affixed the ring gear. The starter drive engages the ring gear, turning the flywheel, which rotates the crankshaft, imparting the initial starting motion to the engine.

FOOT POUND (ft. lbs. or sometimes, ft.lb.): The amount of energy or work needed to raise an item weighing one pound, a distance of one foot.

FUSE: A protective device in a circuit which prevents circuit overload by breaking the circuit when a specific amperage is present. The device is constructed around a strip or wire of a lower amperage rating than the circuit it is designed to protect. When an amperage higher than that stamped on the fuse is present in the circuit, the strip or wire melts, opening the circuit.

GEAR RATIO: The ratio between the number of teeth on meshing gears.

GENERATOR: A device which converts mechanical energy into electrical energy.

HEAT RANGE: The measure of a spark plug's ability to dissipate heat from its firing end. The higher the heat range, the hotter the plug fires.

HUB: The center part of a wheel or gear.

HYDROCARBON (HC): Any chemical compound made up of hydrogen and carbon. A major pollutant formed by the engine as a byproduct of combustion.

HYDROMETER: An instrument used to measure the specific gravity of a solution.

INCH POUND (inch lbs.; sometimes in.lb. or in. lbs.): One twelfth of a foot pound.

INDUCTION: A means of transferring electrical energy in the form of a magnetic field. Principle used in the ignition coil to increase voltage.

INJECTOR: A device which receives metered fuel under relatively low pressure and is activated to inject the fuel into the engine under relatively high pressure at a predetermined time.

INPUT SHAFT: The shaft to which torque is applied, usually carrying the driving gear or gears.

INTAKE MANIFOLD: A casting of passages or pipes used to conduct air or a fuel/air mixture to the cylinders.

JOURNAL: The bearing surface within which a shaft operates.

KEY: A small block usually fitted in a notch between a shaft and a hub to prevent slippage of the two parts.

MANIFOLD: A casting of passages or set of pipes which connect the cylinders to an inlet or outlet source.

MANIFOLD VACUUM: Low pressure in an engine intake manifold formed just below the throttle plates. Manifold vacuum is highest at idle and drops under acceleration.

MASTER CYLINDER: The primary fluid pressurizing device in a hydraulic system. In automotive use, it is found in brake and hydraulic clutch systems and is pedal activated, either directly or, in a power brake system, through the power booster.

MODULE: Electronic control unit, amplifier or igniter of solid state or integrated design which controls the current flow in the ignition primary circuit based on input from the pick-up coil. When the module opens the primary circuit, high secondary voltage is induced in the coil.

NEEDLE BEARING: A bearing which consists of a number (usually a large number) of long, thin rollers.

OHM: (Ω) The unit used to measure the resistance of conductor-to-electrical flow. One ohm is the amount of resistance that limits current flow to one ampere in a circuit with one volt of pressure.

OHMMETER: An instrument used for measuring the resistance, in ohms, in an electrical circuit.

OUTPUT SHAFT: The shaft which transmits torque from a device, such as a transmission.

OVERDRIVE: A gear assembly which produces more shaft revolutions than that transmitted to it.

OVERHEAD CAMSHAFT (OHC): An engine configuration in which the camshaft is mounted on top of the cylinder head and operates the valve either directly or by means of rocker arms.

OVERHEAD VALVE (OHV): An engine configuration in which all of the valves are located in the cylinder head and the camshaft is located in the cylinder block. The camshaft operates the valves via lifters and pushrods.

OXIDES OF NITROGEN (NOx): Chemical compounds of nitrogen produced as a byproduct of combustion. They combine with hydrocarbons to produce smog.

OXYGEN SENSOR: Use with the feedback system to sense the presence of oxygen in the exhaust gas and signal the computer which can reference the voltage signal to an air/fuel ratio.

PINION: The smaller of two meshing gears.

PISTON RING: An open-ended ring with fits into a groove on the outer diameter of the piston. Its chief function is to form a seal between the piston and cylinder wall. Most automotive pistons have three rings: two for compression sealing; one for oil sealing.

PRELOAD: A predetermined load placed on a bearing during assembly or by adjustment.

PRIMARY CIRCUIT: the low voltage side of the ignition system which consists of the ignition switch, ballast resistor or resistance wire, bypass, coil, electronic control unit and pick-up coil as well as the connecting wires and harnesses.

PRESS FIT: The mating of two parts under pressure, due to the inner diameter of one being smaller than the outer diameter of the other, or vice versa; an interference fit.

RACE: The surface on the inner or outer ring of a bearing on which the balls, needles or rollers move.

REGULATOR: A device which maintains the amperage and/or voltage levels of a circuit at predetermined values.

RELAY: A switch which automatically opens and/or closes a circuit.

RESISTANCE: The opposition to the flow of current through a circuit or electrical device, and is measured in ohms. Resistance is equal to the voltage divided by the amperage.

RESISTOR: A device, usually made of wire, which offers a preset amount of resistance in an electrical circuit.

RING GEAR: The name given to a ring-shaped gear attached to a differential case, or affixed to a flywheel or as part of a planetary gear set.

ROLLER BEARING: A bearing made up of hardened inner and outer races between which hardened steel rollers move.

ROTOR: 1. The disc-shaped part of a disc brake assembly, upon which the brake pads bear; also called, brake disc. 2. The device mounted atop the distributor shaft, which passes current to the distributor cap tower contacts.

SECONDARY CIRCUIT: The high voltage side of the ignition system, usually above 20,000 volts. The secondary includes the ignition coil, coil wire, distributor cap and rotor, spark plug wires and spark plugs.

SENDING UNIT: A mechanical, electrical, hydraulic or electro-magnetic device which transmits information to a gauge.

SENSOR: Any device designed to measure engine operating conditions or ambient pressures and temperatures. Usually electronic in nature and designed to send a voltage signal to an on-board computer, some sensors may operate as a simple on/off switch or they may provide a variable voltage signal (like a potentiometer) as conditions or measured parameters change.

SHIM: Spacers of precise, predetermined thickness used between parts to establish a proper working relationship.

SLAVE CYLINDER: In automotive use, a device in the hydraulic clutch system which is activated by hydraulic force, disengaging the clutch.

SOLENOID: A coil used to produce a magnetic field, the effect of which is to produce work.

SPARK PLUG: A device screwed into the combustion chamber of a spark ignition engine. The basic construction is a conductive core inside of a ceramic insulator, mounted in an outer conductive base. An electrical charge from the spark plug wire travels along the conductive core and jumps a preset air gap to a grounding point or points at the end of the conductive base. The resultant spark ignites the fuel/air mixture in the combustion chamber.

SPLINES: Ridges machined or cast onto the outer diameter of a shaft or inner diameter of a bore to enable parts to mate without rotation.

TACHOMETER: A device used to measure the rotary speed of an engine, shaft, gear, etc., usually in rotations per minute.

THERMOSTAT: A valve, located in the cooling system of an engine, which is closed when cold and opens gradually in response to engine heating, controlling the temperature of the coolant and rate of coolant flow.

TOP DEAD CENTER (TDC): The point at which the piston reaches the top of its travel on the compression stroke.

TORQUE: The twisting force applied to an object.

TORQUE CONVERTER: A turbine used to transmit power from a driving member to a driven member via hydraulic action, providing changes in drive ratio and torque. In automotive use, it links the driveplate at the rear of the engine to the automatic transmission.

TRANSDUCER: A device used to change a force into an electrical signal.

TRANSISTOR: A semi-conductor component which can be actuated by a small voltage to perform an electrical switching function.

TUNE-UP: A regular maintenance function, usually associated with the replacement and adjustment of parts and components in the electrical and fuel systems of a vehicle for the purpose of attaining optimum performance.

TURBOCHARGER: An exhaust driven pump which compresses intake air and forces it into the combustion chambers at higher than atmospheric pressures. The increased air pressure allows more fuel to be burned and results in increased horsepower being produced.

VACUUM ADVANCE: A device which advances the ignition timing in response to increased engine vacuum.

VACUUM GAUGE: An instrument used to measure the presence of vacuum in a chamber.

VALVE: A device which control the pressure, direction of flow or rate of flow of a liquid or gas.

VALVE CLEARANCE: The measured gap between the end of the valve stem and the rocker arm, cam lobe or follower that activates the valve.

VISCOSITY: The rating of a liquid's internal resistance to flow.

VOLTMETER: An instrument used for measuring electrical force in units called volts. Voltmeters are always connected parallel with the circuit being tested.

WHEEL CYLINDER: Found in the automotive drum brake assembly, it is a device, actuated by hydraulic pressure, which, through internal pistons, pushes the brake shoes outward against the drums.

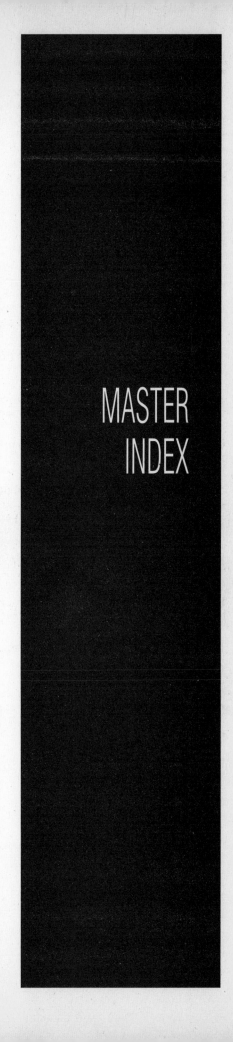

MASTER

INDEX